Running heads indicate the subject being discussed.

Chapter number and sections identify your location in the text.

Annotated icons refer to *The Ready Reference Handbook's* Companion Website.

ESL Grammar Notes provide grammatical support for multilingual writers.

Section headings describe guidelines for writing, revising, and editing.

"How To" boxes provide immediate help for most writing processes.

Writing in the USA notes discuss stylistic and rhetorical characteristics of academic writing in the USA.

Cross-references show where to find related information.

Computer tips provide ways to use computers to facilitate the writing process.

Handwritten corrections show how to revise and edit in a given situation.

Bracketed explanations provide the reasons for the changes.

ESL GRAMMAR NOTE Unnecessary words.

When you combine sentences, take care to avoid unnecessary repetition of subjects, objects, and adverbs. (See 32b.)

21.3
Combining choppy sentences: Exercises

21c Divide loose, rambling sentences into two or more separate sentences

Carefully crafted long sentences can be as clear, emphatic, and easy to read as shorter sentences. But long, rambling sentences may obscure important ideas and be tiresome to read.

1 ▪ Dividing loose sentences at conjunctions or transitions

Omit conjunctions or transitions if possible. Then check to see that your revised sentences are varied and emphatic.

HOW TO . . . Identify the Subjects of Sentences

Ask *who* or *what* + the verb + the remainder of the sentence: *Algae produce their food through photosynthesis*. What produce their food through photosynthesis? *Algae*. Note that not all sentences open with the subject: *Into the room walked the President of the United States*. Who walked into the room? *The President of the United States*.

WRITING IN THE USA Coordinating conjunctions.

English permits the beginning of sentences with coordinating conjunctions (*for, and, nor, but, or, yet, so*) as in the preceding sample sentence revision. (See 32c and 8g1.)

2 ▪ Dividing sentences at subordinating conjunctions or relative pronouns

COMPUTER TIP Using Search and Replace.

Use the Find or Search and Replace command to locate nouns linked by *and, or,* and *nor* and pronouns containing *-body, every-,* and *-one* (see item 2 above).

their prime stands of old-growth timber, ~~although, once~~ *. Once* logging begins, *however,* these forests will last less than a decade.

[To create two sentences, the revision omits a subordinating conjunction, *although,* and adds a conjunctive adverb, *however,* as a transition.]

21.4
Dividing rambling sentences: Exercises

4th EDITION

The Ready Reference Handbook

JACK DODDS

Professor Emeritus

William Rainey Harper College

With the participation of
Carol Numrich
American Language Program, Columbia University

PEARSON
Longman

New York   Boston   San Francisco
London   Toronto   Sydney   Tokyo   Singapore   Madrid
Mexico City   Munich   Paris   Cape Town   Hong Kong   Montreal

SENIOR SPONSORING EDITOR: Virginia Blanford
DEVELOPMENT EDITOR: Lai T. Moy
SENIOR SUPPLEMENTS EDITOR: Donna Campion
MEDIA SUPPLEMENTS EDITOR: Jenna Egan
EXECUTIVE MARKETING MANAGER: Megan Galvin-Fak
MANAGING EDITOR: Robert Ginsberg
PRODUCTION MANAGER: Joseph Vella
PROJECT COORDINATION, PHOTO RESEARCH, TEXT DESIGN, AND ELECTRONIC
    PAGE MAKEUP: Nesbitt Graphics, Inc.
COVER DESIGNER/MANAGER: Wendy A. Fredericks
COVER PHOTOS: Left to right: Digital Vision Ltd.; NASA/Johnson Space Center;
    Altrendo Images/Getty Images, Inc.; and Photodisc Collection/Getty Images, Inc.
MANUFACTURING MANAGER: Mary Fischer
SENIOR MANUFACTURING BUYER: Dennis J. Para
PRINTER AND BINDER: Quebecor World–Taunton
COVER PRINTER: Phoenix Color Corporation

Library of Congress Cataloging-in-Publication Data

Dodds, Jack.
  The ready reference handbook : / Jack Dodds.-- 4th ed.
    p. cm.
  ISBN 0-321-33069-2
  1. English language—Rhetoric—Handbooks, manuals, etc. 2. English
language—Grammar—Handbooks, manuals, etc. 3. Report writing—Handbooks,
manuals, etc. I. Title.
PE1408.D595 2006
808'.042--dc22

                                                                    2004029651

Please visit our website at http://www.ablongman.com

ISBN: 0-321-33069-2

 2 3 4 5 6 7 8 9 10—QWT—08 07 06

A Preface for Teachers

For three editions, *The Ready Reference Handbook* has provided comprehensive coverage of the writing process, grammar and style, research, and the major forms of academic writing. In its new fourth edition, it now meets the needs of an even wider audience of student writers. With more in-depth guidance to the grammar, style, and rhetoric of American academic English than any other brief handbook, it speaks to the increasingly diverse student body in American college classrooms: traditional students, students learning English in addition to their primary language, those whose primary language is English but whose families speak another language at home—often called "Generation 1.5," and those students whose career success requires global communication skills. *The Ready Reference Handbook* is unique in addressing this multicultural audience as one, recognizing whenever possible the similar needs of developing writers.

New Features

- *Special text features for multicultural classrooms: "Writing in the USA" and "ESL Grammar Notes."* Nearly 70 throughout, these notes show how conventions of American English—especially academic English—differ from those of other languages. These notes will be valuable for students whose primary language is not English, for those who have grown up in homes where another language is spoken—even for native English speakers who need more detailed support for effective writing in the college classroom or who are learning to write in a global context.

- *Guide for Multilingual Writers.* Redesigned and renamed for an enlarged multicultural audience, Part V speaks directly to non-native speakers of English and to "Generation 1.5," focusing on the features of standard written English they find most challenging: articles, verb forms, American English syntax, and prepositions.

- *Critical visual literacy (Chapters 1, 58).* Added to the coverage of critical thinking in Chapter 1, this new section introduces students to basic principles of visual design and provides guidelines for the critical "reading" of images, graphs, and charts. In this chapter and throughout, students learn how to use visuals for appeal and impact to help fulfill the purposes for their writing. Chapter 58 introduces visuals as a form of evidence in argument and shows how visual distortions create "visual fallacies."

- *Online brainstorming (Chapter 2).* Because college composition classrooms are increasingly connected to the Internet for networking, online publishing, and research, Chapter 2 shows students how to use online writing, in chat rooms, for example, as a strategy for topic invention and exploration.

- *Oral presentations (Chapter 62).* This section shows students how to use their writing skills to prepare for effective public speaking.
- *Weblog (Chapters 48, 63).* Chapter 48 introduces students to this important new Internet format and emphasizes both the promises and pitfalls of Weblogs as research resources. Chapter 63 provides guidelines for effective Weblog design and style.
- *Companion Website icons.* Listed on the tabbed section dividers and placed marginally throughout each chapter, these annotated icons direct students to important Internet links, expanded topic coverage, and exercises on *The Ready Reference Handbook* Website.
- *Sleek new design.* A streamlined, simplified layout makes *The Ready Reference Handbook* easier for students to read and easier to navigate as a reference tool for writing and revising.

Expanded Features

- *Self-diagnostic exercises.* Unlike many brief handbooks, *The Ready Reference Handbook* includes brief exercises for diagnostic evaluation and editing practice in standard written English grammar, usage, word choice, sentence structure, and punctuation. For the fourth edition, the number of exercises has been increased to over 40. Answers to these exercises appear in an appendix at the end of the handbook. Additional exercises are available both in the *Exercise Book to Accompany The Ready Reference Handbook* and on the Companion Website.
- *Companion Website.* The new Website provides Internet links important to student writers, detailed guides to specific kinds of academic and public writing, additional student sample papers and exercises, and a wide range of other student and instructor resources. Most exciting is the new **ESL Help Desk**, which includes not only general Web resources and practice exams for multilingual writers, but language-specific guidance for speakers of the ten most prevalent languages in the US (Spanish, French, Russian, Polish, Arabic, Farsi, Japanese, Chinese, Thai, and Vietnamese.)
- *"How-To" boxes.* Expanded to meet the needs of both traditional and multilingual students, more than 50 handy, quick-reference boxes provide practical, process-oriented, easy-to-follow tips for writing and revising. Emphasizing "small-steps" instruction, they break the most complex activities into manageable, "do-able" procedures.

Widely Praised Features

- *Comprehensive coverage.* More comprehensive than most compact handbooks, *The Ready Reference Handbook* is filled with detailed guidance showing students how to evaluate the writing situation, understand their audiences, choose an appropriate purpose, find and develop topics, write "revisable" first drafts, and then revise, edit, and proofread so their documents develop the polish appropriate to academic and public writing. Students learn the contents, style, and design requirements for effective research projects, argument and persuasion, writing about literature, business writing, and writing online.

- *Encouraging tone.* The friendly voice and positive advice encourage students throughout the writing process and in a variety of writing situations.

- *"Focus on . . . " boxes.* Located on the tabbed dividers, these boxes focus attention on student writers' most important questions and activities and highlight "must read" sections in each part of the handbook.

- *Many examples, illustrations, and models.* Throughout, students will find full-length examples of student writing that model successful writing strategies: an expository essay, an MLA-style research paper, an APA-style formal report, an argumentative/persuasive essay, a literary analysis, and numerous examples of professional and online writing.

- *Up-to-date research strategies.* The Ready Reference Handbook presents the latest information about library research tools, Internet resources, and documentation guidelines for MLA, APA, CMS, and CBE papers. A separate chapter on avoiding plagiarism (Chapter 51) provides students with guidelines for using sources fairly, effectively, and appropriately when drafting a research paper. Numerous examples of fair, full, and effective documentation are included.

- *Emphasis on the features of effective writing.* Each chapter emphasizes the features of good writing that matter most to writers and readers: clear, accurate sentences; vivid word choice; focus; the writer's voice; audience awareness; economy; and coherence.

- *Integrated technology.* Individual sections cover researching the Internet, evaluating Internet sources, document design, writing online, Netiquette, discussion groups, Weblogs, and Web page creation. Numerous **Computer Tips** show students how to use computers effectively throughout the writing process. And new marginal icons direct students to the robust Companion Website.

Ancillaries

- *Exercise Book.* Separately published, this student supplement is keyed to the handbook and offers more than 100 exercises in critical thinking, reading, and viewing; topic "invention," persona creation, organizing, paragraphing, grammar, usage, diction, punctuation, style, research, Internet use, avoidance of plagiarism, and argument.

- *Companion Website.* This site comes complete with chapter summaries, study questions, teaching resources, sample student papers, and links to related Internet sites, as well as extensive ESL resources.

■ *MyCompLab.* To see the complete list of supplements available upon adoption of *The Ready Reference Handbook,* please visit this book's online catalog page, which can be accessed from www.ablongman.com.

Acknowledgments

As in the three editions preceding, the best features of this fourth edition of *The Ready Reference Handbook* are the result of a warm collaboration. To all those who have given their expertise, care, and critical eyes, I offer heartiest thanks. Many friends and colleagues at Harper College have given me encouragement, wise advice, and lots of classroom testing: Helen Allen, James Andres, Pauline Buss, Barbara Butler, Anne Davidovicz, Julie Fleenor, Tony Hammer, Kurt Hemmer, Jack Hendriksen, Barbara Hickey, Carol Jakimow, Rich Johnson, Meera Kannan, Karen Keres, Tony Laouras, Xilao Li, Fran Martin, Bill Myers, Kurt Neumann, Kris Piepenburg, Rosemary Shellander, Martha Simonsen, Peter Sherer, Joseph Sternberg, Josh Sunderbruch, and Andrew Wilson. I am also grateful for the many helpful suggestions provided by my colleagues at other colleges: James Allen, College of DuPage; Colleen Brice, Grand Valley State University; Kurt Hemmer, William Rainey Harper College; George F. Horneker, Arkansas State University; John Hyman, American University; Kathleen Lazarus, Daytona Beach Community College; Martin Maner, Wright State University; Paul Kei Matsuda, University of New Hampshire; Carol Numrich, Columbia University; Trisha O'Connor, Delta College; Melinda Reichelt, University of Toledo; Christine Tardy, DePaul University; Jo Fauts Zausch, Jefferson Community College; and Laura W. Zlogar, University of Wisconsin-River Falls. Special thanks to all at Longman Publishers whose enterprise, resources, and energy guided this revision: Lai T. Moy (my hard-working development editor now for two editions), Joseph Vella, Ginny Blanford, and Joseph Opiela. And, of course, at home and always, there's Judy.

JACK DODDS

PART I

The Writing Process

FOCUS ON . . . the Composing Process

COMPOSING

PARAGRAPHING

ON THE WEB   www.ablongman.com/dodds

Writing

Composing

1 Becoming a Critical Writer

For many people, "critical" is a word with a bad reputation, associated in their minds with faultfinding, nit-picking, and negativity. But it has a much broader and more positive meaning, one important to writers of all kinds. *Critical* comes from a Greek word meaning "to discern or perceive, to separate, to understand." To be critical, therefore, means to look carefully at something, to discover its parts and what it's made of, and then, sometimes, to evaluate—positively or negatively. And to become a critical writer means applying these critical skills to whatever writing situation you find yourself involved in.

HOW TO . . . Identify a Critical Thinker

Are you a critical thinker? Put a check (✓) before each trait you possess.

- ■ _____ I'm inquisitive. I ask questions of myself or others. I ask questions while I'm reading or looking at things.
- ■ _____ I like to be well informed about all kinds of topics.
- ■ _____ I trust my powers of reasoning to help me think clearly.
- ■ _____ I'm open minded. I like to hear what others have to say, even when I disagree with them.
- ■ _____ I'm flexible. I'm willing to reconsider and even, sometimes, to change my mind.
- ■ _____ I'm usually honest about myself—what I think, want, and feel.
- ■ _____ I challenge my own assumptions.

Researchers have discovered that critical thinkers possess these traits. With practice, you can acquire them and improve your own critical thinking. Here's an incentive: These researchers have learned that critical thinkers have higher GPAs than noncritical thinkers do.

1a Think critically about information, ideas, and opinions

What goes into your writing may come from your own knowledge or experience, or from a book or some other source. Wherever they come from, these details, ideas, and opinions will come to you in clumps or in bits and pieces, and you may be uncertain about their accuracy or meaning or doubtful about their value. To sort things out, see the connections, and decide what things add up to, you'll employ the four methods of critical thinking described on the following pages. You'll use these methods whenever you write—in school, in your career, in your personal life.

🌐 WRITING IN THE USA Academic Goals and Expectations

In many American college classrooms the goal is not only the transmission of knowledge from teacher to student but also critical thinking about that knowledge. Your instructors expect you to reason carefully, form opinions, and present your opinions in class discussion. It is not rude to disagree with others, if you do so politely: *I understand your point, but . . . .* You should also expect that instructors will pose questions for which they don't have ready answers.

1 ▪ Analyzing

When you analyze something, you take it apart and describe it, part by part, according to some specific interest, in order to understand it. If a literature teacher asks you to analyze a short story, you may describe the role that each character plays, divide the plot into a series of related events, or explain why the characters behave as they do. Your interest in character relationships, the action of the story, or human motivation determines what you see as you make your analysis.

- ▪ *Descriptive analysis.* When you describe the roles played by the various characters in a short story, you're making a descriptive analysis. You are assigning each character a part in the story and describing how that character plays his or her part, based on the contents of the story. A botanist who describes a newly discovered plant species part by part—root, stem, leaves, and flower—is also making a descriptive analysis.

- ▪ *Process analysis.* To divide an event or activity into stages or steps and then describe their relationships is to make a process analysis. A recipe for chicken enchiladas is a kind of process analysis: first do this, then this, then this. A sports reporter who writes a play-by-play account of a basketball game is writing a process analysis.

- *Causal analysis.* To examine events as patterns of cause and effect is to make a causal analysis. A naturalist who sets out to explain why the forests of Shenandoah National Park are slowly dying and discovers the reasons in automobile air pollution has made a causal analysis, reasoning backward from effects to causes. An urban planner who considers the traffic consequences of a new highway is reasoning forward, from causes to their potential effects.

To think analytically about something, choose from questions 1, 2, and 3 in the "How to Think Critically" box (pp. 6–7). As you analyze a topic, be sure to describe *all* of its parts and to apply your interests—your principles of analysis—consistently. For example, your analysis of the death of a forest would be incomplete and ineffective if you omitted some of the regions affected or some of the causes, or if you confused the effects of automobile pollution with those of harmful insects.

2 ▪ Interpreting

To interpret means to explain, decode, or bring to light. When you interpret something, you're reading between the lines, whether those "lines" are the actual lines of a difficult short story or poem, the confusing behavior of a person you know, or the reasons for some mysterious phenomenon. You're looking for "hidden meanings" that will remain hidden until you reveal them through interpretation. Where are you likely to find these hidden meanings?

- *Assumptions.* To read printed texts—or people—successfully, try to discover their assumptions, the basic, often untested beliefs that influence their outlook, opinion, or behavior. A person who argues that "The US government should temporarily halt legal immigration because our economy cannot absorb any more new immigrants" is assuming but not actually saying that immigrants drain economic resources rather than adding to them or having no effect.

- *Patterns.* When you're trying to understand something, look for patterns—regularities or repetitions in information, design, language, or occurrence. Patterns often reveal the meaning of what you're studying. Imagine an acquaintance who, you have noticed, speaks constantly about money: how much he has or doesn't have, other people's salaries, the cost of this or that, the dangers of inflation. You probably would base your interpretation of his personality on his overriding concern with money, guessing his values and predicting his future behavior accordingly.

- *Implications.* An implication is a connection, usually unstated, between one thing and another. Often printed texts and people don't come right out and say exactly what they mean. Instead, they imply something—that is, they suggest or point in a certain direction. To discover implications, ask yourself, "Where is this train of thought going? What is the next logical step?" What, for example, are the implications of a national welfare policy that requires single parents to look for a job in order to qualify for financial aid but does not provide day care funds for the children of those parents?

When your subject matter requires interpretation, choose from questions 2 through 7 in the "How to Think Critically" box (pp. 6–7). You'll express the results of your interpretation as an **inference**—that is, a statement of meaning based on your understanding of the available information. To state—or "draw"—an inference, you bring together all assumptions, patterns, and implications to see what they add up to. Using reasoning, you state an idea that didn't exist or wasn't apparent before your interpretation. For example, in a literary essay interpreting a poem (see 60g), student Leslie Kelly investigates the language, assumptions, and actions of a character in the poem to discover why he commits what appears to be a cold, heartless act. What she discovers (her interpretation) is summed up in her inference about what motivates his behavior.

3 ■ Evaluating information and opinions

When you evaluate, you do more than state personal opinions or subjective preferences regarding a topic—a movie, an automobile, a book, a political speech. When you evaluate, you measure something against widely shared **standards of value** that indicate whether it is good or not so good. To write effectively, you'll evaluate all that goes into your writing to see that it is useful and trustworthy.

■ *Facts and statistics.* A fact is something that can be verified. The statement "State governments used public lotteries during the American Revolution to fund the Continental Army" sounds like a fact, as does "Per capita sales of lottery tickets are higher in poor, urban neighborhoods than in the suburbs." You can check these statements in history books and public records to see whether they're true. To decide whether you and other writers are using facts effectively, apply these four standards (known as *Rules of Evidence*):

1. **Sufficiency**—are there enough facts to support the point being made?
2. **Relevance**—do these facts actually apply to the situation being considered?
3. **Timeliness**—are these facts up to date?
4. **Variety**—do these facts come from or are they verified by a variety of sources?

■ *Opinions.* An opinion is a statement of belief or a conclusion. Consider these two statements: "Gambling causes an increase in the same hormones in the blood that are seen in drug addicts. Obviously, gambling, like drug usage, is addictive." Both statements sound like facts. The first can be verified by observation and is a fact. The second, however, is an inference—an opinion—based on the first. In your writing, you'll use both facts and opinions, and you'll have to distinguish between them. When you identify an opinion, evaluate its usefulness with these questions:

1. Is this opinion supported by sufficient facts? Mistrust any opinions that aren't.
2. Is the source of this opinion an expert or eyewitness? Be careful with opinions from unqualified sources.
3. What are the opinions of other experts or eyewitnesses? See how they compare.

■ *Examples and anecdotes.* An **example** describes one member of a group in order to explain the whole group (see also 6b5). Here is an example of an example: In order to explain the economic effects of state lotteries on poor people, a writer focuses on one state, Illinois, as an example. By showing what happens in Illinois, the writer intends to suggest what occurs in other states. An **anecdote** is a brief story that makes a point. Examples and anecdotes are vivid ways to explain or support a point because they help readers see what you mean. To use them effectively, ask yourself this question: Does my example or anecdote really represent what it is supposed to illustrate? Reconsider the example at the beginning of this paragraph and ask yourself: Is Illinois really like other states in its lottery-marketing expenditures, in the amount of money that poor people spend on the lottery, and in the social and economic effects of this type of gambling?

4 ■ Synthesizing

When information and opinions come from a variety of sources, you have to synthesize them to make them useful. *Synthesis* comes from a Greek word meaning "to put together, to integrate, to blend." When you synthesize facts, ideas, and opinions, you choose among them and put together your choices to express *your* ideas and support *your* opinions. *Your* thinking becomes the focus.

To prepare a research paper on overcrowding in US national parks, student Eric Martínez (see Chapter 54) read books, articles, and Internet sources, interviewed US Park Service officials, and drew on his own experiences. He gathered information about the effects of visitors on the environment, on park facilities, and on one another. He also gathered a variety of opinions about what should be done about these crowds. He didn't reject conflicting opinions or eliminate those he disagreed with. He evaluated them, selected the best supported and most reasonable, and showed what was wrong with the others. From all his research, he drew inferences and formed his own opinions about the best solutions to the problem. Like most research papers, his is the result of synthesis.

To synthesize effectively, follow these guidelines:

■ *Make a working bibliography.* When you take materials from two or more sources, list your sources, including complete publication information (see 47e2). You may make this list an annotated bibliography by adding brief statements about the content and quality of each source (see 47e3).

■ *Compare sources.* Notice similarities and differences in your sources' use of key terms, in their thinking, and in their use of facts and opinions. Try to classify or group your sources. To help yourself make useful comparisons, ask question 4 in the "How to Think Critically" box.

■ *Choose the best sources.* Use the guidelines in 49a. Consider how your readers will respond to the sources you've chosen. Decide how to respond to sources you disagree with.

■ As you write, blend your sources smoothly, so they support your ideas and opinions clearly and coherently (see 50c and 51a and b).

Note: When you synthesize, you gather information from a variety of sources to support your ideas. When you summarize, you present a brief digest of another person's ideas in your own words. A good synthesis makes frequent use of summary. (See also 49e2.)

HOW TO . . . Think Critically

Use these questions to guide your critical thinking.

1. What are the parts of (your topic)? How do they fit or work together? What larger topic is (your topic) a part of? How is it similar to or different from other topics?

    In Charlotte Perkins Gilman's short story "The Yellow Wall-Paper," what are the traits of the narrator's relationship with her husband? [a question about parts]

    How do the effects of visitor overcrowding compare to other environmental threats to US national parks? [a question of comparison]

1.1
Critical
thinking:
Web links

2. What is the environment or background of (your topic)? Where does it come from?

    What is the history of government aid to dependent children in the United States?

3. What is happening to (your topic)? What are the causes of its change? What are the effects of this change? Who is affected? How? What will stop the process?

1.2
Critical
thinking:
Exercises

What causes the narrator's insanity in Charlotte Perkins Gilman's "The Yellow Wall-Paper"?

How have poor people in the United States been affected by reform of the welfare laws? Who has benefited most from welfare reform? Who has benefited least?

4. What is known for a fact about (your topic)? What do the experts or eyewitnesses think? What assumptions or biases influence their view of the facts? Where do they disagree? Which opinions are best supported or most reasonable?

Who are the homeless in the United States?

5. What is missing from the information about (your topic)?

Why does the narrator of William Stafford's poem "Traveling Through the Dark" display so little feeling when he discovers the dead deer on the highway?

6. How are you involved with (your topic)? What bias might influence your thinking?

Why do I automatically become suspicious and skeptical when supposedly homeless panhandlers ask me for spare change?

7. What should be done about (your topic)? Who will do it? What will it cost?

What will repair the environmental harm caused by visitors to US national parks?

1b Read critically

Some reading can be done in the relaxed, casual way you watch television. But the reading you do for school, on the job, or about important issues calls for greater attention and care. Ideas won't leap off the page with dramatic clarity, and you won't always be able to tell at a glance whether something that looks plausible really is.

1 ▪ Previewing

Before you begin reading a book or other source, look it over briefly to determine its content and to see whether it meets your needs. Skim the title page, preface, introduction, headings, boxed text, and graphics. Look for the following:

- The major topics of the source.

- Patterns of organization. Common patterns of organization are time order, part by part or step by step, comparison, thesis/support, problem/solution.

- Information about the author. Try to discover the writer's experiences, opinions, or organizational affiliations that reveal point of view or possible bias.

- The purpose of the source and whether it suits your purpose.

- Quality indicators that reveal whether the source is trustworthy and whether readers will respond favorably to it if you refer to it in your writing. Evaluate a source according to the guidelines in 49a.

2 ■ Reading to understand

As you read important or challenging texts, ask yourself questions like the ones in the "How to Think Critically" box (pp. 6–7). Look for answers by following these guidelines:

- *Analyze your reading* by identifying its true topic. Look for the clearest, fullest statement of the writer's point or message. Identify the writer's purpose: to inform, to persuade, to entertain. Note how the writer develops or argues his or her point: with personal experience, facts, reasoning, examples, opinions, or testimony. Gauge how much of the presentation is factual and how much is opinion.

- *Interpret* by slowing down when you come to the "hard" parts. Reread. Look up new words. Read for the meaning hidden between the lines (see 1b3). Restate the writer's ideas in your own words; compare your version with the original source to be sure you've read accurately.

- *Synthesize sources* if you're reading more than one source on the topic. Compare the cases they make for their opinions. Do they agree? If not, where do they disagree? Who seems to have the best information? Do they use the same facts but reach different conclusions? If so, can you explain their reasoning?

- *Evaluate your reading* by asking whether the writer has presented a plausible case. Can you think of other, equally plausible possibilities? Has anything been left out? Look for charged or biased language that may reveal blurred thinking. Test the writer's reasoning by applying the rules of evidence: sufficiency of support for opinions, relevance of support, timeliness, and variety of sources (see pp. 4–5).

1.3
Critical
reading
checklist:
Web link

While reading your source, also "read yourself." The material before you, no matter how fair or objective its author may be, has been selected and organized to represent a point of view or support an opinion. It is not neutral, and neither are you. When you read, you select and organize the materials to make them meaningful by using your own assumptions, outlook, knowledge, and opinions. Therefore, as you read, pay close attention to your responses and to what is causing them. Note what you don't understand, where you agree or disagree, whether your responses are emotional or intellectual. Ask yourself whether your thoughts and reactions are fair, relevant, and complete.

3 ■ Reading between the lines for implied meanings

Many readers see only the surface of what they read. They read in a two-dimensional way, interpreting words literally as they go along, assuming that the writer's sole purpose is to communicate. But much of the reading you'll do in college—and outside, too—is "thick" reading, packed full of opinions, feelings, judgments, and purposes suggested by the words but buried beneath their surface meaning, the way an iceberg's bulk lies mostly beneath the surface of the ocean. To discover this hidden meaning, read in three dimensions, looking between the lines of a text. Look for:

- *References.* Writers develop their ideas by referring to persons, places, or things involved with those ideas. An environmentalist writing about air pollution in national parks will, no doubt, *refer* to specific parks and specific sources of pollution, such as snowmobiles. Ask yourself what "picture" the writer is giving you by making specific references. Is it positive or negative?

- *Associations.* Writers choose words that suggest associations not directly related to the words but involved with their topics. The word *snowmobile* is associated, among other things, with winter, sports, speed, and noise. Ask yourself whether the associations you have with a word are positive or negative.

- *Connotations.* Some words come with what has been called a "halo" of emotional associations (see 25b). If you like tests, the word *quiz* probably has positive connotations for you; if you don't enjoy them, well, the connotations are negative. As you read, ask yourself what feelings are conveyed by the language.

- *Allusions.* Sometimes writers will refer to a person, place, or thing without mentioning it directly. These veiled references, known as *allusions,* help to create positive or negative responses to a topic, but without the commitment and obviousness of direct references. To say, "Peter's life is one long series of 'To be or not to be' speeches" is to make an allusion to Shakespeare's indecisive Hamlet and to suggest, indirectly, that Peter is equally indecisive.

- *Figurative language.* Figures of speech, such as metaphors, similes, and analogies, are nonliteral comparisons that, all at once, can paint a picture, express a feeling, and make a judgment (see 26c and d). To say that bicycles are part of the urban ecosystem is to create a metaphor comparing cities to natural environments and to suggest that bicycles belong naturally in cities, in the same way that plants and animals belong in a forest.

- *Irony and sarcasm.* These are patterns of reversal, words that mean one thing literally but that are expressed in such a way as to convey the opposite meaning. When a batter strikes out in the bottom of the ninth inning, a spectator might taunt sarcastically, "Sweet swing!"

For an example of how to read between the lines, consider the following famous words spoken by Martin Luther King, Jr., as he stood before the Lincoln Memorial, pleading for the passage of new civil rights laws:

An analogy

References to America's founding documents

An allusion to words from The Declaration of Independence.

> In a sense we have come to our nation's capital to cash a check. When the architects of our republic wrote the magnificent words of the Constitution and the Declaration of Independence, they were signing a promissory note to which every American was to fall heir. This note was the promise that all men—yes, Black men as well as white men—would be guaranteed the inalienable rights of life, liberty, and the pursuit of happiness.

Now King could have said simply, "African-Americans are equal to white Americans and deserve the same civil rights." He would have been clear but these words would not have been as vivid nor as meaningful as his actual words. Comparing the campaign for civil rights to cashing a check, King makes his campaign seem natural, a fair demand for what one already possesses. And, by considering these rights as property, something all Americans are "heir" to, he implies that all Americans belong to the same family—one nation. Finally, introducing his allusion to the most famous words of the Declaration as a "promise," a word echoing the term "promissory note" that precedes it, he counts on our association with phrases such as "promises are made to be kept." King uses such "thick" language to declare the justice of his campaign and to locate his actions squarely within American history and American values. To see all that a writer means, you must read in this way, for both implications and literal meanings.

4 ▪ Annotating your reading

People who read a lot know that the best way to understand their reading is to annotate it—highlighting important passages and jotting brief notes. True, they don't annotate everything they read, but if it's important or challenging, they do. So should you. You might jot your notes on a sheet of paper, notecard, "stickie pad," computerized notes file, or photocopy of the sources you're reading. You don't have to be elaborate or use colored highlighters, but you should keep a record of your understanding of a source and your reactions to it.

🌎 WRITING IN THE USA Reading for Writing

Annotating what you read will help prepare you for writing about what you read. On page 12 is an example of one student's annotations. Eric Martínez investigated problems of overcrowding in US national parks and, while doing his research, learned of a controversial proposal to ban snowmobiles from Yellowstone National Park. Looking into the debate over this proposal, he discovered a Web site opposing the ban. Consider how Eric's underlining and marginal notes reveal his critical thinking as he analyzes, interprets, and evaluates the information in the document and synthesizes it with information from other sources. If English is not your primary language, you might consider making annotations in your primary language.

HOW TO . . . Annotate Your Reading

Highlighting. Use the following symbols to highlight sources you own, photocopies, and, when possible, computer files.

_____	Underline key words and phrases. Also underline "clue" words and phrases that indicate relationships between ideas, suggest the importance of a passage, or indicate the author's evaluation: *to conclude, fortunately, in all fairness, on the other hand*, and so forth.
|	Draw a vertical line next to important passages that you may want to quote or summarize in your own writing.
?	Place a question mark next to unfamiliar words or passages you don't understand.
+ or –	Use a plus or minus sign for passages you agree or disagree with.
*	Use an asterisk for passages an author wants you to respond to.
1, 2, 3, etc.	Number ideas in sequence or use arrows to connect related ideas.
ZZZZ	Identify where your attention drifts or you lose interest, and ask yourself why.
X-ref	Note cross-references to other sources containing related ideas. Marginally note the author of the cross-reference or other identifying information.

Notes. In the text's margins or elsewhere if the source does not belong to you, jot brief summaries of important passages, questions you have, musings, reactions, ideas about how you'll use information from your reading in your writing.

1.4
Critical
reading:
Exercises

COMPUTER TIP Annotating Computer Files

Print computer files and annotate them as you would a photocopy. Or, paste these files into a word processing file to open and add highlighting symbols or insert notes as you would to any other text file. However, be
(continued on page 13)

Snowmobiles in National Parks

◁ Back ✕ Stop ▷ Forward ⌂ Home ✉ Mail

Address @ http://www.antc.org

Protect your access to America's public lands.

American Nature Trails Conservancy

Fight the snowmobile ban in Yellowstone National Park!

April 23, 2005

Snowmobiles banned!
If partisan environmental groups have their way in Washington, snowmobiles will be banned from Yellowstone and 385 other US National Parks; over 700 miles of America's most scenic trails will be closed to avid nature lovers.

Rights denied!
Snowmobilers represent the largest group of winter visitors to National Parks. (185,000 visits a year), but legalistic restrictions will reduce our visits to a trickle. Our taxes have bought, paid for, and maintain our cherished public lands. A snowmobile ban denies our right of access.

Freedom threatened!
Alternatives to snowmobiles in Yellowstone are unsatisfactory. The elderly and disabled are unable to cross-country ski. And snow coaches–nothing more than buses on skis–turn park visitors into passive observers, forced to travel with the herd. This isn't outdoor living; this isn't freedom; this isn't exhilaration; this isn't being active.

True facts told!
Modern snowmobiles powered by four-stroke engines are environmentally friendly–cleaner, quieter, more efficient. Mt. Rainier National Park rangers report, snowmobiles "have minimal effects in wilderness areas and create far fewer effects than park officials previously claimed."

Snowmobiling is a $7 billion-a-year sport in the United States. Banning snowmobiles from Yellowstone would be an economic catastrophe for the region, costing millions of dollars of tourist revenue and hundreds of jobs.

Protect your rights!
Join with the American Nature Trails Conservancy, Citizens for Park Access, Wild Forests Preservation, and Wild Paths Forever. Call, write, or e-mail your legislators today. Tell them: Snowmobilers are voters too!

The flag and the colors appeal to patriotism and environmentalism.
[Interpreting graphics]

Note charged language.
[Evaluation]

X-ref. American Council of Snowmobilers identifies 230,000 miles of US snowmobile trails.
[Synthesis]

Does the payment of taxes give people rights?
[Analysis]

A good point! I don't like to be "herded" either!
[Personal response]

What does this term mean?
[Analysis]

These claims don't seem relevant.
[Evaluation]

Who are these organizations?
[Analysis]

sure to use some clearly identifiable method of separating your words from your source's words, such as a row of asterisks (********) or some other keyboard symbol typed at the beginning and end of a note.

Note: some word processing files have "stickie pad" utilities you can use to attach notes to computer files. ▪

1c View images critically

1 ▪ Reading the "language" of images

Perhaps the most famous photograph from America's Great Depression is Dorothea Lange's "Migrant Mother," shot in 1936 at a California migrant workers' camp. Speaking of this photo and others she took during this difficult era, Lange declared, "I am trying here to say something about the despised, the defeated, the alienated. About death and disaster, about the wounded, the crippled, the helpless, the rootless, the dislocated. About finality. About the last ditch." When this photograph appeared in a San Francisco newspaper, it prompted an outpouring of donations earmarked for the camp in which Lange had photographed.

What enabled Lange's photo to "say" what she intended? And what moved its viewers to "read" what she had "said" and respond so sympathetically? The answer is the mother and her children, of course, but also the photographic techniques Lange uses. Together, subject matter and technique constitute a "language" of images employed by image makers of all kinds—photographers, movie makers, advertisers, advocates for a cause, scholars, and Web designers. To "read" an image and understand its message, consider the following.

Subject matter. What do you see in Dorothea Lange's photo? The image is captioned "Destitute peapickers in California. Mother of seven children. Age thirty-two. Nipomo, California." Look closely.

Frame and context. Literally speaking, a frame surrounds an image and helps us focus on what's important. It may be something outside the image—a wooden frame or the border of a photographic print—or it may exist within the image itself. In "Migrant Mother," something vertical on the right side of the image obscures the baby's head and most of the child on the right, so our attention is focused on the woman at the center.

An image is also framed by its context, the background or history that we can use to understand what we're seeing. "Migrant Mother" was the sixth in a series Lange took of the mother and her children at the end of a long day of photography. The two women exchanged few words; Lange did not even get her subject's name. Only later was the woman identified as Florence Owens Thompson, a Cherokee Indian from Oklahoma, who at times during the Depression was involved in farm labor struggles and even acted as a labor organizer. Does knowing this information change your interpretation of Thompson's expression? Do you think she is experiencing despair, uncertainty, determination, or something else?

Point of view. Point of view refers to the physical location from which a viewer views something: in front of, to the side, above, below, near, far. But it may also mean the cultural and psychological background of a viewer. Together, our physical, cultural, and psychological points of view determine what we see as we look at something. If, for example, you are a parent or female, or have experienced despair or uncertainty, you probably view "Migrant Mother" differently than others who are non-parents or male, or who have had happier experiences.

Now consider another image from Lange's series of photos (see below), taken before she came close to the mother. Lange's oblique angle and her distance from her subjects cause her camera to record a very different image. "Migrant Mother" draws attention to the mother and her state of mind. What draws your attention in this other image?

Line, shape, and composition. An image consists of lines and shapes that both present an image and guide our eyes as we look at it. Certain lines and shapes carry with them emotional associations and cul-

tural meanings. In our society, horizontal lines suggest repose, vertical lines suggest stasis, and diagonal lines suggest movement, instability, action, and change. Circles are often associated with what is female, as well as with calm feelings and optimistic attitudes. Triangles are often associated with conflict and tension. What lines and shapes create the figures in "Migrant Mother"? Describe the path your eyes follow as you view Lange's photo. What do you see first? Second? What feelings do these lines and shapes convey?

Color, tone, and texture. *Color*—or the lack of it—helps to focus a viewer's eye and to express specific emotional meanings. We divide colors into warm (red, yellow, orange) and cool (blue and green). Specific colors can have specific associations. Consider the red, white, blue, and green colors in the Web site announcement on p. 12. What messages do these colors suggest? *Tone* refers to the amount of light in an image. Like line and shape, tone guides the viewer's eye. *Texture* refers to our sense that visual objects are rough or smooth. In "Migrant Mother," where is the tone brightest? What feelings do you have for this family as you consider the rough textures of their clothing?

Scale. Scale, the proportion in size between objects in an image, can indicate importance. The larger something is, the greater its importance and power. In Lange's photograph of the family in their tent, the daughter in the rocker and the luggage in the foreground are scaled larger than the mother and the other children in the background. What's important here seems different from what's important in "Migrant Mother."

Focus. The "focus" of an image is created by such features as line, shape, color, and scale, and also by the position of elements within it. Certain points within an image are natural focal points. One is the *optical center,* located about one-third of the way down from the top of the image. In "Migrant Mother," the mother's eyes occupy the optical center of the photo, so her gaze naturally commands much of our attention.

In well-crafted images such as this, other focal points are created by the *rule of thirds,* by which four imaginary intersecting lines divide an image into vertical and horizontal thirds. The points at which these lines meet tend to be points of emphasis. Consider how the "rule of thirds" helps to move our eyes around the family circle that is the subject of the photo.

Nonliteral features. Some images or their parts are meaningful but not meant to be taken literally. Consider the flag in the snowmobiling Web site on p. 12. It represents more than a rectangular, tricolored object, more even than the emblem of the United States. What message does it convey about the creators of this Web site and the value of their opinions? Here the US flag is a *visual symbol* that conveys multiple meanings.

1.5
Persuasive
strategies
on the Web:
Web link

HOW TO . . . View an Image Critically

1. Look at the entire image first. Identify its key features and examine the details of each feature. Identify the physical point of view. What lines and shapes compose the image? How do they guide your eyes? What is the focus of attention?

2. Consider the context of images. Read titles and captions; do additional investigation if necessary. Who created the images? When? Where? Who sponsored them? What points of view, motives, or beliefs guided the creators? Do you share their points of view? If not, how are yours different?

3. Examine the techniques of presentation. What impressions are conveyed by color, texture, light, and scale? Can you tell whether the image has been cropped, omitting features? How does this manipulation change the focus and alter your response? Consider special effects and how they magnify, minimize, distort, or omit features. How do these changes affect your response?

4. Identify the purpose behind the image: to inform, express or stimulate feelings, evaluate, persuade, or entertain. Has the image fulfilled its purpose for you? If not, why not?

5. Sum up the point or message of the image. Does this message seem fair, logical, appropriate? Do you agree with it? If not, why not? If the image accompanies written text, how does it support that text? Does the image or its context contain anything that contradicts the message of the image? If so, how?

2 ■ Reading graphs and charts

In school, on the job, and in your private life, you encounter graphs and charts displaying numerical information for the purposes of explanation and comparison. When you're presented with materials like these, treat them as if they are visual arguments. Analyze and evaluate them to

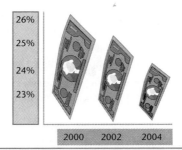

Note. Share of family income among low-income families required for tuition at public universities.

be sure they are accurate, complete, and fair. Here, for example, a special-effects bar graph reports the tuition expenses of college students from low-income families. At a glance, you might conclude that for poorer students, a college education is becoming *less* expensive. But look and think critically: Perhaps these students are using other sources to pay their tuition—grants or scholarships, perhaps, or loans that will need to be repaid at a later date.

Now look more closely and evaluate the message. The height of the dollar bills accurately reflects the two percent decline in family spending from 2000 to 2004—but their comparative sizes falsely suggest that families in 2004 spent *less than half* of what families spent in 2000. That's because the graph only shows a total range of four percent. If it began at 0 rather than at 23%, the size differential between the bills would be much, much smaller. This graph is an example of what's known as a **visual fallacy**. A fair, complete graph would send a very different message about trends in college tuition expenses for low-income people.

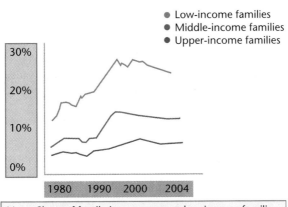

Note. Share of family income among low-income families required for tuition at public universities.

> ## HOW TO . . . Read Graphs and Charts
>
> - Read the accompanying label above or below the graphic. What information is being displayed, and how does it relate to surrounding text?
> - Identify the purpose of the graphic: to inform, evaluate, or persuade. Consider the source of the graphic. Can you identify any bias that might influence its design?
> - Decide the point of the graphic. Avoid drawing conclusions that the graphic does not support.
> - Evaluate the presentation of the information. Is the graphic fair and accurate in design?
> - Evaluate the context of the information. Has information been presented selectively or relevant details omitted?

1d Write critically: survey the writing situation

When you have a writing project, make preliminary plans by considering what you need to do. The following questions will help you analyze and evaluate a project before you actually begin writing. You may not be able to answer all of these questions at once, and some of your answers may change as these project unfolds. That's natural. But use the answers to guide your writing.

1 ▪ The subject and the assignment

- Has your topic been given to you as part of an assignment? Can you adapt the topic to your interests? If you have to choose a topic, what is suitable for the assignment?
- What kind of writing does the assignment require: a letter, essay, report, review, or some other form?
- What is the scope of the assignment? Do you have to cover a broad topic? How focused must your writing be because of reader interest or length and time restrictions? How much detail will you have to use?

🌍 WRITING IN THE USA College Writing Topics

Most writing assignments in US colleges ask you to focus on a limited, specific topic and provide as much detail as the allotted time or space allows.

- What do you know about the topic? According to the assignment, what kinds of information should be included: personal experience, facts and figures, or expert opinion? Where will you get your information: from memory, observation, reading, discussion? What experience or bias may affect your view of what you find? If you borrow others' words or ideas, what system of documentation are you required to use?

2 ▪ Your purpose and role

▪ What purpose does the wording of the assignment set for you? Consider instructions such as "Write a personal narrative," "Write an informative essay," "Explain," "Evaluate," and "Take a position." (To learn to interpret the instructions given in writing assignments, see 61a.)

▪ What writer's role have your knowledge and personal experience prepared you for? Can you play the role of an **autobiographer** writing about yourself, a **reporter** informing readers, a **teacher** explaining ideas or procedures, a **critic** making an evaluation, or a **persuader** arguing for a position, or some combination of these? Deciding on the appropriate role to play in your writing will help you find your writer's voice, strike the appropriate relation with your readers, and choose appropriate strategies for writing.

3 ▪ Audience

When you were younger, your teachers may have instructed you to write for a "general audience." This is good advice for writers first learning to write publicly. But frequent, successful writers know that no audience is "general." Audiences may be large or small, one or a million readers, but all members of an audience bring to their reading specific knowledge, expectations, opinions, and experiences that influence how they read. As you plan your writing, envision the people in your target audience: Who are they? What do they know about your topic? What do they want or need from you? Ask the questions in the "How to Create an Audience Profile" box on p. 20. Then use your answers to plan how you'll express your ideas to meet your audience's interests and needs.

Consider the informative and argumentative essay on bicycle commuting written by John Chen, a student (see 4f). He knew that most members of his college audience would be motorists, and so, as he planned his writing, he had to consider the opinion of many that bicycles and motorists cannot share the same road safely. In his essay, he had to show that the two really could travel safely together.

A cautionary note: Sometimes, it's not a good idea to think too much about your audience early in a project, when you're exploring a topic or trying to discover your opinions. Doing so may cramp your reasoning or creativity. But as soon as you begin thinking of the actual writing you'll do, consider your readers. Your supporting details, focus, organization, style, and word choice—all these depend on who your readers are and the response you want from them.

HOW TO . . . Create an Audience Profile

1. Classify your readers. Are they (1) **allies** who will accept almost any-thing you write, (2) **potential allies** who need only to be informed to accept your ideas, (3) **disinterested observers** who want infor-mation above all else, (4) **skeptics** who expect careful reasoning and detailed support, (5) **opponents** who require abundant proof and may not accept your ideas even if you provide it?

2. Identify what these readers know about your topic. What assump-tions, biases, or knowledge gaps will influence their responses?

3. Determine what your readers expect from you: personal experience, information, explanation, evaluation, proof, or entertainment. What writing style is appropriate for addressing them, informal or formal?

4. Consider what these readers believe about your sources of informa-tion. Which ones will they accept as authoritative? Which might they reject as superficial, biased, or inaccurate?

WRITING IN THE USA Writing to Diverse Audiences

If you are writing for readers whose language or background differs from yours, carefully consider how their background might influence their reading. You may have to investigate before you write. What kinds of documents are they used to reading? What patterns of organization will they expect—a main idea early or late in the text? What style will they expect—formal or informal, personal or distanced, linear or discursive? What *don't* you know about these readers, and how might you find it out? (See also the "How to Write Effectively to International Readers" box on p. 480.) ■

4 ■ The final draft

- Are there length specifications?

- When is the final draft due? How much time do you have for each stage of your writing: gathering materials, planning, writing, revis-ing, typing, and proofreading?

- What is the appropriate format for your final copy? (For academic writing, see 46a; for business writing, see Chapter 62. For online writing, see Chapter 63.)

2   "Inventing" Your Writing

Through experience and practice, successful writers have made two discoveries that can help you succeed with your writing.

- ■ *Writing is a process.* Writers, like inventors, create their work in stages, not all at once from beginning to end but through trial and error, reflection and discovery, writing and rewriting. The result is not the straightforward transcription of thoughts. That would be dull work. It's a more exciting and experimental process of creating thoughts through written words. "How can I know what I think," asked novelist E. M. Forster, "till I see what I say?" If we could visualize this process all at once, from start to finish, we'd see writers engaged in four activities to which they return again and again, until their writing is finished: exploring, planning, writing, and revising.

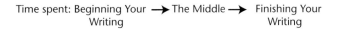

Time spent: Beginning Your ⟶ The Middle ⟶ Finishing Your
Writing   Writing

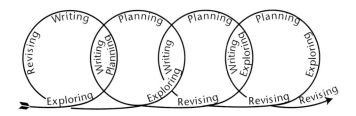

What you write: Notes, Lists, Freewriting, etc. ⟶ Drafts &
Revised Drafts ⟶ the Final Draft

- ■ *There are many ways to write successfully.* It might seem that a book like this teaches one right way to successful writing. But there are many different kinds of writing; writers produce their writing using a variety of technologies, rituals, and strategies; they address many different audiences with a variety of purposes; sometimes they work alone, other times as part of a team. How could one "right" way ever be right for all writers in all situations? What *The Ready Reference Handbook* does is provide you with many writing strategies and information about many writing situations. Explore and experiment; take what you need for the writing you do; find out what works for you.

2.1
Searching
for topics:
Web link

2a Explore possible topics

As you critically survey a writing assignment and begin to see what to do (see 1d), create choices for yourself. Discover what you think about possible topics by doing various kinds of exploratory writing described in the following pages. Find what works best for you in which situations, and adopt these writing strategies to your style and habits.

🖥 COMPUTER TIP Making Templates

For frequent assignments, create master template files that you can reuse every time you begin a new project. Consider templates that will help you explore writing situations and topics: audience profiles, questions to answer about your topics, note taking formats, outline formats, thesis or purpose statements, revision and editing checklists, formats for final drafts. Once you've created and saved an empty template file (named "Audience Profile," for example), all you have to do is open it and begin typing at the appropriate place. Then save your work under a new file name (for example, "Profile 1"). The original, empty template will stay in place for your next project.

1 ▪ Keeping a journal or diary

These daily records of experience, reflection, and opinion can be a valuable source of personally important topics that you may decide to transform into public or academic writing. You may also record quotations or summarize other people's thoughts to reflect upon.

🌏 WRITING IN THE USA Subject Matter in Academic Writing

Cultures differ in what is considered appropriate subject matter for academic writing. In the United States, some composition classes present writing assignments that are personal in nature; you're asked to use your own experiences and opinions to support generalizations about life, or you may use your experience as examples constituting a form of proof in argument—although it is a limited, not a conclusive, form of proof. Personal experience is most useful as evidence when it illustrates a point that can be proven independent of that experience. Make sure you understand whether writing about personal experience is appropriate for a particular assignment.

2.2
Brain-
storming:
Web link

2 ▪ Brainstorming

To brainstorm a topic, simply make free-association lists. Start with a topic or what first comes to mind. Follow wherever your mind leads.

Don't worry if you can't think of much the first time. Lists should be easy and fast. When you finish, underline key words or phrases to explore further.

> Brr! Cold outside
>
> Almost too cold to bike to school this morning-
>
> Snow on the way home-
>
> Wisconsin last spring, caught in a freak April storm
>
> "Just look at you!" cried the woman at the quick mart where I stopped-snow mounded on my helmet, me covered with slush, soaking wet, shaking in the cold
>
> Drivers' strange looks when it's this cold-disbelief, mostly: "What are you doing out there?" their eyes ask.
>
> Actually, I'm doing okay-feeling good in the crisp air. Toes don't get cold till I'm almost to school or home. Easy trip unless there's rain, snow, or headwind.
>
> Pedal, pant, puff-endorphins flowing, a steady 17-18 mph this a.m.
>
> In all that traffic, I'm getting where I'm going just about as fast as the cars are, backed up one after another in endless traffic jams.
>
> Honk, inch ahead, stop, honk, inch ahead
>
> Commuting-bicycle commuting
>
> Good for health, fitness
>
> Good for everybody's health-less pollution, one less car-

This brainstorm may make little sense to anyone but the writer, but if you look, you can see several topics that the writer might explore further, expand, rearrange, and turn into the materials for a full-length writing project.

3 ■ Brainstorming dialogues

The popular image of the writer, working alone, isolated in some private room, is only sometimes accurate. Writers are frequently involved with others, especially at the beginning of a project. As you think about a writing topic, talk to friends, family, fellow students, coworkers, and teachers to get feedback on your ideas. You may discuss your topic face to face—or online, in an e-mail exchange, in an online class discussion, even in a Weblog. (For more about online exchanges, see 63a, b, and c.)

2.3
Collabora-
tive writing:
Web link

Use such discussions not only to lay out and rehearse your ideas but also to sharpen them and find new things to think about. As you talk and listen, consider questions you hadn't asked about your topic, new ways of describing it, opinions or arguments you hadn't heard before, and fresh perspectives. Here, for example, in a composition class chat room, student Jesse Montoya and two fellow students explore Jesse's topic for an upcoming argument paper.

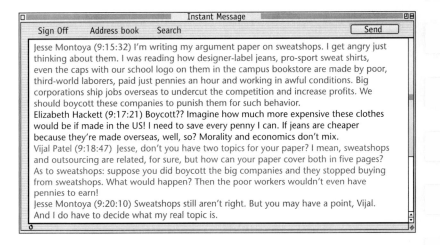

Instant Message

| Sign Off | Address book | Search | | Send |

Jesse Montoya (9:15:32) I'm writing my argument paper on sweatshops. I get angry just thinking about them. I was reading how designer-label jeans, pro-sport sweat shirts, even the caps with our school logo on them in the campus bookstore are made by poor, third-world laborers, paid just pennies an hour and working in awful conditions. Big corporations ship jobs overseas to undercut the competition and increase profits. We should boycott these companies to punish them for such behavior.
Elizabeth Hackett (9:17:21) Boycott?? Imagine how much more expensive these clothes would be if made in the US! I need to save every penny I can. If jeans are cheaper because they're made overseas, well, so? Morality and economics don't mix.
Vijal Patel (9:18:47) Jesse, don't you have two topics for your paper? I mean, sweatshops and outsourcing are related, for sure, but how can your paper cover both in five pages? As to sweatshops: suppose you did boycott the big companies and they stopped buying from sweatshops. What would happen? Then the poor workers wouldn't even have pennies to earn!
Jesse Montoya (9:20:10) Sweatshops still aren't right. But you may have a point, Vijal. And I do have to decide what my real topic is.

4 ■ Topic mapping (clustering and branching)

If you like to visualize what to say before you write, draw a **topic map.** Put a topic in the middle of a sheet of paper, draw a circle around it, and then draw branches that lead to related topics and subtopics. Leave room in case you think of other branches and topics to add later.

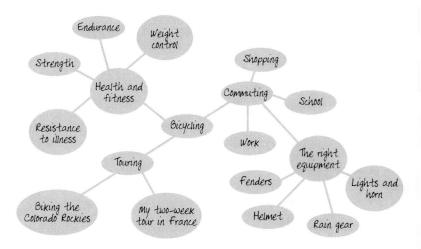

5 ■ Freewriting

Like brainstorming and mapping, **freewriting** is free association on paper. The difference is that, for most people, freewriting expresses thoughts more fully in sentence- and paragraph-length statements and may lead more deeply into a subject. Many writers find freewriting a useful activity throughout the writing process as a way to explore new or challenging ideas. In freewriting, your aims are to loosen up your mind, go where it leads you, and record what it gives you.

Looping, an expanded form of freewriting, will help you focus your thinking and narrow a topic. When you finish a freewriting, read it and look for the central thought or most interesting point. Use that as the opening for a new freewriting. When you finish this second exploration, look again for the central thought or most interesting point. Use that to begin a third exploration. Sometimes you'll circle around a topic, examining it from different perspectives; at other times you'll spiral into a topic, probing it more deeply each time you write.

HOW TO . . . Explore a Writing Topic

1. You can do exploratory writing in two ways. In unfocused explorations, write whatever comes to mind, whether everything connects or not. In focused explorations, try to focus on one topic, unless you get pulled to something more interesting.

2. Set a time limit, usually 7 to 15 minutes. Start writing about whatever comes to mind the moment you begin. Write by hand or use a computer.

3. Don't stop. If your mind suddenly goes blank, write "blank, blank, blank" or repeat your last word until thoughts begin flowing again.

4. Don't censor. Write whatever comes to mind, however strange it sounds. It may lead to something important or powerful. If you don't like what you've written when you finish, you can throw it away.

2.4
Exploring
topics:
Exercises

5. Don't change anything. If you write something one way and think of another way, make a slash (/) and then write the second version.

6. Don't stop to correct mistakes. Don't worry about them. You're only exploring.

 COMPUTER TIP Exploratory Writing

7. If you're having trouble getting started, try darkening the screen and typing your thoughts without looking at them. ▪

---

6 ▪ Choosing a topic

If you've surveyed the writing assignment (see 1d) and explored possible topics, you'll probably see what's best to choose. Or, if you already have a topic, you'll see more clearly what is most interesting about it. A good writing topic has these characteristics:

2.5
Guidelines
for specific
kinds of
writing:
Web link

- *It is important.* A good topic is important to you and your readers.

- *It is fresh.* A good topic is new to you or your readers, or your approach to a familiar topic is fresh. Don't reject topics that at first seem quirky or strange. They may inspire your freshest writing.

- *It is challenging.* Choose topics that challenge your thinking, curiosity, or feeling. Easy topics may lead to boredom for you and your readers.

- *It fits the occasion.* It reflects your interests, meets the assignment, fulfills reader expectations.

2b Focus your writing

Most topics come to writers as an array of possibilities. They are open-ended, broad, general—unfocused. **Focusing** a project means becoming clear about your subject, figuring out what's most important about it, what you want to do with it, and the point you want to make. A reminder: You may not be able to decide everything at once. In fact, if you focus on too much too soon, you may not see important parts of your topic.

1 ■ Narrowing your topic

Most topics discovered in exploratory writing or listed in assignments are too broad for you to cover adequately in the space and time available. Therefore, focus on one narrow part of your topic and on the significance of that part.

2.6
Narrowing
topics:
Exercises

BROAD TOPICS		NARROW TOPICS
My life on the move: from the city to the suburbs	→ What I learned moving 5 times in 18 years	→ What moving has taught me about good people and good communities
My grandmother	→ My grandmother, an old-fashioned artist	→ My grandmother's lost art: bobbin lace making
Bicycling	→ Bicycle commuting	→ How to increase bicycle commuting
America's national parks	→ Snowmobiling in America's national parks	→ The environmental consequences of snowmobiles in America's national parks
Charlotte Perkins Gilman's short story "The Yellow Wall-Paper"	→ The symbolic wallpaper	→ The wallpaper as a reflection of the narrator's state of mind

2 ▪ Writing a purpose statement

After surveying the requirements of the assignment and exploring your ideas, write a tentative **purpose statement**. Briefly tell yourself what you want to accomplish in your writing. This purpose may change as your project unfolds, but writing it out early will guide you.

2.7
Identifying
your
purpose:
Exercises

> *I want to inform urban and suburban readers that, for many, bicycling is a solution to the frustrations of rush-hour commuting.*

This writer's purpose is to inform; the writer's roles are to act as a reporter and a teacher.

3 ▪ Asking questions

Jot down questions based on the reporter's *who, what, when, where, why,* and *how,* or use the critical thinking questions listed in the "How to Think Critically" box (pp. 6–7). Ask other questions relevant to your topic. Your answers might become the materials for your project.

> *Who should become a bicycle commuter?*
> *What problems do bicycle commuters face?*
> *What are the benefits of bicycle commuting?*
> *What are the best conditions for bicycle commuting?*
> *Why do some motorists object to sharing the road with bicyclists?*
> *How can a cyclist begin commuting by bicycle?*
> *How can a community or business begin to encourage bicycle commuters?*

2.8
Asking
questions:
Exercises

2c　Consider your voice (persona)

Everything you write has a **voice**, also called a **persona**. Whether your writing is personal or public, informal or formal, opinionated or objective, whether you appear in your writing (as "I") or not, your writing speaks with your voice. Readers hear it in your words and sentences, in your attitude toward your subject, and in your relationship with them as readers. This voice is the written expression of your personality, and you should write and revise to express that personality. Creating a voice is one of the great pleasures of writing.

But just as you modify the way you speak to suit various occasions, so should you adapt your persona, adjusting it as you would adjust the volume, tone, and balance on a stereo to produce the best sound. Each of these features of a writer's voice can be adjusted toward one or the other end of a spectrum:

FORMALITY	Informal vocabulary ←•→	Formal vocabulary
TONE	Negative attitude ←•→	Positive attitude

| BALANCE | Understatement ←•→ Overstatement |
| MANNER OF ADDRESS | Irony, sarcasm, ←•→ "Straight talk" indirectness |

WRITING IN THE USA Creating a Persona

Writing and speaking are different, but good writing almost always sounds like speech. Write to sound like yourself, speaking in a way that is suitable to the occasion, formal or informal (see 27a–d). Especially if you are not writing in your primary language, establishing your own voice may prove challenging.

- Choose words true to your knowledge and experience. If you are writing in a language other than your primary language, use a learner's dictionary to help you find appropriate words. Worry less about writing impressively than about accuracy.

- Choose positive, negative, and neutral words that accurately communicate your feelings, but also express the objectivity appropriate to the occasion.

- As you revise, read aloud and listen to your sentences. If necessary, rewrite sentences so that they emphasize your most important words and have the rhythms of speech (see Chapter 21).

1 ■ The persona for formal writing

In formal academic and professional writing, aim to sound fair, objective, and relatively serious. Generally, make your style straightforward and to the point. Use "I" to refer to yourself if necessary, but focus on your subject. Avoid slang and most contractions, but don't sound pompous or flowery. Whatever you write should sound like you speaking in a voice suitable to the subject and occasion. (See also 27a.)

2.9
Creating
your voice:
Exercises

WRITING IN THE USA Direct and Linear Writing

Writing in English tends to follow a direct line; the writer establishes a main idea and supports it in a straightforward, linear series of arguments. This way of writing may seem unfamiliar to writers trained in more indirect styles.

2 ■ The persona for personal or informal writing

The more personal your subject, the more informal you can be. In informal writing you have lots of room for variety in vocabulary, attitude, and style of expression. But keep in mind the knowledge and interests of your readers.

2d Write a tentative thesis

When you know enough about the subject and purpose of your writing, write a tentative statement of the point you want to make—your **thesis**. Usually a sentence but sometimes longer, the thesis in its final form will be the primary controlling idea or opinion holding your writing together, the basic message you want your writing to express. It may be any kind of assertion: a factual statement, a generalization, a cause-and-effect statement, an evaluation, a prediction, or a proposal. Consider these thesis statements:

2.10
Developing
a thesis:
Web link

- An informative thesis (an evaluation):

  Bicycles are a safe, practical solution to the problems of rush-hour commuting.

- The theme of an autobiographical essay (cause and effect):

  Moving five times in eighteen years, from a housing project to an apartment building to a house in the suburbs, has given me invaluable knowledge about getting along with people and what makes for good communities.

- A multisentence claim for an argument essay (a proposal):

  Boycotting stores and clothing manufacturers who depend upon sweatshops for their products does not help exploited laborers. To aid these workers, college students should join anti-sweatshop organizations that provide economic aid, publicize the abuses of sweatshops, and identify those who profit from them.

Whatever its topic or assertion, a thesis is usually the most important statement in a piece of writing. At the beginning of a project, it will help you decide what to say. In a later, more detailed version based on the information you've gathered, it will act as a point-to-point map to keep you on course as you write a draft. Still later, as you revise your project, you'll compare your thesis to what you've actually written to see whether your point has remained the same or changed. If it has changed, you'll rewrite the thesis to fit your new discoveries. In the final version the thesis will help readers answer the one question they almost always ask: "So what's the point?"

HOW TO . . . Write a Tentative Thesis

Early in a writing project, begin with the formula *My point is that,* and then follow with a statement that identifies your topic and makes an assertion about it.

My point is that to ease the problems of commuting, federal highway funds and state gasoline taxes should be used to create bicycle lanes on city streets and wide shoulders on secondary roads.

(continued)

If you can't write a thesis early in your project because you don't yet know enough about your topic, write it later, after you've learned what you need to know.

1 ■ Guidelines for writing an effective thesis

As your knowledge grows and your thinking changes, rewrite your thesis following these guidelines:

■ *Making assertions instead of asking questions.* Write a sentence that makes a point or, if necessary, several sentences, but not a question. If all you can write is a question, you're not ready to write a thesis. Answer your question first. Compare these original and revised statements:

ORIGINAL *Are home-schooled students as well educated as students who attend public schools?*

REVISED *Standardized test scores and college graduation rates indicate that home-schooled students are as well educated as students who attend public schools.*

[The revised version is an assertion that answers the question in the original version and identifies the subject matter the writer will cover in her essay.]

■ *Writing a thesis statement instead of a purpose statement.* Be sure to write a thesis statement rather than a purpose statement. A **thesis statement** focuses on your topic and says something about it. A **purpose statement** focuses on your paper and says something about it rather than your topic. Compare these statements:

PURPOSE *In my paper I intend to examine the case against the death penalty.*

THESIS *The death penalty does not deter murderers from their crimes, and it is unfairly applied to the poor and minorities.*

[The purpose statement focuses primarily on the writer and his paper rather than the topic of the paper. The thesis statement makes two assertions that the writer will attempt to prove. The thesis gives his paper focus and direction.]

🌐 WRITING IN THE USA Purpose Statements versus Thesis Statements

In many languages, a purpose statement is necessary to good academic writing. In English, however, purpose statements are rare, and thesis statements are the norm.

■ *Avoiding "So?" statements.* A "So?" thesis is a statement that prompts readers to ask, "So? What's the point?" Do more than announce your topic or state a fact. Make a complete assertion about the cause, consequences, or significance of your topic. Or state what should be done about it. Compare these thesis statements:

SO?   *Mercury poisoning kills many people each year.*

REVISED   *The many deaths each year from mercury poisoning can be prevented by more detailed consumer education, extensive employee training in the handling of mercury, and stricter regulation of mercury waste disposal.*

[The first sentence may state a tragic fact, but it lacks a point. The revised version makes three assertions—or points—about how to prevent this tragedy.]

- *Using accurate and specific words.* Replace broad, vague expressions with specific words that say precisely what you mean. Compare the original thesis and a revised version:

ORIGINAL   *In Charlotte Perkins Gilman's "The Yellow Wall-Paper," the narrator's doctor-husband does many things that drive her crazy.*

REVISED   *The narrator of Charlotte Perkins Gilman's "The Yellow Wall-Paper" is driven insane by her doctor-husband's misdiagnosis of her depression and by his indifference to her need for intellectual and social stimulation.*

[In the original version, the words *many things* and *crazy* are broad and vague. They do not tell readers what the husband does and whether his wife is merely angry or actually insane. The language in the revised version is both specific and accurate.]

- *Matching your thesis and supporting information.* Be sure the facts and other details you've gathered support your thesis. Revise the thesis and the body of your writing until they fit each other point by point.

- *Writing a reader's thesis.* After writing your essay, cut the *My point is that* formula as you revise, keeping only your actual assertion. The formula helps you make a point, but readers won't need it to get your point. With the formula removed, the thesis in the "How to Write a Tentative Thesis" box (pp. 29–30) becomes

To ease the problems of commuting, federal highway funds and state gasoline taxes should be used to create bicycle lanes on city streets and wide shoulders on secondary roads.

2 ▪ Unwritten thesis statements

In some kinds of writing the writer decides not to state a thesis directly. It may be unnecessary, impossible, or unwise to state a point, so the writing makes an implicit point. Readers will still "get the message," because everything supports that unwritten thesis, develops a dominant mood, and fulfills the overall purpose. Note, however, that in most academic writing you will be expected to state your thesis clearly and explicitly.

3 ▪ Placement of your thesis

Thesis statements usually appear early in a writing. If they're clear and especially dramatic, they may come in the first sentence. More often they appear at the end of an introduction, after the writer prepares readers for the main point. Placed in the introduction, the thesis acts to guide writers as they write and readers as they read. (See the introduction to student John Chen's essay in 4f.)

Sometimes the thesis doesn't appear until the conclusion, revealing an important discovery or summing up what has come before. If you place a thesis at the end of a paper, your introduction must point the way to it, perhaps hinting at its message, describing the problem it solves, or posing the question it answers. (See the conclusion to the sample report in 55d.)

WRITING IN THE USA Putting the Main Idea Early

In most public writing—academic, technical, business—American readers favor writing that states a clear thesis early in the text. Your writing will be more effective if you place the main idea of informative, or argumentative, or business writing in the introduction.

---

4 ■ Other thesis-like statements

Thesis statements are usually associated with informative and explanatory essays. But other kinds of writing also depend on thesis-like statements to give them unity, focus, and direction. Most of the writing you do will make a point of some kind or other.

2.11
Writing
thesis
statements:
Exercises

- **Personal narratives** frequently contain a **discovery statement** to sum up the meaning or lesson of the experiences that the writer describes. Often this statement appears near the end of the story, at a moment of discovery or revelation.

- **Reviews** generally contain a **dominant impression statement** that gives the reviewer's overall judgment of the movie, book, product, or other topic under review. This statement may appear at the beginning or the end of the writing.

- **Arguments and persuasive writing** contain a **claim** that the writer intends to prove or to demonstrate as plausible. (See 58a.)

- **Reports** contain a **conclusion** that sums up the meaning, significance, or uses of the information in the body of the report. (See 62f2.)

2e   Gather the materials for your writing

Following are the materials you'll use to develop your ideas and support your points. They will not only provide information about a topic but also help you understand that topic; some will even give you clues for organizing your writing. Using lists, notes, photocopies, or computer files, gather the materials that are suitable for both your purposes and your readers' interests and needs.

- *Facts and figures.* Gather facts and figures to inform, evaluate, or argue. (See 6b4.)
- *Quotations and summaries.* Gather the words or ideas of eyewitnesses, experts, or others involved with your topic. Use quotations to add life, variety, and authority to your writing. (Be sure to credit your sources when you borrow words or ideas. See 51a and b.)
- *Description.* Describe scenes, people, features, traits, processes, and events in autobiographical and informative writing. (See 6b3.) Use these physical details to give your writing impact, and to help readers see, understand, and remember your point.
- *Narration.* Tell stories or anecdotes to add life to your information, to dramatize an idea, or to illustrate a point. (See 6b1.)
- *Examples.* Use individual illustrations or specific members of a group to explain that group or to dramatize a point. Examples help you and your readers "see" what you're saying. (See 6b5.)
- *Definition.* Define terms unfamiliar to you or your readers. Use definition to help you explain what something is or what it does. (See 6b10.)
- *Comparison and contrast.* Use comparison to reveal similarities between things and to establish relationships. Compare something familiar to something unfamiliar to help identify the unfamiliar item. Use contrast to point out unnoticed differences between similar things or to make distinctions in situations that would otherwise be confusing to readers. (See 6b6.)
- *Analysis.* Identify the parts or features of something; describe the stages or steps in a process; tell how something works; or point out causes or effects, taking note of multiple causes and underlying as well as immediate causes. (See 6b2 and 8.)
- *Classification.* Divide up large groups of things into smaller groups, each with its own label and set of traits. Use classification to organize groups of individuals, details, or instances. (See 6b9.)
- *Figurative language.* Invent analogies, comparisons of dissimilar things that will help you explain something or persuade your readers (see 6b7). Create metaphors or similes to make a topic vivid, to express your feelings about it or to convey your judgment about it (see 26c and d).
- *Explanations.* Restate unfamiliar ideas in familiar words, give instructions, or add details to expand a subject and make it clear.

WRITING IN THE USA Supporting a Topic

In the United States, writers are expected to support their opinions with facts and statistics, direct observation, examples or anecdotes, and information from recognized authorities. Communal wisdom, analogies,

(continued)

appeals to intuition, or an implicit style may be less valued than they are in academic writing in other cultures. US readers generally expect writers to explore various sources of information first, then form an opinion, and then support the opinion with the evidence that persuaded the writer.

🖥 **COMPUTER TIP** A Template for Taking Notes

Use the tables feature of your word processing program to create a note-taking template. Adjust the width and height of each note-taking box in the template so that all of your notes will be the same physical size, 4.50 inches high by 3.25 inches wide. Center your template on the printed page, like this:

As you begin taking notes for a new project, save your file under an appropriate name—for example, "Notes1," "Notes: Res.Paper." Be sure to document the sources of your notes (see 49d). When you finish taking notes, print the file and cut the pages into individual slips that you can arrange and rearrange to organize your ideas.

---

3 Planning and Organizing

3a Refocus your writing

Because writing is a creative process of discovery, your topic and what you intend to say about it will probably change as you prepare to write. New information will lead to new ideas, perhaps a new thesis; your original purpose may change; you may change your relationship to your audience.

Therefore, before you begin a first draft—or later, after completing a draft—pause, step back, and reconsider your project in light of all you've learned. Compare what you have so far with the survey you made when you began (see 1d). Answer these questions:

- *Focus.* At this point in your project, what is your exact subject?

- *Contents.* What will your paper contain: facts, feelings, opinions, personal experiences or observations? Are they reliable and suitable to the occasion? (For most kinds of serious informative writing, personal experience or observation may not be suitable or sufficient. Consider your audience's interests and needs.)

- *Purpose.* Do you have what you need to fulfill your purpose? If you do not, should you gather more information or change your purpose?

- *Support.* Do you have enough information to support your point (your thesis) and communicate its message? If you do not, what do you need? Should you rewrite your thesis to fit what you've found?

3b Plan a communications strategy

Experienced writers usually make detailed plans for communicating with readers. You'll write more effectively if you plan a communications strategy that includes the following elements.

1 ■ Organization

Arrange the content of your essay to fulfill your purpose and satisfy readers' needs. You can organize your writing to:

- Tell a story (personal narrative, how-to writing, steps in a process). (See 6b1 and 2.)
- Present causes and effects. (See 6b8.)
- Describe (scenic arrangement, part-by-part analysis). (See 6b3.)
- Compare or contrast (point by point or the block method). (See 6b6.)
- Classify. (See 6b9.)
- Emphasize what is most important (organizing from least to most important or from most to least).
- Give the pros and cons of an issue and then state your opinion.
- Explain a problem and pose a solution.

3.1
In search
of form:
Web link

For additional organizing patterns, see the research project (50b1), the argument (59a3), and the report (62f2).

🌎 WRITING IN THE USA Organizational Patterns in Writing

There are a variety of ways to organize an English essay, but the typical organizational pattern of academic writing in English is based upon a clearly stated thesis, paragraphs with topic sentences, a linear train of evidence and argument, and a clearly stated conclusion. Although this pattern may seem unfamiliar to good writers in other languages, US readers will appreciate reading texts organized in familiar ways.

3.2
Planning
specific
kinds of
writing:
Web link

2 ▪ Introduction

Think of an opening to attract and focus your readers' interest. (See 6c.) It should identify your topic, suggest your purpose, and, usually, state your thesis.

3 ▪ Lead

As you plan an introduction, try to think of an opening line, your **lead**, to start you writing and draw readers into your introduction. Consider the first sentences of the sample student writing projects in Chapters 4f, 54, 55d, 59d, and 60g. Note how these leads variously provide the context for the writing, pose problems to solve, and establish a point of view on the writer's topic.

4 ▪ Title

A good title is informative and may be intriguing, but should not be a baffling mystery. Come up with a word or phrase that makes your readers want to learn more and, if possible, suggests your topic or even your thesis. Consider the titles of the sample student writing projects in Chapters 4f, 54, 55d, 59d, and 60g.

5 ▪ Conclusion

Good writing doesn't abruptly stop, nor does it slowly unravel. Bring your writing to a satisfying close that ties up loose ends and leaves readers feeling that everything has come together. (See 6d.) Also consider the conclusions of the sample student writing projects in Chapters 4f, 54, 55d, 59d, and 60g.

3c Write an outline, if necessary

3.3
Developing
an outline:
Web link

For many kinds of writing, especially on difficult or unfamiliar topics, outlines are essential. For informative, technical, and research writing, you can use outlines to organize ideas, guide your writing, and later reveal the actual design of various drafts. Outlining will even help you write paragraphs and the topic sentences that unify them. Depending on your project, you may write three kinds of outlines, each a version of the others: a sketch, working, and final-draft formal outline. For some papers, a sketch outline is all you'll need; for others, you'll need all three.

1 ▪ Sketch outline

A **sketch outline** is little more than a list of major points in the order you want to cover them. As you begin organizing, experiment with sketch outlines until you find one that is right for your ideas and purpose.

Bicycles are a safe, practical solution to the problems of rush-hour commuting.
  I. The myths and realities of bicycle commuting in America
    A. Bicycling as a safe means of transportation
    B. Bicycling as a practical means of transportation
 II. Becoming a bicycle commuter
    A. How to get started
    B. The benefits of bicycle commuting

2 ■ Working outline

A **working outline** is developed from a sketch outline and is divided into topics and subtopics. It is the most detailed of the three outlines and will function as a map to follow as you write. As a kind of rough draft of a rough draft, a good working outline has a place for nearly everything:

- Introduction
- Thesis or main idea
- Major topics and subtopics, including facts, key details, illustrations, explanations, and quotations
- Major transitional statements
- Conclusion

You will, no doubt, think of other things to say while drafting, but the clearer and more detailed your plans are at this stage, the easier your first draft will be to write.

HOW TO . . . Organize Your Ideas and Write an Outline

1. Look for clues in key words that suggest common organizing patterns: story order, part by part, comparison, grouping, and so forth. Look in the sequence of ideas in your thesis, or in the list of questions readers might ask about your topic.

2. If your exploratory writing doesn't follow a logical sequence, number the topics in the order you'll write about them.

3. Jot down a list of topics you'll cover (a sketch outline).

4. Draw a **flow chart**, a conceptual diagram showing relations and connections. Put topics in boxes arranged in sequence and connected by lines that trace the path of your writing. Use other boxes and lines to insert advice to yourself about details to remember, quotations, facts, transitional statements, and ideas about introductions and conclusions.

(continued)

5. Create a working outline that includes most of what you want to say:

- Sort your materials to see whether everything fits within a list of major points you want to cover. Revise your list if necessary.

- Then arrange your materials in the order you want to follow as you write your paper. Write a detailed working outline that reflects this order.

- Look for relationships among ideas, and group them as subheadings under headings.

- If you can't decide where to put something, put it in two or more places in your outline and trust your writing to show you where it belongs.

- If an important idea doesn't fit, find a place for it in a new outline.

6. Review your outline looking for "red flags" that signal incomplete topic development or disorganization:

- *Headings without subheadings.* Do you know what you'll say about each of your topics?

- *Long "shopping lists" of parallel headings, A–G or 1–7, for example.* Can you see clusters of ideas that should be grouped as subheadings under new headings?

- *Headings without words or ideas from your thesis or main idea.* What does this part of your outline have to do with your topic or main point?

- *Headings that don't seem to follow one another logically or in sequence.* What's the connection here? How can you rearrange to make sense of your ideas?

COMPUTER TIP Outlining with a Computer

Most word processing programs have an outlining function. Select the outlining style appropriate for your document format, MLA, APA, or other. (See 46c and d, 57b.)

---

3 ■ Final-draft formal outline

Your instructor may require you to hand in a **formal outline** with the final draft of some projects. Base the outline on the organization of your finished paper. It probably will be longer than a sketch outline but shorter than a working outline, often about a page. Include your thesis statement, list your major topics, and follow the guidelines for formal outlines listed in the "How to . . . Organize Your Ideas and Write an Outline" box on pp 37–38 and illustrated in 3c4.

- *Be sure at least two subheadings follow each heading.* Because subheadings divide the ideas in a heading, you must have at least two subheadings under each heading. You can't divide a topic into only one subtopic. If you have only one subheading, you may have simply restated the original heading.

- *Be sure your subheadings are logical.* Because subheadings break up or divide ideas in the headings they stand under, they must reflect the ideas and even the language of those broader headings.

- *Be sure your headings are grammatically parallel.* If heading *I.* is a complete sentence, headings *II.* and *III.* must also be complete sentences. If *A.* under heading *II.* is a noun phrase, *B.* must also be a noun phrase, and so forth. (See Chapter 19.)

- *Use standard outline subdivisions.* For the Modern Language Association style, see the sample outline below.

4 ▪ Sample formal outline

Notice how the example follows the guidelines for formal outlines given above in 3c2. (For a sample formal outline arranged in the format for a typed paper, see Chapter 54.)

Thesis statement

Thesis: Bicycles are a safe, practical solution to the problems of rush-hour commuting.

Logical subdivisions: Every heading has two or more subheads clearly related to the headings.

I. The myths and realities of bicycle commuting in the United States

   A. Bicycling is a safe means of transportation.

      1. The fears motorists have about bicycling safety

      2. The facts of bicycling safety

   B. Bicycling is a practical means of transportation.

      1. Motorists' objections to bicycle commuting

Parallel grammatical form: Coordinate headings are grammatically parallel. For example, I and II are noun phrases; IA and IB are complete sentences.

      2. Widespread support for bicycle commuting

         a. Numerous bicycle commuters

         b. Business support

         c. Federal, state, and local government support

II. Becoming a bicycle commuter

   A. How to begin bicycle commuting

   B. The benefits of bicycle commuting

3.4
Outlining:
Exercises

4 Writing, Revising, and Editing

4a Write a first draft

4.1
Overcoming writer's block:
Web link

Like experienced writers, you should expect to write more than one draft of important, complex projects. Each revision provides an opportunity for rethinking, rearranging, and rewording based on the discoveries of the preceding draft. When you write a first draft, let yourself go; you don't have to get everything right the first time. If you have the information you need and have planned your project, writing a first draft should feel almost like doing a freewriting once you get going.

If you're struck by writer's block as you stare at that blank first page, try these tips:

- Reread your plans and start your writing with the first thing that comes to mind, as if you were doing a freewriting. Words and ideas will start to flow.

- If you can't begin at the beginning, begin in the middle. Come back and write your opening later, after you're warmed up.

- Instead of beginning your project, write a letter to your audience. Tell them what you'd like to write about. Or write a letter to yourself about what you want to say and your frustrations.

- Try visualizing something to do with your subject. Start by writing about what you see.

- Write an advance summary of your project: "In this essay I have tried to . . ." Pretend you're finished. Describe what you would like to have written.

HOW TO . . . Write a First Draft

1. Write major sections or a complete draft at one sitting. Give yourself time to get involved with your writing.

2. Whether you write by hand or with a computer, leave lots of room to revise. Double-space or triple-space, and leave wide margins.

3. Don't bother editing or correcting. If you're unsure of a word or phrase, write out several versions separated by slashes (/). Put a checkmark (✔) in the margin to mark passages to fix later.

4. Use a blank line or row of asterisks (******) to mark easy-to-find places to fill in missing words or information as you revise a draft.

5. If you have to stop, give yourself a thread to pick up when you return. Start writing a sentence or paragraph that you know how to finish, and then stop in the middle of it.

COMPUTER TIP Writing to Revise

Write revision notes to yourself surrounded by the pound sign (######) or another easy-to-see symbol. Your word processing program may have a "stickie pad" feature, enabling you to attach notes to your text. Or you can create a "Notes" file as you draft, split your computer screen, and switch between your draft and your notes. If you're unsure whether to keep something you've written, cut and paste it to the end of your file, where you can reconsider it as you revise. Or turn on your "track changes" function so you can compare all the changes you make as you write a project. ■

4b Revise to say what you want to say

Novice writers think they're nearly finished when they complete a first draft. For them, revision is correcting or touch-up work. Experienced writers, however, know that a single draft rarely says all they want it to say or says it in the best way. The discovery process they began with exploratory writing continues as they revise. For them, revision means "reseeing" and then rewriting based on what they've seen. How to revise? Consider these strategies.

4.2
Revising specific kinds of writing: Web link

1 ▪ Letting your writing cool off

Don't confuse the elation you feel when you finish a draft—or your frustration—with a judgment of the quality of your writing. If you can, wait awhile before you revise. Your perspective and objectivity will improve.

2 ▪ Identifying the status of your draft

Ask yourself, "Is this draft a dress rehearsal, complete except for finishing touches? Is it exploratory, still searching for a point or something to hold it together? Is it experimental, trying out topics and styles?" Your answers will help you see what to do next.

3 ▪ Considering the big picture first

Imagine you're a camera with a telephoto lens. Look at the big picture first. Decide on the status of major elements such as your thesis, its support, and your overall design. Add information, cut, rearrange, condense, or substitute to make your point and fulfill your purpose. When you're satisfied with the big picture, zoom in and focus on individual paragraphs, sentences, and words. Don't waste time fixing small problems before you fix the big ones.

4 ▪ Comparing plans and results

- Compare the draft of your paper to the original plans you made as you first surveyed the assignment (see 1d). Did you fulfill the requirements of the assignment or meet your reader's needs? Revise accordingly.

- Compare your original thesis with what you've written in your conclusion. Look for "Aha!" statements. Often, near the end of a draft, writers write something that makes them say "Aha!" They think they've found a conclusion, but what they may have found is the real point of the paper—a new thesis, different from the original. If you find such a statement, rewrite it as your new thesis, move it to the introduction of your essay, and revise your writing to support it.

- Compare your outline to your draft. If the two are different, which makes more sense of your ideas?

COMPUTER TIP Revising with a Computer

1. Revise on hard copy, not on your computer screen. Revision is easier when you can lay your projects out before you, page by page, rather than scrolling back and forth through a document on-screen. Revise and reprint as often as necessary.

2. Save multiple versions. If you make major changes to a draft but are unsure whether they're the right ones, save several versions of your draft under different file names—for example, "Essay 1a" and "Essay 1b." Compare printed versions and choose the one that is the best.

4c Use peer review to help you revise

WRITING IN THE USA Peer Review

Professional writers have reviewers to help them evaluate their writing. You should, too. In many US college classes and on the job at US businesses, peer review is a frequent activity. On your own, you can form readers' groups to share and improve your writing.

---

1 ▪ Reading as a peer reviewer

When you review another person's writing, your most valuable traits are honesty, tact, sensitivity to your experiences of reading, and awareness of the writer's purpose. Your aim is not to tell the writer how *you* would write but to help the writer say what he or she wants to say. As a reviewer, you may play three roles:

- As a **respondent** you give feedback about your experience of reading and help writers see the impact of their writing. Tell what you thought and felt as you read, what you understood or didn't, where you followed or lost the writer's thread.

- As an **editor** you show the writer how to fulfill his or her intentions. If asked, you may give advice about subject matter, organization, style, and grammatical matters. Be specific, detailed, and practical.

- As a **critic** you evaluate. The best critics are descriptive and factual, describing what something is or is not, what it does or doesn't do, rather than whether it is good or not. To paraphrase a famous poet, your aim is to tell the truth in the kindest words possible. Play this role only when asked by writers you know well. Tell writers what you see as the status of their writing. Is it a dress rehearsal, nearly finished? Or does it seem exploratory or experimental? Explain your answer.

2 ▪ Sharing your writing with peer reviewers

If you share your writing with readers outside class, check with your instructor for a definition of fair editorial assistance. If you know what you want, ask for specific feedback. But don't talk too much, don't explain, and don't apologize for what you've written. If you do, you'll color readers' views and hinder honest responses. As you listen, remember that this is your paper and you have the final say. If their advice sounds good, use it. If it doesn't—well, thanks, but no thanks. If you get conflicting advice or you're uncertain whether to take advice, ask two questions:

- What do these readers know about my assignment, the topic, the kind of writing I'm doing, and my intended audience? The more knowledgeable they are, the better their advice.

- What's their stake in my writing? Readers will have differing interests and priorities that affect how they read and the feedback they give. Look for readers who respond with encouraging objectivity.

HOW TO . . . Give—or Get—a Peer Review

Use these questions to help you review others' writing—and your own. Tell reviewers which questions to answer about your writing, or ask them to respond to the ones they think important.

(continued)

1. What is the subject? Does it change from one page to the next? If it does, which subject is right for this project? (See 2a6 and 2b1.)

2. Is the purpose of the writing autobiographical, informative, persuasive, or critical? Does it change? If it does, what purpose is appropriate? (See 1d2 and 2b2.)

3. Given the content, who is the audience for this project? Are readers supposed to respond with sympathy, understanding, evaluation, agreement, or enjoyment? Will this project achieve its purpose? What changes would make it more effective? (See 1d3.)

4. Does this project have a thesis, main idea, or overall mood? Point it out or describe it. Does the writing provide enough detail to illustrate, explain, or support its point? What should be added? (See 2d and e.)

5. Can you follow this project from start to finish? What reorganization would make its ideas clearer or easier to follow? (See 3b and c.) Help the writer see how his/her writing is constructed. Tell what you see happening in each paragraph: "In this paragraph you're talking about _____, and in the next paragraph you talk about _____," and so forth.

6. Does the project have a distinctive writer's voice? What changes would make this voice more emphatic or appropriate? (See 2c.)

7. What does the opening do to attract readers' attention and help them predict the project's subject, purpose, thesis, organization, or style? What changes would make the opening more interesting to readers? (See 6c.)

8. If the project contains visuals, what do they add to the writing: information, explanation, drama, or clarification? Are they properly placed in the text, where readers will want them? Does the writer refer to them in the text? (See 46b.)

4.3
Peer review
questions
for specific
kinds of
writing:
Web link

4d Edit for your readers

1 ▪ The aims of editing

When you revise, you're focusing primarily on your ideas and message. When you edit, you're focusing on your readers and rewriting to help them get your message. Editing is a paragraph-by-paragraph, line-by-line process. Consider the edited paragraph about bicycle commuting that follows. The student writer, John Chen, made typical editorial improvements—the kinds you'll make in your writing:

- Improving accuracy and brevity. The writer cut and added words to increase accuracy and brevity.

- Adding important information and details. He inserted additional information and details to develop and clarify his proposal.

- Adapting the content for the intended audience. He cut a sentence that might offend readers who are motorists.

- Increasing precision and vividness. He cut vague, general words and substituted descriptive details.

- Rearranging for clarity and emphasis. He moved one passage earlier in the paragraph to reorganize for emphasis.

What will end commuters' rush-hour nightmare
~~The cycling solution to the problem of commuters' gridlock~~ ~~already exists in sketch form. What it consists of~~ is not a single *solution for all, however.* ~~one~~ way ~~for all plan~~ Commuting problems and needs differ from community to community, region to region. The best solutions will be local. Each will have a number of parts, and each part will solve a *specific* local travel problem. In some communities, few changes are required. *All that may be needed is public service announcements to encourage bicycle commuting.* In other communities, converting abandoned railroad lines to green-*ways* ~~paths~~ or improving *park paths or* other off-road bikeways is the right solution. In others, parking might be restricted along busy streets during peak travel times. ~~The police might begin ticketing and the courts prosecuting drivers who harass bicyclists exercising their right to the road.~~ In still other*-s,* communities~~, where highways have long been crumbling, aging~~ highways might be widened *repaved with widened* to ~~provide wide~~ shoulders, *dangerous sewer grates might be removed, and high curbs eliminated. Larger,* ~~or eliminate high curbs. Clearer,~~ more frequent signs would guide motorists and cyclists alike. In almost every community, *well-placed* bicycle racks and storage facilities ~~will~~ *would* help encourage more bicycle *commuting.* ~~commuters, as will public service announcements to promote bicycle awareness.~~

2 ■ Editing symbols

As you edit, use the following copyediting symbols to make your final draft easier to prepare.

insért   start a new paragraph: ¶

addspace   remove paragraph: no ¶

delete lettter or word   cAPITALIZE A LETTeR OR word

closе up   Lowercase a Letter or WORD

tranpspse   move left:

let it stand as written: stet   move right:

HOW TO . . . Edit Your Writing

1. Reread your writing looking for passages that seem vague or fuzzy. Rewrite until you're confident your ideas will be clear to your intended readers.

2. Study your paragraphs. Consider whether each focuses on a single topic and says all that needs to be said about it. Make sure that each paragraph supports your thesis or main idea, flows from preceding paragraphs, and connects with following paragraphs. (See Chapters 5–7.)

3. Look for sentences that seem long, choppy, difficult to follow, or unfocused. Or ask a peer editor to read your writing aloud while you follow along. If your editor stumbles, you've probably found a passage that needs rewriting. (See Chapters 20–24.)

4. Look for words your readers might not know or words that you don't use often. Add definitions; substitute familiar words. Search for vague, general, or tired words; substitute precise words. Look for charged words with inappropriate feelings or bias; find alternatives. Find words you can cut without losing your meaning. (See Chapters 25–29.)

5. Be on the lookout for grammar, spelling, or punctuation errors you've had trouble with in previous writing. Make sure your writing is appropriately formatted. (See Chapters 11–19 and 33–46.)

WRITING IN THE USA Editing

6. If you are writing and editing in English and it is not your primary language, look especially for errors in complete sentences (fragments or fused sentences); mistakes in parallel form; repetitious sentence length and structure; grammar errors (verb forms, articles, subject-verb agreement, word order); and word choice errors (unnecessary repetition). See Part V for more guidance. ■

COMPUTER TIP Editing with a Computer

- *Find commands.* Use Search and Replace or Find commands to locate words, punctuation, blank lines, or symbols such as asterisks that you inserted at places where you want to add or change things.

- *Grammar checkers.* Beware of relying too heavily on grammar or style checkers. They can identify repeated words, clichés, wordy or vague phrases, big words, and long or short sentences. But they can't read your intentions, don't know your audience, and can't detect the feelings you want to convey. Be sure a recommended change will actually improve your writing before you accept it.

- *Spell checkers.* Spell checkers can't identify confused words such as *threw* for *through, there* for *they're* or *their, see* for *sea, so* for *sew.* If you misspell a word by typing another, correctly spelled word—*ad* instead of *and*—your spell checker can't identify that error either. Use your spell checker but proofread afterward.

- *Manuscript form.* For information about the manuscript form of computer-produced papers, see 46a1.

4.4
An editing
checklist:
Web link

WRITING IN THE USA Overreliance on Grammar and Spell Checkers

If English is not your primary language, avoid overdependence on grammar and spell checkers, which can be flawed. Trust your own knowledge or, if you are unsure, use a dictionary or talk to a writing tutor.

---

3 ■ How to know when you've finished revising and editing

You may have to write several drafts before you say what you want to say in the way you want to say it. But some writers tinker and tinker, changing and changing, never sure when they've finished. When your changes aren't making your writing noticeably better, you're finished; you've written as well as you can.

4.5
Editing
sentence
errors:
Exercises

4e   Prepare and proofread your final draft

As you prepare your final draft, use the appropriate manuscript form. (See 46d for the Modern Language Association format for writing in the humanities and 46e for the American Psychological Association format for writing in the social sciences.)

Proofread your final copy slowly and carefully. When many writers proofread their own writing, they miss spelling errors and other typos because they read as they normally do, for the meaning, or in anticipation of the parts they like.

HOW TO . . . Proofread a Final Draft

1. Proofread on printed copy. Errors will be hard to detect on a computer screen.

2. Read your final draft aloud, pronouncing each word as it appears on the page. Use a pencil eraser to point at each word, or lay a ruler beneath each line to guide your eyes.

3. After you correct an error, return to the beginning of the line and begin proofreading anew in case you missed a second error on that line.

4. If you find it hard to focus on the spelling of your words or if you're a poor speller, read your writing backward, word by word. Use a dictionary to verify the spelling of any word you don't write frequently (see Chapter 45).

4f   Sample student essay

4.6
More
student
writing:
Web link

The writer of the following project was instructed to "write a 3–5 page informative and explanatory essay about a topic many people misunderstand," formatted in the Modern Language Association style. For other sample student writing the see the research project (Chapter 54), the formal report (55d), the persuasive essay (59d), and the literary essay (60g).

                                                    Chen 1

John Chen   *Modern Language Association format (see 46d)*

Professor Sternberg

English 101-015   *Standard heading information*

September 10, 200-

                  The Highway My Way   *Centered title*

    For most residents of America's cities and sub-

urbs, the worst part of any weekday is the excruciating   *Double-spacing throughout*

time

Chen 2

spent trapped in rush-hour traffic. Morning, night, and
sometimes even at noon, I watch my fellow commuters
lined up, scowling, inching, and honking their way to
work or school. I used to share their fender benders,
foul air, fouler tempers, frazzled nerves, clenched
jaws, high blood pressure, higher insurance premiums,
the same old songs on the radio, the wasted time, and
boredom. But no more. Not since I parked my car and
began commuting by bicycle. What I've discovered in the
process is that bicycle commuting is a safe, practical,
and enjoyable alternative to short-trip car travel. If
other motorists joined me, we could bring an end to
this commuting misery.

Many drivers, however, think of cycling,
especially commuter cycling, as anything but safe. To
them, people who put their fragile bikes and bodies on
rush-hour streets and highways risk instant destruction
by 4,000-pound cars and 40,000-pound trucks and buses.
How could a bicycle commuter survive even one rush
hour, they wonder.

The truth is that cars, trucks, buses, and
bicycles can safely share most roads and streets. As
reported by the National Highway Traffic and Safety
Administration, on-street bicycling is about as safe as
driving. Fewer than fifteen percent of bicycle
accidents involve motorized vehicles, and the number of
deaths from bicycle accidents has dropped by nearly ten
percent in the last ten years (United States). With
increased enforcement of traffic laws, roadway
redesign, the creation of more off-road bike paths
where appropriate, and improved driver and cyclist

*Dramatic
introductory
description
to attract
reader
interest*

*The writer's
informative
thesis*

*Transition to
the first part
of the essay:
the myths
and realities
of bicycle
commuting*

*A topic
sentence: the
realities of
bicycle
safety*

*Information
that
supports
the topic
sentence*

Chen 3

education, the incidence of these accidents will be even lower. If millions upon millions of bicycle commuters can pedal their way safely along the narrow, densely crowded streets and roads of Mexico, the Netherlands, Sweden, India, China, and many other countries, cyclists can easily be accommodated on the United States' wider streets and roads.

Even so, many will object, what happens elsewhere is no guide to the future of America's roads. Large-scale bicycle commuting would be impractical. In America, the car is king. Highway redesign and modification to accommodate cyclists would be too complex and expensive. Another bureaucracy would be created, they argue, and one more governmental body would lean on us for taxes. Where would we begin?

Transition and topic sentence: objections to the practicality of bicycle commuting

The truth is that we have already begun. Nearly thirty percent of Americans go cycling in a thirty-day period, and already seven percent of Americans bicycle or walk to work (Shay 38). Many businesses now encourage bicycle commuting by providing bicycle parking and employee clean-up facilities. In all fifty states, bicycles have for years had the same legal status as motor vehicles, and cyclists have had the same legal rights and responsibilities as motorists. In 2003, the Safe, Accountable, Flexible, and Efficient Transportation Equity Act (SAFETEA) went into effect, providing millions of dollars to state and local governments to develop more ecological modes of transportation, including bicycles. The American Association of State Highway and Transportation Officials has already produced a Guide to the

Parenthetical in-text documentation of borrowed information (see Chapter 52)

The reality of bicycle commuting as a practical alternative

Chen 4

Development of Bicycle Facilities, with highway redesign
recommendations that will enable bicycles and other
vehicles to coexist safely.The federal government and
most state and local governments already have officials
to oversee the integration of bicycles into
transportation programs. And many municipalities--such as
San Diego, Denver, Minneapolis, Chicago, and
Philadelphia--have already laid out networks of bike
routes to aid bicycle commuters. Some, such as Portland,
Seattle, and Washington, DC, equip buses with bike racks
to expand the possibilities for bicycle commuters (Shay).

This kind of business and government support makes
it easy for other commuters to do as I did: park their
cars and ride their bikes instead. Most of the trips we
take by car are under five miles. Most of the routes we
drive are bicycle accessible. These are trips we could
take most of the time in most weather by bicycle. Many
of us already own bicycles. A call to our local
government or a visit to a bike shop will give us
routes and maybe even maps. What else do we need?

-A bicycle tune-up

-A review of the rules of the road (We have to
follow the same regulations motorists do.)

-A few articles of clothing and equipment (a helmet
for sure, bike shorts perhaps, baskets or bags,
rain gear, lights for night commuters, possibly
fenders, and a horn or bell)

-Cycling companions to share the ride with us

For more detailed tips on bicycle commuting, see "The
Bicycle Commuter's Guide" at <http://bicyclinglife.com/
Practical/Cycling/commuteguide.htm>.

*Transition to
the second
part of
the essay:
becoming a
bicycle
commuter*

*A list for
emphasis*

Chen 5

It takes only a little imagination to see the

Topic
sentence

benefits of bicycle commuting. Those who must drive
because of health, their route, or the distance will
benefit from reduced traffic and commuting times.
Bicyclists will benefit from the money they save
cycling instead of driving. According to an Internet
bicycle advocacy site, the overall cost of driving a
compact car one mile is thirty-five cents; the cost of
cycling the same distance, five cents. Commuting
cyclists can save up to $7,000 annually (Benefits).
Even greater are the physical and psychological
benefits. "A UCLA study demonstrated that cycling
relaxes the central nervous system, improves moods and
sharpens mental acuity, while commuting by car raises
blood pressure, lowers frustration tolerance and
fosters negative attitudes" (Benefits).

Obviously, businesses will benefit from the
increased productivity of their healthy cycling
employees and from reduced expenditures for employee
parking facilities. On average, a single parking space
costs up to $10,000 for design, construction,
maintenance, insurance, and taxes (Benefits). And the
communities where these cyclists live and work will
benefit. Short trips by automobile, the largest single
source of air pollution, pour up to 3.6 pounds of
pollutants into the air per mile traveled. By contrast,
say environmentalists with the World Watch Institute,
"Every trip made by a bike reduces the environmental
burden of low-level ozone, nitrous oxides, carbon
dioxide, and soot. Neither electric cars nor high-
mileage gas-powered cars can match that achievement"

Introduction
of a source
of informa-
tion and
in-text
parenthetical
documenta-
tion of the
page number

Chen 6

(Gardener 20). In sum, bicycle commuters are money in
the bank--and a healing power in the environment.

  Imagine a morning or afternoon when the sky is not
brown with smog. Imagine broad, open streets easy and
safe to travel any time of day. Imagine the scent of
flowers and trees instead of gasoline and rubber.
Imagine the songs of birds instead of the blare of
horns, the rumble of engines, the screech of tires.
Imagine feeling relaxed and exhilarated at the end of a
commute, instead of frustrated, tense, angry. This is
what a bicycle rush hour would be like. Instead of the
worst part of the day, it just might be the best.

Descriptive
conclusion
that
contrasts
with the
introduction
and drama-
tizes the
writer's
thesis

Chen 7

Works Cited

"Benefits to Employers of Bicycle Commuting."

  BicycleSource. 2003. BicycleSource Online. 9 Apr.

  2004 <http://bicyclesource.com/you/commuting/

  employer-benefits.shtml>.

Gardner, Gary. "When Cities Take Bicycles Seriously."

  World Watch Sept.-Oct. 1998: 16-23.

Shay, Laura. "Bicycle Commuting." 21st Century

  Alternatives 28 Apr. 2004: 38-40.

United States. National Highway Traffic and Safety

  Administration. Traffic Safety Facts 2002:

  Pedalcyclists. National Center for Statistics and

  Analysis. Washington: GPO, 2003.

In MLA
style, the
Works Cited
section
begins on a
new page.

An alphabet-
ical list of
the sources
of informa-
tion for this
essay (see
53a)

5 Unifying Your Paragraphs

5.1
Paragraph-
ing and
topic
sentences:
Web link

For writers and readers alike, paragraphs chunk ideas and information into distinct, manageable parts and thus make writing and reading easier. Good paragraphs, like full-length pieces of good writing, have a clear purpose, focus on a single topic, and have an overall design. In a word, good paragraphs are unified.

5a Write topic sentences to focus and unify your paragraphs

A **topic sentence** resembles the thesis statement of an essay. It announces a topic or makes a point. Just as everything in an essay supports its thesis, everything in a paragraph supports its topic sentence. Consider this example:

Topic sentence	Calf ropers are the whiz kids of rodeo: they're expert on the horse and on the ground, and their horses are as quick-witted. The cowboy emerges from the box with a loop in his hand, a piggin' string in his mouth, coils and reins in the other, and a network of slack line strewn so thickly over horse and rider, they look as if they'd run through a tangle of kudzu before arriving in the arena. After roping the calf and jerking the slack in the rope, he jumps off the horse, sprints down the length of nylon, which the horse keeps taut, throws the calf down, and ties three legs together with the piggin' string. It's said of Roy Cooper, the defending calf-roping champion, that "even with pins and metal plates in his arm, he's known for the fastest groundwork in the business; when he springs down his rope to flank the calf, the resulting action is pure rodeo poetry." The six or seven separate movements he makes are so fluid they look like one continual unfolding.
Support: Cowboys as expert riders	
Support: Cowboys and horses working together	
Support: An example	
A concluding evaluation	

(Gretel Ehrlich, "Rules of the Game: Rodeo,"
from *The Solace of Open Spaces*)

Topic sentences may appear early in a paragraph, as in the preceding example, or later, to sum up preceding information, as in the following:

Transition to link paragraphs	Girls, on the other hand, play in small groups or pairs; the center of a girl's social life is a best friend. Within the group, intimacy is key: Differentiation is measured by relative closeness. In their most frequent games, such as jump rope and hopscotch, everyone gets a turn. Many of their activities (such as playing house) do not have winners or
Introduction and clarification	

Support: Details about girls' play

losers. Though some girls are certainly more skilled than others, girls are expected not to boast about it, or show that they think they are better than the others. Girls don't give orders; they express their preferences as suggestions, and suggestions are likely to be accepted. Whereas boys say, "Gimme that!" and "Get outta here!" girls say, "Let's do this," and "How about doing that?" Anything else is put down as "bossy." They don't grab center stage—they don't want it—so they don't challenge each other directly. And

A topic sentence explaining girls' play

much of the time, they simply sit together and talk. Girls are not accustomed to jockeying for status in an obvious way; they are more concerned that they be liked.

(Deborah Tannen, "It Begins at the Beginning," from *You Just Don't Understand*)

One key to successful paragraph design is the placement of the topic sentence. Organize your paragraphs to follow from the topic sentence or to lead to it, as in the preceding examples. Another key is emphasis. Whenever possible, put the most important information early in your paragraph, an arrangement known as **dramatic order**, or late, known as **climactic order**. In the following example, the writer opens with a topic sentence but saves her most important example for the end of her paragraph.

Topic sentence

Neat people are especially vicious with mail. They never go through their mail unless they are standing directly over a trash can. If the trash can is beside the mailbox, even better.

Clarifying description

All ads, catalogs, pleas for charitable contributions, church bulletins and money-saving coupons go straight in the trash

Supporting examples

can without being opened. All letters from home, postcards from Europe, bills and paychecks are opened, immediately responded to, then dropped in the trash can. Neat people keep their receipts only for tax purposes. That's it. No senti-

Most important example

mental salvaging of birthday cards or the last letter a dying relative ever wrote. Into the trash it goes.

(Suzanne Britt, "Neat People vs. Sloppy People," from *Show and Tell*)

HOW TO . . . Write Topic Sentences

1. As you organize your writing, consider outline headings or items in lists you have made as potential topic sentences. Compose headings that you can later expand into topic sentences.

2. As you write a first draft and indent for new paragraphs, think of sentences to announce your topics. Where will you put them for best effect? At the beginning, to launch your paragraph? Or at the end, as a destination to aim for?

(continued)

3. As you write the beginning of paragraphs, try to repeat key words or important concepts from your thesis or introduction. You'll help to guide yourself and your readers through the subject matter of your writing.

4. As you edit, look for topic sentences in your writing. They should appear regularly, but sometimes a topic sentence in one paragraph will announce a topic for several paragraphs. Sometimes you can imply your point rather than state it explicitly.

5.2
Writing
unified
paragraphs:
Exercises

5. Reread your writing from your readers' point of view. If you suspect they might ask, "So, what's the point here?" add topic sentences to answer their question.

5b Adjust paragraph length to express your purpose and suit your audience

1 ▪ Paragraph length, purpose, and audience

Paragraphs may be almost any length. Some are necessarily short: speeches in a dialogue, a paragraph to set off a thesis, transition statements, or emphatic paragraphs. These may be only a sentence or two—or even less. Paragraphs that present and develop ideas, such as introductions, body paragraphs, or conclusions, may be much longer.

In any case, you should write paragraphs for your readers' eyes as well as their brains. Too many short paragraphs will make your writing look choppy and disconnected even when it isn't. Too many long paragraphs may make readers think, "I can't read this; it's too difficult." Paragraphs should look readable.

2 ▪ Paragraph length and content

Paragraphs must not only look readable but also be readable, fully expressing their topic and purpose. As you adjust paragraph length when you revise, be sure that each paragraph links to the preceding one, that it clearly announces its topic or purpose, and that it is complete. A paragraph may contain six kinds of sentences, each playing a distinct role.

- *Transitional* sentences linking one paragraph to another
- *Introductory* sentences
- *Topic* sentences
- *Supporting* sentences that present a topic or prove a point
- *Clarifying* sentences that explain or restate
- *Concluding* sentences

Not every paragraph contains every kind of sentence, and some sentences play more than one role, but a good paragraph has all the sentences necessary to make its point.

To see how individual sentences each play distinct roles in complete paragraphs, reread the sample paragraphs in 5a (pp. 54–55), paying attention to the marginal notes.

HOW TO . . . Adjust Paragraph Length

1. To divide a paragraph that seems too long, look for break points at shifts in time or place, between subtopics, or before sentences that signal logical shifts.

2. In double-spaced typescript, common in college writing, break for a new paragraph one to three times per page—every five to fifteen lines or so. Break more often to increase the pace of your writing or for special-purpose paragraphs.

3. In single-spaced typescript, common in business letters, make your paragraphs from four or five to nine or ten lines long. Break more frequently if your information is complex or if your readers may only be skimming your writing for its main ideas.

4. If you are writing in columns, as in technical writing and journalism, break up long paragraphs to make them look readable, usually one to three sentences in length.

5. If you are writing by hand, divide once or twice per page.

6. If you are designing a Web page, shorten paragraphs to look readable in a computer window.

COMPUTER TIP Editing Paragraphs

7. If you're unsure whether a passage belongs in a particular paragraph, select it, cut it, and paste it temporarily at the end of your paper. Read the paragraph without it. If it belongs, move it back. If not, move it or delete it.

   To see how your paragraphs will look to your readers, use your word processor's Print Preview command. As you click through your project, look at each page. Does your paragraphing make your writing look too complex, too choppy? Edit your paragraphs accordingly.

5.3
Paragraph-
ing in
specific
kinds of
writing:
Web link

6 Developing Topics and Paragraphs

6a Include details to support your topic sentence

"God is in the details," said architect Mies van der Rohe. As in a well-designed building, the power of a well-designed paragraph lies in its details. If you're writing to readers familiar with your topic, you may not need to say much. However, in most public writing, especially in college writing, readers want enough detail to understand fully the main idea of your topic sentence. That means writing well-developed paragraphs.

HOW TO . . . Write Well-Developed Paragraphs

1. Do exploratory writing or take notes before beginning a first draft. Give yourself things to put in your paragraphs before you write them. (See 2e.)

WRITING IN THE USA Topic Development and US Audiences

2. As you revise, make sure that the points in your topic sentences are fully supported by the body of your paragraphs. US readers value details that prove your assertions and explain your ideas. Try to reread your paragraphs from your readers' viewpoints. Do your details answer their questions and satisfy their interest in your topic? ■

6b Choose appropriate methods of paragraph development to present a topic

The methods of paragraph development illustrated in this section will enable you to communicate information, experiences, feelings, ideas, and opinions. Sometimes, when an idea needs several kinds of support, you'll combine more than one method in a paragraph, as in the earlier illustration about calf-ropers (see 5a), in which the writer combines narration, description, and example. Sometimes, when subjects are complex or your readers' need for information is great, you may extend one method of development over several paragraphs, all unified by one topic sentence. You may even use one method throughout an entire piece of writing, unified by a thesis statement.

1 ▪ Narration

Narration organizes events in chronological order to tell a story. Use it in personal-experience writing and to illustrate a point in explanatory writing or argument. As in the following example, narrative paragraphs almost always include description to make actions clear and vivid.

Event 1: action and reaction

Dramatizing description

Event 2: a second shot and its effects

Event 3: a third shot and its effects

> When I pulled the trigger I did not hear the bang or feel the kick—one never does when a shot goes home—but I heard the devilish roar of glee that went up from the crowd. In that instant, in too short a time, one would have thought, even for the bullet to get there, a mysterious, terrible change had come over the elephant. He neither stirred nor fell, but every line of his body had altered. He looked suddenly stricken, shrunken, immensely old, as though the frightful impact of the bullet had paralysed him without knocking him down. At last, after what seemed a long time—it might have been five seconds, I dare say—he sagged flabbily to his knees. His mouth slobbered. An enormous senility seemed to have settled upon him. One could have imagined him thousands of years old. I fired again into the same spot. At the second shot he did not collapse but climbed with desperate slowness to his feet and stood weakly upright, with legs sagging and head drooping. I fired a third time. That was the shot that did for him. You could see the agony of it jolt his whole body and knock the last remnant of strength from his legs. But in falling he seemed for a moment to rise, for as his hind legs collapsed beneath him he seemed to tower upward like a huge rock toppling, his trunk reaching skywards like a tree. He trumpeted, for the first and only time. And then down he came, his belly towards me, with a crash that seemed to shake the ground even where I lay.
>
> (George Orwell, "Shooting an Elephant," from *Shooting an Elephant and Other Essays*)

2 ▪ Process

Like narrative paragraphs, **process** paragraphs are organized in chronological order. But they emphasize the sequence of events as much as the events themselves. Process paragraphs are used frequently to explain steps or stages in informative and how-to writing.

Step 1

Step 2

Step 3

> To define a word, then, the dictionary editor places before him the stack of cards illustrating that word; each of the cards represents an actual use of the word by a writer of some literary or historical importance. He reads the cards carefully, discards some, rereads the rest, and divides up the stack according to what he thinks are the several senses of the word. Finally, he writes his definitions, following the hard-and-fast rule that each definition must be based on what the quotations in front of him reveal about the mean-

ing of the word. The editor cannot be influenced by what he thinks a given word ought to mean. He must work according to the cards or not at all.

> (S. I. Hayakawa, "How Dictionaries Are Made," from *Language in Thought and Action*)

3 ▪ Description

Description adds sensory details to personal and informative writing—whenever it is important for writers to "see" a subject. Descriptive paragraphs are usually organized in spatial order: left to right, front to back, top to bottom, and so forth. The following paragraph is organized from the center to the margins of a scene.

Topic sentence	There once was a town in the heart of America where all life seemed to live in harmony with its surroundings. The
Visual details	town lay in the midst of a checkerboard of prosperous farms, with fields of grain and hillsides of orchards where,
Color	in spring, white clouds of bloom drifted above the green fields. In autumn, oak and maple and birch set up a blaze of color that flamed and flickered across a backdrop of pines.
Sound	Then foxes barked in the hills and deer silently crossed the fields, half hidden in the mists of the fall mornings.

> (Rachel Carson, "A Fable for Tomorrow," from *Silent Spring*)

4 ▪ Facts and figures

Factual paragraphs present **facts or statistical information** in some clear pattern to provide information or prove a point in an argument. The following paragraph is organized according to the ways bats are both familiar and strange to human beings.

Facts that make bats familiar	Bats are mammals like we are. They suckle their young, and have such wizened ancient-looking faces that they seem strangely akin and familiar. Yet they find their way and
Facts that make bats strange to human beings	locate food by using sound that we cannot hear. They hunt by night, and in cold weather some migrate and others hibernate. They are odd and alien to us, too, so much so that we have made up fancies about them—that they are evil and ill-omened, or at the very least will fly into our hair. Anyone who has read *Dracula* will remember that young ladies should not moon around graveyards at night, or they will be in big trouble with bats.

> (Sue Hubbell, "Summer," from *A Country Year*)

5 ▪ Examples

An **example** uses individual members of a group (people, events, conditions, objects, ideas, and so forth) to explain or illustrate the whole group. Explanatory writing and argument frequently depend on examples. Occasionally, they are introduced by signal phrases: *for example, for instance,* or *such as.*

Topic sentence and the group to be explained: visible symbols of the consumer society

Examples

Signal phrase

> Since its birth in the United States, the consumer society has moved far beyond its American borders, yet its most visible symbols remain American. The Disneyland near Tokyo attracts almost as many visitors each year as Mecca or the Vatican. Coca-Cola products are distributed in over 170 countries. Each day, a new McDonald's restaurant opens somewhere in the world. Singaporean youngsters can brush their teeth with the Teenage Mutant Ninja Turtle Talking Toothbrush, which says "Hey, Dudes!" in Malay. The techniques of mass marketing first perfected in the United States are now employed on every continent, teaching former East Germans, for example, to "Taste the West. Marlboro."
>
> (Alan Thein Durning, "The Consumer Society," from *How Much Is Enough?*)

6 ■ Comparison/contrast

Comparison/contrast presents subjects according to similarities and differences in order to explain a subject or make an evaluation. Comparison/contrast paragraphs may be organized in two ways. In **block comparison,** as in the first paragraph that follows, one subject is presented and then the other, subject A and then B. In **point-by-point comparison,** as in the second paragraph, the comparison moves back and forth, first to one point of comparison, then to a second, and so forth, $A_1 B_1$, then $A_2 B_2$, and $A_3 B_3$.

Block contrast

Custer's knowledge of his society

Crazy Horse's knowledge of his society

> [George Armstrong] Custer's society was specialized. Thus, despite his range of choices, once Custer settled into an occupation, he knew relatively little about what other men in his society did for their daily bread. After becoming a soldier, Custer knew almost nothing about medicine or law or manufacturing. He never really understood how his society worked. [The Sioux warrior] Crazy Horse knew how to do everything required to make his society function. He could put up a tipi, kill buffalo, skin animals, cook, make war, treat injuries or illness, and so on. Put Crazy Horse down naked and alone on the Great Plains and within a month he would have a full set of weapons, shelter, stocks of food, and be in good shape to face the future.

Point-by-point comparison

Differences in dress

> Beyond their bravery, Custer and Crazy Horse were individualists, each standing out from the crowd in his separate way. Custer wore outlandish uniforms, let his hair fall in long, flowing gold locks across his shoulders, surrounded himself with pet animals and admirers, and in general did all he could to draw attention to himself. Crazy Horse's

individualism pushed him in an opposite direction—he wore a single feather in his hair when going into battle, rather than a war bonnet. Custer's vast energy set him apart from most of his fellows; the Sioux distinguished Crazy Horse from other warriors because of Crazy Horse's quietness and introspection. Both men lived in societies in which drugs, especially alcohol, were widely used, but neither Custer nor Crazy Horse drank. Most of all, of course, each man stood out in battle as a great risk taker.

Differences in bearing

Two similarities

(Stephen Ambrose, from *Crazy Horse and Custer: The Parallel Lives of Two American Warriors*)

7 ▪ Analogy

As a form of comparison, **analogy** uses something simple or familiar to explain something complex or unfamiliar. To help explain what can be observed in newly fallen snow, the writer of the following paragraph compares snow to a book.

Topic sentence

The wind = pages turning

Physical details = the language of the book

To one who lives in the snow and watches it day by day, it is a book to be read. The pages turn as the wind blows; the characters shift and the images formed by their combinations change in meaning, but the language remains the same. It is a shadow language, spoken by things that have gone by and will come again. The same text has been written there for thousands of years, though I was not here, and will not be here in winters to come, to read it. These seemingly random ways, these paths, these beds, these footprints, these hard, round pellets in the snow: they all have meaning. Dark things may be written there, news of others' lives, their sorties and excursions, their terrors and deaths. The tiny feet of a shrew or a vole make a brief, erratic pattern across the snow, and here is a hole down which the animal goes. And now the track of an ermine comes this way, swift and searching, and he too goes down that white shadow of a hole.

(John Haines, "Snow," from *The Stars, the Snow, the Fire*)

8 ▪ Cause-effect

Cause-effect paragraphs divide events into causes and effects in order to explain relationships within a process. They may be organized in two ways: *causes → effects* or, as in the following example, *effects → causes*. Notice how the writer arranges causes into a *causal chain*, from immediate to underlying causes.

Topic sentence: an effect (literacy)

Fortunately, there are many children who manage to become literate despite the way in which they are taught reading. They do so because they are highly motivated by

Two chief causes: home and school

their home environment or because of an attachment to their teacher. Studies show that nothing correlates more highly with a child's future academic success than the academic achievement of his parents. The reason for this is not just that the parents are committed to the merit of reading, a commitment which they pass on to their children, but also

Underlying causes: observation and experience

that from an early age the child can observe how important reading is to his parents and how much they enjoy it. Additionally, parents who are avid readers are more likely to read often—and with enjoyment—to their children. So the child becomes convinced that reading is important and enjoyable long before he is confronted for the first time with a primer in school. And he is then able to distance himself from the stupidity of the primers, since he knows not all

Two additional effects of these causes

books are like those. Still, many years later, that child will remember how disgusted he was with the books he had to read in early grades.

(Bruno Bettelheim, from *Johnny Wants to Read*)

9 ▪ Classification

Classification divides subjects into classes according to characteristics shared by the members of each class. Classification paragraphs are often used in informative and evaluative writing to show how things differ or fit together. They may include examples or description to distinguish the members of one class from another.

Topic sentence

There are three kinds of book owners. The first has all the standard sets and best sellers—unread, untouched.

Class one

(This deluded individual owns woodpulp and ink, not books.) The second has a great many books—a few of them

Class two

read through, most of them dipped into, but all of them as clean and shiny as the day they were bought. (This person would probably like to make books his own, but is restrained by a false respect for their physical appearance.) The

Class three

third has few books or many—every one of them dog-eared and dilapidated, shaken and loosened by continual use,

Descriptive details

marked and scribbled in from front to back. (This man owns books.)

(Mortimer Adler, "How to Mark a Book," in *The Saturday Review*)

10 ▪ Definition

In explanatory writing and argument, **definitions** explain what something is. There are several methods of definition.

- ▪ **Formal definition** puts something into a class of related items and then distinguishes it from other words in that class.
- ▪ **Functional definition** tells how something works.

- **Etymology** traces the history of a term to its origins.

- **Giving synonyms** compares words with similar or related meanings.

- **Providing examples** defines by illustrating the term.

<table>
<tr><td>Definition by
origin, by
synonym</td><td>"Niche" is a word ecologists have borrowed from church architecture. In a church, of course, a "niche" means a recess in the wall in which a figurine may be placed; it is an address, a location, a physical place. But the ecologist's</td></tr>
<tr><td>Definition by
contrast</td><td>"niche" is more than just a physical place: it is a place in the grand scheme of things. The niche is an animal's (or a plant's) profession. The niche of the wolf spider is everything it does to get its food and raise its babies. To be able to</td></tr>
<tr><td>Example and
functional
definition</td><td>do these things it must relate properly to the place where it lives and to the other inhabitants of that place. Everything the species does to survive and stay "fit" in the Darwinian sense is its niche.</td></tr>
</table>

(Paul Colinvaux, "Every Species Has Its Niche,"
from *Why Big Fierce Animals Are Rare*)

6c Write introductions that attract reader interest

6.1
Introductions and conclusions:
Web link

Professional writers frequently spend a lot of time on openings. They know that a good lead will take them in the right direction as they begin a draft. They also know that they have to arouse interest within the first two or three sentences or risk losing their readers. And they know that effective introductions are sometimes challenging to write because these introductions must do several things at once:

- Identify the writer's topic and, often, the purpose of the writing

- Stimulate reader interest

- Create the writer's personality and style

- State the writer's thesis or main idea

- Provide a bridge to carry readers into the body of the writing

Consider how the following introduction attracts reader interest and then focuses it on the thesis statement.

<table>
<tr><td>Dramatic quotation to create interest</td><td>"A name is a prison, God is free," once observed the Greek poet Nikos Kazantzakis. He meant, I think, that valuable though language is to man, it is by very necessity limit-</td></tr>
<tr><td>Explanation that announces the writer's topic</td><td>ing, and creates for man an invisible prison. Language implies boundaries. A word spoken creates a dog, a rabbit, a man. It fixes their nature before our eyes; henceforth their shapes are, in a sense, our own creation. They are no longer</td></tr>
</table>

Thesis
statement

part of the unnamed shifting architecture of the universe. They have been transfixed as if by sorcery, frozen into a concept, a word. Powerful though the spell of human language has proven itself to be, it has laid boundaries upon the cosmos.

> (Loren Eiseley, "The Cosmic Prison," from *The Invisible Pyramid*)

🌐 WRITING IN THE USA Writing Effective Introductions

If getting your introduction to say what you want it to say seems impossible, you may want to draft the body of your paper first; many writers do. You'll almost always want to revisit your introduction after you have completed your paper.

---

1 ▪ Strategies for introductions

- Begin with a **dramatic quotation**, as Loren Eiseley does. Be sure to tell who is speaking and, if necessary, provide explanation to help readers understand how the quotation introduces your topic. (See Chapter 54, the sample research project.)

- Open with **dramatic details or description**. (See 59d, the sample persuasive essay.)

- Open at a dramatic point **in the middle of things** (also referred to as *in medias res*); then flash back to the beginning.

- Write a **strong statement**: a warning, or something that at first seems puzzling or contradictory.

- Pose a **problem** to solve **or question** to answer. (See 4f, the sample essay, and 55d, the sample report.)

- Open with an **analogy or comparison** that describes or illustrates your topic. (See the example paragraph in 6b7.)

- Tell an **anecdote**—a brief story—that illustrates your point. For example:

Topic and purpose for writing

An anecdote that creates reader interest and sets the tone of the essay

He was one of the greatest scientists the world has ever known, yet if I had to convey the essence of Albert Einstein in a single word, I would choose *simplicity*. Perhaps an anecdote will help. Once, caught in a downpour, he took off his hat and held it under his coat. Asked why, he explained, with admirable logic, that the rain would damage the hat, but his hair would be none the worse for its wetting. This knack for going instinctively to the heart of the matter was

The thesis of the essay the secret of his major scientific discoveries—this and his extraordinary feeling for beauty.

(Banesh Hoffman, from "Unforgettable Albert Einstein")

2 ■ Introductions, purpose, and audience

■ *Autobiographical and narrative writing.* Good stories usually begin at a point when something dramatic or important is about to happen. The introduction creates tension or expectation about the events soon to occur. Consider:

> The last inch of space was filled, yet people continued to wedge themselves along the walls of the Store. Uncle Willie had turned the radio up to its last notch so that youngsters on the porch wouldn't miss a word. Women sat on kitchen chairs, dining-room chairs, stools, and upturned wooden boxes. Small children and babies perched on every lap available and men leaned on the shelves or on each other.
> The apprehensive mood was shot through with shafts of gaiety, as a black sky is streaked with lightning.
> "I ain't worried 'bout this fight. Joe's gonna whip that cracker like it's open season."
>
> (Maya Angelou, from *I Know Why the Caged Bird Sings*)

As this scene is set, readers are interested to read on, as interested as the listeners in the story to hear whether "Joe," the great boxer Joe Louis, will indeed win the fight that is about to begin.

■ *Informative and explanatory writing.* Good introductions to informative and explanatory writing do whatever is necessary to help readers understand the information about to follow. They may put the topic in some larger context, describe the background, define key terms, identify the writer's point of view, present a problem to be solved or questions to be answered, state the purpose of the writing, or review what is already known about the topic. Consider this opening to a formal research report:

The context for the writer's research

Religious context

Philosophical context

Social context

> The situation in which one agent commands another to hurt a third turns up time and again as a significant theme in human relations. It is powerfully expressed in the story of Abraham, who is commanded by God to kill his son. It is no accident that [Danish philosopher Søren] Kierkegaard, seeking to orient his thought to the central themes of human experience, chose Abraham's conflict as the springboard to his philosophy.
> War too moves forward on the triad of an authority which commands a person to destroy the enemy, and perhaps all organized hostility may be viewed as a theme and

variation on the three elements of authority, executant, and

The purpose and topic of the report

victim. We describe an experimental program, recently concluded at Yale University, in which a particular expression of this conflict is studied by experimental means.

The research question to be answered

In its most general form the problem may be defined thus: if X tells Y to hurt Z, under what conditions will Y carry out the command of X and under what conditions will he refuse?

(Stanley Milgram, from "Some Conditions of
Obedience and Disobedience to Authority")

■ *Argumentative and persuasive writing.* Frequently, writers who intend to change readers' thinking or behavior begin by establishing a bond with their readers, earning their trust, and presenting their credentials for making the case that they do. (For persuasive introductions, see 59b.)

HOW TO . . . Revise Introductions

1. Avoid repeating your title in your opening line; doing so may make your introduction sound monotonous or unimaginative.

2. Cut unnecessary background or warm-up writing that you used to get yourself started. Advice for movie directors is also good for writers: "Cut to the chase." Open where your readers are, with what will interest them.

3. Although purpose statements are often appropriate in reports and scholarly articles, they are usually unnecessary in essays whose introductions contain a thesis statement. At the beginning of essays, don't tell your readers what you'll do; just do it.

4. Beware of mysterious openings. It's one thing to stimulate curiosity, quite another to mystify readers or plunge them into the dark. Your introduction should help readers make sound predictions about your topic—and even about your design and style.

5. Beware of overworked openings such as "Webster's defines . . ."

6d Write conclusions that signal the fufillment of your purpose

Conclusions are more than stopping places. For writers and readers alike, they create a sense of fulfillment and wholeness. They are not only your final words, they are your final opportunity to answer reader questions that justify their time spent reading: "So what?" "What next?" "Why should I care?" "What should I do?" Consider how this conclusion to an essay celebrating America's cultural diversity leads in the final sentence to a restatement of the writer's main point.

Two examples that illustrate the writer's thesis

Rhetorical questions that explain the examples

Answers that restate the thesis

One of our most visionary politicians said that he envisioned a time when the United States could become the brain of the world, by which he meant the repository of all of the latest advanced information systems. I thought of that remark when an enterprising poet friend of mine called to say that he had just sold a poem to a computer magazine and that the editors were delighted to get it because they didn't carry fiction or poetry. Is that the kind of world we desire? A humdrum homogeneous world of all brains but no heart, no fiction, no poetry; a world of robots with human attendants bereft of imagination, of culture? Or does North America deserve a more exciting destiny? To become a place where the cultures of the world crisscross. This is possible because the United States is unique in the world: The world is here.

(Ishmael Reed, "America: The Multinational Society," from *Writin' Is Fightin'*)

1 ▪ Strategies for conclusions

As the preceding example illustrates, effective conclusions restate, provide food for thought, and challenge reader thinking, feeling, or action. Create a conclusion appropriate to the topic and the occasion.

- Conclude with **your thesis** or other unifying statement. Organize your writing so that it leads naturally and inevitably to your point.

- Conclude by asking a **rhetorical question** for which the body of your paper has suggested the answer.

- Conclude by **challenging readers** to new thinking or action.

- Conclude with a **quotation**. Introduce and explain it if necessary.

- Conclude with an **anecdote** that summarizes your thinking.

- Conclude with a **hook**. Unify your writing by returning to—hooking up with—the subject of your opening and commenting on it in light of what you've written in the body of your paper.

6.2
Good introductions and conclusions: Web link

2 ▪ Conclusions, purpose, and audience

Like introductory strategies, the preceding conclusion strategies may be adapted to almost any writing situation. But certain kinds of writing tend to do certain things as they close in order to emphasize or achieve the writer's purpose.

6.3
Introductions and conclusions for specific kinds of writing: Web link

- *Autobiographical and narrative writing.* These kinds of writing often end with a discovery the writer has made. The story just completed has brought changes of understanding, outlook, or action, and the conclusion announces or dramatizes them.

- *Informative and explanatory writing.* These kinds of writing often end by telling readers what can be done with the information they've just received. These conclusions may state the meaning or significance of the information, offer proposals for action, describe the benefits of action, or predict the consequences of action or inaction. (See 4f and Chapter 54.)

- *Argumentative and persuasive writing.* These kinds of writing often end with an emotional appeal, an attempt to rouse readers' desire to agree with the writer. (See 59c and d.)

HOW TO . . . Revise Conclusions

1. Be sure your conclusion flows smoothly from the body of your writing. If necessary, write transitions or repeat key words.
2. Avoid restating the thesis you wrote in your introduction. If you want to emphasize your main point, do so with fresh language.
3. Avoid stock phrases that tell the obvious, such as *In conclusion, In closing,* and *In summary.*
4. Do not introduce new topics. Refocus attention on your original topic.
5. Be sure your readers will understand a closing quotation. Identify the speaker and, if necessary, explain its point.

7 Creating Coherence

Effective writing is **coherent**, meaning that all of its parts fit snugly together. A more descriptive word is **fluent**. Effective writing flows from idea to idea, paragraph to paragraph, sentence to sentence, and so is easier to read than incoherent writing. Writing unified by a single topic and overall design already has the essential features of coherence. Following are other features of coherent writing and ways to create them.

7.1
Coherence
tips:
Web link

HOW TO . . . Edit for Coherence

1. Look at your writing. Be sure you've written topic sentences and necessary transitions. If not, add them.
2. Mark key words and their synonyms. If you've written coherently, you'll see these words repeated frequently from paragraph to para-
(continued)

graph. If you have marked many different key words, you may have too many topics, and your writing may be disunified or incoherent. Refocus, reorganize, and rewrite to support your thesis and topic sentences.

3. Reread from the beginning of a paragraph. When you finish rewriting a paragraph, go back to its beginning and reread. If your rewrite fits coherently, your original and revised sentences will flow together smoothly.

4. Reread at your readers' pace. Writers read their writing more slowly than readers, pausing frequently to consider and evaluate. At this slower pace, transitions and repetitions may seem appropriate. But if you reread at your readers' swifter pace, you may discover that your momentum will carry you smoothly from one idea to the next without transitions or repetition. Cut unnecessary words.

🖥 **COMPUTER TIP** Checking Coherence

5. As you revise a rough draft, use your word processor's style features (underlining, italics, boldface, even alternative type fonts and sizes) to highlight topic sentences, key words, synonyms, pronouns, and transitions. You can see at a glance whether you've written coherently. Be sure to reformat your final draft before you print it. (See 46a1.) ▪

7a Repeat key words and their synonyms

Some writers believe that repeated words are a sign of monotonous writing. But key words that name your topics are worth repeating, especially key words from your thesis and topic sentences. Readers depend on them just as they depend on highway route markers to tell them they're on the right road. Consider the following paragraphs in which Pulitzer Prize–winning poet and journalist Donald Murray explains how experienced nonfiction writers create voice. Notice how often Murray repeats the word *voice* and related words (emphasis added).

Experienced writers rarely begin a first draft until they **hear** in their heads—or on the page—a **voice** that may be right. **Voice** is usually the key element in effective writing. It is what attracts the reader and communicates to the reader. It is that element that gives **the illusion of speech. Voice** carries the writer's intensity and glues together the information that the reader needs to know. It is the **music** in writing that makes meaning clear.

Writers keep rehearsing possible first lines, paragraphs, or endings, key scenes or statements that will reveal how what is to be **said** may be **said** best. The **voice** of a piece of writing is the writer's own

voice, adapted in written language to the subject and audience. We **speak** differently at a funeral or a party, in church or in the locker room, at home or with strangers. We are experienced with using our **individual voices** for many purposes. We have to learn to do this same thing in writing, and to **hear a voice** in our head that may be polished and developed on the page.

The **voice** is not only rehearsed but practiced. We should **hear** what we're writing as we write it. I **dictate** most of my writing and monitor my **voice** as I'm **speaking**, so that the **pace**, the **rhythm**, the **tone** support what I'm trying to **say**.

("Tricks of the Nonfiction Trade," *The Writer*)

7b Write transitions to connect ideas

Coherent writing not only repeats key words to develop its subject; it also links topics, sentences, and paragraphs with **transitions**. Transitional words, phrases, and sentences are like bridges that carry writers and readers from one idea to the next. They make the following connections:

- Addition: *additionally, again, also, and, as well, equally important, first (second, third), for one thing, further, moreover, next,* and so forth
- Alternation: *or, otherwise, nor, rather, instead*
- Comparison: *also, in the same way, likewise, similarly*
- Concession or agreement: *granted, it is true, of course, to be sure*
- Contrast: *after all, and yet, but, conversely, even so, however, in contrast, instead, nevertheless, nonetheless, on the contrary, on the other hand, yet*
- Examples: *as an illustration, for example, for instance, specifically*
- Explanation and logical relation: *as a result, because, consequently, for, for this reason, so, that being the case, therefore, thus, since*
- Place: *above, at this point, below, beyond, close, elsewhere, farther, here, near, next, on the other side, opposite, outside, within, there*
- Summary, emphasis, or conclusion: *accordingly, in conclusion, in other words, in short, in summary, indeed, on the whole, that is, therefore, thus*
- Time: *after, as, at last, at once, at the same time, by degrees, eventually, gradually, immediately, in a short time, in the future, later, meanwhile, promptly, soon, simultaneously, suddenly, then, when, while*

Consider the following excerpt, in which the writer uses transitions to weave action and description into a story, compare the past to the present, and signal conclusions. (Transitions linking paragraphs, sentences, and clauses are emphasized.)

Time transition

When I was a boy skating on Brooks Pond, there were no grown-ups around. Once or twice a year, on a weekend day or a holiday, some parents might come by with a thermos of hot cocoa. Maybe they would build a fire (which we were forbidden to do), **and** we would gather around.

Addition

Contrast

But for the most part the pond was the domain of children. In the absence of adults, we made and enforced our own rules. We had hardly any gear—just some borrowed hockey gloves, some hand-me-down skates, maybe an elbow pad or two—**so** we played a clean form of hockey, with no high-sticking, no punching, and almost no checking. A single fight could ruin the whole afternoon. **Indeed**, as I remember it, thirty years later, it was the purest form of hockey I ever saw—until I got to see the Russian national team play the game.

Logical relation

Emphasis

Time, contrast

But before we could play, we had to check the ice. We became serious junior meteorologists, true connoisseurs of cold. We learned that the best weather for pond skating is plain, clear cold, with starry nights and no snow. (Snow not only mucks up the skating surface but also insulates the ice from the colder air above.) **And** we learned that moving water, even the gently flowing Mystic River, is a lot less likely to freeze than standing water. **So** we skated only on the pond. We learned all the weird whooping and cracking sounds that ice makes as it expands and contracts, **and thus** when to leave the ice.

Addition

Logical relation

Logical relation

Question link

Contrast

Do kids learn these things today? I don't know. How would they? We don't let them. **Instead** we post signs. Ruled by lawyers, cities and towns everywhere try to limit their legal liability. **But try as they might**, they cannot eliminate the underlying risk. Liability is a social construct; risk is a natural fact. When it is cold enough, ponds freeze. No sign or fence or ordinance can change that.

Contrast

Conclusion

In fact, by focusing on liability and not teaching our kids how to take risks, we are making their world more dangerous. **When we were children**, we had to learn to evaluate risks and handle them on our own. We had to learn, quite literally, to test the waters. **As a result**, we grew up to be savvier about ice and ponds than any kid could be who has skated only under adult supervision on a rink.

Time

Logical relation

(Adapted from Christopher B. Daly, "How the Lawyers Stole Winter," *The Atlantic*)

7c Link sentences with pronouns

Pronouns substitute for nouns and noun phrases—the antecedents of pronouns (see 8b). The result is smoother reading. In the following example, consider how pronouns substitute for key words and, by so doing, link one sentence to another. (Pronouns and antecedents are emphasized.)

In the folklore of the country, numerous superstitions relate to winter weather. Back-country **farmers** examine **their** corn husks—the thicker the husk, the colder the winter. **They** watch the acorn crop—the more acorns, the more severe the season. **They** observe where white-faced **hornets** place **their** paper nests—the higher **they** are, the deeper will be the snow. **They** examine the size and shape and color of the spleens of butchered hogs for clues to the severity of the season. **They** keep track of the blooming of dogwood in the spring—the more abundant the blooms, the more bitter the cold in January.

> (Edwin Way Teale, from *Wandering Through Winter*)

HOW TO . . . Link with Transitions and Pronouns

1. Choose transitions that accurately signal the relationship between ideas and paragraphs—not ones that mean almost what you intend. For example, *and* may mean either "in addition" or "consequently."

2. Choose transitions that suit the formality of your writing. For example, you may use *so* or *but* in informal writing and *therefore* or *nevertheless* in more formal writing.

3. Use pronouns to substitute for nouns and noun phrases. As reminders, occasionally repeat the nouns or phrases to which pronouns refer.

WRITING IN THE USA   Using Transitions Sparingly

4. It can be tempting to use transitions frequently, but effective writing in English uses them sparingly. If you organize effectively, your writing will lead naturally from one topic to the next.

7d Write "old/new" sentences: include material from preceding sentences in each new sentence

Fluent sentences repeat "old business" from earlier sentences—words, ideas, or structural patterns—and add "new business" to develop a topic one step further. Read the following paragraph and consider how each sentence is linked to those that precede it. (Sentences are numbered; "old business" in each sentence is emphasized.)

(1) Be willing to make radical changes in your second draft. (2) If your thesis **changed** while you were writing your first draft, you will

base your **second draft** on this new subject. (3) **Even if your thesis
has not changed**, you may need to shift paragraphs around, eliminate
paragraphs, or add new ones. (4) Inexperienced writers often suppose
that **revising** a paper means **changing** only a word or two or adding
a sentence or two. (5) **This kind of editing** is part of the writing
process, but it is not the most important part. (6) **The most important part of rewriting** is a willingness to turn the paper upside
down, to shake out of it those ideas that interest you the most, to set
them in a form where they will interest the reader, too.

(Adapted from Richard Marius, "Writing
Drafts," from *A Writer's Companion*)

Sentences 1
and 2

Changes/changed . . . second draft are key words used in
both sentences.

Sentences 2
and 3

If . . . in sentence 2 is grammatically parallel with *Even if*
. . . in sentence 3 (parallel structure), and the words *thesis . . .
changed* are key words used in each sentence.

Sentences 3
and 4

Revising in sentence 4 connects with *shift paragraphs
around, eliminate paragraphs, or add new ones* in sentence 3
(key words).

7.2
Writing
coherent
paragraphs:
Exercises

Sentences 4
and 5

The key words *This kind of editing* in sentence 5 refer to
an activity described in sentence 4.

Sentences 5
and 6

In sentence 6, *The most important part* repeats key words
from sentence 5, and a dramatic description of revision reminds readers of the key words *radical changes* in sentence 1.

As you rewrite, examine your sentences to see whether they repeat
words, ideas, and patterns from earlier sentences. Without these links,
your sentences will seem to jump around, disconnected. With them, your
sentences will flow.

🌎 WRITING IN THE USA Varying Sentences

If you repeat words or sentence patterns unnecessarily, your writing will
sound choppy or wordy. Vary the kinds of sentences you use and the
sentence openings. (See 21b and 28a–c.)

Sentence Editing

FOCUS ON . . . Recognizing Key Sentence Parts

- How to identify nouns and verbs   76
- How to identify dependent clauses   88
- How to use the "yes/no test" to identify complete sentences   91
- How to identify agreement trouble spots   114 and 122

II Grammar & Editing

ON THE WEB   www.ablongman.com/dodds

Identifying Grammar

Grammar describes how native speakers and writers of a language produce their sentences. But this description is not what people have in mind when they say, "Watch your grammar!" What they mean is a set of language do's and don'ts known as **usage**: the conventions and language etiquette that the members of specific language groups follow. Grammar says, in effect, "This is what a native speaker or writer *does*." Usage says, "This is what a speaker or writer *ought* to do."

8.1
Useful
grammar
sites:
Web link

🌎 WRITING IN THE USA Standard English

The grammar presented in the following pages is actually a combination of the grammar and usage for one version or dialect of English, **Standard Written English**. This is the dialect generally written in schools, the professions, the business world, and the media. It is worth knowing because it is so widely shared, and it will give you editorial skills useful for improving your writing. For more detailed coverage of some of the points made in the following chapters, see Part V, Guide for Multilingual Writers.

8 Parts of Speech

The term **parts of speech** refers to a system for classifying English words according to their functions in sentences. Traditionally, words have been divided into eight parts of speech: nouns, pronouns, verbs, adjectives, adverbs, prepositions, conjunctions, and interjections. But some words change classes as their functions change. Consider the word *present.*

- A verb that describes action: *A geologist will* present *the next report.*
- A noun that describes an object: *Larry gave his sister a* present.
- An adjective that describes a feature: *This verb is in the* present *tense.*

8a Nouns

Nouns name persons, places, and things, including ideas, activities, qualities, conditions, and materials: *Confucius, brother, Baghdad, justice, baseball, tenderness, intelligence, paper.* We classify these nouns in a variety of ways, as

- **Proper** or **common nouns**: *King Juan Carlos* or *a king* (see 40b).
- **Abstract** or **concrete**: *flower* or *hope* (see 26b).
- **Count** or **noncount nouns**: *an apple* or *snow* (see 30a and b).
- **Collective nouns**: *jury* and *class* (see 14g and 15c).
- **Compound nouns**: *attorney general, grandmother,* or *brother-in-law.*

HOW TO . . . Identify Nouns and Verbs

Nouns

1. Nouns may be preceded by *a, an,* or *the: a computer, an apple, the president.*
2. Most nouns may be singular, plural, or possessive: *horse* [singular], *horses* [plural], *horse's* [possessive].
3. Nouns formed from other words end in *-ance* (guid*ance*), *-ation* (don*ation*), *-dom* (free*dom*), *-ence* (refer*ence*), *-hood* (neighbor*hood*), *-ice* (just*ice*), *-ion* (incis*ion*), *-ist* (tour*ist*), *-ity* (generos*ity*), *-ment* (judg*ment*), *-ness* (busi*ness*), *-ship* (friend*ship*).

Verbs

1. If you change the time of an action, a verb changes its form (known as **tense**) and reveals itself: *Aaron opened the book. Aaron is opening the book.* (For more on tense, see 8c3.)
2. Verbs formed from other kinds of words end in *-ize* and *-ify: realize, identify.*

ESL GRAMMAR NOTE   Placement of Adverbs

The adverbs *already, always, ever, not, often, only,* and *very* are sometimes placed in the middle of verbs—not after them—to provide additional information: *Larry has already written the report,* not *Larry has written already the report.* ■

8b   Pronouns

A **pronoun** refers to a noun, called its **antecedent**, that gives the pronoun its meaning. Pronouns change form to signal their function in a sentence.

8.2
Complete
guide to
pronouns:
Web link

	personal pronoun	possessive pronoun	reflexive pronoun
antecedent			

The little boy boasted that he could tie his shoes for himself.

1 ▪ Personal pronouns

Personal pronouns refer to specific persons, places, or things. (See also 17a–d.) Singular: *I, me, you, he, she, him, her, it.* Plural: *we, us, you, they, them.*

2 ▪ Possessive personal pronouns

In contrast to possessive nouns, **possessive personal pronouns** have no apostrophe. Singular: *my, mine, your, yours, his, her, hers, its.* Plural: *our, ours, your, yours, their, theirs.* (See also 17d; for ESL, see 32f.)

3 ▪ Demonstrative pronouns

A **demonstrative pronoun** (*this, that, these, those*) points to the noun it replaces.

pronoun   antecedent

These are the grapes my mother uses to make jelly.

4 ▪ Indefinite pronouns

An **indefinite pronoun** refers to a nonspecific person or thing. (See also 14f and 15d.)

all	anything	everyone	nobody	several
another	both	everything	none	some
any	each	few	no one	somebody
anybody	either	many	nothing	someone
anyone	everybody	neither	one	something

5 ▪ Interrogative pronouns

An **interrogative pronoun** begins a question: *who(ever), which(ever), whom(ever), whose, what(ever). Who wrote this poem?*

6 ▪ Relative pronouns

A **relative pronoun** (*who, which, whom, whose, that, whoever, whomever*) connects a relative clause to a noun in the main clause. (See also 10b3 and 16d.)

Note: Except for *that,* all relative pronouns begin with *wh-.*

antecedent   relative clause
                    pronoun

We asked directions from a man who was selling newspapers.

7 ▪ Intensive and reflexive pronouns

Intensive and **reflexive pronouns** consist of a personal pronoun plus *-self* or *-selves: myself, yourself, himself, herself, itself, ourselves, yourselves, themselves.* (See also 17g.)

- An **intensive pronoun** emphasizes a noun: *Joan designed the house herself.*

- A **reflexive pronoun** identifies the receiver of an action as identical to the doer of the action: *Peter rewarded himself with a day off.*

8 ■ Reciprocal pronouns

A **reciprocal pronoun** (*each other, one another*) refers to an individual part of a compound subject: *Pedro and Jack read each other's essays.*

8c   Verbs

Verbs express action or a state of being: *run, wish, is, appear, become, taste.*

Carol Morales **is campaigning** for a seat in the legislature.

He **seems** content.

1 ■ Helping verbs

Twenty-six **helping verbs** (also called **auxiliary verbs**) help to complete the meaning of a main verb: *They have arrived. They may arrive.*

HAVE, DO, BE	MODALS
have, has, had	can, could, may, might, must, shall,
do, does, did	should, will, would, ought to, had better, had to
be, am, is, are, was, were, being, been	

The verbs *have, do,* and *be* may also be the main verb of a sentence: *I had the answer. They were amazed.* **Modals** act only as helping verbs: *We might leave early.* (See also 13d; for ESL, see 31a–c.)

2 ■ Main verb forms

Except for the verb *be,* the main verb of a sentence has five forms:

- Base or infinitive form: *I often* (*play, speak*).

- *-s/-es* or third-person form: *He often* (*plays, speaks*).

- Past tense: *Then I* (*played, spoke*).

- Past participle: *I have* (*played, spoken*) *before.*

- Present participle: *I am* (*playing, speaking*) *now.*

Note: When accompanied by helping verbs, participles act as verbs: *They are playing my song.* When they stand without helping verbs, participles act as nouns or as adjectives: *Playing is sometimes hard work. Playing softly, the guitarist sang a sad song.* (See 10a3; for ESL, see 31f.)

3 ■ Tense

Helping verbs and main verb forms combine to indicate **tense**, the time when an action occurs. Standard English has six tenses, and each of these tenses has a progressive *-ing* form to indicate continuous action. (See also 13b; for ESL, see 31a.)

■ Present tense: action taking place now. *I sigh. He speaks. You/we/they are working.*

■ Past tense: past action. *I sighed. He spoke. You/we/they were working.*

■ Future tense: action that will take place. *I will sigh. He will speak. You/we/they will be working.*

■ Present perfect tense: past action continuing or completed in the present. *I have sighed. He has spoken. You/we/they have been working.*

■ Past perfect tense: past action completed before another past action. *I had sighed. He had spoken. You/we/they had been working.*

■ Future perfect tense: action that will begin and end in the future. *I will have sighed. He will have spoken. You/we/they will have been working.*

🌐 ESL GRAMMAR NOTE Additional Help with Verbs

Verbs are the heart of effective English sentences. They are also the most complex word form in English grammar. For additional help with verbs, see Chapter 31.

8d Adjectives and articles

An **adjective** modifies a noun or pronoun. It answers the questions *which one, what kind,* or *how many.* (See also 18a–d; for ESL, see 32g.)

which one   how many
That rock contains three fossils.

what kind   what kind
The dark clouds warned of a dangerous storm.

🌐 ESL GRAMMAR NOTE Articles

The articles *a, an,* and *the* are considered adjectives. *The* is a **definite article** referring to specific persons, places or things: *the dancer, the house. A* and *an* are **indefinite articles** referring to nonspecific persons, places, or things: *a dancer* (any dancer), *a house* (any house). Unlike many languages, articles in English do not change based on gender or number of the noun they precede. (See Chapter 30.)

ESL GRAMMAR NOTE Adjectives in a Series

Standard English requires that adjectives in a series follow a particular order. For guidelines, see 32g3.

8e Adverbs

An **adverb** modifies verbs, adjectives, and other adverbs. It answers the questions *how, when, where, why, under what circumstances,* and *to what extent.* (See also 18a and c; for ESL, see 32g.)

adverb modifying the adverb *softly*: how

The old man whispered very softly.

adverb modifying the verb *revise*: when

Revise your paper later.

adverb modifying the verb *are camping*: where

The scouts are camping nearby.

HOW TO . . . Identify Adjectives and Adverbs

Adjectives

1. Adjectives can be compared using *-er/-est, more/most, less/least: happier, most beautiful.*

2. Adjectives formed from other words end with *-able* (enjoy*able*), *-ar* (spectacul*ar*), *-ent* (depend*ent*), *-ful* (power*ful*), *-ial* (colon*ial*), *-ible* (respons*ible*), *-ing* (disgust*ing*), *-ish* (fool*ish*), *-ive* (invent*ive*), *-less* (use*less*), *-ly* (kind*ly*), *-ous* (gener*ous*), *-y* (leaf*y*).

 ESL GRAMMAR NOTE Adjective Word Endings

3. Unlike adjectives in many other languages, English adjectives take word endings only when used in comparative statements.

[adjective]

She was the *happiest* person in the room. ▪

Adverbs

1. Many adverbs end with *-ly: happily, evenly, smoothly.* But some also have other forms: *far, fast, first, not, very,* and *well.* Furthermore, not all *-ly* words are adverbs.

[adjective]

She gave him a *friendly* glance.

2. Most adverbs can be compared using *-er/-est, more/most, less/least: faster, more slowly.*

The couple walked *more slowly* the closer they came to the front door.

3. Adverbs may often be moved within a sentence to shift emphasis or focus.

She smiled *slyly. Slyly,* she smiled. She *slyly* smiled.

(See also 21a and 23a.)

8f Prepositions

A **preposition** usually precedes a noun or pronoun called the **object of the preposition**. Together the preposition and its object form a **prepositional phrase**, which modifies other words in a sentence. (See also 10a2; for ESL, see 32h.)

preposition   object   preposition object

The children ran into the room and knelt before the fire.

As the following list indicates, some prepositions consist of two or more words.

COMMON PREPOSITIONS

about	before	down	of	till
above	behind	during	off	to
according to	below	except	on	together with
across	beneath	for	opposite	toward
after	beside	from	out	under
against	besides	in	over	underneath
along	between	in addition to	past	unlike
among	beyond	in spite of	regarding	until
around	by	instead of	respecting	up
as	concerning	into	round	upon
as many as	considering	like	since	with
as well as	despite	near	through	within
at	different from	next	throughout	without

🌏 ESL GRAMMAR NOTE Prepositions and Verbs

Certain prepositions appear with certain verbs in two-word combinations, called collocations. There are no rules that govern these combinations; they must be memorized. For more on two-word verbs, see 31g.

8g Conjunctions

A **conjunction** links words, phrases, or clauses and signals their relationship as grammatically equal or unequal.

1 ■ Coordinating conjunctions

Coordinating conjunctions (*and, but, for, so, or, nor, yet*) link grammatically equal words and word groups. To remember coordinating conjunctions, think of the word *FANBOYS: For, And, Nor, But, Or, Yet, So.* (See also 11b6, 14d, 15a, and 19a; for ESL, see 32b3.)

> Kim **and** Jean played their best tennis of the season, **but** they lost to superior opponents.

2 ■ Correlative conjunctions

Correlative conjunctions are word pairs (*both/and, either/or, neither/ nor, not/but, not only/but also, whether/or*) that link grammatically equal words and word groups. (See also 14e, 15b, and 19c.)

> **Both** the Earl of Oxford **and** Ben Jonson have been proposed as the true author of William Shakespeare's plays.

3 ■ Subordinating conjunctions

Subordinating conjunctions begin adverb clauses and link them to independent clauses. They specify *how, when,* or *where* or introduce a qualifying statement. (See also 10b2.)

In the following example, the subordinating conjunction *after* introduces an adverb clause that tells when the action of the main verb (*began*) occurs.

subordinate clause	independent clause

> **After** they finished breakfast, the campers began loading their gear into the canoes.

COMMON SUBORDINATING CONJUNCTIONS

after	before	provided that	unless
although	even if	rather than	until
as	even though	since	when
as if	how	so	where
as long as	if	than	wherever
as soon as	in order that	that	whether
as though	just as	though	while
because	once	till	why

4 ■ Conjunctive adverbs

Conjunctive adverbs are used with a semicolon to link independent clauses. They signal logical relations. (See also 12b3 and 35b.)

It rained five inches in the last week; **however**, the drought is far from over.

COMMON CONJUNCTIVE ADVERBS

also	furthermore	likewise	otherwise
anyhow	hence	meanwhile	similarly
anyway	however	moreover	still
besides	incidentally	nevertheless	then
consequently	indeed	next	therefore
finally	instead	nonetheless	thus

8.3
Identifying
parts of
speech:
Exercises

8h Interjections

An **interjection** is a strong expression of feeling or a call for attention, followed by a comma or exclamation point: *Oh, I'm sorry to hear that. Ouch! I've pinched my hand in the door.*

9 Sentence Parts

A sentence has two parts: a subject and a predicate. Together they make a complete statement, question, exclamation, or command. In most commands, the subject *you* is not stated.

<u>subject</u> <u>predicate</u>

- Statement: The sonnet has two forms, the Italian and the Elizabethan.

<u>predicate</u>

- Command with unstated subject *you*: Be sure to bring the volleyball to the picnic.

9a Subjects

The **subject** of a sentence names the person, place, or thing that acts, is acted on, or is described. The subject may precede or follow the predicate but usually precedes it.

She works as a pathologist.

Algae produce their food through photosynthesis.

The batik technique for dyeing fabric was developed in Malaya.

In a box under the porch slept **four tiny kittens**.

9.1
Sentence
parts and
their
functions:
Web link

1 ■ Simple subjects

The **simple subject** of a sentence is a noun or pronoun by itself, without modifying words, phrases, or clauses: *she, algae, technique, kittens.*

2 ■ Complete subjects

The **complete subject** is the noun or pronoun and all of its modifiers: *algae, the batik technique for dyeing fabric, four tiny kittens.*

3 ■ Compound subjects

A **compound subject** consists of two or more simple subjects linked by a conjunction.

Muscle **strength and** aerobic **efficiency** are essential to physical fitness.

HOW TO . . . Identify the Subjects of Sentences

Ask *who* or *what* + the verb + the remainder of the sentence: *Algae produce their food through photosynthesis.* What produce their food through photosynthesis? *Algae.* Note that not all sentences open with the subject: *Into the room walked the President of the United States.* Who walked into the room? *The President of the United States.*

9b Predicates

1 ■ Simple predicates

The **simple predicate** of a sentence consists of a verb and any helping verbs.

The locksmith **is resetting** the tumblers of the lock.

9.2
Identifying
subjects
and
predicates:
Exercises

2 ■ Complete predicates

A **complete predicate** consists of the simple predicate and all words associated with it: modifiers, objects, and complements.

$$\overset{\text{verb}}{\overbrace{\text{The locksmith is resetting}}} \overset{\text{object}}{\overbrace{\text{the tumblers of the lock.}}}$$

3 ■ Compound predicates

A **compound predicate** consists of two or more predicates with the same subject.

$$\overset{\text{subject}}{\overbrace{\text{The locksmith}}} \overset{\text{predicate}}{\overbrace{\text{reset the tumblers of the lock}}} \overset{\text{predicate}}{\overbrace{\text{and made a new key.}}}$$

9c Objects

1 ▪ Direct objects

A **direct object** is the person, place, or thing that receives the action of a **transitive verb**, a verb that does something to someone or something.

transtive verb   direct object

Judy is growing a new variety of hosta in her garden.

To identify the direct object in a sentence, use the subject and verb in a question ending with *what?* or *whom?* *Judy is growing what?* The answer is the complete direct object.

2 ▪ Indirect objects

An **indirect object** is the person to whom or for whom an action occurs.

                    transitive   direct
        subject   verb   indirect object   object

Dr. Watson gave Sherlock Holmes a clue.

To identify the indirect object in a sentence, look for the words *to* or *for* or see whether you can insert them before the person to or for whom an action is done. You may have to rearrange the sentence. *Dr. Watson gave a clue to Sherlock Holmes.*

9d Complements

Complements complete the meaning of a verb and provide additional information about a subject. (See also 14c and 18b.)

1 ▪ Subject complements

A **subject complement** is a noun or adjective that renames or describes the subject of what is called a **linking verb**, such as *become, be, feel, taste.* Subject complements are also called *predicate adjectives* or *predicate nouns.*

            subject complement: adjective

The sunset is beautiful.

                    linking verb subject complement: noun

The prince will soon become king.

2 ▪ Object complements

An **object complement** is a noun or adjective that follows a direct object and renames or describes it. Object complements only appear with certain verbs, such as *name, call, elect, find, make.*

subject   verb   direct object   object complement: noun

The proud parents named their daughter Stephanie.

subject   verb   direct object   object complement: adjective

The jury found the defendant guilty.

9.3
Diagram-
ming
sentences:
Web link

Note: Verbs without objects or complements are called **intransitive verbs**. These verbs may, however, be followed by other words such as adverbs: *The engine hummed. The engine hummed softly.*

10 Phrases, Clauses, and Sentence Types

10a Phrases

A **phrase** is a grammatically related group of words lacking a subject, a verb, or both. Within a sentence a phrase may act as a noun, verb, adjective, or adverb.

phrase as a noun   phrase as an adjective

Kevin's decision to return the lost wallet was not very difficult to make.

1 ■ Noun phrases

A **noun phrase** consists of a noun plus all of its modifying words. These modifiers may precede or follow the noun.

modifiers noun   noun   modifiers

A good essay contains topics worth reading about.

Note that complete noun phrases may contain other phrases or even clauses.

noun   adjective clause

The man that I met last night is surely a genius.

You can identify complete noun phrases by substituting personal pronouns such as *it, he, they, one,* and so forth: *A good essay contains topics worth reading about* becomes *It contains them. The man that I met last night is surely a genius* becomes *He is surely one.*

2 ■ Prepositional phrases

A **prepositional phrase** consists of a preposition plus a noun or pronoun (the object of the preposition) and any modifiers. (See also 8f; for ESL, see 32h.)

preposition modifiers   object

at the morning roll call

Prepositional phrases may act as adjectives (telling *which one* or *what kind*), as adverbs (telling *how, when,* or *where*), or as nouns.

prepositional phrase as an adjective: which one

The man in the gray suit is my father.

prepositional phrase as an adverb: where

Sally is studying in the biology lab.

prepositional phrase as a noun: subject complement

The best time to see your instructor is before class.

WRITING IN THE USA Idiomatic Prepositional Phrases

English prepositional phrases often possess idiomatic meanings: *She arrived on time. He arrived just in time.* See 32h for guidance.

---

3 ▪ Verbal phrases

A **verbal phrase** is a verb and its related words acting as a noun, adjective, or adverb. There are three kinds of verbal phrases.

▪ A **gerund phrase** consists of the *-ing* form of a verb and any related words: *campaigning for office, swimming in the ocean, exercising regularly.* In a sentence, a gerund phrase acts as a noun. (For ESL, see 31f.)

gerund phrase as a subject

Campaigning for office requires energy and money.

gerund phrase as a direct object

I enjoy swimming in the ocean.

gerund phrase as a complement

One key to good health is exercising regularly.

▪ A **participial phrase** consists of the present or past participle of a verb (ending *-ing, -ed, -d, -en, -n,* or *-t*) and any related words. A participial phrase always acts as an adjective modifying a noun or pronoun. (See also 11b2.)

participial phrase modifying a subject

Gazing at the painting, she recalled the house where she was born.

participial phrase modifying the direct object *uniform*

The soldier put on a uniform covered with ribbons and medals.

▪ An **infinitive phrase** consists of the word *to* plus the base form of the verb plus any related words. It may act as a noun, adjective, or adverb.

infinitive phrase as a noun: direct object

Paul wanted to learn silk screening.

infinitive phrase as an adjective modifying *place*

Unfortunately, the library is no longer a place to find peace and quiet.

infinitive phrase as an adverb modifying *use*

Use a spell checker to help you proofread your writing.

4 ■ Appositive phrases

An **appositive phrase** renames or describes a preceding noun or noun phrase. It usually acts like a noun or noun equivalent.

noun   appositive phrase

Shiraz, the ancient capital of Persia, is now a pilgrimage center for Shiite Muslims.

5 ■ Absolute phrases

10.1
The garden
of phrases:
Web link

An **absolute phrase** consists of a noun or noun phrase plus the present or past participle of a verb and is preceded or followed by a comma. An absolute phrase modifies an entire sentence or clause.

Hands waving, the children clamored for the teacher's attention.

The sailors raised the sails eagerly, **their minds filled with dreams of home**.

10.2
Identifying
and writing
phrases:
Exercises

10b Clauses

A **clause** is a group of words with a subject and a predicate: *roses are red, where the buffalo roam, which essay is best.*

- ■ An **independent clause** (often called a **main clause**) can stand alone as a complete sentence: *Roses are red.*

- ■ A **dependent clause** cannot stand alone: *where the buffalo roam, which essay is best.* Within a sentence a dependent clause may act as a noun, an adjective, or an adverb: *We were told to decide which essay is best.* The dependent clause *which essay is best* acts as a noun, the direct object of the sentence.

HOW TO . . . Identify Dependent Clauses

Independent and dependent clauses both contain a subject and a verb:

subject   verb

Independent clause: The rain was falling.

subject   verb   subject   verb

Dependent clauses: Because the rain was falling . . . which was falling . . .

But dependent clauses *always* begin with a "subordinator word," a subordinating conjunction such as *because* (see 8g3 for a complete list), or a relative pronoun such as *which* (see 8b6). In certain kinds of sentences, these subordinator words function to link one clause (a dependent clause) to the main or independent clause: *Because the rain was falling so heavily, we decided to postpone our trip. The rain, which was falling steadily, soon filled the birdbath.* By itself, a dependent clause is not a complete sentence. (See also 11b3 and 4.)

1 ▪ Noun clauses

A **noun clause** may act as a subject, object, complement, or appositive. Noun clauses usually begin with *how, that, which, who, whoever, whom, whomever, what, whatever, when, where, whether, whose,* or *why.*

<u>subject</u>
Where he went is a mystery to me.

<u>direct object</u>
Researchers have discovered what causes depression.

2 ▪ Adverb clauses

An **adverb clause** (often referred to as a **subordinate clause**) begins with a subordinating conjunction such as *after, because, since, when* (see 8g3 for a list). Adverb clauses modify verbs, adjectives, or adverbs, and tell *how, when, where, why,* or *under what conditions.* (See also 11b3.)

<u>adverb clause that tells *when*</u>
After the hailstorm ended, the farmers inspected their damaged crops.

3 ▪ Adjective clauses

An **adjective clause** (also called a **relative clause**) begins with a relative pronoun (*who, whoever, which, that, whose, whom, whomever*) or, occasionally, with the adverbs *when, where,* or *why.* Relative clauses act as adjectives and tell *which one* or *what kind.* (See also 11b4.)

We plan to hire someone **who can do technical writing**.

The land **where the buffalo roam** has been shrunk to a few national parks and preserves.

10.3
Identifying
clauses:
Exercises

10c Sentence types

1 ▪ Classifying sentences by their clauses

▪ A **simple sentence** has one independent clause and no dependent clauses. It may have a compound subject and compound predicate and one-word or one-phrase modifiers.

10.4
A sentence
type quiz:
Web link

independent clause

The Roman poet Virgil is the author of the *Aeneid*.

independent clause

Adam and Eve left the Garden of Eden and entered a treacherous new world.

■ A **compound sentence** has two or more independent clauses and no dependent clauses. Its clauses are linked by a coordinating conjunction (*and, or, but, yet, so, for, nor*) or by a semicolon. (See also 34a and 35a.)

independent clause   independent clause

A penny saved may be a penny earned, but the earnings don't amount to much.

■ A **complex sentence** has an independent clause and at least one dependent clause.

dependent clause   independent clause

When the wind changed direction, the temperature began to drop.

■ A **compound-complex sentence** has at least two independent clauses and at least one dependent clause.

independent clause   independent clause

dependent clause   dependent clause

Imran knew that he should help, but he wasn't sure what he should do.

2 ■ Classifying sentences by their purpose

■ A **declarative sentence** makes a statement: *Bumblebees hummed in the doorway of the abandoned house.*

■ An **interrogative sentence** asks a question: *Where is Lake Agassiz located?*

10.5
Practicing
with
sentence
types:
Exercises

■ An **imperative sentence** issues a command, makes a direct request, or gives advice: *When you come to the meeting, bring your copy of the annual report.*

■ An **exclamatory sentence** makes an exclamation of excitement or emotion: *That's the best performance of* Othello *I've seen!*

Editing Grammar and Usage

11 Editing Sentence Fragments

HOW TO . . . Identify Sentence Fragments

1. *Look for clue words.* Look for clue words that sometimes signal sentence fragments:

   - present participles (the *-ing* verb form) without helping verbs (see 11b2);

   - a subordinating conjunction, such as *although, because, when, after,* or *if* at the beginning of a word group (see 11b3);

   - a relative pronoun—*who, which, whom,* and so forth—at the beginning of a word group that is not a question (see 11b4).

COMPUTER TIP Using Search and Replace Commands

2. Use the Find or Search and Replace command of your word processing program to look for the clue words that sometimes signal fragments. ▪

3. *Use the yes/no test.* If you're unsure whether a word group is a complete sentence, try the yes/no test. If a word group is not already a question, turn it into a yes/no question. Rearrange words if necessary.

   She is going to buy a new computer → Is she going to buy a new computer?

   If the word group contains a single-word verb, add a helping verb. Change verb forms as necessary to complete the question.

   She bought a new computer → Did she buy a new computer?

   If the yes/no question makes sense and sounds complete, as in the preceding examples, the original word group is an independent clause, which can be punctuated as a complete sentence. Otherwise, the word group is a sentence fragment.

   Because she is going to buy a new computer → Is because she is going to buy a new computer?

   [The question doesn't make sense; therefore, the original is a fragment.]

   (continued)

Buying her first computer, a laptop → Is buying her first computer, a laptop?

[The question sounds incomplete; therefore, the original is a fragment.]

4. *Read from the end of your paper.* Begin at the end of your paper and read each sentence aloud. Isolating each sentence in this way will help you hear the incomplete thoughts that signal fragments.

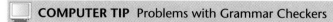 **COMPUTER TIP** Problems with Grammar Checkers

5. Grammar checkers may misidentify complete sentences as fragments or miss actual fragments. Use the tips above to identify fragments.

11a Connect fragments to complete sentences, or rewrite them as complete sentences

11.1
Identifying
and editing
fragments:
Web link

A **sentence fragment** is an incomplete sentence. To be complete, a sentence must have an independent clause—a subject and verb that can stand alone. (See 9a and b, 10b.) In the following examples, fragments are italicized.

The individual most responsible for making Texas part of the United States was Sam Houston. *War hero, president of Texas, and its first senator.*

[The italicized word group is a series of noun phrases without a verb.]

Last night I opened my window to enjoy the autumn air. *Which unfortunately was filled with ragweed pollen from the vacant lot next door.*

[The italicized word group has a subject and verb, *which . . . was filled*, but the relative pronoun *which* cannot be the subject of an independent clause.]

If you sometimes write fragments, you can learn to identify and rewrite them as complete sentences. (See the "How to Identify Sentence Fragments" box, pp. 91–92.) Most fragments can be fixed in one of two ways.

1 ▪ Connecting fragments

Connect the fragment to a nearby complete sentence. Repunctuate if necessary. Use this method if your main idea is expressed in the complete sentence rather than in the fragment.

The individual most responsible for making Texas part of the United

States was Sam Houston, War hero, president of Texas, and its first senator.

2 ▪ Rewriting fragments

Rewrite the fragment as a complete sentence. Add words or change word forms; if necessary, rearrange for clarity or emphasis. Use this method to emphasize an idea in the fragment or to create two sentences where one would be too long.

Last night I opened my window to enjoy the autumn air. ~~Which unfortunately~~ *Unfortunately, it* was filled with ragweed pollen from the vacant lot next door.

[The relative pronoun *which* cannot be the subject of a sentence. The revision substitutes the personal pronoun *it,* which can be a subject, and rearranges for emphasis.]

11b Learn the clues that signal sentence fragments

Certain word groups are sometimes written and punctuated as if they were complete sentences. Learn to recognize them as sentence fragments.

1 ■ Appositive phrases without verbs

Look for noun phrases—**appositive phrases**—that describe a word at the end of the preceding sentence. An appositive phrase standing alone, without a verb, is a fragment. Usually you can attach these fragments to the preceding sentence with a comma. (See also 10a4.)

The first African American to earn widespread fame as a novelist was Richard Wright~~, Author~~ *, author* of <u>Native Son</u> and <u>Black Boy</u>.

🌍 **ESL GRAMMAR NOTE** Omitting Verbs

In formal written English, complete sentences must contain a complete verb (a main verb and any necessary helping verbs). (See 31a2.) However, intentional fragments or incomplete sentences—word groups without verbs—are sometimes appropriate in less formal or more personal writing. (See 11c.)

---

2 ■ Phrases with present participles and no helping verbs

Phrases with *-ing* verbs—present participles—and no helping verbs are participial phrases, which cannot be punctuated as complete sentences. They lack subjects and complete verbs. (See 10a3.) Usually you can connect these fragments to the preceding sentence.

The greatest environmental threat to equatorial Africa is the Sahara~~, Spreading~~ *, spreading* southward during ten years of severe drought.

[Use the yes/no test to identify the fragment: *Is spreading southward during ten years of severe drought?* This sounds incomplete and is therefore a fragment.]

3 ■ Word groups beginning with subordinating conjunctions

Standing by itself, a word group beginning with a subordinating conjunction, such as *after, because,* and *when,* is a sentence fragment. Even though it contains a subject and a verb, the subordinating conjunction creates a dependent clause—an incomplete sentence. Connect a dependent clause to a complete sentence nearby. If necessary, move it next to the words it modifies, as in this example.

Because his paintings appeal to nostalgia and sentimentality,
∧Norman Rockwell is an artist admired by many. ~~Because his paintings~~

~~appeal to nostalgia and sentimentality~~,

[Use the yes/no test to identify the fragment: *Is because his painting appeals to nostalgia and sentimentality?* The result is a nonsense question, and the original is therefore a fragment.]

Note: Introductory phrases and clauses are usually set off from the main part of the sentence with a comma. (See 34b.)

4 ■ Word groups beginning with relative pronouns

Relative pronouns (*who, whom, which, that*) link a group of words—an adjective clause—to an independent clause. (See 10b3.) If it stands by itself, an adjective clause is an incomplete sentence, even though it contains a relative pronoun as its subject and a verb. If you find a capitalized relative pronoun at the beginning of a word group that is not a question, you may have found a fragment. If so, connect it to a complete sentence nearby.

, who
Each judge gave a long speech praising the contestants. ~~Who~~ stood near
∧
the podium, smiling nervously, waiting for the winner to be announced.

[Use the yes/no test to identify the fragment: *Is who stood near the podium smiling nervously, waiting for the winner to be announced?* The result is a nonsense question, and the original is therefore a fragment.]

5 ■ Lists punctuated as sentences

Connect fragmentary lists to the clause that introduces them. Use a colon, a dash, or an introductory phrase such as *for example, such as,* or *including.* (See 36a and 39a3.)

: two
Plans for rehearsing the play should be precise. ~~Two~~ weeks for
∧
memorizing the script, two weeks for learning the music, one month for

practicing the dance routines.

[To identify the fragment, apply the yes/no test to the list.]

6 ▪ Disconnected compound predicates

A fragment results when one part of a compound predicate (see 9b3) is separated from the other part and punctuated as a complete sentence. Connect the fragment to the preceding sentence.

Most viewers praise the artistry in <u>Birth of a Nation</u>. ~~But~~ *but* condemn the

movie for its racism and distortions of American history.

Their engines groaning, several cars slowly climbed the steep mountain

road. ~~Then~~ *, then* disappeared over the summit.

[To identify the fragments in these examples, apply the yes/no test to each group of words punctuated as a sentence.]

 ESL GRAMMAR NOTE Omitting Subjects

Unlike many other languages, standard English does not allow subjects to be omitted from sentences, except for the implied *you* of imperative sentences. (See 32a1.)

---

7 ▪ Long prepositional phrases

Look for phrases beginning with *during, concerning, except, in addition to, instead of.* (See 8f for a list of prepositions.) A phrase that is not connected to an independent clause is a fragment. Connect it to the preceding sentence.

The senator from Ohio proposed that all welfare recipients receive job

training or education. ~~In~~ *in* addition to welfare checks.

[To identify the fragment, apply the yes/no test to each statement punctuated as a sentence.]

11c Occasionally use fragments for special effect

Most writing for school, business, and the professions requires complete sentences. But occasionally, in personal, informal, or emotionally charged writing, fragments help to emphasize an idea, avoid repetition, or duplicate speech rhythms. To decide whether a fragment is appropriate, consider whether the situation permits informal or emotionally charged writing. Use fragments sparingly. (Fragments are italicized in the following examples.)

1 ■ A fragment for emphasis and economy

A beautiful woman, we say in English. *But a handsome man.* "Handsome" is the masculine equivalent of—and refusal of—a compliment which has accumulated certain demeaning overtones, by being reserved for women only.

> (Susan Sontag, "A Woman's Beauty: Put-down or Power Source?" emphasis added)

2 ■ Fragments for emphasis, feeling, and speech rhythms

Family language, my family's sounds: the voices of my parents and sisters and brother. Their voices insisting: You belong here. We are family members. *Related. Special to one another.* Listen! *Voices singing and sighing, rising and straining, then surging, teeming with pleasure which burst syllables into fragments of laughter.* At times it seemed there was steady quiet only when, from another room, the rustling whispers of my parents faded and I edged closer to sleep.

> (Richard Rodriguez, "Aria: A Memoir of a Bilingual Childhood," *American Scholar,* emphasis added)

11.2
Fixing
sentence
fragments:
Exercises

EXERCISE 11.1   Fixing Fragments

Fix sentence fragments by connecting them to nearby sentences or by rewriting them as complete sentences. If an item is correct, write "correct." See the answers in the appendix.

1. The causes of social status are many. The possession of money, education, relationship to political power, the accidents of birth or geography, even physical appearance.

2. Strategies in chess are determined by the designated movements of each piece. As well as the initial arrangement of the pieces on the board.

3. In most games, the winner earns the most points, but in some games, the object is to end with the fewest points. One example is darts.

4. The majority of smokers begin to smoke as teenagers. Seventy-five percent by age seventeen, eighty-nine percent by age nineteen.

5. Gena lay awake throughout the storm. Listening to the branches of the ancient crabapple scratching the side of her house.

12 Fixing Comma Splices and Fused Sentences

12a Fix comma splices by repunctuating or rewriting

A **comma splice** results when two or more independent clauses (grammatically complete word groups) are linked by a comma. They are spliced together as if they were parts of one sentence instead of being punctuated as separate statements. For example:

> Ramon performed well on the first test, he expected to do even better on the second.

> [*Ramon performed . . . test* is one independent clause with its own subject and predicate; *he expected . . . second* is another.]

🌐 WRITING IN THE USA Comma Splices

Some languages, and some varieties of English, permit comma splices. Standard Written American English, however, does not.

HOW TO . . . Identify and Edit Comma Splices

1. To identify comma splices, apply the yes/no test to word groups preceding and following a comma. (The yes/no test is explained in the "How to Identify Sentence Fragments" box, pp. 91–92.) If these word groups make sense and sound complete by themselves, they are independent clauses linked by a comma: a comma splice.

   John had told a lie, he knew he had to apologize. → Had John told a lie? Did he know he had to apologize?

   > [The two questions make sense and sound complete, so they are two independent clauses linked by a comma: a comma splice.]

   Because John had told a lie, he knew he had to apologize. → Had because John told a lie? Did he know he had to apologize?

   > [The first question doesn't make sense, so it is not a complete sentence. The first word group is a dependent clause followed by an independent clause. Therefore, the example is a complete sentence, not a comma splice.]

   The weather forecaster predicted sunshine for our picnic, however, it rained all day. → Did the weather forecaster predict sunshine for our picnic? Did it rain all day, however?

   (continued)

[The yes/no test identifies two word groups linked by a comma and the conjunctive adverb *however* that make sense and sound complete. Even with the adverb, they are independent clauses linked by a comma: a comma splice.]

2. Eliminate comma splices by repunctuating with a period, semicolon, colon, or dash. Or rewrite, turning one independent clause into a dependent clause or a phrase.

Having told a lie, John knew he had to apologize.

The weather forecaster predicted sunshine for our picnic; however, it rained all day.

1 ▪ Repunctuating

▪ Use a **period** to make each clause a separate sentence.

Ramon performed well on the first test, he expected to do even better on

the second.

[margin correction: . He]

▪ Use a **semicolon (;)** to join related independent clauses when they are nearly equal in importance. (See 35a.)

Ramon performed well on the first test, he expected to do even better on

the second.

[margin correction: ;]

▪ Use a **colon (:)** to join independent clauses when one clause introduces or explains the other. (See 36a.)

Professor Li is the best instructor I've had, he knows his subject and

how to present it in an imaginative way.

[margin correction: :]

▪ Use a **dash (—)** to join independent clauses when the second clause makes a surprising or abrupt response to the first. (See 39a.)

Alison asked Betsy if she knew where the car keys were, she didn't.

[margin correction: —]

2 ▪ Adding a coordinating conjunction

Add a coordinating conjunction (*and, but, or, nor, so, yet, for*) after the comma that joins two independent clauses. The result is a compound sentence. (See 10c1.)

Ramon performed well on the first test, he expected to do even better on

the second.

[margin correction: and]

3 ▪ Rewriting to create one complete sentence

▪ *Adding a subordinating conjunction.* Add a subordinating conjunction (*because, although, when,* and so forth) to one clause to connect it grammatically to the other. (See 8g3.) The result is a complex sentence that emphasizes one clause and deemphasizes the other. (See 10c1.)

Because
Ramon performed well on the first test, he expected to do even better on
∧
the second.

▪ *Turning a clause into a phrase.* Turn one clause into a phrase that modifies the remaining independent clause. The result is a simple sentence. (See 10c1.)

After performing   *Ramon*
~~Ramon performed~~ well on the first test, ~~he~~ expected to do even better on
∧   ∧
the second.

12b Learn the clues that signal comma splices

1 ▪ Independent clauses on both sides of a comma

Examine the words on both sides of a comma. If you can put a period after both word groups, you have two independent clauses incorrectly connected with a comma. Fix the comma splice by repunctuating or rewriting.

I'm not going to college because my parents told me to*;* there are specific

subjects I want to study.

[To the left of the comma, *I'm not going to college* is an independent clause; to the right, *there are specific subjects* is an independent clause.]

12.1
Editing
comma
splices:
Web link

2 ▪ A second clause that begins with a pronoun

In some comma splices the subject of the second independent clause is a pronoun referring to the subject of the first.

. He
Julian refused the award for heroism, ~~he~~ said he had only done what
∧
anyone would.

[The *he* following the comma is the subject of the second independent clause; it also refers to the subject of the first, *Julian.*]

3 ▪ Independent clauses joined by a comma and a transition or conjunctive adverb

Transitions and conjunctive adverbs link words and word groups (see 7b and 8g4).

COMMON TRANSITIONS AND CONJUNCTIVE ADVERBS

accordingly	conversely	in fact	otherwise
after all	even so	in other words	similarly
also	finally	in the first place	specifically
anyhow	for example	likewise	still
anyway	for instance	meanwhile	subsequently
as a matter of fact	furthermore	moreover	that is
as a result	hence	nevertheless	then
at any rate	however	next	therefore
at the same time	indeed	now	thus
besides	instead	of course	
certainly	in addition	on the contrary	
consequently	in conclusion	on the other hand	

These words seem similar to the coordinating conjunctions (*and, but, for, nor, or, so,* and *yet*) but are grammatically different. Joining independent clauses with a comma plus a transition or conjunctive adverb produces a comma splice. Use a semicolon instead.

Mass transit offers many environmental benefits, for example, the

nitrogen emissions responsible for smog are greatly reduced.

[The linking of two independent clauses with a comma and the transition *for example* produces a comma splice. To join independent clauses, use a semicolon before a transition.]

John did not enjoy mathematics, however, if he was going to study

economics, he had to understand statistics.

[The linking of two independent clauses with a comma and the conjunctive adverb *however* produces a comma splice. To join independent clauses, use a semicolon before a conjunctive adverb.]

Note: A comma plus a transition or conjunctive adverb does not always signal a comma splice: *Both parents may work part-time, however, to share the care of their children.* The word group before *however* is an independent clause; the word group after *however* is a phrase. The commas before and after *however* signal a pause within a single independent clause. (See also 34f.)

12.2
Fixing
comma
splices:
Exercises

EXERCISE 12.1   Fixing Comma Splices

Fix comma splices by repunctuating or by rewriting. If an item is correct, write "correct." See the answers in the appendix.

1. As we stood at the grave side, we had no words to share with one another, we had only our silent sorrow.

2. During my sophomore year of high school, I was involved in a serious accident, ironically, it occurred on the last day of driver's ed.

3. After four hours of skiing, Michael was starving for a bratwurst, a hot dog—anything hot, spicy, and fast.

4. Women and girls have little reason to fear hemophilia, or bleeder's disease, usually only males are affected.

5. As the motorist knelt beside the badly injured German shepherd, all he could hear were its agonized howls.

12c Fix fused sentences by punctuating or rewriting

A **fused sentence**, sometimes called a **run-together** or **run-on**, results when two or more grammatically complete sentences are joined with no punctuation between them. They are joined—fused—so tightly that they appear to be a single sentence, not two sentences.

Consider this example:

Soon the holidays will be here once more many will miss an opportunity to share themselves and their possessions with the less fortunate.

Did you stumble as you read this example? If you did, you experienced the effect of fused sentences.

HOW TO . . . Identify and Edit Fused Sentences

1. Reread your writing aloud at a steady pace. If you have written a fused sentence, you may stumble where two separate thoughts blur together. Pause and study your words. Divide them into separate word groups.

   In 1900, there were few forests in Vermont now the state is covered with woodlands. → [1] In 1900, there were few forests in Vermont [2] now the state is covered with woodlands.

2. Can each word group be punctuated as a complete sentence? To find out, use the yes/no test (see the "How to Identify Sentence Fragments" box, pp. 91–92).

   Were there few forests in Vermont in 1900? Is the state now covered with woodlands?

   [The yes/no test reveals two word groups that sound complete and make sense: independent clauses that could be punctuated as complete sentences. Linking them without punctuation creates a fused sentence.]

3. To fix fused sentences, put a period, semicolon, colon, or dash between independent clauses. Or rewrite to create two complete sentences.

   In 1900, there were few forests in Vermont. Now the state is covered with woodlands.

1 ■ Adding punctuation

■ *Periods.* Use a period to separate one independent clause from another.

Soon the holidays will be here _∧ ~~once~~ more many will miss an opportunity

. Once

to share themselves and their possessions with the less fortunate.

[In this example, *the holidays will be here* is one independent clause; *many will miss an opportunity* is the second.]

■ *Semicolons and colons.* Use a semicolon to link related independent clauses roughly equal in importance. (See 35a.) Use a colon to link independent clauses when one clause introduces or explains the other. (See 36a.)

The Grand Canyon is not the first choice of travelers familiar with

canyon scenery _∧ that honor goes to Zion National Park or Bryce Canyon.

;

It all began like this _∧ I had a new computer and needed help installing

:

the software.

■ *A comma plus a coordinating conjunction.* Insert a comma before a coordinating conjunction (*and, but, or, nor, so, yet, for*) to link related independent clauses.

I enjoy cooking _∧ but cleaning up afterward is another matter.

,

■ *A semicolon plus a transition or conjunctive adverb.* Insert a semicolon before a transition or conjunctive adverb linking independent clauses. (For a list of transitions and conjunctive adverbs, see 12b3.)

The Jensens knew that starting a business would not be easy _∧ however _∧

;   ,

they did not imagine how difficult it would be.

[The semicolon links two independent clauses; the comma is added following *however* to signal a pause. For more on punctuating transitional words and phrases, see 34f.]

2 ■ Rewriting to make one clause subordinate to the other

Add a subordinating conjunction (*because, although, when, since,* and so forth) to an independent clause to make it a dependent clause. Connect the dependent clause to the remaining independent clause to make one complete sentence. (For a list of subordinating conjunctions, see 8g3.)

The witness did not understand the lawyer's question about South

because

Carolina _∧ he had never been to South Carolina.

[Adding the subordinating conjunction *because* turns the second independent clause, beginning with *he had,* into a dependent clause.]

3 ■ Compressing two independent clauses into one sentence

Omit words or change word forms to make one shorter sentence out of two independent clauses.

Travelers

~~The Grand Canyon is not the first choice of travelers~~ familiar
     ∧

prefer
with canyon scenery ~~that honor goes to~~ Zion National Park or
                                    ∧

     to the Grand Canyon
Bryce Canyon.
             ∧

The Jensens ~~knew that starting a business would not be easy however~~

~~they~~ did not imagine how difficult it would be. *to start a business.*

EXERCISE 12.2 Fixing Fused Sentences

Fix fused sentences by adding punctuation or by rewriting. If an item is correct, write "correct." See the answers in the appendix.

12.3
Fixing fused
sentences:
Exercises

1. Pessimists never hope for the best they always expect the worst.

2. Losing her second job in six months didn't seem to bother Charlene she took the disappointment with her usual wisecrack and a grin.

3. When they were less than two years old, the Fox children were put in a foster home and they grew up knowing nothing of what had happened to their parents.

4. My background is similar to Irene's my mother is Spanish and came to the US just before I was born.

5. Pollution is particularly common in valleys and is densest when hot air rises and traps cool, polluted air beneath it.

13 Choosing Verb Forms

13a Use the standard forms of irregular verbs

1 ■ Identifying main verb forms

Except for the verb *be,* the main verb of a sentence has five forms:

13.1
Verbs:
Web link

- Base or infinitive form: *I often (play, speak).*

- *-s/-es,* or third-person form: *He often (plays, speaks).*

- Past tense: *Then I (played, spoke).*

- Past participle: *I have (played, spoken) before.*

- Present participle: *I am (playing, speaking) now.*

2 ■ Identifying regular and irregular verbs

Regular and irregular verbs can be distinguished by their past tense forms and past participles. **Regular verbs** form the past tense and past participle in predictable ways, by adding *-d* or *-ed.* **Irregular verbs** form the past tense and past participle in various and unpredictable ways.

	PRESENT TENSE	PAST TENSE	PAST PARTICIPLE
Regular verbs	play believe	played believed	played believed
Irregular verbs	begin eat	began ate	begun eaten

The past-tense forms of regular and irregular verbs can stand alone, without any helping verb, as the main verb in a sentence: *The pianist played softly. The pianist began her solo.* The past participles of regular and irregular verbs cannot stand alone as the main verb in a sentence; they need a helping verb such as *is, has, had, were,* or *does* to complete their meaning: *She had played this song many times before. The concert has begun.*

3 ■ Identifying frequently used irregular verbs

If you're unsure about the form of an irregular verb or about whether a verb is irregular, consult this list of frequently used irregular verbs or your dictionary.

13.2
A complete irregular verb list: Web link

PRESENT TENSE	PAST TENSE	PAST PARTICIPLE
awake	awoke, awakened	awakened
be	was, were	been
beat	beat	beaten
begin	began	begun
bend	bent	bent
bite	bit	bitten, bit
blow	blew	blown
break	broke	broken
bring	brought	brought
build	built	built
burst	burst	burst
buy	bought	bought
catch	caught	caught
choose	chose	chosen

PRESENT TENSE	PAST TENSE	PAST PARTICIPLE
come	came	come
cost	cost	cost
do	did	done
draw	drew	drawn
drink	drank	drunk
drive	drove	driven
eat	ate	eaten
fall	fell	fallen
find	found	found
flee	fled	fled
fly	flew	flown
forget	forgot	forgotten
freeze	froze	frozen
get	got	gotten
give	gave	given
go	went	gone
grow	grew	grown
hang (to suspend)	hung	hung
hang (to execute)	hanged	hanged
hear	heard	heard
hide	hid	hidden
hold	held	held
keep	kept	kept
know	knew	known
lay (to place something)	laid	laid
lead	led	led
leave	left	left
lend	lent	lent
lie (to recline, to rest on a surface)	lay	lain
lose	lost	lost
pay	paid	paid
ride	rode	ridden
ring	rang	rung
rise	rose	risen
run	ran	run
say	said	said
see	saw	seen
set (to place)	set	set
shake	shook	shaken
shrink	shrank	shrunk
sing	sang	sung
sink	sank	sunk
sit (to be seated)	sat	sat
slide	slid	slid

PRESENT TENSE	PAST TENSE	PAST PARTICIPLE
speak	spoke	spoken
spend	spent	spent
spring	sprang	sprung
stand	stood	stood
steal	stole	stolen
strike	struck	struck
swim	swam	swum
take	took	taken
teach	taught	taught
tear	tore	torn
tell	told	told
throw	threw	thrown
wear	wore	worn
weave	wove	woven
write	wrote	written

4 ▪ Avoiding switched verb forms

WRITING IN THE USA Dialect and Standard Verb Forms

Some speakers of English use verb forms different from those of Standard English. They add regular endings to irregular verbs (*blowed* instead of *blown*), treat regular verbs as if they were irregular (*drug* instead of *dragged*), or use the past participle in place of the past tense (*seen* instead of *saw*). In your writing, use the appropriate standard forms for the past tense and past participle of regular and irregular verbs.

NONSTANDARD ENGLISH	STANDARD ENGLISH	NONSTANDARD ENGLISH	STANDARD ENGLISH
brung	brought	drived	drove
binded	bound	drug	dragged
blowed	blew	growed	grew
catched	caught	snuck	sneaked
creeped	crept	sweared	swore
costed	cost	had went	had gone
drawed	drew		

In your writing, use the appropriate standard forms for the past tense and past participle of regular and irregular verbs.

dragged
They ~~drug~~ the sandbags onto the levee.

[*Drag* is a regular verb that forms the past tense with *-ed*.]

blew
The wind ~~blowed~~ from the northeast for fourteen days.

[As an irregular verb, *blow* forms the past tense irregularly.]

saw
We ~~seen~~ him in his garage last night.
^

[The past tense of *see* is *saw*, not *seen*, which is the past participle.]

given
My brother had ~~gave~~ his keys to the mechanic so he could start the car.
^

[The past participle is required for action begun and completed in the past.]

5 ■ Using *lie/lay, sit/set,* and *rise/raise* correctly

The words in each of these pairs are often confused. One is an intransitive verb, the other a transitive verb (see also 9c and d). **Intransitive verbs** do not require direct objects; they indicate states of being or conditions: *The basket is sitting on the table.* **Transitive verbs** take direct objects; they do something to someone or something: *The boy set the basket on the table.* Avoid confusing one kind of verb with the other.

- *Lie, lay, lain, lying* (intransitive) means "to rest on or to recline": *He lay down to take a nap. The book is lying on the table. The cat had lain in the basket for an hour.*

- *Lay, laid, laid, laying* (transitive) means "to put or place something": *I will lay the pillow on the bed. He laid the book on the table.*

- *Sit, sat, sat, sitting* (intransitive) means "to be seated": *She sat down at the piano.*

- *Set, set, set, setting* (transitive) means "to put or place something in a particular position": *The student set the pen on the desk.*

- *Rise, rose, risen, rising* (intransitive) means "to get up from a lying, sitting, or kneeling position": *She rose from the chair.*

- *Raise, raised, raised, raising* (transitive) means "to move something or someone to a higher position": *He raised his hand to speak.*

6 ■ Spelling irregular verbs correctly

Because of their similarity to other words, the following irregular verbs are sometimes misspelled.

13.3
Editing
irregular
verbs:
Exercises

- *Laid/"layed."* The past tense of the verb *lay* is *laid*, not "layed."

laid
He ~~layed~~ the book on the table.

- *Led/lead.* The past tense of the verb *lead* is *led*, not "lead."

led
The leader ~~lead~~ the soldiers into battle.
^

[When *lead* is pronounced like *led*, it refers to the soft gray metal or to pencil lead.]

■ *Lose/loose. Lose* is a verb; *loose* is an adjective.

If he doesn't improve his grades, he may ~~loose~~ his scholarship.
                                            lose

■ *Paid/"payed." *The past tense of the verb *pay* is *paid,* not "payed."

The workers were ~~payed~~ weekly.
                    paid

13b Choose verb tenses that put events in sequence

Tense is the time when the action of a verb takes place. Verbs change form to indicate tense: present (*she is studying*), past (*she studied*), and so forth. Sometimes it is difficult to know which tense to use to describe an action, especially when more than one action is involved. The following guidelines will help you decide. (To review the six tenses of English verbs and the way to create them, see 8c3; for ESL, see 31a.)

1 ■ Using the present tense in special situations

■ *Writing about literature. *Authors of fiction, poetry, and nonfiction usually write in the past tense—for example: *When Paul went down to dinner, the music of the orchestra came floating up the elevator shaft to greet him* [Willa Cather]. But to summarize action in a literary paper, use the present tense. (See 60f2.)

When Paul ~~went~~ down to dinner, he ~~heard~~ the orchestra through the
          goes   *hears*
elevator shaft.

■ *Introducing quotations, summaries, and paraphrases. *In research writing, use present-tense verbs such as *reports, suggests,* and *argues* in signal phrases that introduce quotations, summaries, and paraphrases. Follow this convention whether the writer you cite is living or dead. (See also 50c1 for a list of these verbs.)

In the essay "Violent Crime," Bruce Shapiro ~~argued~~ that current
                                              argues
anticrime legislation is based on "a delusion, a myth" about criminals.

Note: If you include a date in the text of your writing, as the American Psychological Association style requires, use the past tense to introduce your borrowing: *In the essay "Violent Crime," Shapiro (1995) argued that current anticrime legislation is based on "a delusion, a myth" about criminals.* Use the present tense to discuss what information reveals and to draw conclusions: *The results of the surveys suggest that the majority of students require increased Internet access.* (See also 55a1.)

- *Describing scientific principles and general truths.* Use the present tense to describe accepted scientific principles or general truths.

   describes
   Ohm's law ~~described~~ the amount of resistance in an electrical circuit.
   ^

   declares   *are*
   The Declaration of Independence ~~declared~~ that all people ~~were~~ created
                                          ^   ^

   equal.

2 ▪ Using the present perfect tense to describe past action continuing in the present

Use the present perfect tense (*has/have* + the past participle: *has laughed, have eaten*) when actions begin in the past and continue in the present or occur at no specific time.

   have never forgotten
   I ~~never forgot~~ my mother's words of wisdom.
        ^

   [Because the writer still remembers these words, the present perfect tense is appropriate.]

3 ▪ Using the past perfect tense to describe past action completed before some other past action

Use the past perfect tense (*had* + the past participle: *had laughed, had eaten*) when a past action begins and is completed before some other past action.

   had been
   The police officer stated that my brother ~~was~~ in an accident.
                                                     ^

   [The accident occurred before the officer informed the writer.]

                                                          had
   When the hikers reached the lake, they found that someone camped
                                                                            ^

   there recently.

   [Others had camped there before the hikers arrived.]

4 ▪ Using infinitives and participles in a sequence of events

Use infinitives and participles to refer to actions that are related in some way to the action expressed by the main verb.

- *Simultaneous actions: the present infinitive.* Use the present infinitive (*to* + the base verb form: *to laugh, to eat*) for actions occurring at the same time as or immediately after the action of the main verb.

   spray
   Park officials tried to ~~have sprayed~~ for mosquitoes after every rain.
                                    ^

   [The action of the infinitive *to spray* occurred at the same time as the action of the main verb *tried*.]

■ *One action and then another: the present perfect infinitive.* Use the present perfect infinitive (*to have* + the past participle: *to have laughed, to have eaten*) for actions occurring before the action of the main verb.

The mayor would like to ~~give~~ *have given* a speech before the council voted on the resolution.

[The speech would have occurred in the past before the mayor's wish. Therefore, the present perfect infinitive (*to have given*) is required.]

■ *Simultaneous actions: the present participle.* Use the present participle (*-ing*) for an action occurring simultaneously with that of the main verb: *Pulling into the parking lot, he saw a thief smashing a car window.*

■ *One action and then another: the past participle or present perfect participle.* Use the past participle (*laughed, eaten*) or the present perfect participle (*having* + the past participle: *having laughed, having eaten*) for an action occurring before that of the main verb.

Having finished
~~Finishing~~ his exam before the period was half over, Kim asked to be excused.

13.4
Editing verb
tenses:
Exercises

EXERCISE 13.1 Editing Verb Tenses

Edit the following sentences to correct errors in verb tense. If a sentence is correct, write "correct." See the answers in the appendix.

1. We returned home from California by the same route that took us there.

2. More movies were made of *Romeo and Juliet* than of any other Shakespeare play.

3. At Matt and Joe's funeral, we laughed as much as we cried, remembering all the good times we had with them.

4. It wasn't until a year later that Mia discovered what had caused her friends to abandon her without a word.

5. Throughout the history of the United States, minorities and women were discriminated against.

13c Use *-s/-es* endings on present-tense verbs that have third-person-singular subjects

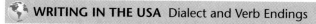

WRITING IN THE USA Dialect and Verb Endings

Some speakers of English drop the *-s* or *-es* from third-person-singular verbs in the present tense: *he work* instead of *he works*. In your writing, take care to add *-s* or *-es* to third-person verbs following the types of words listed here.

- Singular nouns: *Joan hikes. The baby cries.*
- Singular personal pronouns: *She hikes. He sings. It flies.*
- Indefinite pronouns, which are usually singular: *Everyone hikes. Each sings. No one qualifies.*

He try to come home early, but his job often keep him out late.
[*tries* above *try*; *keeps* above *keep*]

13d Use the Standard English forms of the verbs *be, have,* and *do*

🌐 WRITING IN THE USA Dialect and Standard Verb Forms

Some speakers of English use the forms of *be, have,* and *do* in ways different from Standard English. In your writing, use Standard English verb forms. (See 31b.)

1 ▪ Be

The eight forms of *be* (*be, am, is, are, was, were, been, being*) make it the most complex English verb.

	SINGULAR	PLURAL
First person	I am/am being/ was/have been	we are/are being/ were/have been
Second person	you are/are being/ were/have been	you are/are being/ were/have been
Third person	he, she, or it is/is being/ was/has been	they are/are being/ were/have been

To use *be* in its Standard English forms, follow these guidelines:

- ***Events in progress or habitual events.*** Use the third-person-singular *-s* form (*is*) plus the present participle (*-ing*) to indicate events in progress and habitual or continuous events: *is laughing.*

He going to school. [*is* above *going*]

[He is on his way to school.]

He be going to school. [*is* above *be*]

[He is currently attending school.]

- ***Using* am, is, *and* was *with first-person-singular and third-person-singular verbs.*** Use *am, is,* and *was* with first- and third-person-singular verbs. Otherwise, use *are* and *were.*

was

She ~~were~~ trying to get her essay published in the campus magazine.

[The third-person-singular pronoun *she* takes a third-person-singular verb, *was*.]

■ *Omitted verbs.* In informal Standard English, forms of the verb *be* are sometimes shortened and combined with their subjects: *I'm, you're, she's, we're, they're.* But these verbs must not be omitted entirely. (See also 31a2.)

'*m*

I working forty hours a week.

is

The actress on stage now.

2 ■ *Have*

Use the *-s* form *has* for the third-person singular (*John has*). Use *have* for all other present-tense and present-perfect forms (*we have*). Do not omit *has* or *have* when these forms are used as helping verbs: *John has worked, we have lived.* (See also 31a2.)

has

She ~~have~~ come to every meeting of the drama club.

has

He been a successful businessman for twenty years.

have

They been going to Canada every summer for five years.

3 ■ *Do*

Use the *-es* form *does* for the third-person singular (*she does*). Use *do* for all other present-tense forms. (See also 31b.)

doesn't

Merrilee ~~don't~~ want to go to the party this weekend.

Does

~~Do~~ he ever consider other people's feelings?

13e   Beware of omitting or misusing verb endings in words such as *used to, supposed to, asked,* and *would have*

1 ■ *Used to* and *supposed to*

"Use to" and "suppose to" are nonstandard. Write *used to* and *supposed to.*

supposed

Polly was ~~suppose~~ to fly to Memphis at the beginning of the month.

used

Scientists ~~use~~ to believe that outer space was filled with ether.

2 ▪ Past and past perfect endings

The *-d* and *-ed* endings signal the past and perfect tenses of regular verbs.

The little boy ~~frighten~~ *frightened* the ducklings.

My mother has ~~ask~~ *asked* me to call her every week.

Robert Goddard was the American who ~~develop~~ *developed* the rocket engine.

3 ▪ *Would, could, should*

"Would of," "could of," and "should of" are nonstandard. Write *would have* or *would've, could have* or *could've, should have* or *should've.*

We would ~~of~~ *have* won the tournament if we had practiced harder.

13.5
Editing verb
forms:
Exercises

13f Use the subjunctive mood for wishes and other nonfactual statements

The **mood** of a verb is a verb form that indicates how the writer or speaker views the action expressed by the verb. The **indicative mood** is used to make statements of fact and to ask questions: *She looked happy. They would have won. Are you sad?* The **imperative mood** is used for commands or direct requests: *Come home. Try again.*

The **subjunctive mood** is used for statements contrary to fact: wishes, speculations, assumptions, recommendations, indirect requests, and hypothetical situations.

To form the **present-tense subjunctive**, use the base form of the verb (*be, give, arrive*).

It is important that everyone **arrive** by nine o'clock.

To form the **past-tense subjunctive**, use *were*, not *was*.

If I **were** better organized, I would get more done.

Though slowly disappearing from English, the subjunctive is still used in certain phrases and situations.

1 ▪ Wishes and desires

Use the subjunctive to express wishes and to follow verbs expressing a wish or desire: *ask, insist, move, recommend, request, suggest,* and *urge.*

We recommend that the dean ~~awards~~ *award* an honors certificate to Carlos

Montoya.

[present-tense subjunctive]

were
Gena wished that the instructor ~~was~~ finished with his lecture.

[past-tense subjunctive]

2 ■ Nonfactual statements

Use the past-tense subjunctive after *if* or *as if* to express hypothetical
or nonfactual situations.

were
If I ~~was~~ you, I would study harder for tomorrow's quiz.

3 ■ Indirect requests

Use the subjunctive to express indirect requests.

be
It is important that you ~~are~~ in your seat before the concert begins.

[present-tense subjunctive]

4 ■ Speculation

Use the subjunctive to make a speculation.

13.6
Subjunctive
verbs:
Exercises

were
If James ~~was~~ going with us, he would be here by now.

[past-tense subjunctive]

14 Making Subjects and Verbs Agree

14.1
Agreement
guidelines:
Web link

Agreement is the correspondence of one word to another in number, person, and sometimes gender. Subjects and verbs must agree in
number (singular or plural) and person (first, second, and third), as in
the following examples.

	SINGULAR	PLURAL
First person	I run	we run
Second person	you run	you run
Third person	he/she/it runs, Pauline runs	they run

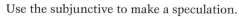

third-person-singular agreement

On weekends Penny volunteers at a homeless shelter.

third-person-plural agreement

Two homeless shelters were opened during last month's severe weather.

HOW TO . . . Identify Subject-Verb Agreement Trouble Spots

1. Look for long sentences where agreement may be a problem.
2. Look for clue words that may accompany agreement errors: the sentence openers *there is/are, here is/are* (14b); the conjunctions *and, or, nor* (14d and e); indefinite pronouns, such as *every, anyone, everybody* (14f); collective nouns, such as *team, committee, group, number* (14g); plural nouns considered as a single unit, such as *economics* and *glasses* (14h); and the relative pronouns *who, which, that* (14i).
3. To decide whether a subject and verb agree, first identify the subject and verb. (See 8c and 9a for guidelines.) Then read the subject and verb, omitting any words that come between. Rewrite if they do not have the same number (singular or plural) and person (first, second, or third person).

 COMPUTER TIP Using Search and Replace

Use the Find or Search and Replace command to locate clue words that may accompany agreement errors (see item 2 above). ▪

14a Make separated subjects and verbs agree

Subjects and verbs are sometimes separated by other words. But no matter how far apart they are, subjects determine the person and number of their verbs.

plural subject   plural verb

The tapestries on the walls of the palace were woven by children.

believes

Not one of the scientists investigating Alzheimer's disease believe a cure

will be found in this decade.

[The subject of the sentence is *one*. *Scientists* is the object of the preposition *of* and cannot be the subject of the sentence.]

are

The beneficial effects of her enthusiastic work is apparent everywhere.

[The subject is the plural noun *effects*. *Work* is the object of the preposition *of* and cannot be the subject of the sentence.]

Note: Prepositional phrases that begin with *accompanied by, along with, as well as, except, in addition to, including, no less than, together with,* or *with* do not add to a subject to make it plural. Identify the noun, pronoun, or noun phrase that is the true subject.

was

The valedictorian, together with her major professors, ~~were~~ asked to stand for the audience's applause.

[The subject, *valedictorian*, is singular; *her major professors* is the object of the preposition *together with* and is not part of the subject. To form a plural subject, use a coordinating conjunction: *the valedictorian and her major professors*.]

14b Make subject and verb agree when the subject follows the verb

Normal English word order is subject followed by verb: *The geese were flying*. Occasionally, however, normal word order is inverted, and the verb precedes the subject: *On a pine bough sat two large bluejays*. Whatever its position, the subject determines the number of the verb. Compare these two examples:

plural verb   plural subject

Seated in the front row were the parents of the bride and groom.

are

In his backpack is enough food and clothing for two weeks of camping.

[*Backpack* is the object of the preposition *in*; it is not the subject of the sentence. The subject is a compound, *food and clothing*, so the verb must be plural.]

🌎 ESL GRAMMAR NOTE *There* and *Here*

In sentences beginning *there is, there are, here is,* and *here are,* the subject follows the verb. Compare these two examples:

plural verb   plural subject

There are three reasons to elect Alice Brown to the student council.

were

Last night there was a dictionary and a thesaurus on my desk.

[The compound subject, *a dictionary and a thesaurus*, is plural, so the verb must be plural.]

🌎 ESL GRAMMAR NOTE The Pronoun *It*

At the beginning of a sentence, the pronoun *it,* like *here* and *there,* often moves the subject of a sentence into the predicate: *It was the first day of vacation.* The verb following *it* is always third-person singular. (See 32a2.)

14c Make a linking verb agree with its subject, not with a subject complement

Linking verbs (such as *am, is, are, was, were, seem, become, appear, feel, smell, sound, taste*) link a subject to an adjective or a noun—a subject complement—that describes the subject: *Becky is a social worker.* Do not confuse the subject with the subject complement. In most sentences, the subject precedes a linking verb. (See 9c and d.)

A loving family, loyal friends, and interesting work is *are* my definition of happiness.

[The three-part subject is plural, so the verb must be plural even though the subject complement, *definition*, is singular.]

The most attractive feature of the house are *is* the large, arched windows.

[The subject, *feature*, is singular, so the verb must be singular.]

If a grammatically correct sentence seems awkward, rewrite it to turn the subject complement into the subject: *My definition of happiness is a loving family, loyal friends, and interesting work. The large, arched windows are the most attractive feature of the house.*

14d With most compound subjects, use a plural verb

Compound subjects are linked by the coordinating conjunctions *and, but, or, so, for, yet, nor.*

    plural subject   plural verb

Cairo and Alexandria are the two largest cities in Egypt.

The dress and equipment for racquetball is *are* similar to those for tennis.

Note: If a compound subject is thought of as a unit, refers to one person, or begins with *each* or *every*, use a singular verb.

The **horse and buggy is** the primary mode of transportation among the Amish.

The **company's president and chief operating officer has announced** her retirement.

Fortunately, **every man, woman, and child was rescued** from the sinking ship.

14e When the parts of a compound subject are linked by *or* or *nor*, make the verb agree with the closer part

When both parts of a compound subject joined by *or* or *nor* are singular or plural, agreement is an easy match of subject and verb forms.

    singular noun + singular noun = singular verb

Neither Alice nor Gary plays chess well enough to be on the chess team.

plural noun + plural noun = plural verb

Either tulips or daffodils are a good choice for early spring flowers.

But when one part of the compound subject is singular and the other is plural, the part closer to the verb determines whether the verb is singular or plural. When the closer word is singular, the verb is singular. When the closer word is plural, the verb is plural.

Neither the children nor their mother ~~were~~ was happy when the parade ended.

[The singular *mother* is closer to the verb, so the verb must be singular.]

Either the lawyer or her clients ~~has~~ have been available each day for interviews.

[The plural *clients* is closer to the verb, so the verb must be plural.]

To avoid awkwardness, rewrite using *and: The children and their mother were unhappy when the parade ended.* But note that *or* may be necessary to signal alternates, either one subject or the other: *The children or their mother carries an umbrella to every parade.*

14f Treat indefinite pronouns as singular

Indefinite pronouns, such as *anyone, everybody*, and *everything*, refer to indefinite, unspecified persons or things (see 8b4). These words may seem to be plural and often are treated as such in speech. *Everybody* seems to refer to more than one person. But because their form is singular—there is only one *body* in *everybody*—indefinite pronouns take singular verbs. (See also 15d.) Compare these examples:

Each of the flowers **is** blooming.

Anyone who wants to be a good writer must also be a good editor.

None of the students in our dorm ~~have~~ has signed up for intramural sports.

[*None* means "not one," so the verb must be singular.]

Either of the mechanics ~~are~~ is able to repair the car.

[*Either* means "one or the other," so the verb must be singular.]

Note: The indefinite pronouns *all, any, most,* and *some* may be singular or plural, depending on the sense of the sentence or the words they refer to.

All of the volunteers **have** arrived.

[*All* refers to more than one volunteer; the sense is plural.]

All that she has left **is** twenty-five dollars.

[*All* refers to the twenty-five dollars as a unit; the sense is singular.]

Most of the speakers **have supported** the proposal.

[The sense of *most* is plural.]

Most of the snow **has** melted.

[*Most* refers to snow, which is usually singular.]

14g Treat collective nouns as singular unless their individual members act separately

Collective nouns are words such as *class, committee, couple, dozen, family, group, herd, jury, number, public, remainder,* and *team*. If their members act collectively, as a unit, collective nouns take a singular verb. If their members act separately, they take a plural verb. Compare these examples:

The senior **class is** about to sing the national anthem.

The class *are* ̷i̷s̷ in their seats.

[In the first example, the class sings together as one, and the verb is singular. In the second, the individual members of the class take their own seats, the sense of the subject is plural, and the verb must be plural.]

The **jury is deliberating**.

The jury *are* ̷i̷s̷ divided over the verdict.

[In the first example, the jury members collectively deliberate as one, and the subject is singular. In the second, the individual members of the jury hold separate opinions, the sense of the subject is plural, and the verb must be plural.]

ESL GRAMMAR NOTE Noncount Nouns and Singular Verbs

English count and noncount nouns are often troublesome, particularly to native speakers of other languages. Noncount nouns, such as *advice, crime, coffee, luggage,* and *machinery,* are almost always singular and require singular verbs: *Our luggage is in the trunk of the car.*

Note: The phrase *the number* is singular in meaning and takes a singular verb; *a number,* referring to individuals acting separately, is plural and takes a plural verb.

The number of students who prepare writing portfolios **is** increasing.

A number of these students **have** prepared portfolios.

14h With plural nouns singular in meaning, use singular verbs

Some plural nouns are singular in meaning or are understood as a unit: *athletics, economics, mathematics, measles, news, physics, statistics.* These words take singular verbs. Compare these examples:

After last night's dinner, **three dollars was** all he had in his wallet.

Fifteen miles is a long way to hike through mountainous terrain.

> *causes*
Mathematics sometimes ~~cause~~ a disturbance known as "math anxiety."

> *has*
The measles ~~have~~ affected half of the third graders.

Some plural words thought of as a unit take a plural verb: *glasses, scissors, tweezers, jeans.*

The **scissors were** lying on the table.

Note: If units of measure refer to separate persons or things, use a plural verb. Otherwise, the verb is singular.

Three-fourths of the students **are** doing A or B work.

Three-fourths of the school year **has** passed.

[In the first example, the students work individually, the sense of the subject is plural, and the verb is plural. In the second, *three-fourths* refers to one part of the year, and the verb is singular.]

14i With *who, which,* and *that,* use verbs that agree with their antecedents

To decide whether a relative pronoun is singular or plural, identify its **antecedent**, the noun or pronoun it refers to. (To learn to recognize nouns and pronouns, see 8a and b.)

> noun   pronoun verb
The Atlas Mountains, which extend from Morocco to Tunisia, are among the highest in western Africa.

[The relative pronoun *which* refers to the Atlas Mountains, a plural noun, so the verb *extend* must be plural.]

1 ■ *One of the . . . who/which/that*

The construction *one of the . . . who/which/that* usually precedes a plural verb. Compare these examples:

> plural   plural   plural
Leslie is one of the few members of this class who understand quadratic equations.

[*Who* refers to members, not *Leslie* or *one*; therefore, *who* is plural, and the verb *understand* is plural.]

have

White Pines is one of many state parks that ~~has~~ scenery worth a second visit.

[*That* refers to *parks*; therefore, the verb must be plural.]

2 ▪ Only one of the . . . who/which/that

The construction *only one of the . . . who/which/that* usually precedes a singular verb. Compare these examples:

singular   singular   singular   singular

Leslie is the only one of these students who understands quadratic equations.

lives

The manatee is the only one of the elephant's relatives that ~~live~~ underwater.

[*That* refers to *one*, not *relatives*. Only one relative lives underwater.]

Here is another version of the same construction: *I am the only person I know who actually enjoys airports.*

14j With titles, words mentioned as words, company names, and gerund phrases, use singular verbs

When I was a child, *Alice's Adventures in Wonderland* **was** one of my favorite books.

[One book, singular, takes a singular verb.]

Wharves **is** the plural of *wharf*.

[A word used as a word takes a singular verb.]

Learning foreign languages **becomes** more difficult as a person grows older.

[The singular gerund *learning* is the subject of the sentence, and so the verb *becomes* is singular.]

was

Tales of the Grotesque and Arabesque ~~were~~ written by Edgar Allan Poe.

is

Kline and Keys ~~are~~ one of the largest corporations in the United States.

EXERCISE 14.1 Editing Subject-Verb Agreement

Edit the following sentences to correct errors of subject-verb agreement. If a sentence is correct, write "correct." See the answers in the appendix.

1. People who have been laid off or downsized know why economics are referred to as "the dismal science."

14.2
Editing
subject-verb
agreement:
Exercises

122 **15** www.ablongman.com/dodds
Making Pronouns and Antecedents Agree

2. John Knudsen's paintings and sculpture is varied in technique but always devoted to urban themes.

3. The silence of the brooding, majestic pines and firs create a somber mood in the park's visitors.

4. In recent months, there has been several cases of Dengue fever reported in Texas.

5. Commerce Secretary Ron Brown, in addition to his staff and the plane's crew, were killed in the crash.

15 Making Pronouns and Antecedents Agree

A pronoun refers to a noun or another pronoun, called the **antecedent** (see 8b). Whether appearing in the same sentence or in different sentences, pronouns and antecedents must match (agree) in person (first, second, or third), number (singular or plural), and gender (masculine, feminine, or neuter).

third-person-singular feminine agreement

The **mother** cradled **her** child in **her** arms.

third-person-plural agreement

The **students** exchanged **their** essays to read and discuss.

The **Colorado River** flows from northern Colorado to the Gulf of

third-person-singular neuter agreement

California. During **its** 1,450-mile journey, **it** loses most of **its** water.

HOW TO . . . Identify Noun-Pronoun Agreement Trouble Spots

1. Look for long sentences or passages in which your ideas are complex.

2. Look for the antecedents that may cause noun-pronoun disagreement: nouns linked by *and, or, nor* (15a and b); nouns referring to groups, such as *committee* or *audience* (15c); words referring to individuals without regard to gender, such as *student* or *everyone* (15d); the names of organizations (15e).

3. To hear noun-pronoun disagreement, read a pronoun and its antecedent aloud, omitting any words between them.

4. Use singular pronouns to refer to singular antecedents; use plural pronouns to refer to plural antecedents.

COMPUTER TIP Using Search and Replace

Use the Find or Search and Replace command to locate nouns linked by *and, or,* and *nor* and pronouns containing *-body, every-,* and *-one* (see item 2 on p. 122). ▪

15a With compound antecedents linked by *and*, use plural pronouns

David and **Darrell** congratulated **themselves** for their good luck.

15b With compound antecedents linked by *or* or *nor*, make the pronoun agree with the closer antecedent

Neither **Alicia** nor **Louise** uses a computer to write **her** papers.

[*Neither* means "not one or the other"; the pronoun must be singular.]

Either the **Cardinals** or the **Cubs** have a chance to win the World Series if **they** improve **their** pitching.

[Both antecedents are plural; the pronoun must be plural.]

Neither **Mrs. Newton** nor her **daughters** visit as often as **they** would like.

[The second antecedent, *daughters*, is closer to the pronoun than *Mrs. Newton*; the pronoun must be plural, *they.*]

Note: When one antecedent is singular and the other plural, put the plural antecedent last to avoid awkwardness, as in the third example here: *Neither Mrs. Newton nor her daughters.*

15c With collective nouns, use singular pronouns unless individual members act separately

Collective nouns are words such as *audience, class, committee, couple, crowd, dozen, group, herd, jury, number, public, remainder,* and *team.* Compare these examples:

The **audience** gave **its** approval.

[The audience acted together, as a unit, so the pronoun is singular.]

The **jury** refused to discuss **their** opinions of the defendant.

[Each member of the jury had a separate opinion, and so the pronoun that refers to *jury* is plural.]

its
The jury delivered ~~their~~ verdict.

[The members of the jury function together as a unit, so the pronoun that refers to *jury* must be singular.]

 ESL GRAMMAR NOTE Noncount Nouns and Singular Pronouns

Noncount nouns, such as *advice, crime, coffee, luggage,* and *machinery,* are almost always singular and require singular pronouns: *We brought our luggage to the car, and my father packed **it** in the trunk.*

15d With generic nouns and indefinite pronouns, avoid disagreement and stereotyping

Generic nouns and **indefinite pronouns** refer to individuals without regard to gender.

SAMPLE GENERIC NOUNS

person, student, professor, lawyer, chemist, secretary, doctor, athlete, bicyclist, firefighter, flight attendant

SAMPLE INDEFINITE PRONOUNS

anyone, each, everybody, nobody, none, someone, something, and so forth (For a complete list, see 8b4.)

Using a third-person-singular pronoun (*he, she, his, her, him*) to refer to a generic noun or to an indefinite pronoun can create gender stereotyping. Consider this example: *A doctor owes his primary loyalty to his patients.* The pronouns in this sentence suggest that all doctors are male. In casual speech we sometimes avoid such stereotyping by using plural pronouns: *A person who goes out of their way to help others is a Good Samaritan. Did everybody remember to bring their skis?* But in your writing, pronouns and antecedents should agree in number. To solve the problem of lack of pronoun-antecedent agreement and to avoid gender stereotyping, follow these guidelines:

- When possible, use plural nouns and pronouns.

  Good Samaritans are people   *go*
  ~~A Good Samaritan is a person~~ who ~~goes~~ out of their way to help others.

  [The plural generic noun *people* takes a plural pronoun, *their.*]

  the students
  When ~~everyone~~ had finished studying, they picked up their books and left.

  [Replacing the indefinite pronoun *everyone* with a plural generic noun *students* makes the plural personal pronoun *they* agree.]

- When possible, omit the generic noun or the pronoun.

  Good Samaritans make sacrifices to help others.
  ~~A Good Samaritan is a person who goes out of their way to help others.~~

  [With rewording, this sentence omits the pronoun *their.*]

a
Someone had walked off and left ~~their~~ backpack under a tree.

- When the sense of a sentence must be singular, use *he or she, his or her, him or her* to refer to a singular generic noun or an indefinite pronoun.

his or her
Each committee member should bring ~~their~~ copy of the report.

Avoid awkward chains of paired pronouns: *Everyone in the building was angry when he or she received his or her latest rent increase.* In public writing do not use the slash to link pronouns, as in *he/she* and *his/her.* (See 39e.)

15e With nouns that name organizations, use singular pronouns

It may be logical to think of an organization in terms of its members and to refer to it with a plural pronoun. But use *it* and *its* to refer to a single organization.

its
Mercy Hospital cares for ~~their~~ patients' emotional as well as physical

health.

[*Its* refers to the organization, *Mercy Hospital*.]

EXERCISE 15.1 Editing Pronoun-Antecedent Agreement

Edit the following sentences to correct errors of pronoun-antecedent agreement. If a sentence is correct, write "correct." See the answers in the appendix.

15.1
Editing
pronoun-
antecedent
agreement:
Exercises

1. When my parents sat me down to tell me of their divorce, I heard their words, but none of it made any sense.

2. Everyone experiences depression at some point in their lives.

3. Hideaway Resort is widely known for their inexpensive but comfortable and activity-filled vacations.

4. Neither Eric nor the other swimmers could remember when they last saw Jean with them near the raft.

5. Unable to speak the language and knowing little about local customs, we did what anyone would do to protect themselves from con artists and thieves.

16 Making Pronoun Reference Clear

A pronoun refers to a noun or another pronoun, the **antecedent**, that gives the pronoun its meaning.

As *Stephanie* watched quietly, **she** saw a red *fox* emerge from **its** den.

When pronouns lack clear, specific, and logical antecedents, the result is faulty pronoun reference and writing that is vague and hard to understand.

HOW TO . . . Clarify Pronoun Reference

1. Locate your pronouns, and see whether each refers to a specific noun or pronoun. (See 16a.)

2. Look for nouns that refer to organizations and for possessive nouns (ending *-'s* or *-s'*). Then look for nearby pronouns and decide whether they can logically refer to these nouns. (See 16a1 and 2.)

   When my brother's car broke down in the Nevada desert, he had to hitchhike two hundred miles.

   > [The antecedent of *he* cannot be the possessive noun *brother's*, which functions here as an adjective.] Revision: *When his car broke down . . . , my brother had to . . .*]

3. Look for the pronouns *you, it, this, who, which,* and *that,* especially at the beginning of sentences or clauses. Decide whether they have clear, specific antecedents.

4. To decide whether pronoun reference is faulty, substitute the antecedent for the pronoun and reread. You'll hear the problem if there is one. (See 16a and b.)

5. Add a specific noun, indefinite pronoun, or noun phrase to be the antecedent for a pronoun.

6. Rewrite to replace an unclear pronoun with a clarifying word or phrase.

🖥 COMPUTER TIP Using Search and Replace

7. Use the Find or Search and Replace command to locate *it, this, that, which,* especially at the beginning of sentences. Decide whether each pronoun has a clear antecedent. ▪

16a Make pronouns refer to specific antecedents

You should be able to point to the antecedent that a pronoun refers to. If you can't identify the specific word or phrase, rewrite to supply the missing antecedent or to omit the pronoun.

My grandfather may have been seriously ill, but he declared that he

wasn't dead yet and wasn't afraid of *it*.
                                    dying
                                       ^

[The pronoun *it* cannot refer to the adjective *dead*. To hear the faulty reference, try rereading the sentence using *dead* in place of *it*. The revision substitutes the noun *dying*, which completes the meaning of the sentence.]

                                              prisoners are squeezed
American prisons are now so crowded that in some states ~~they squeeze~~
                                                                    ^
~~them~~ in, four or five to a cell.

[In the original version, *they* and *them* have no antecedents. The revision omits *they*, replaces *them* with the noun *prisoners*, and changes the verb form.]

1 ■ Not using *they, them,* and *their* to refer to organizations

A pronoun that takes the place of an organization should refer to the organization (*it, its*), not to its members (*they, them, their*).

On May 3, Manor Drugstore announced that **it** was closing **its** last store.

To revise faulty references to organizations, omit the faulty pronoun, substitute the appropriate pronoun, or add the name of the organization.

           manufacturers
In the last decade ~~they~~ have begun to build televisions with studio-quality
                      ^
sound systems.

[The revision replaces a pronoun lacking an antecedent with an identifying noun.]

2 ■ Not using pronouns to refer to possessive nouns

Nouns that end in *-'s* or *-s'* act as adjectives and cannot be the antecedents for pronouns. Rewrite to supply a noun antecedent for each pronoun or to correct faulty pronoun reference.

              its
As Lucy admired ~~the motorcycle's~~ sleek design, she knew she wanted to
                                ^
the motorcycle.
own ~~it~~.
      ^
[*Motorcycle's* cannot be the antecedent of *it*. To hear the faulty reference, reread the sentence, replacing *it* with *motorcycle's*.]

Jill bent to hear the old woman's ~~voice, who was~~ mumbling of old friends

long dead.

[*Woman's* cannot be the antecedent of *who*. To hear the problem, try replacing *who* with *woman's*.]

3 ▪ Not using *you* as an indefinite pronoun

You is a personal pronoun, not an indefinite pronoun referring to persons in general. In public writing, use *you* only to address readers directly. To refer to people in general, use *people, one,* or some other appropriate word. If these words make your writing sound stuffy, rewrite to omit the pronoun.

Even in remote wilderness, ~~you~~ *a hiker* will find pollution, litter, and

environmental damage.

Even in remote wilderness, ~~you can find~~ pollution, litter, and

environmental damage *can be found*.

4 ▪ Not using *it* to refer to authors or their writing

In summarizing, do not use the personal pronoun *it* to refer to authors or their writings in phrases such as *it says that*.

~~In~~ Henry David Thoreau's <u>Walden</u>, ~~it says~~ *argues* that people should simplify

their lives.

[Logically, the author does the saying, not the book. This revision emphasizes the book. Another revision emphasizes the author: *In* Walden, *Henry David Thoreau argues that people should simplify their lives.*]

16b Avoid ambiguous reference

Pronoun reference is ambiguous when a pronoun seems to refer to more than one antecedent. Rearrange or rewrite so that each pronoun has one specific antecedent.

~~Abusive~~ *When abusive* parents often hit their children *are angry, they* ~~when they are angry~~.

[In the original sentence, it is unclear who is angry, the parents or their children. The revision clarifies the antecedent for *they.*]

16c Generally avoid using *it, this, that,* and *which* to refer to whole sentences

If you use *it, this, that,* and *which* to refer broadly to whole sentences or clauses, you may confuse readers. Replace these pronouns with their antecedents, or rewrite to clarify meaning.

When prices rise, consumers purchase less and production decreases.

pattern

This leads to higher unemployment.
   ^

[In the original, the antecedent for *this,* the cause of higher unemployment, is unclear.]

In Everglades National Park, hundreds of species of nonnative plants

. *Such carelessness illustrates*

grow from seeds scattered by picnickers, ~~which is~~ ᶺwhy antilittering

regulations are needed.

[In the original, the pronoun *which* does not identify the reason regulations are needed: the number of nonnative plants, the actions of picnickers, or both.]

16d Use *who, that, whose,* or *whom* to refer to people and to animals with names

Standard English does not use the relative pronoun *which* to refer to people. Use *who, that, whose,* or *whom* instead.

whom

Many early blues musicians, few of ~~which~~ could read or write music,
   ^

who

are remembered today only because of the historians ~~which~~ recorded them.
   ^

Note: Use *that, which,* and *whose* to refer to objects and unnamed animals.

The planets **that** orbit farthest from the sun are Neptune and Pluto.

The deer, **whose** food was threatened by drought, began foraging in suburban backyards.

EXERCISE 16.1 Editing Pronoun Reference

Edit the following sentences to correct errors in pronoun reference. If a sentence is correct, write "correct." See the answers in the appendix.

16.1
Editing
pronoun
reference:
Exercises

1. Karen had no desire to taste the goat's milk, and she was certain she didn't want to milk it.

2. Betty told Adele the exciting news about her winning lottery ticket.

3. Morale at my company is low because employees don't know one another or understand any job besides their own. This makes it difficult to increase productivity.

4. Avid readers should stop at the Book Nook; they have weekly specials on adult and children's books of all kinds.

5. In today's highly mobile society, you can easily lose touch with family members which have been forced to relocate as part of their jobs.

17 Choosing Pronoun Case Forms

Nouns and pronouns change **case form** to signal their functions as subjects, objects, and possessives. Deciding the correct case form of nouns is rarely a problem because they change form only in the possessive:

subject   possessive   object
form   form   form

That little dog just bit your dog's tail.

Personal pronouns and the relative pronouns *who* and *whoever* change form to signal each function.

SUBJECT FORMS	OBJECT FORMS	POSSESSIVE FORMS	
I	me	my	mine
you	you	your	yours
he/she/it	him/her/it	his/her/its	his/hers/its
we	us	our	ours
they	them	their	theirs
who/whoever	whom/whomever	whose	

HOW TO . . . Edit Pronoun Case Forms

1. The "drop" test. When a pronoun is part of a compound or identifies a nearby noun, use the "drop" test to identify the correct case form. Drop everything from the compound except the pronoun in question or drop the nearby noun.

   The limousine brought Alice and I to our hotel. → The limousine brought . . . I to our hotel.

   [The "drop" test reveals that *I* should be *me*, the direct object of the verb *brought*: *The limousine brought Alice and me to our hotel.*]

   Us students have to work full time to pay our tuition → Us . . . have to work full time.

   [The "drop" test reveals that *us* should be the subject pronoun *we*: *We students have to work full time to pay our tuition.*]

2. Pronouns before gerunds (*-ing* verb forms used as nouns). Use the possessive form (*my, your, her, our,* and so forth) before a gerund: *I appreciate his loaning us his car.* (See 17d.)

3. *Who* or *whom*. When you're trying to decide between *who/whom* or *whoever/whomever,* follow the four steps described in 17e.

4. Pronouns in comparisons. When a pronoun follows *than* or *as* in a comparison, mentally complete the thought to hear the correct form: *She is a much better tennis player than I [am].* (See 17f.)

5. Reflexive pronouns. Use reflexive pronouns (*myself, yourself,* and so forth) only when the receiver of an action or the object of a preposition is identical to the doer of an action: *I did it myself.* (See 17g.)

17a Use the subject case form for pronouns that are subjects or that identify subjects

Singular pronoun subjects seldom cause a problem.

When **she** saw her nephew playing with the puppy, **she** laughed so hard **she** almost cried.

1 ▪ Using pronouns in compound subjects

To identify the correct case form in a compound subject, use the "drop" test. Drop everything from the compound except the pronoun in question, say the sentence, and trust your ear to guide you.

17.1
Choosing
pronoun
case:
Web link

Kim and ~~me~~ spent spring vacation in Vancouver.
                I

[Drop *Kim* to hear the error in *me spent.* The first-person subject pronoun *I* is correct.]

                                              he and I
We took this path because ~~me and him~~ were told it was open to bicyclists.

[Drop one half of the compound at a time to hear the errors in *me . . . were told* and *him were . . . told.* In a compound construction, put the other person before yourself.]

2 ▪ Using pronouns as subject complements

Use the subject case form for pronouns that identify the subject of a linking verb such as *be, is, was,* or *were.* (See also 9d1.)

                                                   I
The only one to read the complete report was ~~me~~.

[*One* is the subject of the verb *was. I* complements—identifies—the subject and is in the subject form.]

In Standard English, subject complements always take the subject case form. If this usage sounds stuffy, try another version of the sentence: *I was the only one to read the complete report.*

3 ▪ Using pronoun appositives that identify subjects

An appositive renames or describes a preceding noun (see 10a4). Use the subject case form for pronoun appositives that rename or describe subjects.

At the end, only two spectators, Sally and me, remained to mourn our

(I above me)

team's loss.

[Use the "drop" test to remove everything from the subject and appositive except the pronoun: *only . . . me remained. I* is the correct form.]

4 ▪ Using *we*, not *us*, before subjects

Use the subject case form *we*, not the object form *us*, to refer to the subject of a clause.

Professor Desai knows that us students want to postpone the exam.

(we above us)

[Use the "drop" test to omit the subject and hear the error in *that us . . . want to postpone the exam. We* is correct.]

17b Use the object case form for pronouns that are objects

Single direct objects, indirect objects, or objects of prepositions seldom cause a problem.

Lisa's parents saw **her** sitting on the porch.

To choose the correct case form for compound objects, use the "drop" test. Drop everything from the object except the pronoun, read the sentence, and trust your ear to guide you.

1 ▪ Using pronouns in compound direct and indirect objects

When a pronoun acts as a direct or indirect object to complete the meaning of a verb, use the object case form. (See 9c.)

Please help my friend and I with this calculus problem.

(me above I)

[Drop *my friend and* to hear the error in *help . . . I. Me* is correct.]

2 ▪ Using pronouns as objects of prepositions

Use the object case form for pronouns following prepositions. (See 10a2.)

I wish someone would settle a friendly debate between my father and I.

(me above I)

[*Between* is a preposition. Drop *my father and* to hear the error in *between . . . I. Me* is correct.]

3 ▪ Using pronouns in appositive phrases that describe direct or indirect objects

Use the object case form in an appositive phrase that describes a direct or indirect object.

Professor Konewski chose two new research assistants, John Park and I.
^{me}

[Drop *two new research assistants, John Park and* to hear the error in *chose . . . I. Me* is correct.]

17c Use the object case form in the compound subjects and objects of infinitives

An **infinitive** consists of *to* plus the base form of the verb: *to bake* (see 10a3). Both the subject and the object of an infinitive take the object case form. To hear the correct pronoun form for compound subjects and objects of infinitives, use the "drop" test.

Our English instructor has asked Oscar and I to critique each other's

essays.

[Drop *Oscar and* to hear the error in *has asked . . . I to critique.* The object case form in *has asked . . . me* is correct.]

Penny volunteered to tutor John and I.

[Drop *John and* to hear the error in *to tutor . . . I.* The object form in *to tutor . . . me* is correct.]

17d Use the possessive case form for nouns and pronouns before gerunds

A gerund is an *-ing* verb used as a noun: *Flying is safer than driving* (see 10a3). Use the possessive case form for nouns and pronouns that precede gerunds: *the pilot's flying, his flying.*

Roger appreciated ~~Celeste~~ Celeste's helping him learn Spanish.

Dorothy received the credit for ~~him~~ his being elected to the senate.

🌐 ESL GRAMMAR NOTE Participles and Gerunds

Distinguishing between participles and gerunds can be troublesome for both native and non-native English speakers. A participle is the *-ing* or *-ed* verb form used as an adjective: *The flying hawk searched for prey.* Here *flying* is an adjective describing *hawk.* A gerund is the *-ing* verb form used as a noun: *Flying is her favorite thing.*

- Do not use a possessive before a participle: *Kevin observed a hawk flying above the field*; not *Kevin observed a hawk's flying above the field.*
- Do use a possessive before a gerund; *Amelia Earhart's flying made her an American hero*; not *Amelia Earhart flying made her an American hero.*

Note: Possessive pronouns do not contain apostrophes: *yours, hers, its, ours, theirs,* and *whose.* (See 37a.)

17e Use *who* and *whoever* for subjects and subject complements, *whom* and *whomever* for objects

Follow these four steps to decide when to use *who, whoever, whom,* and *whomever.**

- Step 1: Consider the words following *who/whom.* In the sentence *The reporter was uncertain who/whom she should interview,* consider *she should interview.*

- Step 2: Rearrange the words you're considering to make a complete sentence. Leave a blank where the pronoun should go: *She should interview _____.*

- Step 3: In the blank put *he, she, him, her, they,* or *them,* whichever is correct: *She should interview him.*

- Step 4: Replace *he, she,* or *they* with the subject case form *who* or *whoever.* Replace *him, her,* or *them* with the object form *whom* or *whomever*: *The reporter was uncertain whom she should interview.*

Other examples:

Voters want to know who/whom the Democratic candidate will be.

[Step 1: Consider the words following *who/whom.* Step 2: Rearrange them to make a sentence, with a blank where the pronoun should be: *The Democratic candidate will be _____.* Step 3: In the blank, put *he, she, him, her, they,* or *them,* whichever is correct: *The Democratic candidate will be she* (use the subject form *she* for a subject complement following the linking verb *be*). Step 4: Replace *he, she, they* with *who* or *whoever*; replace *him, her, them* with *whom* or *whomever*: *Voters want to know who the Democratic candidate will be.*]

Who/whom do you think should receive the award?

[Step 1: Consider the words following the pronoun. Step 2: Rearrange them to make a sentence, with a blank where the pronoun should be: *Do you think _____ should receive the award?* Step 3: In the blank, put *he, she, him, her, they,* or *them,* whichever is correct: *Do you think they should receive the award?* Step 4: Replace *he, she, they* with *who* or *whoever*; replace *him, her, them* with *whom* or *whomever*: *Who do you think should receive the award?*]

---

*For the formula to discover pronoun case, I am grateful to Maxwell Nurnberg, *Questions You Always Wanted to Ask about English* (New York: Pocket Books, 1983).

17f For the correct case form in comparisons using *than* or *as*, mentally complete the sentence

Informal spoken English often uses an object pronoun after *than* and *as*: *Brenda likes jazz more than me.* But this construction is ambiguous. Does it mean that Brenda likes jazz more than I like jazz or that Brenda likes jazz more than she likes me? In your writing, use the correct subject or object form following *than* or *as* to make your meaning clear. To choose the correct form, complete the thought: *Brenda likes jazz more than I* [*like jazz*].

Fran may be younger than her supervisor, but she is as qualified as ~~him.~~ *he*

[*He* is the subject of the unstated verb *is qualified: as qualified as he* [*is qualified*]. If ending a sentence with *he* sounds stuffy, add the verb: *she is as qualified as he is.*]

I think my art history professor likes old buildings more than ~~we~~ students. *us*

[*Us* is the direct object of the verb *likes: more than* [*she likes*] *us students.*]

17g Use reflexive (-*self*) pronouns only to refer to a preceding noun or pronoun

Reflexive pronouns—such as *myself, yourself, itself, himself, herself, ourselves, themselves*—are correct when the receiver of an action or the object of a preposition is identical to the doer of the action: *The baby scratched himself. I am going for a walk by myself.* (See 8b7.) When a reflexive pronoun is part of a compound, use the "drop" test to hear the correct case form.

Maria and Carlos invited Barbara and ~~myself~~ to the concert. *me*

[Drop *Barbara and* to hear *invited myself. Invited me* is correct.]

🌎 **WRITING IN THE USA** Nonstandard Pronouns

Hisself, themself, theirself, or *theirselves* are not correct forms of Standard English. Use *himself, herself,* or *themselves.*

EXERCISE 17.1 Editing Pronoun Case Forms

Edit the following sentences to correct errors in pronoun case. If a sentence is correct, write "correct." See the answers in the appendix.

1. It should be obvious that we students prefer a more generous scholarship program.

17.2
Editing
pronoun
case forms:
Exercises

2. Janet, Jeffrey, Patricia, and myself will be pleased to help with the Oxfam Fund Drive.

3. As me and my two friends were setting up our tents at sunset, we looked up and saw four or five black bears near the edge of the woods.

4. We will sell the antique telephone to whomever makes us the best offer.

5. I was delighted when Edward gave my husband and I two tickets to the new Tom Stoppard play.

18 Choosing Adjectives and Adverbs

18a Use adjectives to modify nouns and pronouns; use adverbs to modify verbs, adjectives, and other adverbs

1 ▪ Using adjectives

Adjectives modify—provide information about—nouns and pronouns and indicate *which one, what kind,* or *how many.* (See 8d.)

which one   what kind

That tall, heavyset man is an excellent dancer.

Note: Two or more adjectives with no commas separating them must be arranged in a specific order. (See 34d; for ESL, see 32g3.)

🌎 **ESL GRAMMAR NOTE** Adjectives and Plural Forms

While some languages (including Spanish and French) add *-s/es* to adjectives to make them agree with plural nouns, standard English does not: *red brick buildings,* not *reds bricks buildings.* Descriptive adjectives used in place of nouns—even if they represent more than one thing—generally remain singular: *The strong and brave too often die young,* not *The strongs and the braves too often die young.*

18.1
Choosing
adjectives
and
adverbs:
Web link

2 ▪ Using adverbs

Adverbs modify verbs, adjectives, and other adverbs and indicate *how, when, where, why,* or *under what conditions: She spoke enthusiastically.* (See 8e.) Many adverbs, as in this example, end in *-ly,* but not all: *always, here, nearby, there,* and *very.* And some *-ly* words are adjectives: *friendly* and *lovely.*

In casual speech adjectives are sometimes substituted for adverbs, usually by dropping the *-ly* from the end of an adverb. In writing, however, use adverbs to modify verbs, adjectives, and other adverbs.

Stock market investors in 1929 ~~sure~~ *surely* did not expect the market to crash.

[The adverb *surely* is necessary to modify the verb *expect*.]

Second-parent adoption is a ~~rapid~~ *rapidly* growing phenomenon.

[The adverb *rapidly* is necessary to modify the verbal adjective *growing*.]

It was a ~~real~~ *very* beautiful morning, perhaps the best of the summer.

[In casual speech *real* is sometimes used to modify adjectives such as *beautiful*. But in Standard English use *very*.]

🌍 ESL GRAMMAR NOTE   Placement of Adverbs

Adverb placement differs greatly in different languages. In standard English, avoid placing adverbs between verbs and direct objects: *I wrote my essay quickly,* not *I wrote quickly my essay.*

18b   Use adjectives as complements

Adjectives usually appear before nouns. But they may also follow certain verbs as complements, words that complete the meaning of a noun or pronoun.

1 ▪ Using adjectives as subject complements

Subject complements describe or rename the subjects of linking verbs such as *be, become, feel, look, smell, seem, sound,* and *taste* (see 9d1). Use an adjective as a subject complement following a linking verb.

She *became* **angry**; he *felt* **sick**.

Does anything smell as ~~sweetly~~ *sweet* as a freshly mowed lawn?

[*Sweet,* an adjective, modifies the subject *anything,* not the linking verb *smell.* It describes a thing, not an action.]

2 ▪ Using adjectives as object complements

Object complements give information about the direct objects of verbs such as *call, consider, create, elect, find, keep,* and *make.* (See 9c1 and 9d2.) Use adjectives to modify noun and pronoun direct objects.

A safe-deposit box will keep valuable papers **secure**.

The personnel manager considered the applicants ~~equally~~ *equal*.

[*Equal* is an adjective describing the direct object *applicants.* In the original sentence, *equally* modifies *considered* and describes the action of the manager.]

18c Use *good/well* and *bad/badly* correctly

WRITING IN THE USA Confusing Word Pairs

Native and non-native speakers of English frequently find *good/well* and *bad/badly* difficult to use correctly in their writing. Pay particular attention to the distinctions in the following sections.

1 ▪ Using *good* and *bad* as adjectives

Use *good* and *bad* as adjectives after linking verbs (see the list in 18b1): *The fresh bread smelled good. The music from those speakers sounds bad.*

As the coach studied her players, she thought how ~~well~~ *good* everyone looked.

[*Good* is a subject complement accompanying the linking verb *looked* and describing the appearance, not the health, of the subject *everyone*.]

Bill felt ~~badly~~ *bad* about his behavior.

[Following the linking verb *felt, bad* is an adjective, a subject complement describing the subject *Bill*. It does not describe the act of feeling.]

2 ▪ Using *well* as an adjective or an adverb

Use *well* as an adjective to refer to health or well-being. Otherwise, use it as an adverb modifying verbs, adjectives, and other adverbs.

After three weeks' rest, I feel ~~good~~ *well* again.

[Here *well* is an adjective following a linking verb and modifying the subject *I*.]

After its tuneup, the car runs ~~good~~ *well*.

[Here *well* is an adverb modifying the verb *runs*.]

3 ▪ Using *badly* as an adverb

Use *badly* as an adverb: *The team played badly.*

18d Use the comparative and superlative forms of adjectives correctly

1 ▪ Forming comparatives and superlatives

Adjectives and adverbs have three forms to indicate degree or intensity: **positive**, **comparative**, and **superlative**.

POSITIVE	COMPARATIVE	SUPERLATIVE
good	better	best
bad	worse	worst
happy	happier	happiest
beautiful	more beautiful, less beautiful	most beautiful, least beautiful

To form comparatives and superlatives, follow these guidelines:

- *One-syllable adjectives and adverbs.* One-syllable adjectives and adverbs generally use *-er* and *-est* (*taller, tallest; faster, fastest*).

- *Two-syllable adjectives.* Two-syllable adjectives accented on the first syllable generally use *-er* and *-est* (*happier, happiest; lovelier, loveliest*).

- *Three-syllable adjectives.* Three-syllable adjectives use *more/most, less/least* (*more beautiful, most beautiful; less beneficial, least beneficial*).

- *Two- and three-syllable adverbs.* Two- and three-syllable adverbs, especially those ending *-ly,* use *more/most, less/least* (*more slowly, most slowly; less happily, least happily*).

- *Irregular adjectives and adverbs.* Memorize these irregular words: *good/better/best; bad/worse/worst; far/farther/farthest; far/further/furthest; little/less/least; many/more/most.*

2 ■ Choosing between comparative and superlative forms

Use the comparative form to compare two things, the superlative to compare three or more.

Although Ernest Hemingway and William Faulkner are considered

major novelists, Hemingway has been ~~most~~ *more* influential.

[Two writers are compared; the comparative form is necessary.]

My chores were weeding, planting, and, ~~worse~~ *worst* of all, emptying garbage.

[Three activities are compared; the superlative form is necessary.]

3 ■ Avoiding repetition of comparative or superlative forms

Use either *-er/-est* or *more/most,* not both.

Increasing the number of pedestrians will lead to a ~~more~~ healthier environment.

That was the most ~~unkindest~~ *unkind* remark I have ever heard.

4 ■ Avoiding comparison of absolutes

Absolutes are words describing characteristics that cannot be compared. *Unique,* for example, means one of a kind; something cannot be more unique ("more one of a kind") or most unique ("most one of a kind"). Other absolutes: *absolute, boundless, circular, complete, definite, empty, eternal, enough, favorite, final, full, inevitable, mutual, perfect, perpendicular, priceless, round, square, sufficient, supreme, total, triangular, universal, vacant.* Avoid the comparison of absolutes.

Your story will be ~~more~~ complete when you add an exciting ending.

Of all the old jazz bands, the Count Basie Orchestra is my ~~most~~ favorite.

18e Avoid double negatives

WRITING IN THE USA Double Negatives

Some languages (like Spanish) use double negatives regularly, and they also appear frequently in some English dialects. However, they appear infrequently in academic English. In your writing, avoid using *not, never,* or *no* with other negative words such as *no one, another, none, nothing, barely, hardly, scarcely.*

Eighteen-year-olds without jobs ~~don't~~ have nothing to lose by joining the military.

can barely
She ~~can't hardly~~ swim a stroke.

a
Despite what some may think, welfare recipients don't live ~~no~~ life of ease.

Note: You may use a double negative to soften the intensity of a positive statement or to suggest irony: *Karen was not unhappy to learn she would graduate with honors.*

18.2
Editing
adjectives
and
adverbs:
Exercises

EXERCISE 18.1 Editing Adjectives and Adverbs

Edit the following sentences for the correct use of adjectives and adverbs. If a sentence is correct, write "correct." See the answers in the appendix.

1. Judy's chocolate chip holiday cookies smell wonderful and taste delicious.

2. The man in the clown suit and greasy makeup looked at me peculiar.

3. The man in the clown suit and greasy makeup looked peculiar.

4. Joshua had the most happiest of childhoods.

5. On the balance beam, Sharon performed good.

19 Putting Linked Words in Parallel Form

Parallel form (also known as **parallelism** or **parallel structure**) refers to a similarity in the grammatical structure of two or more words, phrases, or clauses that are linked by coordinating conjunctions or in some other way. In the phrase *Rosario or Maria, Rosario* and *Maria* are parallel nouns linked by a coordinating conjunction. Similarly, *revise and edit* is a pair of linked, parallel verbs. Abraham Lincoln's *government of the people, by the people, for the people* is a series of parallel prepositional phrases. And in President John Kennedy's inaugural address, *ask not what your country can do for you—ask what you can do for your country* is a pair of parallel clauses. Parallelism is a way to join and emphasize equally important ideas.

19.1
Parallel
form:
Web link

Faulty parallelism occurs when linked words do not have the same grammatical form. *To hike or skiing* links a verb and a noun. *Tall, dark, handsome, and with a sly wit* links three adjectives to a prepositional phrase. To make your sentences emphatic and grammatical, put linked words in parallel form. (See also 20c.)

 COMPUTER TIP Using Search and Replace

Use the Find or Search and Replace command to locate conjunctions. Then determine whether the linked words are parallel in form.

19a Make words linked by a coordinating conjunction parallel in form

Coordinating conjunctions (*and, but, yet, for, so, or, nor*) link grammatically equal words. (See 8g1.) Use parallel forms before and after these conjunctions.

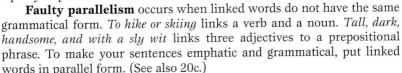

Among her favorite sports, Jill likes ~~to jog~~ jogging and racquetball the most.

[In the original, the verb form *to jog* is linked to a noun, *racquetball*. The revision links a noun to a noun.]

Nearing thirty-five and ~~with~~ having only a high school diploma, Alan is

pessimistic about his future.

[In the original, an adjective phrase, *nearing thirty-five*, is linked to a prepositional phrase, *with only a high school diploma*. The revision links two adjective phrases, *nearing thirty-five* and *having only a high school diploma*.]

19b Make words in a series or a list parallel in form

Words in series may be linked by a conjunction, or they may be in a list. In either case, make each item in the series grammatically parallel to the others.

As I plan this semester, I am dividing my life into three categories:

school
academic, work, and pleasure.
     ^

[In the original, the adjective *academic* is linked with two nouns. The revision links three nouns.]

Representative Cairns criticized her opponent as soft on crime,

quick to raise taxes
indifferent to voters, and a tax-and-spend politician.
                                       ^

[The original links two adjective phrases (*soft on crime, indifferent to voters*) to a noun phrase (*a tax-and-spend politician*). The revision links three adjective phrases.]

19c Make words linked by a correlative conjunction (*either . . . or*) parallel in form

Correlative conjunctions are linking phrases that come in two parts: *either . . . or, neither . . . nor, not only . . . but also, both . . . and, whether . . . or.* (See 8g2.) Make words linked by correlative conjunctions grammatically parallel. Do not use a comma after the first part.

When it comes to fast food, I love not only old favorites like hamburgers but also ethnic foods like falafel make my mouth water.

[The original links a noun phrase *old favorites like hamburgers* to a clause *ethnic foods like falafel make my mouth water*. The revision links two noun phrases, *old favorites like hamburgers* and *ethnic foods like falafel*.]

camping
Cassie was undecided whether to go white water rafting or camp.
                                                          ^

[The original links a verbal noun—the gerund *rafting*—to the verb *camp*. The revision links two gerunds, *rafting* and *camping*.]

19d Make comparisons using *than* or *as* parallel in form

to compose
Many students find it easier to write a research paper than composing a
                                                             ^
poem.

[The original links the infinitive *to write* and the gerund *composing*. The revision links two infinitives, *to write . . . to compose*.]

The Anasazi ruins of Mesa Verde are as impressive as ~~at the~~ in Athens ^*the Acropolis* at the Acropolis.

[The original links the noun phrase *the Anasazi ruins* to a prepositional phrase, *in Athens at the Acropolis*. The revision links two noun phrases.]

19e Repeat function words to achieve parallel form

Readers depend on function words to signal grammatical forms and relations. Function words are prepositions (*to, by, in,* and so forth), articles (*a, an, the*), the infinitive *to,* and introductory words at the beginning of clauses (*that, who, which, because, when, if,* and so forth). If readers are likely to misunderstand you, repeat function words before parallel statements. To see the effect of repetition, read the following examples in their original versions and then in revision.

The climbers deserved praise for risking their lives to save their injured friend but not ^*for* the recklessness that led to his fall.

The keys to academic success, Jana decided, were to attend class as if she were going to work and ^*to* study as if she were playing a sport.

Senator Cohen said that he opposes the Cartwright Dam project and ^*that* the Fremont River must remain unobstructed.

EXERCISE 19.1 Editing Faulty Parallelism

Edit the following sentences to correct faulty parallelism. If a sentence is correct, write "correct." See the answers in the appendix.

19.2
Editing
faulty
parallelism:
Exercises

1. The campsites in many national parks have electric and running water.

2. According to a recent Canadian study, the keys to financial success are education, to work hard, and not take risks.

3. Today, many college students use the Internet to register for classes and reserve seats for special on-campus events.

4. As my father's cancer worsened, he debated whether to end the painful chemotherapy or continuing to battle his terrible disease.

5. Erin would rather spend her weekend surfing the Internet on her computer than dance the night away at a fancy club.

Crafting Sentences

III Sentences

III Sentences

Crafting Sentences

20 Writing Emphatically

20a Use the active voice when possible

20.1
Sentence
style sites:
Web link

Voice refers to verb forms that show whether a subject performs an action or is acted on. In the **active voice,** an active subject—an actor—performs the action of a transitive verb. Note that this actor-subject may be human or nonhuman.

subject verb   subject verb
Jane mailed the letter.   The sun scorched the lawn.

In the **passive voice,** a passive subject receives the action of the verb. Note that passive voice sentences may retain or omit the actor that commits the action of the verb.

subject verb actor   subject verb
The letter was mailed by Jane.   The lawn was scorched.

🌐 **ESL GRAMMAR NOTE** Transitive Verbs

Only transitive verbs—verbs that do something to someone or something (the direct object)—appear in active voice and passive voice constructions. (See 9c and d.)

---

1 ▪ Using the active voice for emphasis

20.2
Active and
passive
voice:
Web link

In the active voice, a sentence becomes a little story: *Jane heaved a sad sigh and dropped the letter in the mailbox.* Someone or something performs an action. This kind of sentence is usually the simplest to write, the shortest, and the easiest to read. And simplicity and brevity usually make main ideas stand out.

As you edit your writing, look for two kinds of sentences to rewrite in the active voice.

▪ Unemphatic, action-less sentences. Look for forms of the verb *be* (*be, am, is, are, was, were, being, been*) and an action suggested by another word in the sentence. Think of an action verb and rewrite.

recognizes
This award is in recognition of your months of hard work.
        ^

[The revision moves the action of the sentence to the verb.]

■ Unemphatic, wordy passive voice sentences. Rewrite to make the actor the subject of the sentence, or, if necessary, to identify the actor.

The Board of Trustees is considering tuition
~~Tuition~~ increases of ten percent ~~are being considered~~ for next year.
∧
[The revision adds the actors who perform the action of the sentence.]

2 ■ Using the passive voice effectively

Three situations require the passive voice:

■ When actors are unknown or unimportant, use the passive voice.

Nearly half of the world's fresh water **is locked** in the Antarctic ice sheet.

■ When actors are the most important information, use the passive voice to move the actor from the beginning of the sentence to the end, where it will receive the greatest emphasis.

During the last Ice Age, the landscape of Wisconsin and northern Illinois **was gouged and shaped** by a gigantic moving ice sheet.

■ When two sentences written in the active voice are incoherent, use the passive voice in the second sentence to link its subject to words that end the first sentence.

If we fight a war and win it with H-bombs, what history will remember is not the ideals we were fighting for but the methods we used to accomplish them. These methods **will be compared** to the warfare of Genghis Khan who ruthlessly killed every last inhabitant of Persia.

(Hans A. Bethe)

[The end of the first sentence, *the methods we used to accomplish them,* links with the passive voice opening of the sentence: *These methods will be compared . . . .* If the second sentence had opened in the active voice, *People will compare these methods,* the two sentences would not link coherently.]

To put a verb in the passive voice, use a form of the helping verb *be* plus the past participle of the main verb: *is mailed, was loved, will be chosen.* Put the original actor-subject in a *by*-phrase or omit it if it is unnecessary. Thus, *A specialist examined him* (active voice) becomes *he was examined by a specialist* (passive voice). Don't confuse voice and tense; the passive voice may appear in any tense. (See also 31d.)

20.3
Editing
active and
passive
voice:
Exercises

EXERCISE 20.1   Editing the Active and Passive Voice

Edit the following sentences for ineffective uses of the active and passive voice. If a sentence uses the active or passive voice effectively, write "correct" after it. See the answers in the appendix.

1. Care should be taken by writers of arguments to use only facts and generally accepted truths.

2. An iceberg the size of Rhode Island has recently broken away from the coast of Antarctica and may drift northward for ten years before melting.

3. The massive iceberg is estimated to tower 100 to 160 feet above the water and 1,000 feet below.

4. A polyester gene has been inserted into a cotton plant by genetic engineers in order to grow wrinkle-free fibers as warm as wool.

5. Between 1900 and 1972, US courts condemned more than 150 innocent men to die, and executioners executed at least 23 of them.

20b Subordinate less important ideas

To emphasize important ideas, put them in an independent clause, the main part of a sentence. To deemphasize less important ideas or add supporting details, subordinate them in dependent clauses or phrases connected to the independent clause. What you choose to emphasize will depend not only on what is most important about your topic but also on the way one sentence fits with the sentences that precede and follow it. (For more on subordination, see 21b and 28c.)

1 ▪ Subordinating with dependent clauses

You can deemphasize an idea by expressing it in a **dependent clause,** a group of words with a subject and verb that cannot stand by itself as a complete sentence.

▪ *Dependent clauses beginning with subordinating conjunctions.* Add a subordinating conjunction, such as *after, although, because, when,* and so forth, to create a dependent clause. Connect it to a related independent clause. (For a list of subordinating conjunctions, see 8g3.)

Because
Oahu was once a social center for Hawaii's kings, ~~so~~ it is now called
∧
"The Meeting Place."

[By subordinating the first half of the sentence as a dependent clause, the revision emphasizes the title given to Oahu.]

▪ *Dependent clauses beginning with relative pronouns.* Add a relative pronoun, such as *who, which,* and *that,* to act as the subject of a dependent clause. Use it to modify a word in the main clause or to act as part of the main clause. (See also 10b1 and 3.)

, which
Oahu was once a social center for Hawaii's kings, ~~so it~~ is now called
∧
"The Meeting Place."

[The dependent clause deemphasizes the history of Oahu; the independent clause emphasizes the title based on that history.]

2 ■ Subordinating with phrases

You can reduce the importance of an idea further by putting it into a **phrase,** a word group lacking a subject, a verb, or both.

20.4
Emphasizing
with
subordina-
tion:
Exercises

■ *Appositive phrases.* Put a less important idea in an appositive, a nounlike word or phrase that describes a nearby noun.

Oahu ~~was~~ once a social center for Hawaii's kings, ~~so it~~ is now called
"The Meeting Place."

■ *Participial phrases.* Put a less important idea in a phrase headed by the *-ing* or *-ed* participial forms of the verb. Put the phrase near the noun or pronoun it modifies.

Called "The Meeting Place,"
Oahu was once a social center for Hawaii's kings, ~~so it is now called~~
"~~The Meeting Place.~~"

[By deemphasizing the second half of the sentence in a participial phrase, the revision emphasizes Oahu's history, now part of an independent clause.]

20c Use coordination to emphasize equal ideas

20.5
Creating
parallelism:
Web link

Coordination (also called **parallel form**) refers to linked words having the same grammatical form (see Chapter 19). It is a way to emphasize the equality of related words and ideas.

1 ■ Coordinating with a conjunction or with a comma and a coordinating conjunction

■ Use a coordinating conjunction (*and, but, or, so, for, yet, nor*) to link and emphasize equally important words and phrases.

linked words
Horns and sirens announced the ship's arrival.

linked phrases
The violin evolved from ancient Asian fiddles and medieval stringed instruments.

■ Use a comma and coordinating conjunction to link equally impor-tant independent clauses. (See also 34a.)

, but its
The old cabin looked warm and cozy, ~~Its~~ roof leaked even in a gentle rain.

■ Use correlative conjunctions (*both/and, either/or, neither/nor, not/ but, not only/but also, whether/or*) to focus attention on important word pairs and to give greater emphasis to the second half of the pair.

Both

*∧*Politicians and the news organizations that report on them are heavily influenced by money from corporate sponsorship.

2 ■ Coordinating with a semicolon and a transition or conjunctive adverb or with a semicolon alone

■ Use a semicolon and a transition or conjunctive adverb such as *however* or *therefore* to link related and equally important independent clauses. (For a list of transitions and conjunctive adverbs, see 12b3; see also 35b.)

; however, they

Some say American workers are unproductive. ~~They~~ now work more

∧

than forty-five hours per week.

■ Use a semicolon standing alone to balance equally important clauses that are similar in structure. (See 35a.)

; artificial

Natural air pollutants include dust, gases, spores, and pollens. ~~Artificial~~

∧

air pollutants include smoke and gases from industries, vehicles, and households.

🌐 WRITING IN THE USA Coordination and Parallelism

To achieve emphatic sentences, avoid stringing together coordinate word groups that are loose and rambling. (See 21c.) To achieve parallelism, link together words that are grammatically equal. (See 19a–c.)

EXERCISE 20.2 Emphasizing with Subordination and Coordination

Using coordination and subordination, combine or rewrite the following sentences. When appropriate, use both in one item. For some items more than one correct revision is possible. See the answers in the appendix.

20.6
Emphasizing
with
subordina-
tion and
coordina-
tion:
Exercises

1. In one version of her story, Lady Godiva was observed by only one person. This was a tailor. He was the original Peeping Tom. He was struck blind by what he saw.

2. Lightning is usually associated with thunderstorms. It may also be produced by snowstorms, sandstorms, even the clouds over erupting volcanoes.

3. Ball lightning is a spherical flash. The flash varies in size from three to three hundred feet in diameter. It lasts less than five seconds.

4. The abominable snowman is a giant creature. It is also known as the "yeti." It supposedly roams the mountains at night. It is looking for victims.

5. It is described as having an upright posture. It has a covering of black to reddish hair. And it has the appearance of a bear, ape, or human.

20d Repeat key words to emphasize ideas

To affirm your beliefs, express feelings, or give special emphasis, repeat key words in grammatically equal (parallel) structures. Parallel key words are italicized in the following passages.

> Men in great places are thrice *servants*: *servants* of the sovereign state; *servants* of fame; and *servants* of business.
>
> (Francis Bacon, emphasis added)

> *Study* without *thought* is vain; *thought* without *study* is dangerous.
>
> (Confucius, emphasis added)

> If all you saw of life was the Iowa State Fair on a brilliant August day, when you hear those incredible crops ripening out of the black dirt between the Missouri and Mississippi rivers, you would believe that this is surely the best of all possible worlds.
>
> You would have *no* sense of the destruction of life, only of its rich creativeness: *no* political disasters, *no* assassinations, *no* ideological competition, *no* wars, *no* corruption, *no* atom waiting in its dark secrecy to destroy us all with its exploding energy.
>
> (Paul Engle, "The Iowa State Fair," *Holiday*, emphasis added)

20.7
Emphasizing
with
repetition:
Exercises

In the first example, the repetition of *servant* emphasizes the ironic constraints on people in positions of power. In the second example, to emphasize a contrast, the words *study* and *thought* are reversed when they are repeated, a strategy known as **chiasmus**. In the third example, each repeated *no* helps emphasize just how safe the writer believes Iowa to be from the threats of the modern world.

Note: Although repetition can emphasize important points, excessive repetition will make your writing sound choppy or overemotional. (See 21b and d.)

20e Place important ideas at the end of the sentence

When people listen to jokes, what they most want to hear is the punch line. When they study business documents, they're looking for the bottom line. When they read a story, they anticipate the climax. In each case, what's most important comes near the end. So, too, with effective sentences. The rhythms of spoken English and the pattern of information flowing from old to new information give the end of a sentence the greatest emphasis. As you edit your writing, aim to follow this same pattern.

1 ■ Emphasizing compounds and lists at the end of a sentence

When you end a sentence with a compound (words joined with conjunctions such as *and, or, but*) or a list, put the most important item last. Study these examples:

> Genius is one percent inspiration and ninety-nine percent perspiration.
>
> (Thomas A. Edison)

> Music expresses, at different moments, serenity or exuberance, regret or triumph, fury or delight.
>
> (Aaron Copeland)

How much less impact these compounds would have if reversed: *Genius is ninety-nine percent perspiration and one percent inspiration. Music expresses, at different moments, fury or delight, regret or triumph, serenity or exuberance.*

2 ■ Placing modifiers before the main clause of a sentence

Open a main clause with modifying phrases or clauses, but be sure these modifiers stand near the words they modify (see Chapter 23). As noted earlier, emphasize a main clause by putting it at the end of a sentence. Consider these examples:

> When you get to the end of your rope, *tie a knot and hang on.*
>
> (Franklin Delano Roosevelt, emphasis added)

[Note how much less encouraging, how much less powerful and imaginative this sentence would be if the main clause came at the beginning: *Tie a knot and hang on when you get to the end of your rope.*]

> Having laid waste the wilderness, skunked the waterways with toxins, and decimated animal and Indian alike in the name of economic progress, *we now indulge ourselves in an orgy of sentimentalism for whatever comes labeled "natural."*
>
> (Jonathan Evan Maslow, "Stalking the Black Bear," *Saturday Review*, emphasis added)

[This example, known as a *periodic sentence*, puts the main clause at the end of the sentence and saves the most important word for last.]

3 ■ Using "cleft formulas" to move subjects toward the end of a sentence

English employs several strategies known as *cleft formulas* to move the grammatical subject of a sentence to a position of greater emphasis within its predicate (the words that follow the verb). These formulas begin a sentence or main clause with *it, what, here,* and *there: It* was the best of times, *it* was the worst of times. *What* surprised me most was how gracefully he dances. *There's* the answer I'm looking for. Consider another example in which cleft formulas and subjects are italicized.

> Twice in my life I have seen the expression on the face of a person who was soon to die by suicide. *It* was not *the look of depression or despair. It* was more *the look of a person watching life from a great distance. It* was *an absorbed attention,* as if the person were reviewing an elaborate show, of which he or she had once been the star. I hope I never see it again.
>
> (Hugh Drummond, "The Masked Generation," *Mother Jones,* emphasis added)

20.8
Emphasizing
with end
focus:
Exercises

Use the *it, what, here,* and *there* cleft formulas as this writer has done: to move grammatical subjects to places of emphasis near the end of a sentence. But use them sparingly and carefully. Without a clear purpose for using them, you'll write wordy, unemphatic sentences. In those cases, edit your writing to eliminate cleft formulas. (See also 28b3.)

~~There was~~ a documentary on PBS Television this week ~~reporting~~ *reported* that human beings' appetite for food is controlled both by the brain and by sensors in the mouth and stomach.

🌎 **ESL GRAMMAR NOTE** Cleft Sentences and Subject-Verb Agreement

In cleft sentences beginning with *it,* the verb is singular: *It was her first victory.* In cleft sentences beginning with *what,* the verbs in the *what*-clause and the main clause may be singular or plural, depending upon the number of the subject or complement in each: *What we want from our nation's leaders is a higher regard for truth. What she wants are more true-to-life movies.* Following *here* and *there,* the verb agrees with the grammatical subject of the sentence: *It was my first computer. There is only one correct answer to my question.* (See also 14c and 32a2.)

---

21 Adding Variety

21a Vary the length of your sentences

21.1
Creating
sentence
variety:
Web link

Effective writing is like music. Repeated words and sentence patterns create an emphatic rhythm, and varied patterns make a melody that adds surprise, moves readers ahead, and prevents monotony. One of the most important creators of this musical style is variety in sentence length. Consider the following example. The numbers to the left indicate the number of words per sentence:

19 The point of going somewhere like the Napo River in Ecuador is not to see the most spectacular anything. It is
8 simply to see what is there. We are here on the planet only
18 once, and might as well get a feel for the place. We might as
60 well get a feel for the fringes and hollows in which life is lived, for the Amazon basin, which covers half a continent, and for the life that—there, like anywhere else—is always and necessarily lived in detail: on the tributaries, in the riverside villages, sucking this particular white-fleshed guava in this particular pattern of shade.

(Annie Dillard, "In the Jungle," from *Teaching a Stone to Talk*)

As you write, use short sentences to emphasize important ideas. The topic sentences of paragraphs are often shorter than those that follow; so are emotionally charged sentences and climactic sentences that make a point. Use longer sentences to explain, describe, and restate. As you edit your writing, check to see that your sentences follow these patterns.

HOW TO . . . Edit Sentences for Variety

1. Count the number of words in your sentences. If you find passages in which sentences repeatedly have nearly the same number of words or sentences that all have the same structure, you may have found a choppy or monotonous passage to rewrite.

2. When you finish editing, reread to check for coherence. Be sure that your sentences flow smoothly from one to the next.

COMPUTER TIP Analyzing Sentence Variety

3. Create a separate file for sentence editing for each project (e.g., *Project 1, sentence edits*). Then search your writing for end punctuation. After each period, question mark, or exclamation point, hit the return key to begin each sentence on a new line. Or use your Find or Search and Replace command to change each end punctuation mark to a hard return. Then study your sentences, comparing their length and structure. ■

21b Combine short, choppy sentences

One or two short sentences will emphasize important ideas, but several choppy ones may create a monotonous, singsong effect. To combine choppy sentences, do the following: eliminate unnecessary words, reword, rearrange, and repunctuate.

1 ▪ Subordinating less important ideas

Combine choppy sentences by reducing one sentence to a subordinate phrase or clause. (See 20b.)

The protestors surrounded city hall, ~~They believed~~ ⌃*, believing* incorrectly that the Mayor was still in her office.

[The revision combines two sentences into one, subordinating the second sentence as a participial phrase.]

Although many ~~Many~~ people try to avoid jury duty, ~~But~~ those who serve often praise their experience, ⌃*for the* ~~They speak of~~ new insights into human nature they have gained.

[The revision combines three sentences into one, subordinating the first sentence as a dependent clause and the third as a phrase.]

2 ▪ Coordinating equal ideas

Use parallel forms to coordinate related, equally important ideas. (See 20c.)

Most high school students watch television several hours a day. ⌃*,* ~~They~~ spend little time on homework, ~~They~~ ⌃*,* seldom read ⌃*,* and never write for pleasure.

[The revision eliminates pronouns and repunctuates to link the uses of high school students' time into an emphatic series.]

3 ▪ Restating ideas to subordinate one related sentence to another

Combine related but choppy sentences by introducing a now-subordinate phrase or clause with a word that repeats or summarizes something important from the main clause. Repetition will help guide your readers to the main point of your new combined sentence.

It's difficult for writers at the beginning of the new millennium to imagine a time before computers. ~~Then~~ ⌃*, a time when* writers had to plan carefully before they began writing. ⌃*and* ~~Their~~ errors were tedious to correct~~, too~~.

21.2
Sentence-
combining
skills:
Web link

[The revision combines three sentences by repeating the word *time* to emphasize the contrast in eras and by coordinating two sentences to emphasize the differences.]

21.3
Combining
choppy
sentences:
Exercises

> 🌐 **ESL GRAMMAR NOTE** Unnecessary Words

When you combine sentences, take care to avoid unnecessary repetition of subjects, objects, and adverbs. (See 32b.)

21c   Divide loose, rambling sentences into two or more separate sentences

Carefully crafted long sentences can be as clear, emphatic, and easy to read as shorter sentences. But long, rambling sentences may obscure important ideas and be tiresome to read.

1 ▪ Dividing loose sentences at conjunctions or transitions

Omit conjunctions or transitions if possible. Then check to see that your revised sentences are varied and emphatic.

Some cigarette advertisements use cartoons to make smoking a playful

activity, ~~and~~ others present attractive models to make smoking

glamorous, ~~but if~~ *. But if* you examine these ads closely, you will discover more complicated messages about smoking.

> 🌐 **WRITING IN THE USA** Coordinating Conjunctions

English permits the beginning of sentences with coordinating conjunctions (*for, and, nor, but, or, yet, so*) as in the preceding sample sentence revision. (See 32c and 8g1.)

2 ▪ Dividing sentences at subordinating conjunctions or relative pronouns

Too many dependent clauses in a sentence make reading difficult, especially when they come at opposite ends of the sentence. Rewrite dependent clauses as complete sentences.

As the soil of privately owned tree farms in the Pacific Northwest has

become less fertile, lumber companies have turned to federal lands and

their prime stands of old-growth timber, ~~although, once~~ *. Once* logging begins,

however, these forests will last less than a decade.

[To create two sentences, the revision omits a subordinating conjunction, *although,* and adds a conjunctive adverb, *however,* as a transition.]

21.4
Dividing
rambling
sentences:
Exercises

21d   Vary your sentence types

Sentences can be classified according to the clauses they contain: simple, compound, complex, and compound-complex. (See 10c1.) Varying sentence types will help you emphasize important ideas, vary sentence length, and match the order of your ideas with the structure of your sentences. Consider the varied sentences in the following example.

<table>
<tr>
<td>Compound
Simple, simple</td>
<td rowspan="7">The Puritans were a daring lot, but they had a mean streak.They hated the theater and banned Christmas. They punished people in a cruel and inhuman manner. They killed children who disobeyed their parents. When they came in contact with those whom they considered heathens or aliens, they behaved in such a bizarre and irrational manner that this chapter in the American history comes down to us as a late-movie horror film. They exterminated the Indians, who taught them how to survive in a world unknown to them, and their encounter with the calypso culture of Barbados resulted in what the tourist guide in Salem's Witches' House refers to as the Witchcraft Hysteria.</td>
</tr>
<tr><td></td></tr>
<tr><td>Complex</td></tr>
<tr><td></td></tr>
<tr><td>Complex</td></tr>
<tr><td></td></tr>
<tr><td>Compound-
complex</td></tr>
</table>

(Ishmael Reed, "America: The Multinational Society," from *Writin' Is Fightin'*)

21e   Vary the structure of your sentences

1 ▪ Varying sentence openers

Most sentences, like this one, open with their subjects. But too many of these sentences in a row can be monotonous. Vary your sentence openers occasionally to create new rhythms and to direct readers to the ideas you want to emphasize.

- ▪ *Adverbs and adverbial openers.* Adverbs can appear almost anywhere in a sentence.

Slowly, the
~~The~~ bicyclist pedaled ~~slowly~~ up the steep hill.
  ^

When runners   *exercise, they*
~~Runners~~ and bicyclists should not wear portable stereos ~~when they~~
  ^   ^   ^
~~exercise.~~

- ▪ *Participial openers.* Open with a participial phrase beginning with the *-ing* or *-ed* form of the verb. Follow it with the noun or pronoun that it modifies.

Churning the brown river, the
~~The~~ paddle-wheel steamer, ~~churning the brown river~~ pulled away from
  ^
the dock.

- *Prepositional phrases.* Open with a prepositional phrase, often a modifier of the main verb of the sentence.

In November, the
The city of Bloomington opened its first homeless shelter ~~in November~~.
^   ^

- *An appositive.* Open with a noun or noun phrase that modifies a nearby noun.

The loneliest of athletes, ultramarathon   *compete*
Ultramarathon runners ~~are the loneliest of athletes, competing~~ in events
^   ^
with few prizes and even fewer spectators.

- *An infinitive phrase.* Open with a *to* verb and its related words.

To study unwritten languages, linguists
Linguists go to Alaska, Africa, and South America ~~to study unwritten~~
^   ^
~~languages~~.

2 ■ Inverting sentence order

The most common English word order is subject plus verb plus object, complement, or verbal modifier. If you invert this order, putting the verb or other later words before the subject, you will change the rhythm of a sentence and create variety.

On the east wall hung a
A small painting of a French river ~~hung on the east wall~~.
^   ^

[This revision moves the verb and a prepositional phrase to the beginning.]

Among
~~The Chippewas of central Minnesota are among~~ the first Native
^
                                        are the Chippewas of central Minnesota
Americans to govern themselves outside federal government authority.
                                                                    ^

[This revision moves the subject and verb to the end of the sentence.]

Vivid language, a fluent style, and a writer's voice—these are traits both
Both writers and readers enjoy ~~vivid language, a fluent style, and a~~
^
~~writer's voice~~.

[This revision moves a closing list to the beginning of the sentence and connects it to the main clause with a dash and linking words.]

Note: Too many inverted sentences make your writing sound awkward or pretentious.

21.5
Varying
sentence
structure:
Exercises

21f Ask an occasional question

Most sentences you write are declarative sentences that provide information. (See 10c2.) You can increase sentence variety and attract readers if you alternate declarative sentences with questions. This strategy is italicized in the following examples.

1 ▪ Using a question to begin a paragraph

Placed at the beginning of a paragraph, questions give direction to your writing and involve readers in a search for answers.

> *But does imprisonment deter crime?* Deterrence requires that potential offenders think about the consequences of their actions, as many fail to do. More important, deterrence requires that those who do think about the consequences see some real risk that they will be caught and punished—a risk that must outweigh the benefits they expect from the crime. Unfortunately for deterrence, potential offenders think that the threat of capture and punishment applies to others but not to them.
>
> (Paul H. Robinson, "Moral Credibility and Crime," *The Atlantic Monthly*, emphasis added)

2 ▪ Using rhetorical questions

Rhetorical questions, assertions phrased as questions, vary the expression of your ideas and opinions.

> We need to recognize that ideas have consequences. By granting a special status to children, we go far toward ensuring that they will be self-occupied and all too often, irresponsible. *If children are fundamentally different from you and me, how could we possibly expect them even to begin to measure up to the same standards? How can you discipline them when, by definition, they are supposed to be creative, natural, and free?*
>
> (R. Keith Miller, "The Idea of Children," *Newsweek*, emphasis added)

22 Avoiding Mixed and Incomplete Messages

HOW TO . . . Edit Sentences for Accuracy and Clarity

1. Identify subjects and verbs. When possible, choose actor-subjects (human or nonhuman) and action verbs. Make sure that subjects and verbs go together logically and stand as closely together as possible. Consider this example:

subject verb subject verb

Watching television, *you'd think we lived* at bay, in total jeopardy, sur-

rounded on all sides by human-seeking germs, shielded against infec-

subject verb

tion and death only by chemical technology *that enables* us to keep killing them off.   (Lewis Thomas)

2. Examine the opening words of your sentence. Unless you have good reasons for doing otherwise, put subjects and verbs early, whether in independent or dependent clauses. And make the opening parts of your sentences short; put the long parts later. In the preceding example, the main part of the sentence comes early and is short: *Watching television, you'd think we lived at bay.*

3. Look for modifiers and the words they modify. Consider words immediately preceding and following commas. Be sure they go together logically and stand as closely together as possible. Consider the modifiers in the sample sentence. An arrow points to the words they modify. *Watching television, → you'd think we lived at bay, ← in total jeopardy, surrounded on all sides by human-seeking germs, shielded against infection and death only by chemical technology ← that enables us to keep killing them off.*

22.1
Improving
sentence
clarity:
Web link

4. Make sure that only one thing at a time is happening. "Chunk" your sentences into easily readable parts. Your sentences may occasionally be long, but their parts should be short, as in the sample sentence above.

22a Write subjects and predicates that make sense together

In clear, accurate sentences, subjects fit logically with their predicates, consisting of the main verb and any associated words. When they do not, the error is known as **faulty predication.** Subjects must be able to do what their verbs say they are doing. Subjects and subject complements must fit together naturally and appropriately.

inspires few
Today the ideal of national service ~~has dwindled among many~~ young
                                    ∧
Americans.

[Logically, an ideal cannot dwindle, which means "to become smaller." The problem is not the size of the ideal but people's awareness of or opposition to it.]

1 ▪ Using a subject that does not fit part of a compound predicate

A subject must make sense with all of its verbs.

Hot air ballooning experienced a renaissance

~~The renaissance of hot air ballooning came~~ in the early 1960s and since

then has grown increasingly popular.

[The original version says that a *renaissance . . . came . . . and . . . has grown . . .
popular.* But the renaissance did not grow popular. The writer means to say that
hot air ballooning has grown popular.]

2 ■ Using an illogical subject complement

An adjective or noun that follows a verb must logically describe or
rename the subject of the sentence.

A   is an organization

~~The hospice concept is a program~~ that provides skilled and compassionate

care to dying patients.

[The original says that a concept is a program. The assertion is illogical, and neither word accurately describes a hospice.]

3 ■ Using *is when, is where*

These phrases are common in casual speech, but often, especially in
definitions, they create statements that are not grammatical or logical.

the

Algophobia is ~~when a person has~~ excessive fear of pain.

[*When* is an adverb of time, but *algophobia* is a condition. The revision connects
the term to its definition.]

in which

Cubism was an early twentieth-century artistic style ~~where~~ painters

presented multiple perspectives of three-dimensional objects.

[*Where* is an adverb of place, but Cubism was an artistic movement.]

22b Avoid mixed constructions that say one thing in two ways

Many ideas can be expressed in more than one way. A **mixed construction** occurs when two ways of saying the same thing are combined
in one sentence. To rewrite a mixed construction, identify the two patterns of expression and choose the one that best fits the surrounding sentences and most clearly expresses your ideas.

The   has

~~According to a report by the~~ Center for U.S.-Mexican Studies ~~uncovered~~

changed immigration patterns in California.

22.2
Editing
mixed
construc-
tions:
Exercises

[In the original, a prepositional phrase, *according to a report*, seems to be the subject of the sentence—a grammatical impossibility. The revision uses a noun
phrase, *the Center for U.S.-Mexican Studies*, as the subject. Another revision might
follow the pattern begun by the original opening: *According to a report by the Center
for U.S.-Mexican Studies, immigration patterns in California have changed.*]

22c Make comparisons logical and complete

1 ▪ Comparing noncomparable items

To write logically, compare subjects that are genuinely comparable.

Cosmetic manufacturers have experimented with rabbits because they

have eyes similar to ~~the membrane of the~~ human eye. *eyes.*

[The original sentence compares eyes to a membrane: *eyes similar to the membrane of the human eye.* The revision compares eyes with eyes.]

2 ▪ Using incomplete formulas

Comparisons are made with certain verbal formulas that bring the terms being compared into relationship with each other. To be logical, supply all words necessary to complete the formula. (See also 19d.)

Alcoholics often spend more time drinking with friends than *they spend with* their families.

[The original seems to say that alcoholics drink with friends and families alike. Inserting *they spend with* distinguishes time spent with friends from time spent with families.]

3 ▪ Making incomplete comparisons

To be complete, comparisons must mention all items being compared.

The Miami Dolphins are not only a bigger and faster football team *than the Chicago Bears*. Man for man, they are also more experienced.

4 ▪ Mixing comparative and superlative forms

Use the comparative *-er/more* form to compare two items, the superlative *-est/most* form to compare three or more items. (See also 18d2.)

The United States has ~~the highest~~ *a higher* divorce rate than any other country.

[The original sentence uses the superlative form to compare the United States to any other country. The revision uses the correct form for comparing two items.]

22d Include all necessary key words and function words

1 ▪ Checking for omitted key words

The omission of key words may produce illogical statements. As you rewrite, be sure your sentences have all the words necessary to express your ideas completely.

When we reached a clearing in the forest, we found ourselves knee-deep

lost in six-foot   *blinded by*
in green slime, weeds ~~six feet tall,~~ and clouds of flying insects.
                    ^   ^   ^

[In the original, the hikers improbably appear to be knee-deep in six-foot weeds and clouds of insects, as well as slime. The added verb phrases describe their situation accurately.]

2 ■ Checking for omitted function words

Function words help to identify the grammatical functions performed by the key words of sentences. Include all the function words necessary to signal the direction your sentences are taking.

- ■ *The articles* **a, an,** *and* **the.** Include articles before nouns to make series or compounds grammatically complete.

                        an   *the*
  Onto the stage walked a doctor, astronaut, and president of the university.
                              ^   ^

  [It is necessary to add *an* before a word beginning with a vowel sound and the definite article *the* before the title of a specific person.]

🌐 ESL GRAMMAR NOTE Articles

The use of articles in English differs from that in many other languages. For specific guidance about using articles appropriately, see Chapter 30.

- ■ *The subordinating conjunction* **that.** You may often omit *that* from your sentences: *Leslie stuffed her backpack with all [that] she would need for two weeks.* But include *that* if readers may not see that a clause follows a verb instead of a phrase.

                that
  Kevin found the historic house he wanted to photograph had been
              ^
  demolished.

  [Adding *that* indicates that the historic house is the subject of a clause, not the direct object of *found.*]

- ■ *Verbs in compound structures.* Even though a verb may be common to both parts of a compound structure, you must repeat the verb to signal tense changes.

                                                    recruited
  Without generous scholarships, our university has not and never will
                                                          ^
  recruit the best students.

  [The original is ungrammatical: *has not . . . recruit. Recruited* is necessary to signal that the tense of the first verb differs from that of the second.]

- ■ *The relative pronouns* **who** *and* **whom.** If a relative pronoun changes case from one part of a compound structure to another, use both case forms. (See 17e.)

22.3
Writing
clear,
accurate
sentences:
Exercises

whom
Arthur Ashe was a man many thought the greatest male tennis player of
    ^
his generation but who should be remembered as a social activist.

[*Whom* must be added to the first half of the compound to signal that it is in the object case as the direct object of the verb *thought*. In the second half, *who* is in the subject case as the subject of the verb *should be remembered*.]

23 Placing Modifiers

23a Move misplaced modifiers near the words they modify

A **misplaced modifier** is a word or phrase that is located incorrectly in relation to the words it modifies. The result may be an illogical sentence that is difficult to follow. If you spot a misplaced modifier, rearrange the sentence to make sense and make reading easier.

23.1
Placing
modifiers:
Web link

, which hummed quietly,
A small fan stood on the desk ~~which hummed quietly~~
                          ^   ^
[In the original, the desk appears to hum quietly. The revision moves the modifier next to the word it modifies, *fan*.]

, driving through eastern Pennsylvania,
I knew I was near my destination when I tuned in a New York radio
                                    ^
station ~~driving through eastern Pennsylvania~~
      ^
[In the original, the New York radio station appears to be driving through Pennsylvania. Locating the modifier next to *I* makes clear who is driving.]

1 ■ Using limiting modifiers correctly

Limiting modifiers restrict or limit the meaning of the words they modify: *almost, even, exactly, hardly, just, merely, nearly, only, scarcely, simply.* To make your meaning clear and unambiguous, place these modifiers before the words they modify.

only
Barry ~~only~~ chose the chocolate-covered caramels.
        ^
[In the original, *only* may seem to refer to Barry, as in *Barry alone did the choosing.* Moving the modifier emphasizes that he chose only one kind of candy.]

almost
On average, Americans ~~almost~~ work as many hours per week as the
                        ^
Japanese.

[In the original, the location of *almost* seems to suggest that Americans don't quite work. Moving the modifier emphasizes how much Americans work.]

2 ■ Avoiding squinting modifiers

Squinting modifiers appear to modify both preceding and following words, creating ambiguous meaning. Move the modifier before the word it modifies or rewrite to eliminate ambiguity.

Because she wanted to work for the National Park Service, Nancy

seriously
considered ~~seriously~~ studying for a degree in botany.
∧

[The original seems to say that Nancy considered doing some serious studying. The revision says that the way she considered was serious.]

in the evening
The owner required his tenants ~~in the evening~~ to play their music quietly.
∧

[The original seems to say that the landlord made his requirement in the evening. The revision says that the tenants must be quiet in the evening.]

3 ■ Avoiding split infinitives

An infinitive is the *to* form of a verb: *to run.* **Split infinitives** occur when a modifier comes between *to* and the verb: *to quickly run.* Avoid split infinitives when they sound awkward or may confuse readers.

quickly
Dean's mother told him to ~~quickly~~ run to the store and buy a newspaper.
∧

without much preparation
Sheri hoped to~~, without much preparation,~~ pass her French final exam.
∧

It is, however, appropriate to write split infinitives in some circumstances:

- ■ *To avoid ambiguity.* Consider the difference between these two sentences, the first containing a split infinitive: *The President proposed to further delay agricultural reforms. The President proposed to delay further agricultural reforms.* In the first sentence, the President proposed to increase the delay. In the second, the President proposed to delay more reforms.

- ■ *To avoid awkwardness.* Consider this sentence containing a split infinitive: *With more practice, the relay team was able to nearly equal their best time.* This version is clearer and more natural than *With more practice, the relay team was able nearly to equal their best time.*

EXERCISE 23.1 Editing Misplaced Modifiers

Edit the following sentences to correct misplaced modifiers. More than one correct revision is possible. See the answers in the appendix.

1. Albert only intended to just eat one chocolate-covered doughnut.

2. Dust began to thicken as the months passed on bookcases, file cabinets, and desks.

23.2
Editing
misplaced
modifiers:
Exercises

3. None of us thought night would ever come after paddling our canoes for twelve hours.

4. On the walls of the restaurant are large frames containing records and CDs plated with silver, gold, and platinum of famous musical artists.

5. I was walking back to the courthouse after a lunch break where I was serving on jury duty.

23b To connect dangling modifiers, rewrite or add missing words

A **dangling modifier** has no words to modify. It "dangles" disconnected or appears to make an illogical connection.

1 ■ Rewriting dangling participles

A participle is the *-ing* or *-ed* verb form acting as an adjective. A **dangling participle** "dangles" because it has no logical actor to perform the action that it names. Rewrite to identify the actor; you also will have to change the form of the verb.

As I pedaled

~~Pedaling~~ around a sharp curve on the steep mountain road, the warning
of other bicyclists echoed in my head.

[In the original, the warning itself seems to be pedaling around a curve. The revision adds a subject and changes the verb to turn a phrase into a dependent clause.]

we finally saw

After drifting down the river for an hour, the bridge ~~came into view~~.

[In the original, the opening phrase seems to modify *bridge*. Adding an actor-subject to the main clause and changing its verb clarifies the meaning of the sentence.]

2 ■ Rewriting a modifier that appears to modify a possessive

Modifiers that provide information about nouns or pronouns cannot modify possessive *-'s* words, which act as adjectives rather than nouns. Rewrite to omit the possessive or to supply a noun or pronoun.

Although recognized by many for her fundraising, Lucille Allen's ~~name~~
didn't become well known until she married the mayor.

[In the original, the opening phrase seems illogically to modify *Lucille Allen's name*. Dropping the possessive *-'s* and *name* makes all parts of the sentence fit together.]

3 ■ Rewriting dangling appositives

A noun or noun phrase functioning as an appositive must stand near the noun or equivalent form that it can logically modify. Rewrite to create logical relations.

The actress's sensitive performance revealed the mother's ~~character,~~ a strong, courageous person.

to be

[In the original, the appositive *a strong, courageous person* illogically modifies *character*. Adding *to be* turns the appositive into a complement describing *mother*.]

EXERCISE 23.2   Editing Dangling Modifiers

Edit the following sentences to correct dangling modifiers. More than one correct revision is possible. See the answers in the appendix.

1. Chef Edgar has served dinners throughout Europe, including royalty.

2. From watching people toss it around in the park, playing with a Frisbee must be very relaxing.

3. Hopefully, when the championship game is over, the victory flag will be hoisted over our stadium.

4. After reaching what lawyers call the age of accountability, life becomes more difficult for most young people.

5. Some jobs are not satisfying or glamorous but do pay good wages, a supermarket, for instance.

23.3
Editing
misplaced
and
dangling
modifiers:
Exercises

---

24 Avoiding Faulty Shifts

24a Maintain a consistent point of view

24.1
Verb and
pronoun
consistency:
Web link

Point of view is the perspective of a piece of writing: **first person** (*I* or *we*), **second person** (*you*), or **third person** (*he, she, it, one,* or *they*). A faulty shift in point of view frequently involves a shift from first or third person to second person—from *I* or *they* to *you*. As you write, settle on a point of view appropriate to the subject and occasion. For informal writing, first-person point of view is usually appropriate; for formal writing, third person is often appropriate. Once you decide on your point of view, maintain it consistently.

My job washing dishes may be damp and dirty, but at least no one ever

me   *I am*
bothers ~~you~~ while ~~you are~~ working.

Pedestrians stared suspiciously as the Jeffreys searched for the right

they   *they*
address. Wherever ~~you~~ turned, ~~you~~ were inspected from head to foot.

🌐 WRITING IN THE USA Direct Address

Academic English permits the writer to address the reader directly, as in instructions or advice: *When you finish a rough draft, let it sit for a while before you begin revising.* (See 16a3.) *You* may also be used in less formal writing to represent people in general: *When you go to the movies in New York City, you always have to stand in line.*

24b Avoid inconsistent shifts in number

If you begin using the plural to write about a subject, stick to the plural; if you begin using the singular, stick to the singular.

homes
Televised violence makes many viewers afraid to leave their ~~home~~.

24c Stay in one tense unless the time of the action changes

When you use more than one verb to describe an action, put all verbs in the same tense. A faulty tense shift between past and present sometimes occurs in narratives about past events.

When General Picket was ordered to prepare his men to charge, the

could not
young officer ~~cannot~~ contain his anticipation.

[The original version shifts from the past tense, *was ordered*, to the present, *cannot contain*. The revision makes both verbs past tense.]

At the beginning of Shirley Jackson's short story, Mr. Johnson is in love

wants   *does*
with the world. He ~~wanted~~ to make others feel as good as he ~~did~~.

[The original, from a student paper about a short story, shifts from present to past tense. The revision makes all the verbs present tense, the appropriate tense for writing about literature and the events that take place in individual stories, novels, and plays. (See also 13b1.)]

24d Maintain a consistent mood and voice

1 ▪ Avoiding shifts in mood

Mood identifies the kind of statement a verb makes: an expression of fact (**indicative mood**), a command or advice (**imperative mood**), and wishes or speculation (**subjunctive mood**). Stick to one mood unless you have reason to change. (See also 13f.)

plant marigolds
For best growth and color, ~~it is important that marigolds be planted~~ in full
                                                                        ∧
sun. Water them often and pinch back the blooms.

[The original shifts from the subjunctive mood in the first sentence, *be planted,* to the imperative mood in the second, *water . . . and pinch back.* The revision puts both sentences in the imperative mood appropriate for instructions.]

2 ▪ Avoiding shifts in voice

Voice refers to the relationship between a subject and verb. (See 20a.) In active voice expressions, an active subject performs the action of the verb: *The child hit the ball.* In passive voice expressions, a passive subject is acted on: *The ball was hit.* Maintain a consistent voice unless you have reason to change.

she had achieved
Jane congratulated herself because all of her goals ~~had been achieved.~~
                                                     ∧   ∧

[The original shifts from the active voice, *congratulated,* to the passive, *had been achieved.* The revision maintains the active voice throughout.]

24e Avoid inconsistent shifts from indirect to direct discourse

Direct discourse consists of word-for-word quotations and questions addressed directly to listeners or readers. **Indirect discourse** summarizes quotations and questions. Be consistent in the form of discourse you use. (For ESL, see 32d.)

Last week Dr. Lambert told us that we were behind schedule, ~~and~~

and would   our
"~~You'll~~ have to finish ~~your~~ report by the end of the month."
     ∧   ∧

[The original shifts from summary to direct quotation. The revision maintains indirect discourse throughout. An alternative revision would quote all of Dr. Lambert's remarks: *Last week Dr. Lambert told us, "You're behind schedule. You'll have to finish your report by the end of the month."*]

Doctors in the nineteenth century were uncertain whether the causes of

whether they should
mental illness differed for men and women and ~~if so, should they~~ be
                                               ∧

treated differently~~?~~
                   ∧

[The original opens with an indirect question and shifts to a direct question. The revision maintains indirect discourse throughout.]

24.2
Editing
faulty shifts:
Exercises

ON THE WEB   www.ablongman.com/dodds

Choosing Words

25 Choosing Exact Words

25a Denotation: Choose words that say exactly what you mean

The **denotation** of a word is its literal, dictionary definition. Although writers don't intend to choose the wrong word, even the best occasionally choose a word that is not quite right. As you write, experiment to find words that have your exact meaning. Whenever possible, choose words you know well. If you use a word that doesn't seem exact, try several alternatives. If you don't find the right word, put a check mark (✓) in the margin to remind you to reconsider your choice later. Then, as you revise, use a dictionary or thesaurus to look up words outside your everyday vocabulary. Look for mismatches between what you mean to say and what your words actually mean.

25.1
Vocabulary:
Web link

1 ▪ Checking for ambiguous words

Writers sometimes choose words that, in the context of their writing, have multiple, or ambiguous, meanings. To write unambiguously, choose specific words that express only the meaning you intend. (See 26a.)

Although many were dissatisfied with Judge Tanaka's decision, they did
impartial
agree that it was ~~fair~~.
                    ∧

[*Fair* may mean that the judge ruled without favoritism, the meaning of *impartial*. But *fair* may also mean in the best interests of each person involved or without self-interest. The exact meaning of *fair* is unclear in the original sentence.]

2 ▪ Checking for approximate words

Some words are near synonyms of other words. But, as Mark Twain observed, the difference between the right word and the almost-right word is the difference between lightning and a lightning bug. To distinguish between words with similar meanings, use the synonym section of dictionary entries or a thesaurus. (See 25c and d.)

                              ~~quietly~~ ~~weakly~~ faintly
At dawn, the cardinal's song echoed ~~feebly~~ over the roof tops.
                                     ∧

25b Connotation: Choose words that convey appropriate feelings and attitudes

The **connotation** of a word is the emotional associations and attitudes that the word calls up. Words similar in dictionary definition often differ widely in connotative meaning. Consider the connotations of the word pairs in the following sentences. The words in each pair are similar in denotation but differ in connotation. Is the connotation of each word positive, negative, or neutral?

On the dining room table was a vase filled with *artificial/fake* flowers.

The old *cabin/shack* stood near the edge of a forest.

Political parties aim to *educate/indoctrinate* voters.

1 ▪ Matching connotation and the writer's attitude

Choose words whose positive, neutral, or negative connotation matches your attitude toward your subject. Find the right word in the synonym section of a dictionary entry or in a thesaurus. (See 25c and d.)

$\qquad$ scent
The ~~odor~~ of burning leaves reminds me of childhood.
$\qquad$ ^

[*Odor* generally has negative, unpleasant associations. If the writer's memories are positive, *scent,* associated as it is with perfume, is the better choice.]

2 ▪ Expressing connotation in public writing

Decide whether words with strong connotations are suitable. Not all situations permit such expressions of feeling or attitude, either positive or negative. Informative writing in school and on the job usually requires neutral or subdued words.

$\qquad$ crowd $\qquad\qquad$ rushed to
A ~~mob~~ of reporters ~~stormed~~ the rooming house where President Lincoln
$\qquad$ ^ $\qquad\qquad$ ^
lay dying.

[The strong negative connotations of the original words are inappropriate for writing from an objective perspective.]

25c Learn to use all parts of a dictionary entry

25.2
Dictionaries:
Web link

A good college desk dictionary does more than give spelling, pronunciation, and basic definitions. To choose the exact words for your meaning, you need to know—and use—all that a dictionary entry contains. Here is an entry from *The American Heritage Dictionary.*

Pronunciation   Grammatical labels   Word endings

Spelling —— **af·fect**[1] (-ə-fĕkt´) *tr.v.* **-fect·ed, -fect·ing, -fects.** **1.** To
and word   have an influence on or effect a change in: *Inflation*
division   *affects the buying power of the dollar.* **2.** To act on the
emotions of; touch or move. **3.** To attack or infect,
Definitions—— as a disease: *Rheumatic fever can affect the heart.*
—**affect** (-ə-fĕkt´) *n.* **1.** *Psychology.* **a.** A feeling or   ─Usage label
emotion as distinguished from cognition, thought, or
action. **b.** A strong feeling having active conse-
quences. **2.** *Obsolete.* A disposition, feeling, or ten-   ── Etymologies
dency. [Latin *afficere, affect-* : *ad-,* ad- + *facere,* to do;   (word
see **dhē-** in Appendix.]   origins)

SYNONYMS: *affect, influence, impress, touch, move,*
strike. These verbs are compared as they mean to
produce a mental or emotional effect. To *affect* is to
act upon a person's emotions: *The adverse criticism*
the book received didn't affect the author one way or
Examples   *another. Influence* implies a degree of control or   Synonyms
illustrating   sway over the thinking and actions, as well as the   (related
the contexts   emotions, of another: *"Humanity is profoundly*   words)
appropriate —   *influenced by what you do"* (John Paul II). To
for each   *impress* is to produce a marked, deep, often endur-
synonym   ing effect: *"The Tibetan landscape particularly*
impressed him" (Doris Kerns Quinn). *Touch* usually
means to arouse a tender response, such as love,
gratitude, or compassion: *"The tributes* [to the two
deceased musicians] *were fitting and touching"*
(Daniel Cariaga). *Move* suggests profound emotional effect that sometimes leads to action or has a
further consequence: *The account of her experiences*
as a refugee moved us to tears. Strike implies keenness
or force of mental response to a stimulus: *I was*
struck by the sudden change in his behavior.

Usage ——— **USAGE NOTE:** *Affect*[1] and *effect* have no senses in
common. As a verb *affect*[1] is most commonly used
in the sense of "to influence" (*how smoking affects*
health). *Effect* means "to bring about or execute":
An example ——— *layoffs designed to effect savings.* Thus the sentence
of appropriate   *These measures may affect savings* could imply that
usage   the measures may reduce savings that have already
been realized, whereas *These measures may effect*
savings implies that the measures will cause new
savings to come about.

1 ■ Locating spelling, word division, and pronunciation

Words are divided by syllables: **af·fect.** Two words with the same
spelling but different meanings are numbered to signal their difference.

Compounds are written as one word (*multimedia*), with a hyphen (*multiple-choice*), or as two words (*multiple sclerosis*). When two or more spellings or pronunciations are correct, the preferred appears first. The phonetic alphabet (as in ə-fĕkt´) is explained in the dictionary's introduction and in the pronunciation key, usually found at the bottom of each page. Accent marks (´) indicate the most heavily stressed character or syllable.

2 ▪ Locating grammatical labels and word endings

Labels indicate the grammatical function (part of speech) of a word and its various endings: *tr.v.* **-fect·ed, -fect·ing, -fects.**

adj. adjective	*interj.* interjection	*prep.* preposition
adv. adverb	*n.* noun	*pron.* pronoun
aux. auxiliary	*pl.* plural	*sing.* singular
conj. conjunction	*pl. n.* plural noun	*tr.* transitive
def. art. definite article	*pref.* prefix	*intr.* intransitive
indef. art. indefinite article	*suff.* suffix	*v.* verb

Whenever a word changes grammatical function, alternatives are listed in boldface accompanied by a grammatical label:—**affect** (ăf´ ĕkt´) *n.* All abbreviations are defined in the dictionary's introduction (see the table of contents after the title page).

3 ▪ Locating definitions and etymologies

Definitions are numbered and arranged by frequency of use or according to meaning clusters. Letters following numbers identify closely related definitions. Examples occasionally illustrate a word's use. The **etymology** of a word (its origin or history) is often an important guide to its meanings and associations. **Affect,** for example, comes from Latin words (Latin *afficere, affect-* : *ad-, ad-* + *facere,* to do).

4 ▪ Locating usage labels

Labels preceding a definition tell under what conditions that definition is appropriate: *Informal, Slang, Nonstandard, Offensive, Archaic, Obsolete, Chiefly British.* Field labels identify special areas such as music, art, computer science, and medicine where specific definitions apply (see *Psychology* in the sample entry).

5 ▪ Locating synonyms and usage

Following the main entries of many words are notes that distinguish among related words (see the synonyms of *affect*) or that compare actual uses of words with what experts consider correct uses (see the Usage Note on *affect* and *effect*).

25d Use a thesaurus to find the exact word, not necessarily the biggest or fanciest

A **thesaurus** (from the Latin word for "treasure") lists words together with their synonyms, antonyms, and related words. A thesaurus may be a printed reference work such as *Roget's II: The New Thesaurus*, or *Webster's Collegiate Thesaurus*, or a data file accompanying a computer word processor. Here is an entry from *Webster's Collegiate Thesaurus.**

25.3
Thesauruses:
Web link

Headword   Grammatical label   ┌Numbers identifying different senses of the headword

believe *vb* **1** to have a firm conviction in the reality of   Illustration
Synonyms   something < *believes* in ghosts > ──────   of the core
listed   **syn** accept, ‖ buy, swallow   meaning of
    the headword
Related words ─ **rel** accredit, credit, trust; admit
that are not   **idiom** have no doubts about, hold the belief that, take (or
synonyms   accept) as gospel, take at one's word, take one's word for
Idiomatic   **con** discredit, distrust, doubt, mistrust, question, suspect; ┌Cross refer-
equivalents   challenge, dispute; reject, turn down   ence number
Contrasting   **ant** disbelieve, misbelieve
words that are   **2 syn** FEEL **3.** consider, credit, deem, hold, sense, think   A signal to
not antonyms   **3 syn** UNDERSTAND **3.** assume, expect, gather, imag-   check usage
Antonyms   ine, ‖ reckon, suppose, suspect, take, think   labels in a
    dictionary

1 ■ Matching words to contexts

Although a thesaurus groups words having related meanings, it cannot identify the specific contexts in which each word is appropriate. As you decide between synonyms or related words, consider the denotation and connotation of each word, your readers' vocabulary, and the formality of the occasion. (See 27a and b.) In most contexts, synonyms are not interchangeable with one another.

anxious desirous *eager*
We were dying to share our experiences from our vacation in Egypt.
                ^

[*Dying* is too informal for academic and most public writing. *Desirous* sounds too stuffy. And *anxious* suggests apprehension. *Eager* combines the senses of anticipation and desire in a word appropriate for public writing.]

2 ■ Choosing exact words instead of impressive words

Many writers use a thesaurus because they doubt that their words sound polished or impressive enough. But consider how you respond to people who try to impress you with their vocabularies. Use a thesaurus to help you find exact but familiar words. (See 27a and 27d1.)

interest   began   a vacation
My absorption in archaeology commenced with an excursion in Egypt.
        ^   ^   ^

──────────
*By permission. From *Merriam-Webster's Collegiate® Thesaurus* ©1994 by Merriam-Webster, Incorporated.

25e Distinguish between frequently confused words

Writers confuse one word with another for several reasons.

- **Homophones** sound alike but are spelled differently and have different meanings: *there, their, they're; affect, effect; complement, compliment.*

- **Near homophones** sound enough alike to be confused with each other: *adapt, adopt; allusion, illusion, delusion; ambiguous, ambivalent; lie, lay.*

- **False synonyms** are related but different words often used in similar contexts: *imply, infer; fewer, less; contagious, infectious; number, amount.*

- Some words have similar roots but different prefixes or suffixes: *disinterested, uninterested; empathize, sympathize; incredulous, incredible; assume, presume; nauseous, nauseate; sensuous, sensual.*

To avoid confusion, look up words outside your everyday vocabulary and memorize differences between words that you have confused. (For a list of frequently confused words, see the guide to usage in Chapter 29.)

**25.4
Often
confused
words:
Web link**

integral
Movies have become an ~~intricate~~ part of American culture.

[*Intricate*, meaning complex or elaborate, and *integral*, meaning essential or necessary, are near homophones differing greatly in their denotations.]

25f Use words idiomatically

An **idiom** is a word or expression given special meaning by native speakers of a language. It cannot be understood by knowing the meanings of the individual words alone. For example, native speakers of English say "Good evening" as a greeting but "Good night" as a farewell. Although they appear synonymous, these phrases are idiomatic expressions, each with its own meaning. Generally, idioms take three forms.

1 ■ Choosing individual words with idiomatic meaning

Some words are frequently used in some situations but not in others that may appear similar.

buried
The murderer ~~lodged~~ his victims in the crawl space beneath his house.

[*To lodge* may mean "to place, leave, or deposit an item," as in *The bone lodged in his throat.* Living persons may be "lodged," as in *We lodged our uncle at our neighbor's house.* But in idiomatic English, people are not "lodged" in anything but a residence.]

2 ▪ Using stock phrases

Stock phrases are tired expressions, such as *sitting pretty, comes in handy, travel light, take your time, as good as, heavy-handed, make do, take stock, keep company,* and *change of heart,* which are overused. (See also 26d1.)

3 ▪ Using phrases with prepositions

Prepositions (*in, by, on, according to,* and so forth) and preposition-like words called **particles** following verbs (*agree with/to, abide by, argue with/about, consist in/of*) are idiomatic, appearing only in specific situations and with certain words.

A quiet walk through autumn leaves is always preferable ~~than~~ weaving

to

~~in~~ the crowded aisles of some department store.

through

[Idiomatic English uses *better than* but *preferable to. Weaving through* is necessary to describe a person's path through a crowd.]

🌐 WRITING IN THE USA Idioms

Native speakers of a language typically use words and phrases idiomatically, but nonnative speakers and native writers who choose words outside their everyday vocabularies may encounter difficulties.

- ▪ If you're uncertain of a word or phrase, check the usage notes in Chapter 29 and in dictionary entries.

- ▪ For phrases not listed in dictionaries, check special learners' dictionaries, like the *Longman Dictionary of American English,* or dictionaries of idioms, often found where materials for learners of English as a second language are sold.

- ▪ For prepositions, often particularly problematic, look up the word preceding the preposition (*preferable* or *weaving* in the example above) in a dictionary. (See also 31g.)

- ▪ Keep in mind that idioms are often culture-bound and do not translate meaningfully to other languages.

25.5
Choosing
exact
words:
Web link

26 Choosing Vivid Words

26a When possible, choose specific rather than general words

Words can be classified as specific, general, or somewhere in between. **General words** are umbrella terms that refer to many things. **Specific words** refer to individual persons, places, things, actions, or qualities.

GENERAL WORDS	←			→	SPECIFIC WORDS
artist		painter			Mary Cassatt
urban area		city			Calcutta
vegetation	tree	evergreen	fir		spruce
observe		look			stare
textured	uneven	rough	coarse		scratchy

Because they are precise in meaning and feeling, specific words tend to be more pictorial than general words and to make a subject clearer and easier to grasp. Choose them for these reasons.

Consider the italicized specific words in this passage from a memoir of childhood.

> The bodies of the men I knew were twisted and maimed in ways visible and invisible. The *nails* of their *hands* were *black* and *split*, the *hands tattooed* with *scars*. Some had lost *fingers*. Heavy lifting had given many of them *finicky backs* and *guts* weak from *hernias*. Racing against *conveyor belts* had given them *ulcers*. Their *ankles* and *knees* ached from years of *standing on concrete*. Anyone who had worked for long around machines was *hard of hearing*. They *squinted*, and the *skin of their faces* was *creased like the leather of old work gloves*. There were times, studying them, when I dreaded growing up.
>
> (Scott Russell Sanders, from *The Paradise of Bombs*, emphasis added)

As you write, create the rhythm of general and specific language illustrated by the preceding passage. Use general words to identify a subject, make assertions, and provide background. Use specific words to support assertions and bring ideas to life.

Drivers are becoming increasingly ~~dangerous~~/hostile. They tailgate at seventy miles an hour, drag race from stop signs, curse, and honk at whatever they think threatens their right to the road.

[*Dangerous* is a general word that may refer to unskilled drivers or, as the writer intended, to driver hostility. The added specific examples prove the point and dramatize it.]

26b When possible, choose concrete rather than abstract words

Concrete words refer to things you see, hear, taste, touch, and smell: *rock, trumpet, tomato, fur, rose.* **Abstract words** refer to conditions, qualities, and ideas: *democracy, justice, mercy, misery, hope, independence.* Use concrete words to make your writing pictorial and to bring abstractions to life. In the following passage, the emphasized concrete words explain and illustrate *entropy,* the principle of disorder.

> Because of its unnerving irreversibility, entropy has been called the *arrow* of time. We all understand this instinctively. *Children's rooms,* left on their own, tend to get messy, not neat. *Wood rots, metal rusts, people wrinkle and flowers wither.* Even *mountains wear down;* even the *nuclei of atoms decay.* In the *city* we see entropy in the *rundown subways* and *worn-out sidewalks* and *torn-down buildings,* in the increasing disorder of our lives. We know, without asking, what is old.
>
> (K. C. Cole, "Entropy," *New York Times,* emphasis added)

1 ▪ Using concrete words for description

As you write and revise, think of concrete nouns to describe your subject and concrete verbs to dramatize its actions.

An autumn bicycle tour in western Wisconsin ~~is a wondrous sensory~~ *offers a sensory feast:* ~~journey/~~ the intense red and yellow of maples, musty aromas of just-harvested corn and beans, sounds of cattle and roosters, and the texture and taste of apples mounded in baskets at roadside stands.

2 ▪ Avoiding the seven deadly nouns

When possible avoid *area, experience, factor, field, situation, thing,* and *type*—words so abstract and vague that they deaden almost any idea.

Urban public schools suffer from ~~a lack of funds, a situation caused by~~ *the unequal distribution of local property taxes.* ~~unfortunate property tax factors.~~

3 ▪ Choosing alternatives to forms of the verb *be*

When you can find alternatives to *is, was, were,* and so forth, your writing will become more vivid and pictorial.

26.1
Choosing
vivid words:
Exercises

Americans ~~are concerned about~~ *protest* dwindling natural resources only when
^

~~there are long lines at~~ *lines of autos jam* gas stations, home construction costs ~~are high~~ *soar*, and
^   ^

monthly utility bills ~~are also high.~~ *run into the hundreds of dollars.*
^

26c Use figurative language to dramatize ideas, opinions, and feelings

Figurative language (also called **figures of speech**) uses words imaginatively and nonliterally to describe, evaluate, and express feelings. The most frequently used figure of speech is **figurative comparison,** which reveals hidden similarities between dissimilar subjects by transferring the features of one subject, called the **vehicle,** to the writer's true subject, called the **tenor.** Consider these lines from Robert Burns's famous love poem:

> O, My Luve's [love's] like a red, red rose
> That's newly sprung in June

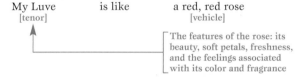

My Luve   is like   a red, red rose
[tenor]   [vehicle]

The features of the rose: its
beauty, soft petals, freshness,
and the feelings associated
with its color and fragrance

In two short lines, the poet describes his beloved, praises her beauty, and expresses his feeling for her. Because figurative comparisons say so much in so few words, they are an especially vivid use of language, one that can make your writing colorful and powerful, a pleasure for you and your readers.

26.2
Creating
figurative
language:
Web link

🌎 WRITING IN THE USA Using Figurative Language Appropriately

In some languages, figurative language is an especially important part of graceful, effective expression. In academic writing in the United States, however, figurative language is used primarily to aid in analysis, description, and persuasion and is less common than in other languages or other varieties of English, such as Indian English.

1 ▪ Using similes

As in the preceding example, a **simile** explicitly compares two unlike subjects using *like, as, as if,* or *as though.* Describing an early morning walk on an ocean beach, essayist David Black tells how "the waves, as they slid up the sand, foamed and hissed like butter sizzling in a frying pan" (waves

= sizzling butter). Along the way, he fills his pockets with water-polished rocks "shaped as perfectly as eggs" (rocks = eggs) and pauses to watch seagulls that "stood in crowds, each gazing over the heads of the others, like guests at a chic party on the lookout for celebrities" (gulls = guests). Here similes describe concrete subjects by adding details of sound, shape, texture, appearance, and action. But they may also describe less tangible subjects, as in this description of how Pueblo people speak:

> The structure of Pueblo expression resembles something like a spider's web—with many little threads radiating from a center, crisscrossing each other. As with the web, the structure will emerge as it is made and you must simply listen and trust, as the Pueblo people do, that meaning will be made.
>
> (Leslie Marmon Silko, "Language and Literature from a Pueblo Indian Perspective," in Leslie A. Fiedler and Houston A. Baker, Jr., eds., *English Literature: Opening Up the Canon*)

[Comparing the structure of Pueblo speech (tenor) to a spider web (vehicle) dramatizes the organization of the language but also suggests something of its delicacy and sensitivity.]

2 ▪ Using metaphor

A **metaphor** compares implicitly: not *X is like Y,* but *X is Y.* Tenor and vehicle are fused; one becomes the other.

> Superstition seems to run, a submerged river of crude religion, below the surface of human consciousness.
>
> (Robertson Davies, "A Few Kind Words for Superstition," *Newsweek*)

[*Superstition* (tenor) becomes *a submerged river* (vehicle) and acquires the river's traits: depth, darkness, cold, and power.]

> The bristlecone pine of American Indians, Hopis live where almost nothing else will, thriving long in adverse conditions: poor soil, drought, temperature extremes, high winds. Those give life to the bristlecone and the Hopi.
>
> (William Least Heat-Moon, *Blue Highways*, 1982)

[The *Hopis* (tenor), described as *bristlecone pine* (vehicle), acquire the bristlecone's traits of hardiness, longevity, and the ability to thrive in adverse conditions.]

HOW TO . . . Create Similes and Metaphors

If you're unsure how to create a metaphor or simile, use the following figurative language formula. Try several alternatives until you find one that is accurate, original, and appropriate. Then, as you write and revise, omit the formula and work the figure of speech into your sentences.

(continued)

If (*my subject*) were (*choose from one of the following categories*),

it would/would not be (*make up a term to complete the formula*).

a movement	a road	a piece of furniture
a place	a shape	an article of clothing
a toy	a sound	a means of
a person	a work of art	transportation
a smell	a beverage	an animal
a color	a building	the weather
an object	a musical	vegetation
a food	instrument	music

If *skydiving* were a *movement*, it would be a *dandelion seed drifting in the wind*.

When the parachute opened above me, I lost my prejump jitters, relaxed, and felt how graceful I was, floating as gently as a dandelion seed drifting in the wind. [a simile]

(Nancy Lee, student)

If *grammar* were *a musical instrument*, it would be *a piano played by ear*.

Grammar is a piano I play by ear, since I seem to have been out of school the year the rules were mentioned. All I know about grammar is its infinite power. [a metaphor]

(Joan Didion, "Why I Write," *New York Times Book Review*)

26d Avoid clichés and mixed metaphors

1 ■ Avoiding clichés

26.3
Clichés to
avoid:
Web link

Clichés are overused, worn-out figures of speech or other expressions that have lost their power to communicate. How many of these clichés do you recognize?

avoid it like	the ladder	since the dawn
the plague	of success	of time
beat around	the last straw	stop and smell
the bush	light as a feather	the roses
blind as a bat	off the beaten path	water over the dam
the bottom line	on the brink	without a shadow
crystal clear	playing with fire	of a doubt
fresh as a daisy	sadder but wiser	white as a ghost

If you write a catchy metaphor or simile that you've heard others use, chances are it is already a cliché. Create your own fresh, original figurative language. The figurative language formula in the "How to Create Similes and Metaphors" box (p. 179–180) will help.

2 ▪ Avoiding mixed metaphors

A **mixed metaphor** brings together two or more comparisons that don't make sense and is often unintentionally humorous. To write effective metaphors and similes, make a single figurative comparison.

26.4
Editing
clichés and
mixed
metaphors:
Exercises

The Abbey Road album ~~was the springboard that~~ reignited the Beatles' musical career.

[According to the original, the album is compared to a springboard and, through the verb *reignited,* to something that could start a fire. But a springboard cannot start a fire. The revision omits the illogical metaphor.]

27 Choosing Appropriate Words

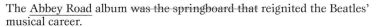

27a Choose words that fit the occasion

Choose an informal or a formal vocabulary appropriate for your subject and the occasion. An **informal vocabulary** will make your writing personal and give it a conversational style. A **formal vocabulary** will convey a serious and more objective attitude. Once you decide what vocabulary is appropriate, use these lists to guide your writing and editing:

	FEATURES OF INFORMAL VOCABULARIES	FEATURES OF FORMAL VOCABULARIES
CONTRACTIONS	*can't, shouldn't, won't,* etc.	None
SLANG AND REGIONAL EXPRESSIONS	*broke, strapped, dirt poor, beat my brains, brainy,* etc.	No slang; *poor, destitute, concentrate, study, intelligent,* etc.
FREQUENT USAGES	*I, we, us,* and *you*—to express writer's closeness to the reader	Emphasis on the subject matter rather than author
FAMILIAR WORDS	In conversation: *poor, smart, my place, my house, think,* etc.	In writing: *impoverished, intelligent, residence, speculate,* etc.
CONNOTATIVE MEANING	Obvious: *fake, phony, bright,* etc.	Subtle: *artificial, clever,* etc.

1 ■ Choosing words in academic and professional writing

Generally use a formal vocabulary for informative or persuasive writing about serious subjects. You shouldn't sound stuffy or use words you're uncomfortable with, but choose words that convey the importance of the occasion. Refer to yourself as *I* if you are involved with your subject, but focus on your subject rather than yourself. Avoid using "you" unless you mean to address readers directly. Avoid slang and most contractions. Use an informal vocabulary for personal narratives, nonserious informative writing, and humorous writing.

2 ■ Maintaining consistent formality

Maintain a consistent attitude toward your subject and a consistent relationship with readers. As you edit, look for shifts from one vocabulary to another. Because you talk more than you write, take special care in serious writing to look for shifts from formal to informal words.

Contemporary religious philosophers have ~~come down hard on~~ *severely criticized*

American society as selfish and materialistic.

[*Come down hard on* is slang. Its conversational tone makes this expression inappropriate for academic writing on serious subjects.]

~~Right now, though,~~ compressed natural gas has several ~~bugs~~ in its *Currently, however,* *problems*

storage that prevent its wide use as an alternative to gasoline.

[*Right now, though,* is too conversational and imprecise for serious academic writing. *Bugs* is slang and a cliché, inappropriate in objective writing.]

27b In most academic and public writing, avoid slang, regionalisms, and nonstandard words

1 ■ Avoiding slang

Slang is the informal vocabulary of a group or subculture. It is colorful, rapidly changing, strong in feeling, and often not understood by outsiders. Consider the slang popular among young Americans during the last fifty years; note how dated some words sound: *cool, hot, downer* (to describe bad news), *dank, schwag, geek, groovy, gizmo, heavy* (meaning "serious"), *later* (for "goodbye"), *out of sight, razzle-dazzle, I read you.*

Some slang becomes widely accepted and proves so durable that it becomes part of the language: *movie, muckraker, handout.* More often slang is incomprehensible to outsiders, has a life of only a few months or years, and is more often spoken than written. For these reasons it is appropriate only for informal writing to readers you know well.

27.1
Some basics about diction: Web link

2 ▪ Avoiding regionalisms

Regionalisms are words and expressions used by speakers from a specific geographic region. For example, in the south-central Midwest *considerable* means a large amount. In the upper Midwest *eat razor soup* means to make a wisecrack. In the eastern United States, cottage cheese is frequently called *smearcase.* In some parts of Texas, *borrego* (borrowed from Spanish, "a young lamb") refers to sheep and to fleecy-looking clouds. Like slang, regional expressions are often colorful and strong in feeling. But because their use is restricted, they may be misunderstood, and you should avoid them in serious writing for diverse audiences.

3 ▪ Avoiding nonstandard words

WRITING IN THE USA Dialect and Nonstandard Words

Nonstandard words and usages such as *nowheres, done told, theirselves,* and *don't never* occasionally appear in spoken English dialects. Each dialect has its own grammar and vocabulary, and both are considered correct for speakers of that dialect. However, these nonstandard words and constructions are inappropriate for academic writing and for most other public writing in English. (See Chapter 29. See also 13c–e, 17g, and 18e.)

27c Use jargon and neologisms only with specialized audiences

Jargon is the technical language of a profession, craft, trade, or activity. Computer operators, for example, use acronyms such as *VGA;* metaphors such as *motherboard* and *cookie;* words derived from people's names, such as *baud;* compounds such as *online* and *login;* shortened words such as *e-mail, blog,* and *modem;* and old words with new meaning, such as *server.*

A **neologism** is a newly invented word. Many neologisms begin their lives as jargon, slang, or media expressions: *vaporware, cyberspace, CAT scan, morphing, disco.* Many neologisms, such as *radar* and *scuba,* prove useful and eventually become part of standard English; the rest disappear.

Jargon and neologisms enable members of special-interest groups to communicate with one another clearly, economically, and efficiently. They cause problems, however, when addressed to outsiders. Therefore, follow these guidelines.

1 ▪ Writing for a nontechnical audience

When writing for a nontechnical audience, avoid jargon and neologisms. Choose accurate, widely understood words. If only jargon will say what you mean, provide definitions.

The design of the university's new Web site requires ~~applets~~ *programs* that ~~enable~~ *transform* ~~the morphing of~~ images as users navigate the site.

2 ■ Academic writing

In academic writing for readers who understand your subject, choose words appropriate to the field or discipline. Demonstrate your knowledge of technical language, but avoid using technical words merely to impress. If in doubt about the proper vocabulary, check with your instructor.

3 ■ Technical writing

In technical writing for knowledgeable readers—for example, in on-the-job memos and e-mail or reports—a technical vocabulary is appropriate. But carefully consider your audience's knowledge. (See also Chapter 62.)

🌐 WRITING IN THE USA Jargon

The term *jargon* is sometimes used broadly to refer to difficult words used primarily to impress readers. These words are not usually appropriate in American academic writing, although sometimes specialized vocabulary is necessary.

27d Avoid pretentious words, doublespeak, and most euphemisms

1 ■ Avoiding pretentious words

Pretentious writing aims to impress more than communicate. Most readers are annoyed by it. Therefore, avoid the following kinds of words:

■ Unfamiliar "big" words, often with Latin roots

Some ~~educators in the~~ *teachers* humanities have been ~~dilatory in their cognizance~~ *slow to recognize how* ~~of the pedagogical ramifications of~~ new instructional technologies *can improve their teaching*.

■ Flowery words

The warm sunrise promised ~~Rising into azure heavens flecked with billowy clouds, the warm sun~~ ~~foretold a wondrous autumnal~~ *a fine autumn* day.

2 ▪ Avoiding doublespeak

Doublespeak, a term invented by George Orwell in his novel *1984,* refers to deliberately misleading words and expressions that aim to create a favorable impression opposite that of the truth. It is an essential feature of political propaganda, but you can find it wherever writers disguise the truth: in advertisements; in government, military, and business writing; even, occasionally, in academic writing. Some examples of doublespeak:

downsizing = layoffs	revenue enhancements = tax increases
terminated = fired	sanitize = censor
final solution = kill	substandard housing = slum
preowned = used	fees for product testing = bribe

Remember Abraham Lincoln's axiom that you can't fool all the people all the time. Avoid misleading language.

3 ▪ Avoiding euphemisms

Like doublespeak, euphemisms hide the truth. But a **euphemism,** from Greek words meaning "good speech," is a pleasant-sounding word or expression that aims to soften a topic that some readers may consider distasteful, ugly, or difficult to speak of. Euphemisms usually appear in discussions of emotionally charged subjects such as death (*to pass away, expire*), bodily functions (*go to the bathroom*), and sex (*make love, sleep together, adult entertainment*). Unless your audience will be offended or hurt by direct language, avoid euphemisms. They will make you seem prudish or mealy mouthed.

27e Avoid biased and offensive language

Ethical writing recognizes the dignity and individuality of all people, regardless of background, race, gender, or physical capacities. Choose words that respect the equality of men and women, nationalities, and regional and ethnic groups.

1 ▪ Avoiding sexist and racist words

Sexist words describe men or women, but more often women, in demeaning, often physical terms (*chick, stud, bitch*) or deny men and women equal status (*gals, the girls in the office, woman doctor*). **Racist words** and **ethnic slurs** belittle or abuse members of races, nationalities, or ethnic groups. Every group has the right to decide what it wants to be called. Some Americans, for example, refer to themselves as *African American,* others as *persons of color,* and still others as *Black;* most reject *Negro* or *colored.* Fairness obliges you to adopt the words each group uses to describe itself.

27.2
Using
unbiased
language:
Web link

2 ▪ Avoiding stereotypes

Stereotypes are occupational titles, generic terms, or common expressions that exclude women or men, refer to a person's gender where it is irrelevant, deny equality, or describe restrictively. Omit biased language or replace stereotypes with nonrestrictive substitutes.

STEREOTYPE	ACCEPTABLE SUBSTITUTE
businessman	businessperson, executive
chairman	chair, head, moderator, chairperson
congressman	representative, legislator
fireman	firefighter
foreman	supervisor
handicapped	physically disabled
landlord/landlady	owner, manager
mailman	letter carrier, postal worker
mankind	humankind
policeman	police officer
salesman	salesclerk, salesperson
steward/stewardess	flight attendant
workman	worker

🌐 WRITING IN THE USA Special Problems with Biased Language

▪ Writers may unintentionally stereotype audiences. As you write, keep in mind the differences in your readers' genders and background.

Employees are invited to bring their ~~wives~~ *spouse or friend* to the company picnic.

[Not all employees may be men; not all may be married. The revision recognizes the diversity of the audience.]

▪ The use of *he, him,* and *his* to refer collectively to men and women may seem to exclude women. Instead, use both masculine and feminine pronouns or, when possible, change the sentence from singular to plural. (See also 15d.)

Each candidate must write an essay explaining ~~his~~ *his or her* qualifications for admission.

When a ~~teenager~~ *teenagers* first receives ~~his~~ *their* driver's license, ~~he wants~~ *they want* to drive everywhere.

EXERCISE 27.1 Editing for Words Appropriate to Academic and Public Writing

Edit the following sentences to make them appropriate for academic and public writing. Eliminate slang, regionalisms, and nonstandard words. See the answers in the appendix.

27.3
Choosing
appropriate
words:
Exercises

1. The years following the stock market crash of 1929 were tough for most all Americans.

2. Isn't it funny how slick politicians say they're all in favor of changing the way elections get paid for—until they get elected.

3. My low aptitude test scores almost messed up my chances for getting into college. I did get accepted at two state schools, though.

4. The writer Oscar Ramírez goes deep into the way in which American culture sort of blends with immigrant cultures and ends up different somehow.

5. President Nixon really messed things up for himself and a bunch of his friends when he put tape recorders in his office at the White House.

28 Editing Wordiness

HOW TO . . . Edit Wordiness

28.1
Eliminating
wordiness:
Web link

1. Don't be concerned about wordiness as you plan and write a first draft. But if you're having trouble saying what you mean, look for words that get in the way of your message. Cutting extra words often clarifies meaning.

2. As you edit, cut:

   - Needless repetitions (*the reason why is because*)

   - Empty sentence openers (*In my opinion . . .*), needless intensifiers (*really, very*) or qualifiers (*somewhat, seems*), and unnecessary impersonal constructions (*there is, there are, it is*).

   - Padded transitions that link sentences or sentence parts (*because of the fact that*), unnecessary clause openers (*which is/are, who is/are*), and nouns ending in *-ence, -ance, -ment,* and *-tion* that could be transformed into the main verb of the sentence.

(continued)

3. Bracket words that may be unnecessary. Read the sentence without the bracketed words. If you don't lose any meaning, cut.

Each of these quilts is ⌊truly⌋ unique; no pattern has been duplicated ⌊twice.⌋

28a Eliminate redundancy

Redundancy is unnecessary repetition, as in *first and foremost* or *crisis situation*. One word in each of these examples implies the meaning of the other. Eliminate redundancy from your writing, but remember that sometimes you need to repeat for emphasis or clarity. (See 20d and 22d.) Here are some repetitions to avoid.

1 ▪ Needlessly repeated words

what most impressed

As I watched her skate, ~~the impression that was most impressed on~~ me was her athletic grace.

The man turned the pages of the magazine for a moment or two, then

it

laid ~~the magazine~~ on the end table.

[Use pronouns to avoid unnecessary repetition of nouns and to create variety.]

2 ▪ Needlessly repeated ideas

Cut unemphatic words that merely repeat the meaning implied by other, more important words.

Future

~~The reason why future~~ airline hijackings are unlikely in the United States

~~is~~ because the federal government has greatly improved passenger

screening ~~procedures.~~

[*Reason, why,* and *because* mean the same thing in this sentence; two of the three words can be cut. *Passenger screening* implies *procedures;* this word can be omitted.]

3 ▪ Redundant pairs

Writers sometimes pair words with the same meaning: *first and foremost, hopes and aspirations, hopes and desires, goals and objectives, honest and true,* and so forth. If you pair redundant words, cut one.

The ~~basic and~~ fundamental right to free speech is guaranteed by the US Constitution.

4 ▪ Redundant modifiers

Some modifiers are unnecessary because their meaning is contained in the words they modify: *basic fundamentals, the color blue, crisis situation, end result, past memories, period of time, personal opinion, shiny appearance, square in shape, true facts,* and so forth.

If the supplier expedites our order ~~as quickly as possible~~, we will ~~completely~~ finish the project before the deadline.

[*To expedite* means "to speed a process," and to finish something is to complete it; *as quickly as possible* and *completely* are redundant.]

28b Cut empty words and phrases

1 ▪ Cutting empty sentence openers

The meaning of an opening phrase may be implied by the rest of the sentence. Generally cut openers such as *I think that, in some ways, needless to say, in some respects, for the most part, as everyone knows, the fact is, obviously,* and *as we see.*

~~The purpose of the meeting is to~~ inform employees about changes in their benefits. *[The meeting will]*

[Information about the subject of the meeting identifies its purpose.]

2 ▪ Cutting empty qualifiers and intensifiers

Intensifiers and **qualifiers** are modifiers that express degree: *very, definitely, really, truly, uniquely, wonderfully, apparently, may, seems, perhaps, probably, somewhat, quite,* and so forth. You may need them to indicate the strength of a statement or shade your meaning. More often, they suggest that writers doubt the force of their ideas. Prefer the plain truth.

After two semesters, ~~it seems~~ I ~~really~~ am a veteran college student.

3 ▪ Cutting unnecessary impersonal constructions

Impersonal constructions begin with *there is/are* or *it is.* They enable writers to move ideas to the end of a sentence or to emphasize actions that lack actors: *There are four reasons that General Lee lost the Battle of Gettysburg,* or *It is raining.* But when impersonal constructions are unnecessary, cut them and rewrite.

~~There is some~~ urban land ~~that~~ is set aside each year for new parks but not enough to equal the acres buried under new subdivisions and shopping centers. *[Some]*

Businesses

~~It is clear that businesses~~ have a social obligation to support nonprofit
∧
organizations in their communities.

28c Compress padded writing

Wordiness sometimes results not only from extra words but also
from **padding,** the use of inflated or indirect expressions. Look for and
eliminate the following wordy expressions in your writing.

1 ▪ Cutting padded phrases

Compress inflated phrases to one or two words.

INFLATED	CONCISE	INFLATED	CONCISE
as a matter of fact	in fact	for the reason that	because
at the present time	now, currently	in order to	to
because of the fact that	because	in spite of the fact that	although, even though
by means of	by	in the event that	if
due to the fact that	because	in the neighborhood	approximately, about
for the purpose of	for, to	in today's world	now, today
		prior to	before
		with regard to	about

We were impressed ~~by the fact~~ that the courthouse had been renovated
so quickly.

2 ▪ Cutting padded clauses

Compress padded dependent clauses to a phrase or word. (To learn
to recognize clauses, see 10b.)

In front of the troops stood their duffle bags, ~~which had been~~ packed
with all their gear for the next twelve months.

Unable

~~Because they don't know how~~ to handle their new freedom, some recent
∧
high school graduates have difficulty adjusting to college life.

3 ▪ Cutting padded sentences

Combine two padded sentences. (For sentence-combining strategies,
see 21b.)

The most scenic tour of Mammoth Cave is a four-mile , four-hour walk that ~~lasts~~
~~about four hours. This tour~~ includes lunch in the Snowball Room and
ends at Frozen Niagara.

4 ■ Avoiding indirect use of the passive voice verb form

As a grammatical term, *voice* refers to the relation between a subject
and verb. The passive voice often requires more words than the active.
Use the active voice to make your writing concise and direct. (To learn
when the passive voice is appropriate, see 20a2.)

The judges   *first prize*
~~First prize was~~ awarded ~~by the judges~~ to a poem, "Violet Voices."

5 ■ Avoiding indirect use of nominals

A **nominal** is a noun derived from a verb, often ending *-ence, -ance,
-ment, -tion: dependence/depend, guidance/guide, argument/argue, adapta-
tion/adapt.* Nominals often appear in wordy, indirect writing. When you
can do so, transform a nominal into its verb form, eliminate empty
words, and rewrite.

The   can be repaired only after it is removed
~~Repairs to the~~ compressor ~~are possible only after its removal~~ from the
refrigerator.

[Turning two nominals, *repairs* and *removal,* into verbs eliminates the empty verb
are, and the sentence becomes direct and emphatic.]

EXERCISE 28.1 Editing for Wordiness

*Edit the following sentences for wordiness. More than one effective revision
is possible. See the answers in the appendix.*

28.2
Editing
wordiness:
Exercises

1. Some elderly people have a resistance to seeing themselves as old.

2. When the Christmas holidays come, I purchase all of my gift items
   from catalogs.

3. Bide-a-Wee Resort has a wide variety of campsites. There are pull-
   through sites with electricity and water, electricity-only sites, and
   primitive sites carved into bluffs.

4. Many different kinds of waste toxins can linger around in landfills,
   polluting the soil and ground water for dozens, even hundreds of
   years on end.

5. The position of an executive secretary falls more in the category of
   administrative assistant than mere clerk or typist.

A Guide to Usage

29 Troublesome Words and Phrases

29.1
Usage list:
Web link

This glossary contains commonly confused words (such as *less* and *fewer*); words frequently misused (such as *aggravate*); nonstandard words (such as *hisself*); pretentious or needlessly technical words, often referred to as jargon (such as *finalize*); wordy phrases (such as *reason why*); and colloquialisms inappropriate for formal writing (such as *okay*).

a, an. Use *a* before words beginning with a consonant sound or an *h* that is pronounced: *a student, a sparrow, a happy man, a hospital.* Use *an* before words beginning with a vowel sound (*a, e, i, o, u*) or silent *h*: *an apple, an investment, an honor, an honorable person.*

a lot (*not* **alot**). *A lot* is two words, not one. *We have had a lot of rain this spring.*

a while, awhile. *A while* is an article and a noun that mean "a period of time": *Stay with us for a while.* *Awhile* is an adverb and means "a short time": *He visited awhile and then left.* *Awhile* is never preceded by a preposition such as *after, for, in.*

accept, except. *Accept,* a verb, means "to receive, agree, or believe": *The singer accepted the bouquet from an admirer.* As a preposition, *except* means "but" or "other than": *Everyone is here except James.* As a verb, *except* means "to leave out, exclude": *The last three names were excepted from the list.*

adapt, adopt. *Adapt,* a verb, means "to adjust or to become accustomed": *Some wild animals have adapted to urban environments.* *Adopt,* also a verb, means "to take up and make one's own": *Many childless parents wish to adopt children.*

advice, advise. *Advice* is a noun, *advise,* a verb: *The lawyer advised her client to accept her advice.*

affect, effect. *Affect* is usually a verb meaning "to influence or act on." *Effect* is usually a noun meaning "a result"; occasionally it is a verb meaning "to bring about." *Smoking affects the body in many ways. Smoking has many harmful effects. Negative advertising may effect a decrease in tobacco use.*

aggravate. *Aggravate* means "to make worse or more troublesome": *High-sugar diets often aggravate childhood misbehavior.* In formal writing, avoid the colloquial use of *aggravate,* "to annoy or irritate." *The traffic was irritating* [not *aggravating*].

agree to, agree with. *Agree to* means "to consent": *The lawyers agreed to the proposed settlement. Agree with* means "to be in accord or to match": *She didn't agree with him about the causes of the problem.*

ain't. *Ain't* is nonstandard. Use *am not, is not, has not, have not,* and so forth: *They have not* [not *ain't*] *repaired the motor yet.*

all ready, already. *All ready* means "fully prepared." *Already* means "before" or "by this time." *By the time everyone was all ready to leave, it was already too late.*

all right (*not* **alright**). *All right* is two words; *alright* is nonstandard.

all together, altogether. *All together* means "in a group": *They stood all together near the doorway. Altogether* means "entirely, completely, totally": *They were altogether drenched by the sudden rain.*

allusion, illusion. An *allusion* is an indirect reference: *Writers and speakers make frequent allusions to Shakespeare.* An *illusion* is a false perception of reality: *A mirage is an optical illusion created by alternate layers of hot and cool air.*

among, between. Use *among* to refer to three or more things, *between* to refer to two: *There was little agreement among the members of the jury. It is so difficult to choose between strawberry and butter pecan ice cream.*

amount, number. Use *amount* with things that cannot be counted; use *number* with things that can: *The amount of happiness people enjoy is often related to the number of their friends.*

and etc. *Et cetera* (*etc.*) means "and so forth"; *and etc.* is wordy. (See also *etc.*)

and/or. Avoid *and/or* except in technical writing, where it may be necessary for precision.

angry at, angry with. *Angry at* is nonstandard; use *angry with: I was angry with* [not *at*] *him because he had cheated.*

anxious, eager. *Anxious* means "uneasy or worried." In formal writing, avoid using *anxious* to mean "eager." *We are eager* [not *anxious*] *to meet our new president.*

any one, anybody, anyone. *Any one* refers to a specific person or thing in a group: *Any one of our staff will help you. Anybody* and *anyone* mean "any person at all": *I have not found anyone who knows the answer. Anybody* and *anyone* are singular.

anyplace. *Anyplace* is appropriate for informal writing. For formal writing, use *anywhere.*

any way, anyway. *Any way* means "by whatever means or manner." *Any way you choose to travel will bring you unimagined adventures. Anyway* means "nevertheless, at least": *We asked them not to bother us, but they did anyway.*

anyways, anywheres. *Anyways* and *anywheres* are nonstandard forms of *anyway* and *anywhere.*

as, as if, like. *As if* is a subordinating conjunction that joins a subordinate clause to a main clause: *The last runners to finish looked as if* *they were in a trance. Like* is a preposition that should be followed only by a noun or noun phrase: *The last runner looked like a zombie.* In informal speech, *like* is often substituted for *as* or *as if,* but in formal writing, use *as: As* [not *like*] *the Bible says, it is easier for a camel to pass through a needle's eye than for a rich man to enter heaven.*

awful, awfully. The precise meaning of the adjective *awful* is "inspiring awe," but it also has the colloquial meaning of "extremely bad or terrible": *Modern technology has increased the awful power of military weapons. Julia was involved in an awful accident.* As an adverb, *awfully* has the colloquial meaning of "very"; avoid this sense of the word in formal writing: *Most unwed teenage mothers are very* [not *awfully*] *poor.*

awhile, a while. See *a while.*

bad, badly. *Bad* is an adjective that often follows linking verbs: *A bad storm is approaching. I feel bad today. Badly* is an adverb that modifies verbs, adjectives, and other adverbs: *He played badly.* (See 18c.)

basis, bases. *Basis* is singular, *bases,* plural.

being as, being that. *Being as* and *being that* are nonstandard; use *because* or *since: Because* [not *being that*] *I work overtime every day, I have almost no social life.*

beside, besides. *Beside* is a preposition meaning "at the side of or next to": *They walked beside the river. Besides* is a preposition meaning "in addition to" or "except for": *Besides jazz, I also enjoy bluegrass and gospel music. Besides* is also an adverb meaning "also" or "furthermore": *My pen has run out of ink; besides, my mind has run out of ideas.*

between, among. See *among.*

breath, breathe. *Breath* is a noun, *breathe* a verb: *Relax; take a breath; now breathe again.*

bring, take. Use *bring* when the action is toward the speaker: *Please bring me a cup of coffee.* Use *take* when the action moves away from the speaker: *Be sure to take traveler's checks on your vacation.*

but what, but that. *But what* and *but that* are colloquial phrases following expressions of doubt; use *that* instead: *I do not doubt that* [not *but what*] *they intend to do the right thing.*

can, may. *Can* expresses ability, knowledge, or capacity: *I can speak. May* expresses possibility or permission: *It may snow tomorrow. You may borrow my calculator.* In formal writing, avoid using *can* to mean permission: *May* [not *can*] *we send you a brochure?*

capital, capitol. *Capital* refers to a city, *capitol* to a building.

cite, site. The verb *cite* means "to mention as proof or to quote as an authority": *If you wish to be believed, cite your sources.* As a noun, *site* means "a place or setting for something": *They visited famous battlefield sites.*

cloth, clothe. *Cloth* is a noun, *clothe,* a verb: *The best cloth for sportswear pulls perspiration away from the skin. A compassionate government will feed, clothe, and house citizens who cannot care for themselves.*

coarse, course. *Coarse* means "rough in texture or unrefined": *The coarse fabric of his jacket scratched his skin. Course* usually refers to a unit of study, a direction of movement, a playing field, or part of a meal. *Of course* means "naturally" or "certainly." *Next semester I plan to take a course in Asian art. Of course, we are coming to the party.*

compare to, compare with. Use *compare to* when showing that two things are similar or belong in the same category: *In height, the Alps compare to the Rocky Mountains.* Use *compare with* when you intend to examine things side by side to discover similarities and differences: *Compared with the defense budget, the United States foreign aid budget is quite small.*

complement, compliment, complementary, complimentary. *Complement* means "to go with" or "complete" or "something that makes up a whole": *His artistic skill complements his creativity. A complement of marines led the attack. Compliment* means "to praise or flatter": *She complimented him for his tact. Complementary* means "completing" or "offsetting": *She chose complementary colors for the design. Complimentary* means "expressing a compliment" or "given freely, as an act of courtesy": *He received complimentary software with his new computer.*

conscience, conscious. *Conscience* refers to "moral awareness or the source of moral judgment": *Lying gave him a guilty conscience. Conscious* means "mentally aware or alert": *Before my morning coffee, I am barely conscious.*

continual, continuous. *Continual* means "recurring regularly or frequently": *The dog's continual barking kept him awake. Continuous* means "uninterrupted in time or sequence": *The siren rose and fell in a continuous wail.*

could care less. People generally use *could care less* when they really mean *couldn't care less.* The latter expression is logical and correct: *She couldn't care less* [not *could care less*] *about the lives and loves of Hollywood celebrities.*

could of. Nonstandard for *could have* or *could've*: *With his talent, John could have* [not *could of*] *been very successful.*

criteria. *Criteria* is the plural of *criterion,* which refers to a standard or rule for a decision or judgment. *One criterion for success is hard work. Two other important criteria are preparation and imagination.*

data. *Data* is the plural of *datum,* meaning "a fact or piece of information used to make a decision." Some readers object when *data* is used with singular verbs and modifiers; use plural verbs and modifiers instead: *These* [not *this*] *data show* [not *shows*] *that soil erosion is increasing.*

different from, different than. *Different from* is always correct: *Is a man's thinking process different from a woman's?* You may use *different than* when it is followed by a clause: *Television has made our thinking process different than it was fifty years ago.*

differ with, differ from. To *differ with* is to disagree with someone: *The student differed with her professor about the meaning of the poem.* To *differ from* is to contrast or be unlike: *The student's interpretation differed from her professor's.*

disinterested, uninterested. *Disinterested* means "unbiased, impartial, objective": *An umpire is supposed to be a disinterested observer.* *Uninterested* means "without interest": *He was uninterested in their opinion.*

done. In formal writing, avoid the imprecise use of *done* to mean "finished or complete": *By 1914, work on the Panama Canal was nearly complete* [not *done*].

don't. *Don't* is the contraction for *do not.* Avoid using *don't* as a contraction for *does not,* which is *doesn't*: *She doesn't* [not *don't*] *waste any time.*

due to. *Due to* means "because of." It is correct when used to introduce a subject complement following a linking verb: *The airplane's crash was due to icy weather.* Some readers object to the use of *due to* as a preposition: *The airplane crashed because of* [not *due to*] *icy weather.*

each. *Each* is singular. (See 14f and 15d.)

easy, easily. *Easy* is an adjective: *She makes a mile run look easy.* Do not use *easy* as an adverb modifying a verb; use *easily*: *She won the race easily* [not *easy*].

effect, affect. See *affect.*

elicit, illicit. *Elicit* means "to draw out or bring out": *With a little coaxing, she was able to elicit the right answer.* *Illicit* means "unlawful": *He was convicted of the illicit use of drugs.*

emigrate from, immigrate to. To *emigrate from* means "to leave one country or area for another": *During the 1840s many people emigrated from Ireland because of famine.* To *immigrate to* means "to enter and settle in another country or region": *During the 1840s many Irish immigrated to the United States.*

enthused, enthusiastic. Some readers object to the use of the informal *enthused* as an adjective. In formal writing, use *enthusiastic*: *I am an enthusiastic* [not *enthused*] *collector of 1950s movie posters.*

etc. Avoid *etc.* (*et cetera*, "and so forth") in formal writing; end a list with a specific example or *and so forth.* (Also see *and etc.*)

every body, everybody. See *every one.*

every day, everyday. *Every day* is the noun *day* preceded by the adjective *every*: *I try to exercise every day.* *Everyday* is an adjective meaning "appropriate for ordinary days or routine occasions": *Wear your everyday clothes to the party.*

every one, everyone. *Every one* is the pronoun *one* preceded by the adjective *every*, meaning "each individual or thing in a particular group": *Every one of the students was prepared for the exam. Everyone* is an indefinite pronoun meaning "every person": *Everyone was prepared for the exam.* Both are singular. (See 14f and 15d.)

except, accept. See *accept*.

explicit, implicit. *Explicit* means "fully and clearly expressed, with nothing implied": *I was given explicit instructions. Implicit* means "not directly expressed but understood": *We made an implicit agreement to avoid the issue.*

farther, further. *Farther* refers to physical distance: *I can run farther now than I could six weeks ago. Further* refers to quantities or degree and means "more or to a greater extent": *When we inquired further, we found he had changed jobs twice within a year.*

fewer, less. Disregard the supermarket signs that say "Ten items or less." Use *fewer* with items that can be counted, *less* with things that are not counted: *Fewer* [not *less*] *students now major in business. We had less snow this winter than last.*

finalize. Many readers object to *finalize*, meaning "to put into final form, complete or conclude," as jargon. Find more precise alternatives: *The baseball players' union completed* [not *finalized*] *negotiations for a new contract.*

firstly. *Firstly* sounds pretentious, as do *secondly, thirdly,* and so forth; use *first, second, third.*

further, farther. See *farther*.

goes. *Goes* is nonstandard for *says*: *When he says* [not *goes*], *"Folks, I'm not making this up," I know that he is making it up.*

good, well. *Good* is an adjective: *This salsa tastes good. Well* is an adverb: *This old watch still runs well.* Use *well* to refer to someone's health: *After a long rest, he is well again.* (See 18c.)

got, have. *Got* is the past tense of *get*. Do not use the colloquial *got* in place of *have*: *They have* [not *got*] *the best reputation for reliability.* Do not use *got, got to, has got to,* or *have got to* in place of *must*: *They must* [not *have got to*] *change their priorities.*

hardly, scarcely. Avoid the colloquial double negatives *can't hardly, not hardly, can't scarcely, not scarcely*: *I can hardly* [not *can't hardly*] *explain what it felt like.* (See 18e.)

have, got. See *got*.

have, of. Use *have* following the modal verbs *could, should, may, might, must,* and *would*: *They should have* [not *of*] *received an invitation.* (See 13e3.)

he/she, his/her. Many readers object to the awkward expressions *he/she, his/her*; use *he or she* or one of the alternatives in 15d.

hisself. *Hisself* is nonstandard; use *himself*.

hopefully. *Hopefully* means "in a hopeful manner": *He looked hopefully toward the clock.* Many readers object to its use, especially at the beginning of a sentence, to mean "it is to be hoped": *Hopefully, job opportunities for graduates will soon improve.* Indicate instead who is doing the hoping: *We hope job opportunities for graduates will soon improve.*

if, whether. Use *if* to introduce statements of condition and *whether* to introduce alternatives: *If we have enough volunteers, we can finish; it makes no difference whether they are young or old.*

impact. Many readers object to the use of *impact* as a verb: *The recent election will have an impact on* [not *will impact*] *proposed antipollution laws.*

implicit, explicit. See *explicit.*

imply, infer. *Imply* means "to express indirectly": *She glanced at her watch to imply that it was time to leave. Infer* means "to draw a conclusion": *After studying the evidence, we inferred that the fire was caused by lightning.*

infer, imply. See *imply.*

irregardless. Nonstandard for *regardless.*

is when, is where, is why, is because. Avoid these imprecise and illogical expressions in writing definitions and explanations: *A paceline is a line of cyclists tightly grouped* [not *A paceline is when cyclists group together tightly*] *to reduce wind resistance.*

its, it's. *Its* is a possessive pronoun: *The dog twitched its tail. It's* is the contraction of *it is*: *It's good to hear that they arrived safely.*

kind(s), sort(s), type(s). *Kind, sort,* and *type* are singular: *This kind of words is* [not *these kind of words are*] *known as "fighting words." Kinds, sorts,* and *types* are plural, referring to more than one kind or sort: *These kinds of flowers grow well in the shade.*

kind of, sort of. Avoid using *kind of* and *sort of* to mean "somewhat": *I was somewhat* [not *kind of*] *disappointed by the novel's conclusion.* Do not use *a* following either phrase: *It was the same sort of* [not *sort of a*] *speech politicians always make.*

lay, lie. *Lay,* a transitive verb meaning "to put or set down," always takes a direct object: *Lay the pencil on the table.* Its other forms are *laying, laid, laid. Lie,* an intransitive verb meaning "to rest on a surface or occupy a position," does not take a direct object: *The pencil lies on the table.* Its other forms are *lying, lay, lain.* (See 13a5.)

lead, led. *Lead* (the metal) sounds like *led* (the past tense of the verb *to lead*); do not confuse them: *The officer led* [not *lead*] *his men into battle.*

leave, let. *Leave* means "to go away"; *let* means "to give permission or allow." Do not use *leave* when you mean *let*: *Let* [not *leave*] *him clean up the mess he has made.*

less, fewer. See *fewer.*

like, as. See *as.*

loose, lose, losing. *Loose* is an adjective meaning "not fastened or contained"; *lose* is a verb meaning "to misplace." Do not use one word when you mean the other, and do not write "loosing" when you mean *losing.* (See 13a6.)

lots, lots of. In formal writing, avoid the colloquial expressions *lots* and *lots of,* meaning "many, much, or a lot": *Many* [not *lots of*] *medicines are produced from rain forest plants.*

mankind. Many readers object that *mankind* excludes women. Use *humankind, humanity, humans,* or *the human race* instead.

may be, maybe. *May be* is a verb phrase: *The computer may be unplugged. Maybe* is an adverb meaning "possibly": *Maybe the computer is unplugged.*

may, can. See *can.*

media, medium. *Media* is the plural of *medium*: *Among the news media, television is the most popular medium but the least informative.*

most. In formal writing, avoid using *most* as a substitute for *almost*: *Almost* [not *Most*] *everyone arrived on time.*

must of. See *have, of.*

nauseous, nauseated. *Nauseous* means "sickening": *A nauseous gas filled the room. Nauseated* means "to feel nausea, loathing, or disgust": *I felt nauseated as soon as I smelled the gas.*

number, amount. See *amount.*

of, have. See *have, of.*

off of, off from. *Off of* and *off from* are redundant; write *off*: *The cat jumped off* [not *off of*] *the table.*

ok, O.K., okay. All three spellings are acceptable, but avoid these colloquial expressions in formal writing. Use the adjectives *acceptable, satisfactory,* or *all right* or the verbs *approve of, agree to,* or *authorize*: *If my application is satisfactory* [not *okay*], *will you authorize* [not *okay*] *my loan?*

passed, past. *Passed* is the past tense of the verb *pass*: *The sports car passed the truck. Past* refers to a time before the present or a place farther than another: *The old man spoke nostalgically of his past. He lives two houses past the grocery store.*

plus. In formal writing, avoid using *plus* to mean "and," "in addition," or "as well as": *Culture consists of the shared knowledge and beliefs of a human community, as well as* [not *plus*] *the tools that use and express culture.*

precede, proceed. *Precede* means "to come before"; *proceed* means "to go forward": *Preceded by her parents, the bride proceeded down the aisle.*

presently. *Presently* means "in a short time, soon"; do not use it to mean "now": *Currently* [not *presently*], *factory output is ninety percent of capacity. We will arrive presently.*

principal, principle. As a noun, *principal* means "the head of a school or organization" or "a sum of money"; as an adjective it means "first or most important." *Principle* is a noun meaning "a basic truth or law": *My principal taught me the principle known as the Golden Rule.*

proceed, precede. See *precede.*

quote, quotation. *Quote* is a verb, *quotation* a noun. Do not use *quote* as a substitute for *quotation: I have several good quotations* [not *quotes*] *supporting my opinion.*

real, really. *Real* is an adjective, *really* an adverb. In formal writing, do not use *real* as a substitute for *really: He was really* [not *real*] *pleased to receive the award.*

reason is because, reason why. *Reason is because* is illogical; use *that* instead of *because: The reason they lost was that* [not *because*] *they rarely ever practiced. Reason why* is redundant: *The reason* [not *reason why*] *the economy has improved is technological advance.*

scarcely, hardly. See *hardly.*

set, sit. *Set,* meaning "to put or place," has the principal parts *set, set, set.* It is a transitive verb that takes a direct object: *Set the computer on this desk. Sit,* an intransitive verb meaning "to be seated or to rest," has the principal parts *sit, sat, sat: Sit here next to me.*

shall, will. *Shall* has nearly disappeared as a helping verb used with *I* or *we* to signal action in the future. It now appears mainly in polite requests, legal documents, and emphatic statements: *Shall we go? Both parties shall agree. I shall return. Will* is appropriate for most future statements.

should of. See *have, of.*

since. Some readers object to *since* as a substitute for *because.* Use *since* to mean "from then until now" or "between then and now": *Because* [not *since*] *it rained so hard last night, the game has been postponed. We have been waiting since six o'clock.*

sit, set. See *set.*

site, cite. See *cite.*

so. In formal writing, avoid using *so* as a substitute for the intensifier *very: Lake Constance is very* [not *so*] *beautiful.*

someone, somebody, something. *Someone, somebody,* and *something* are singular. (See 14f and 15d.)

some time, sometime, sometimes. *Some time* is the adjective *some* modifying the noun *time: She wants to spend some time with her grandparents. Sometime* is an adverb meaning "at an indefinite or unstated time": *We'll be there sometime soon. Sometimes* is an adverb meaning "at times, now and then": *Sometimes we don't understand each other.*

sort, kind. See kind(s), sort(s), types(s).

suppose to, use to. Write *supposed to* and *used to.* (See 13e1.)

sure. In formal writing, avoid using *sure* as an adverb; use *surely* instead: *We were surely* [not *sure*] *pleased by the news.*

take, bring. See *bring.*

than, then. *Than* is a conjunction that links unequal comparisons: *Harry types faster than Kevin. Then* is an adverb meaning "at that time or next in time": *He turned first one way and then another.*

that. See *who, which, that.*

that, which. Many writers use *that* to introduce essential or restrictive clauses, *which* to introduce nonessential or nonrestrictive clauses. (See 34e.)

theirself, theirselves, themself. *Theirself, theirselves,* and *themself* are nonstandard for *themselves*: *They decided to go by themselves* [not *theirselves*].

then, than. See *than.*

this kind. See *kind(s), sort(s), type(s).*

to, too, two. *To* is a preposition; *too* means "very" or "also"; *two* is a number.

try and. *Try and* is nonstandard for *try to*: *Try to* [not *try and*] *remember where you last saw your keys.*

unique. *Unique* is an absolute meaning "one of a kind"; do not use *unique* with qualifiers such as *more* and *most*: *She is a unique* [not *the most unique*] *writer.* (See also 18d4.)

use to, suppose to. See *suppose to.*

ways. In formal writing, avoid the use of *ways* to mean "distance": *They have come a long way* [not *ways*] *to get where they are today.*

well, good. See *good.*

where. In formal writing, avoid using *where* to substitute for *that* or *when*: *I recently read that* [not *where*] *the news media are more balanced than critics claim. Surprisingly, Christmas is a time when* [not *where*] *many people are most unhappy.*

where . . . at/to. Redundant; omit *at/to*: *Where did they say we would find them* [not *find them at*]?

which. See *that, which,* and *who, which, that.*

who, which, that. Use *who* to refer to people, *which* to things, and *that* to groups of people or to things: *The man who just left carried a heavy suitcase, which he shifted from one hand to the other. I want a book that tells me something new.* (See 16d; see also *that, which.*)

who, whom. *Who* is used with subjects and subject complements, *whom* with objects. (See 17e.)

whose, who's. *Whose* is a possessive pronoun; *who's* is a contraction of *who is*: *Whose essay is this? Who's ready for dessert?*

will, shall. See *shall.*

would of. See *have, of.*

your, you're. *Your* is a possessive pronoun: *Your time is up. You're* is a contraction of *you are*: *You're our first choice.*

ON THE WEB   www.ablongman.com/dodds

Guide for Multilingual Writers

This section is designed for writers who are learning English in addition to their primary language and for those who have grown up speaking two or more languages fluently, including English, but who are less confident in their written English. The complexities of English grammar and idiomatic expression sometimes puzzle even advanced multilingual speakers and writers of English. For immediate answers to your questions about English, see Chapters 30–32. For additional help with your writing, consider the following resources.

- *Dictionaries: Longman Dictionary of American English* (New York: Longman, 2000); *New Horizon Ladder Dictionary of the English Language* (New York: Signet, 1997); or *Oxford Advanced Learner's Dictionary* (New York: Oxford, 2000). For more choices visit < http://www.longman.com >.

- *Phrase books and idiomatic dictionaries:* NTC's *American Idioms Dictionary* (Lincolnwood, IL: National Textbook Company, 2000) or *The American Heritage Dictionary of Idioms* (Boston: Houghton Mifflin, 1997).

- *Practice for advanced English language learners:* Betty Azar, *Understanding and Using English Grammar* (New York: Longman, 2004).

- *Internet resources for ESL students:*
  < http://owl.english.purdue.edu/handouts/esl/eslstudent.html >.

- *Grammar checkers:* Use computer grammar checkers cautiously. They may identify some trouble spots in your writing, but they frequently fail to recognize errors. Other times they highlight expressions that are not errors. If your grammar checker identifies a possible error in your writing, double check it against *The Ready Reference Handbook* or the advice of a reader whose knowledge you trust.

- *Your instructors' responses to your writing:* As writers and speakers learn a new language, they expect to be corrected as they develop their fluency. But in the United States, instructors sometimes avoid correcting errors in student writing, especially in preliminary writing, where the goal is the development of a writer's ideas rather than flawless expression. Even when responding to finished writing, instructors may prefer to focus only on certain kinds of errors or those that most affect successful expression. If you're concerned about specific trouble spots in your writing and want help with mistakes, talk to your instructor and identify the kind of assistance you want. Or visit your college's tutoring or writing center.

30 Articles and Quantifiers

Many languages use articles differently than English does, and some do not use them at all. Japanese, for example, uses no articles, so a common transfer error is a dropped article: *I eat apple.* Many European languages— French, Spanish, German, among others—use an article for generalizations: *The television is bad for children.*

In standard English, articles (*a, an, the*) and quantifiers (*a few, many, some,* and so forth) introduce nouns, which may follow immediately or be preceded by other words.

article + noun
The snow lay in gentle drifts.

article + adjective + noun
A wet snow bent the boughs of the tree.

quantifier + noun
Some snow fell last night.

30a Use *a/an* with nonspecific singular count nouns

Count nouns name persons, places, or things that can be counted; they may be singular or plural: *student/students, forest/forests, computer/computers.*

Nonspecific count nouns name a class of things or something not specifically identified: *A computer makes writing easier.* The indefinite articles *a* and *an* are used to introduce nonspecific singular count nouns.

1 ■ Matching *a* with consonant sounds, *an* with vowel sounds

■ Use *a* before words beginning with a consonant sound: *a book, a happy man, a pen.*

■ Use *an* before words beginning with a vowel sound (*a, e, i, o, u,* or silent *h,* as in *hour*): *an apple, an episode, an impossible task, an operator, an understanding, an honor.*

2 ■ Knowing when to use *a* or *an*

Use *a* or *an* in these following situations:

■ To mean "one of a certain type": *A banana will give you more energy than an apple.*

Most moral issues have _a gray area where right and wrong become cloudy.

- To refer to something not specifically identified: *Choose an apple from this bowl.*

I have just received _{an} exciting job offer.

- To mention something for the first time: *A dish* [first mention] *fell from the shelf and broke. The dish* [second mention] *belonged to my grandmother.*

Note: Exception. The article *the* is used in a generic sense with certain nonspecific singular count nouns to mean "one of a certain type of thing":

- Species of animals: *The woolly mammoth lived in Siberia 6,000 years ago.*

- Inventions: *The computer is indispensable for most students.*

- Musical instruments: *The koto, a stringed instrument similar to the zither, is important to Japanese sacred music.*

30b Never use *a/an* with noncount nouns

Noncount nouns name things that are not countable in English. Noncount nouns cannot be made plural and are never preceded by *a* or *an*.

- Whole groups of similar items: *baggage, clothing, equipment, furniture, garbage, hardware, jewelry, junk, luggage, machinery, mail, makeup, money/cash/change, postage, scenery, traffic,* and so forth

When I return home next time, I will take only _{one piece of} a luggage.

[To refer to countable units of otherwise noncount nouns, use quantifiers like *one piece* or *a little*. See 30e3.]

- Abstractions: *advice, beauty, courage, education, grammar, happiness, health, homework, honesty, importance, information, knowledge, laughter, music, news, peace, progress, sleep, time, violence, wealth, work, vocabulary,* and so forth

On American television, ~~a~~ violence is presented as attractive and exciting.

- Liquids: *water, coffee, tea, milk, oil, soup, gasoline, blood,* and so forth
- Solids: *ice, bread, butter, cheese, meat, gold, iron, silver, glass, paper, wood, cotton, wool,* and so forth
- Gases: *steam, air, oxygen, hydrogen, smoke, smog, pollution,* and so forth

- Particles and powders: *rice, chalk, corn, dirt, dust, flour, grass, hair, pepper, salt, sand, sugar, wheat,* and so forth

- Languages: *Arabic, Chinese, English, Polish, Sanskrit, Spanish, Urdu,* and so forth

- Fields of study: *chemistry, engineering, history, mathematics, psychology,* and so forth

- Recreation: *baseball, bridge, chess, soccer, tennis,* and so forth

- General activities: *driving, studying, traveling,* and other gerunds (*-ing* nouns)

- Natural phenomena: *darkness, dew, electricity, fire, fog, gravity, hail, heat, humidity, lightning, rain, sleet, snow, thunder, weather, wind,* and so forth

Note: Some nouns can be either count or noncount nouns.

- *Please bring us two coffees.* [count noun]
  African coffee is very strong. [noncount noun]

- *We had two big snows this winter.* [count noun]
  I love snow! [noncount noun]

  Nouns of this kind must be learned; see an ESL dictionary.

30c Use *the* with nouns whose specific identity your readers know

The definite article *the,* indicating "this" or "that," introduces a specific person, place, or thing singled out from others. Use *the* in these situations:

- When readers know the identity of the noun: *I enjoy going to the bank on payday.*

  Many societies have abandoned ⌃the death penalty.

- When the noun refers to a unique person, place, or thing: *Last year, the Pope visited my country.*

  In this poem, ⌃the poet asks us to praise God for His creation.

- When the noun is mentioned for the second time: *Last night I went to a new restaurant* [first mention]. *The restaurant* [second mention] *is called La Chosa.*

- When the words following the noun specify its identity:

  The notes on your experiment *are detailed and complete.*

  The student who won the chess championship *was David Wu.*

■ When the noun is modified by a superlative adjective (see 18d):

The tallest player *on the team is Nestor Wozny.*

When I finally got married, **the most relieved person** *in the room was my mother.*

30d Do not use *the* with most proper nouns and with statements meaning "all" or "in general"

1 ■ Proper nouns

Do not use *the* before most singular proper nouns, including languages (*Arabic, English*), a person's name (*Juan Ramírez*), organizations (*Environmental Technologies*), holidays (*New Year's*), continents (*South America*), countries (*Mexico*), states (*New Jersey*), cities and towns (*Dallas*), streets and roads (*42nd Street, Fifth Avenue*), squares (*Herald Square*), parks (*Central Park*), single lakes (*Lake Geneva*), bays (*Tampa Bay*), islands (*Easter Island*), and specific mountains (*Mount Kilimanjaro*).

In ~~the~~ Japanese, the saying "Look up into the sky" means "Stop and smell the roses."

Exceptions: Some singular proper nouns require *the*:

■ *Specific languages*: Use *the* before phrases identifying a specific language: *the Chinese language, the language spoken by newcomers,* and so forth.

■ *Certain country names and organizations*: Use *the* before the names of certain countries and organizations: *the United Nations, the Netherlands, the United States, the Philippines, the Ukraine, the People's Republic of China, the Commonwealth of Independent States.*

■ *Regions*: Use *the* before the names of regions (*the East Coast*), deserts (*the Sahara*), peninsulas (*the Malay Peninsula*), and bodies of water other than lakes (*the Pacific Ocean, the Mediterranean Sea, the Mekong River*).

Use *the* before plural proper nouns, such as *the Himalaya Mountains, the Great Lakes, the Sunda Islands.*

2 ■ General statements

Do not use *the* before plural or noncount nouns used in a general sense.

Students
~~The students~~ today are drinking less but smoking more.

In dangerous situations, ~~the~~ courage may not be as important as ~~the~~ patience.

3 ▪ Certain place expressions

Do not use *the* before general uses of the words *school, class, work, church, town,* and *bed.*

This semester I go to ~~the~~ school three days each week.

4 ▪ Games

Do not use *the* before the names of games: *chess* [not *the chess*], *baseball, soccer.*

5 ▪ Subjects of study

Do not use *the* before subjects of study: *economics* [not *the economics*], *history, mathematics, political science, sociology,* and so forth.

When I took ~~the~~ art history, I studied both Western and Asian painters.

30e Match quantifiers with appropriate count or noncount nouns

Quantifiers are words or phrases that tell *how much* or *how many: two inches of rain, a few students.* Use certain quantifiers with certain kinds of nouns.

1 ▪ Using quantifiers with singular count nouns

Use *one, each,* and *every* with singular count nouns: *one apple, each student, every computer.*

2 ▪ Using quantifiers with plural nouns

Use the following quantifiers with plural nouns to tell *how many:* numbers of two or more, *both, a couple of, a few, many, a number of* (*the*), *a percentage of* (*the*), *quite a few, several, too many.* For example: *two apples, many apples, a majority of the students, a number of computers.*

3 ▪ Using quantifiers with noncount nouns

Use *a little, much,* and *a great deal of* with noncount nouns to tell *how much: a little baggage, much snow, a great deal of progress.*

4 ▪ Using quantifiers with plural and noncount nouns

Use the following quantifiers with plural and noncount nouns to tell *how many* or *how much: all, almost all, almost no, a lot of, enough, hardly any, lots of, a majority/minority of* (*the*), *most, not any/no, plenty of, some.* For example: *all the apples, all the snow, hardly any students, hardly any progress, some computers, some fog.* When count nouns follow these quantifiers, be sure to make them plural.

Some ~~university~~ *universities* make an extra effort to help international students feel at home.

Note: In general, do not use an article before a quantifier.

The zoo in my hometown had ~~a~~ one large animal, an old bear.

A favorite pastime of ~~the~~ many older people is going out to eat and talk.

Exceptions include *a few, a little, the most, all the, a number of, a majority of* and so forth: *a few days ago, the most important discovery, all the time, a number of students, a majority of women.*

EXERCISE 30.1 Editing Articles and Quantifiers

Edit the following sentences for errors in the use of articles, quantifiers, and nouns. If a sentence is correct, write "correct." See the answers in the appendix.

30.1
Editing
articles and
quantifiers:
Exercises

1. After hiking two more miles, we found a easy way down the mountain.
2. The territorial behavior is expressed by the humans and the animals alike.
3. Finally, the soccer is becoming popular game in the United States.
4. Every Friday evening I go out to eat with the several of my friends.
5. Although I'm not the musician, I enjoy the music very much, and the music I enjoy most is the jazz.

31 Verbs

Languages have a variety of rules governing verb use. Some—Chinese, Vietnamese, and others—have no tense inflection; others—Japanese, Korean, Russian, and others—have no inflection for person or number. Many (French, Greek, Russian, among others) have no progressive form, and some (Urdu and Hindi) use the progressive form much more freely than English does.

This chapter focuses on features of English verbs frequently troublesome to nonnative speakers of English. Features that may be troublesome to native and nonnative speakers alike are treated elsewhere:

- Irregular English verbs: see 13a.

- Specific uses of English verb tenses: see 13b.

- Subject-verb agreement: see 13c and Chapter 14.

- The helping verbs *be, have,* and *do*: see 13d.

- *-d, -ed,* and *-ve* verb endings: see 13e.

- The subjunctive mood for wishes and nonfactual statements: see 13f and 24d1.

- Voice: see 20a, 24d2, 28c4.

31a To express tense correctly, match appropriate helping and main verb forms

1 ▪ **Forming tenses**

31.1
Verb tenses:
Web link

Tense is the time of the action expressed by the verb: past, present, and so forth. Standard English has six tenses, and each of these tenses has a progressive form (a form of *be + ing*) to indicate continuous or ongoing action. To form each tense correctly, use the following combinations of helping verbs and main verbs.

- Present tense: action that takes place now. Use the base or *-s/-es* form of the main verb: *I sigh. He speaks. She confesses. I am working. He is working. You/we/they are working.*

- Past tense: past action. Use the past tense form of the main verb: *I sighed. He spoke. I/he/she was working. You/we/they were working.*

- Future tense: action that will take place. Use *will* plus the base form of the main verb: *I will sigh. He will speak. You/we/they will be working.*

- Present perfect tense: past action continuing or completed in the present. Use *has/have* plus the past participle form of the main verb: *I have sighed. He has spoken. He/she has been working. I/you/we/they have been working.* For information on past participles of irregular verbs, see 13a.

- Past perfect tense: past action completed before another past action. Use *had* plus the past participle form of the main verb: *I had sighed. He had spoken. I/he/she/you/we/they had been working.* (See 13a.)

- Future perfect tense: action that will begin and end in the future. Use *will* plus *have* plus the *-d/-ed/-n/-en/-t* past participle form of the main verb: *I will have sighed. He will have spoken. I/he/she/you/we/they will have been working.* (See 13a.)

As you revise, be sure to use the correct combination of helping and main verbs to express tense.

changing
She is ~~change~~ her major from biology to botany.
                     ^

[The progressive *-ing* verb form is necessary to form the present progressive tense, indicating present ongoing action.]

have
Scientists ~~had~~ now demonstrated that some animals are capable of reason.
              ^

[*Has* or *have* is necessary to form the present perfect, indicating past action completed in the present.]

Note: Tense consistency. Two or more verbs that refer to the same action must be in the same tense: *I read the book, and I enjoyed it.* (See 24c.)

2 ▪ Including helping verbs

Always include helping verbs even when the meaning or verb tense seems clear without them.

are
So far, they ˏ the friendliest students in my dorm.
             ^

[The helping verbs *be, have,* and *do* may stand alone as main verbs. Here *are* is necessary to connect the subject *they* to its complement, *the friendliest students.*]

has
She ˏ been a member of Amnesty International for five years.
     ^

[*Has* is necessary to create the present perfect tense.]

3 ▪ Identifying verbs that lack progressive forms

The following types of verbs do not generally appear in the progressive *-ing* form.

- Verbs referring to mental states: *believe, doubt, feel, forget, imagine, intend, know, mean, need, prefer, realize, recognize, remember, suppose, understand, wish.*

  have known
  I ~~am knowing~~ the Patel family for seven years.
     ^

- Verbs referring to emotional states: *appreciate, care, dislike, envy, fear, hate, like, love, mind.*

- Verbs referring to the act of possessing: *belong, have, own, possess. Have,* an exception, is sometimes used in an active sense: *She is having a baby.*

- Verbs referring to sense perceptions: *feel, hear, see, smell, taste.* Exceptions: These verbs may appear in progressive tenses with a change of meaning. For example, in *I can feel the soft ground beneath my sleeping bag, feel* refers to tactile experience. But in *I'm feeling good this morning, feeling* refers to the speaker's mood.

31b After the helping verbs *do, does,* and *did,* use only the base form of the verb

The helping verb *do* appears in questions, in negatives with *not* or *never,* and in emphatic statements. Use the appropriate form to signal tense and number (singular or plural): *do* is the base form, *does* is the *-s* form (third-person singular), and *did* signals the past tense. After *do, does,* or *did,* use the base form of the main verb. Do not omit these helping verbs even if the meaning is clear without them.

- A question: *Do you have the DVD I requested?*

- A negative statement: *He doesn't* [present tense: *does not*] *know what he wants for dinner.*

- An emphatic statement: *We did* [past tense] *offer to help whenever we could.*

31c Use modal verbs to indicate your attitude toward the action of a main verb

The modal helping verbs *can, could, may, might, must, shall, should, will, would, ought to, had better,* and *had to* express the writer's attitude toward an action.

- Capability: *I can help you with your calculus.*

- Intention: *I will finish by tomorrow.*

- Possibility: *They might go to the party.*

- Probability: *She must have gone home already.*

- Permission: *You may leave when you finish the exam.*

- Advisability: *He should edit his writing more carefully.*

- Necessity: *We must finish the book by this weekend.*

Use only one modal before a main verb.

They might ~~could~~ take a Spanish class next semester.

1 ▪ Using present/future modals

For action in the present or future, use *can, may, might, must, should, had better, ought to, will* plus the base form of the main verb: *Next semester I had better take fewer classes.* Do not add an *-s* to the modal even when the subject is *he, she,* or *it.*

Natasha says she ~~will~~ come to the party this evening.

[The modal verb *will* is required to express future action even though the closing phrase, *this evening,* indicates future time.]

can
Tamiko assured her supervisor that she ~~cans~~ finish the project by Tuesday.

[Modal verbs never take the *-s* verb ending.]

volunteer
With a little encouragement, Henry might ~~volunteers~~.

[To signal future action, the modal *might* is followed by the base form *volunteer.*]

play
Lucia might ~~to play~~ a Chopin sonata at her next recital.

[Following the future tense modal *might,* the base form of the main verb *play* is required rather than the infinitive *to play.* (For uses of the infinitive, see 31f.)]

2 ■ Using past modals

For past action, use *would, could, might, had to* plus the base form of the main verb: *Carlos had to leave early in order to be home by midnight.* Do not use the past tense of the main verb.

could
As she listened to their explanation, she ~~can~~ understand their motives.

be
When I saw how pale she was, I thought she might ~~been~~ sick.

3 ■ Using past perfect modals for potential past action

For past action that did not actually occur, use *could* (*not*) *have, should* (*not*) *have, would* (*not*) *have* plus the past participle of the main verb: *Edgardo should have covered his roses to protect them from frost.* (See also 31e.)

died
With regular feeding, the fish would not have ~~die~~.

have
They should waited a week or two before planting the flowers.

31d Use the passive voice when a subject receives the action of a transitive verb

In passive voice expressions, a passive subject receives the action of a transitive verb. The subject is acted on instead of performing an action.

a subject being acted on
In ancient Ethiopia, coffee was consumed as a food rather than a beverage.

1 ■ Confusing voice and tense

Do not confuse the passive voice with the past tense. A passive voice verb may appear in the past, present, or future tense. To form the passive, use the appropriate form of *be* to signal number and tense plus the past participle of the main verb. Note that *be, being,* and *been* must be preceded by another helping verb.

TENSE	EXAMPLE
Present passive	The music *is played.*
Present progressive passive	The music *is being played.*
Present perfect passive	The music *has been played.*
Past passive	The music *was played.*
Past progressive passive	The music *was being played.*
Past perfect passive	The music *had been played.*
Future passive	The music *will be played.*
Future perfect passive	The music *will have been played.*

2 ■ Misusing the passive voice

■ To form the passive voice, use the past participle form of the main verb, not the base or past tense form.

released
The movie will be ~~release~~ in China early next year.
                    ^

driven
The emigrants who left Ireland in the 1840s were ~~drove~~ by famine.
                                                  ^

■ Include the appropriate form of *be* in all passive voice expressions.

is
In our culture today, too much emphasis placed on material goals.
                                        ^

■ Use the passive voice sparingly. (See 20a and 28c4.)

31.2
Editing for
correct verb
forms:
Exercises

EXERCISE 31.1   Editing for Correct Verb Forms

Edit the following sentences for the correct use of helping verbs, main verbs, modal verbs, and the passive voice. See the answers in the appendix.

1. By the time I receive my flu shot I am already having the flu twice this year.

2. When the hurricane struck, our car was sat under two huge palm trees.

3. Hasn't anyone ever tell you that cigars can be as deadly as cigarettes?

4. When handling HIV patients, you do not suppose to work with your bare hands.

5. We would have love to attend the party.

31e Use correct verb tenses in conditional (*if . . .*) sentences

Conditional sentences usually consist of two parts: (1) an *if* dependent clause stating conditions and (2) a main clause stating results.

conditions   results
If we have time, we'll go bicycling this weekend.

results   conditions
We used to go bicycling when we had the time.

results   conditions
We would go bicycling this weekend if we had enough time.

conditions   results
If we had had enough time, we would have gone bicycling last weekend.

31.3
Conditional
sentences:
Web link

These examples illustrate three features of conditional sentences: (1) the *if* clause may appear before or after the main clause stating results; (2) not every conditional sentence contains *if*; and, most important, (3) the kind of conditional statement determines the tenses of the verbs.

1 ■ Describing habitual past and present conditions

For conditions that occur again and again in the past or present, use the same tense in the *if* clause and the "results" main clause.

present tense (*if* clause)   present tense (*results* clause)
If we have enough time, we go bicycling on weekends.

past tense (*if* clause)   past tense (*results* clause)
When we had enough time, we went bicycling on weekends.

2 ■ Describing possible future conditions

To predict future conditions and results:

■ In the *if* clause, use *if* or *unless* plus the present tense (not the future tense).

■ In the "results" clause, use *can, may, might, should,* or *will* plus the base form of the verb.

present tense (*if* clause)   *may* + base form (*results* clause)
If we have enough time, we may go bicycling this weekend.

will + base form (*results* clause)   present tense (*if* clause)
We will go bicycling this weekend unless it rains.

3 ■ Speculating about present or future conditions

To speculate about imagined conditions in the present or future:

■ In the *if* clause, use *if* plus the past tense (not the present tense).

Note: If you use a form of the verb *be* in the *if* clause, use *were* instead of *was,* whether the subject is singular or plural. (See also 13f.)

■ In the "results" clause, use *could, might,* or *would* plus the base form of the verb.

past tense (*if* clause)   *would* + base form (*results* clause)

If the weather were better today, we would go bicycling.

might + base form (*results* clause) past tense (*if* clause)

We might go bicycling if it stopped raining.

4 ■ Speculating about past conditions

To speculate about what might, could, or should have happened in the past:

■ In the *if* clause, use *if* plus the past perfect tense (*had* + the past participle).

■ In the "results" clause, use *could have, might have,* or *would have* plus the past participle.

past perfect tense (*if* clause)   *would have* + past participle

If it had stopped raining, we would have gone bicycling.

could have + past participle (*results* clause) past perfect tense (*if* clause)

We could have gone bicycling if the weather had been better.

31.4
Using
conditional
verb forms:
Exercises

EXERCISE 31.2   Editing Conditional Sentences

Edit the following conditional sentences for the correct use of helping verbs, main verbs, and modal verbs. See the answers in the appendix.

1. Whenever I am most absorbed by my work, the telephone will ring.

2. If Carol was less outspoken, she would offend fewer people.

3. Yueng would be a better musician if he would spend more time practicing.

4. If I leave my house by six o'clock I would arrive at your house by seven.

5. You would have seen a spectacular meteor shower if you went for a walk with us.

31.5
Verbs taking
infinitives
and
gerunds:
Web link

31f Learn which verbs may be followed by an infinitive, gerund, or either verb form

An infinitive is the base form of a verb preceded by *to: to study.* A gerund is the *-ing* form of a verb used as a noun: *Studying is difficult after a full day's work.* Following certain verbs, infinitives and gerunds may appear as objects.

1 ■ Verb + infinitive

■ Some verbs are followed by an infinitive (*to* + base form) but not by a gerund:

agree	claim	deserve	offer	refuse
appear	come	hope	plan	seem
arrange	decide	intend	pretend	wish

The group agreed **to study** [not *studying*] in the library after dinner.

■ When used in the active voice, a related group of verbs follows this pattern: verb plus noun or pronoun plus infinitive:

advise	convince	force	permit	tell
allow	encourage	instruct	persuade	urge
ask	expect	invite	remind	want
cause	forbid	order	require	warn

verb + noun + infinitive

We have invited Gary to join us for dinner.

verb + pronoun + infinitive

Brigit advised me to apply for a scholarship.

■ A small group of verbs may be followed either by an infinitive or by a noun or pronoun plus an infinitive:

allow	cause	get	promise
ask	expect	help	want
beg	force	need	would like

verb + infinitive

The lawyer asked to address the court.

verb + noun + infinitive

Mercedes asked Luis to bring his laptop computer to class.

■ When the verbs *have* ("cause"), *let* ("allow"), and *make* ("force") are followed by a noun or pronoun plus an infinitive, the *to* is omitted:

Please have the carpenters finish [not *to finish*] their work by Thursday.

2 ■ Verb + gerund

■ These verbs may be followed by a gerund but not by an infinitive:

admit	deny	imagine	postpone	resist
appreciate	discuss	keep	practice	risk
avoid	enjoy	mention	put off	suggest
consider	escape	mind	quit	tolerate
delay	finish	miss	recall	

Keiko recalled **leaving** [not *to leave*] her gloves in the car.

■ The following expressions with prepositions often take a gerund or a possessive noun or pronoun plus a gerund:

accuse someone of	be used to	insist on
apologize for	believe in	keep someone from
approve of	concentrate on	look forward to
be accustomed to	depend on	object to
be capable of	dream of	prevent someone from
be excited about	feel like	stop someone from
be fond of	forgive someone for	succeed in
be interested in	get around to	talk about
be responsible for	have an influence on	think about
be tired of	help in	

verb + preposition + gerund

For more than a year Anne and Judy have dreamed of traveling to Italy.

verb + preposition + pronoun + gerund

I depend on his arriving on time.

3 ■ Verb + infinitive or gerund

■ Certain verbs may be followed by infinitives or gerunds with little or no change of meaning: *begin, continue, hate, like, love, prefer, start.*

Ali **loves playing** the guitar.

Ali **loves to play** the guitar.

■ After the verbs *forget, remember, stop,* and *try,* the infinitive and gerund have different meanings:

A Good Samaritan is someone who **stops to help** those in need. [provides assistance]

Concerned with his own problems, Felix **has stopped helping** those in need. [no longer provides assistance]

31.6
Using
infinitives
and
gerunds:
Exercises

EXERCISE 31.3   Editing Infinitives and Gerunds

Edit the following sentences for the correct use of infinitives and gerunds. If a sentence is correct, write "correct" after it. See the answers in the appendix.

1. After the way they embarrassed me, I refuse speaking to them any more.

2. You can depend on me to help you in any way possible.

3. My family and I are planning going to the Grand Canyon next summer.

4. We are looking forward to see lions, elephants, and zebras in the wild game parks of Kenya.

5. I object to spending so much money for a car that I'm only going to drive back and forth to work.

31g Use two-word verbs correctly

31.7
Two-word
verbs:
Web link

Two-word verbs (also called **phrasal verbs**) consist of a verb and a preposition that together mean something different from the meanings of their individual words. Consider two-word verbs using *call*:

I promise to **call up** my parents this weekend. [to telephone]

When I get the information, I'll **call** you **back**. [to return a telephone call]

The Army **is calling up** its reserves. [to report for service]

The instructor **called** the student **in** for a conference. [to ask to come to a specific place for a specific purpose]

I'm going to **call on** you tomorrow. [to ask to speak, to visit]

The umpire **called off** the game because of darkness. [to cancel]

1 ▪ Using a dictionary or phrase book

Because English two-word verbs are so numerous and their meanings are almost always idiomatic, use a dictionary or phrase book of idioms as you write and edit. Two reference books are the *Oxford Dictionary of Phrasal Verbs* (New York: Oxford UP, 1993) and the *Cambridge International Dictionary of Phrasal Verbs* (New York: Cambridge UP, 1997). A Web site list of two-word verbs may be found at < http://owl. English.purdue.edu/handouts/print/esl/eslphrasal.html >. Check to see that you've used the correct verb and preposition combination for the meaning you intend.

2 ▪ Placing objects and prepositions after the verb

The preposition in a two-word verb, called a **particle**, is either inseparable or separable from the verb:

▪ An **inseparable particle** follows the verb immediately.

The instructor **called on** Jigna to answer the question.

Today's college students often **drop out** of school for a few years and then return.

Rosendo **goes out** to dinner tonight to celebrate his promotion.

▪ A **separable particle** may be separated from a transitive verb in either of two ways:

Noun objects. If the object of a two-word verb is a noun, place the noun after the particle or between the verb and particle.

verb + particle + noun

The umpire called off the game.

verb + noun + particle

The umpire called the game off.

Pronoun objects. If the object of a two-word verb is a pronoun, place the pronoun between the verb and particle.

verb + pronoun + particle

The umpire called it off.

31.8
Completing
two-word
verbs:
Exercises

EXERCISE 31.4 Completing Two-Word Verbs

In each sentence, fill in the blank with the correct preposition to complete the two-word verb. See the answers in the appendix.

1. Please turn _____ your assignments by Friday afternoon at the latest.

2. Shut _____ the engine so that we don't run _____ of gas.

3. I was so angry that I tore _____ the letter and threw it _____.

4. Timothy and Angela left an hour ago; we'll never catch _____ with them.

5. When my best friends come home in the evenings, the first thing they do is turn _____ their stereo and turn _____ the volume so that all their neighbors can hear them.

32 More Grammar

32a Include all necessary words

1 ■ Including subjects

Except for imperatives, all English sentences must have a subject. Be especially careful to include personal pronoun subjects that refer to antecedents in preceding clauses or sentences. Compare these examples:

The Hindu god Brahma is considered equal to Vishnu and Siva. However, **he** has had only one temple dedicated to him, at Pushkar in India.

Because Carlos practices speaking into a tape recorder, *he* has excellent
pronunciation.

[*Carlos* is the subject of the opening dependent clause; the personal pronoun *he* is required as the subject of the independent clause.]

She says
Takao is such an optimist. ~~Says~~ that problems are only clouds hiding the
  ⌃
sun.

[Even though both sentences refer to the same person, the personal pronoun *she*
is required to provide a subject for the second sentence.]

2 ■ Including the expletives *it, here,* and *there*

Expletives are words used primarily to provide a subject for a sentence that doesn't logically have one or to introduce a subject following the verb. Usually an expletive is followed by a form of *be*:

It *is* raining again.

delayed subject
⌐‾‾‾‾‾‾‾‾‾¬
There *are* many Andean mountains higher than 6,700 meters.

Do not omit *it, here,* and *there* even though they contribute little meaning to your sentences, and be sure the verb agrees with its actual subject. (See also 14b and 20e3.)

It is
~~Is~~ necessary to take health precautions before traveling in tropical countries.
⌃

[*It* is required to introduce the subject of the sentence, *to take health precautions.*]

, *there*
Ten years ago was a severe drought in my country.
       ⌃

[The subject of the sentence is not *ten years ago* but *a severe drought* following the verb *was*. *There* is required to introduce it.]

Here are
~~Is~~ two solutions to the problems created by illegal immigration.
⌃

[The subject of the sentence, *two solutions,* requires the plural verb *are.*]

32b Avoid unnecessary repetition

1 ■ Avoiding unnecessary repetition of a subject

Do not repeat a subject within its own clause, even when the subject and verb are separated.

American cigarette manufacturers ~~they~~ now advertise heavily throughout Asia.

[The personal pronoun *they* repeats the subject, *American cigarette manufacturers,* and is therefore unnecessary.]

The Wei River, at flood stage for nearly three weeks, ~~it~~ began to recede at last.

[Although the subject of the sentence, *Wei River,* is separated from the verb *began,* the pronoun *it* is unnecessary.]

2 ■ Avoiding unnecessary repetition of objects or adverbs

Do not repeat an object or adverb in an adjective clause beginning with a relative pronoun (*who, which, whom, whose, that*) or relative adverb (*where, when*).

Ahmed is the one person whom I can always trust ~~him~~ to tell the truth.

[The relative pronoun *whom* is also the object of the verb *trust*; the objective pronoun *him* is unnecessary. Even if *whom* were omitted, *him* would be unnecessary: *Ahmed is the one person I can always trust to tell the truth.*]

Marrakech sits on a high plain where the air is thin and the sun is

brilliant ~~there~~.

[*There* repeats the meaning of the relative adverb *where* and is therefore unnecessary.]

3 ■ Avoiding unnecessary repetition of conjunctions

Conjunctions link words, phrases, and clauses. Coordinating conjunctions (*and, or, but,* and so forth) link words of equal value. Subordinating conjunctions (*although, because, if, when,* and so forth) link dependent clauses to main clauses. To link clauses, use only one conjunction. (See also 8g.)

Although I'm happy here, ~~but~~ I miss the sweet sounds and smells of home.

[The subordinating conjunction *although* links the first clause, *I'm happy here,* to the main clause; *but* is unnecessary. To emphasize the clauses equally, the writer would omit *although* and retain *but*: *I am happy here, but I miss the sweet sounds and smells of home.*]

32.1
Editing
omissions
and
repetitions:
Exercises

EXERCISE 32.1 Editing Omissions and Repetitions

In the following sentences, include necessary subjects and expletives; delete any repeated subjects, objects, adverbs, or conjunctions. See the answers in the appendix.

1. I know this is true because has happened to me.

2. Are many orchards and gardens in the Nile River valley.

3. In some parts of Saudi Arabia, ten years may pass there without rainfall.

4. Because all of Nigeria lies within the tropics, so there are only two seasons, wet and dry.

5. The Amazon Valley of eastern Ecuador it constitutes about half the country's area.

32c Begin dependent clauses with correct linking words

Whatever their role in a sentence, dependent clauses always begin with a "subordinator" word that links them to the main clause of the sentence. Such words may be relative pronouns such as *who* or *that*, question words such as *what* or *how*, and subordinating conjunctions such as *although* or *because*. (For lists of linking words, see 8b5 and 6, 8g3.) To express your meaning effectively, choose "subordinator" words that fit grammatically in your sentence and that say what you intend.

Angela mentioned ~~about~~ ^that^ international students make frequent use of

college writing centers.

[*About* is a preposition, used for prepositional phrases; it cannot begin a clause. A linking pronoun is required to begin a noun clause functioning as a direct object.]

1 ▪ Creating accurate *wh-* clauses

Wh- dependent clauses are headed by a connecting word usually beginning with *wh-*: *who, which, whom/about whom, whose, where, when, what, why, whether,* and *how. Wh-* clauses may function as subjects, objects, adjectives, and adverbs.

A subject	*Why she behaved that way* he could not explain.
An object	Peter could not predict *what his decision would be.*
An adjective	Part-time students *who work full-time jobs* generally have lower grade-point averages than full-time students.
An adverb	Most people wish to work *where loyalty is rewarded.*

Choose the *wh-* word that best fits the meaning of the clause it begins and that links with the word in the main clause that it modifies.

It was her aunt ~~which~~ ^who^ loaned Mary the money to go to Gale College.

[Used to refer to objects or unnamed animals, *which* is inappropriate to introduce an adjective clause modifying *aunt. Who* or *that* is correct.]

The building ~~what~~ ^where^ Heriberto lives ~~in~~ is very old.

[*Where* is appropriate for identifying a place, *the building.*]

2 ▪ Creating effective adverbial clauses

Adverbial dependent clauses (known as **subordinate clauses**) modify verbs and begin with subordinating conjunctions that indicate time (*after, when*), place (*anywhere*), reason (*because*), comparison (*although*), and manner or condition (*as, if*). (See the complete list in 8g3.) As you edit your sentences, check to be sure that subordinating conjunctions fit the clauses they introduce and that subordinate clauses contain a subject and verb.

Mark Twain's *Huckleberry Finn* is controversial primarily ~~for so~~ *because* it seems

to portray African-Americans negatively.

[*Because* is appropriate to introduce a clause that states a reason.]

I attended my political science class for three weeks before *I began* to feel

comfortable with my instructor.

[A subordinate clause must contain a subject and verb: *I began.* As an alternative version, *before* may introduce an adverbial phrase: *before feeling comfortable with my instructor.*]

Note: Sentence fragments are word groups that are incomplete for some reason. Avoid fragments in academic writing. Link dependent clauses to independent clauses (see 11b3). Also avoid the pairing of coordinating and subordinating conjunctions to link a dependent clause to the main clause of a sentence: *Although I liked that movie, ~~but~~ I didn't like it as much as the one we saw last weekend.* (See 32b3.)

32.2
Editing
dependent
clauses:
Exercises

EXERCISE 32.2 **Editing Dependent Clauses for Correct Linking Words**

Edit the following sentences for appropriate linking words (relative pronouns and subordinating conjunctions) that introduce dependent clauses and connect them to the main clause of the sentence. If a sentence is correct, write "correct" after it. See the answers in the appendix.

1. I like Seyung's research project the fact that he used so many quotations to support his opinions.

2. To strangers, I usually present myself as someone which is afraid of nothing.

3. Beate is someone whom many people misunderstand.

4. Barbara returned to the Ukraine, even the rest of her family remained in the United States.

5. When Darina arrived at the airport, a kind police officer showed her what her departure gate was located.

32d Follow these guidelines to summarize questions and speech

1 ■ Summarizing questions

Summarized questions (also called **indirect questions**) are usually part of a longer statement of fact; therefore, they follow the word order and punctuation of declarative sentences (see 10c2).

■ *Subject plus verb.* After the question word (*who, which, when, why, where, how,* and so forth) that introduces the summarized question, place the subject before the verb.

The panel considered where <s>is</s> air pollution ˄is the most severe.

■ *Using* **whether** *for yes/no and or questions.* Use *whether* to introduce summarized *yes/no* questions and *or* questions that pose alternatives.

I have not decided ˄*whether I will* <s>will I</s> go home for the summer or attend summer school.

■ *Omitting* **do, does, did.** Omit *do, does, did* from summarized questions; signal tense (the time of the action) with the correct form of the main verb.

He asked me ˄*whether* <s>did</s> I ˄*needed* <s>need</s> help with my experiment.

[*Needed* matches the past tense form of the main verb *asked.*]

■ *Punctuation.* Punctuate summarized questions in a way appropriate to the complete sentence.

The judge asked the jury whether it had reached a verdict˄. <s>?</s>

2 ■ Summarizing speech

In **summarized speech** (also called **reported speech** or **indirect quotation**), a writer restates a direct quotation in his or her own words, without quotation marks.

■ *Summarizing in a noun clause.* Write the summarized speech as a noun clause within your own sentence.

DIRECT QUOTATION	SUMMARIZED SPEECH
She said, "A monsoon is a strong seasonal wind."	She said that a monsoon is a strong seasonal wind.

[*That* may be omitted from certain noun clauses. (See 22d2.)]

■ *Changing present tense to past tense and present progressive to past progressive.* Change the present tense or present progressive of a direct quotation to the past tense or past progressive in summarized speech.

An exception: Use the present tense if the summarized speech is a general truth or habitual action, as in the preceding example.

DIRECT QUOTATION	SUMMARIZED SPEECH
She said, "My report is finished."	She said that her report was finished.
She said, "I am finishing my report."	She said that she was finishing her report.

- *Changing past tense or present perfect to past perfect.* Change the past tense or present perfect of a direct quotation to the past perfect of summarized speech.

DIRECT QUOTATION	SUMMARIZED SPEECH
She said, "They arrived an hour ago."	She said that they had arrived an hour ago.
She said, "I have tried to help him."	She said that she had tried to help him.

- *Changing modal verbs.* When summarizing speech, change *can* to *could, will* to *would, may* to *might, must* to *had to.*

DIRECT QUOTATION	SUMMARIZED SPEECH
She said, "I will call him next week."	She said that she would call him next week.

- *Summarizing commands.* To summarize commands, use *to* plus the base form of the verb (the infinitive).

DIRECT QUOTATION	SUMMARIZED SPEECH
She told her students, "Go to the lab."	She told her students to go to the lab.

32.3
Editing
summarized
questions
and speech:
Exercises

EXERCISE 32.3   Editing Summarized Questions and Speech

Edit the following sentences to correct errors in summarized questions and speech. Consider word choice, word order, verb forms, and punctuation. If a sentence is correct, write "correct" after it. See the answers in the appendix.

1. When I called, Natalia told me she is getting dressed and will be ready in fifteen minutes.

2. An old man sitting next to me on a park bench said that once he was wealthy and powerful.

3. After the plane had been in the air for an hour, Sergio nervously asked how long will it be before he arrives in Los Angeles?

4. In my environmental ethics class we spent a whole week debating should the federal government act to preserve wetlands.

5. Yesterday, my supervisor asked me would I like to attend this year's COMDEX computer convention in Las Vegas?

32e   Choose the correct word endings for your meaning

1 ▪ Forming plural nouns

- *Count nouns.* Count nouns refer to countable things and may, therefore, be either singular or plural: *apple/apples, joy/joys.* Do not omit the -*s*, -*es*, and other plural endings from nouns that are plural in meaning, even when other words indicate that your meaning is plural.

Middle Eastern cuisine makes frequent use of grape, pine nut, and chickpea. *[-s -s -s marked above grape, nut, chickpea]*

- ■ *Noncount nouns.* Noncount nouns refer to the whole of something that is not counted and, therefore, cannot be made plural: *snow, air.* (See also 8a and Chapter 30.)

I enjoyed the movie because of its elaborate science fiction machineries. *[-y marked above]*

[*Machine* is a count noun and can be made plural, *machines,* but *machinery* is a noncount noun and cannot be made plural.]

- ■ *Nouns as modifiers.* When nouns and numbers are used as modifiers preceding other nouns, they are singular in form.

Throughout college I lived in my relatives' guests room. *[deletion mark on -s of guests]*

Because I had to work after finishing high school, I am now a

twenty-two-years-old freshman. *[deletion mark on -s of years]*

2 ■ Choosing correct word endings for nouns, verbs, adjectives, and adverbs

English nouns, verbs, adjectives, and adverbs can change their forms—and often their meanings—by changing their endings (known as **derivational suffixes**). Thus, the verb *believe* may be transformed to a noun (*belief* or *believer*), an adjective (*believable*), or an adverb (*believably*). As you edit your writing, consider word endings to be sure each word fits your intended meaning and its grammatical function as a noun, verb, adjective, or adverb. Use a dictionary to check words you have written that are not in your everyday speaking vocabulary. (For endings that create nouns and verbs, see the "How to Identify Nouns and Verbs" box, p. 76; for endings that create adjectives and adverbs, see the "How to Identify Adjectives and Adverbs" box, pp. 80–81.)

I have lived among isolated villagers and sophisticated urban residence. *[-ts marked above residence]*

[Because of their similar sounds, the writer has confused the noun for a building, *residence,* with the noun for its inhabitants, *residents.*]

Because he was so young, he was vulnerable and easily influential. *[-ced marked above, deletion of influential]*

[This sentence confuses the adjective meaning the power to influence (*influential*) with the participial adjective meaning to experience influence (*influenced*).]

I want my instructors to response to my work in detail. *[-d marked above response]*

[This sentence confuses the noun form, *response,* with the base form of the verb, *respond.*]

32.4
Choosing
correct
word
endings:
Exercises

EXERCISE 32.4 Choosing Correct Word Endings

Edit the following sentences to correct errors in the endings of nouns, verbs, adjectives, and adverbs. If a sentence is correct, write "correct" after it. See the answers in the appendix.

1. Ana is a person who is usually able to give good reasons for her believes.

2. Couple today marry at a later age than they did two or three decades ago.

3. Unfortunately, the victims of many crimes choose to keep silence and not call the police.

4. The times and energy that farmers devote to advanced fertilization techniques will go far to reducing world hunger.

5. Ironically, just one little mistake or misjudge by the tragic hero is responsible for his dead.

32f Show possession with an apostrophe or an *of* phrase

English signals a possessive noun with an apostrophe or a phrase beginning with *of: India's president, the president of India.* In some cases, as in the preceding examples, the forms are interchangeable; often they are not.

1 ▪ Indicating possession with an apostrophe

To make a singular noun or an indefinite pronoun possessive, usually add an apostrophe followed by *s* (*-'s*): *the student's book, someone's book.* To make a plural noun ending in *-s* possessive, usually add only an apostrophe: *the students' request.* An apostrophe is generally used with nouns referring to persons and other living beings: *the president's address, the lions' roar.* (For more on the possessive form and the apostrophe, see 17d and 37a.)

2 ▪ Indicating possession with *of*

To signal possession when referring to things, you would typically use an *of* phrase: *the body of the car, the soles of my feet.* An *of* phrase may also be used to emphasize what is possessed: *the novels of Chinua Achebe.* Do not use possessive *of* phrases with personal pronouns: *her book,* not *the book of her.*

effect of
Many parents do not consider the ˄ TV violence ~~effect~~ on their children.

his
Without ~~the~~ help ~~of him~~, we could not have afforded the trip.
                       ^

Exceptions: The apostrophe form of the possessive appears frequently in references to time (*an hour's drive, a month's time*), natural phenomena (*the sun's rays, Earth's atmosphere*), political organizations (*the city's parks, the nation's tax system*), and groups of people working together (*the ship's crew, the company's employees*).

32g   Use adjectives and adverbs with care

1 ■ Forming adjectives

Adjectives modify nouns by telling *which one, what kind, how many: the tall man, a new student, four flowers.* (See 8d and 18a.) Some languages add singular and plural endings to adjectives so that they match the nouns they modify, but in English adjectives are neither singular nor plural. Do not add *-s* to adjectives even when they precede plural nouns:

> After only four full~~s~~ days of work, Zahid knew this job was the one he
>
> wanted.

Note: Pronoun-like adjectives such as *this, that, these,* and *those* (called demonstrative adjectives) must agree in number with the nouns they modify: *these professors,* not *this professors.*

2 ■ Using participles (-*ing* and -*ed* verb forms) as adjectives

To form some adjectives, English uses the present participle (-*ing*) and past participle (-*ed, -en, -n,* or *-t*) of verbs: *a terrifying story, a crowded street.* Both kinds of participles may appear before a noun or after a linking verb: *The terrifying story is true. The story is terrifying. The terrified child could not speak. The child seemed terrified.* But present and past participles may not be used interchangeably.

- Use **present participle adjectives** (ending in -*ing*) to describe something causing or stimulating an experience: *The survivors told a terrifying story to their fearful listeners* [the story caused terror in the listeners].

  breaking
  They jumped in surprise at the sound of ~~broken~~ glass.
                                              ^

- Use **past participle adjectives** (ending in -*ed, -d, -en, -t*) to describe a person or thing undergoing an experience: *The listeners shuddered, terrified by the survivors' story* [the listeners experienced terror].

I felt ~~embarrassing~~ *embarrassed* when my instructor read my paper aloud.
                    ^

EXERCISE 32.5 Editing *-ing* and *-ed* Adjectives (Participles)

Edit the following sentences for the appropriate use of present and past participles. If a sentence is correct, write "correct" after it. See the answers in the appendix.

32.5
Editing *–ing*
and *–ed*
adjectives:
Exercises

1. I had just finished eaten breakfast when the telephone rang.

2. She thought he was the most fascinated person she had ever met.

3. Casey said she was not interesting in attending the urban planning lecture.

4. We were pleased to see that the finished product turned out the way we had planned.

5. After the police used riot control gas, the demonstrators were nauseating for several hours.

3 ▪ Arranging cumulative adjectives

Cumulative adjectives are two or more adjectives that are not separated by commas and that modify the whole phrase following them: *the large round Persian rug.* To use cumulative adjectives correctly, arrange them in this order:

32.6
Cumulative
adjectives:
Web link

1. Article, possessive, or quantifier: *the, my, Teresa's, some, four,* and so forth

2. Comparative and superlative: *younger, older, best, worst, least*

3. Evaluator (a word that can be preceded by *very*): *beautiful, courageous, responsible*

4. Size: *large, small, gigantic, tall*

5. Length or shape: *long, round, oval, square, triangular*

6. Age: *young, old, new, antique, modern, twentieth-century*

7. Color: *green, yellow, violet*

8. Nationality: *Peruvian, Iranian, Polish, Canadian*

9. Religion: *Baptist, Buddhist, Christian, Hindu, Muslim, Protestant*

10. Material: *wood, walnut, metal, gold, wool*

11. Noun used as an adjective: *guest* (as in *guest room*), *history* (as in *history class*)

12. Noun modified: *room, class, truck, table*

Compare these examples:

Four old wooden clocks will be sold at the auction.

The baby was being entertained by her older ~~two~~ sisters.
(two)

Note: Avoid long series of cumulative adjectives—generally use no more than two or three adjectives between an article, possessive, or quantifier and the noun that they modify: *an old Hindu temple, Kevin's famous buttermilk pancakes, several well-known European scientists.*

4 ■ Placing adverbs

Adverbs that modify verbs may appear at the beginning, end, or in the middle of a sentence. However, do not place an adverb between a verb and a direct object. (See also 23a.) Compare these examples:

Carefully, she took her daughter's hand.

He turned the dial **carefully**.

He walked **carefully** along the ledge.

To complete my art history project, I examined ~~carefully~~ Mayan
(carefully)

architecture.

EXERCISE 32.6   Arranging Cumulative Adjectives and Placing Adverbs

Edit the following sentences for the correct arrangement of cumulative adjectives and the correct placement of adverbs. If a sentence is correct, write "correct" after it. See the answers in the appendix.

32.7
Cumulative
adjectives:
Exercises

1. When my rich aunt comes to visit, she brings often little gifts to remind us just how rich she is.

2. Some kind of yellow thick slime was oozing rapidly from a pipe into the small stream.

3. In front of the tiny green cottage stood two tall pine trees, the boughs heavy with freshly fallen snow.

4. Waiters like to see Armand stroll through a restaurant door because he leaves always large tips.

5. During the Vietnam War, several Buddhist devout monks burned themselves to death to protest the conflict.

32h Choose the appropriate preposition for your meaning

English prepositions can be especially troublesome to speakers of English as a second language, no matter what their first language. There are many prepositions to remember, their meanings are often idiomatic, and certain prepositions seem glued to some words but not to others.

Taiwo is so busy with school and work that he can scarcely keep track ^*of* the

time.

Mountain biking has inspired new trends ~~to~~ ^*in* clothing.

Although Avani is surely in love, she is not yet ready to make a

commitment ~~with~~ ^*to* Dhaval.

1 ■ Using reference sources to choose prepositions

32.8
Prepositions:
Web link

To choose prepositions appropriately, see the guidelines for two-word verbs in 31g, consult an ESL dictionary (see p. 203), use an English dictionary to look up the meaning of the word preceding the preposition, or check reference sources on English idioms and prepositions, such as *The Ins and Outs of Prepositions* (Hauppauge: Barrons Educational Series, 1999). Eventually, however, your effective use of prepositions will depend upon the powers of your memory.

2 ■ Choosing prepositions to indicate place

- Use **at** before a location, meeting place, the edge of something, the corner of something, or a target: *arriving at school, seated at the table, turning at the corner of Fifth and Maple streets, aiming at the bull's eye.*

- Use **in** before an enclosed space or geographic location: *growing in the garden, standing in the phone booth, hiking in the desert, living in Mexico City.*

- Use **on** before a surface or street: *lying on the table, hanging on the wall, walking on Fifth Avenue.*

3 ■ Choosing prepositions to indicate time

- Use **at** before specific expressions of time: *She arrived at 2:30. They left at dawn.*

- Use **in** before a month, year, century, period of time, or part of a twenty-four-hour period: *in May, in 1865, in the twentieth century, in an hour, in the morning.*

- Use **on** before a day or date: *on July 20, on Thursday.*

Note: Arranging place and time phrases. In most English expressions, *place* comes before time: *My relatives arrived at my house in the early morning.* However, a prepositional phrase indicating the time may appear at the beginning of a sentence: *In the early morning, my relatives arrived at my house.*

32.9
Editing
prepositions:
Exercises

EXERCISE 32.7   Editing Prepositions

Edit the following sentences for the correct prepositions. If a sentence is correct, write "correct" after it. See the answers in the appendix.

1. I meet so many interesting people in work.

2. For four long blocks a suspicious person followed me in the other side of the street.

3. Happy people are usually content on the things they have, whether a little or a lot.

4. The phrase "age of accountability" refers to the age when children are treated as responsible of themselves.

5. In most American restaurants, smokers and non-smokers are seated at different areas.

Punctuating

🖥 **COMPUTER TIP** Using Search and Replace to Edit Punctuation

Use the Find or Search and Replace command of your word processing program to locate and review specific punctuation marks in your writing.

33 End Punctuation

33a Use a period to mark sentences and abbreviations

1 ■ Marking sentences

Use a period to end all sentences except direct questions and genuine exclamations. Use a period to end sentences that summarize questions, make polite requests not phrased as questions, and give commands that are not exclamations.

33.1
End
punctuation:
Web link

> Edyta called the ticket office to ask whether the concert had been canceled.

> Return the rental car by Friday at noon.

Note: In writing that follows the Modern Language Association format, you may follow end punctuation with one space or two spaces.

2 ■ Marking abbreviations

The punctuation of abbreviations varies. When in doubt, consult a dictionary, style manual, or publication guide appropriate to your subject or audience. The Modern Language Association provides these guidelines.

■ *Abbreviations ending in lowercase.* Use a period after most abbreviations ending in lowercase letters. Do not put a space between lowercase letters that represent separate words.

Mr.	Dr.	Sept.	etc.	p.m.
Mrs.	Inc.	Capt.	introd.	e.g.
Ms.	Jan.	Maj.	a.m.	i.e.

- *Abbreviations that end sentences.* When an abbreviation ends a sentence, do not add a second period.

- *All-capital abbreviations.* Do not use a period in all-capital abbreviations or after US Postal Service abbreviations of state names.

ALL-CAPITAL ABBREVIATIONS				US POSTAL SERVICE ABBREVIATIONS
NATO	FBI	IQ	CAT scan	CA
UNESCO	USA	COD	BA	MA
NAACP	NRA	IOU	PhD	TX

3 ▪ Writing about literature

When citing a passage from a literary work, use a period with no intervening spaces between the divisions of the work.

Hamlet 3.2.16–23 or *Hamlet* III.ii.16–23 [act, scene, lines]

Paradise Lost 10.55–57 or *Paradise Lost* X.55–57 [book, lines]

4 ▪ Avoiding unnecessary periods

- *Paper titles.* Do not use a period after the titles of your papers, even if they are complete sentences.

- *Second periods.* When an abbreviation ends a sentence, do not add a second period.

The shipment will be delivered by 9 a.m./

- *Sentence within a sentence.* Do not use a period after a sentence within a sentence.

"Cure the disease and kill the patient" was a statement made by Francis Bacon, not Benjamin Franklin.

By 1893, fewer than a thousand buffalo remained in the United States (at the beginning of the century there had been 20 million).

33b Use a question mark to signal questions, requests, and doubts

1 ▪ Signaling questions

Use a question mark after direct questions.

How long did Henry David Thoreau live at Walden Pond**?**

Do not use a question mark after indirect or summarized questions. (See 38a; for ESL, see 32d1.)

She asked when the order would be delivered?

You may use question marks after questions in a series even when they are not complete sentences.

> Will reducing income taxes stimulate savings**?** Encourage investment**?** Weaken social programs**?** Enlarge the federal budget deficit**?**

2 ■ Signaling expressions of doubt

Use a question mark to signal doubt.

> Professor Isaacs is not giving a final exam this semester**?**

3 ■ Signaling polite requests

Use a question mark after a polite request phrased as a question.

> Will you please send me an admissions application**?**

4 ■ Punctuating a question within a sentence

When a question within a sentence is followed by other words, put a question mark after the question and a period at the end of the sentence.

> "What time does the play begin**?**" he asked**.**

33c Use an exclamation point for an outcry, emphasis, and irony

1 ■ An outcry

> "A horse**!** A horse**!** My kingdom for a horse**!**" cried the desperate king.

2 ■ An expression of emphasis

> Alderman Paddy Bauler became famous for declaring, "Chicago ain't ready for reform**!**"

3 ■ An expression of irony

> Standing in the mud, shivering in the rain, she muttered, "I keep reminding myself that this is the vacation of a lifetime**!**"

Note: Avoid overusing exclamation points. They rarely appear in academic writing, especially in serious informative writing. Even in personal or narrative writing, too many will create a melodramatic or false tone.

EXERCISE 33.1   Editing End Punctuation

Edit the following sentences to correct errors in the use of periods, question marks, and exclamation points. If a sentence is correct, write "correct" after it. See the answers in the appendix.

1. Was Thomas Jefferson the first to declare that human beings have the right to "life, liberty, and the pursuit of happiness?"

33.2
Using end
punctuation:
Exercises

2. Because most of the Earth is covered in a liquid mantle, science writer Dava Sobel says a more appropriate name for our planet would be "Water".

3. According to one medical professor, laughter has such powerful health benefits that if it were bottled "it would require FDA approval."

4. The Japanese fliers began their surprise attack on Pearl Harbor at 7:50 a.m. and concluded their devastating bombardment by 10 a.m..

5. Most Americans believe that the federal government has hidden proof of UFOs from the public (a surprising twenty percent believe UFOs represent alien life forms.).

34 The Comma

34a Use a comma before a coordinating conjunction (*but, and*) that links independent clauses

When the coordinating conjunctions *and, but, or, nor, so, for,* and *yet* link independent clauses—word groups that can be punctuated as complete sentences—they are preceded by a comma. (To identify independent clauses, use the yes/no test in the "How to Edit Sentence Fragments" box, pp. 91–92.)

Groups of sharks attack their prey ferociously, but they never bite one another.

If the meaning of a compound sentence is clear and the independent clauses are short, you may omit the comma before the conjunction.

The whistle bellowed once and the boat left the dock.

Do not use a comma before conjunctions that link phrases or dependent clauses. (To learn to identify phrases and dependent clauses, see 10a and b.)

The musicians played sad songs marching to the funeral/but joyful songs

on their return.

[The *but* in this sentence joins two phrases, *sad songs . . . but joyful songs . . .* , so the comma is unnecessary.]

WRITING IN THE USA Comma Usage

Comma usage varies from language to language, and even among varieties of English (American, British, Indian, and so on). When writing for U.S. readers, follow the guidelines in this chapter.

34b Use a comma after introductory words

34.1
Commas:
Web link

Use a comma to set off an introductory word, phrase, or dependent clause from the rest of the sentence. (To learn to identify phrases and clauses, see 10a and b.)

> Unfortunately, exotic species introduced to new habitats often threaten native species.

> Growing up in Africa, she had been entertained by storytellers of all kinds.

> After Harriet Tubman escaped the South, she became a "conductor" on the Underground Railroad that carried slaves north.

You may omit the comma following a brief introductory phrase or clause.

> By noon the storm had passed.

But be sure to use commas to prevent misreading.

> When Carol returned , her baby's joyful smile greeted her.
>   ∧

34c Use a comma between items in a series

Use a comma to separate three or more words, phrases, or clauses written as a series. The Modern Language Association and the American Psychological Association require a comma before the conjunction preceding the last item in the series.

> Winter drivers should carry a scraper, shovel, sand, flares, extra washer fluid, and a blanket.

Note: If one or more items in a series contain internal punctuation, such as commas, use a semicolon between items. (See 35c.)

34d Use a comma between coordinate adjectives but not between cumulative adjectives

1 ▪ Using a comma between coordinate adjectives

Two or more adjectives are **coordinate** if each one modifies the noun by itself. Use a comma after each adjective to signal its separate function.

> Muhammad Ali was a **skilled, fierce, imaginative** boxer.

[Each adjective—*skilled, fierce, imaginative*—modifies *boxer* by itself.]

34.2
Proofread-
ing for
comma
errors:
Exercises

2 ■ Avoiding a comma between cumulative adjectives

Two or more adjectives are **cumulative** if each one modifies all the words that follow it, adjectives and noun together. Because meaning accumulates as the phrase unfolds, do not separate the adjectives with commas.

Muhammad Ali was **the most famous war** protestor to refuse military service during the Vietnam War.

[*War* modifies *protestor, famous* modifies *war protestor,* and *most* modifies *famous war protestor.* Meaning accumulates as the phrase unfolds.]

🌐 ESL GRAMMAR NOTE Cumulative Adjectives

In standard English, cumulative adjectives must be placed in a particular order. See 32g3 for guidance.

3 ■ Identifying coordinate and cumulative adjectives

Two tests will help you distinguish between coordinate adjectives and cumulative adjectives.

■ *The* **and** *test.* If you can put *and* between the adjectives, they are coordinate and require a comma between them to signal their separate functions. Consider the two preceding examples: *A skilled and fierce and imaginative boxer* signals coordinate adjectives that require commas to separate them. But you would not write *most and famous and war protestor,* so these are cumulative adjectives not separated by commas.

■ *The reversal test.* If you can reverse the order of the adjectives, they are coordinate and require a comma between them (*skilled, fierce, imaginative boxer* may become *fierce, skilled, imaginative boxer*). But you would not write *war famous most protestor.*

34e Use commas to set off nonessential modifiers; do not use commas to set off essential modifiers

1 ■ Using commas with nonessential modifiers

Nonessential modifiers (also called **nonrestrictive modifiers**) are words, phrases, or clauses that add extra information but are not essential to the basic meaning of a sentence. Omitting nonessential modifiers does not drastically alter the meaning. Use commas to signal their nonessential nature.

Arthur Jensen, **my minister,** has volunteered to head the Heart Fund drive.

[Because it is nonessential, *my minister* is set off by commas.]

The Ferris wheel, **named for the man who invented it,** was first erected in 1892 at the Chicago World's Fair.

[Information about the inventor of the Ferris wheel is nonessential to a sentence about the wheel's first location and is set off by commas.]

Many nineteenth-century pioneers came first to Kansas City, **where one branch of the Oregon Trail began.**

[Information about the Oregon Trail is important but not essential to a sentence about Kansas City, so it is set off by a comma.]

2 ▪ Avoiding commas with essential modifiers

Essential modifiers (also called **restrictive modifiers**) restrict the meaning of the words they modify to a special sense. If they are omitted, the meaning of the sentence changes. To signal their essential nature, do not set off essential modifiers with commas. Consider how commas change the meaning of this sentence:

My brother **who lives in Little Rock** often comes to visit. [essential modifier]

[The modifier *who lives in Little Rock* identifies which of the writer's brothers often comes to visit. Because it is essential to the basic meaning of the sentence, it is not set off by commas.]

My brother, **who lives in Little Rock,** often comes to visit. [nonessential modifier]

[The writer's only brother, who happens to live in Little Rock, often comes to visit. The brother's location is not essential to the basic meaning of the sentence, so it is set off by commas.]

3 ▪ Identifying nonessential and essential modifiers

To tell whether a modifier is nonessential or essential, try reading the sentence without the modifier. If the basic meaning is unchanged, the modifier is nonessential and needs to be set off by commas. If the sentence changes or loses meaning, the modifier is essential and should not be set off. Compare:

Ernest Hemingway's story "Hills Like White Elephants" portrays a couple debating the consequences of an abortion.

Ernest Hemingway's story . . . portrays a couple . . .

[Without the title of the story and *debating the consequences of an abortion,* the sentence has no meaning. These are both essential modifiers not set off by commas.]

If after rereading you're still not sure whether a modifier is nonessential or essential, use these clues.

- Modifiers of proper nouns (see 8a) are usually nonessential and set off by commas.

Nimi speaks Hindi, **the official language of India**.

- Clauses beginning with *although, even though,* and *whereas* are usually nonessential and set off by commas.

The burglar was captured within hours, **even though he was sure he had left no clues**.

- Modifiers of indefinite pronouns such as *anyone* and *something* are usually essential and are not set off by commas.

Anyone **who studies the textbook** can pass this course.

[The clause *who studies the textbook* is essential to identify *anyone* and is therefore not set off by commas.]

- Relative clauses beginning with *that* are essential modifiers and are not set off by commas.

The cars **that require the fewest repairs** have the highest resale value.

- If you can substitute *that* for *who, whom,* or *which,* the clause is an essential modifier and is not set off by commas. (For when to use *that,* see 16d.)

The painter **whom/that** I admire most is Edward Hopper.

- If you can omit *who, whom,* or *that,* the clause is an essential modifier and is not set off by commas.

The painter [**whom**] I admire most is Edward Hopper.

- Concluding adverb clauses beginning with *as soon as, before, because, if, since, unless, until,* and *when* are essential to the basic meaning of a sentence and are not set off by commas.

Students should sign up for flu vaccinations **as soon as they arrive on campus**.

34f Use commas to set off transitions, parenthetical expressions, and contrast statements

1 ▪ Commas with transitions

Set off conjunctive adverbs such as *however* and transitional phrases such as *for example* with commas. (For a complete list of conjunctive adverbs and transitional phrases, see 12b3.)

Most people refuse to think about pain. Some kinds of pain**, however,** are important to recognize and understand.

Some common painkillers have harmful side effects. **For example,** aspirin may cause internal bleeding.

Note: When you connect independent clauses with a transition, use a semicolon before the transition and, usually, a comma following it. (See 35b.)

Professional athletes must often play in pain; **consequently,** they turn to trainers for strong pain suppressants.

If little or no pause follows a transition, you may omit the comma.

We have never planned a long bicycle trip; **therefore** we're asking for your suggestions.

2 ▪ Commas with parenthetical expressions not enclosed in parentheses

Use commas to set off parenthetical expressions that add supplemental or explanatory information. Notice that a parenthetical expression is not necessarily enclosed in parentheses.

Riverboat gambling**, once an example of social decay,** is now a tax resource eagerly sought by politicians.

Beth was the first to arrive**, as usual**.

Note: When the word *too,* meaning "also," appears in the middle or at the end of a sentence, it is usually set off with commas.

Muslims, too, believe that Jesus was born of the Virgin Mary.

3 ▪ Commas with contrast statements

Use a comma to set off statements of contrast or contradiction, usually beginning with *not, nor, never, but,* or *unlike.*

Jan's stepfather**, unlike her father,** is relaxed and jovial.

Mom gave the last piece of pie to Jerry**, never one to refuse an extra dessert.**

34g Use commas to set off signal statements, direct address, and mild interjections

1 ▪ Commas with signal statements

Use a comma to set off a signal statement at the beginning or end of a sentence.

As George Bernard Shaw wrote, "In the arts of peace Man is a bungler."

"I'll do it tomorrow," **Kevin said lazily.**

Do not use a comma if the quotation is the subject or complement of the sentence.

"I shall return," was General MacArthur's vow on leaving the Philippines.

2 ▪ Commas in direct address

Use commas to set off words that signal you are addressing readers directly: names or titles, tag questions, the words *yes* or *no*.

Thank you**, Professor Thoreson,** for writing a recommendation for me.

The book is better than the movie**, don't you think?**

Yes, the overdue books have been returned to the library.

3 ▪ Commas with mild interjections

Use commas to set off mild expressions of feeling.

Well, I'm not surprised to see her receive a promotion.

34h Use commas with titles and degrees, dates, addresses, place names, and numbers

1 ▪ Titles and degrees

Use commas to set off titles or degrees that follow a person's name.

Martin Luther King, **Jr.,** campaigned for peace as well as civil rights.

The keynote address will be given by Jean Payne, **president of Springfield College.**

2 ▪ Dates

In dates, use a pair of commas to set off the year from the rest of the sentence. Do not use commas if the date is inverted or only the month and year are given.

On March 6**, 1837,** General Santa Anna defeated the Texans at the Alamo.

The blizzard of **27 January 1967** was the worst in the state's history.

In **April 1942** the United States began building the Alaskan Highway.

3 ▪ Addresses and place names

Use commas in addresses and place names. Do not use a comma before a zip code.

The regional community center is now located at 238 West Spring, Seneca, IL 61360.

The Women's Christian Temperance Union was founded in Cleveland, Ohio, in 1874.

4 ■ Numbers

In numbers of more than four digits, use commas to divide the numerals into groups of three, counting from the right. The comma is optional in four-digit numbers.

1,466 *or* 1466

186,000

6,286,836

> ### WRITING IN THE USA Commas in Numbers
>
> Unlike many other languages, American English generally does not use commas within street numbers (*6206 Main Street*), ZIP codes (*17701*), telephone numbers (*914-555-4785*), or years (*2005*).

Note: In standard English when units of measure are written as words, use commas to separate feet and inches, pounds and ounces, and so forth.

My Labrador puppy stands **one foot, two inches** tall and weighs **twenty pounds, four ounces.**

34i Use commas to signal omissions and prevent misreading

The hikers took the right fork in the path; their rescuers, the left.

To Paul, Carlos remained a puzzle.

34j Follow these guidelines to use commas with quotation marks, parentheses, and brackets

1 ■ Commas with quotation marks

Place commas inside closing quotation marks, single and double, whether the quotation is a word, phrase, sentence, or several sentences. (See 38b.)

It is "time to stop thinking of wild animals as 'resources' and 'game,'" claims Joy Williams in her argument against hunting.

2 ■ Commas with parentheses and brackets

Place commas outside closing parentheses and brackets.

Caused by an extra number 21 chromosome (three instead of the usual two)**,** Down's syndrome is characterized by mental retardation and a flattened facial profile.

34k Avoid unnecessary commas

1 ■ Unnecessary comma dividers

■ Do not use a comma between a subject and its predicate.

Taxes that communities receive from legalized gambling⁄ are often offset by the losses of local gamblers.

■ Do not use a comma between a verb and its object or complement.

People in their thirties often protest⁄ their limited career choices.

■ Do not use a comma before conjunctions joining phrases or dependent clauses. (To learn to identify phrases and dependent clauses, see 10a and b.)

The coach warned her team that their next opponents were not only tall and fast⁄but also very smart.

■ Do not use a comma before the conjunction *than* in comparison statements.

I'd rather visit the ancient ruins of Egypt and Greece⁄than go to Disney World.

■ Do not use commas between cumulative adjectives or between adjectives and nouns. (See also 32g3.)

Eddie fished all day but caught only one⁄ small⁄ red snapper.

[*One* and *small* and *red* are cumulative adjectives and should not be separated by commas.]

One wrong turn after another led him into difficult, nearly impassable⁄ terrain.

[*Impassable* is an adjective modifying the noun *terrain,* so no comma is needed.]

■ Do not use a comma before a summarized or indirect quotation.

A famous philosopher once wrote⁄that anything worth saying can be said clearly.

2 ■ Unnecessary introductory commas

■ Do not use a comma after *such as* or *like* to introduce a list.

Many people, such as/Arabs, Indians, and southern Europeans, have personal space requirements different from those of northern Europeans.

- Do not use a comma after the subordinating conjunction *although*.

  The mayor continued the sprinkler ban, although/rain had fallen weekly for a month.

- Do not use a comma after a phrase that opens an inverted sentence.

  On the highest hill/stands a house designed by Frank Lloyd Wright.

- Do not use commas before the first or after the last item in a series (but do use commas between items in a series).

  Laura's favorite flowers are/hollyhocks, day lilies, and irises.

  Someone who enjoys camping, hiking, and cycling/shouldn't mind a little rain.

3 ▪ Unnecessary commas to set off essential modifiers

Do not use commas to set off modifiers essential to the basic meaning of a sentence.

The friends/whom Lacy trusted the most/repaid her faith in them.

[Readers need the modifier *whom Lacy trusted the most* to know which friends are referred to. It is essential and not set off by commas.]

The wagon train crossed the river/where it was shallowest.

[Readers need the modifier *where it was shallowest* to know where the wagon train crossed the river. It is essential and not preceded by a comma.]

4 ▪ Unnecessary commas with other punctuation

- Do not use a comma before parentheses, only afterward.

  Although critics of rock and roll often quote Plato/(who favored the strict regulation of music), few have examined his argument carefully.

- Do not use a comma after a question mark or exclamation point.

  "What's a thousand dollars?"/asked Groucho Marx. "Mere chicken feed. A poultry matter."

EXERCISE 34.1 Editing Commas

Add necessary commas in the following sentences. If a sentence does not require additional punctuation, write "correct." See the answers in the appendix.

1. Ralph reached for his pocket calculator which he carried everywhere and quickly added up the long list of figures.

2. The Luddites were early 19th-century weavers who wrecked their looms because they believed the machinery responsible for their low wages and unemployment.

3. Francis Bacon said "Some books are to be tasted others to be swallowed and some few to be chewed and digested."

4. Des Moines Iowa the state capital was founded in 1843 and originally called Fort Des Moines.

5. Some of the most intricately designed oriental rugs actually come from Kurdistan a region of northern Iraq and southern Turkey.

34.3
Punctuating
with
commas:
Exercises

EXERCISE 34.2 Editing for Missing and Misused Commas

Add necessary commas and delete unnecessary commas in the following sentences. If a sentence requires no changes, write "correct." See the answers in the appendix.

1. Most people associate bagpipes with Scotland but, they originated in Greece and Asia.

2. If the "big bang" theory is correct the universe is about 10 billion years old.

3. According to the Catholic doctrine of papal infallibility, the Pope is an imperfect human being but he cannot lead the church into religious error.

4. Air pollution is severe in Albuquerque, because the city is located in a broad shallow valley.

5. To challenge someone in authority, who disagrees with me, is not easy to do.

35 The Semicolon

35a Use a semicolon to join closely related independent clauses

35.1
Semicolons:
Web link

A semicolon usually links grammatically equal word groups. Use it in place of a comma and coordinating conjunction (*and, but, so, or, nor, for, yet*) to link independent clauses closely related in subject or structure. To identify independent clauses, use the yes/no test. (See the "How to Edit Sentence Fragments" box, pp. 91–92.)

> Few people will admit to being superstitious; it implies naiveté or ignorance.
>
> (Robertson Davies, "A Few Kind Words for Superstition," *Newsweek*)

Note: Joining independent clauses with a comma instead of a semicolon creates an error known as a comma splice. (See 12a.)

Students of the 1960s were activists and dreamers; students of the 1990s were less idealistic and more practical.

35b Use a semicolon before a conjunctive adverb or transition joining independent clauses

Conjunctive adverbs and transitional phrases such as *however* and *for example* are linking words. (For a complete list, see 12b3.) Use a semicolon before conjunctive adverbs or transitions that link independent clauses. To use a comma instead is to make a comma splice. (See 12a.)

The runner slid into second base certain he was safe; however, the umpire called him out with a swift jerk of his thumb.

There is still no treatment for smallpox; even so, a vaccination against the disease has been in use since 1796.

Note: If the conjunctive adverb or transition comes in the middle of the second independent clause, use a semicolon between clauses and enclose the conjunctive adverb or transition with commas.

The runner slid into second base certain he was safe; the umpire, however, called him out with a swift jerk of his thumb.

35c Use a semicolon between items in a series if one or more items contain internal punctuation

Use semicolons to separate internally punctuated items in a series.

Exotic species posing severe threats to native American wildlife are the ruffe, which may drive the Great Lakes perch to extinction; the Muscovy duck, which has ousted the Florida mallard; Mute Swans, which kill related species' goslings and ducklings; and the starling, which has displaced flickers, wrens, swallows, and bluebirds.

35d Avoid unnecessary semicolons

1 ■ Avoiding semicolons between dependent and independent clauses

Do not use a semicolon between a dependent clause and the rest of the sentence. Use a comma instead. (See 34b.) To identify dependent and independent clauses, use the yes/no test. (See the "How to Edit Sentence Fragments" box, pp. 91–92.)

Although New Jersey has numerous oceanside resorts, they are too close to home for many easterners.

2 ▪ Avoiding semicolons between a nonessential dependent clause and the rest of the sentence

If a nonessential dependent clause ends a sentence, precede it with a comma, not a semicolon. (See 34e1.)

The smallpox vaccine was developed by Edward Jenner, who discovered that a mild infection acquired from cows would give immunity to smallpox.

3 ▪ Avoiding semicolons between an appositive and the word it explains

Do not use a semicolon between an appositive (a nounlike modifier) and the word it explains. Use a comma instead. (See 34e1.)

To build furniture, you need a doweling jig, a tool for drilling straight holes.

4 ▪ Avoiding semicolons between a list and the words that introduce it

Do not use a semicolon to introduce a list. Use a colon instead. (See 36a.)

States now use five methods of execution: hanging, the firing squad, the electric chair, the gas chamber, and lethal injection.

5 ▪ Avoiding semicolons between independent clauses linked by a coordinating conjunction

Do not use a semicolon between independent clauses linked by a coordinating conjunction such as *and* or *but.* Use a comma instead. (See 34a.)

The gap between the highest- and lowest-paid workers has been

increasing for years, so the President has proposed an increase in the minimum wage.

35.2
Using
commas
and
semicolons:
Exercises

EXERCISE 35.1   Editing Commas and Semicolons

Edit the following sentences for the misuse of commas and semicolons. If a sentence is correct, write "correct" after it. See the answers in the appendix.

1. The old log cabin stood five feet from the ground; on a stone foundation; its log steps leading up to an open doorway.

2. Vince pulled into the gas station for a fill-up; and as he stood at the pump, his eyes fell on the huge dent in his rear fender.

3. People with heart disease are strongly cautioned to control their anger; instead of venting their emotions and risking a heart attack.

4. According to the Center on Addiction and Substance Abuse, women get drunk more quickly than men; become addicted to drugs more quickly; and develop substance-abuse illnesses more quickly.

5. The contest for energy resources is now the primary cause of international conflicts; in the near future, however, the lack of safe drinking water will increasingly cause strife between thirsty nations.

36 The Colon

36a Use a colon following an independent clause to introduce a list, quotation, appositive, or explanation

36.1
Colons:
Web link

A colon signals that what follows it depends on what comes before it. It is a compressed way of saying "for example," "that is," or "this is what I mean." To punctuate correctly, use a colon *only* if you can put a period where you wish to put a colon.

Many national parks are threatened with air pollution, for example, Grand Canyon, Shenandoah, and Yellowstone.

[You would not put a period following *for example,* and so a comma should replace the colon.]

1 ■ Using a colon with a list

Use a colon to introduce and emphasize a list or series.

It is by the goodness of God that we have in our country three unspeakably precious things: freedom of speech, freedom of conscience, and the prudence never to practice either.

(Mark Twain, from *The Perpetual Pessimist*)

2 ■ Using a colon with a quotation

Use a colon to introduce a quotation.

Animal trainer Vickie Hearne describes the brutal brevity of life in the wild: "In Africa, 75 percent of the lions cubbed do not survive to the age of two. For those who make it to two, the average age at death is ten years."

3 ▪ Using a colon with an appositive

Use a colon to emphasize an appositive that explains a preceding noun.

Many hyperactive children eat only one kind of food: junk food.

4 ▪ Using a colon with an explanation

Use a colon to introduce an explanation of what comes before.

Humanity does not pass through phases as a train passes through stations: Being alive, it has the privilege of always moving yet never leaving anything behind.

(C. S. Lewis, from The Allegory of Love)

Note: If a complete sentence follows a colon, begin with a capital letter.

36b Use a colon to separate related formal elements

1 ▪ Using colons in business letters

Use a colon to separate the salutation from the body of a business letter. (See also 62a.)

Dear Director of Admissions:

2 ▪ Using colons in bibliographic citations

In bibliographic citations, use a colon to separate the title from the subtitle, and the city of publication from the name of the publisher.

Lopez, Barry. *Arctic Dreams: Imagination and Desire in a Northern Landscape.* New York: Scribner's, 1986.

3 ▪ Using colons with numbers

Use a colon to separate hours and minutes (9:36 A.M.), ratios (15:1), volume and page numbers (4: 98–115), and biblical chapter and verse (John 3:16).

Note: The Modern Language Association requires a period instead of a colon in biblical citations (John 3.16).

36c Avoid unnecessary colons

A colon usually is appropriate if you can place a period where you intend to use the colon. Do not use a colon where no punctuation should be used.

1 ■ Avoiding colons after *such as, like,* or *including*

Do not use a colon after words that introduce items in a series.

The children took whatever they could eat while they played, such as⫽

candy bars, carrots, and sandwiches.

[Because the sentence cannot end with *such as,* a colon is inappropriate. Do not separate a list from an introductory phrase.]

2 ■ Avoiding colons between a verb and its object or complement

Do not use a colon to separate a verb from its object or complement. (To identify objects and complements, see 9c and d.)

Two unnecessary animal experiments are⫽ poisoning rats to test drugs

and injuring monkeys to test helmet safety.

3 ■ Avoiding colons between a subordinating conjunction and the clause that follows

Do not use a colon to introduce a clause following a subordinating conjunction. (For a list of subordinating conjunctions, see 8g3.)

Researchers report that⫽ the death penalty does not deter murderers.

4 ■ Avoiding colons between a preposition and its object

Do not use a colon to separate a preposition and its object. (For a list of prepositions, see 8f.)

Jason slowly packed his collection of⫽ tapes, posters, and comic books.

EXERCISE 36.1   Editing Commas, Semicolons, and Colons

Edit the following sentences for the misuse of commas, semicolons, and colons. If a sentence is correct, write "correct." See the answers in the appendix.

36.2
Punctuating
with
commas,
semicolons,
and colons:
Exercises

1. Barbara's allergies make her so sensitive to food that she can eat only one kind; beige food.

2. Some of the most dangerous sports include: climbing, cycling, swimming, skiing, and football.

3. Where is it stated in the Constitution that: all Americans are guaranteed happiness and a life as comfortable as the next person's?

4. The best description of big-city life is the definition of *pluralism:* "a condition of society in which numerous ethnic, religious, or cultural groups coexist."   *(continued)*

5. Victims of AIDS suffer a variety of symptoms, such as: coughing, shortness of breath, skin lesions that do not heal, seizures, cramps, diarrhea, and memory loss.

37 The Apostrophe

37a Use an apostrophe to signal possession by nouns and indefinite pronouns

37.1
Apostrophes:
Web link

As a grammatical term, **possession** refers not only to actual possession or ownership, as in *the student's book,* but also to relationships, associations, amounts, and duration: *the flower's scent, Pike's Peak, your money's worth,* and *two days' journey.* To decide whether a noun should be written as a possessive, use two tests.

■ *The **of**-**phrase** test.* Try to turn the words into an *of* phrase: *the scent of the flower, the worth of your money, a journey of two days.* (To learn when to use an apostrophe for the possessive and when to use an *of* phrase, see 32f.)

■ *The **noun-plus-noun** test.* In most cases, if two nouns appear together and the first noun ends in *-s,* add an apostrophe to the first noun to make it possessive: *students* (noun) + *book* (noun) = *student's book; Pikes* (noun) + *Peak* (noun) = *Pike's Peak.* (To learn to identify nouns, see 8a.)

1 ■ Forming possessives of singular nouns

To form the possessive of singular nouns, add an apostrophe plus *s* (*-'s*):

sun's rays	television's influence	Dr. Benton's lecture
girl's bicycle	Aesop's fables	Arkansas's governor
hour's work	John Keats's poems	IBM's new computer

Exceptions:

■ Awkward pronunciation. Add an apostrophe but no *-s* to singular possessive nouns that already end with an *s* or *z* sound if pronunciation would be awkward: *Moses' commandments, Aristophanes' plays, Joan Rivers' wisecracks.*

■ Institutional and place names. The apostrophe is frequently omitted from institutional and place names: *Nags Head, North Carolina; Grants Pass, Oregon; Governors Island, New York; The Boys Club; Teachers College of Columbia University.* Check a dictionary, an atlas, or encyclopedia.

2 ■ Forming possessives of plural nouns

To form the possessive of plural nouns ending in *-s,* add only an apostrophe.

planets' orbits	players' coach	drivers' licenses
machines' noise	the Johnsons' car	Yankees' uniforms

Note: To form the possessive of irregular plural nouns, add an apostrophe plus *s* (*-'s*): *children's games, women's health, news media's accuracy.*

3 ■ Forming possessives of indefinite pronouns

Most indefinite pronouns (*everyone, everybody, no one, something*) are singular. To form the possessive, add *-'s.* (For a complete list of indefinite pronouns, see 8b4.)

To **no one's** surprise, the Bears won the championship game.

A democratic government must represent **everyone's** interest.

4 ■ Indicating joint and individual possession

To signal joint possession, make only the last noun possessive. To signal individual possession, make each noun possessive.

■ Joint possession:

Ben and Jerry's Ice Cream

Carol, Shuli, Mari, and Yae's group project

■ Individual possession:

Mai's and **Anwer's** skis

Plato's and **Gandhi's** philosophies

5 ■ Forming possessives of compound nouns

To form the possessive of compound nouns, add *-'s* to the last word if it is singular, *-s'* to the last word if it is plural.

my **father-in-law's** birthday

the **Board of Supervisors'** report

37b Use an apostrophe to signal contractions

Use an apostrophe to signal omissions of letters or numbers.

It's [it is] not easy to read by candle light.

Rock **'n'** [and] roll sounds best when the volume is turned way up.

The blizzard of **'79** [1979] was not as bad as the blizzard of **'67** [1967].

Note: Contractions are inappropriate in most serious academic writing.

Note: The possessive pronouns *its* and *your* are not contractions and do not take an apostrophe. (See 37d3.)

its

The tree is losing it's leaves because of a fungus.
                 ∧

Your

~~Your'~~ father was the last to hear about the accident.
   ∧

37c Use an apostrophe plus *s* for plural letters and plural words used as words

Conventions vary regarding the use of the apostrophe to form the plurals of letters and of words used as words. The Modern Language Association guideline is to use *-'s*.

The *A's* and *B's* on this assignment outnumber the *C's* and *D's*.

Let's finish this project without any more *if's*, *and's*, or *but's*.

Note: Individual letters and words used as words are italicized or underlined.

37d Avoiding unnecessary apostrophes

1 ▪ Avoiding apostrophes with plural numbers and abbreviations

Conventions vary on the use of apostrophes with plural numbers and abbreviations. The Modern Language Association guideline is to omit the apostrophe.

The winning hand was a pair of **8s** and three **3s**.

This season Berenson has a batting average in the high **280s**.

In the **1990s**, not even people with **MAs**, **PhDs**, and high **IQs** could be sure of finding jobs.

Two **IDs** are required for customers to pay by personal check.

2 ▪ Avoiding apostrophes with possessive pronouns

Possessive personal and relative pronouns (*hers, his, its, ours, theirs, yours, whose*) do not take an apostrophe.

The hurricane unleashed it's wind and rain on the coastal lowlands.

[*It's* is the contraction of *it is*.]

whose

~~Who's~~ backpack is sitting under the desk?
  ∧

[*Who's* is the contraction of *who is*.]

3 ▪ Avoiding apostrophes with nouns that are not possessive

Not all nouns that end in *-s* take an apostrophe. Use the apostrophe only when it is required to signal possession.

The Bates╱ family is away on vacation.

[*The Bates* do not possess the family; *Bates* is the family name.]

The decision of the judges╱ will be final.

[Possession is signaled by the preposition *of*; the apostrophe is unnecessary.]

4 ▪ Avoiding possessives that sound like contractions

Do not confuse contractions with similar-sounding pronouns that do not take an apostrophe: *you're* (*you are*) with *your, it's* (*it is*) with *its, they're* (*they are*) with *their, who's* (*who is*) with *whose.*

You're
~~Your~~ going to thank me for this advice.
      ⌄

EXERCISE 37.1   Editing Apostrophes

Edit the following sentences to correct errors in the use of apostrophes. If a sentence is correct, write "correct." See the answers in the appendix.

37.2
Editing
apostrophes:
Exercises

1. Greshams Law refers to peoples preference for spending overvalued currency and hoarding undervalued currency.

2. Stacys sister works as a field investigator in the FBIs Dallas office.

3. The summers of 88 and 89 were Americas driest since the dust-bowl years of the Great Depression.

4. The childrens delighted cries echoed from the playground.

5. The Old Mill Inn's best menu items are fresh catfish, steak, and taco's.

38 Quotation Marks

38a   Enclose direct quotations in double quotation marks (" ")

Use double quotation marks at the beginning and end of all word-for-word quotations of speech or writing.

38.1
Quotation
marks:
Web link

In his inaugural address President John F. Kennedy redefined citizenship in a democracy: **"**Ask not what your country can do for you; ask what you can do for your country.**"**

Henry David Thoreau emphasizes the message of *Walden* with one word: **"**Simplicity, simplicity, simplicity!**"**

WRITING IN THE USA Punctuating Quotations

Different languages punctuate quotations following different rules and using various punctuation marks. Even British and American English differ in their rules for single and double quotation marks and the placing of quotation marks with other punctuation. If English is not your primary language, and you have learned British English, you will want to pay particular attention to the following rules.

1 ▪ Avoiding quotation marks in indirect quotations

Do not use quotation marks around indirect (summarized) quotations.

According to President Kennedy, Americans should not ask what their country can do for them; they should ask what they can do for their country.

2 ▪ Using quotation marks in paragraphing

In writing dialogue, begin a new paragraph to signal a change in speaker, no matter how brief each person's speech.

> "Girl number twenty," said Mr. Gradgrind, squarely pointing with his square forefinger, "I don't know that girl. Who is that girl?"
> "Sissy Jupe, sir," explained number twenty, blushing, standing up, and curtseying.
> "Sissy is not a name," said Mr. Gradgrind. "Don't call yourself Sissy. Call yourself Cecilia."
>
> (Charles Dickens, from *Hard Times*)

If one person's speech runs for two or more paragraphs, open each paragraph with quotation marks, but do not use closing quotation marks until the end of the speech.

When quoting from several sources to prove or explain a point, as in research writing, introduce each quotation with its own signal statement, but group the quotations in a single paragraph. (See 50c3.)

3 ▪ Quoting accurately

When quoting someone's actual spoken or printed words, quote accurately, even if the quotation contains a factual or grammatical error. To note your recognition of such error, follow the guidelines in 39c3.

38b Follow these guidelines to punctuate quotations correctly

1 ▪ Periods and commas

Put periods and commas inside quotation marks, even when the quotation is less than a sentence.

"Writing is a very painful process," says essayist and novelist Tom Wolfe. "I never understand writers who say it's enjoyable."

The Supreme Court ruled that school integration should proceed "with all deliberate speed."

Note: When you use the Modern Language Association's in-text documentation format, place the period after the quotation marks and parenthetical documentation. (See 52a.)

Flannery O'Connor's "Greenleaf" is a story dramatizing "the divine harmony that embraces nature, man, and God" (Asals 330).

2 ■ Colons and semicolons

Put colons and semicolons outside quotation marks.

Murphy's Law ought to be called "Murphy's Threat": If something can go wrong, it will.

Shakespeare wrote, "All the world's a stage"; if he were a member of today's music video generation, he'd write, "All the world's a sound stage."

3 ■ Question marks and exclamation points

Put question marks and exclamation points inside quotation marks if they are part of the quotation. Otherwise, put them outside.

Mark Twain wrote an essay surprisingly titled "Was Shakespeare Famous?"

What famous mystery writer said, "Where there is no imagination there is no horror"?

Note: When you use the Modern Language Association's in-text documentation format, punctuate quoted questions and exclamations according to the preceding guidelines, followed by the parenthetical documentation and a period.

Mr. Lengel, the antagonist of John Updike's short story "A & P," gives the hero one last chance when he asks, "Did you say something, Sammy?" (133).

4 ■ Introducing quotations

To introduce a quotation, use a colon, comma, or no punctuation, whichever is appropriate to the context. (See also 50c and d.)

■ *Introductory independent clauses.* Use a colon after an introductory independent clause.

Sue Hubbell explains that bees communicate by dancing: "Bees tell other bees about good things such as food or the location of a new home by patterned motions."

- *Opening signal statements.* After opening quotation signals like *he said* or *she observes,* use a comma.

  Scientist Carl Sagan warns, "There are severe and previously unanticipated global consequences of nuclear war—subfreezing temperatures in a twilit radioactive gloom lasting for months or longer."

- *Capitalizing quotations following signal statements.* Capitalize the first words of dialogue and other quotations that are complete sentences, as in the preceding example. Otherwise, do not capitalize. (See also 40a.)

- *Closing signal statements.* When a signal statement closes a quotation, use a comma after the quotation unless it ends with a question mark or exclamation point.

  "The other America, the America of poverty, is hidden today in a way that it never was before," **argues** social critic Michael Harrington.

  "Dr. Livingstone, I presume?" **asked** explorer H. M. Stanley when he found the doctor on the shores of Lake Tanganyika in 1871.

- *Quotations woven into a sentence.* Use no punctuation before a quotation that is the object or complement of a verb, a clause following a subordinating conjunction, a modifying phrase, or the object of a preposition.

  The American Psychological Association **notes that** "80% of people who fall victim to depression fail to recognize the illness."

  Describing the origins of barbecue, poet Amiri Baraka praises West Africans **for** "developing the best sauce for roasting whole oxen and hogs, spicy and extremely hot."

5 ▪ Interrupted quotations

If you interrupt a quotation with a signal statement in the middle of a sentence, set off the statement with commas.

  "God is subtle," **quipped Einstein,** "but he is not malicious."

If you interrupt a quotation at the end of a complete sentence, use a comma before the signal statement and a period following. Then resume the quotation.

  "We are born knowing how to use language," **remarks Lewis Thomas.** "The capacity to recognize syntax, to organize and deploy words into intelligible sentences, is innate in the human mind."

6 ▪ Long quotations

Guidelines for presenting long quotations vary. For the MLA guidelines, see 50d; for the APA guidelines, see 46e4.

38c Use single quotation marks (' ') only to enclose quotations within quotations

As Phillip walked into trigonometry class, he muttered, "Someone should post a sign outside this room that quotes Dante: 'Abandon hope, all ye who enter here.' "

Note: Some writers assume that quotations of single words or brief phrases should be enclosed with single quotation marks. Not so. Use single quotation marks only for quotations within quotations.

Note: If you must quote a passage that contains a quotation, alternate quotation marks: double, single, double ("" ' . . . '""). Be sure to use as many closing as opening quotation marks.

Kerry continued, "Then Lisa whispered, 'Don't forget the old saying, "If at first you don't succeed, try, try again." ' "

38d Use quotation marks to enclose the titles of short works

Use quotation marks around the titles of magazine and newspaper articles, essays and book chapters, short stories, poems, songs, and episodes of radio and television programs.

Nathaniel Hawthorne's "Young Goodman Brown" is the story of what happens to a man who is not as good as he thinks.

At next week's church service, our choir will sing "Amazing Grace."

Note: Italicize or underline the titles of books, plays, long poems, films, television and radio series, and the names of magazines and newspapers. (See 41a.)

38e Occasionally use quotation marks to signal words used in a special sense

Although italics or underlining is the preferred method to signal a word used as a word or in a special sense, you may use quotation marks. Be consistent throughout your writing.

The word "Dutch" in "Pennsylvania Dutch" refers to the *Deutsche*, people from Germany.

The word *Dutch* in *Pennsylvania Dutch* refers to the *Deutsche*, people from Germany.

Note: Foreign words are underlined or italicized. (See 41c.)

38f Avoid unnecessary quotation marks

1 ■ Omitting quotation marks around the titles of your own papers

On the title page or first page of the papers you write, do not put quotation marks around the title unless it is an actual quotation.

2 ■ Avoiding quotation marks for emphasis or slang

Do not use quotation marks for emphasis or slang.

Store owners who sell liquor to teenagers often receive only a ⸻slap on the wrist.⸻

3 ■ Avoiding quotation marks with indirect quotations

Do not use quotation marks with indirect (summarized) quotations.

The lawyer warned the team owner that ⸻his players would sue him for breach of contract.⸻

38.2
Punctuating
quotations:
Exercises

EXERCISE 38.1 Editing Quotations

Make necessary punctuation changes in the following sentences. Consider quotation marks, periods, commas, colons, semicolons, question marks, and exclamation points. See the answers in the appendix.

1. The beggar asked Jeff whether he had any "spare change."
2. "Are these bags yours or his," the ticket agent asked?
3. The funeral director indicated that "cremation was not as expensive as burial."
4. Midwives provide assistance with what is called 'natural childbirth,' a process involving no anaesthesia or surgery.
5. "All rise", the bailiff called out to the courtroom.

39 Other Punctuation Marks

39a Use a dash for a change of thought, parenthetical remarks, or faltering speech

Type a dash as two hyphens, with no space before or after (*word--word*). Use the dash to send the following signals.

COMPUTER TIP Typing *Em* Dashes

Most word processing programs enable you to type a dash, called an **em dash,** distinct in its appearance from a hyphen.

---

1 ▪ Indicating an emphatic change in thought or feeling

Use a dash to signal an emphatic change in thought or feeling.

> I don't make jokes—I just watch the government and report the facts.
> (Will Rogers, "A Rogers Thesaurus," *Saturday Review*)

2 ▪ Setting off parenthetical material

Use a pair of dashes to set off and emphasize parenthetical material.

> It seems possible that more than 3 billion people—almost half of all the humans on earth—would be destroyed in the immediate aftermath of a global thermonuclear war.
> (adapted from Carl Sagan, "The Nuclear Winter," *Parade*)

Note: As the preceding example illustrates, a dash is the strongest mark of parenthetical punctuation: dashes emphasize what they enclose; parentheses and commas deemphasize. (See 39b.)

3 ▪ Displaying lists

Use a dash to introduce a list or to connect a list to the main part of the sentence.

> It is almost a ghost forest, for among the living spruce and balsam are many dead trees—some still erect, some sagging earthward, some lying on the floor of the forest.
> (Rachel Carson, from *The Edge of the Sea*)

> Choosing, defining, creating harmony, bringing that clarity and shape that is rest and light out of disorder and confusion—the work I do at my desk is not unlike arranging flowers.
> (May Sarton, from *Plant Dreaming Deep*)

Note: A colon may also introduce a list (see 36a1); a dash is less formal but more emphatic.

4 ▪ Setting off parenthetical modifiers containing punctuation

Modifiers rename, explain, or add information about nearby words. Often they are set off by commas; but if they contain internal punctuation,

39.1
Punctuation:
Web link

commas may be confusing. Use dashes to set off modifiers that contain internal punctuation.

> The sun—like a hot, luminous magnet—happened to be shining powerfully that antique afternoon.
>
> (Al Young, "Java Jive," *Harpers*)

5 ▪ Indicating faltering speech

Use a dash to signal faltering speech.

> "I—I—don't know how it could have happened," he said, astonished by the accident.

6 ▪ Avoiding unnecessary dashes

Avoid the dash unless you want to create an informal tone. In serious academic writing, prefer the comma, colon, or parentheses. Too many dashes will make your writing unclear or choppy.

A majority of students surveyed—/71 percent /—favored the elimination *(71 percent)*

of classes beginning at 7 a.m.

39b Use parentheses to enclose parenthetical remarks and numbers that mark items in a series

1 ▪ Using parentheses for parenthetical remarks

Use parentheses around supplemental or explanatory information.

> Already we have childproof (and, often, adultproof) containers for virtually everything.
>
> (Philip Sellinger, "Mother Hen," *Newsweek*)

Note: Of all the punctuation marks used to enclose, parentheses signal the greatest separation between the supplemental or explanatory material and the material that precedes and follows it. Unlike dashes, parentheses deemphasize. (See 39a2.)

2 ▪ Using parentheses for numbers or letters to mark a series

Use parentheses to enclose letters or numbers that identify items in a series.

> Touring bicyclists should carry what they need to cope with unpleasant surprises: (1) a ground cloth for their tent, (2) waterproof matches, (3)

water purification tablets, **(4)** twine and tape, **(5)** extra flashlight batteries, **(6)** a folding tire, **(7)** extra inner tubes.

3 ▪ Using parentheses correctly and effectively

▪ *Parentheses and other punctuation.* Put parentheses before commas and semicolons, not after them. (See 34k4.)

Colleges have begun to try new methods of evaluation/(portfolios, self-evaluation, and peer evaluation)' but teachers' grades are still the most common.

▪ *A sentence within a sentence.* If one sentence contains a second sentence enclosed by parentheses, do not open the parenthetical sentence with a capital letter or end it with a period.

Brian Delaney and Rita Kim have the best chances to win the downhill skiing competition (they currently hold the conference records).

▪ *A parenthetical sentence by itself.* When a parenthetical sentence stands by itself, open with a capital letter and close with appropriate end punctuation.

The nursery rhyme about Little Jack Horner pulling a plum from his Christmas pie has historical sources. (The real Jack Horner was a cunning sixteenth-century Englishman who helped King Henry VIII seize land from the Catholic Church.)

▪ *Unnecessary parentheses.* Avoid unnecessary parentheses. Readers tend to skip parenthetical remarks. Parentheses may also make your sentences overly complex and difficult to read.

To test the effects of overpopulation, researchers (in 2001) released a 300-acre small herd of fifteen deer (15) in a forest preserve (it was 300 acres and surrounded by subdivisions).

39c Use brackets for insertions

Use brackets, typed or handwritten, to insert explanations, clarifications, or corrections within direct quotations and to enclose parenthetical material that appears within parentheses.

1 ▪ Using brackets for explanations

Use brackets to insert information that readers need to understand a quotation.

"More than 33,000 cases [of skin cancer] leading to nearly 7,000 deaths are expected this year alone."

2 ▪ Using brackets for clarifications

Use brackets to insert the antecedent nouns that quoted pronouns refer to or to take the place of omitted words.

"Many state legislators view this [tax revenues from riverboat gambling] as free money, but it is not."

"Many French-speaking Canadians believe they will disappear as a distinct people if [Quebec] does not become independent."

[The original version of this quotation is *Many French-speaking Canadians believe they will disappear as a distinct people if the province does not become independent.* For clarity, *the province* was replaced with *[Quebec].*]

3 ▪ Using brackets for corrections

Always quote accurately. If a quotation contains an error, insert *sic* (Latin for "so," "thus," "in this manner") in brackets immediately following the error.

"On his second expedition to the New World, in 1943 [sic], Columbus made landfall in the Lesser Antilles."

4 ▪ Using brackets within parentheses

In research papers that follow the Modern Language Association format for in-text documentation, use brackets to enclose documentation within parenthetical remarks.

Where wolves have been released in the wild, their numbers have increased slowly (see National Park Service reports [Johnson 23 and Lopez 29–36]).

39d Use ellipsis points to signal omissions

Ellipsis is the omission of words, phrases, or sentences from quoted material. Use ellipsis points to signal omissions from direct quotations.

▪ *Spacing.* Type an ellipsis as three evenly spaced periods with a space before and after each period.

"The flock of geese turned . . . in a large circle above the lake."

[The original sentence reads, *The flock of geese turned slowly, sweeping in a large circle above the lake.*]

▪ *End punctuation.* If an ellipsis comes at the end of a quoted sentence, use a period or other end punctuation *before* the ellipsis points and quotation marks following. No space precedes the period or the closing quotation marks.

"The flock of geese turned slowly. . . ."

- *Internal punctuation.* When ellipsis points precede or follow internal punctuation, reproduce the internal punctuation exactly as it appears in the original.

"The flock of geese turned . . . , sweeping in a large circle above the lake."

Note: In the *MLA Handbook for Writers of Research Papers*, 6th edition (2003), the Modern Language Association, with one exception, no longer requires that brackets enclose ellipsis points to signal that they have been added to a quotation. The exception: If you quote part of a passage that already contains ellipsis points, use brackets to enclose your ellipsis points and distinguish them from the author's punctuation.

"The horrible thoughts of impending war. . . . [. . .] I spend my nights in wakeful agitation."

[The original passage reads. *The horrible thoughts of impending war. . . . All those televised images of death and destruction from wars past flood my mind, and I spend my nights in wakeful agitation.* In the original, the opening fragmentary sentence ends in a period plus three ellipsis points. In the revision, bracketed ellipsis points signal the omission of part of the next sentence.]

1 ■ Using ellipsis points in prose quotations

- *Omissions.* Use ellipsis points to signal the omission of an unnecessary word, phrase, sentence, or longer passage from a quotation.

According to essayist Lewis Thomas, "It begins to look **. . .** as if the gift of language is the single human trait that marks us all genetically, setting us apart from all the rest of life. **. . .** Language is, like nest-building or hive-making, the universal and biologically specific activity of human beings."

[The first ellipsis points signal the omission of a phrase; the second ellipsis points, with an added period, signal the omission of a complete sentence.]

To use ellipsis points effectively, follow these guidelines:

- *Grammar.* A quotation containing an ellipsis must be grammatically correct. You would not write *According to essayist Lewis Thomas, "the gift of language . . . setting us apart from the rest of life."* The quotation is not grammatical. Use brackets to insert words that make elliptical quotations grammatically correct: *"the gift of language . . . [sets] us apart from the rest of life."* (See 39c.)

- *Omissions at the beginning and end of a quotation.* Do not use ellipsis points at the beginning of a quotation. Use ellipsis points at the end only if you have omitted words from the end of the last sentence quoted.

According to essayist Lewis Thomas, "language is the single human trait that marks us all genetically. **. . .** "

■ *Fragmentary quotations.* Do not use ellipsis points if the quotation is an obviously incomplete sentence.

> Essayist Lewis Thomas calls language the "biologically specific activity of human beings."

■ *MLA documentation and ellipsis points.* To use the Modern Language Association in-text format to document a quotation that ends in an ellipsis, follow this pattern: space + three periods + quotation marks + a space + parenthetical documentation + a final period.

> According to essayist Lewis Thomas, "language is the single human trait that marks us all genetically . . ." ("Social Talk" 105).

■ *Ellipsis points and end-of-line breaks.* Do not put one or two ellipsis points at the end of one line and the rest on the next. Put all three ellipsis points, and the final period (if needed) on the same line.

2 ■ Using ellipsis points in poetry quotations

When quoting poetry, use three periods to signal the omission of less than a line. To omit a line or more, use a line of spaced periods equal to the length of a complete line.

> The world is too much with us; . . .
> Getting and spending, we lay waste our powers;
>
> . . . .
> We have given our hearts away, a sordid boon!
> > (William Wordsworth)

3 ■ Using ellipsis points to indicate pauses, interruptions, or incomplete thoughts

Use ellipsis points in narratives or dialogue to signal pauses, interruptions, or incomplete thoughts. At the end of a sentence intentionally left incomplete, use the three ellipsis points and omit the final period.

> "It has to be . . . ," he worried, shuffling the papers on his desk. "I'm sure I saw it sitting on top of . . ."

39e Use the slash with poetry and paired words

1 ■ Using slashes with run-in quotations of poetry

Use a slash to separate two or three lines of poetry run into your text. Add a space before and after the slash.

Boasting of his poetic powers, Shakespeare opens one of his most famous sonnets with "Not marble, nor the gilded monuments / Of princes, shall outlive this powerful rhyme."

Note: When quoting more than three lines of poetry, use the indented quotation format. (See 50d.)

2 ■ Using slashes with paired words

Use the slash to separate paired words or abbreviations: *AC/DC, CAD/CAM, true/false, introvert/extrovert.* Do not use a space before or after the slash. Overuse of the slash in this way will make your writing seem finicky or complex. Especially avoid *and/or, he/she, his/hers.*

EXERCISE 39.1   Editing the Dash, Parentheses, Brackets, the Ellipsis, and the Slash

Edit the following sentences to correct errors in the use of the dash, parentheses, brackets, the ellipsis, and the slash. If a sentence is correct, write "correct" after it. See the answers in the appendix.

39.2
Editing
sentence
punctuation:
Exercises

1. Ernest Wynder identifies the paradoxical goal of modern medicine as helping ". . . people die young as late in life as possible."

2. With Shakespeare, I believe that fate is more than the sum of our choices: "There's a divinity that shapes our ends, / Rough-hew them how we will."

3. The terrain of China rises (almost like steps) from the lowlands of the east coast to the high mountains of the west.

4. Reducing welfare payments to poor families, without providing funds for job creation, job training, and day care, will do nothing to reduce the number of poor people.

5. The aurora australis—the southern lights—glow as brightly and dynamically in the southern hemisphere as the aurora borealis glow in the northern hemisphere.

PART VII

Mechanics, Spelling, and Document Design

FOCUS ON . . . Effective Document Formatting

ON THE WEB www.ablongman.com/dodds

Mechanics

40 Capital Letters

40a Capitalize the first word of sentences, deliberate fragments, and lines of poetry

1 ▪ Sentences

The wind blew the snow in swirling circles.

Capitalize the first word of quoted dialogue and other quotations that are complete sentences. But do not capitalize the first word of a quoted sentence you have woven into your own sentence.

Of his duties as president, Harry Truman said, "The buck stops here."

President Harry Truman's motto "the buck stops here" is a vow of personal responsibility many people admire but seldom practice.

If a complete sentence follows a colon, capitalize the first word.

Stars are not all that twinkle in the night sky: The brightest lights may be reflections from satellites or the space shuttle.

Do not capitalize the first word of a parenthetical sentence contained within another sentence.

Western ranchers claim that wolves reintroduced to the wild will kill their livestock (conservation groups, however, have pledged to repay them for losses).

2 ▪ Deliberate fragments

Capitalize the first words of deliberately written sentence fragments.

The Pueblo people believe that lightning strikes bring death to evildoers. **A**nd magical powers to persons of good will.

3 ▪ Poetry

When you quote poetry, capitalize the first word of a line unless the original is not capitalized.

FIRST WORDS CAPITALIZED

Gather ye rosebuds while ye may,
Old time is still a-flying;
And this same flower that
    smiles today
Tomorrow will be dying.
            (Robert Herrick)

FIRST WORDS UNCAPITALIZED

Fiesta laughed with me in San Juan
many compas fired their rifles
   at the stars
music played on radios till dawn
where Venus danced the *cumbiá*
   with Mars
           (Rex Burwell)

40b Capitalize proper nouns and words derived from them

Proper nouns name specific persons, places, and things (*Confucius, Grand Canyon, the US Constitution*). Proper nouns and their derivatives are capitalized. Common nouns name a general category of persons, places, and things (*a religious leader, a canyon, a government document*) and are not capitalized unless they are part of a specific name, as in *Grand Canyon*.

1 ▪ Capitalizing the names and titles of people

- ▪ *The names of people.* Capitalize the names, nicknames, and initials of real and imaginary persons, and words derived from names: *William Shakespeare, Shakespearean, Abraham Lincoln, Honest Abe, the Great Emancipator, Lincolnesque, Dwight D. Eisenhower, Ike, Mickey Mouse.*

- ▪ *Races and nationalities.* Capitalize races, nationalities, geographic groupings of people, languages, and words derived from them: *Asian, Spanish, Hispanic, African, English, Native American, Polish-American.*

- ▪ *Titles of persons.* Capitalize civil, military, religious, and professional titles immediately preceding a personal name: *President Lincoln, General Grant, Pope Paul, Queen Victoria, Senator McCain.* Capitalize titles used in place of names in introductions, toasts, and direct address: *Dear Senator.* Do not capitalize titles following a name: *Abraham Lincoln, sixteenth president of the United States; Victoria, queen of England.*

- ▪ *Kinship names.* Capitalize kinship names followed by a given name or used in place of the name; otherwise, lowercase. Compare these examples:

  This year **Aunt Jennifer** is helping to pay my tuition.

  When she was first married, ~~mother~~ *Mother* worked in a furniture factory.

  Rebecca's ~~Father~~ *father* has just been admitted to the hospital.

- ▪ *Abstractions.* Capitalize abstract words if they have been personified with the attributes of people; otherwise, lowercase.

All **N**ature wears one universal grin.

(Henry Fielding, from *Tom Thumb the Great*)

In **n**ature there are no rewards or punishments; there are consequences.

(Horace Annesley Vachell, from *The Face of Clay*)

2 ▪ Capitalizing religious terms

Capitalize the names of religions, deities, holy persons, holy writings, religious groups and movements, religious events and services, and words derived from these terms.

Islam, Islamic	the Bible	the Crucifixion
the Lord, our Lord	the Ten	Holy Communion
Christ, the Savior	Commandments	the Sermon on
Buddha, Buddhism	Catholicism	the Mount

Note: The adjective *biblical* is usually not capitalized, and the word *bible* is not capitalized when it refers to a book considered authoritative: *When Judy is in the kitchen,* The Joy of Cooking *is her bible.*

3 ▪ Capitalizing cultural and historical terms

Capitalization of cultural and historical terms varies; check your dictionary. In general, follow these guidelines.

▪ *Events and documents.* Capitalize the names of historical, political, and cultural events and documents; capitalize historical periods only when proper nouns or to avoid ambiguity.

Boston Tea Party	the Fall of Rome	*but:* ancient Rome
Reconstruction	the Renaissance	*but:* the sixteenth century
Prohibition	the Roaring Twenties	*but:* the twenties

▪ *Archaeological periods.* Capitalize time periods recognized by archaeologists and anthropologists: *Bronze Age, Neolithic era, Paleolithic times.* Lowercase recent periods: *the space age, the cold war, the civil rights era.*

▪ *Literary and artistic terms.* Capitalize philosophical, literary, and artistic terms derived from proper nouns; otherwise, lowercase: *Platonism* but *existentialism*; a *Gothic novel* but a *horror story.*

4 ▪ Capitalizing geographic regions, place names, and structures

▪ *Countries, regions, continents.* Capitalize geographic names of countries, regions, and continents: *Spain, Europe, the Arctic, the Southern Hemisphere, the South, New England, North Pole, the Badlands of South Dakota, the Texas Panhandle, the New World.* Do not capitalize terms that indicate direction:

When they retire, Peter and Becky plan to move ~~South~~. *south*

- *Place names.* Capitalize the names of cities, counties, states, empires, colonies, locales, and popular place names: *New York's Lower East Side, the City of Brotherly Love, the Loop (Chicago), Cook County, Louisiana, the Buckeye State, Soweto Township, Land of the Rising Sun.*

- *Geographic names.* Capitalize the names of rivers, lakes, oceans, islands, and other specific geographic places: *the Fox River, Lake Itasca, the Indian Ocean, Long Island, the San Juan Mountains, the Nile Delta.*

- *Structures.* Capitalize the names of buildings, streets, highways, bridges, and monuments: *the White House, the Capitol, the Pyramids, New York Thruway, Fifth Avenue, Forty-Second Street, Woodfield Mall.*

Note: Generic place names that precede a name or stand alone are usually lowercase: *the city of New York.*

5 ■ Capitalizing the names of objects and trademarks

- *Celestial bodies.* Capitalize the names of celestial bodies: *Earth, the North Star, Halley's Comet, the constellation of Orion, the Big Dipper.*

- *Means of transportation.* Capitalize the names of ships, trains, aircraft, and spacecraft: USS *Constitution, Voyager II.*

- *Trademarks and brand names.* Capitalize trademarks and brand names but not the generic products associated with them: *Coca-Cola, Coke,* but *cola; Levi's jeans; Kleenex tissue; Tylenol,* but *aspirin.*

Note: The names of software and other high technology products sometimes contain "intercaps," capital letters in the middle of the word. Capitalize where appropriate: *WordPerfect, QuarkXPress.*

6 ■ Capitalizing dates and time designations

Capitalize days of the week, months, and holidays: *Tuesday, July, Halloween, Lent, Ramadan.* Lowercase seasons, decades, centuries, and time zones that are spelled out: *spring, the nineties, the nineteenth century, central daylight time.*

7 ■ Capitalizing the names of organizations

Capitalize the names of companies, civic organizations, institutions, and government agencies: *Hudson's Bay Company, La Chosa Restaurant, United States Congress.* Lowercase generic organization names and plural generic names that follow organization names: *adoption court, the president's cabinet, the legislative branch, Barnes & Noble* and *Borders bookstores.*

8 ■ Capitalizing academic terms

Capitalize the names of specific courses: *I'm taking two literature courses, Literature of the Nonwestern World and Fiction 115.* Lowercase school terms (*spring semester*), generic degrees, and the names of academic subjects except foreign languages: *bachelor's degree, political science,* but *Spanish.*

9 ■ Capitalizing plants and animals and medical terms

Capitalization of the names of plants and animals and of medical terms is varied; see your dictionary. Generally capitalize only a proper noun that is part of the name and lowercase the common noun: *Canada thistle, Virginia creeper, an Irish setter, a Dalmatian puppy, Down's syndrome;* but *cocker spaniel, rheumatic fever.*

10 ■ Capitalizing acronyms

Acronyms are all-capitals abbreviations formed from the first letters of words, such as names of organizations, government agencies, companies, and institutions (*OPEC, IBM*) and technical, scientific, and military terms (*CD-ROM, HIV*).

11 ■ Capitalizing Internet addresses

Some parts of e-mail and Internet addresses (URLs) that follow the single forward slash mark combine upper- and lowercase letters. Capitalize these addresses exactly to ensure reliable Internet communication. For example:

> < http://www.inform.edu/EdRes/ARHU/Depts/English/Programs/ FreshmanWriting > (See also 48a2 and 63a.)

40c Capitalize the first, last, and all major words in the titles of works

1 ■ General guidelines

■ *Titles and subtitles.* Capitalize the titles and subtitles of written works such as books and essays, performances such as plays, visual works such as painting and sculpture, and media productions such as television and radio programs: *Moby-Dick, Adam's Task: Calling Animals by Name,* "The Murders in the Rue Morgue," *Hamlet,* the *Mona Lisa.*

■ *First, last, and major words.* Capitalize first, last, and major words. Do not capitalize articles (*a, an, the*), prepositions (*in, from, on,* and so forth), coordinating conjunctions (*and, but, for, yet, so, or, nor*), and the *to* in infinitives (*How to Repair Almost Anything*).

- *Compounds.* Always capitalize the first word of a compound in a title (*The Modern City-State*); capitalize the second word only if it is important. Compare *Twenty-First Century, A-Bomb,* and *Citizen-Soldier* with *Medium-sized.*

- *Newspapers and news stories.* Do not capitalize, italicize, or underline *the* before a newspaper name.

When I can afford it, I buy ~~The~~ the *New York Times.*

In newspapers usually only the first word and proper nouns are capitalized in a headline: *"Destruction of the last smallpox virus delayed."* But when you give the title of a newspaper article in your writing, capitalize according to the preceding guidelines: *"Destruction of the Last Smallpox Virus Delayed."*

2 ▪ APA guidelines

These are the American Psychological Association guidelines for writing in the social sciences.

- *Titles in the text of your writing.* Capitalize the first and last words. Also capitalize all words of four letters or more and both words of a hyphenated compound: *Landscape, History, and the Pueblo Imagination.* Lowercase articles (*a, an, the*). Also lowercase prepositions and conjunctions of one to three letters (e.g., lowercase *to, in,* and *why,* but capitalize *Toward, Into,* and *When*).

- *Titles in a list of references.* Capitalize only the first word of a title, the first word of a hyphenated compound, the first word after a colon, and proper nouns: *Landscape, history, and the Pueblo imagination; Modern media: The electronic transformation of America.*

40d Avoid unnecessary capital letters

1 ▪ Avoiding capitals with *a, an,* and *the*

Do not capitalize the articles *a, an,* and *the* before proper nouns unless they are the first or last words of a title. Compare these examples:

Gene Kelly did his best dancing in An American in Paris.

Today there are few genuine luxury liners like ~~The~~ the Queen Elizabeth II.

2 ▪ Avoiding capitals for emphasis

Do not capitalize words for emphasis.

greatest

Fantasia is the ~~GREATEST~~ cartoon ever produced by the Disney studio.
                          ^

[Create emphatic sentences by rewording and rearranging: *The greatest cartoon ever produced by the Disney studio is* Fantasia.]

graduated income tax.

The fairest system of taxation is the ~~Graduated Income Tax~~.
                                                          ^

3 ▪ Avoiding capitals with common nouns derived from proper names

Do not capitalize personal, national, or geographic names when used with special meanings. Common nouns derived from proper nouns are often not capitalized: *french fries, diesel engine, venetian blinds,* and *arabic numerals.* But other such common nouns are capitalized: *Homeric poetry* and *Russian dressing.* See your dictionary for correct capitalization.

EXERCISE 40.1 Editing Capital Letters

Edit the following sentences to correct errors in capitalization. If a sentence is correct, write "correct" after it. See the answers in the appendix.

40.1
Capitalizing
correctly:
Exercises

1. Many hispanics would prefer to be referred to as latinos or latinas.

2. My Aunt and Uncle have invited me to live with them if I attend school near their home.

3. This evening's speech on anti-drug legislation will be given by attorney general Alberto Gonzalez.

4. Zachary Taylor, twelfth President of the United States, died of cholera after serving for less than one year.

5. The country town where I grew up was so small that its Downtown consisted of only a General Store and a tiny Post Office.

41 Italics/Underlining

41.1
Using
italics/
underlining:
Web link

 COMPUTER TIP MLA and APA on Italics and Underlining

Virtually all computers have the ability to produce easily recognizable and readable italics. But note that the Modern Language Association recommends underlining, while the American Psychological Association requires italics.

41a Italicize or underline the titles of separately produced works

1 ■ Italicizing written works

Italicize or underline the titles and subtitles of books and pamphlets, the names of magazines and newspapers, and the titles of long poems: *The Invisible Man* or The Invisible Man, the *New York Times* or the New York Times (do not italicize or underline *the* before newspaper titles).

2 ■ Italicizing visual and performing arts

Italicize or underline the titles and subtitles of movies and plays, television and radio programs, paintings, sculpture, and cartoons: *Hamlet* or Hamlet, Picasso's *The Bather* or The Bather, *Star Trek* or Star Trek (specific episodes of television and radio programs are enclosed by quotation marks and neither italicized nor underlined: "The Trouble with Tribbles").

3 ■ Italicizing long musical compositions, recordings, and choreographic works

Italicize or underline the titles of long musical compositions, recordings (records, tapes, and compact discs), and choreographic works: *Sgt. Pepper's Lonely Hearts Club Band* or Sgt. Pepper's Lonely Hearts Club Band, *Swan Lake* or Swan Lake.

Note: Individual song titles are enclosed in quotations marks: "Heartbreak Hotel." Do not italicize, underline, or use quotation marks around musical compositions identified by form, number, or key: Beethoven's Symphony no. 5 in C minor.

4 ■ Exceptions

Do not italicize or underline the titles of sacred writings (including all books and versions of the Bible), the titles of legal documents, descriptive titles, or the titles of your own writing.

the King James Version of the Bible	the Constitution
Genesis	the Declaration of Independence
the Talmud	Lincoln's Gettysburg address
the Koran	Kennedy's inaugural address

41b Italicize or underline the names of ships, trains, aircraft, and spacecraft

Mayflower or Mayflower	*Spirit of St. Louis* or Spirit of St. Louis
Dixie Flyer or Dixie Flyer	*Apollo 8* or Apollo 8

41c Italicize or underline foreign words and phrases

Italicize or underline foreign words or phrases, whether part of a quotation or your own words. Translate or explain foreign words if readers may not understand them.

> Special effects in the ancient Greek theater included the *deus ex machina* ("the god from the machine"), an actor suspended above the stage.

Note: (1) Do not italicize or underline foreign words used frequently in English: ad hoc, cliché, laissez-faire, per diem, sauerkraut, status quo, versus, and so forth. (2) Do not italicize or underline quotations entirely in another language and non-English titles enclosed in quotation marks.

41d Italicize or underline letters, words, and numbers used as nouns

> With grade inflation, *A's* have become as common as *B's* and *C's*.

> Freud's term *narcissism* has nothing to do with the flower; it refers to the myth of the Greek youth Narcissus who fell in love with his reflected image.

> The number *3* has symbolic meaning in many religions.

Italicize or underline the apostrophe or *s* following letters, words, and numbers used as nouns: *p's* and *q's* or p's and q's; *7s* or 7s; *yea's* or *nay's*, yea's or nay's. (See 37c.)

Note: Quotation marks are sometimes used to set off words used as words: "narcissism." (See 38e.)

41e Occasionally italicize or underline for emphasis

> Many travelers are uncomfortable when foreign countries feel like *foreign* countries.

Too many italics or too much underlining will make your writing sound strained or false. Find emphatic words and sentence patterns that emphasize important ideas. (See Chapter 20.)

most offensive

The TV announcers ~~I can't stand most~~ are the gushing, friendly types.

41.2
Editing
italics:
Exercises

EXERCISE 41.1   Editing Italics/Underlining (MLA Style)

Edit the following sentences to correct errors in the use of italics. Underline to signal italics. If a sentence is correct, write "correct" after it. See the answers in the appendix.

1. NASA's Pathfinder spacecraft is scheduled to land on Mars on July 4, 1997.

2. Willa Cather's most popular novel is probably "My Antonia."

3. The conductor directed the violin section to play *con brio,* with fire and vivacity.

4. The Supreme Court's decision in Gideon v. Wainwright gave the right to legal counsel to all accused persons.

5. The first three books of the *New Testament—Matthew, Mark,* and *Luke*—are believed to be based on an earlier account of Jesus's life.

42 Abbreviations

42a General guidelines

1 ▪ Using abbreviations correctly

42.1
Abbrevia-
tions:
Web link

▪ *Parenthetical statements.* In the text of most formal writing, use abbreviations only in parenthetical statements. Compare:

The first insecticides were naturally occurring plant products, **for example**, pyrethrum from dried chrysanthemum flowers.

The first insecticides were naturally occurring plant products (**e.g.**, pyrethrum from dried chrysanthemum flowers).

▪ *Familiar abbreviations.* You may use familiar abbreviations in the text of your writing: *MTV, HIV, CAT scan,* and so forth.

▪ *Repeated terms.* Use abbreviations for repeated names and technical terms. For the first use, write out the term completely and include the abbreviation in parentheses. From then on, use the abbreviation alone.

The **Race Across America (RAAM)** is sponsored annually by the **Ultra-Marathon Cycling Association (UMCA)**. The **UMCA** sponsors other races as well.

▪ *Visual aids and documentation.* Use abbreviations in tables, graphics, notes, and documentation. (See 46b3 and 46c. For MLA documentation, see 53a. For APA documentation, see 55b.)

▪ *E-mail messages.* For guidelines to abbreviations commonly used in informal e-mail messages, see 63a3.

2 ▪ Punctuating abbreviations and acronyms

- ▪ *Personal names.* Use a period and a space following initials: *H. L. Mencken.*

- ▪ *Acronyms.* Do not use periods or spaces between the letters of acronyms: *USA, NY, COD, IQ, NAACP, PhD, rpm.*

- ▪ *Abbreviations ending in lowercase letters.* Use a period after most abbreviations that end in lowercase letters: *intro., e.g., pp., assn.*

42b Titles with personal names

Generally avoid titles in academic writing except to give the qualifications of people whose opinions or information you use. You may use titles more frequently in other kinds of writing.

1 ▪ Abbreviated titles

- ▪ *Titles always abbreviated.* Always abbreviate *Mr.* and *Mrs.,* as in *Mr. Edward O'Connell* or *Mr. O'Connell, Mrs. Judy Chang* or *Mrs. Chang.*

- ▪ *Titles before or after full names.* Abbreviate titles before or after a full name. *Prof. Elizabeth Hull, Gen. Colin Powell, William Wrigley, Sr.; Darlene Clark Hine, PhD.* Do not use abbreviations without names; avoid redundant titles.

My English ~~prof.~~ professor plans to travel the route of the European Grand Tour.

The speaker at this year's honors convocation will be Dr. Barbara Hickey, ~~PhD.~~

2 ▪ Unabbreviated titles

Spell out titles used with surnames (last names) alone: *Professor Hull, General Powell, Doctor Spock, Saint Joan, Senator Simon.* Do not abbreviate given names: not *Benj. Franklin* but *Benjamin Franklin.*

42.2
Acronyms
and
abbrevia-
tions:
Web link

42c Dates and time

1 ▪ Abbreviating date and time markers

Always abbreviate *a.m., p.m., AD, BC, BCE* ("Before the Common Era"), and *CE* ("Common Era"). Place *AD* (*anno Domini,* or "in the year of the Lord") before the date: *AD 1066.* Place *BC* ("before Christ") after the date: *461 BC.* Use date and time markers only with specific times and dates: *3:30 p.m., 1066 CE.*

I study best in the early ~~a.m.~~, when everyone else is asleep. *(morning)*

2 ■ Spelling out months, days, and other time designations

■ *Months and days.* In the text of formal writing, spell out months and days: *Thursday, October 31. Exception:* In notes and documentation, abbreviate days and months except May, June, and July.

■ *Other time designations.* Spell out other time designations in the text of your writing: not *hrs.* but *hours*; not *wks.* but *weeks*; not *Xmas* but *Christmas.*

42d Geographic terms and place names

1 ■ Spelling out place names and addresses in text

In the text of your writing, spell out place names such as the names of continents, countries, states, territories, and cities, as well as the names of streets, cities, and states in addresses: *South America; United States; Michigan; Virgin Islands; Fort Wayne; 150 State Street, Boston, Massachusetts; Herald Square.*

2 ■ Abbreviating place names in notes and documentation

In notes and documentation, abbreviate the names of states, territories, countries, and continents: *MS* for *Mississippi, Ecua.* for *Ecuador, Gr.* for *Greece, No. Amer.* for *North America,* and so forth.

42e Organization names

1 ■ Abbreviating familiar organizations

Use familiar organizational abbreviations in the text of your writing: *IBM, IRS, NBC, YMCA.* Spell out the names of organizations unfamiliar to your readers: *Littman Brothers, Chicago and North Western Railroad, Eastridge Neighborhood Organization,* and so forth. *Incorporated* is usually written *Inc.* or omitted.

2 ■ Abbreviating in notes and documentation

In notes and documentation abbreviate consistently: *Assoc., &, Co., Corp., Bro., Bros., Inc., Ltd., RR,* and so forth: *Capstone Corp., Littman Bros.*

42f Units of measure

1 ▪ Spelling out the names of units of measure in text

Spell out most units of measure in the text of your writing: *inches, cubic foot, gallons, kilograms, meter, megabytes, square yards,* and so forth. Exceptions: *mph, mpg, rpm, Hz (Hertz).*

2 ▪ Abbreviating in technical writing and notes

Abbreviate in technical writing and notes: *in., kg, sq. yds., cu. ft., gal, MB,* and so forth.

3 ▪ Spelling out plural terms

Always spell out the plural terms *inches, feet, meters,* and *gallons: 25 inches, 540 square feet, 47 meters, 300 gallons.*

42g Latin and other scholarly abbreviations

Avoid Latin and other scholarly abbreviations in the text of your writing, unless they appear in material enclosed in parentheses. Such abbreviations are appropriate in tables, notes, and documentation. In text, use the English equivalents of the Latin terms and spell out ordinary English words. (See also 53b and 55b3.)

42.3
Latin
abbrevia-
tions:
Web link

cf.	*confer,* "compare"	i.e.	*id est,* "that is"
e.g.	*exempli gratia,* "for example"	NB, n.b.	*nota bene,* "note well"
		n.d.	no date of publication
et al.	*et alii,* "and others"	p., pp.	page, pages
		UP	University Press
etc.	*et cetera,* "and so forth"	vs., v.	versus, "against"

EXERCISE 42.1   Editing Abbreviations

Edit the following sentences to correct errors in the use of abbreviations. If a sentence is correct, write "correct" after it. See the answers in the appendix.

42.4
Editing
abbrevia-
tions:
Exercises

1. NASA's *Clementine* spacecraft has used radar to locate ice in a giant lunar volcano twice the size of Puerto Rico and higher than Mount Everest.

2. According to Dr. Herman Tyroler, PhD, heart disease is no longer an illness primarily afflicting the affluent.

3. Returning from a night reconnaissance following the Battle of Chancellorsville, Gen. Jackson was wounded by some of his own men, who mistook him for the enemy.

4. One of the most famous photographs of World War II shows Gen. Douglas MacArthur wading ashore upon his return to the Philippines.

5. Computers that will process video signals should have at least one or two gigabytes of memory.

43 Numbers

43a Write numbers as words or figures according to the following guidelines

1 ■ Spelling out numbers that begin a sentence

Spell out numbers that begin a sentence. If the number is large, rewrite or rearrange the sentence. Compare these examples:

Three hundred students visited the state capitol on a field trip.

The strike involves
465 employees ~~are on strike.~~

2 ■ Using Modern Language Association guidelines for numbers

■ *Numbers expressible in one and two words.* Spell out whole numbers from one to ninety-nine, including zero if the figure "0" would be confusing; and spell out large whole numbers expressible in two words: *seven, eighteen, twenty-six, two hundred, fifteen thousand.* Use a hyphen for numbers from twenty-one to ninety-nine.

Note: When using numbers frequently in technical or business writing, use figures for all numbers except those beginning a sentence.

■ *Numbers expressible in more than two words.* Use figures for numbers of more than two words: *340; 1,650; 2,989,000.* Counting from the right, use commas to separate groups of three digits, except in addresses, telephone numbers, dates, and page numbers: *22,560* but *7201 South Locust.*

3 ■ Using American Psychological Association guidelines for numbers

■ Spell out numbers from one to nine.

■ Use figures for numbers over nine: *10; 68; 200; 3,462.*

4 ■ Using numbers in addresses

Always use figures in addresses: *PO Box 14; 15 West Pine Street; 137 North Maplewood; Route 59.*

5 ■ Using numbers for time, dates, and time periods

■ *Time.* Spell out the time except when using *a.m.* or *p.m.*: *seven o'clock in the morning, twelve midnight, half past four, 6:30 a.m., 9:45 p.m.*

■ *Decades.* Spell out decades or use figures: *the nineties, the 90s, the 1990s.*

■ *Centuries.* Spell out centuries; hyphenate when used as adjectives.

In the **twentieth century**, major wars were fought in nearly every decade.

Next semester I'm taking a **twentieth-century** American history course.

■ *Historical dates with abbreviations.* Use figures with *AD, BC, BCE* ("before the Common Era"), and *CE* ("Common Era"): *AD 1066, 461 BC, 32 BCE, 1456 CE.* Notice that *AD* (*anno Domini*) precedes the date, *BC* ("before Christ") follows the date.

■ *Inclusive dates.* For inclusive dates, write both years in full unless they are in the same century: *1895–1910* but *1941–45.*

6 ■ Writing fractions, ordinal numbers, and ratios

■ Common fractions and ordinal numbers. Spell out common fractions (*one-half, two-thirds*) and the ordinal numbers *first* to *ninth.*

Nearly **one-half** of our employees have been sick since the **first** of the year.

■ Decimal fractions, numbers followed by fractions, and ratios. Use figures for decimal fractions, numbers followed by fractions, and ratios: *a 3.8 grade average, a hat size of 7¾, a ratio of 4:1* [or *four to one*].

7 ■ Writing numbers with abbreviations and symbols

Use figures with abbreviations and symbols.

$29.00	4 MB	62 km
14 mi. (miles)	65 mph	4" × 6"
8 hrs.	9 V battery	32°–43°
18% or 18 percent	50 lbs.	35-mm film

Note: According to MLA style, if your writing contains few numbers, spell out one-, two-, and three-word percentages and amounts of money: *twenty-six percent, sixty-nine cents, fifteen dollars, three hundred dollars.*

8 ▪ Writing well-known phrases containing numbers

Generally spell out well-known phrases containing numbers: *the Ten Commandments, the Twelve Apostles, the Fourth of July.*

9 ▪ Writing page numbers and divisions of written works

Use figures for page numbers, book divisions, and acts, scenes, and lines of plays: *page 7, paragraph 47, volume 5, chapter 16; Hamlet 3.2.46* or *Hamlet III.ii.46.*

Note: According to MLA style, to cite inclusive page numbers, give the second page number in full, through *99: 7–23, 85–96.* For higher numbers, give only the last two digits of the second page number unless more are necessary to prevent confusion: *122–34, 200–05, 1220–32* but *98–103, 287–303, 1238–1342.*

In APA style, to cite inclusive numbers, give all the digits of both numbers: *23–32, 458–467, 1152–1158.*

43b When one number modifies another, write one as a figure, the other as a word

1 ▪ Writing large rounded numbers

Write large rounded numbers as a combination of figures and words.

The population of China today is **1.25 billion**.

Congress proposes to cut **$375 million** from the national parks budget.

2 ▪ Writing back-to-back numbers

Write back-to-back numbers as a combination of figures and words.

Last year Maria taught a class with **34 ten-year-olds**.

The order requests **seventy-five 8 × 10 glossy prints**.

Each of the **first 10** customers was given a potted plant.

43c Write related numbers alike, as words or figures

Related numbers that appear together in the same sentence or paragraph should be written alike, as words or figures. If, according to the guidelines in 43a, you write some numbers as figures, be consistent and write all the numbers in your series as figures.

Within two decades, the university has grown from ~~ten thousand~~ to 25,550 students.
_{10,000 ^}

EXERCISE 43.1 Editing Numbers

Edit the following sentences to correct errors in the use of numbers. If a sentence is correct, write "correct" after it. See the answers in the appendix.

43.3
Editing
numbers:
Exercises

1. Montana has imposed a seventy-five mph speed limit on its highways.
2. The most prolific builder of ancient Egyptian temples was probably King Ramses the 2nd.
3. A small Swedish postage stamp has just been sold at auction for more than two million dollars.
4. On a clear night, the average number of stars visible from an American suburb is 250; from the wilderness, the average is 2,500.
5. A Chia bust of the late Jerry Garcia of the Grateful Dead rock group, already seeded to grow green hair, sells for twenty-one dollars, ninety-five cents.

44 The Hyphen

Type a hyphen as one keystroke, with no space before or after: *student-athlete.* Do not confuse a hyphen (-) with a dash (—). (See 39a.) To use hyphens correctly, note how your dictionary lists words:

- Use a hyphen to join words listed with a hyphen (*half-life*).
- If you must divide a multisyllable word listed with dots between syllables, use a hyphen. The word **har•mo•nize** may be divided *har-monize* or *harmo-nize.*
- Compounds listed as two words (*half note*) are written without hyphens.

44a Avoid word division at the end of a line

The Modern Language Association and American Psychological Association guidelines forbid word division at the end of a line, and this is good advice for most writing. If a whole word won't fit, leave the line a little short and begin the word on the next line. Most word-processing programs have automatic word wrap to do this for you.

44.1
Hyphens:
Web link

- Divide already hyphenated words only at the hyphen.

Downhill skiing became more frightening than exciting for me after my ~~bro-~~ *brother-*

in-law
~~ther-in-law~~ broke his leg in a bad fall.

- Divide personal names (1) between first and last names: Mary / Cassatt; (2) after the middle initial: Susan B. / Anthony; (3) if necessary, between initials and the last name: H. L. / Mencken. Never divide between initials.

💻 COMPUTER TIP Breaking Internet Addresses

- If an Internet address (URL) must be broken at the end of a line, divide after a period or a forward slash. Do not use a hyphen.

44b Use a dictionary to hyphenate compounds

A **compound** is a word made up of two or more words. Compounds may be hyphenated (*cross-stitch, cross-reference, cross-examine*), written as separate words (*cross hair, cross section, cross matching*), or written as one word (*crossbow, crossroad, crossword*). Your dictionary will show you the correct forms. If you don't find a compound listed, write the word as two words.

Note: To produce easily readable lines in a column format—in a résumé, brochure, or newsletter—you may have to hyphenate at line ends. In your word processing program, turn on automatic hyphenation and proportional spacing.

Note: Technical terms, especially those associated with computers, are usually written as closed compounds: *logon, homepage, startup*.

44c Hyphenate compound adjectives before a noun but not following a noun

Compare the following pairs of sentences.

I've written a **first-rate** essay. My essay is **first rate**.

Darrell uncorked a **seven-year-old** bottle of wine. Darrell uncorked a bottle of wine that was **seven years old**.

The film received **less-than-enthusiastic** reviews. The reviews were **less than enthusiastic**.

- **-ly *adverbs and adjectives.*** Do not hyphenate a compound modifier consisting of an *-ly* adverb and an adjective.

  Heavily-traveled mountain paths contribute to significant soil erosion.

- **Series of hyphenated adjectives.** In a series of hyphenated adjectives, use the second word of the compound only with the last modifier: *We plan to rent a two-, three-, or four-bedroom cottage for our vacation.*

44d Hyphenate after the prefixes *all-, ex-, great-,* and *self-* and before the suffix *-elect*

all-American athlete	great-grandson	self-respect
ex-mayor	great-great-grandmother	senator-elect

44e Hyphenate spelled-out fractions, numbers from twenty-one to ninety-nine, and combinations of figures and words

one-half	eighty-eight
two-thirds	100-yard dash
seven-eighths	mid-1800s
forty-seven	pre-1960
fifty-two	twentieth-century artist

44f Hyphenate to prevent misreading

Without hyphens, some words might be misread or confused with other words.

> Until a fertilized ovum is implanted in the uterus, it exists in a
>
> *pre-embryonic*
> ~~preembryonic~~ state.
>
> [Without a hyphen, readers may pronounce one long *e* sound instead of a long *e* followed by a short *e*.]
>
> *re-sign*
> The lawyer asked her client to ~~resign~~ the agreement.
>
> [Without a hyphen, *re-sign*, "to sign again," could be confused with *resign*, "to relinquish."]

EXERCISE 44.1   Editing Hyphens

Edit the following sentences to correct errors in the use of the hyphen. If a sentence is correct, write "correct" after it. See the answers in the appendix.

1. The "either/or" fallacy treats a many sided issue as if it had only two sides.

2. Seated in front of me at the theater last night was a well known television actor.

3. The highway overpass cave-in was caused by a moderately severe earthquake.

4. When a reward was offered for information about the escaped prisoners, the police switch-board was flooded with calls.

5. One problem with modern housing developments is that street lay-out prevents the formation of genuine neighborhoods.

44.2
Editing
hyphens:
Exercises

Spelling

45 Spelling

45a Use a word guide, electronic dictionary, or spell checker

As you edit your writing, look up any words that are not part of your everyday writing vocabulary. Use one of the following aids.

🌐 WRITING IN THE USA British Spelling

If English is not your primary language and you studied British English, check with your instructor about the acceptability of British spelling, which differs occasionally from American.

45.1
Spelling:
Web link

1 ■ Using word guides

Word guides such as *Webster's Instant Word Guide* are pocket-sized books that list words without definitions, pronunciations, or grammatical information. If you're sometimes so unsure of a spelling that you can't look up the word, consider a word guide such as *Webster's Pocket Bad Speller's Dictionary,* which lists words by their correct spellings and by their most frequent misspellings.

2 ■ Using electronic dictionaries

Pocket-sized electronic dictionaries such as the *Franklin Wordmaster* and the *American Heritage Dictionary* will confirm an accurate spelling, correct a misspelling, or provide alternatives for unrecognized words you've typed in. Look for one with a word list of at least eighty thousand words.

3 ■ Using spell checkers

If you write with a computer, your word processing program probably has a spell checker. Use it. Many writers who seem to be poor spellers are, in fact, poor typists who forget to run their spell checkers. But even if you use yours faithfully, proofread carefully when you finish to guard against the limitations of these software programs.

🖥 COMPUTER TIP Using Spell Checkers

■ Spell checkers do not distinguish between sound-alike words. If you type *their* when you mean *there,* your spell checker will not correct you.

45.2
Spelling
help:
Web link

- Spell checkers do not correct mistakes that produce correctly spelled words. If you mean to type *band* but type *hand* or *and,* your spell checker will not recognize your mistake.
- Most spell checkers will permit you to add specialized technical terms to the word list. You may also be able to add these and other frequently misspelled words to your word processor's "quick correct" feature.

45b Make a checklist of your spelling errors

Make a personalized checklist of your spelling errors. Buy a small alphabetically arranged address book or a pocket notebook. Find out which words you misspell and list them there. Write the word down, first as you misspelled it (to help you spot errors as you proofread) and then correctly spelled. To help yourself see the error, underline it.

WRONG	RIGHT
for*fill*ing	ful*fill*ing
gove*r*ment	gove*r*nment
gramm*er*	gramm*ar*
rec*on*ize	rec*og*nize
th*ie*r	th*ei*r
were	*where*

HOW TO . . . Edit Spelling When You Don't Have a Dictionary or Spell Checker

1. Compare spellings. Write out alternate spellings to compare. Correctly spelled words often look and feel right.

2. Disassemble words. Divide them into syllables and sound them out. Try to see and hear the word as you've actually spelled it. Is it *tra-deg-y* or *tra-ged-y? lon-li-ness* or *lone-li-ness? nec-cess-ary* or *ne-cess-ary? di-satisfied* or *dis-satisfied? tom-morrow* or *to-morrow?*

3. Find related words to help you spell the unaccented vowels that often sound like *uh* no matter what their spelling.

   comp ? tition + comPETE
     = competition
   gramm ? r + gramMARian
     = grammar
   infin ? te + fiNITE
     = infinite

   prev ? lent + VALue
     = prevalent
   rel ? tive + reLATE
     = relative
   sep ? rate + PARE
     = separate

   (continued)

4. Use memory aids. Make up phrases or sentences to associate with the correct spelling of words—the sillier the better. Everyone knows "The princiPAL is my PAL." How about "I get all A's in grAmmAr" or "A secretAry never tArries"? You can think of others.

45c Learn the most important spelling rules

1 ■ Putting *i* before *e*

Almost everyone knows the beginning of this rhyming rule: *i* before *e* except after *c.* Not many know the remainder.

> *i* before *e* except after *c*
> or when sounding like *a*
> as in *neighbor* and *weigh*

- *i* before *e* = *believe, chief, field, relief, siege, yield*

- *i* before *e* except after *c* = *ceiling, conceive, deceive, receive*

- *e* before *i* when pronounced like the letter *a* = *eight, freight, neighbor, weigh, vein*

- *i* before *e* exceptions: *conscience, financier, science, species, sufficient*

- *e* before *i* exceptions: *counterfeit, either, foreign, forfeit, height, leisure, neither, seize, sheik, sovereign, weird*

2 ■ Adding silent *e* at the end of a word

English generally requires a silent *e* at the end of a word to keep a preceding vowel long in sound: *mat/mate, met/mete, kit/kite, hot/hotel, cut/cute.* To add a suffix to a word that ends with a silent *e*, follow these rules.

- Drop the silent *e* when the suffix begins with a vowel: *cute/cutest, desire/desiring, fame/famous, imagine/imaginary, love/lovable, prime/primal, retrieve/retrieving.* An exception: *mileage.*

- Keep the silent *e* when a suffix begins with a consonant: *achieve/achievement, care/careful, live/lively, lone/lonely, sincere/sincerely.* Exceptions: *argument, judgment, awful, truly, duly, wholly.*

- Keep the silent *e* when a word ends in *-ce* or *-ge* and the suffix begins with *a* or *o*: *service/serviceable, change/changeable, courage/courageous.*

- Exceptions to avoid confusion or mispronunciation: *dying/dyeing, hoeing, toeing, shoeing, singing/singeing.*

3 ■ Changing *y* to *i*

- When a word ends with a consonant plus *y*, change *y* to *i* and add the suffix: *busy/business, community/communities, embody/embodi-*

ment, lonely/loneliness, modify/modifier, penny/penniless. Exceptions: *babyish, cityless, fairylike.*

■ When the suffix is *-ing* or *-ist,* do not change the *y* to *i: copy + ing = copying, essay + ist = essayist; lobby + ing = lobbying; study + ing = studying.*

■ When a word ends in a vowel plus *y,* add the suffix: *boy/boyish, buy/buyer, obey/obeying, sway/swayed, valley/valleys.* Exceptions: *daily, gaily, laid, paid, said.*

4 ■ Doubling consonants

Double the consonant at the end of a word when the word meets all three of these tests:

■ The word ends in a vowel plus a consonant: *begin, cut, fog, glad, occur, prefer, regret.*

■ The suffix begins with a vowel: *-ed, -en, -ing, -y.*

■ The word has one syllable or is accented on the final syllable: *begínning, cutting, foggy, gladden, occúrrence, preférring, regrétted;* but *bénefited, concealed, gláddened, láboring, préference.*

5 ■ Adding the suffix -ly

■ When a word ends with one *-l,* add *-ly.* Do not drop the *-l* at the end of the word: *casual/casually, formal/formally, real/really, usual/usually.*

■ When a word ends *-ll,* add only *-y: chill/chilly, hill/hilly.*

6 ■ Adding suffixes to words ending in -ic

■ When a word ends in *-ic* and the suffix begins with *-e, -i,* or *-y,* add *-k. Traffic + ed =* add *-k: trafficked; picnic + ing =* add *-k: picnicking. Panic + y =* add *-k: panicky.*

■ Some words ending in *-ic* take the suffix *-ally: heroically, logically, tragically.*

7 ■ Forming plurals

■ To form the plural of most nouns, add *-s* to the singular: *boat + s = boats; glove + s = gloves; shoe + s = shoes; Johnson + s = Johnsons.*

■ When a noun ends *-s, -sh, -ch, -x,* or *-z,* form the plural with *-es: Jones + es = Joneses; dish + es = dishes; church + es = churches; box + es = boxes; buzz + es = buzzes.*

■ When a noun ends in a consonant plus *o,* the plural varies:

ADD -S ONLY	ADD -ES ONLY	ADD -S OR -ES
autos	echoes	zeros, zeroes
memos	heroes	cargos, cargoes
pianos	tomatoes	
	potatoes	

- When a noun ends in *-f* or *-fe,* add *-s* to some words: *roofs, safes, chiefs.* To form the plural of others, change the *f* to *v* and add *-es*: *hoof/hooves, thief/thieves, wharf/wharves, wife/wives.*

- Some words have irregular plurals: *child/children, ox/oxen, goose/geese, mouse/mice.*

- Some words have the same form for singular and plural: *deer, jeans, glasses* (for the eyes), *pliers, rice, sheep, swine, trousers, wheat.*

- To form the plural of letters, add an apostrophe plus *s*: *the three* R's, *dot your* i's *and cross your* t's.

- To form the plural of numbers and abbreviations, omit the apostrophe unless it is needed to prevent confusion: *1990s, BAs.*

- To form the plural of most compound nouns, add *-s* to the last word unless the first word is more important: *checkbooks, masterminds, student-athletes;* but *mothers-in-law, attorneys general, courts martial, editors-in-chief, passers-by.*

- To form the plural of most English nouns that originally were Latin, Greek, or French words, use the plural from the original language.

SINGULAR	PLURAL	SINGULAR	PLURAL
alumna (female)	alumnae	datum	data
alumnus (male)	alumni	medium	media
antenna	antennae	memorandum	memoranda
basis	bases	phenomenon	phenomena
chateau	chateaux	psychosis	psychoses
criterion	criteria	radius	radii
crisis	crises	thesis	theses

 WRITING IN THE USA Differences in American, British, and Canadian Spelling

American spelling varies slightly from the British and Canadian in the use of *a/ae, e/oe, o/ou,* silent *e, c/qu, ck/que, ct/x, l/ll, ter/tre,* and *z/s.* Consult your dictionary, and use American spelling in the United States.

45.3
British and American spelling: Web link

AMERICAN SPELLING	BRITISH AND CANADIAN SPELLING	AMERICAN SPELLING	BRITISH AND CANADIAN SPELLING
anemia	anaemia	honor	honour
apologize	apologise	judgment	judgement
check	cheque	licorice	liquorice
connection	connexion	theater	theatre
fetus	foetus	traveled	travelled

45.4
Editing spelling: Exercises

Document Design

46 Formatting Your Writing

46a Give your writing a professional, easy-to-read appearance

1 ▪ Following principles of effective document design

As your ideas take shape in the course of a writing project, begin thinking about your format: the physical arrangement of your text, the use of highlighting features that clarify or emphasize your ideas, and the use of visuals. After all, if you're writing with a computer, you'll probably format your project as you write a rough draft. But don't let yourself become distracted by all the fancy features of your computer. The layout of your writing should serve your ideas and reasons for writing—not the opposite. As you plan your format, be guided by these principles of effective document design:

Note: With the wide availability of computers, handwritten work is unacceptable for most academic writing, except in-class writing such as notes or examinations (see Chapter 61) and preliminary writing such as laboratory notes, outlines, and rough drafts. But even in this writing, using basic format principles will make information clearer and important points stand out.

- *Purpose.* All of your format decisions about text, graphics, and their physical arrangement should support your specific purposes for writing, whether to inform, instruct, persuade, or entertain. Remember, too, that the "look" of a document is expressive; it helps set the tone of your writing and creates an image of you in readers' minds. How do you want readers to feel about you and what you have to say? The serious purpose and subjects of most academic writing urge a format that looks equally serious.

- *Simplicity.* As you format your writing, make your reader's work as easy as possible. A simple format works best. The more cluttered your layout, the more things that are happening at once on your page, the harder it will be for readers to figure out exactly what you're trying to say. Use the fewest number of format features possible to make your meaning and purpose clear. For academic writing, ask your instructor about the appropriateness of headings, visuals, and highlighting devices such as **bold text**.

- *Focus.* Think of a page as a distinct unit, with its own focus of attention. As you design your pages, use format to keep readers' eyes moving naturally from left to right, from the top to the bottom of the page. Consider how readers might view this sample page of text, with its centered heading at the top, clear paragraphing, graphics on the right margin, and a bulleted list that arranges a topic vertically.

- ***Emphasis.*** The most important features in your writing can be given prominence by headings, font selection, color, visuals, and highlighting devices, such as underlining and boldface. But remember the principle of simplicity. Too many devices of emphasis will make your writing seem cluttered and unemphatic.

■ *Consistency.* To unify your writing and clarify ideas, be consistent in the use of fonts, font sizes, headings, white space, color, and page layout. Parts of your writing that are equal in importance should look equal on the page; those that differ in importance should look different. Inconsistent presentation is distracting and confusing. If your project will be long or visually complex, spend a few minutes before you begin a rough draft preparing a "style sheet," a list of your decisions about all the features of your format: page headers or footers, fonts and font sizes, in-text headings, your use of colors, and your use of visuals and boxed text. As you write a draft, a style sheet will help keep you focused on what's most important—your ideas.

HOW TO . . . Design a Page of Academic or Professional Writing

1. "Chunk" your text into parts that look easy to read by adjusting paragraph length, listing, and inserting headings. But avoid paragraphs that look too short or choppy.
2. Organize your writing to group related items together.
3. Unless instructed otherwise, place visuals with the texts they illustrate.
4. Avoid placing headings at the bottom of a page.
5. Avoid unnecessary text breaks that may mislead readers about where you are in your development of a topic. If, for example, a paragraph at the bottom of one page continues to the next, run the last line of text on the first page all the way to the right margin. Do *not* end one sentence on one page and wait till the next page to begin the next sentence.
6. Avoid "widows" (single last lines of a paragraph at the top of a page) and "orphans" (single first lines of a paragraph at the bottom of a page).

---

2 ■ Preparing your computer and printer

■ *Templates.* For some types of writing—especially business documents such as letters, memos, and e-mail messages—your word processor may contain templates that will format your writing appropriately as you work. Some word processors even contain Modern Language Association and American Psychological Association style guides. See your File menu or Help screen. For the writing you do frequently, you can make your own templates. (See the "Computer Tip: Making Templates" on p. 22.)

■ *Automatic settings.* If you are not using a template, set automatic formatting commands in advance, including spacing, tabs, margins, line justification, automatic paging, word wrap, and headers (most word processing programs do this for you with default settings). If your computer has "smart quotes," use them for all quotation marks instead of the symbols for feet (') and inches ("). (See your Preferences or Tools menu.)

- *Printers.* Check that your printer is set up to produce clean letter-quality text.

- *Paper.* For the final drafts of academic and other public writing, use high quality, white, 8½ x 11 inch bond paper. For résumés, parchment or cream-colored paper may be appropriate. For projects such as newsletters, brochures, or informal writing, colored paper may be appropriate.

3 ▪ Choosing type fonts

When printing documents, writers have three large font categories to choose from: Serif fonts, such as Times Roman, **New Century Schoolbook,** and Palatino have little lines at the top and bottom of letters that make this type of font easiest to read. Sans serif fonts, such as **Geneva, Arial,** and **Helvetica** lack these little lines. Novelty fonts, such as *Brush Script,* have unusual appearances. Avoid writing an entire document in any font that looks too "artful." Fonts may be printed in many sizes, or "points": 10 point, 14 point, and 18 point, for example. Computers and printers have default fonts and font sizes appropriate for most of your writing. If you wish to choose from the many fonts and font sizes available to you, follow these guidelines:

- *Academic writing.* Choose an easily readable serif font in standard 10- or 12-point size. The American Psychological Association recommends Times Roman or Courier. Use one font and font size for all text, including titles and headings.

- *Other public writing.* In newsletters, brochures, and résumés, you may wish to vary font and font size. But use no more than two fonts per document: serif fonts for text and sans serif in headings, when you want to slow reading speed. For the text of your document, vary font size according to line length: the smaller the font, the shorter the line. For headings, increase font size, with one size for major headings and a smaller size for subheadings.

- *Highlighting.* Avoid the all-capitals format, even in most headings. In academic writing, avoid such features as font outlining or shadowing. (For italics and underlining, see Chapter 41.) If you have a color printer, print text in black ink.

4 ▪ Setting margins and spacing

Margin width and spacing within a document are powerful design elements for creating readability, focus, and emphasis. Too little white space surrounding or within a text will make a document look cluttered and hard to read. Too much white space may create a sense of unimportance or wasted space. To use space effectively, follow these guidelines.

- *Academic writing.* In most academic writing, use a one-inch margin around your text and double-space between lines. Set your computer to justify lines flush (aligned) left. For Modern Language Association requirements, see 46d; for the American Psychological Association guidelines, see 46e.

- *Other public writing.* Spacing conventions vary. Much business writing uses single spacing or a mixture of single and double spacing (see Chapter 62). For brochures and newsletters, you have opportunities to experiment with white space surrounding headings, visuals, and boxed text to create focus and emphasis. If you print these documents with columns, use right and left justification to create readable text.

5 ■ Using color

With the wide availability of color printers, you can now use color to achieve four effects in your writing. First, color can link related parts, features, or ideas. See how the pie chart on p. 305 uses four colors to link similar recreational activities pursued by college students. Second, color creates contrasts between different elements, as in the pyramid diagram on p. 307. Third, color supports symbolic or metaphorical messages, as the red, white, blue, and green does in the Web site on p. 12. Fourth, color emphasizes what's important, focuses attention, or divides a space, as in the bar graph on p. 305. To use color effectively, follow these guidelines:

- *Text and graphics.* For academic writing, print text in black, including headings. Use color for color photographs and drawings or to highlight charts and graphs—but the fewer the colors, the easier your readers will see their meanings. (See 46c.)

- *Color and tone.* When appropriate, use color to convey feelings and attitudes about your topics. Cool colors (blue, green, violet) are calming; warm colors (red, orange, yellow) are stimulating.

- *Consistency and contrast.* Use the same color for similar headings, text boxes, or graphics (as illustrated by the headings in *The Ready Reference Handbook*). Use color to group and simplify related elements. Choose complementary (opposite) colors to set off adjacent elements in a document. When possible, avoid placing text on images, and make sure the text on a colored background is visible.

6 ▪ Preparing your final draft

▪ *Punctuation.* Never begin a line with a comma, colon, semicolon, hyphen, dash, end punctuation, or one or two ellipsis points. Never end a line with opening quotation marks, parentheses, or brackets standing alone, not connected to a word.

▪ *Print preview.* Use the print preview feature of your word processor to give your format a "visual proofreading." Look for "widows" and "orphans" at the top or bottom of a page, headings at the bottom of a page, broken lists or text boxes, misplaced graphics, errors in section or page numbering, and appropriate white space. Check to see that what's most important stands out and that your design leads your eye down the page.

▪ *Proofreading.* Run your spell checker before you print; then proofread your final draft carefully. Correct and reprint, if necessary. Give your paper a last check to be sure that everything has printed correctly.

▪ *Binding of an academic writing project.* Paperclip the pages. Do not use staples or pins.

Note: You may be asked to submit a project on disk or as an e-mail attachment. Before proceeding, check with your instructor to determine the system or application compatibility to open your documents. If your writing will be read on screen, place a bracketed number followed by a space at the beginning or end of each paragraph to make reading and discussion easier. Do not send a fax unless directed to do so by your instructor. (For more about academic writing online, see Chapter 63.)

46b Use headings, lists, and tables to clarify ideas

Word processing programs provide powerful tools for enhancing your ideas with headings, lists, tables, and other special effects. But be aware that too many extra features will disrupt your flow and distract readers. To be effective, these format features should

▪ Add to rather than duplicate your text

▪ Convey essential information, not be merely decorative

▪ Be easy to understand

▪ Make your subject easier to understand

Note: Specific subject areas may have specific formats for visual aids. Ask your instructor.

1 ▪ Formatting in-text headings

Essays and many other kinds of writing do not require headings. However, reports and other technical documents such as proposals and grant requests are divided by headings that identify topics and guide readers. (See the sample report in 55d.) If headings are appropriate for your writing, use the following format based on American Psychological Association (APA) guidelines:

▪ *Heading levels.* Use from one to five levels of heading, depending on the complexity of your writing. The following headings are arranged from most to least important and show the position and capitalization style to use. The phrase *capital and lowercase letters* directs you to capitalize the first, last, and all major words in the heading (see 40c).

CENTERED ALL CAPITAL LETTERS

Centered Capital and Lowercase Letters

Centered, Italicized, Capital and Lowercase Letters

Flush Left, Italicized, Capital and Lowercase Letters

    Paragraph indent, italicized, sentence-style capitalization and punctuation. The text immediately follows the heading on the same line.

▪ *Numbering.* Headings are not numbered except in scientific writing.

▪ *Punctuation and capital letters.* Do not end centered and flush-left headings with a period. For run-in heads at the beginning of paragraphs, capitalize the first letter of the first word, lowercase the remaining words, and end with a period. Italicize as in the preceding examples.

▪ *Spacing.* Double-space above and below headings that appear on a line by themselves. Double-space within multiline headings.

▪ *Length and consistency.* Keep headings brief and grammatically parallel (see Chapter 19). Headings at a particular level should have the same grammatical form: noun phrases, verb phrases, questions, and so forth.

▪ *Grammar.* Make the grammar of a heading suggest the content of the section. Use nouns or noun phrases to introduce information or explanation (e.g., *Exotic Species*); *-ing* verbs to introduce processes, actions, or events (e.g., *Preserving Native Species*); commands to introduce instructions (e.g., *Reintroduce Natural Predators*); questions to interest readers (e.g., *How May Endangered Songbirds Be Saved?*).

■ *Multiple headings.* Avoid using only one subsection heading within a section. Note that too many headings on one page will make your writing look cluttered.

■ *Format.* Do not put each heading on a new page. But if a heading comes at the bottom of a page, move it to the next page unless it is followed by at least two lines of text.

2 ■ Formatting lists

Use lists to clarify steps in a process, materials, ingredients, parts, advice, or items to be covered. To make a list, follow these guidelines:

■ *Introduction.* Write a lead-in followed by a colon, as in the preceding sentence.

■ *List marker.* Precede each item in the list with a marker: a number or letter plus a period and 2 spaces; or a dash or bullet (•) plus 1 space. Use numbered or lettered lists if chronology or the ordering of information is important, as in step-by-step instructions. Use bullets for presenting items that lack chronological or procedural relationship.

■ *Margins.* Begin each item flush with the left margin. Indent runover lines one-half inch or 5 spaces to form a hanging paragraph. For greater emphasis, indent the first line of each item 5 spaces and runover lines 1 inch or 10 spaces.

■ *Grammar.* Make items grammatically parallel: a phrase, sentence, or other grammatical form.

■ *Punctuation.* Do not use periods after items in a vertical list unless one or more items are complete sentences.

3 ■ Formatting tables

46.1
Using tables
and
graphics:
Web link

Tables present information in a systematic way, usually in columns. Use tables sparingly to eliminate complex, number-filled text. Place each table close to the text to which it relates. Give each table a number: *Table 1, Table 2,* and so forth. Briefly introduce each table in a sentence or refer to it in parentheses: (*see Table 1*).

HOW TO . . . Create a Table

Modern Language Association (MLA) Style

1. Double space throughout each table. Do not use all capital letters.

2. Position the table number (e.g., *Table 1*) flush left on a line by itself. Then double-space and provide a descriptive caption, also flush left. If the caption is long, indent each additional line a quarter-inch or 3 spaces from the left. Do not use all capital letters. Double-space the caption.

3. Between ruled lines, write descriptive headings for each column.

4. Arrange each column beneath its heading.

5. Double-space below the last line of the table and make a ruled bottom line.

6. If the table needs a source note, double-space below the bottom line, type the word "Source" followed by a colon and 1 space, and then give the source of the table written as one sentence: author or producer, title, (publication information or date in parentheses) followed by the page number in the original source, if available. Double space throughout. Indent additional lines (if any) a quarter-inch or three spaces.

7. Use superscript lowercase letters (e.g, [a], [b], [c], and so forth) for notes to the table.

American Psychological Association (APA) Style

1. Italicize the descriptive caption preceding the table (e.g, *2003 Recreational Visits to Selected Areas Administered by the National Park System*).

2. After the table, in place of the word *Source*, use *Note* italicized and followed by a period (*Note.*) and then one space.

3. Then type "From" and give the source of the table followed by the author's name, date of publication, and publication information following APA reference guidelines (see 55c).

Table 1

2003 Recreational Visits to Selected Areas Administered by the National Park System

Classification	Recreational Visits (Millions)
National Parks	63.5
National Monuments	20.1
National Historical Sites	34.4
National Battlefields	32.3
National Parkways	31.1
National Recreation Areas	47.8
National Seashores, Lakeshores, and Rivers	26.7
National Preserves and Reserves	2.2
National Capital Parks[a]	8.0
National Total	266.1

Source: Adapted from National Park Service, "Recreation Visits by Type of Area," Statistical Abstract: 2003. (Denver: WASO-TNT, 2004) 1.

[a]National Capital Parks include National Capital Park, National Mall, and the White House.

46.2
Graphics
resources:
Web link

46c Display graphics to clarify and emphasize

Graphics, or figures, include charts, drawings, maps, graphs, clip art, and photographs. Use them to reveal relationships among data, to draw attention to details, and to dramatize important points. Draw them by hand, cut and paste reproductions, use a computer graphics program, or download images from the World Wide Web. Introduce each graphic, place it appropriately on the page near related text, and document its source.

HOW TO . . . Document Graphics

Modern Language Association (MLA) Style

1. Double space below your graphic. Flush left, write the label "Fig." and an Arabic numeral followed by a period (see Figure 1, p. 305).

2. On the same line write a caption using an initial capital and lower-case letters followed by a comma, the word *from,* and documentation of the source, written as one sentence: author or producer, title (publication information or date in parentheses), followed by the page number in the original source, if available. Double-space throughout. (See Figures 2 and 3, pp. 305–306.)

3. You must cite the source of each image that you borrow, but take special care with images downloaded from the World Wide Web. If the image is copyrighted (identified with a ©) and you intend to distribute the image outside of class or use it on a Web site, you must ask for permission to use it. For a guide to permission requests, see 51c.

American Psychological Association (APA) Style

1. Below the graphic, write and italicize the word *Figure,* the number, and a period (*Figure 1.*); leave one space and write a caption, using sentence-style punctuation.

2. If necessary, type "From" and document the source of the graphic following APA reference guidelines (see 55c).

---

1 ▪ Preparing charts, graphs, and diagrams

Pie charts. Pie charts enable you to divide the whole of something (100%) into portions of varying sizes. Arrange the portions clockwise, beginning with the largest, or use colors, as in the following example, to indicate relationships between individual portions. Label the portions inside or outside the circle.

Bar graphs. Bar graphs enable you to show relationships between groups and make comparisons, as in the following figures comparing student GPA and alcohol consumption. To construct a bar graph, begin

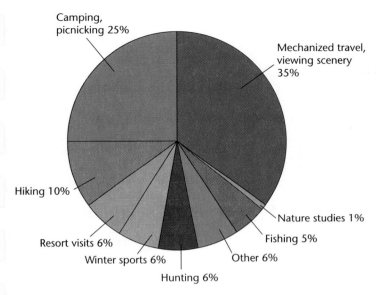

Fig 1. Harper College student recreational use of national and state parks, 2004.

quantity scales at zero if possible, make proportions fair, use grids, marks, or graphic icons (as in Figure 3 on p. 306) to signal amounts, and arrange the bars in a logical sequence. If the writing situation is serious or formal, use simple lines and bars; less formal situations or those requiring dramatic impact allow you to be more creative. Beware of using 3-dimensional bar images; they can be difficult for readers to interpret.

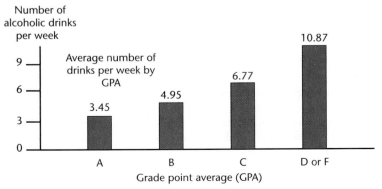

Fig 2. The relationship between alcohol consumption and grade point average.

Grade Point
Average
(GPA)

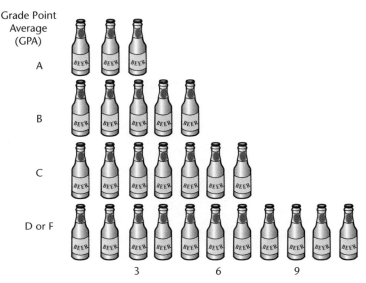

A

B

C

D or F

3   6   9

Number of Alcoholic Drinks per Week

Fig 3. The relationship between alcohol consumption and college student
grade point average, from "Choices," Eagle Eye, 1997, University of
Wisconsin-La Crosse, 1 June 2004 http://www.uwlax.edu/StudentLife/
choice.html>

Line graphs. Line graphs enable you to chart trends or relationships through time, as in Figure 4 on p. 307, comparing twenty-five-year changes in family income among various economic groups. To construct a line graph, begin quantity scales at zero if possible, and focus on only one comparison, as Figure 4 focuses only on family income.

Diagrams. Diagrams enable you to identify and locate the parts of both physical objects and concepts. See Figure 5 on p. 307.

2 ▪ Using photos, clip art, drawings, and maps

Visual images will help you to display spatial information (for example, see the map in the research paper on p. 402), make comparisons, provide narrative sequences, or dramatize points in an argument. Whether you create them yourself, copy and paste them, or download them from the Web, you'll probably have to edit these images to give them focus and to omit irrelevant details.

For example, in his research paper on the impact of overcrowding in US National Parks (see Chapter 54), student Eric Martínez planned to include a photo he took on a visit to New Mexico's Bandelier National

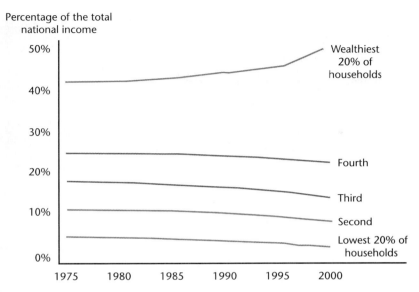

Fig 4. Share of total US income received by each fifth of households, US Census Bureau, Money Income in the United States: 2000 (Washington: GPO, 2001) 21.

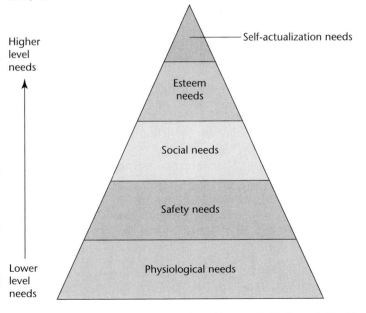

Fig. 5. Maslow's Needs Hierarchy, from Abraham H. Maslow, Motivation and Personality, 2nd ed. (New York: Harper, 1970).

Monument to see its ancient Indian cliff dwellings. He wanted to dramatize his point that crowds of park visitors make it difficult for individuals to see what they came to see, in this case, rare archeological sites. Before he could use this photo, however, he had to trim it in a computer video editor to focus it on the crowds that were his subject instead of the scenery and the ancient dwelling places.

Note: As you create tables and graphics, take care that what you produce tells the truth about your subject. Be sure that you include all relevant details and that your representations are accurate, fair to the originals, and properly sized. (See also 1c2.)

46d Use the Modern Language Association format for writing in the humanities

46.3
MLA:
Web link

The following format, based on the *MLA Handbook for Writers of Research Papers,* 6th ed. (New York: MLA, 2003), is appropriate for writing in English composition, literature, and foreign language courses; it is also used in the humanities, philosophy, religion, and history.

1 ■ Formatting the identification heading and title

Most college writing does not require a title page. Use an identification heading instead. On your first page, 1 inch from the top and left margins, list your name, your instructor's name, course title and section number, and date, double-spacing throughout. Double-space to reach the title line; center your title. If the title runs more than one line, double-space the lines; use a colon between a title and subtitle. Capitalize the first and last words and all words except articles, prepositions, conjunctions, and the *to* in infinitives (e.g., *to Write*). Do not use underlining, italics, and quotation marks unless your title contains another title or a direct quotation. Double-space between your title and the first line of text. (See 4f, Chapter 54, and 59d for sample papers in the MLA format.)

2 ▪ Formatting the title page

If your instructor requires a title page, center the title one-third of the way down the page. In the center of the page, write "by," double-space, and give your name. Two-thirds of the way down the page and centered on separate lines, write the course name, your instructor's name, and the date, double-spacing between lines. On the first page of text, repeat the title, centered on the first line. Double-space between the title and first line of text. (See the sample title page in Chapter 54.)

3 ▪ Indenting

▪ *Paragraphs.* Indent the first word of a paragraph one-half inch or 5 spaces from the left margin. If you write by hand, indent 1 inch.

▪ *Long quotations.* If a prose quotation runs more than four typed lines, indent it 1 inch or 10 spaces from the left margin. If an indented quotation runs longer than one paragraph, indent the first line of successive paragraphs an additional quarter-inch or 3 spaces. Indent more than three lines of poetry 1 inch or 10 spaces from the left margin, or center the poetry so that it looks balanced on the page. Do *not* enclose indented quotations with quotation marks. (See 50d.)

4 ▪ Spacing

Double-space between all lines, including titles, headings, indented quotations, and outlines. Space once after a colon and after end punctuation (periods, question marks, and so forth). Leave no space between end punctuation and closing quotation marks, parentheses, and brackets. Space once after periods following initials or abbreviations and after periods within bibliographic citations.

5 ▪ Paging

If your paper does not have a title page, begin numbering with arabic numeral one (1) on the first page. In the upper right corner, one-half inch from the top of the page, put your last name followed by 1 space and the page number (e.g., *Lopez 1*). Do not use the word *page,* the abbreviation *p.,* parentheses, dashes, or other punctuation. Number consecutively to the end of your paper, including notes and documentation. Double-space beneath the page heading or position the first line of text 1 inch from the top of the page.

If your paper has a title page and other **preliminary pages** such as an outline, leave the title page unnumbered and use lowercase roman numerals for the other preliminary pages. Count the title page as page i, but begin page-numbering on the following page, which is page ii. In the upper right corner, one-half inch from the top, put your name followed by 1 space and roman numeral two (e.g., *Lopez ii*). Use lowercase roman numerals for all of the preliminary pages: ii, iii, iv, and so forth. Then, on the first page of text, begin a new series of numbers; put your last name followed by 1 space and arabic numeral one (e.g., *Lopez 1*). Double-space beneath the page heading or position the first line of text 1 inch from the top of the page.

 COMPUTER TIP Using Headers

Create a page header that will automatically insert your name and page numbers at the top of each page. If necessary, turn on the consecutive page numbering feature.

---

6 ▪ Headings

Identify the parts of your paper by appropriate section headings: *Outline,* the paper's title on the first page of text, *Notes,* and *Works Cited.* Center the heading 1 inch from the top of the page and capitalize it correctly. Double-space to the first line of text. (See the sample research paper in Chapter 54.)

In-text topic headings to divide the body of an essay are seldom necessary. However, headings may be useful or required for complex technical writing such as reports (see 46b1).

7 ▪ Order of pages

Arrange your paper in this order:

Title page, if required
Acknowledgments page, if required
Outline, if required
Body of the paper
Notes, if necessary
Works Cited, if necessary

 46e Use the American Psychological Association format for writing in the social sciences

46.4
APA:
Web link

The following format, based on guidelines for student writing in Chapters 5 and 6 of the *Publication Manual of the American Psychological Association,* 5th ed. (Washington, DC: APA, 2001), is appropriate for writing in the social sciences, education, business, linguistics, biology, and earth sciences. Note that the APA format for student papers differs slightly from that of papers to be published in APA journals. See your instructor for the appropriate format for your writing.

1 ■ Formatting the title page

Prepare a title page for your paper. (See the APA sample report in 55d.)

- *Page head.* In the top right corner, one-half inch from the top of the page, put a short form of your title (the page head) followed by one-half inch or 5 spaces and the page number. The page head and page number will appear at the top of all pages of your paper. If you use a computer, you can probably insert the heading and page numbers automatically.

- *Title.* Center the complete title in the middle of the page. Capitalize the first and last words and all words of four letters or more. If your title runs more than one line, double-space; use a colon between a title and subtitle.

- *Identifying information.* On separate, double-spaced lines beneath the title, put your name, the course title and section number, your instructor's name, and the date.

2 ■ Formatting preliminary pages

In addition to the title page, you may be required to include some other **preliminary pages:** acknowledgments, a table of contents, a list of tables and figures, or an abstract. On each preliminary page, type your page header and page number at the top right. Type the heading for each page centered, in capital and lowercase letters: *Table of Contents, Abstract,* and so forth. Double-space beneath the heading.

3 ■ Formatting an abstract

An **abstract** is a brief, comprehensive summary (100–120 words) of your paper. Write the abstract after you have written the paper itself. Report rather than evaluate or comment. Do not use *I* or *we.* Define all terms and abbreviations; write all numbers as figures. Type the abstract in one double-spaced paragraph beginning two spaces beneath the heading (*Abstract*). Do *not* indent the first line. (See the example in the sample APA report in 55d.)

4 ■ Indenting

- *Paragraphs.* Indent the first word of a paragraph one-half inch or 5 spaces from the left margin.

- *Long quotations.* If a quotation runs more than 40 words, indent it one-half inch or 5 spaces from the left margin, none from the right. If an indented quotation runs longer than one paragraph, indent the first line of successive paragraphs an additional one-half inch or 5 spaces. Do not use quotation marks unless they appear in the original.

5 ■ Spacing

Double-space throughout, including titles, headings, indented quotations, tables, graphics captions, notes, and references. Space once after commas, semicolons, colons, and punctuation at the end of a sentence. Leave no space between end punctuation (periods, question marks, and so forth) and closing quotation marks, parentheses, and brackets. Space once after periods following a person's initials and within reference citations.

Note: If your instructor permits, you may single-space within titles, headings, tables, and references to improve readability, and you may triple- or quadruple-space before major in-text headings and before and after in-text tables.

6 ■ Placing tables and figures

Unless instructed otherwise, place tables and figures in the body of your paper, near the text they illustrate. (See also 46b3.)

7 ■ Paging

Unless instructed otherwise, number the pages of your paper consecutively, beginning with the title page and continuing to the end, including notes, references, and appendices. Use arabic numerals (*1, 2, 3,* and so forth). At the right margin, one-half inch from the top of the page, put the page header followed by one-half inch or 5 spaces and the page number. Double-space below the page number.

Note: Your instructor may require you to use lowercase roman numerals (*i, ii, iii,* and so forth) on preliminary pages such as the title page and abstract.

8 ■ Formatting in-text headings

APA-style papers frequently contain in-text section and topic headings. See 46b1 for placement and capitalization information.

9 ■ Arranging the order of parts

Arrange an APA paper in this order:

Title page
Acknowledgment page, if required
Table of Contents, if required
List of Tables and Figures, if required
Abstract, if required
Text of the paper
References
Appendices, if required

FOCUS ON . . . Responsible Research—Avoiding Plagiarism

ON THE WEB   www.ablongman.com/dodds

The Research Project

47 Choosing a Topic, Finding Sources, Preparing a Bibliography

For many writers, the research project is a daunting assignment. But consider: if you've ever shopped for a car, tried to decide what college to attend, or looked for a new job—you've already developed a number of skills necessary for successful college-level research writing. The differences between everyday research and academic research are differences of degree rather than kind. Research is an activity as natural as breathing, a part of nearly everyone's life, useful whenever facts, ideas, good judgments, and sound decisions are important.

Here's something else: the research paper may be one of the biggest assignments given in a college course, but you don't have to do it all at once. Your instructor has made time for you to do everything you need to do:

1. Choosing and focusing a topic.

2. Identifying and locating sources; evaluating their suitability for your project.

3. Gathering information about your topic; evaluating its soundness and suitability.

4. Taking stock of what you discover and planning your project.

5. Writing and revising your project so that it meets the requirements of the assignment: a report, a review of others' findings (the "review of research"), a thesis-support essay, or a literary research paper.

6. Preparing the final draft of your project and documenting the sources you've used to write your paper.

Note: Managing your research project. To smooth your way through the six steps to successful research listed here, take a few minutes to get yourself organized. Print materials: Get a three-ring notebook, manila envelope, or several folders to hold notes, photocopies, and other print documents. Computer materials: Create a folder to hold your electronic files such as downloads, notes, and drafts of your project. Put each kind of file in its own folder within your larger project folder.

47a Choose a researchable topic

1 ■ Identifying possible topics

In most respects, choosing a research paper topic is like choosing any topic. The one you choose should interest you and stimulate your curiosity. (See the guidelines for choosing topics in 2a6.) Research projects, however, follow an additional guideline. Your topic must be genuinely researchable: reliable information and trustworthy opinions must be available to you.

HOW TO . . . Find "Researchable" Topics

1. *Ask the experts.* If you don't already have a list of topics given to you as part of an assignment, ask your professor or other experts for recommendations.

2. *Check reference sources.* Read about interesting topics in encyclopedias or other reference works. Look for problems, questions, or controversies that have stimulated the writing of scholars and others. A librarian will help you locate these sources.

3. *Check source lists.* Skim bibliographies, indexes, and other source lists in your library. The titles of books and articles may suggest topics that have received the serious attention necessary for your research.

4. *Check Internet topic guides.* Visit the North Harris College Topics Resources Guide at < http://nhclibrary.nhmccd.edu/research/subject/controversial/guide.html > .

5. *Beware of "headline" topics.* Current popular topics like abortion, terrorism, and the legalization of marijuana may attract lots of attention, but they may not yet have received the expert attention that usually leads to the most reliable information. If you choose a "hot topic," make sure your information sources are trustworthy. Chapter 49a will help you evaluate your sources.

---

2 ■ Narrowing and focusing your topic

Professional researchers rarely investigate a whole topic in one project. They choose a part, a single issue, or a key question to investigate in depth in the time available. Do the same. Begin with a topic map of the kind described in 2a4 to subdivide a large topic into smaller, more manageable parts. Once you have your actual research topic, narrow it further and draw the line of inquiry you'll follow in your research.

- *Writing baseline notes.* Before you begin research, write brief notes exploring your current thinking about your topic and establishing a baseline for investigation. Write down what you feel, believe, and know—or don't know. Remind yourself where your ideas come from. Are your sources trustworthy? Your notes may raise research questions for you to answer. They may also reveal assumptions that influence your thinking. Knowing your biases will help you evaluate information more objectively.

- *Thinking critically about your assignment and audience.* Clarify what you're looking for and what you'll do with it by analyzing the "operator" terms in your assignment. These are words such as *analyze, explain, persuade,* and *review* that define your approach to a topic (see 61a for a list of these terms). Then consider your audience's knowledge and interests by writing an audience profile (see the "How to Profile an Audience" box on p. 20).

- *Reading background materials.* If you haven't already read encyclopedias or other reference sources, do so now. Look for enduring issues, questions, or problems having to do with your topic. Your librarian will help you locate these sources.

- *Posing key questions or describing a problem.* Pose questions to answer. They may combine the reporter's six questions: *who, what, when, where, why,* and *how.* Or briefly describe a problem for your research to solve. For example:

      The widespread popularity of America's national parks is reducing
      the enjoyment of visitors and harming the environment. What can be
      done to protect park environments and at the same time increase the
      enjoyment of these beautiful attractions?

- *Stating your purposes.* Your purposes may change as you investigate a topic, perhaps transforming you from a reporter of information to an advocate for a position. But thinking about your purpose will reveal what you're looking for and why. Write a brief statement about why you're investigating your topic. For example:

      My purposes are to investigate interpretations of Charlotte
      Perkins Gilman's "The Yellow Wall-Paper" to discover the symbolism of
      the wallpaper and the causes of the narrator's insanity.

- *Writing a tentative thesis.* What do you expect to discover by your research? If you know little about your subject, you'll have little to say here, but if your purposes are critical or argumentative, you may already have opinions. Research may lead you to revise your thesis, even disprove it, but stating it now will point the direction of your investigation. Write your thesis as a declarative sentence:

I expect to discover/prove/explain/demonstrate/show that [*make an assertion about your subject*].

I expect to prove that the wallpaper in Charlotte Perkins Gilman's "The Yellow Wall-Paper" symbolizes the narrator's suffocating life and the causes of her deepening insanity.

HOW TO . . . Focus a Research Project

Help yourself focus your project by writing the following exercise. Complete as many items as possible.

1. My general subject area:

2. My specific research topic:

3. My key question:

4. My purposes (to report, explain, evaluate, or persuade):

5. My tentative thesis (if possible):

6. Key words I'll use to research my topic:

7. What words in my topic, question, or thesis are vague or unclear? What opposing opinions or questions could be offered in response to my thesis? Do my stated purposes fit the language of my questions or thesis?

8. The date this project is due:

    a. Number of days for researching:

    b. Number of days for organizing:

    c. Number of days for writing:

    d. Number of days for revising and preparing the final draft:

47b Choose a variety of appropriate sources

1 ▪ Locating background, general, and scholarly sources

The sources you'll read for your project may provide background, general, or scholarly knowledge. Choose those appropriate to your knowledge and the assignment. **Background sources**, such as encyclopedias and biographical dictionaries, are valuable for the foundation knowledge necessary to investigate complex subjects. For example, if you were investigating Charlotte Perkins Gilman's story "The Yellow Wall-

Paper," you might begin by reading an encyclopedia to gain a basic understanding about schizophrenia, one of the topics of the story.

General sources are written for a general audience by experts, investigative journalists, or first-person observers. They may be book-length or appear in periodicals such as *The Atlantic Monthly*. These are books and periodicals that you'll find in local libraries and major bookstores such as Barnes & Noble or Borders. Such sources are often appropriate for undergraduate research projects.

When you have the background knowledge and resources, locate as many **scholarly sources** as possible for your project. Published by government bodies, research organizations, and academic institutions and appearing in books, scholarly periodicals, and Internet resources, these are sources written by experts for experts. Usually they will provide you with the most detailed, insightful treatment of a subject. Depend upon them as much as possible.

2 ▪ Locating primary and secondary sources

Primary sources provide the raw materials of a subject, unfiltered and unexplained. Charlotte Perkins Gilman's story "The Yellow Wall-Paper," like all literary works, is a primary source. So are statistics about visits to America's national parks. So, too, are interviews, eyewitness accounts, personal papers, court records, news stories, and the results of surveys and experiments. Part of your work as a researcher is to give raw materials the evaluation and explanation that will make them meaningful.

Secondary sources explain and interpret primary sources and present opinions. A scholar's essay interpreting "The Yellow Wall-Paper" is a secondary source, as is an essay proving the damage caused to national park environments by large numbers of park visitors. Secondary sources use primary source information to fulfill a purpose.

In your research, you'll use both kinds of sources. For research topics in the humanities, you'll depend heavily on secondary sources. In the social sciences, you'll depend on both primary and secondary sources. In the sciences, many of your sources may be primary. But whenever possible, use primary sources to form your own opinions.

3 ▪ Locating balanced sources

If you've chosen a controversial topic, such as federal funding of abortions for the poor or granting resident status to undocumented immigrants, look for sources to represent all sides. Rarely will you find individual sources that are each perfectly balanced, objective, and unbiased in their treatment of a topic. The best correction for undue bias in one source—which you may not see if you read only one side of an issue—is a voice from the other side. Divide your research among competing opinions. Read those you disagree with as well as those you agree with. You'll end up with a fairer, clearer presentation of your topic and opinions.

4 ■ Choosing print and electronic sources

With the rapid development of computer technology, a vast number of sources are now available electronically. CD-ROM publications available in your library or for purchase will, among other things, provide you with reference sources, such as dictionaries and encyclopedias. Sources available through the Internet include book-length sources, electronic versions of print sources, electronic periodicals and newspapers, government resources, primary research sources of all kinds, announcements of special-interest organizations, and personal communications. The computer has become a nearly indispensable component of speedy, in-depth, efficient research.

However, with Internet sources, it is sometimes difficult to determine their creators' credentials and whether their information is trustworthy. Major publishers and libraries, on the other hand, act as filters or referees. While they don't positively guarantee that something is true or accurate, their professional reputations give them an incentive to ensure the truth and accuracy of what they publish or place on their shelves. It is also true that many excellent sources are available *only* in print versions. To complete your research project successfully, you'll probably depend upon both kinds of sources.

5 ■ Using a checklist of sources

The following list indicates the range of sources available to you. Look it over at the beginning of a project, and check off appropriate sources. Return to the list later, in the middle of your research when you know more about your topic, to identify other sources.

Source-locating tools

_____ *Bibliographies, abstracts, indexes, and Internet search engines and directories.* These references provide the publication information to locate books, articles, and other sources. Examples: *MLA International Bibliography, Art Abstracts, Social Sciences Index, Google,* and *Yahoo!* Available in print or electronically.

_____ *Library information services and databases.* Like bibliographies and indexes, these references provide publication information about sources. Often, they also provide abstracts or the full texts of sources. Examples: *Infotrac, LEXIS-NEXIS Universe, EbscoHost, FirstSearch, Literature Resource Center,* and *Newsbank.* Available electronically, through your library's computer network.

Reference sources

_____ *Encyclopedias.* General encyclopedias such as the *Encyclopedia Britannica* will provide background information on your topic. Specialized encyclopedias such as the *Encyclopedia of American History, Encyclopedia of Psychology,* and *Encyclope-*

dia of Biological Sciences provide more specific information. Available in print or electronically.

_____ *Other references.* Similar to encyclopedias are biographical guides such as the *Dictionary of American Biography*; almanacs and yearbooks such as *Facts on File* or *World Almanac* and *Book of Facts*; atlases such as the *National Geographic Atlas of the World*; and dictionaries. Available in print or electronically.

Information and opinion sources

_____ *Books.* Indispensable for most academic research, books give the long and broad views of a subject. Book-length works are increasingly available as e-books on the Internet.

_____ *Essays in anthologies.* Scholars frequently compile the best essays on a particular topic and publish them together in book form. These anthologies are frequently available on literary and controversial topics.

_____ *Book reviews.* Full-length book reviews are available in periodicals and in summarized form in *Book Review Digest, Book Review Index,* or *Current Book Review Citations.* Check these sources in print or on the Internet to evaluate a book's quality and coverage of a topic.

_____ *Articles.* Periodical articles are often more current and focused than books. Available in print and electronically.

_____ *Businesses, government organizations, and other organizations.* Businesses and other special-interest organizations may provide you with print or electronic sources of information related to your topic, or experts to interview.

Fact sources

_____ *Newspapers.* Complete editions of major newspapers such as the *New York Times* are available at your library in microfilm form. Daily editions and archived stories are available electronically. Individual news stories from local newspapers are available through *Newsbank,* available electronically. (Note, however, that the editorial pages of newspapers and feature articles contain opinion as well as facts.)

_____ *Government documents.* Government sources contain legislative and judicial information, scientific reports, statistics, cultural and historical information, recreational and health information, and practical how-to information. Available in print and electronically.

Special resources

_____ *Archival materials.* Most libraries have special collections of letters, diaries, rare books, and local historical materials. Available in print and electronically.

_____ *Audio-visual materials.* Maps, charts, photos of visual art, films, musical recordings, tapes, or recorded television and radio programs may be appropriate for your topic. Many are available both in print and electronically.

_____ *Special online sources.* E-mail, news groups, and discussion groups may provide you with expert or personal sources of information.

_____ *Field research.* You may develop your own sources of information by making direct observations or conducting interviews or surveys.

47c Follow a systematic search strategy to identify sources

1 ■ General search guidelines

■ *Consult reference librarians.* Whenever you have a research question you can't answer on your own, turn to these experts on libraries and research. They may even have handouts and tutorials to help you with your project.

■ *List key words.* You'll use these words to search for sources. Choose nouns whenever possible. For example, key words for research on Charlotte Perkins Gilman's "The Yellow Wall-Paper" might include her name and the title of the story, *mental illness* (one of the topics of the story), *nineteenth-century medicine* (another topic), and *feminism* (an intellectual movement that considers Gilman's work important). Use the *Library of Congress Guide to Subject Headings,* available in your library's reference section, to identify headings for your topic. Your reference librarian will show you how to use it.

■ *List synonyms and related terms.* As you list key words, think of synonyms to expand or narrow your search. Research on overcrowding in national parks might use such related terms as *government lands, federal lands, national forests, national monuments, wilderness, conservation,* or *environmentalism.*

■ *Expand or narrow the search.* If key words are not leading to sources, expand your search with more general words, or narrow it with more restrictive ones. A researcher getting nowhere using "The Yellow Wall-Paper" as a search term might expand his search with the author's name. Another researcher, not finding what she wants using the term *national parks,* might narrow her search to specific parks such as Grand Canyon or Yellowstone.

■ *Learn the abbreviations for search terms.* Nearly every search tool, print or electronic, uses abbreviations in its description of sources. Learn what these stand for by checking introductory glossaries or help screens.

■ *Take advantage of special library services.* Many libraries will reserve sources for you on request or order them through interlibrary loan. See your reference librarian early in your research process.

2 ■ Special guidelines for electronic searches

Finding help electronically. Most electronic search tools come with instructions for their use. Look for introductory screens, welcome messages, help screens, or files with names such as "?", "Readme," "About . . . ," "FAQ [frequently asked questions]," or "Formulating a search with . . ."

Using word variations. In addition to key words and synonyms, try singular or plural word forms, different word combinations (*parks, national parks, government land,* and so forth), different disciplines (botany instead of biology, psychology instead of literature), and truncated words in which an asterisk (*) or a pound sign (#) replaces part of a word (*environ** will help you search for sources containing key words such as *environment, environmental, environmentalist, environmentalism,* and *environmental movement*).

Boolean searching. A **Boolean search** (named after George Boole, a nineteenth-century mathematician and logician) uses the terms *AND, OR, NOT,* and *NEAR* (written in all capital letters) to expand or restrict a search.

47.1
Boolean
searching:
Web link

■ *AND.* If you tell an electronic search tool to look for *national parks* alone and *pollution* alone, it will list all works having to do with either subject. But if you tell it to search for *national parks AND pollution,* it will narrow your search to only those sources in which both terms appear.

■ *OR.* If you wish to expand a search, use *or.* Telling a search tool to look for *preservation OR conservation* will lead to all sources that contain either term.

■ *NOT.* Using *not* will narrow a search. Telling a search tool to look for *national parks NOT Yosemite* will lead to all sources about national parks except those mentioning Yosemite National Park.

■ *NEAR, ADJACENT, or FOLLOWED BY.* In some electronic search tools, especially those used for searching the Internet, you can use *near, adjacent,* or *followed by* to narrow a search. Telling a search tool to look for *National Parks NEAR pollution* will lead you only to those sources in which these terms appear within a few words of each other.

Note: Not all electronic search tools recognize the Boolean operators described above. Some use symbols like plus or minus signs: + or − (see 48d3).

Choosing and accessing sources. Some search tools include abstracts briefly summarizing sources. Check these to decide whether a source is worth reading. When you identify potentially useful sources, many of these tools provide options for viewing all or part of a source, downloading it to your computer, or printing it out as hard copy.

47d Use library search tools to identify sources

1 ■ Using library catalogs

Whether your library catalogs its holdings in a computerized database, on cards in file drawers, or on microfilm, you'll search for sources about your topic in three ways, according to key words for your topic, author names, or source titles. At the beginning of a search, you'll probably use key words.

Note: Literary research topics: Look up the author's name to find information about the work you're studying.

If you use a computerized library catalog, you will be presented with a series of successively restricted screens: first an initial search screen, then lists of sources, and finally a screen containing detailed publication and availability information about a single source. See the sample screen below.

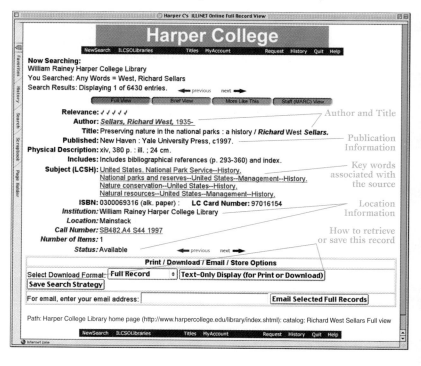

- *Expanding or narrowing a search.* To expand or narrow your search, combine search terms and use the Boolean operators *AND, OR, NOT,* and *NEAR.* (See 47c2.)

- *Partial title or author names.* To search for sources when you have only a partial title or name, type in what you know, and the catalog will list all sources with titles or author names that contain what you've typed.

- *Noting bibliographic information.* When you identify a potential source, record complete publication information by hand, or copy and paste the citation in a computer file. In either case, arrange each citation in the appropriate documentation style for your paper. (See 53a and b for the MLA style and 55b and c for the APA style.)

- *Checking availability.* After you've recorded publication information for a source, use the computer to check for availability (whether it's on the shelf or checked out) and location (in the main stacks, on reserve, or at a branch library).

2 ▪ Using electronic indexes

Indexes list sources alphabetically. Some, such as *The Readers' Guide to Periodical Literature,* list only periodical articles; others, such as *EbscoHost,* include books, articles, and other sources. Some, such as *NewsBank,* list sources on a broad range of topics; others, such as the Modern Language Association's *International Bibliography,* are devoted to one general subject area. Many of these indexes are available in your library through a network link in your library's computer catalog.

- *Years of coverage.* Electronic indexes usually cover several years of publication, making them more comprehensive than a single print volume of an index. If an electronic index does not go back far enough for the sources you need (for literary or historical research), use the print versions of the index.

- *Search strategy.* Search for sources as you would in any electronic catalog, by key words, title, author, or combinations of these.

- *Noting bibliographic information.* When you identify a potential source, record complete publication information by hand, or copy and paste the citation in a computer file. In either case, arrange each citation in the appropriate documentation style for your paper. (See 53a and b for the MLA style and 55b and c for the APA style.)

- *Viewing and recording information.* Most indexes will permit you to copy and paste, print, or e-mail abstracts or complete texts.

See the sample screens on pp. 324 and 325, illustrating a search for sources on the topic of standardized testing: a keyword search screen, a results screen listing sources, and an abstract screen briefly summarizing

A search in an online library database

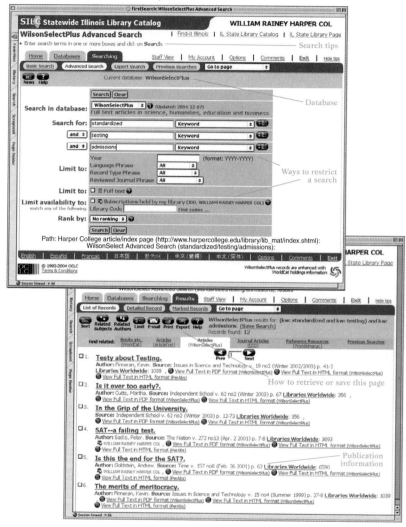

A results page listing sources on a topic, with links to those sources

one source. The results and abstract screens contain links leading to the actual source.

3 ▪ Using print indexes

Print versions of many of these indexes are located in the reference section of a library. Issued annually, they list publications for a single

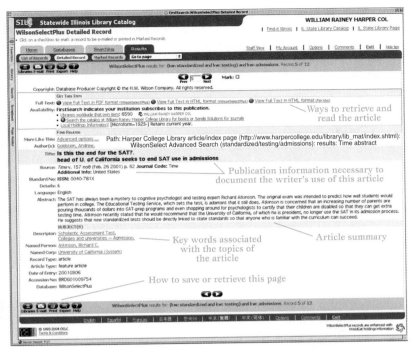

An abstract summarizing an article

year. To investigate what has been published over a number of years, you would have to search several volumes. Search for sources as you would in any index—by subject, author, or title.

47e Compile a bibliography of sources

A **bibliography** is a systematic list of sources. You'll use this list to locate sources and, as you write your paper, to document borrowed information and give credit to your sources.

1 ■ Noting bibliographic information

As you identify a source on your topic, record publication and location information for it. At the beginning of your research, you may simply print this information from electronic catalogs and indexes. Later you'll turn it into individual bibliographic citations, each in a format appropriate to your discipline or subject area.

Writing note slips. If you write bibliographic information by hand, use slips instead of lists on sheets of paper. Individual slips, each with its own source, will be easier to use as you search for titles, add and drop sources, and arrange these slips for documentation. To take a shortcut, divide sheets of notebook paper into quarters, write a citation in each quarter, and cut the sheets into individual slips as you search for the sources themselves or prepare a bibliography.

Using a computer. If you write with a computer, you may compile bibliographic information in a file that you alphabetize, update, and correct as you go along. You won't need note slips. At the end of your project, you can rework this file to become the list of works cited or list of references accompanying the final draft of your paper.

What to include. Note the author's name, title of the individual work, other relevant identifying information such as editor and edition, publication information, page numbers, and call numbers for locating a source in the library. If it is an electronic source, note the medium—for example, *CD-ROM* or *online*—the computer service, the date of your search, and the URL, or electronic address.

Incomplete information. If a catalog or index does not provide complete information, leave blanks to be filled in later when you have the actual source.

Documentation styles. As you write bibliography notes, follow the documentation style assigned by your instructor or preferred by the discipline in which you are writing. Use the Modern Language Association (MLA) style for papers in the humanities, including literature, history, religion, and the arts. (For sample MLA citations, see 53b.) Use the American Psychological Association (APA) style for writing in the social sciences. (For sample APA citations, see 55c. For a list of style manuals in other disciplines, see 57b.)

Comparing publication information. When you actually locate a source, compare the publication information on its title page or in its preliminary pages with the publication information in your notes. Correct or complete your citation. The following is a bibliography note for a book written in the MLA documentation style.

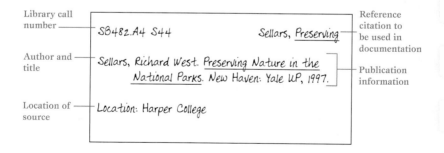

Library call number ⟶ SB482.A4 S44   Sellars, *Preserving* ⟵ Reference citation to be used in documentation

Author and title ⟶ Sellars, Richard West. *Preserving Nature in the National Parks.* New Haven: Yale UP, 1997. ⟵ Publication information

Location of source ⟶ Location: Harper College

🖥 **COMPUTER TIP** Copying and Pasting Bibliographic Information

If you use online search tools, you will probably be able to copy and paste online bibliographic citations into your bibliography. Be sure to rearrange these citations to fit the required documentation style for your paper, capitalizing and punctuating as necessary. (See 53a and b for the MLA style and 55b and c for the APA style.) Here is an example.

A newspaper citation as it appears in an online index.

The Chronicle of Higher Education, June 8, 2001 v47 I39 pB11(2)

How admission tests hinder access to graduate and professional schools. Peter Sacks

The same citation reformatted in the MLA style. (See 53b.)

Sacks, Peter. "How Admission Tests Hinder Access to Graduate and Professional Schools." The Chronicle of Higher Education 8 June 2001, sec. B: 11.

Note how reformatting in the MLA style has (1) organized the citation into a double-spaced hanging paragraph, (2) reversed the author's first and last names to permit alphabetical arrangement, (3) added appropriate punctuation, (4) capitalized the title, (5) underlined the journal title, and (6) omitted unnecessary information. The way you reformat your citations will depend upon the documentation style required by your assignment.

A computer program known as a bibliography generator, such as Citation, Nota Bene, Reference Manager, or EndNote Plus, can arrange publication information for you in the appropriate bibliographic style. Two online bibliography generators are available at < http://www.easybib.com > and < http://www. landmark-project.com/citation_machine/index.php > .

2 ▪ Writing a working bibliography

At the beginning of your research, your instructor may ask you to prepare a **working bibliography** listing all the sources you plan to read. When you finish your paper, you'll use an updated and corrected version to prepare the Works Cited or reference list accompanying your finished project.

To prepare a working bibliography, arrange your note slips in the order required by the documentation system you're using and copy your entries on a sheet of paper following the appropriate format. Or, if you've compiled a computerized bibliography file, format your citations appropriately and print them. See 53a for Modern Language Association guidelines and the sample MLA papers in Chapter 54 and 59d. See 55b for American Psychological Association reference list guidelines and 55d for a sample reference list.

3 ▪ Writing an annotated bibliography

Your instructor may assign an **annotated bibliography**, a list of sources in which each entry is followed by a brief descriptive and evaluative paragraph. Such a bibliography will inform readers of the content,

47.2
Writing an annotated bibliography: Web link

relevance, and quality of the sources you cite. To prepare an annotated bibliography, do the following:

47.3
Writing
bibliographic
citations:
Exercises

- Select sources that provide a variety of perspectives on your topic.

- Cite each work in the appropriate documentation style, such as MLA or APA style.

- After each citation, write a brief descriptive paragraph in which you evaluate the credentials of the writer, identify the intended audience, compare the work to similar works, and explain what it contributes to your topic.

48 Searching the Internet

48.1
Internet
tutorial:
Web link

If you're a college student, you're probably among the nearly ninety percent of US college students who now use the Internet to find out what's new or news, to communicate, to shop, to enjoy yourself—and to prepare classroom assignments. With its vast number of electronic documents, its democratic format that allows almost anyone to say almost anything, its speed, convenience, and increasing ease of use, the Internet is now an invaluable tool of modern living.

48a Manage your Internet search

1 ▪ Keeping track of Internet addresses

48.2
Under-
standing
URLs:
Web link

The addresses that enable you to navigate the Internet, also known as **URLs (Uniform Resource Locators)**, are composed of three parts: a "protocol" identifying the computer language used to gain access to a site, the "domain" identifying the owner of a site, and a "directory path" indicating where this address leads on the Internet. Here are the parts of the address for the National Park Service's home page:

protocol   domain   directory path

http://www.nps.gov/parks.html

Because these addresses are essential for locating a site, revisiting it, and documenting online information—but sometimes difficult to remember—it's important to keep track of them as you make your way from site to site. Here are two methods.

- *Using Internet Bookmarks or Favorites files.* You can set an electronic bookmark. Select the "Add Bookmark" option from the Bookmarks menu in Netscape Communicator or the "Add to Favorites" option from the Favorites menu in Internet Explorer. Communicator

immediately adds the address to the Bookmarks menu. Internet
Explorer pops up a window that allows you to edit the address and
organize your bookmarks into folders.

■ *Preparing an Internet address file.* Create a file in your word processor in which you store addresses that you've copied from your browser's
"Address" or "Go" box as you visit individual Internet sites. Also copy
non-hypertext addresses that you find unhighlighted in electronic documents or addresses that appear in print documents. Later, you can visit
or revisit sites by copying and pasting these addresses from your word
processing file back into your browser's address window. To make this
file especially useful, include the name of each site, a word or two about
its contents or your intended use of it, even a full citation of the site in
the appropriate documentation format. For a list of required publication
information, see 47e1. (For more on documenting Internet sources, see
53b for MLA guidelines and 55c for APA guidelines.)

2 ■ Writing Internet addresses in the MLA style

■ *Using URLs in the text of your writing.* Enclose Internet and e-
mail addresses in angle brackets. Do not leave internal spaces or
drop internal punctuation or capitalization. For example:

Further information about the increase in air pollution at the

Grand Canyon is available at the Environmental Defense Fund site:

<http://www.edf.org>.

■ *Using URLs in bibliographies.* Do not italicize or underline URLs
or e-mail addresses in the list of Works Cited. Enclose them with angle
brackets. For example: < http://www.edf.org > . If necessary, turn off
the "links" or "HTML citation" feature of your word processor so that
Internet addresses print in plain text and black instead of blue ink.

■ *Breaking addresses.* If you must break a URL or e-mail address, follow these MLA guidelines: (1) Break only after a slashmark (/).
(2) Never add a hyphen when you must break an address. (3) Do
not break the protocol (*http://*). (4) Add a period after a URL at the
end of a sentence. For example:

The US Forest Service environmental impact statement is

now available at <http://www.canyonforestvillage.com/

eis.htm>.

■ *Working with missing or long URLs.* Occasionally, an online
source may lack a URL (the case with documents from services such
as America Online) or may have a URL that is long, complex, and
difficult to transcribe (often the case with files in online library databases). In case of missing URLs, give the URL of the site's home
page and then list the search words you used to locate the document.

In the case of long URLs, give the URL of the site's search page. For more on working with such sources, see items 38 and 39 in 53b.

3 ■ Identifying suitable sites for your research

Identify site sponsors. Individuals and organizations have all kinds of motives and biases that influence the design and contents of their Internet sites. Sometimes these motives will serve your interests as a researcher, sometimes not. Begin to identify site sponsors and their motives by considering the suffixes in the domain (middle) portion of Internet addresses: *.com* (commercial or for profit), *.edu* (educational), *.gov* (government), *.mil* (military), *.net* (network management), *.org* (noncommercial, nonprofit organization).

Classify Internet sites. From a research perspective, Internet sites may be classified in five ways. As you consider a site, decide what category it fits and whether something in that category is likely to be helpful to your research. Then, as you actually investigate a site, evaluate its usefulness according to the guidelines in 49a.

- *Advocacy sites* aim to influence your opinion or behavior. Frequently their Internet addresses end in *.org.* But other sites whose addresses end in *.com, .edu,* or *.gov* may also contain documents advocating positions associated with topics of interest to them.

- *Business/marketing sites* want to sell something. Usually their Internet addresses end in *.com*—but not always. If you use such sites, identify what the site is selling and decide how any information it contains helps to market the product.

- *News sites* such as *CNN,* the *New York Times,* or the Google search tool's *News* page provide current events coverage and, sometimes, editorial opinion.

- *Informational sites* provide factual information. Their addresses frequently end in *.edu* and *.gov.* Some sites that appear informational, especially those with addresses ending in *.com* or *.org,* may actually argue for a particular opinion.

- *Personal sites* represent one person's personality, interests, knowledge, and opinions—expert or non-expert. Such sites may appear as part of an organizational site whose address ends in *.com, .edu,* or *.org* and frequently contain a tilde (~) as in < http://www.harpercollege.edu/ ~ tthoreson > .

4 ■ Reading and saving Internet sources

When you find a site that looks promising, you have several options.

- Read the source on screen and take notes. Take computerized notes by creating a file in your word processor and splitting your computer screen between the Internet site and the notes file. (See the computer tip in 2e.)

- Print the source and read it later, highlighting the text or taking notes. To save time (and printer ink or toner), turn off images in the text by clicking the appropriate link.

- Copy the source; then paste it into a file in your word processing program. Write a statement to introduce your borrowing, surround it with quotation marks (what you've cut and pasted is now a direct quotation), and provide complete publication information for the source. (See the "How to Avoid Copy-and-Paste Plagiarism" box on pp. 349–350.)

- You can save many sources on your own computer by performing a download using your browser software. To save other sources, you may need special software such as Adobe Acrobat Reader or FTP software.

48.3
Download
software:
Web link

48b Search the World Wide Web

In the vast cyberspace of the Internet, the largest portion and the one you're probably most familiar with is the World Wide Web, with its Web page combinations of text, graphics, links to other Web pages, even sound. Its size, ease of use, information contents, and gateways to other parts of the Internet make it the place where you'll do most of your online research. Here are just some of the Web sites you can investigate and ways to get to them:

- *Archives* of print documents and images. Find online books at Project Bartleby < http://www.bartleby.com >, Project Gutenberg < http://www.promo.net/pg/index.html >, and the Electronic Text Center < http://etext.lib.virginia.edu >. For back issues of scholarly journals, go to the Scholarly Journal Archive < http://www.jstor.org >. For images, go to the American Memory digital image collection < http://lcweb2.loc.gov/amhome.html >.

- *Newspapers and periodicals.* Some newspapers and periodicals are published only online, such as *Slate* < http:slate.msn.com > and *Salon* < http://www.salon.com >. Others are online versions of print publications, such as the *New York Times* < http://nytimes.com >. For links to many newspapers and periodicals, go to NewsLink at < http://www.newslink.org >, the Internet Public Library at < http://www.ipl.org/div/serials >, or the Newspaper and Current Periodical Reading Room at the Library of Congress < http://www.loc.gov/rr/news >.

- *Government sites* at every level of government:
  Bureau of the Census < http://www.census.gov >
  Department of Justice Statistics < http://www.ojp.usdoj.gov/bjs >

Bureau of Labor Statistics < http:// stats.bls.gov >
Department of Education < http://www.ed.gov >
National Institutes of Health < http://www.nih.gov >
Library of Congress < http://lcweb.loc.gov >

■ *Academic and municipal libraries,* many with online collections.

■ *Nonprofit, professional, and business organizations.*

■ *Discussion groups* on a vast array of topics.

You can visit all of these sites directly if you know their addresses, or you can reach them indirectly by investigating your research topic with the following search tools.

1 ■ Using search engines for key word searches

If you have a clear idea of your research topic and have key terms to describe it, then you should do a key word search using a search engine such as Google or HotBot. A **search engine** scans the texts of documents in its database looking for the key words you've told it to search for. (See 48b4 for a list of these search tools.)

If, for example, you tell a search engine to look for sources about *standardized testing* and *gender bias,* it will give a list of all sources containing these key words. The sources are arranged in order of their relevance to your topic: how many times a source uses your key words or how closely a source matches what you're looking for. When you first use a particular search engine, be sure to check its FAQs file ("Frequently Asked Questions") or help screens for guidance to its use. See the sample Google screen illustrating a key word search.

2 ■ Using classified subject directories for browsing

If you're hazy about a topic or unsure of its key words, then you should browse the Internet with a subject directory such as Yahoo!, the Librarians' Index to the Internet, or InfoMine. A subject directory will carry you down through a series of menus from general to more narrow topics until you find the specific topic you want to investigate and a list of sources written about that topic. (See 48b4 for a list of these tools.)

If, for example, you are investigating the effects of air pollution on US national parks but are unsure how to look for sources, you might turn to a directory like the Librarians' Index to the Internet. In your browser's address window, you'll type its URL and be taken to its home page. There, as in the search illustrated on p. 334, you'll see a number of hypertext links: *Arts, Crafts, & Humanities, Government & Law, Science, Technology & Computers.* Beneath each are more specific links. For example, under *Science, Technology & Computers* are *Animals, Environment, Geography,* and so forth. Click on *Environment* and you'll be taken to a list of even more specific topic links, all having to do with the environ-

48.4
Web guides
and search
tools:
Web link

Key words used in search

Link

Text containing key words

Title and source

Address

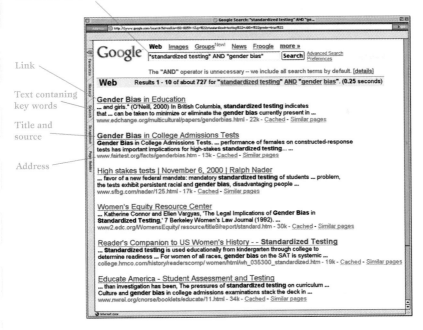

ment, among them, *air pollution.* Browsing through the Librarians' Index to the Internet in this way, you'll move through successively restricted topics, coming eventually to individual Web sites.

Note: Some search engines like Google also contain classified directories, and subject directories like Yahoo! and the Librarians' Index to the Internet generally permit key word searches, as the search on p. 334 illustrates. Explore the features of your search tools as you proceed with your research.

3 ■ Using other search tools

If you have the time, try **multi-tool searching**. Search for sources on your topic using both a search engine and a subject directory. Or choose a multi-engine (also called a "meta-search") tool such as Metacrawler or Vivísimo. (See 48b4 for a list of these tools.)

Note: Because no search tool, not even a multi-search tool, lists all the sources on a topic and because no two search tools list the same sources, you should always use more than one search tool. The more search tools you use, the greater your chance of success in finding sources.

A sample subject directory search

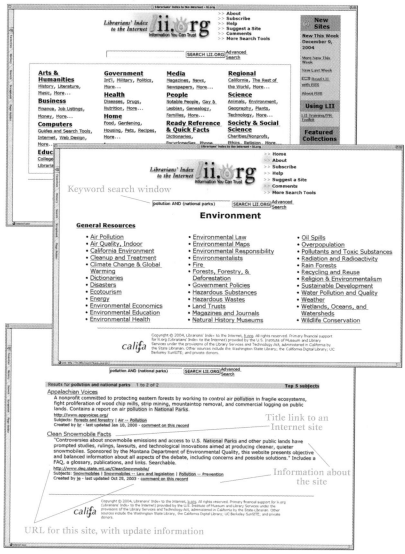

Directory home page; Subtopics page; Results page

4 ■ Web guides and search tools

Master Web sites with guides to searching and links to search tools

Noodle Tools Choose the Best Search:
http://www.noodletools.com/debbie/literacies/information/5locate/adviceengine.html

Southern Oregon University guide to Internet Searching Tools: *http://www.sou.edu/library/searchtools*

Some good search engines

Google (a huge database, uncluttered screens, excellent source ranking): *http://www.google.com*

Teoma (another huge database): *http://www.teoma.com*

HotBot (results sorted by date or media type): *http://www.hotbot.com*

Some good classified subject directories

About.com (directories compiled by subject experts): *http://www.about.com*

Ask Jeeves (answers to natural-language questions): *http://www.ask.com*

Infomine (directory compiled by academic librarians, annotations): *http://infomine.ucr.edu*

Librarians' Index (highest quality listings, annotations): *http://www.lii.org*

Yahoo! (many subdirectories to guide searching): *http://www.yahoo.com*

Some multi-search tools

Easy Searcher: (links to topic-specific search tools): *http://www.easysearcher.com*

Vivísimo: *http://vivisimo.com*

Metacrawler: *http://www.metacrawler.com*

People finders

Bigfoot (e-mail addresses): *http://www.bigfoot.com*

InfoSpace: *http://www.infospace.com*

Switchboard: *http://www.switchboard.com*

Yahoo! People Search: *http://people.yahoo.com*

Image searching

About.com: *http://websearch.about.com/cs/imagesearch*

Yahoo! (maps): *http://maps.yahoo.com*

48c Search discussion groups, Weblogs, and other Web spaces

1 ▪ Reading newsgroup postings

News groups are electronically connected groups of people and their collections of messages, called "postings." These discussions, arranged in topic "threads," are made available for a specified length of time through a network variously called Usenet or Netnews. The many thousands of these "threads" are organized under ten broad headings: *alt.,* any conceivable topic; *biz.,* business-related topics; *comp.,* computer information; *humanities.,* art, literature, philosophy; *misc.,* employment, health, and more; *news.,* information about news groups; *rec.,* sports and recreation; *sci.,* science; *soc.,* social issues; *talk.,* current events. To investigate discussions on your research topic, go to the Google search engine home page and click on "Google Groups."

Note: Evaluate news group sources with care. Anyone and everyone can join a news group, and the quality of the contributions varies widely. (For guidelines on evaluating information, see 49a.)

2 ▪ Subscribing to listservs

48.5
Listserv
discussion
lists:
Web link

A **listserv** is a subscription-based e-mail discussion of a particular topic. The postings of each subscriber are sent by a list owner to the e-mail addresses of all other subscribers, who may then reply, creating a topic "thread." The many thousands of these groups are divided into "public" or "open" discussions, available to anyone who wishes to subscribe, and "private" or "closed" discussions, requiring permission to participate. To search for listservs, visit the directories at < http://topica.com > or < http://tile.net/lists >.

To join or contribute to a listserv that interests you, send a subscription message to the listserv's subscription e-mail address, usually accompanying the name of the discussion list itself, or click on a link named "Subscribe." In the body of your subscription message, not the subject heading, include the word *SUBSCRIBE* in all capitals. For example, if you wanted to subscribe to the National Parks Pollution listserv, you would type "SUBSCRIBE National Parks Pollution" plus your name and e-mail address. To receive reference cards containing general user commands, or to ask questions, include the words *HELP* or *INFO.*

Note: (1) Never send a subscription message to the listserv e-mail address itself; that is reserved for the listserv discussion. Send subscription queries to the subscription address. (2) Evaluate listserv contributions as carefully as you would newsgroup postings, especially those that appear in public or unmoderated listservs. (For guidelines on evaluating information sources, see 49a.).

3 ▪ Reading Weblogs

48.6
A Weblog
directory:
Web link

A **Weblog,** commonly referred to as a "blog," is a Web page of chronologically arranged and dated entries, an online journal of sorts. The Weblog writer or "blogger" writes a brief entry on a topic of interest to him or her to which readers respond in posted comments. Some blogs are very personal, like diaries, but others are professional, concerned with public issues, like the blog on political issues sponsored by the

Columbia Journalism Review. The latter become a kind of newsletter and, through the "post comments" feature, provide a way for researchers to contact experts in a field they're researching. Also of interest to researchers is the "blogroll," a list of links to other Internet sites that is a feature of nearly every blog. The blogger provides links to sites that he or she finds interesting, and functions thereby as a kind of filter to the rest of the Web, leading you to important sites you might not otherwise find. To locate Weblogs, type "Weblogs" and your topic in a search engine's search window.

Note: Evaluate Weblogs and their linked Web sites with care. Anyone can create a blog. Many blogs contain an "About" page that provides information about the blog's author. (For evaluation guidelines, see 49a).

4 ▪ Searching the "Invisible Web"

Search tools like Google and Yahoo! index billions and billions of electronic documents, but they don't list everything. Many documents exist in what has been called the "deep" or "invisible" Web, out of sight of search tools, deep in academic, organizational, governmental, or municipal library databases. Many of these contain detailed information about topics interesting and important to academic researchers. To locate such sources, try the following strategies:

- Use search tools specifically designed to search the "Invisible Web." Gain access to them through < http://www.invisibleweb.com > or < http://www.completeplanet.com > .

- Choose search tools that routinely index databases, such as Librarians' Index to the Internet or Infomine.

- Focus your Google or Yahoo! search by including the word *database* with the key words for your topics, for example: "*US National Parks AND database*" or "*standardized testing AND admissions AND database.*"

48d Use effective search techniques

1 ▪ Using help screens and FAQs

Develop an understanding of the search tools you use. Every search tool comes with guides to its use. Examine the home page or first screen for links to a help screen or a "Frequently Asked Questions" (FAQs) file. As you experiment with a search tool, don't be intimidated by links called "advanced," "super search," or "expert searching." If you want help, consult one of the many online tutorials available (see the Internet tutorial links listed on *The Ready Reference Handbook* Web site, for example).

48.7
Internet
search
guide:
Web link

2 ▪ Focusing and narrowing your search terms

▪ Avoid general terms except when they are modified by more specific ones. Searching for *parks* will give you millions of sources. *National parks* will limit your sources somewhat, but you'll still get citations for parks in Canada, New Zealand, and Australia, as well as the United States. Limiting yourself to *US national parks* will focus your search further.

▪ Use Boolean search operators to link key words (see 47c2). Searching *Grand Canyon AND visitors AND air pollution* will lead to a focused search. Whenever possible, use a unique phrase as your search term; you'll see listed only those documents in which that phrase appears.

▪ Search for organizations associated with your topic. They will provide you with hypertext links to other sites containing additional information. If your topic is controversial, however, remember to search for organizations on all sides of an issue. For example, search for both the National Right to Life and the National Abortion and Reproductive Rights Action League sites.

▪ Narrow the field of your search. When appropriate to your topic, click on the buttons that allow you to restrict your search by date or geographic location.

3 ▪ Using search operators with Internet search tools

48.8
Search
operators:
Web link

In 47c2, you learned to use Boolean search operators to narrow a search for sources: *AND, OR, NOT, NEAR,* and so forth. Be sure to type these operators in all capital letters between the terms you're searching for. Be aware that not all search tools will accept these operators; some use punctuation marks or symbols instead. See the search tool help screens for further information.

▪ Use double quotation marks (". . .") to treat a group of words as a phrase—for example, *"automobile pollution in national parks."*

▪ If your search tool accepts them, use " + " (plus) as you would the Boolean *AND;* use "–" (minus) as you would the operator *NOT.* For example: *+ Yosemite + pollution – automobile.*

▪ Use an asterisk "*" to truncate a key word to its base, so you can search for variants of the word. For example, shorten *pollution* to *pollut** to search for variants such as *pollution, pollute, polluter,* and *polluting.*

▪ Use capitalization to treat adjacent words as proper names; use a comma between proper names—for example, *Aldo Leopold, John Muir, Gifford Pinchot.*

4 ▪ Solving common search problems

Typing URLs correctly. It's easy to mistype a computer address. If you're not finding the source you're looking for, check the address to be sure you've typed all the letters, numbers, and punctuation correctly. Look carefully for incorrect capital letters and unnecessary spaces.

Narrowing a topic that is too broad. If your topic is too broad, begin by searching in a subject directory. When you find a more restricted topic, switch to a key word search. You'll limit yourself to the last topic category and produce a shorter list of sources to examine.

Coping with sources. If your search is giving you too many sources, concentrate on the top ten or so. Examine them to see whether their hypertext links lead to more relevant sources. Google's "Similar pages" option is useful here. If your search is not leading to enough sources, broaden it by omitting the least-required key word. Or try another search engine; not all search tools list the same sources. If you want to print or download a lengthy file and can live without graphics, click on the "text only" option if it exists at that site. You'll get only the text of the file, and you'll get it more quickly.

Guessing relevant sites with unknown addresses. If you are unable to find relevant sources, try to guess the URL (address) of an organization associated with your topic. In the "Address" box of your browser, type in a basic Web template beginning < *http://www.* Then add the name or abbreviation of a relevant organization. Conclude with the appropriate domain suffix: *.com* (commercial); *.edu* (educational); *.gov* (government); and so forth. For example, if you are researching standardized tests, you might guess that the URL of the Educational Testing Service would look something like < http://www.ets.org > , and you'd be right.

Locating sites that have moved. Ocasionally, Internet sources move from one host computer to another. When they do, their addresses change. To find a source that has moved without leaving a forwarding address link, type a URL into a browser "Address" box; then delete parts of it, beginning at the right and stopping at each slashmark. If, for example, you're searching without success for an article on pollution in US National Parks called "Effects of Visual Air Quality on Visitor Experience," which was originally located at < http://www.aqd.nps.gov/ard/visitexp.htm > , begin by omitting *visitexp.htm* to see whether you can locate the article at another site.

Locating publication information. Sometimes it is difficult to locate all the publication information necessary to document Internet sources. See how this information is displayed on the sample Web page, p. 340.

▪ *Author names and publication dates.* Look for author names and publication dates in file headers and footers. Also, authors may have included e-mail addresses containing their names (look for the @ symbol to identify e-mail addresses)

Web page title

Site sponsor

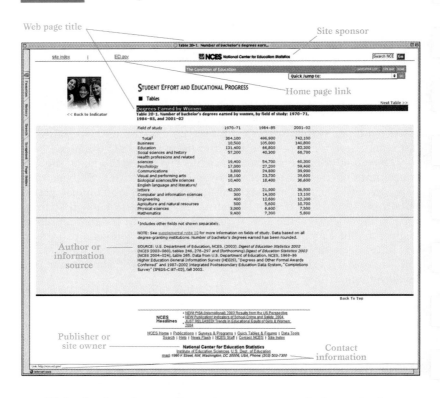

Author or
information
source

Publisher or
site owner

Home page link

Contact
information

- *Titles.* Look at the top of your browser screen window or in the upper corner of text. If a title seems incomplete, go to the Document or Source Information window. If a document is untitled, create an appropriate title enclosed in square brackets [. . .].

48.9
Gathering
Web site
information:
Exercises

- *Publishers or site owners.* For information about publishers, see the "About this Site" or home page link. Also, you may be able to reach a home page by shortening the URL to the domain name. For example, if you can't locate publication information at < http://www.mla.org/main_stl.htm > , shorten the address to < http://www.mla.org > .

48e Use Internet sources fairly and responsibly

1 ▪ Deciding on your intentions, observing copyright protection

Internet sources are considered published works. Like print works, most Internet sources are protected by copyright laws against misuse by others, even when these sources lack the copyright symbol (©). You may, of course, borrow copyrighted materials to use in your own writing, but you must follow certain guidelines, depending on what you will do with your project. (For more on copyright, see 51a.)

Unpublished research projects. If you borrow print or Internet materials solely for classroom use, without publishing your project (that is, copying it for distribution outside of class or displaying it on the Internet), you may use limited parts of copyrighted works, provided that you acknowledge your borrowing in the text of your paper and give complete publication information. (See Chapters 52–57.)

Published research projects. If you distribute your work outside of class or display it on the Internet, your work is considered "published." Just as your words are now protected by copyright, you must also respect the copyright of materials that you borrow.

- *Using non-copyrighted sources.* Certain sources are considered in the "public domain" and are not covered by copyright protection: older print sources published before the 1920s (and sometimes posted on the Internet), government materials, and print and Internet materials explicitly labeled as free for distribution without restrictions. You may borrow from these sources without official permission, although you must document your borrowing.

- *Using copyrighted sources.* All other sources are considered copyrighted: works published after the 1920s, personal communication (letters and e-mail), poetry, music, and images or graphic illustrations. You may use these sources in a project that you distribute or display on the Internet, but you may need to ask written permission to do so. (For guidelines on deciding whether written permission is necessary see 51a; 51c will show you how to make your request.) If you need to ask permission, do so immediately. The process can be time consuming.

2 ■ Recognizing student Internet sites and commercial term paper sites

In the course of your research, you may come across student papers posted online. Student essays such as these might help clarify your thinking about your own topic. You may even want to borrow ideas from these papers. But remember, these student writers are probably in the same position you are—at the beginning of their academic careers. Scholars and other professionals usually provide more reliable information. Evaluate student sources carefully (see 49a). If you do borrow from them, document your borrowing as you would any other source.

Commercial term paper sites are another matter. You can spot them easily enough; if you've done much Internet searching, you've probably already seen them, with names that run from the pseudo-serious to the cynically comic: "Academic Research Group," "Superior Term Papers," "Term Paper Genie," or "Cheathouse.com." You should know several things: (1) No matter how much these sites protest that they provide only research assistance, your instructors consider the submission of purchased papers to be plagiarism. (2) As for content quality, papers sold by these sites are usually not worth their often high prices. (3) Your instructors can usually identify these papers for what they are.

49 Evaluating Print and Electronic Sources, Writing Research Notes

49a Evaluate sources with the "CASE" method

49.1
Evaluating
Web sites:
Web link

Not all sources are equal in value. Some may not suit your purposes; others may have inaccurate information or flawed reasoning. To decide which sources to investigate for your project, think of the word *case*. In order to make your case and support your thesis, be sure that each of your sources meets the standards represented by the letters C, A, S, E: *C*urrency, *A*uthority, *S*uitability, and *E*ase of Use. Use particular care in evaluating Internet sources.

1 ■ Currency: Is this source up-to-date?

Print sources

When was this source published? Is it a first edition, reprint, or revision? For most research topics, you want current sources that contain the most recent information and opinion. For literary and historical topics, however, currency is not always a relevant standard. Primary sources published hundreds of years ago, and secondary sources published decades ago, may still provide valuable insights. But for technical and social science topics, in which information and opinion are changing rapidly, currency is important.

Internet sources

Most Internet sources have three dates associated with them: publication date, file date (when they are placed on a particular host computer), and revision date. Look at the beginning or end of a file for publication and revision dates. Prefer sites with the most recent dates.

2 ■ Authority: Is this source authoritative and trustworthy?

Print sources

- What are the author's credentials for writing about this topic? Is this person an expert or eyewitness? What political, religious, or social beliefs may influence this person's view of the facts or objectivity? What organizational affiliations reveal this person's point of view? A biased source is not necessarily a bad source, but you need to know what the biases are and how they influence objectivity.

- Is the publication source (e.g., a university press, scholarly journal, major publisher) known for publishing reliable information? Are submissions to this publication source checked for their quality— "refereed"—by a panel of experts?

- What do reviews say about the author or the source? If a source is long or controversial, take a few minutes to read reviews in periodicals such as *Current Biography, Book Review Digest,* or *Book Review Index.* Your reference librarian will guide you to these resources.

Internet sources

Because the Internet, newsgroups, and e-mail are open to anyone with a computer, online sources vary widely in the expertise of their authors. With few editorial review boards in cyberspace to vouch for quality, you must use these sources with care.

- Examine Internet addresses for their domain abbreviations: *.com, .edu, .org,* and so forth. The domain of a source doesn't guarantee quality, but it may suggest purpose or point of view, or the likelihood that a source has been checked for accuracy.

- Check an author's home or "About" page. Use an author's name to search for his or her home page, which may contain information you can use to evaluate trustworthiness. Look for organizational affiliations that suggest point of view or bias. A " ~ " (tilde) in a URL indicates a personal Web site.

- Send an e-mail message. Online authors often include e-mail addresses with their names. Explore their qualifications or the background of their opinions. You can locate e-mail addresses with a people finder or "fingering" program. (See the Web sites in 48b4.)

- Trace an author's postings. Evaluate the trustworthiness of an author by tracing his or her various contributions to a newsgroup or listserv. Check whether the newsgroup or listserv has a moderator to screen postings for quality and suitability.

- Follow hypertext links. See whether the source you are viewing is linked to quality sites. Do these sites verify the claims of the source you are considering? Do they have the same outlook? Two sites connected by hypertext links are not equally authoritative. And one source does not necessarily authorize another. Evaluate each site separately.

3 ▪ Suitability: Does this source meet your needs and those of your readers?

Print sources

- Does this source contain the materials that you want and that your readers need: facts, explanation, opinion, statistics, examples, eyewitness accounts, narratives? What are its main idea, thesis, and major supporting points? Will they lead you away from your topic?

- What is the purpose of this source: to inform, entertain, evaluate, or persuade? Does its purpose match your own or the needs of your readers?

- Do you and your readers share the point of view of this source? A source that your readers may reject as biased will probably not suit your purposes.

- What is this source's coverage of your topic? Is it broad in scope, presenting detailed background information? Is it narrow in scope, focusing on a specific topic? Does it present its topics in depth or superficially? Is it complete or partial in its coverage? Answering these questions will help you decide whether a source has the kinds and amount of information suitable for you and your readers.

Internet sources

Like a print document, an Internet site should have a purpose and topic coverage suitable for you and your readers. Identify the type of site. Is it informational, business or marketing, news, advocacy, or personal? Is this type of site likely to have the information and coverage you need? Do the purpose and outlook suit your readers' interests and outlook?

4 ▪ Ease of use: Will you and your readers find this source and its contents easy to use?

Print sources

- Can you locate this source, read it, and understand it in the time available for your project?

- Who is the audience for this source, experts or general readers? Is it written at a level appropriate for your readers? Will they be able to understand its contents if you quote or summarize it in your writing?

Internet sources

- Do you and your readers have the equipment and software necessary to gain access to the source?

- Is the site user friendly? Do you understand how to gain access to the site and use it to its fullest capacity? Can you make your way through it easily, using hypertext links or key word searches?

- Is this site linked to other up-to-date, authoritative, and suitable sites?

- Do you and your readers have the background information necessary to understand the contents of the site?

COMPUTER TIP Internet Evaluation Sites

Some Internet sites claim to evaluate online sources, but they are often concerned with whether a site is "cool," "fun to use," or visually appealing, not whether its information is accurate or complete. Such sites are seldom useful to serious researchers.

49b Follow effective strategies for gathering information

1 ▪ Reading for research

As you read your sources, gather whatever information seems relevant. If you're like most researchers, you'll end up gathering more information than you need, especially in the beginning. The deeper you dig into your subject, however, the more perceptive you'll become about what is right for you.

- *Where to begin.* Before you begin reading, arrange your sources according to difficulty. Read general or introductory sources first, as background for more specialized or technical sources.

- *Previewing your reading.* Before you begin reading a source, even if you're going to read only a chapter or a paragraph or two, put your reading in context by skimming the table of contents, the introduction, and surrounding paragraphs. See how the part fits into the whole document. Use the guidelines and questions in 1b1.

- *What to look for.* Look for facts, of course, but also for explanations or interpretations, expert opinions, evaluations, and examples that illustrate ideas.

  Note: Take note of any controversies involved with your topic. If you already have an opinion, pay attention to the other side. Use this opportunity to test the quality of your opinion or to make up your mind.

- *Reading by the paragraph.* Finish reading a paragraph before taking a note about something you've found in it. In this way you'll see how the information that interests you fits into its context.

■ *Thinking critically as you read.* To understand what you read, use the methods of critical thinking described in 1a: analysis (to see how things fit together), interpretation (to find the meaning of your reading), evaluation (to measure quality), and synthesis (to see how sources fit together and suit your purposes). Follow the guidelines in the "How to Evaluate the Contents of Your Reading" box, below.

49.2
Evaluating
Web sites:
Exercises

> **HOW TO . . .** Evaluate the Contents of Your Reading with the "FLAGS" Method
>
> Use the CASE method (currency, authority, suitability, and ease of use) to choose research sources. Then, as you read these sources, look for red flags that signal unreliable information. Think of the word FLAGS, whose letters will help you evaluate your reading: Fairness, Logic, Accuracy, Grammar, and Source citations.
>
> 1. *Fairness.* Are the authors fair to their opponents? Look for name-calling, emotional characterizations of other's opinions, distortions, and the failure to acknowledge other ways of thinking. Also look for relations between authors and the people they write about that may create bias.
>
> 2. *Logic.* Do the authors reason logically about their topics? Are their opinions supported by facts and reasoning or by emotional appeals? Is the information old and possibly unreliable? Is there enough information? Can you think of other explanations that sound as plausible as those you're reading? Do you spot wild claims and broad generalizations? Most logical arguments have up-to-date facts to back them up and appear reasonable.
>
> 3. *Accuracy.* Do you spot factual errors? As you read sources, compare the information they contain. If you spot discrepancies, decide which source is more accurate and reliable.
>
> 4. *Grammar.* Check for grammar, spelling, and punctuation errors. Is the writing well edited and polished? Reliable sources have usually been carefully edited.
>
> 5. *Source citations.* Do the authors give the sources of their information? Trustworthy authors usually tell where they've gotten their facts and statistics. Look for citations in the text of your reading or in source citations at the end. Then evaluate the quality of these citations using the CASE method. (See 49a.)

2 ■ Gathering information with surveys, observations, and interviews

Conducting surveys. Plan survey questions carefully to avoid personal bias or charged language. Avoid asking yes/no questions whenever possible;

they are often not very informative. Guard against overly personal questions that may hinder respondents from answering truthfully. Ask one question at a time; don't combine two or more questions in one sentence.

Observations. If your research project would benefit from direct, in-the-field observation, plan the time and location of your observation to give you representative information. For example, you probably would not get reliable information about parking problems at your college if you stood in a remote parking lot and observed students arriving for class very early in the morning. Position yourself in an unobtrusive location. Record the date, time, and place of your observation. Take detailed descriptive notes of what you see and hear; give yourself room later to draw conclusions about your observations.

Interviewing. Make appointments with your sources and keep them promptly. Be clear about your purposes for the interview. Prepare your questions in advance using the preceding guidelines to surveys; ask clarifying or follow-up questions as necessary. As you listen, take careful notes; double-check quotations to be sure they're accurate. If necessary, ask your sources whether they are speaking "for the record" and may be cited by name. Tape-record sources only with their permission. Offer to send them a copy of your completed project.

49c Take notes in an easy-to-use format

1 ▪ Taking notes on paper or with a computer

For brief papers drawing from only a few sources, you can gather information informally. You may photocopy and highlight important information or copy and paste it into a computer file. You may jot notes in the margin or on a sheet of paper. If you have more than a few sources and your paper is longer than a page or two, you'll have to take separate, individual notes to handle your information effectively.

- ▪ *Size.* Make note slips easy to sort by using only one size. Avoid slips that are too small for complete notes or so large you may write too much on one slip. Buy a package of 4 × 6 inch cards, or make your own by dividing notebook sheets into four slips each. Cut the sheets into individual notes after you've finished your research.

⬜ **COMPUTER TIP** Taking Notes

To computerize your note taking, create a "Notes" file with four note-taking boxes per page. Using your Table menu, make each "notes" box 4.5 inches high and 3.25 inches wide. While you do Internet or CD-ROM research, you can keep this file open and switch between your sources and your notes. When you finish your research, you can print this file and cut up your evenly sized note slips.

- *Length.* Generally, the shorter the note is, the better. Put one piece of information in each note. More than one idea makes a note difficult to sort and organize. When in doubt, divide an idea in two and put each idea in a separate note. Never write on the backs of note slips. If you have a long note that won't fit on one slip, write *Note 1 of 2, Note 2 of 2,* and so forth on the appropriate slips.

- *Plagiarism.* Use quotation marks around all word-for-word quotations. Compare summaries and paraphrases with the original to be sure you haven't quoted unintentionally. (See 49d and Chapter 51.)

2 ▪ Formatting notes

Every note should contain the following information, which you'll use as you think about your topic, organize your paper, write your paper, and document your borrowing.

- A subject heading to identify the topic of the note.

- A reference citation for identifying the source of the note parenthetically in the text of your paper (the author and a short version of the title).

- A page number, if a print source.

- An introduction that provides a context for the note: *who, what, when, where, why,* or *how.*

- The note itself: quotation, summary, paraphrase, or a combination.

- Your comments on the note, if necessary, explaining it, evaluating it, cross-referencing to other notes, or telling how you intend to use it.

Here is a sample note slip for an environmental research paper based on Aldo Leopold's *A Sand County Almanac*:

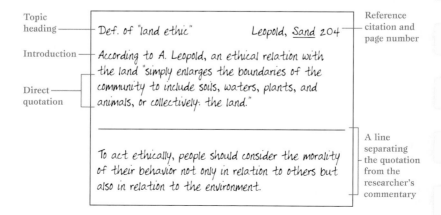

Topic heading — Def. of "land ethic"   Leopold, *Sand* 204 — Reference citation and page number

Introduction — According to A. Leopold, an ethical relation with the land "simply enlarges the boundaries of the

Direct quotation — community to include soils, waters, plants, and animals, or collectively: the land."

To act ethically, people should consider the morality of their behavior not only in relation to others but also in relation to the environment.

A line separating the quotation from the researcher's commentary

49d Take notes by an appropriate method: quotation, summary, or paraphrase

1 ■ Note-taking by direct quotation

A direct quotation is a word-for-word reproduction of an original source. Quote often but briefly as you take notes. Remember that long quotations may be difficult to weave into a paper and difficult for readers to use. What to quote:

- *Key points.* Quote passages that sum up a key point in a condensed, emphatic way.

- *Expert opinions.* Quote sources when they offer an expert's opinion.

- *Powerful passages.* Quote dramatic, memorable, or well-known passages.

- *Subtle ideas.* Quote passages whose meaning may be lost in a summary.

- *Concise passages.* Quote passages whose meaning cannot be expressed in fewer words.

For a sample direct quotation note slip, see 49c2. To quote effectively, you'll need to know how to use quotation marks (see 38a–d), commas and colons to introduce quotations (see 34g and 36a), brackets to insert editorial comments within a quotation (see 39c), and ellipsis points to signal omitted words (see 39d).

Note: If an e-mail message looks and functions like other quotations, correct any typographical errors. But if it observes the style of e-mail, quote exactly, including emoticons and e-mail abbreviations, punctuation meant to signal italics, all-capital words, and typographical errors. (See the "How to Format an E-Mail-Message" box, p. 492.)

HOW TO . . . Avoid Copy-and-Paste Plagiarism

1. Before you copy and paste from the Internet, gather as much publication information as you can for an Internet or other electronic source. (See 47e1.)

2. After you paste borrowed materials into your computer file, place quotation marks around printed text. For copied images, add the copyright symbol © if it existed in the original.

3. Write a heading to help you identify the contents of your borrowing.

4. Cite the publication information you'll use for in-text documentation in your paper: author's name and shortened title, plus page, paragraph, or section numbers.

(continued)

5. Write a signal statement to introduce the borrowing. (See 50c1.)

Here is an example of electronic note taking for a paper on US immigration:

Original electronic source		A reformatted copy-and-paste e-note
Jaret, Charles, "Troubled by Newcomers," *The Journal of American Ethnic History* (Spring, 1999): 9-12.	Topic head ⟶	High-achieving immigrants
	Publication ⟶ information	Jaret, "Troubled," 10.
	Signal statement →	Jaret counteracts the stereotype of uneducated immigrants with statistics and a quotation from
Industries vary in their employment of immigrants, with many in low-skill services and many also in medicine (in 1990, 20 percent of all physicians were immigrants) and high-tech industries. Business Week says, "The next generation of scientists and engineers at United States high-tech companies will be dominated by immigrants" (35).	Title underlining and quotation ⟶ marks added

Single quotation marks for a quotation within a quotation ⟶

Original source page numbers omitted ⟶ | Business Week: "Industries vary in their employment of immigrants, with many in low-skill services and many also in medicine (in 1990, 20 percent of all physicians were immigrants) and high-tech industries. Business Week says, 'The next generation of scientists and engineers at United States high-tech companies will be dominated by immigrants.'" |

2 ▪ Note-taking by summary

A **summary** condenses an original in your own words, reducing a passage as short as a sentence or as long as a paragraph or a chapter to its central meaning and essential details. What to summarize:

- Background information
- Commentaries, explanations, and evaluations
- Arguments or a line of thinking
- Facts
- In literary works: description, events, episodes, and lengthy speeches or dialogue

Here is an original passage about the impact of pollution on national parks, followed by a note summarizing it.

But scientists at Sequoia and other national parks are finding that forests, though enduring and resilient, are increasingly vulnerable to the influence of modern civilization. For example, plant and insect pests, often introduced by humans, have blighted and killed trees and forests in many parks, from conifers in California to palms in Biscayne Bay. Ozone, a common component of smog, is slowing tree growth at Virginia's Shenandoah National Park and along the Blue Ridge Parkway and threatens the health of conifers in Sequoia, Kings Canyon, and Yosemite National parks.

(Steve Nash and Mike Spear, "Ghost Forest," p. 20)

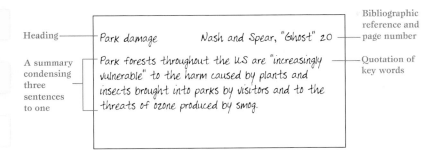

Heading —— Park damage   Nash and Spear, "Ghost" 20 —— Bibliographic reference and page number

A summary condensing three sentences to one —— Park forests throughout the US are "increasingly vulnerable" to the harm caused by plants and insects brought into parks by visitors and to the threats of ozone produced by smog. —— Quotation of key words

---

HOW TO . . . Write a Summary

1. When you come to a passage you want to summarize, consider the surrounding sentences or paragraphs. Avoid taking information or opinions out of context; avoid distorting the author's purpose to suit your own.

2. Read the passage carefully and then look away to write your summary. In your own words and sentence style, present the author's main ideas and most important details. Omit examples, explanations, and statistics.

3. Compare your summary to the original to be sure that your words accurately reflect the original.

4. Check to see whether you have quoted from the original. If you must quote single words or phrases, enclose them in double quotation marks (see 38a and b).

---

3 ■ Note-taking by paraphrase

A **paraphrase** restates a passage in your own words and phrasing. Usually about as long as the original, it includes examples and explanations from the original. Paraphrase what readers might otherwise misunderstand. Avoid a word-for-word "translation" of the original into your words and phrases; that is plagiarism (see Chapter 51). If you quote key words or phrases, enclose them in quotation marks. Here is an original passage about the role the land plays in the natural life cycle, followed by a note paraphrasing it.

49.3
How to
paraphrase:
Web link

Land, then, is not merely soil; it is a fountain of energy flowing through a circuit of soils, plants, and animals. Food chains are the living channels which conduct energy upward; death and decay return it to the soil. The circuit is not closed; some energy is dissipated in decay, some is added by absorption from the air, some is stored in soils, peats, and long-lived forests; but it is a sustained circuit, like a slowly augmented revolving fund of life.

(Aldo Leopold, *A Sand County Almanac*, p. 212)

49.4
Quoting,
summariz-
ing, and
paraphras-
ing:
Exercises

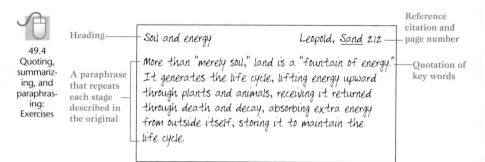

Heading———

A paraphrase that repeats each stage described in the original

Reference citation and page number

Quotation of key words

Soil and energy   Leopold, <u>Sand</u> 212

More than "merely soil," land is a "fountain of energy." It generates the life cycle, lifting energy upward through plants and animals, receiving it returned through death and decay, absorbing extra energy from outside itself, storing it to maintain the life cycle.

50 Planning, Writing, Using Sources, and Revising

50a As you finish your research, take stock of it

Making planning notes

As you do research, your initial thoughts about your topic and paper will change. That's natural. You should expect to change your mind as the result of new information. To keep your thoughts straight and keep track of changing plans for your paper, write them down in planning notes. What should you write down?

- New ideas. Keep track of your new thinking as the result of research.

- New versions of key questions or statements of your problem.

- Audience reassessment. In light of your research, tell yourself what you've discovered that will be most interesting or important to your intended readers.

- New versions of your thesis. Rewrite your thesis until it fits your research. Avoid overgeneral or incomplete thesis statements.

Note: If you're writing a formal report (see 62f), draw conclusions about the results of your research.

- Organizing plans. Write lists of ideas or brief sketch outlines to help you organize your research.
- Good lines. Write brief passages you might use to begin your paper, introduce parts, or explain key ideas.

Your aim is to write down as much as possible about your paper before you write it. The more you write now, the less you'll have to think of later as you write a draft.

HOW TO . . . Refocus Your Research Project

As you near the end of your research, do the following exercise to help yourself refocus your thinking and see your project more clearly.

1. I can now state my specific research topic as:
2. My key question or problem to be solved is now:
3. What I've discovered about my topic from my sources:
   a. What did I expect to find? What have I found instead?
   b. What are the controversies? Who agrees with whom?
   c. Which sources are the best? Why? What sources do I have left to check? (Reconsider the checklist in 47b5.)
4. What parts of my research will be most interesting or important to my intended readers?
5. My tentative thesis: "What I want to prove/explain/demonstrate/ show about [my topic] is that. . . . What I mean to say is that . . ."
6. I now have _____ days left to organize, write, and revise my paper.

50b Plan a communications strategy

1 ■ Organizing

One of the biggest challenges of a research paper is organizing all your materials to support your thesis or, if you're writing a report, to lead logically to your conclusion. Avoid organizing source by source, one after another. Your paper is about the point *you* want to make, not about your sources. Its design should support that point and reflect the logic of your thought. Here are organizing patterns traditionally used by researchers. See whether one is right for you.

- *Thesis support.* State your thesis early and then support it systematically, point by point.

- *Classical organizing patterns.* Arrange your ideas by *order of importance, classification, part by part (analysis), cause-effect,* or *comparison/contrast.*

- *Persuasion.* If you aim to persuade readers to change their beliefs or behavior, see the organizing patterns in 59a3.

- *Review of research.* If you're writing a survey of research, classify your sources into groups, explain their differing views, and then evaluate them to determine the most informative, insightful, and useful.

- *Problem/solution.* First describe the problem in detail; then pose a solution for it, if necessary explaining how the solution might be implemented.

- *Tracing a historical pattern.* Give necessary background information and then trace the unfolding of an event from one episode to the next. Be sure to show how one relates or leads to the next. Conclude by describing the consequences of the event.

- *Formal report.* For guidelines to organizing a formal report see 62f2. If your report will use in-text subject headings, see 46b.

Note: For a paper as complex as a research project, outlining is usually essential to discover an effective pattern of organization. (See 3c for guidelines.)

2 ■ Planning for readers

Focusing intently on their research, learning new information and developing new understanding, researchers sometimes lose sight of their eventual audience, what these readers need to know, and what will interest them. As you begin planning the actual paper you'll write, think carefully about this audience. (See 1d3.)

- *An introduction.* Many kinds of introductions are appropriate for research projects. (See 6c1.) Be sure that your topic and purpose are clear from the outset. Unless you have good reasons for doing otherwise, your opening should lead directly to your thesis, key question, or problem.

- *Illustrations.* Plan for examples and, if necessary, visual aids to explain or dramatize your ideas. (For more on visual aids, see 46b and c.) Think of figurative language, especially analogies. (See 6b7 and 26c.)

- *Conclusions.* The following are appropriate ways to conclude research projects: warn about the need to act on your topic; pose solutions or make recommendations; show how your topic relates to some larger subject; identify a path that future researchers should take. (See 6d1 for other strategies.)

🌐 **WRITING IN THE USA** Effective Style in Research Papers

The style in which you write your research project will depend upon your subject, the discipline in which you're writing, and your audience. In some instances, especially in the humanities, it is appropriate to refer to yourself as "I" and occasionally to develop your topic with personal examples. In other situations, particularly when writing in the sciences, a less personal style is required, with greater emphasis on your sources.

Consider the experience of Eric Martínez, a student in a composition course emphasizing argument and persuasion, who was required to write two papers on the same topic. One (see Chapter 54) is a formal research paper focusing on the logic of his argument. The second (59d) is more personal, addressed to fellow college students and focusing on changing their opinions and behavior. Eric's purpose and audience determined his style in both situations.

50c Blend source materials into your project

The following guidelines, based on the Modern Language Association style, will help you blend information and quotations from your sources with your own ideas to create a coherent, easy-to-follow research paper. (For tips about the American Psychological Association style, see 55a.)

1 ▪ Presenting borrowed material

When you summarize and quote effectively, you have three powerful effects on your readers: You set clear boundaries between your ideas and those that you borrow, thus helping readers keep things straight as you read. You guide readers smoothly through your paper, helping them understand how to interpret the materials you're presenting. And you demonstrate fairness to your sources and your responsibility as a researcher. Effective presentation of borrowed materials is generally a four-step process that, with practice, you'll learn to vary in artful, interesting ways.

Step 1: Use a signal statement. Whenever you quote, give another's opinions, or provide disputed information, write signal statements to introduce your borrowing. Use them to earn readers' acceptance of a source or to help readers understand or see the value of a source. To write a signal statement, do one or more of the following in an introductory phrase or sentence:

▪ Identify the author or sponsor of the source.

▪ Summarize the writer's credentials.

▪ Give the title.

- Announce the subject matter of the borrowing, provide its context, or suggest the writer's purpose.

- Evaluate the contents of the borrowing.

Consider these sample signal statements:

Critic Mary Beth Pringle points out that . . .

[credentials, author, purpose]

Barry Herr, president of Bio-Systems International, assumes . . .

[author, credentials, purpose, and an implied evaluation]

The National Park Service has recently reported statistics on the

alarming number of wild animals killed yearly by motorists on national

parks roadways: . . .

[sponsoring source, purpose, subject matter, evaluation]

. . . warns Aldo Leopold in *A Sand County Almanac*, one of the most

important documents of the environmental movement.

[purpose, author, title, evaluation]

To signal a writer's purpose accurately, choose from the following list of verbs.

acknowledges	claims	emphasizes	objects	reports
adds	comments	endorses	observes	responds
admits	compares	explains	offers	reveals
advises	confirms	grants	opposes	says
agrees	considers	hints	points out	states
allows	contends	holds	presents	suggests
analyzes	criticizes	hopes	proposes	supports
answers	declares	illustrates	reasons	tells
argues	defines	implies	recognizes	thinks
asserts	denies	indicates	refutes	urges
assumes	describes	insists	regards	warns
believes	discusses	interprets	remarks	wonders
charges	disputes	notes	replies	

Note: Choose the present tense for signal verbs in MLA-style papers, the past tense for signal verbs in APA-style papers. (For guidelines, see 13b1.)

Step 2: Present the quotation, summary, or paraphrase.

Step 3: Document the borrowing. Provide enough information about the source to guide readers to complete publication information in the list of works cited or list of references at the end of your paper. (See MLA style, 53a and b; APA style, 55a and c; endnotes or footnotes, 56a; or the appropriate style manuals listed in 57b.)

Step 4: Explain the borrowing, evaluate it, or show how it supports your thesis. Don't assume readers will see what you do or get your message without assistance.

For example:

Signal phrase

```
                  The problems created by the popularity of U.S. national

                  parks begin with the numbers themselves. As the nineteenth-

                  century naturalist and author George Perkins Marsh warned,

                  "Man is everywhere a disturbing agent. Wherever he plants

                  his foot, the harmonies of nature are turned to discords"

                  (qtd. in Stegner 38). Each park has its own "carrying

                  capacity" and can accommodate only so many visitors before

                  their pleasures and the environment are adversely affected.
```

- Signal phrase
- Direct quotation
- Parenthetical documentation
- Explanation

2 ▪ Quoting briefly

Quote whenever you need a source's exact words. But be brief; use only the words you need. More may only mislead. Try to keep quotations to a sentence or less, punctuate them correctly, and connect them grammatically to your own words. (See 38b.) Here are three examples.

- ▪ A full-sentence quotation:

```
    Most old growth forest has disappeared from the Northwest: "Less
    than one-fifth of the old growth that once covered the landscape of
    western Oregon and western Washington still stands" (Ervin 4).
```

- ▪ A quotation of a phrase:

```
    The cliff faces of many mountain parks are so covered by bolts
    drilled to make climbing routes that, according to Claire Martin, they
    are becoming the "equivalent of artificial climbing walls" (37).
```

- ▪ The use of the ellipsis to omit unnecessary words and compress a quotation (see 50c6).

```
    In the winter at Yellowstone National Park, according to Elaine
    Robbins, air pollution from snowmobile engines is so bad that, at park
    entrance stations, "supplemental fresh air has to be pumped in . . .
    to protect employees' health" (44-46).
```

WRITING IN THE USA Quoting Excessively

Although readers in the United States and elsewhere value the authority given to ideas by direct quotations, many people object to reading numerous quotations one after another—especially numerous long quotations. Such a pattern becomes monotonous and may suggest that you haven't thought carefully about the meaning of your borrowing or that you have failed to synthesize information to serve your purposes or support your thesis.

3 ▪ Quoting grammatically and coherently

As you write and revise your research project, be sure that your signal statements and quotations fit together grammatically and coherently. Consider these examples:

> According to Zion National Park Superintendent Don Falvey, up to five
>
> thousand cars a day drove into the canyon, "results in "a degraded
>
> _and caused_
>
> visitor experience" (28).

[The verb phrase in the original quotation does not indicate a subject, and therefore does not connect to the signal statement. The changes connect the quotation to the subject of the sentence, "*up to five thousand cars a day,*" and harmonize the verb tenses.]

> Researchers studying noise have found, "The results show "not a single
>
> _that_
>
> location recorded in Grand Canyon National Park to be totally free of
>
> [is]
>
> aircraft noise" (228).

[To fit a signal statement to a quotation, the writer has omitted extra words, added a linking word, and used brackets to enclose a grammatical change.]

4 ▪ Taking credit for your ideas

Occasionally you'll have an idea about your topic and then find that a source has had a similar idea. To take credit for original thinking yet be fair to others, present your source's version of your idea, quoting if necessary, but also give your version, if necessary explaining how yours differs.

An idea that a writer shares with a source

> Where overcrowding is most intense and harm to the environment greatest, officials should adopt the suggestion of former National Park Service director James M. Ridenour and adopt a reservations system for regulating entry

Citation of the source

> ("Crocodiles" 71). This system need not be permanent or universal, nor operate throughout the year. It would,

The writer's version of the idea

> however, permit the NPS to reduce the flow of visitors to the "carrying capacity" of individual parks and give harmed environments time to heal themselves.

5 ▪ Working with several sources at once

▪ *Presenting one source at a time.* The standard procedure is to present your sources one at a time, documenting each as you borrow from it, as in the preceding examples.

- *Summarizing sources as a group.* A second method, useful when sources agree, is to summarize all of them at once, without mentioning names. After the summary, document them in one citation. But be aware that lengthy citations can be distracting.

    > Throughout America's national parks, environmental damage from automobile air pollution is severe and well documented (McMahon 26; Coates, "Threat" 1; Craig 42).

- *Selecting a spokesperson.* A third method is to select a spokesperson to speak for all your sources. Document the person you quote or summarize.

    > As many recognize, the great popularity of our national parks threatens, in James Coates's words, "to hit delicate natural resources particularly hard" ("Threat" 16).

6 ▪ Using ellipsis points to signal omissions

Use three evenly spaced periods to signal the omission of words from a quotation.

- *The omission of less than a sentence.* Use ellipsis points for omissions within a sentence or at the end of a sentence. The remaining words must be grammatically complete. Do not use ellipsis points before or after fragmentary quotations or for an omission at the beginning of a sentence.

    > Bruce Craig, a former park ranger, argues that "national parks . . . are not able to withstand the daily assaults of thousands upon thousands of visitors without experiencing change or degradation" (42).

    [The writer omitted the words *which preserve unique and delicate ecosystems and fragile historic treasures.* The remaining words make a grammatically complete statement.]

- *The omission of more than a sentence.* If you omit more than a full sentence, place a period before the three ellipsis points, as in the indented block quotation in 50d1.

Note: The Modern Language Association no longer requires that square brackets enclose ellipsis points inserted in quotations (see 39d).

7 ▪ Using brackets for insertions

Use typed or hand-drawn brackets (not parentheses) to insert your own words into a quotation to explain a reference or complete the grammar of the sentence (see 39c).

```
Nature writer Wallace Stegner believes that "recreation could be as
dangerous [to wilderness areas] as logging or extractive use" (43).
```

50.1
Quoting
effectively:
Exercises

Note: If you spot an error of fact, grammar, or spelling in a direct quotation, quote the error exactly as you found it. Immediately following, insert brackets containing *sic,* meaning "thus" or "so," as in "When Columbus came to the Caribbean in 1942 [sic], his crew brought with them new diseases to the Western Hemisphere."

50d Indent long quotations of prose and poetry

1 ▪ Indenting prose quotations

These are the Modern Language Association guidelines for long quotations. (For American Psychological Association guidelines, see 46e4.)

- ▪ *Length.* To make quotations longer than four typed lines easy to read, set them off in an indented block, separate from your words.

- ▪ *Introduction and punctuation.* Introduce the quotation in your own words. If your introduction is an independent clause that could be punctuated as a complete sentence, follow it with a colon. If it is a signal statement such as *According to philosopher Susan Sontag,* follow it with a comma. If no grammatical break occurs between your words and the quotation, use no punctuation.

- ▪ *Indentation.* Indent 1 inch or 10 spaces from the left margin.

- ▪ *Quotation marks and spacing.* Do not enclose indented quotations with quotation marks. The block format signals word-for-word quotation. Double-space the quotation.

- ▪ *Paragraphing.* If you quote part of a paragraph or only one paragraph, do not indent the first line more than 1 inch or 10 spaces. To quote two or more paragraphs in block format, indent the first line of each paragraph an additional quarter-inch or 3 spaces (a total of 13 spaces from the left margin). After a block quotation, begin a new paragraph of your own writing only if you change subjects.

- ▪ *Documentation.* One space after the punctuation ending the quotation, cite the source parenthetically. (For more on MLA in-text documentation, see 52b.)

```
The portrait of Thomas Gradgrind that Charles Dickens presents in
Hard Times satirizes defects in the nineteenth-century philosophy of
utilitarianism:
```

> Thomas Gradgrind, sir. A man of realities. A man of
> facts and calculations. A man who proceeds upon the
> principle that two and two are four, and nothing over, and
> who is not to be talked into allowing for anything over. . . .
> With a rule and a pair of scales, and multiplication tables
> always in his pocket, sir, ready to weigh and measure any
> parcel of human nature, and tell you exactly what it comes
> to. (2)

Note: If you omit words from a quotation, signal the omission with ellipsis points. (See 39d.)

2 ■ Indenting quotations of dialogue in fiction

If you quote dialogue between two or more speakers, use the indented format and follow the paragraphing of the original, even if you quote fewer than four typed lines. One space after the quotation, cite the source parenthetically (see 52b9).

3 ■ Indenting quotations of dialogue in drama and film

If you quote dialogue between two or more speakers, use the indented quotation format. Indent 1 inch or 10 spaces from the left margin. Introduce each speaker by his or her name written in all capital letters followed by a period: *OTHELLO.* Use quotation marks only if they appear in the original. Indent subsequent lines in a character's speech an additional quarter-inch or 3 spaces. When a new character speaks, start a new line 1 inch or 10 spaces from the left margin. One space after the punctuation ending the quotation, cite the source parenthetically (see 52b9).

> As Iago incites him, Othello plots Desdemona's murder:
>
> > OTHELLO. Get me some poison, Iago, this night. I'll not
> > > expostulate with her, lest her body and beauty unprovide
> > > my mind again. This night, Iago!
> >
> > IAGO. Do it not with poison. Strangle her in bed, even the
> > > bed she hath contaminated. (4.1.200-04)

4 ■ Indenting quotations of poetry

For quotations of more than three lines of poetry, use the indented quotation format.

- *Indentation.* Indent 1 inch or 10 spaces from the left margin. If the poem looks unbalanced on the page, indent it more or less as necessary.

- *Spacing and formatting.* Double-space the quotation and arrange the passage to look as much like the original as possible. If a quotation begins in the middle of a line, match the alignment in the original and do not shift the line to the left or right.

- *Line length.* If a long line of poetry would extend beyond the right margin, continue it on the next line, indenting an extra quarter-inch or 3 spaces.

- *Quotation marks.* Use quotation marks only if they appear in the original.

- *Line numbers.* Include line numbers in parentheses 1 space after the last line.

- *Omissions.* If you omit words or lines from a quotation, use ellipsis points. (See 39d.)

```
William Blake's "The Tiger" questions the origins of that part of

creation which is not innocent but not necessarily evil, either.

          Tiger, Tiger, burning bright

          In the forests of the night,

          What immortal hand or eye

          Could frame thy fearful symmetry? (1-4)
```

Note: If you are quoting only two or three lines of poetry, incorporate them in your text, using a slash (/) to indicate the start of a new line (see 39e).

HOW TO . . . Revise and Edit a Research Project

Use the following questions to guide your revision and editing. Or ask peer reviewers to read your draft with these questions in mind and answer the most important. (For more on revision, see 4b and c.)

1. Does the paper's thesis appear somewhere in the introduction? Is it clear and complete? Does the introduction to a formal report describe a problem or pose a key question?

2. Does the paper include all the information, explanation, and interpretation needed to support its thesis or, in a formal report, to justify its conclusion? Will your support satisfy your readers' needs and interests?

3. Does the paper introduce and explain borrowed materials? Is the documentation complete and appropriate to the discipline in which the paper is written? Are all direct quotations enclosed by quotation marks?

4. Do the paper's ideas make sense and fit together logically and smoothly? Does the paper follow its outline? If it does not, which is more logically organized, the paper or the outline? Would another design improve the paper?

5. If the project uses subject headings, as in a report, are they formatted correctly? Do headings clearly identify the sections they introduce? (See 46b1.)

6. Is the language appropriate to research writing: accurate, precise, objective, and appropriately formal? (See 27a and c.) Is the style appropriate for the intended audience?

7. Does the paper include appropriately formatted drafts of a title page, outline page, acknowledgments, or abstract, if required? (See 46d for MLA format, 46e for APA format.) Has the writer prepared a Works Cited or Reference list? (See 53a to prepare an MLA Works Cited list, 55b to prepare an APA reference list.)

For a sample MLA research project with a title page and outline page, see Chapter 54.

51 Avoiding Plagiarism in Your Project

Simply put, plagiarism is theft—taking another's words, ideas, or images and failing to acknowledge that taking. Most academic readers, your professors among them, consider the following to be acts of plagiarism:

- Presenting the whole of another person's work as your own: turning in a purchased term paper or a paper written by another student, or asking someone to write a paper for you.

- Presenting words (paragraphs, sentences, even individual key words), ideas, or images you've taken from print or online sources as if they are yours, without acknowledging that you've borrowed them.

- Presenting a paper as your own work that has been rewritten or heavily revised by family or friends.

- Presenting copyrighted material in a paper you distribute publicly or publish online without receiving permission to use that material.

- Giving incomplete citations to document your borrowing: missing page numbers, titles, author or source names, or publication information.

- Failing to enclose direct quotations, however long or brief, with quotation marks.

- The writing of what might be called "paraquotations," paraphrases that use words from the original passage without quotation marks or that follow its structure too closely.

In the United States and many other countries, in college and out, plagiarism is considered a serious breach of the writer's code of ethics. However, to borrow fairly from the words, ideas, or images of others—to avoid plagiarism—all you have to do is treat these materials as you would want your own words to be treated. That means full, accurate acknowledgment and documentation of your borrowing, a practice that not only puts you on the right side of academic honesty policies and civil law but also gives credibility and authority to your writing. (For the MLA style of documentation, see Chapters 52 and 53; for the APA style, see Chapter 55. For other styles, see Chapters 56 and 57.)

🌐 WRITING IN THE USA Culture and Intellectual Property

Cultures vary dramatically in their attitude toward knowledge and the ownership of words, ideas, and images. In some, knowledge is communal rather than any one person's intellectual property. In such cultures, there are greater obligations to share and cooperate. But American higher education places a particularly high value on independent thought. Writers and speakers may borrow others' ideas or information, but they must acknowledge their sources. Using information or ideas originated by others without appropriate attribution is considered plagiarism.

51a Treat your sources fairly

To be fair to your sources, you need to know several terms that apply to people's words and their creations.

- *Copyright.* The legally protected right of a copyright owner (a creator or some other person or organization) to reproduce, publish, or sell a written, musical, or artistic work. A work is protected for a specific number of years; for example, works published after January 1, 1978, are protected for the life of the author plus seventy years. A work may be copyrighted even if it lacks the copyright symbol ©.

   Note: Internet sources and personal communication (letters and e-mail) are considered to be copyrighted unless accompanied by an explicit statement permitting unrestricted use.

- *Fair use.* The limited right of researchers and others to borrow small portions of a copyrighted work without obtaining official permission. However, fair use requires researchers to acknowledge their borrowing by documenting their sources.

- ***Public domain.*** A term applied to written works and other creations that lack copyright protection: older print sources published before the 1920s (and sometimes posted on the Internet), government materials, and print and Internet materials explicitly labeled as free for distribution without restrictions. Works that exist in the public domain may be freely copied by anyone without permission. However, fair and effective researchers place quotation marks around direct quotations and document their borrowing.

- ***Common knowledge.*** Facts and ideas commonly known by experts in a field, such as biographical or scientific information. Common knowledge is in the public domain and may be used without documentation.

- ***Permission.*** Official, written permission by a copyright owner allowing another to reproduce, publish, or sell copyrighted material.

- ***Documentation.*** Written citation of the source of borrowed materials.

What do these terms mean to you as you're writing your research project? When you use someone else's words, ideas, or graphics, or mention facts that are not common knowledge, you must *always* credit your sources, first by giving in-text citations and then by listing your sources in a Works Cited or References list at the end of your paper. Newspaper reporters and magazine journalists are not always required to document their sources in this way, but in academic writing, you *must* acknowledge your sources. Chapter 47e shows you how to record complete and accurate publication information; 48e presents guidelines for Internet borrowing; 49e explains how to take accurate, fair notes. The following pages illustrate how to present research fairly and effectively in the text of your paper.

🌐 WRITING IN THE USA Recycled Papers

Many instructors do not allow submission of papers that have previously been submitted for another course. Check with your instructor.

🌐 WRITING IN THE USA Collaborative Writing

In school and on the job, writers are often required to write collaboratively. This is especially true of work on electronic documents such as Web pages. Fairness, graciousness, and even policy statements require you to acknowledge the work of your collaborators and any other assistance you receive. You may do so in an acknowledgments page preceding the text of your writing or in a note at the end. In either case, acknowledge collaborators by name, identify their contributions, and thank them. (For an example of an acknowledgment, see the end of the Preface to this book.)

51b   Document the words, ideas, facts, and graphics of others

1 ▪ Documenting factual information

Always document the sources of direct quotations, opinions, explanations, and interpretations. Facts are sometimes more difficult to handle. A fact is "common knowledge" and need not be documented if educated men and women could be expected to know it or if experts repeat it from one source to the next without documentation.

51.2
Avoiding
plagiarism:
Exercises

That Christopher Columbus first sailed to the Western Hemisphere in 1492 is a fact that requires no documentation. But what should a researcher do with the fact that automobile emissions are damaging vegetation in many US national parks and forests? If many sources cite this development without documentation, it is common knowledge and need not be documented. However, if only one source presents it, the fact is original information and must be documented. When in doubt, document.

Note: If you quote or paraphrase a writer's statement of common knowledge, you must document that.

2 ▪ Documenting quotations

Enclose direct quotations with quotation marks and document your borrowing.

▪ *The original source:*

> In Maine's Acadia National Park, needle rot on eastern white pines may be the result of acid fog and ozone pollution moving up the Eastern seaboard from the megalopolis to the south.
>
> (Steve Nash and Mike Spear, "Ghost Forest,"
> *National Parks*, p. 20)

▪ *Plagiarism:*

> In Maine, white pines are being killed by *acid fog and ozone pollution moving up the Eastern seaboard from the megalopolis to the south* (Nash and Spear 20).

[Even though this example is documented, the writer has quoted half of the original without using quotation marks. Take care to prevent summaries from drifting into quotations without quotation marks.]

▪ *Fair use:*

> Steve Nash and Mike Spear declare that "in Maine's Acadia National Park, needle rot on eastern white pines may be the result of acid fog and ozone pollution moving up the Eastern seaboard from the megalopolis to the south" (20).

COMPUTER TIP Avoiding Internet Plagiarism

If you cut an excerpt from an Internet file and paste it into your paper, be sure to enclose it in double quotation marks, introduce it with a signal statement, and document your borrowing at the end. (See the "How to Avoid Copy-and-Paste Plagiarism" box on pp. 349–350.)

51.3
How to
document
borrowing:
Web link

3 ▪ Documenting key words

Even if you take only one or two key words from a source, enclose them with quotation marks and document your borrowing.

▪ *The original source:*

> In short, a land ethic changes the role of *Homo sapiens* from conqueror of the land-community to plain member and citizen of it. It implies respect for his fellow-members, and also respect for the community as such.
>
> (Aldo Leopold, *A Sand County Almanac*, p. 204)

▪ *Plagiarism:*

Americans must enlarge their concept of morality to include a "*land ethic*" to guide their relationship with the natural world.

[Even though the borrowed words are enclosed in quotation marks, the writer has not documented the source.]

▪ *Fair use:*

Americans must enlarge their concept of morality to include what naturalist Aldo Leopold calls a "land ethic" to guide their relationship with the natural world (204).

4 ▪ Documenting opinions

You must document an author's opinion or line of thinking. Writers have rights to their ideas as well as to their words.

▪ *The original source:*

> At the heart of the issue is the fact that the welfare of the national parks is inextricably linked to the lands around them.
>
> (John Kenny, "Park Boundaries," *National Parks*, p. 22)

▪ *Plagiarism:*

Unfortunately for US national parks, they do not exist like islands in a sea, separate from urban America and its ecological threats. Their fate is shaped by the lands that surround them.

[Although this passage is in the writer's own words and even imaginatively written, its ideas are based on those of the original source and must be documented.]

■ *Fair use:*

Unfortunately for US national parks, they do not exist like islands in a sea, separate from urban America and its ecological threats. As John Kenny argues, their fate is shaped by the lands that surround them (22).

5 ■ Documenting a paraphrase

To paraphrase effectively, restate the author's words and phrasing in your words and phrasing. Avoid the mere substitution of synonyms for the author's original.

■ *The original source:*

In the East, to "waste" water is to consume it needlessly or excessively. In the West, to waste water is not to consume it—to let it flow unimpeded and undiverted down rivers.

(Marc Reisner, *Cadillac Desert: The American West and Its Disappearing Water,* p. 16)

■ *Plagiarism:*

Americans from the East say they "waste" their water when they consume it unnecessarily. In the West, however, water is wasted when it is not consumed but allowed to flow uninterrupted down rivers (Reisner 16).

[The writer has documented the source of the original but has merely substituted synonyms for the original words and retained the original sentence structure.]

■ *Fair use:*

Americans define the "waste" of water in contradictory ways. To those in the East, waste means using water unnecessarily, while to those in the West, waste means leaving water in rivers, unused (Reisner 16).

6 ■ Documenting a graphic or image

If you wish to borrow a graphic or image that is accompanied by the copyright symbol (©), include the symbol in your paper, located near the image, as well as complete publication information in an accompanying source note. (For documentation guidelines, see 46c.)

51c If you will publish your research project, request permission to use copyrighted material

If you intend to distribute your project outside of class or post it on the Internet, for example, as part of a class Web site, your work is officially considered published. Therefore, the words, ideas, and graphics you borrow for your project are covered by the copyright laws and fair use guidelines described in 51a, and you may need written permission to use these materials. To decide whether to seek permission, follow two guidelines:

- If you borrow up to 150 words from articles and 400 words from books and you document your sources, you do not need permission.

- If you borrow longer passages of articles or books, passages of poetry, music, and images or graphic illustrations, you do need written permission and documentation.

To request permission, write or e-mail the copyright holders. If yours will be a not-for-profit publication (displayed on a class Web site or appearing in an academic publication), copyright holders will usually respond with a letter or other document that allows you to use their creations for free. To identify copyright holders, look for the copyright symbol ©; examine title pages and credit lines for authors or organization names; look for e-mail addresses at the ends of Internet sites; find publisher addresses at their Web sites. (For sample copyright statements, see the page following the title page of this book and the credit lines on p. C-2.)

In your letter or e-mail request, begin by indicating that you would like permission to use . . . [specifically describe what you want to borrow—a passage of text, a graphic, a photograph, a song lyric, and so forth—and the source in which it appears]. Describe who you are (for example, a student in _____ class at _____ college or university), what your project is, your purposes in your project, its intended audience, how it will be distributed or published. Provide the citation you intend to use to document your borrowing. Conclude with this query: "If you do not control these rights in their entirety, would you please tell me who does?" (See sample MLA citations in 53b and APA citations in 55c.)

ON THE WEB www.ablongman.com/dodds

MLA Documentation

52 Writing MLA In-Text (Parenthetical) Citations

In papers for humanities courses, the preferred way to cite borrowed materials is the Modern Language Association (MLA) system of in-text citation. (For a list of style manuals used in various fields, see 57b.)

52a Follow MLA citation guidelines

As you write the first draft, document your borrowing at three places in your paper.

- *In a signal statement.* Name your source in an introductory signal statement when you quote directly or borrow an explanation, opinion, interpretation, or disputed fact. Give the author's full name for first references and last name only thereafter. (See also 50c1.)

- *In a parenthetical citation.* In parentheses following your borrowing, provide enough information to guide readers to full publication information in the Works Cited list at the end of your paper. Give page numbers if your sources have them. Place the citation after the borrowing, following quotation marks, but before the period at the end of a sentence.

  Note: In block quotations, place the parenthetical reference 1 space after the last punctuation mark.

- *In the Works Cited list.* At the end of your paper, in a list titled "Works Cited," provide full publication or source information for each source you've used.

52b Follow parenthetical citation formats

1 ▪ Naming an author in a signal statement

If you name an author in a signal statement and use only one source by that author, cite the page number of your borrowing in parentheses.

Ann J. Lane suggests that "The Yellow Wall-Paper" is the "most directly, obviously, self-consciously autobiographical" of all of Charlotte Perkins Gilman's short stories (16).

52.1
Writing parenthetical citations: Exercises

2 ▪ Naming a corporate author in a signal statement

Cite a corporate author as you would a person.

```
The Wilderness Preservation Society has proposed reservation systems
to regulate access at fourteen national parks (32).
```

3 ▪ Omitting the author name and signal statement

If you do not name the author in a signal statement and use only one source by that author, cite the author's last name and the page number in parentheses. No punctuation separates the author's name and the page number.

```
At the present time, vegetation at more than seventy national parks is
severely affected by automobile air pollution (McMahon 26).
```

4 ▪ Citing two or more sources by the same author

If your paper includes two or more sources by the same author, follow these guidelines for parenthetical citation.

▪ *Author named in a signal statement.* If you name the author in a signal statement, give a short form of the title and the page number in parentheses. Enclose article titles in quotation marks; underline book titles.

```
Gene Rose has revealed that during the last decade, logging on
National Forest Service lands has declined by seventy-five
percent, from twelve million board feet per year to just three
million ("Wood Cutting" 35).
```

▪ *Author and title in a signal statement.* If a signal statement includes the author's name and the title of the source, give only the page number in parentheses.

```
In A Sand County Almanac, Aldo Leopold explains the necessity of a
"land ethic" to guide human relationships with the land (204).
```

▪ *Author and title not named in a signal statement.* If you do not give the author or title in a signal statement, include both in the parenthetical citation, separated by a comma. Write brief titles in full; give shortened versions of longer titles.

```
In the Florida Everglades, picnickers have left behind the seeds
of 221 nonnative species that are now driving out native species
(Coates, "Threat" 16).
```

5 ▪ Citing more than one author of a source

▪ *Two or three authors.* If a source has two or three authors, name them in the signal statement or parenthetical citation.

```
Campers who show up at national parks to claim the daily campsites

may wait in line for hours (Adler and Glick 48).
```

■ *Four or more authors.* If a source has four or more authors, you may indicate multi-authorship in your signal statement (*Mary Peters and her colleagues report . . .*) or give only the first author's name followed by *et al.* ("and others") in the parenthetical citation.

```
Only recently have detailed proposals been made showing how to

preserve spotted owl habitats without costing loggers their jobs

(Peters et al. 48).
```

6 ■ Citing an unknown author

If an author's name is not given in the source, use the complete title in a signal statement or the first key words in the parenthetical citation.

```
In Minnesota's Voyageurs National Park, snowmobilers have disturbed

the habitat of the endangered gray wolf ("Shattering" 140).
```

7 ■ Citing authors with the same last name

If you cite two or more authors with the same last name, include each author's first and last name in signal statements, or in parenthetical documentation include each author's first initial (full first name if the initial is shared, too) and last name.

```
Handsome park lodges entice visitors to such national parks as

Mt. Rainier, Yellowstone, Bryce Canyon, and Grand Canyon

(James Adams 19).
```

8 ■ Citing a multivolume source

If you cite more than one volume of a multivolume source, give the volume number followed by a colon, 1 space, and the page number in the parenthetical citation.

```
Thoreau describes in his Journals how, in the natural world, humans

"behave like oxen in a flower garden" (8: 110).
```

9 ■ Citing literary and religious works

Provide enough information in the parenthetical citation to enable readers to locate the material you are citing even if they use an edition different from yours. For **undivided** works such as short stories, include the page number in the parenthetical citation. For works **divided** into chapters, acts, verses, and so forth, provide additional information.

■ *Novels.* Parenthetically cite the page number in the edition you used, followed by a semicolon and the part, section, or chapter number.

> In Light in August, novelist William Faulkner traces the complex
>
> process by which his protagonist's childhood memories are
>
> transformed into knowledge and then belief: "Memory believes
>
> before knowing remembers" (104; ch. 6).

■ *Poetry.* To cite poetry that is divided into books or other numbered sections, give the part and line numbers, as in this example from William Wordsworth's "Ode, Intimations of Immortality."

> Our birth is but a sleep and a forgetting:
>
> The Soul that rises with us, our life's Star,
>
>   Hath had elsewhere its setting,
>
> And cometh from afar. . . . (5.59-62)

■ *Plays.* Cite modern plays as you would a book, including page numbers. Cite verse and classic plays by act, scene, and line. Use arabic numerals unless instructed otherwise.

> As Othello plots Desdemona's murder, he confesses her enduring
>
> power over him: "I'll not expostulate with her, lest her body and
>
> beauty unprovide my mind again" (4.1.200-01).

■ *Religious works.* Cite references to the Bible, the Quran, and other religious works as you would literary works. In the text of your paper, do not underline the names of sacred writings nor enclose their parts with quotation marks. But underline individual published editions. Titles for books of the Bible are often abbreviated.

> Throughout the Bible, God's chosen people are promised that they
>
> will be led to what can only be called an environmental paradise,
>
> "a good land and large, . . . a land flowing with milk and honey"
>
> (Holy Bible: Standard Text Edition, Exod. 3.8).

10 ■ Citing an indirect source

If you quote a writer whose words appear in a source written by someone else, name the source you are quoting in a signal statement. Begin the parenthetical citation with *qtd. in* ("quoted in") and identify the source where you found the quotation.

> As historian Kenneth Clark has observed, "Nothing except love is so
>
> universally appealing as a view" of beautiful scenery (qtd. in
>
> McMahon 26).

11 ▪ Citing an entire work

To cite an entire work, give the author's name and the title, if necessary, in a signal statement or parenthetical citation.

```
Henry David Thoreau's Walden is the source of many of the attitudes
Americans hold about the value of wilderness.
```

12 ▪ Citing two or more sources in parentheses

When citing two or more sources in parentheses, separate the citations with a semicolon. Be aware, however, that multiple citations may be distracting. For other ways to document multiple sources, see 50c5.

```
Many who oppose restricting access to national parks profit
economically from that access (Coates, "Comfort" 14; Stapleton 34).
```

13 ▪ Citing an interview

To document an interview, name the source in a signal statement or parenthetical citation.

```
Raymond Marks, an official at Rocky Mountain National Park, reports
that visitors' most frequent complaints have to do with overcrowding.
```

14 ▪ Citing Internet sources

Cite Internet sources as you would print documents. Include enough information to direct readers to the appropriate citation in your Works Cited list. If an Internet source includes section headings, page numbers, or paragraph numbers, include them. (*Pars.* is the abbreviation for *paragraphs; chs.* for *chapters.*) Do not include page numbers from printouts because they may vary from one printout to another.

```
Tonnie G. Maniero, of the National Park Service, reports an alarming
increase in the death of national parks wildlife from heavy metal
pollution ("Nonacidic Particulates," pars. 2-3).
```

To cite Internet addresses in the text of your paper, see 48a2.

Note: If you intend to publish your paper on line, for example, as part of a class Web site, you may wish to use hyperlinks as part of your documentation. In the text of brief or informal writing, set authors, their titles, or Web site titles as links leading directly to these Internet sources. Be aware, however, that hyperlinks in the text of your writing can disrupt the flow of your ideas if readers click on these links and pause to read your sources. On the Works Cited page of longer or more formal papers, set titles of Internet sources as links. If you wish to use hyperlinks, be sure to check with your instructor.

52c Include content and bibliography notes when necessary (optional)

Use notes in an MLA-style research paper only when you must provide additional information that cannot be worked into the text of your paper. Put raised, superscript numbers in your text to refer readers to a **footnote** at the bottom of the page or to an **endnote** on a page headed "Notes" immediately preceding the list of Works Cited. Number your notes consecutively throughout the paper. (For more on the use of notes, see Chapter 56.)

1 ▪ Writing content notes

Use content notes for definitions, formulas, explanations, and translations that would interrupt the flow of ideas if placed in the text of your paper.

▪ *Text:*

In 2003, the 388 units of the national parks system received nearly 267 million recreational visitors, a majority visiting the 55 national parks.[1]

▪ *Note:*

[1] Among the national parks receiving the heaviest use--nearly ten percent of total visits--were Great Smoky Mountains, 9.4 million; Grand Canyon, 4.1 million; Yellowstone, 3 million; Yosemite, 3.4 million; and Olympic, 3.2 million.

2 ▪ Writing bibliography notes

Use bibliography notes to cite several sources at once without a lengthy parenthetical citation, make cross-references, or refer readers to sources relevant to a topic.

▪ *Text:*

Throughout America's national parks, environmental damage from automobile air pollution is severe and well documented.[3]

▪ *Note:*

[3] For examples of this damage, see McMahon 26; Coates, "Threat" 1; "Haze" 95; "Tools" 14; and Craig 42.

53 Preparing the MLA Works Cited List

53a Follow MLA general guidelines

53.1
MLA Works
Cited guide:
Web link

The list of Works Cited gives full publication information for all sources cited in an MLA-style research paper (see the example in Chapter 54). Your instructor may ask you to provide a "works-consulted" list that includes all the works you've read, whether you cite them parenthetically or not.

1 ■ Placement of the Works Cited list

Begin the Works Cited list on a separate page at the end of your paper, after other concluding materials. (See 46d7 for the order of pages in an MLA paper. See the sample Works Cited list on pp. 406–407.)

2 ■ Works Cited—list format

- *Title.* Center the title "Works Cited" (without italics, underlining, or quotation marks) 1 inch from the top of the page. Continue page numbers from the text of your paper.

- *Spacing.* Double-space before the first entry and throughout all entries.

- *Indentation.* Begin each entry flush with the left margin. Indent second and successive lines one-half inch or 5 spaces.

- *Numbering.* Do not number the entries.

- *Alphabetical order.* Arrange entries alphabetically according to the author's last name as it appears on the title page of the sources you are borrowing from. Use square brackets to identify the true name when a pseudonym is given: *Mark Twain [Samuel Langhorne Clemens].* If an entry has no author, alphabetize according to the first word of the title, ignoring *A, An,* and *The.*

Manning, Robert E. "What to do about Crowding and Solitude in

Parks and Wilderness?" Journal of Leisure Research 35.1

(2003): 107-18.

National Park Service Information Office (Rocky Mountain National

Park). Telephone interview. 15 July 2004.

"Ten Most Endangered." National Parks May 2000: 28-30.

3 ■ Citation formats

See 53b for sample MLA citations.

■ *Two or more sources by the same author.* List two or more sources by the same author alphabetically by title. List the author's name for the first entry only. For the remaining entries, in place of the name type three hyphens followed by a period.

```
Lane, Ann J., ed. The Charlotte Perkins Gilman Reader: "The Yellow
     Wall-Paper" and Other Fiction. New York: Pantheon, 1980.

---. Introduction. Herland. By Charlotte Perkins Gilman. New York:
     Pantheon, 1979.

---. To "Herland" and Beyond: The Life and Work of Charlotte
     Perkins Gilman. New York: Pantheon, 1990.
```

■ *Punctuation of entries.* Place a colon followed by one space between titles and subtitles. Place a period followed by 1 space after each part of a citation.

```
Author. Title: Subtitle. Editorial information. Publication
     information. Page numbers.
```

■ *Publication dates.* For books, use the most recent publication date. For periodicals, abbreviate all months except May, June, and July.

■ *Page numbers.* For inclusive page numbers, give only the last two digits unless more are necessary (e.g., *1–21, 88–93, 95–121, 141–61, 198–213*). When a periodical or newspaper article is not printed on consecutive pages, give the first page number and a plus sign (e.g., *36 +*).

■ *Incomplete entries.* If an entry is incomplete, use the following abbreviations in the appropriate places: *n.p.* = no publisher given; *n.p.* = no place of publication; *n.d.* = no date of publication; *n. pag.* = no page numbers.

53b Sample MLA citations

Citing books

The basic citation for a book

```
Author's last name, first name. Title: Subtitle Underlined or
     Italicized. Place of publication: Publisher, date of
     publication.
```

Cite the city of publication as it appears on the title page of the book. If several cities are listed, use only the first. If the location of the city is ambiguous, add an abbreviation for the state. For cities outside the US, add a country abbreviation (or a province for Canadian cities).

Shorten publisher names: Use the publisher's last name (e.g., *Knopf* for *Alfred Knopf*). Use the first last name if the publisher's name includes more than one person (e.g., *Farrar* for *Farrar, Straus and Giroux*). Or use the first key word (e.g., *Random* for *Random House*). Abbreviate *University Press* as *UP* (without periods).

1. *Book with one author*

author name reversed   title with subtitle
Freeberg, David. The Eye of the Lynx: Galileo, His Friends, and the

place of
publication   publisher
   Beginnings of Modern Natural History. Chicago: U of Chicago P,
date of publication
   2004.

2. *Two or three authors.* List authors in the order in which their names appear on the title page. Reverse the name of only the first author. Use commas to separate three authors' names.

first author's name reversed   second author   third author
Hine, Darlene Clark, William C. Hine, and Stanley Harrold. African-

   American Odyssey. Upper Saddle River: Prentice, 2004.

3. *Four or more authors.* Cite only the first author, followed by *et al.* ("and others"), or cite all authors in the order in which they appear on the title page.

first author   abbreviation indicating four or more authors
Medhurst, Martin J., et al. Cold War Rhetoric: Strategy, Metaphor, and

   Ideology. New York: Greenwood, 1990.

4. *Corporate or institutional publication.* Give the name of the corporation or institution as the author, even if it is also the publisher.

corporate author
The Bronte Society. A Bronte Walking Tour. London: Hodgkinson, 1980.

5. *Title within a title.* If a book title appears with the title of another book, do not underline or italicize the shorter title. If the shorter title is normally enclosed with quotation marks, retain the quotation marks and underline the complete longer title.

a book title containing a shorter book title
Vanderham, Paul. James Joyce and Censorship: The Trials of Ulysses.

   New York: New York UP, 1997.

a book title containing a story title
Julie Bates Dock, ed. Charlotte Perkins Gilman's "The Yellow Wall-

   Paper" and the History of Its Publication and Reception.

   University Park: Pennsylvania State UP, 1998.

6. *Introduction, foreword, preface, or afterword.* To cite an introduction, foreword, preface, or afterword, begin with the author of the element being cited; then identify the element. Place the author of the book after the title. Conclude with the page numbers for the part being cited.

author of the part   part   book title
Duncan, Jeffery L. Introduction. Thoreau: The Major Essays. By
        author of the book   page numbers of the part
    Henry David Thoreau. New York: Dutton, 1972. viii-xiii.

7. *Author and editor.* Cite the author's name, the title, and then the editor. Use *Ed.* for one or more editors.

author
Douglass, Frederick. Narrative of the Life of Frederick Douglass, an
                            editor
    American Slave. Ed. David W. Blight. Boston: Bedford, 1993.

8. *Editor or editors.* Name the editor(s), followed by *ed.* or *eds.*

         editors
Anaya, Rodolfo, and Francisco Lomeli, eds. Aztlán: Essays on the
    Chicano Homeland. Albuquerque: Academia, 1989.

9. *Edition other than the first.* Include the number of the edition after the title and after the name of the translator or editor (if any).

                                    edition
Harmon, William, and C. Hugh Holman. A Handbook to Literature. 8th ed.
    Chapel Hill: U of North Carolina P, 2000.

10. *Republished edition.* Give the original publication date before the place of publication.

                      original publication date
Roberts, Elizabeth Madox. The Time of Man. 1926. Lexington: UP of
       republication date
    Kentucky, 2000.

11. *Book in series.* After the title, include the name of the series and the series number.

                        series
Howard, Lillie. Zora Neale Hurston. Twayne's United States Authors
   series number
    Ser. 381. Boston: Twayne, 1980.

12. *Translation.* After the title, write *Trans.* ("translated by") and the name of the translator.

                    translator
Camus, Albert. The Stranger. Trans. Matthew Ward. New York: Knopf, 1988.

13. *Multivolume work.* Give the number of volumes before the place of publication.

number of volumes
Blotner, Joseph. <u>Faulkner: A Biography</u>. 2 vols. New York: Random,

1976.

14. *Volume in a series, each volume titled separately.* If you borrow
from only one volume of a multivolume series, give its number and
the name of the series to which it belongs following the place of publication. Give the total number of volumes preceding the inclusive
dates of publication.

one volume in series
Durrell, Lawrence. <u>Mountolive</u>. New York: Dutton, 1959. Vol. 3 of

total volumes   series publication
series title   in the series   dates
<u>The Alexandria Quartet</u>. 4 vols. 1957-60.

15. *Selection in a multivolume reference work.* Cite the number of the
volume following the title or the editor's name and publication
information. Give publication information only for that volume.

selection author   title of selection   volume title   volume editor
Howard, Wayne. "Vedic Chant." <u>South Asia</u>. Ed. Alison Arnold. New York:

title of multivolume work
Garland, 2000. Vol. 5 of <u>The Garland Encyclopedia of World Music</u>.

page numbers
10 vols. 238-45.

16. *Anthology selection.* If a book contains selections by a number of
authors, give the author and title of the selection you are citing, followed by the title of the book, the editor's name, the edition if appropriate, and the publication information.

author of the selection   selection title
Oates, Joyce Carol. "To Invigorate Literary Mind, Start Moving

title of the book   editor of the book
Literary Feet." <u>Writers on Writing</u>. Ed. John Darnton. New York:

page numbers of the selection
Times, 2001. 165-71.

17. *A selection reprinted in an anthology.* If an anthology selection
was reprinted elsewhere, cite the original source first. Follow with
Rpt. in ("reprinted in") and a citation for the anthology. Original
publication sources are usually listed on acknowledgment pages at
the beginning or end of a book or at the bottom of the first page of a
selection.

author of the selection   selection title   original book title
Naipaul, V. S. "Traveller's Prelude: A Little Paperwork." <u>An Area of</u>

original publisher   anthology title
<u>Darkness</u>. London: Aitken, 1964. Rpt. in <u>The Norton Book of Travel</u>.

editor of the anthology   page numbers of the selection
Ed. Paul Fussell. New York: Norton, 1987. 783-97.

18. ***Selection reprinted in a multivolume reference work.*** Provide publication information for the original source first. Follow with *Rpt. in* ("reprinted in") and a citation for the reference work.

author of the selection   selection title   original publication information
Taylor, Henry. "Gwendolyn Brooks: An Essential Sanity." Kenyon Review

title of the reference work
13.4 (1991): 115-31. Rpt. in Contemporary Literary Criticism. Ed.

editor of the   page numbers of the selection
reference   volume number   in the reference work
Jeffrey Hunter. Vol. 125. Detroit: Gale, 2000. 88-97.

19. ***Cross-references to an anthology.*** If you cite more than one source from an anthology, provide full publication information for the anthology in its own citation. Cross-reference individual selections, giving author, title, editor's last name, and page numbers.

Bone, Robert. "Ralph Ellison and the Uses of Imagination." Cooke 45-63.

Editor of the book as author of the introduction
Cooke, G. C. Introduction. Cooke 1-11.

Cooke, G. C., ed. Modern Black Novelists. Englewood Cliffs: Prentice,
1971.

Tibble, Anne. "Chinua Achebe." Cooke 122-32.

20. ***Anonymous or unknown author.*** Alphabetize the entry according to the first word of the title, ignoring *A, An,* or *The.*

Sir Gawain and the Green Knight. Ed. J. A. Burrow. Baltimore: Penguin,
1972.

21. ***Encyclopedia or dictionary.*** Give the author (if any) of the entry, then the entry title, title of the encyclopedia or dictionary, edition number (if any), and the date.

"Mexico." The Encyclopedia Americana. 1998 ed.

22. ***A religious work, such as the Bible or the Quran.***

The Bible: King James Version. Standard text ed. New York: Cambridge
UP, 1998.

Al-Qur'an: A Contemporary Translation. Trans. Ahmed Ali and Ali Jimale
Ahmed. 2nd ed. Princeton: Princeton UP, 1988.

23. ***Publisher's imprint*** (a specialized name for a group of books). Give the imprint name followed by a hyphen and the publisher's name.

Coles, Robert. The Moral Intelligence of Children: How to Raise a
Moral Child. New York: Plume-Random, 1997.

Citing periodicals and newspapers

24. ***Article in a monthly magazine.*** Give the author's name, the title of the article enclosed by quotation marks, the name of the magazine

underlined or italicized, the month and year of publication, and the page numbers on which the article appears. If the pages are not consecutive, cite the first page number followed by a plus sign (+).

author   title of the article   magazine   date of publication
Wittes, Benjamin. "Enemy Americans." The Atlantic Monthly July/Aug.
      page numbers
    2004: 127-35.

25. *Article in a weekly magazine.* Cite the full date of publication, not only the month.

                              publication information: day, month
Quinn, Jane Bryant. "Colleges' New Tuition Crisis." Newsweek 2 Feb.
    year
    2004: 49.

26. *Article in a journal paged by volume.* For scholarly journals paged consecutively throughout a volume, give the volume number after the name of the periodical and then the date in parentheses.

Richardson, Mark. "A Newly Discovered Robert Frost Poem." Robert Frost
    volume number publication date
    Review 11 (Fall 2001): 70-71.

27. *Article in a journal paged by issue.* For scholarly journals paged separately by issue, give the issue number after the volume number.

Knight, Denise D. "Charlotte Perkins Gilman and the Shadow of Racism."

    American Literary Realism 32.2 (2000): 159-69.

28. *Signed newspaper article.* Cite the author, title, name of the newspaper, and date of publication as you would an article in a weekly magazine. If the city of publication is not given in the newspaper name, add the city in square brackets following the name. (See item 30.) If an edition is given on the masthead of the paper, include it in your citation after the date. If each section of the paper is numbered separately, include the section number or letters before the page number.

Villarosa, Linda. "More Teenagers Say No to Sex, and Experts Aren't
                                  section and non-
                        edition   consecutive paging
    Sure Why." New York Times 23 Dec. 2003, late ed.: F6+.

Note: Following the page numbers of the original source, add the relevant microfilm publication information: name of the microfilm source and cataloging information, such as file, fiche, and location numbers.

29. *Unsigned newspaper article.* If no author is given for an article, begin the citation with the title.

30. *Editorial.* Identify the element by writing *Editorial* after the author's name, or if no author is given, after the title.

city and state of publication
"Charter Schools." Editorial. <u>Herald-Palladium</u> [Benton Harbor, MI]
section letter and page number
7 Oct. 2001: A10.

31. *Letter to the editor.* Write *Letter* after the author's name.
identification of the source
Spingarn, Adena. Letter. <u>The New Yorker</u> 29 Mar. 2004: 8.

32. *Review of a book, movie, or play.* After the author's name and title of the review, write *Rev. of* and then name the work reviewed. Give important information about the work reviewed, such as the name of the author (preceded with *by*) or director (preceded with *dir.*).
author of the review   title of the review   the book being reviewed
Leonard, John. "New Books." Rev. of <u>Circles and Lines: The Shape of</u>
author of the book
<u>Life in Early America</u>, by John Demos. <u>Harper's</u> July 2004: 84.
author of the review   title of the review   movie title
Kauffman, Stanley. "In the Same World." Rev. of <u>Control Room</u>,
director
dir. Jehabe Noujaim. <u>New Republic</u> 21 June 2004: 24-25.

Citing Internet sources

HOW TO . . . Write MLA Internet Citations

In the *MLA Handbook for Writers of Research Papers,* 6th edition (2003), the Modern Language Association has published a template to guide students and scholars when citing Internet sources. As you prepare an MLA-style Works Cited list, include as many items from the following list as are relevant or can be found, in the order in which they are listed here. For information about writing URLs, see 48a2. For tips about locating publication information in an Internet source, see 48d4.

Author, editor, title, original print publication information
1. Author, editor, compiler, or translator of the source (last name first, followed by an abbreviation such as *ed.* or *trans.* when appropriate).
2. Title of article, short story, poem, or chapter (in quotation marks); or the title of a posting to a news group, listserv, or other discussion group (taken from the subject line and put in quotation marks), followed by the description *Online posting.*
3. Title of book or report (underlined).
4. Editor, compiler, or translator (if not cited earlier), preceded by an abbreviation such as *Ed.* or *Trans.* (when appropriate).
5. Publication information for print versions of the source (arranged according to the guidelines elsewhere in 53b).

Online publication information

6. Title of periodical, professional or personal site, database, or scholarly project (underlined); or for an untitled professional or personal site, a description such as *Home page.*
7. Editor of the site (if available).
8. Volume number, issue number, or other identifying number for a journal; or the version number of a source when not part of the title.
9. Date of electronic publication, of the latest update, or of posting.
10. The name of the library database or information service (e.g., *InfoTrac* or *EBSCO*), followed by the name and city (and state abbreviation, if necessary) of the library.
11. The name of the news group, listserv, or other discussion group.
12. The number range or total number of pages, paragraphs, sections, or chapters, if they are numbered.
13. Name of any institution or organization sponsoring or associated with the site.

Internet access information

14. Date when the researcher accessed the source. Do not use a period between items 14 and 15.
15. Electronic address (URL) of the source (in angle brackets, followed by a period). For guidelines to citing Internet addresses, see 48a2.

33. *A book or lengthy document.*

original
book publication
author   title of a chapter   title date
Thoreau, Henry David. "Where I Lived and What I Lived For." Walden. 1854.

name of most   URL broken
database recent update site sponsor access date after slash mark
Eserver. Oct. 2001. U of Washington. 30 Sept. 2001 <http://eserver.org/

thoreau/walden02.html>.

         document title
Reclaiming Our Heritage: What We Need to Do to Preserve America's

     posting date number of chapters   site sponsor
National Parks. 1997. 5 chs. Natural Resources Defense Council.

access date   URL enclosed with brackets followed by a period
7 Dec. 2003 <http://www.nrdc.org/land/parks/roh/rohpre.asp>.

34. *Journal article reprinted online, with online page or paragraph numbers.*

<pre>
    author   article title
Denman, Kamilla. "Emily Dickinson's Volcanic Punctuation." Emily
    original publication   Internet
    information   publication date length   site sponsor
    Dickinson Journal 2.1 (1993). 29 Jan. 1998. 33 pars. U of Colorado.
    access date
    9 Sept. 2001 <http://www.colorado.edu/EDIS/journal/articles/
    11.1.Denman.html>.
</pre>

35. *Online magazine article, without page or paragraph numbers.*

<pre>
    author   title of the work   online publication Internet publication date
Langewiesche, William. "A Sea Story." The Atlantic Online. May 2004.
    access date
    1 July 2004 <http://www.theatlantic.com/issues/2004/05/
    langewiesche.htm>.
</pre>

36. *Work at a professional, scholarly, business, or organizational site.*

<pre>
            authors   title of the work
Chatterjee, Pratap, and A.C. Thompson. "Private Contractors and
                        most recent update   site owner   access date
    Torture at Abu Ghraib." 7 May 2004. CorpWatch. 21 June 2004
    <http://www.corpwatch.org/article.php?id=11285>.
</pre>

37. *Professional, scholarly, business, or organizational site.*

<pre>
    name of the site   site sponsor   most recent update
    FairTest. National Center for Fair and Open Testing. 5 Oct. 2001.
    access date
    10 Oct. 2001 <http://www.fairtest.org>.
</pre>

38. *Sources lacking URLs.* If you retrieve Internet materials from services such as America Online that have not been assigned URLs, at the end of your citation write *Keyword:* or *Path:*, followed by the keyword used or search path you followed to locate the materials.

<pre>
                                                                    most
    title of material   name of the database   recent update
    "Ecosystem." Merriam-Webster Dictionary: Collegiate Edition. 2001.
        online service   access date   keyword used to access the material
        America Online. 6 June 2000. Keyword: Collegiate.
</pre>

<pre>
    author of material   title of the material   name of the database
    Scruggs, Otey M. "Sojourner Truth." World Book Online Americas Edition.
most recent update online service   access date   search path followed to access the
        2001. America Online. 8 Oct. 2001. Path: Research and Learning;
    material punctuated with a colon and semicolons
        History and Biography; Biography.
</pre>

39. ***Work in an online library database.*** Works in online databases such as InfoTrac, Wilson FirstSearch, EBSCO, Literature Resource Center, NewsBank, or SIRS may have long, complex URLs. Include the name of the database, the library you used to access the database, your access date, and the URL of the database home page (rather than the URL for the work) in angle brackets. If the database supplies only the starting page number for original print sources, give the number followed by a hyphen, a space, and a period, for example, *52-* .

author of the work   title of the work
Carroll, Rachel. "Foreign Bodies: History and Trauma in Flannery
                                original publication information
     O'Connor's 'The Displaced Person.'" Textual Practice 14.1 (2000):
        name of the library database   library and its location
     97-114. Literature Resource Center. Harper Coll. Lib., Palatine,
       access date   database homepage URL
     IL. 5 July 2004 <http://galenet.galegroup.com/servlet/LitRC>.

40. ***Article in an online newspaper.***

author   title of the article
Hafner, Katie. "Old Search Engine, Library, Tries to Fit Into a Google
       original publication information   online division of the newspaper
     World." New York Times 21 June 2004: Technology. NYTimes.Com.
  publication date   access date
     21 June 2004. 22 June 2004 <http://www.nytimes.com/2004/06/21/
     technology/21LIBR.html>.

41. ***Letter to the editor of an online publication.***

  identification of the source   publication   publication date   access date
Mieszkowski, Katherine. Letter. Salon 15 June 2004. 23 June 2004
     <http://www.salon.com/tech/leters/2004/06/15/more_wolves/index.html>.

42. ***Work in an online reference.***

author   work   online reference   most recent update
Kjeilen, Tore. "Iraq." Encyclopedia of the Orient 4 May 2004.
   site sponsor   access date
     LexicOrient. 21 June 2004 <http://lexicorient.com/cgi-bin/
     eo-direct.pl?iraq.htm>.

43. ***A government document.*** If the source lacks an author name, begin with the name of the government first, followed by the agency and office. If the author is identified, begin with the author's name, followed by the title of the document.

body of government   agency   office
United States. Environmental Protection Agency. Office of Air and
                        title of the source
     Radiation. Visibility Impairment from Air Pollution, Olympic
       most recent update   access date
     National Park. 5 Sept. 2001. 7 Oct. 2001 <http://www.epa.gov/air/
     vis/olympic.html>.

44. *Literary work in scholarly project or database.*

original date of publication

Gilman, Charlotte Perkins. "The Yellow Wall-Paper." 1892. The Online

name of the project or database   project editor

Archive of Nineteenth-Century U.S. Women's Writings. Ed. Glynis

posting date   access date

Carr. Fall 1999. 6 June 2004 <http://www.facstaff.bucknell.edu/

gcarr/19cUSWW/CPG/TYW.html>.

45. *A newsgroup posting.* Identify the source as *Online posting.* In angle brackets, cite the name of the newsgroup, beginning with the prefix *news:,* or cite the URL used to access the posting.

author of posting   title   identification of the source   posting date

Beno, Tom. "Wolves in the Backcountry." Online posting. 26 May 2004.

name of the newsgroup   access date

Rec.outdoors.national-parks. 30 May 2004 <http://www.google.com/

groups>.

46. *A posting to an e-mail listserv discussion.* Identify the source as *Online posting.* Conclude the citation with the URL for the discussion group or the e-mail address for the group's moderator or supervisor.

author of posting   title   identification of the source   posting date

Boatner, Fred. "Air Pollution Proposal." Online posting. 20 April

name of the discussion group

2004. National Parks Conservation Association: Endangered Parks

access date   URL for the discussion group

Discussion Forum. 3 May 2004 <http://www.npca.org/take_action/

posts/Topicsasp?LngForumID=27>.

47. *Weblog post and comment.* As of summer 2004 the Modern Language Association had yet to issue a citation format for Weblogs. The following citations for a Weblog post and comment, treating both as online postings, are adapted to the MLA style from proposals made in a *Kairosnews* Weblog exchange between Dennis Jerz and Janice Walker of the *Columbia Guide to Online Style.*

author of posting   title of posting   identification of the source

Jerz, Dennis G. "Citing a Weblog in MLA Style." Weblog posting. 11

name of   sponsoring   access
posting date   the Weblog   organization, if any   date

Dec. 2003 Jerz's Literacy Weblog. Seton Hill University. 23 June

2004 <http://jerz.setonhill.edu/weblog/permalink.jsp?id=2000>.

author of the   title or first few   identification
comment   words of comment   of the source

Walker, Janice. "Basically, a blog is cited . . ." Weblog comment.

date comment   title of   author of
was posted   Weblog entry   Weblog entry

13 Dec. 2003. "Citing a Weblog Comment in MLA Style." Dennis Jerz.

name of the
Weblog

sponsoring
organization

date Weblog
was posted

Jerz's Literacy Weblog. Seton Hill University. 10 Dec. 2003.

access date

23 June 2004 <http://jerz.setonhill.edu/weblog/

permalink.jsp?id=2001>.

48. *A synchronous communication (MOO, MUD, or IRC discussion).* To cite synchronous communication, give the name of the speaker, a description of the event, the date of the event, the forum for discussion, and the URL. Whenever possible, cite an archival version of the communication so that readers can more easily access the source.

speaker

description of the event

Choi, Tom. Discussion of narrative point of view in O'Connor's

date of
the event

name of
the forum

access date

"Greenleaf." 3 July 2000. CompMOO. 23 Sept. 2004

<http://www.harper.cc.il.us/~sherer/comp_archive/pov.txt>.

49. *Personal sites, academic course home pages, and academic department sites.* Include a descriptive label to identify the site.

Neumann, Kurt. Home Page. 27 Aug. 2003 <http://www.harpercoll.edu/

~kneumann>.

Thoreson, Trygve. English 200: Grammar and Style. Course home page.

Aug. 2004-Dec. 2004. Dept. of English, Harper Coll. 11 Nov. 2004

<http://www.grammar.harpercoll.edu/~tthoreson/ENG200/Index.htm>.

History. Dept. home page. Lake Michigan Coll. 13 Feb. 2004

<http://www.depts.lmu.edu/history>.

50. *Electronic mail.* To cite electronic mail, give the sender's name, a description of the document that includes the recipient, and the date of the document.

Buss, Pauline. "Choosing a New Computer for Your Office." E-mail to

Joseph Sternberg. 18 Jan. 2004.

51. *Online image or graphic.*

artist

title of the work

date of creation

owner of the work

Hopper, Edward. Railroad Sunset. 1929. Whitney Museum of American Art.

title of the online database

posting date

Surroundings: Responses to the American Landscape. 6 June 1999

sponsor of the site

access date

San Jose Museum of Art. 5 May 2001 <http://www.sjmusart.org/

body_surroundings.html>.

52. *A television or radio program.*

reporter   title of the report   name of the program

Stamberg, Susan. "The Making of Seurat's 'La Grande Jatte.'" Morning

station call letters
radio network   and location   broadcast date

Edition. National Public Radio. WBEZ, Chicago. 18 June 2004.

type of Internet
document   access date

Transcript. 22 June 2004 <http://www.npr.org/features/

feature.php?wfId=1963623>.

Citing other sources

53. *Indeterminate electronic medium.* If you cannot determine the medium of a source you retrieve electronically, for example, a work retrieved through a library network, use the term *Electronic* to identify the medium. Provide as much publication information as possible, including the name of the network or sponsoring organization.

title of the work   publication information for the source of the work

"Ecosystem." Columbia Encyclopedia. 6th ed. New York: Columbia UP,

identification of   sponsoring
the medium   organization   access date

2001. Electronic. Harper College Lib., Palatine, IL. 12 Oct. 2004.

54. *Pamphlet.* Cite a pamphlet as you would a book.

Schubert, John. The Tandem Scoop: An Insider's Guide to Tandem

Cycling. Eugene: Burley Design Coop., 1993.

55. *CD-ROM publication.*

"Grand Canyon National Park." Grolier Multimedia Encyclopedia. 2002

medium of publication

ed. CD-ROM. 2 discs. Danbury: Grolier Interactive, 2002.

56. *Government publications.* The formats for government publications are many and varied. The order of an entry is as follows:

Government body. Subsidiary body. Title of Document. Type and number

of document. Publication information.

Note: If you know the author's name, place it at the beginning of an entry or after the title, following the word *By.*

President's Commission on the Assassination of President Kennedy.

Hearings before the President's Commission on the

Assassination of President Kennedy. 26 vols. Washington:

GPO, 1964.

United States. Cong. House. Subcommittee on Science, Research, and

    Technology. <u>Genetic Engineering, Human Genetics and Cell Biology</u>.

    96th Cong., 2nd sess. Washington: GPO, 1980.

57. *Legal references.* Do not italicize or underline the titles of laws, acts, or legal documents or enclose them within quotation marks; give the section and, if appropriate, the year. Italicize or underline the names of cases in the text of your paper but not in the list of Works Cited. No Works Cited entry is necessary for familiar historical documents or the United States Code (USC); parenthetical citations in your text are sufficient.

Brown v. Board of Ed. 347 US 483. US Sup. Ct. 1954.

58. *Published dissertation.* Identify a dissertation with the abbreviation *Diss.* If the dissertation was published by University Microfilms, add the order number at the end of the citation.

author   title

Butler, Carol Ann. <u>Images against the Sun: The Monument in Willa</u>

    type of   date of

    document   university   degree   publisher   order number

    <u>Cather</u>. Diss. Kent State U, 2000. Ann Arbor: UMI, 2000. 9976632.

59. *Dissertation abstract.* Place the dissertation title in quotation marks, followed by the abbreviation *Diss.*, the institution granting the degree, the date the degree was granted, the abbreviation *DA* or *DAI* (*Dissertation Abstracts* or *Dissertation Abstracts International*), the volume number, the date of publication, and the page number.

Cullen, Elaine Marie. "Women Coming to Voice through Writing." Diss. U

    of Minnesota, 1999. <u>DAI</u> 60 (2000): 2473A.

60. *Published proceedings of a conference.* Cite the published proceedings of a conference as you would cite a book. After the title of the publication, give information about the conference. Give the editor's name if available, followed by the publication information.

Spinner-Halev, Jeff. "Cultural Pluralism and Partial Citizenship."

    <u>Multicultural Questions: Multiculturalism, Minorities, and</u>

                  information about the conference

    <u>Citizenship</u>. Proc. of Conf. on Multiculturalism,

      date and location of the conference   editors

    13-16 Apr. 1996, Florence, Italy. Ed. Christian Joppke and

                            page numbers

              publication information   of the work cited

    Steven Lukes. New York: Oxford UP, 1999. 65-86.

61. *Speech or lecture.* If necessary, identify the occasion or the type of presentation: *Speech, Address, Reading, Lecture,* and so forth.

the occasion or sponsoring organization
Gandhi, Indira. "What Educated Women Can Do." Golden Jubilee
place
Celebrations of the Indraprastha College for Women. Delhi, India.
date of the presentation
23 Nov. 1974.

62. *Interview.* To cite an interview that you conducted, name the person interviewed followed by *Personal interview* or *Telephone interview* and the date. To cite a radio or television interview, name the person interviewed followed by *Interview* or *Interview with* and the name of the interviewer.

O'Connell, Edward J. Personal interview. 4 May 2001.

McPherson, James. Interview with Terry Gross. Fresh Air. Natl. Public

Radio. WVPE, South Bend, IN. 22 June 2004.

Paz, Octavio. Interview. Paris Review Interviews: Writers at Work. Ed.

George Plimpton. 9th ser. New York: Viking, 1992. 81-108.

63. *Personal letter.* Cite a letter addressed to you as follows.

Linville, Alicia M. Letter to the author. 4 June 2001.

64. *Radio or television program.* When appropriate, identify those involved with the production preceded by these abbreviations: *Narr.* (narrator), *Writ.* (writer), *Dir.* (director), *Perf.* (performer), *Introd.* (introducer), *Prod.* (producer).

"The Way the Music Died." Frontline. Narr. Jim Gilmore. Writ., Prod.,

and Dir. Michael Kirk. PBS. WTTW, Chicago. 27 May 2004.

65. *Play performance.* Give the title underlined, followed with *By* and the author's name, *Dir.* and the director's name, *Perf.* and the leading actor's name.

playwright   director
A Raisin in the Sun. By Lorraine Hansberry. Dir. Kenny Leon. Perf.
major performers
Sean Combs, Phylicia Rashad, and Audra McDonald. Royale Theatre.

New York. 17 May 2004.

66. *Film or video recording.*

It's a Wonderful Life. Dir. Frank Capra. Perf. James Stewart, Donna

Reed, Lionel Barrymore, and Thomas Mitchell. RKO, 1946.

67. *DVD, videocassette, laser disc, slide program, or filmstrip.* Cite the work as you would a film, but give the original release date and the medium before the name of the distributor.

David Copperfield. By Charles Dickens. Dir. Delbert Mann. Perf.

original release date

    Richard Attenborough, Edith Evans, and Laurence Olivier. 1970.

medium

    DVD. Brentwood Communications, 2000.

The End of the Buffalo. Videocassette. Prod. Society of American

    History, 1987.

68. *CD, audiocassette, or record.* Within the citation, identify the recording date, publication medium if not a CD (*Audiocassette, LP*), publisher, and date of publication.

Vaughn, Sarah. "Snowbound." Jazz Profile. Rec. 23 July 1962. Blue

    Note, 1998.

69. *A work of art.*

Hopper, Edward. Railroad Sunset. Whitney Museum of American Art, New York.

70. *Map or chart.*

Mt. Rainier National Park, Washington. Map. Reston: Dept. of the

    Interior, US Geological Survey, 1975.

71. *Cartoon or comic strip.* Provide a descriptive label, *Cartoon* or *Comic strip,* to identify the material.

McGruder, Aaron. "Boondocks." Comic strip. Chicago Tribune 14 Mar.

    2003, sec. 5: 7.

72. *Advertisement.*

American Friends Service Committee. Advertisement. New York Times 7

    Oct. 2001, natl. ed., sec. 1: 17.

54 MLA Research Project (with Title Page and Outline)

The writer of the following problem-solution project was instructed to include title and outline pages. The paper follows MLA guidelines for parenthetical in-text documentation and the Works Cited list given in Chapters 52 and 53. Marginal notes indicate important features of research projects and MLA documentation. For an MLA paper without a title page or an outline page, see 4f.

Modern Language Association format, with title and outline pages added.

America's Crowded Parks

Center title one-third down the page

by

Eric Martínez

Double-space

Professor J. Lindsay

English 102

30 Oct. 200-

Center course information two-thirds down the page

Martínez ii

Outline

Thesis: At US national parks where overcrowding and harm to the environment are greatest, officials should adopt a reservation system to control park use and aid environmental recovery.

I. The popularity of US national parks has damaged park environments.

   A. The popularity of US national parks is increasing.

   B. Overcrowding causes problems for visitors.

      1. Visitors experience delays and inconveniences.

      2. Visitors are unable to enjoy the views.

   C. Overcrowding harms national park environments.

      1. Indirect harm: automobile air pollution damages vegetation.

      2. Direct harm: visitors cause erosion and pollution, deface natural sites, and disrupt ecosystems.

   D. Current Park Service budgeting will increase the problems of overcrowding.

II. A reservation system is one obvious solution.

   A. A reservation system at the most threatened parks would reduce overcrowding.

   B. Opposing arguments are flawed.

      1. A reservation system is democratic, not elitist.

      2. Free access does not mean use without restrictions.

      3. Opponents make a faulty comparison of public lands and private property.

   C. A reservation system is an effective method to meet the threats to US national parks.

Use lower-case Roman numerals for preliminary pages.

Center heading 1 inch from top of page.

Double-space throughout.

For guidelines on formal outlines, see 3c.

Martínez 1

America's Crowded National Parks

As historian Kenneth Clark has observed, "Nothing
except love is so universally appealing as a view" (qtd.
in McMahon 26). And the views Americans seem to love most
are views of the forests, mountains, and waters of the US
National Parks. In 2003, almost 270 million people--a
number nearly equal to the total population of the United
States--visited the 388 parks, monuments, and historic
sites administered by the Park Service (United States).
More than 58 million visited the 55 national parks alone,
more than half, over 36 million, visiting the 10 most
popular parks. Each year, the Great Smoky Mountains and
Grand Canyon are visited by the combined population
equivalents of New York, Los Angeles, and Chicago (Hill
par. 1).

These figures have increased nearly every year during
the more than nearly ninety years of the National Park
Service (NPS) and will only continue to increase. One
million additional visitors are anticipated for 2005, and
by the year 2010, annual park visits are projected to
reach 90 million (National). If these nature lovers were
religious pilgrims, their journeys would constitute one of
the great pilgrimages in human history.

The problem of such devotion begins with the numbers
themselves. As the 19th century naturalist and author
George Perkins Marsh warned, "Man is everywhere a
disturbing agent. Wherever he plants his foot, the
harmonies of nature are turned to discords" (qtd. in
Stegner 38). Each park has its own "carrying capacity" and
can accommodate only so many visitors before their
pleasure and the environment are adversely affected. Such

Title centered, double-spaced, if necessary, and typed 1 inch from top of page

Introduction: a dramatic quotation cited from an indirect source

Part I: Essential information about the topic

Internet source with paragraph numbering

Double-spacing throughout

Part IA: Essential information about the topic

A source identified in a signal statement

Martínez 2

is often the case at many of the most popular parks, which receive the most destructive use. These national parks are now burdened beyond their carrying capacity. The adverse effects, both social and environmental, are evident throughout the park system.

Visitors come to national parks seeking escape from civilization, the "tranquility, peace, and silence" of nature, and recovery from stress (Mace, Bell, and Loomis 229), but what they find instead is "an urbanised [sic] environment pervaded by the automobile and its greed for space in the form of roads and parking" (McGregor). At the entrances to the most popular parks, cars are lined up in overflow lots waiting, sometimes half a day, for entrance. The roads within Yosemite are almost always in a state of "gridlock"; at Grand Canyon, up to 6,000 cars a day vie for just 2,500 spaces. Outside their cars, this "crush" of visitors crowds the rim of Bryce Canyon so densely that no one can see the views. At Acadia, the annual three million visitors are crowded in on an average of sixty people per acre. In Utah, outside Moab, 100,000 bikers a summer, rarely out of sight of one another, ride the Slickrock Trail (Hill par. 10). "Getting that snapshot of the Grand Canyon means elbowing aside almost five million people; cruising through the Smoky Mountains involves competing with a whopping 21 million" (Beattie). For dramatic images of the year-round crowds at Yellowstone, see Figure 1.

Few of these visitors travel silently. From the roar of hundreds of thousands of summer airplane and helicopter park overflights to the "incessant whining" of tens of thousands of winter snowmobilers, US national parks are filled not with the "magical sounds of nature"

An expert source's warrant (see 58b2) introducing the first half of the thesis: the claim for an argument

Part IB: The problems overcrowding causes for visitors

An Internet source with no page numbers

A quotation without a signal statement

An in-text reference to a graphic

Quotations blended into the writer's sentences

Martínez 3

Summer crowds await an Old Faithful eruption. (NPS photo)

Snowmobiles on the West Yellowstone Entrance Road. (NPS photo)

Traffic jam caused by visitors viewing wildlife. (NPS photo)

Fig. 1. Crowd photos at Yellowstone from "Images of Park Special Issues," Yellowstone National Park. 23 Dec. 2003. 27 June 2004 <http://www.nps.gov/yell/press/images/issues/index.htm>.

Martínez 4

(Kiernan, "Parks") but with a cacophany of as many as "forty-three noise events in a twenty-minute period," so much noise and such loud noise, that back-country hikers in such parks as Yellowstone, Bryce, Grand Canyon, Cedar Breaks, and Lake Mead are never out of earshot of human-created noise (Mace, Bell, and Loomis 225).

Instead of what one park ranger calls "the national park experience," what these crowded visitors find instead is often more like Times Square on New Year's Eve (National). Not only is there none of the hoped-for "tranquility, peace, and silence," but even the views they gaze upon, clouded by crowds and noise, seem less lovely (Mace, Bell, and Loomis 225). More serious than the diminished visitor experience, however, is the "diminished ecosystem, damaged resources, and diminution of the natural resource base" caused by these visitors and their style of recreation (Ewert 62). As nature writer, poet, and novelist Wallace Stegner speculates, this "recreation could be as dangerous [to national parks] as logging or extractive use [such as mining]" (43).

The most visible danger is air pollution, often caused by the vehicles that bring visitors into the wilds. At many of the most popular parks, visibility has been reduced, down from 140 miles in western parks and 90 miles in eastern parks to only 35-90 miles and 18-40 miles, respectively (Hill par. 12). At Acadia National Park, Grand Canyon, Cape Cod National Seashore, and the Great Smoky Mountains, air quality is so poor that the parks receive the same pollution warnings as Denver, Los Angeles, Washington, and Boston (Wilkinson, "At More Parks" 3; Hill par. 12). For dramatic evidence of this

Citation of an author who provides more than one source for this paper

A source with three authors

Transition to Part IC: Harm to the environment

Brackets used to insert clarifying information within a quotation

Topic sentence

Supporting examples

A multi-source citation

Martínez 5

haze, see the digital photos updated every fifteen minutes
on the Park Service's seventeen Webcams stationed in
national parks throughout the US (go to
<http://www2.nps.gov/air/WebCams/index.htm>).

    The most famous example of National Parks air
pollution is Yellowstone, whose west entrance has the
highest carbon monoxide levels in the US and where, during
the winter, supplemental oxygen must be pumped into ranger
booths because pollution from snowmobiles produces more
noxious gases in one weekend than automobiles emit in the
park throughout a whole year ("Administration"). As
pollution particulates settle out of the air, they increase
the acidity and toxicity of snow, streams, and soil,
thereby making harmful plant and animal diseases more
potent. In some parts of Tennessee's Great Smoky Mountains,
for example, large stands of once-green trees are now gray
skeletons, killed by ozone (<u>Reclaiming</u>, ch. 2).

    Visitors also cause more direct harm. According to
environmental activist Dave Foreman, "the army of
wilderness destruction drives on roads" (94), and for
improved auto, RV, and SUV access, new roads are being cut
into formerly roadless park areas in Alaska and Utah. The
consequence is more traffic, disrupted ecosystems, and the
loss of wildlife (Hill, par. 14). Elsewhere, in
Yellowstone, where one-quarter of the park's road budget
goes for new road construction, visiting motorists
annually kill hundreds of antelope, bighorn sheep, bison,
bear, elk, and moose and frighten uncounted numbers of
other animals (National). Off road, from Golden Gate
National Recreation Area in California to parks in Utah,
Colorado, and Florida, hikers, mountain bikers, horses,

An Internet
source cita-
tion without
page num-
bers

Topic
sentence

Several
kinds of
supporting
detail

Martínez 6

and motorized all-terrain vehicles are wearing new trails,
defacing cliff faces with climbing bolts, gouging graffiti
on the walls of ancient native American dwellings,
pilfering petrified wood and prehistoric artifacts,
trampling fragile alpine vegetation, spreading the seeds
of non-native plant species, and threatening habitats of
such creatures as the desert tortoise, sea turtle, and
gray wolf ("Snowmobile"; "Annual Report"; Hill, par. 10;
Kiernan, "Parks"). Drawn to the national parks for
relaxation and enjoyment, park visitors have, instead,
become something like a huge invading army, waging ironic
war against the objects of their affection.

Unfortunately, the National Park Service is not in a
good position to mount an effective defense of national
park resources. Although the current federal
administration promised $4.9 billion of extra spending on
national parks projects, after nearly four years it has so
far added only $662 million of new money, and the Park
Service must limp along with only two-thirds of necessary
funding ("Fixing"). Because of the growing numbers of
visitors, ninety-eight percent of this new money has been
allocated for such visitor projects as roads and building
construction rather than for the science and preservation
projects necessary for the environmental health of the
parks (Wilkinson, "At More Parks"). As a result, nearly
seventy percent of NPS cultural landscapes will remain in
their current poor condition, and, over the next five
years, sixty-eight percent of threatened or endangered
species are predicted to decline (Kiernan, "Promises"). At
Chaco Culture National Historical Park, Ranger Andy Morris
remarked, "There's no money for park development, no money

Multi-source citation

Part IID: Park budgeting

Citation of a 1-page article

Martínez 7

for archeological research, no money to expand visitor

facilities . . . and only the barest minimum for

maintenance and preservation."

What should be done? The first non-native American

visitors journeyed to what would become our nation's

natural monuments attracted by their wonders and beauties

(Stegner 40). In 1916, the National Park Act set aside

these "pleasuring grounds" for contemporary visitors and

"to conserve the natural and historic subjects in such

manner as will leave them unimpaired for the enjoyment of

future generations." But many of America's national parks

have been so severely damaged and the funds to repair the

damage are so few that the promise of the National Parks

Act is being broken.

Many reforms are needed to rescue our parks from the

excess of adoration they have received. But one would

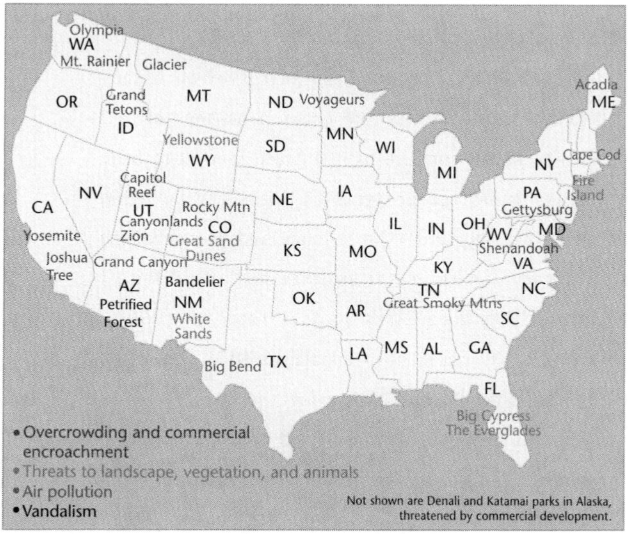

Fig. 2. Some of America's most threatened national parks.

Ellipsis points to signal an omission from a quotation

Transition to Part II. The Solution

A warrant (a federal law) that requires action to solve the problem

Martínez 8

specifically meet the problem of overcrowding: Where
overcrowding and harm to the environment are greatest,
officials should adopt the proposal of the Natural
Resources Defense Council and institute a reservation
system for regulating entry (Reclaiming, ch. 4). As Mike
Soukup, NPS Associate Director for Natural Resource
Stewardship and Science, argues, "we have to learn how to
manage visitors in a much better way" (Mace, Bell, and
Loomis 225). More pointedly, Robert E. Manning, of the
School of Natural Resources, University of Vermont, argues
that "use limits" are appropriate "when social and resource
impacts diminish qualities important to visitors and
threaten [NPS] objectives. . ." (107). Such a system need
not be permanent or universal, nor operate throughout the
year. It would, however, allow officials to reduce the flow
of visitors to the "carrying capacity" of individual parks
and give harmed environments time to heal themselves.

Among the opponents to such a proposal are those who
benefit economically from national parks and their
resources, including park hotel and restaurant
concessionaires, ranchers who graze cattle on park lands,
and mining and logging companies. To them, unrestricted
access to national parks and, in the case of
concessionaires, unrestricted numbers of visitors, are
essential to their economic success. But as Kevin Collins
argues, we accept in other areas of our lives that "some
things just don't belong together." We don't put prisons
near elementary schools; we don't open McDonald's in
cemeteries. "National parks," he maintains, "were not
created to guarantee access for any and all purposes, even
if those purposes are totally appropriate in another

Part II. A.
The second
half of the
writer's the-
sis: a claim
proposing
action

Ellipsis
points to sig-
nal an omis-
sion at the
end of a quo-
tation

Martínez 9

context. . . . We may have to accept that although
everyone should be able to enjoy the national parks, we
can't all go at once." A 1978 federal law requires the NPS
to establish the carrying capacities of national parks and
to limit the number of visitors in order to protect
resources and the quality of everyone's visit (42-43). A
reservation system is the simplest method to achieve the
aims of this law. More, it is a democratic system,
applying equally to all, first come, first served.

The use of an author's name and a parenthetical citation to frame a borrowing

Freedom involves responsibilities. It is time for
Americans to take what Aldo Leopold, one of the founders of
the modern environmental movement, calls the next step in
"ecological evolution," an "extension of ethics" into the
human relationship with the natural world. As he explains
in A Sand County Almanac, what is needed is a "land ethic":

A second rebuttal of opposing arguments: an expert opinion

> An ethic, ecologically, is a limitation on
> freedom of action in the struggle for existence.
> An ethic, philosophically, is a differentiation
> of social from anti-social conduct. These are
> two definitions of one thing. . . . A land ethic
> changes the role of Homo sapiens from conqueror
> of the land-community to plain member and
> citizen of it. It implies respect for his
> fellow-members, and also respect for the
> community as such. (202-204)

A block quotation stating a warrant

A period and ellipsis signaling the omission of a sentence or more

Documentation of a block quotation following the final punctuation

A national parks reservation system, limiting admission to
environmentally threatened parks, pays respect to the land
and to our membership in the community of nature. It is a
gesture of cooperation and an ethical act that meets the
"use without impairment" requirements of the National
Parks Act.

An explanation showing how the quotation supports the thesis

Martínez 10

Opponents of a reservation system have fallen into the fallacy of faulty analogy in a flawed comparison of national park lands to private property. They reason that just as private land owners pay property taxes and enjoy rights to their property, paying federal taxes gives them the right to use government lands as they wish. But the payment of property taxes does not convey land rights or ownership to tax payers. And private land owners are bound by zoning laws restricting the uses they make of their property. Americans pay a portion of their taxes to preserve and maintain parks, not as the purchase price of ownership but as a duty of citizenship. A parks reservation system is equivalent to a zoning regulation established for the common good.

In times of crisis, such as during World War II, Americans have accepted rationing as a way to meet that crisis. Our national parks are in crisis. If a reservation system--entry rationing--were presented as a way to meet such a crisis, park visitors would accept it, especially when they understood the benefits they would receive from the reduced numbers of visitors. In fact, a recent National Parks Conservation Association survey found that ninety-five percent of those surveyed favored a limit on visits to overcrowded, environmentally threatened parks ("National Park Survey"). Fairly applied to all users of the most severely threatened parks, it would lighten the burdens on these parks, maintain and preserve the environment, and ensure that the pleasures of natural beauty that brought the first visitors long ago would remain to be enjoyed by new visitors when it was their time to visit.

A third rebuttal of opposing arguments: explaining an error in reasoning

Part IIC. Conclusion: the benefits of adopting the writer's proposal

Martínez 11

Works Cited

"Administration Chooses Snowmobiles over a Healthy
Yellowstone." 8 Nov. 2002. The Greater Yellowstone
Coalition. 6 Sept. 2004 <http://
www.greateryellowstone.org/news/news_archives/
snowmobiles/snowmobiles_in_yellowstone.html>.

"Annual Report: Protecting Parks for Future Generations."
Dec. 2002. National Parks Conservation Association. 8
Sept. 2004 <http://www.npca.org/about_npca/
annual_report/protecting_parks.asp>.

Beattie, Rich. "America's Loneliest Parks." 5 Dec. 2003.
Gorp: The Away Network. 5 Sept. 2004 <http://
gorp.away.com/gorp/resource/topten/lonely.htm>.

Collins, Kevin. "Access or Excess?" National Parks July
2000: 42-43.

Ewert, Alan W. "Outdoor Recreation and Natural Resource
Management: An Uneasy Alliance." Parks & Recreation
34.7 (July 1999): 58-67.

"Fixing Up the National Parks." Editorial. New York Times.
26 June 2004. NYTimes.Com. 1 Sept. 2004 <http://
www.nytimes.com/2004/06/26/opinion/26sat2.html>.

Foreman, Dave. "The Case Against Roads." Backpacker May
2000: 94.

Kiernan, Thomas C. "Parks in Danger." National Parks May
2000: 6.

---. "Promises to Keep." National Parks May/June 2001: 4.

Hill, Rebecca. "National Parks in Peril" WildSites. 20
July 2004. 15 pars. 30 July 2004 <http://
www.wildsite.org/hill/peril.html>.

Leopold, Aldo. A Sand County Almanac and Sketches Here and
There. 1949. New York: Oxford UP, 1987.

Title centered 1 inch from top of page

Alphabetical arrangement of sources

First lines flush left, second and successive lines indented 5 spaces

A signed article at a commercial Internet site

Magazine article

Journal article with volume and issue numbers

Newspaper editorial from an online source

Two sources by the same author. Second source is preceded by three dashes and a period

An article in an online magazine

Citation of a book

Martínez 12

McGregor, Graeme. "The American Way: Are There Lessons for
    Us?" National Parks Journal 45.1 (Feb. 2001). 18 Aug.
    2004 <http://dazed.org/npa/npj/200102/indexhtm>.

Mace, Britton L, Paul A. Bell, and Ross J. Loomis.
    "Aesthetic, Affective, and Cognitive Effects of Noise
    on Natural Landscape Assessment." Society & Natural
    Resources 12.3 (Apr./May 1999): 225-41.

Manning, Robert E. "What to Do about Crowding and Solitude
    in Parks and Wilderness?" Journal of Leisure Research
    35.1 (2003): 107-18. WilsonSelectPlus. H. W. Wilson.
    Harper Coll. Lib., Palatine, IL. 3 Sept. 2004
    <http://www.oclc.org/firstsearch/periodicals/
    results_title_search.asp>.

McMahon, Edward T. "The Point of a View." National Parks
    Mar./Apr. 1992: 26-27.

Morris, Andy. Personal interview. 10 June 2004.

National Park Service Information Office (Rocky Mountain
    National Park). Telephone interview. 25 Sept. 2004.

"National Park Survey." Earthwatch 2001: 53.

Reclaiming Our Heritage: What We Need to Do to Preserve
    America's National Parks. 1997. 5 chs. Natural
    Resources Defense Council 1 Oct. 2004 <http://
    www.nrdc.org/land/parks/roh/rohinx.asp>.

"Snowmobile Damage in Yellowstone and Grand Teton Will
    Continue." 8 Dec. 2003. The Wilderness Society. 6
    Sept. 2004 <http://www.wilderness.og/Where_We_Work/
    Montana/orv.cfm>.

Stegner, Wallace. "It All Began with Conservation."
    Smithsonian. Apr. 1990: 34-43.

Source with three authors

Source in an online library database

Two interview sources

An Internet source published by an organization

Unsigned Internet article published by an organization

Martínez 13

United States. Department of the Interior. National Park
Service. Public Use Statistics Office. <u>Statistical
Abstract: 2003</u>. (Denver: WASO-TNT, 2004) 1.
Wilkinson, Todd. "At More Parks, Visitors Leave the Car
Behind." <u>Christian Science Monitor</u> 24 May 2001: 3.

Government
source

PART X

APA and Other Documentation Styles

APA DOCUMENTATION

ON THE WEB www.ablongman.com/dodds

Web Links

APA Documentation

55 Using the APA In-Text Citation Style

The American Psychological Association (APA) recommends an author-date style of documentation for papers written in the social sciences. This style is also used in anthropology, the biological sciences, business, economics, education, linguistics, and political science. For guidelines to formatting APA papers, see 46e.

55a Follow APA citation guidelines

1 ■ Citing a summary or paraphrase

To summarize or paraphrase a source, use a signal statement containing the author's last name followed by the publication date in parentheses, or give the author's last name and the date in parentheses at the end of the borrowed material, preceding the period. Use the past tense with signal verbs: *explained, reported,* and *argued* (see 13b1).

■ *Author and date preceding the borrowing:*

Sanchez (1993) reported that students from small, often rural schools do not fare as well on standardized tests as students from urban areas with large economic bases.

■ *Author and date in parentheses following the borrowing.* Use a comma between items in parentheses.

Students from small, often rural schools do not fare as well on standardized tests as students from urban areas with large economic bases (Sanchez, 1993).

2 ■ Citing a quotation or specific reference

To quote directly or refer to a specific part of a source, include page numbers in the parenthetical citation, preceded by *p.* or *pp.* ("page" or "pages").

Among education experts, there is now "virtually unanimous agreement . . . that no single measure should decide a student's academic fate" (Kohn, 2001, p. 350).

Note: If an Internet document does not provide page numbers, use the ¶ symbol or the abbreviation *para.,* followed by the specific paragraph number. If paragraph numbers are not given, provide the heading followed by the number of the paragraph within the section.

```
(Elert, 2003, ¶ 4)
```

```
(Elert, 2003, Validity Statistics, para. 2)
```

3 ▪ Citing authors' names

▪ *A source by one author.* Follow the examples given in 55a1 and 2.

▪ *A source by two authors.* For a source by two authors, give both last names in all signal statements and parenthetical citations. In parentheses, join the two authors' names with an ampersand (&).

As they are currently designed and administered, standardized "high stakes" tests have "pernicious effects on students' learning and motivation" (Paris & McEvoy, 2000, p. 145).

▪ *A source by three to five authors.* For a source with three to five authors, give all last names in the first signal statement or parenthetical citation.

Liu, Lopez, Smith, and Breen (2000) have systematically documented the social bias in standardized tests.

In later citations, give the last name of the first author, followed by *et al.* ("and others").

Liu et al. (2000) have proposed greater minority involvement in the design of standardized tests.

▪ *A source by six or more authors.* When a work has six or more authors, give the last name of the first author followed by *et al.* in signal statements and parenthetical citations.

▪ *Corporate authors.* Generally, spell out corporate names. Always spell out all corporate names in the reference list at the end of your paper. If a corporate name has a well-known abbreviation, spell out the name in the first citation and abbreviate thereafter:

First citation: (National Educational Association [NEA], 2003)

Subsequent citations: (NEA, 2003)

▪ *Unknown author.* When the author of a work is not identified in the source, use the complete title in a signal statement or the first few words of the title in a parenthetical citation.

Standardized testing puts students from rural, often poor areas at a great disadvantage ("Opportunity for All," 2004).

■ *Two or more sources in parentheses.* To cite two or more sources in parentheses, put the citations in the order in which they appear in the list of references at the end of the paper. Separate them with semicolons.

(Anastasi, 1996; Paris & McEvoy, 2000; "Test Bias," 43)

If two or more sources are by the same author, give the author's last name once followed by the dates of publication in chronological order.

(Anastasi, 1996, 2001)

■ *Authors with the same last name.* When two or more authors have the same last name, include initials in all signal statements and parenthetical citations:

(G. B. Dukes, 2000)

(L. K. Dukes, 2004)

■ *Personal communication.* To cite personal communication such as a letter or e-mail, give the author's initial(s) and last name, followed by the words *personal communication* and the date.

W. Hine (personal communication, October 8, 2004) has proposed three

reforms for standardized tests.

55b Prepare the APA reference list

55.1
APA
references
guide:
Web link

The reference list gives full publication information for all sources cited in a research paper. See the sample citations in 55c and the complete reference list at the end of the sample research project in 55d. For more information, see *The Publication Manual of the American Psychological Association*, 5th ed., 2001 (Chapters 4 and 6).

1 ■ Placement of the reference list

Begin the reference list on a separate page at the end of your paper.

2 ■ Reference-list format

■ *Title.* Center the title "References" (without italics, underlining, or quotation marks) at the top of the page. Continue page numbers from the text of your paper.

■ *Spacing.* Double-space throughout, unless instructed to single-space within entries.

■ *Indentation.* Begin each entry flush with the left margin. Indent second and successive lines up to one-half inch or from 3 to 5 spaces.

- *Alphabetical order.* Arrange entries in alphabetical order according to the last names of first authors or corporate names. If the author is not given, alphabetize by the first word of the title, ignoring *A, An,* and *The.*

- *Two or more works by one author.* If you use two or more works by the same author, arrange them by date of publication, with the earliest first.

3 ▪ Citation formats

- *Author names.* Invert the names of all authors: write the last name first, followed by a comma and the person's initials, separated by 1 space. When there are two or more authors, use an ampersand (&) instead of *and.* Separate three to six names with commas. Abbreviate the names of seventh and successive authors with "et al." (not italicized and with a period after "al").

- *Date of publication.* Put the date of publication in parentheses after the author's name.

- *Punctuation.* Space once after punctuation within an entry. Underline periods and commas following the titles of books, the names of periodicals, and volume numbers.

- *Capitalization.* Capitalize the names of periodicals as you would ordinarily. Capitalize only the first word of article and book titles, the first word of a subtitle (if any) usually following a colon, and proper nouns.

  Journal: `Journal of Personality and Social Psychology`

  Article: `Pollution damage in America's national forests`

  Book: `National park environments: An ecological guide`

- *Quotation marks and italics.* Do not enclose article titles in quotation marks. Set book titles and the names of periodicals in italics. Italicize the volume number of periodicals, but not the issue number.

- *Abbreviations.* Use standard bibliographic abbreviations when appropriate: *chap.* (chapter), *Ed.* (editor), *ed.* (edition), *n.d.* (no date), *p.* or *pp.* (page or pages), *Rev. ed.* (revised edition), *Trans.* (translator), *Vol.* (a single volume), *vols.* (a number of volumes), *No.* (number).

- *Publisher names.* You may shorten publisher names, so long as they remain recognizable. Retain words such as *Books* and *Press.*

- *Page numbers.* Write out inclusive page numbers completely: *341–344* (not *341–44*).

55c Sample APA citations

Citing books

1. *One author.*

<small>author name   publication   title and subtitle
reversed   date   (only first words and proper nouns capitalized)</small>

Lemann, N. (1999). *The big test: The secret history of the American*

<small>place of
publication   publisher</small>

    meritocracy. New York: Farrar.

2. *Two or more authors.* An ampersand (&) not "and" links two authors.

<small>revised edition</small>

Owen, D., & Doerr, M. (1999). *None of the above* (Rev. ed.). Lanham,

    MD: Rowman.

3. *Corporate or institutional reports, monographs, or pamphlets.* In parentheses, include the appropriate document number. If the sponsoring organization is both author and publisher, write *Author* in place of the publisher's name.

American Psychiatric Association. (1997, March). *Mental health of the*

    elderly (No. 2254). Washington, DC: Author.

4. *Unknown author.* Begin with the title. If the author is designated as "Anonymous," write *Anonymous*, followed by a period and the date.

Justice: Alternative political perspectives (2nd ed.). (1992).

    Belmont, CA: Wadsworth.

5. *Edited book.*

<small>editor</small>

O'Riordan, T. (Ed.). (2000). *Globalism, localism and identity.* London:

    Earthscan.

6. *An edition other than the first.*

<small>edition</small>

Bersoff, D. N. (1999). *Ethical conflicts in psychology* (2nd ed.).

    Washington, DC: American Psychological Association.

7. *A work in an anthology source or chapter in an edited book.*

Reinecke, M. A., & Freeman, A. (2003). Cognitive therapy. In A. S.

    Gurman & S. B. Messer (Eds.), *Essential psychotherapies: Theory*

    and practice (pp. 224-271). New York: Guilford Press.

8. *A work reprinted in an anthology or collection of materials.*
   Enclose the original publication information in parentheses at the
   end of the citation. For works reprinted from a periodical, give the
   title of the periodical, the volume, and, if necessary, the issue, followed by page numbers and date of original publication. For works
   reprinted from books, give the book title, the page numbers, the editors, if any, the date, the place of publication, and the publisher.

   Bly, R. (1991). The long bag we drag behind us. In C. Zweig &

   J. Abrams (Eds.), *Meeting the shadow: the hidden power of the dark*

   side of human nature (pp. 6-12). New York: Jeremy P.

   Tarcher/Putnam. (Reprinted from *A little book on the human shadow*,

   pp. 1-7, by R. Bly, 1988, New York: Harper-Collins.)

9. *Article in a multivolume reference work, such as an encyclopedia.* Begin with the author's name; for unsigned articles, begin with
   the title, followed by the date.

   Shepard, L. (1992). Uses and abuses of testing. In M. C. Alkin (Ed.),

   Encyclopedia of educational research (Vol. 4, pp. 1477-1485). New

   York: Macmillan.

10. *Article in one volume of a multivolume work, separate titles for
    each volume.*

    selection author   title of selection   volume editor   multivolume title
    Howard, W. (2000). Vedic chant. In A. Arnold (Ed.), *The Garland*
                       italicized volume number + volume title
    encyclopedia of world music: Vol. 5. South Asia (pp. 238-245).

    New York: Macmillan.

11. *Translation.*

                                  translator
    Mahfouz, N. (1995). *Arabian nights and days.* (D. Johnson-Davies,

    Trans.). New York: Doubleday.

12. *Foreword, preface, introduction, or afterword.*

    Benjamin, M. (2001). Foreword. In A. Fung, D. O'Rourke, & C. Sabel,

    Can we put an end to sweatshops? (pp. 1-15). Boston: Beacon.

13. *A book with a title within a title.* Place quotation marks around
    incorporated titles of short works such as articles; do not italicize
    incorporated titles of longer works such as books.

incorporated title of longer work

Jones, S. (2001). *Darwin's ghost:* The Origin of Species *updated.* New

York: Ballantine.

14. *A technical report from the National Technical Information Service (NTIS) or Educational Resources Information Center (ERIC).* Following the citation, enclose NTIS and ERIC numbers in parentheses.

Campbell, P. B. (1989). *The hidden discriminator: Sex and race bias in*

educational research. Groton, MA: Women's Educational Equity Act

information service identification number

Program. (ERIC Document Reproduction Service No. ED322174)

Citing periodicals and newspapers

15. *Journal article, one author, paged by issue.* Type the volume number in italics; type the issue number in non-italic type, enclosed with parentheses. For articles that skip pages, include all page numbers, separated by commas (see item 19).

Thomas, E. A. (2002, Spring). Standardized testing. *Georgetown Journal*

of Gender & the Law, 3(2), 481-487.

16. *Journal article, two authors, paged by volume.*

Low, K. G., & Feissner, J. M. (1998). Seasonal affective disorder in

college students: Prevalence and latitude. *Journal of American*

italicized
volume number   page number

College Health, 12, 135.

17. *Journal article, three, four, or five authors.*

Nolen-Hoeksema, S., Grayson, C., & Larson, J. (1999). Explaining the

gender difference in depressive symptoms. *Journal of Personality*

and Social Psychology, 77(5), 1061-1072.

18. *Magazine article.* Follow the citation style for authored journal articles. For unsigned articles, begin with the title.

year, month of publication

Cooney, E. (2001, October). Death in slow motion: A descent into

Alzheimer's. *Harper's Magazine, 303,* 43-58.

unsigned article

Seasonal affective disorder. (2000, March 1). *American Family*

Physician, 61(5), 1523.

19. *Newspaper article, signed, skipped pages.* Separate all page numbers by commas. Include section numbers before pages. If sections are identified alphabetically, include the letter with the page numbers, for example: *pp. A1, A6* or *pp. B10-12.*

    year, month, day of publication
    Purdum, T. S. (2001, October 7). What's classified? Sorry. It's a

    secret. *The New York Times,* Section 4, pp. 1, 4.

20. *Review.* Following the review title, enclose in square brackets what is being reviewed.

    Sacks, P. (2003, May 5). Class struggle [Review of the book *The early*

    admissions game: Joining the elite]. *The Nation, 276*(17), 29-34.

21. *Letter to editor.* Note that personal letters, interviews, and memos, which are not easily recovered, are not cited in the reference list.

    heading for the letter   description of the work
    Lanier, J. (2001, October). One flew over the cuckoo's nest [Letter to

    the editor]. *Harper's Magazine, 303,* 4-5.

Citing Internet sources

HOW TO . . . Write APA Internet Citations

1. For sources with print counterparts, cite the print publication and the location of the Internet version.

2. When necessary, identify the type of document or source in square brackets [. . .].

3. Do *not* enclose Internet addresses (URLs) with angle brackets (< . . . >); do not end URLs with periods.

   Note: If you must break a URL at the end of a line, break after a slash mark or before a period. Do not add hyphens.

4. Use capitals and italics as you would with print sources. (See 55b2.)

22. *A work from an online library database such as InfoTrac, EbscoHost, PsycINFO, SIRS, or MEDLINE.* Cite the original print publication information for the source. Add a retrieval statement giving access date, the database, and the item number of the source.

    author   original publication date   title of the work
    Atkinson, R. C. (2001/2002, Winter). Achievement versus aptitude in

                        original print source
    college admissions. *Issues in Science & Technology, 18*(2), 31-37.

retrieval statement date of retrieval   database
    Retrieved December 10, 2003, from Academic Search Premier database
item or accession number
    (AN5455751).

23. *An online article with a print counterpart.*

author   original publication date   title of article
Freedle, R. O. (2002, Fall). Correct the SAT's ethnic and social-class
                                        version of the article used
    bias: A method for reestimating SAT scores [Electronic version].
            original print source   retrieval statement
    Harvard Educational Review, 72(3), 1-43. Retrieved June 22, 2004,
                        no punctuation following a URL
    from http:gseweb.harvard.edu/hpeg/freedle.html

24. *An online newspaper article.* If you access a newspaper article through an online library database such as InfoTrac, supply an item identification number in place of the URL, as in item 22.

                original publication date   newspaper article title
Langone, J. (2004, June 22). The secrets of the happy life. *New York*
                                        URL divided after a slash
    Times Online. Retrieved June 23, 2004, from http://www.nytimes.com/

    2004/06/02/health/22book.html

25. *An article in an Internet-only periodical.* If no author is given, begin with the title, followed by the date, the name of the periodical, and the volume number. If the source has an identifying number, include it in non-italic text following the volume number.

Smith, D. L. (1998, August). Free-associations and honeybee dancers:
    article title   journal title
    The unconscious and its place in nature. *The Electronic Journal of*
            volume number, no identifying number
    Communicative Psychoanalysis, 1. Retrieved July 17, 2004, from

    http://www.ejcpsa.com

26. *An online report from a government body, university, or private organization.* Begin with the sponsoring organization, followed by the date, the title of the source, a description of the source in square brackets, and retrieval information.

Centers for Disease Control and Prevention. (2000, July). *Tobacco use*
                                        description of the report
    among US racial/ethnic minority groups [A report of the Surgeon

    General]. Retrieved October 7, 2003, from http://www.cdc.gov/

    tobacco/sgr-minorities.htm

27. *An online report from an information service such as Educational Resources Information Center (ERIC).*

Childs, R. A. (1990). Gender bias and fairness. *ERIC Digest.* Retrieved

May 3, 2004, from http://ericae.net/edo/ED328610.htm

28. *An online abstract of a work.* Identify the work as an abstract within the retrieval statement.

Lupton, D., & Tulloch, J. (2001). Border crossings: Narratives of

movement, "home" and risk. *Sociological Research Online, 5*(4).
a description of the source
Abstract retrieved May 1, 2004, from http://www.socresonline

.org.uk/5/4/lupton.html

29. *Text such as a book that exists in an electronic version*

Martin, E. D. (1920). *The behavior of crowds: A psychological study.*

Retrieved February 9, 2004, from http://www.undergroundmind

.com/oldsite/bcrowdsf.html

30. *Chapter or section of an online document written by a corporate author.*

corporate author   chapter title
Natural Resources Defense Council. (1997). Finding the solutions. In
title of online document
Reclaiming our heritage: What we need to do to preserve America's
chapter number
national parks (chap. 4). Retrieved March 20, 2002, from

http://www.nrdc.org/land/parks/roh/rohinx.asp

31. *Newsgroup posting.* Use brackets to enclose the number of the posting.

message number
Wilken, P. (2000, December 27). The contents of consciousness [Msg. 1].

Message posted to http://groups.google.com/groups/sci.psychology

.journals.psych

32. *Listserv discussion group posting.*

title of posting   number of posting
deMause, L. (2001, October 10). Conspiracy theories [Msg. 1134].
name of the discussion group
Message posted to Psychohistory electronic mailing list, archived

at http://www.topica.com/lists/psychohistory/read/message

.html?mid=1708546146&sort=d&start=1134

33. *E-mail.* Because e-mail is not easily recoverable, it is not cited in the reference list. Cite e-mail and other personal communications only in the text of your paper. (See 55a3.)

Citing other sources

34. *Article from an encyclopedia on CD-ROM.* Provide complete information about the article and its source. In the retrieval statement, give the name of the database provider and, in parentheses, the medium and publication or identification information.

unsigned article   database   database provider
Taboo. (2001). Grolier multimedia encyclopedia. Retrieved from Grolier

                 no punctuation following retrieval statement
    Interactive database (CD-ROM, 2002 release)

35. *Conference proceedings.* Conference presentations are available as journal articles, online textfiles, information service documents, or in book form. Follow the appropriate citation format. Here is a conference presentation as part of a book.

Lawler, P. A., & Wilhite, S. C. (1997). Catching up with the

    information age: A new paradigm for faculty development. In *The*

    Proceedings of the 22nd International Conference on Improving

    University Learning and Teaching (pp. 369-378). College Park, MD:

    University of Maryland.

36. *Dissertation abstract.*

Martin, K. (1995). Attachment style, depression and loneliness in

                    description of the source
    adolescent suicide attempts (Doctoral dissertation,

    institution granting the degree
    American University, 1997). *Dissertation Abstracts International,*

    volume number, page number, and volume
    57, 5924B.

37. *Audiovisual media.* In parentheses, provide relevant descriptive terms such as *Writer, Producer, Director,* and so forth. In square brackets following the title, identify the medium: audio cassette, motion picture, videocassette, filmstrip, and so forth. Identify the country or city of origin and the name of the studio.

Belinsky, J. (Writer). (1967). *The terrible fear of cancer* [Sound

    filmstrip]. United States: American Medical Journal.

Elloie, P. H. (Interviewer). (1994). *Interview with K. Ellis*

    [videocassette]. Durham, NC: Duke University.

38. *An episode from a radio or TV program.*

Loeterman, B., & Kotlowitz, A. (Writers), & Loeterman, B. (Director).

episode title

(2002, November 14). Let's get married [Television series episode].

program title

In B. Loeterman (Producer), *Frontline*. Washington, DC: Public

Broadcasting Service.

55d Sample APA research project

The following report has been written in the APA manuscript format for student papers (see 46e), with APA author-date in-text documentation and a reference list. (For more on reports, see 62f. For more about the headings often used in reports, see 46b1.)

Standardized Testing   1

The Problems of Standardized Testing

Ashley Sheffer

English 201: Advanced Composition

William Rainey Harper College

May 1, 200-

American Psychological Association (APA) Format

Page header and page number 1 inch from top of page

Number pages consecutively from the title page to the end of the paper, including references.

Center title, author, and other identifying information.

Standardized Testing   2

Abstract

This report investigates social bias in standardized educational placement tests such as the SAT and ACT. According to the most recent sources, such tests are being required by a diminishing number of colleges and universities. Whether expert sources favored or opposed standardized testing for college admissions, they generally agreed that these tests are flawed. They measure only a narrow range of skills; they do not accurately predict student success; and they are biased against minorities, women, students of low socioeconomic status, and students from disadvantaged backgrounds. Recommendations include decreasing reliance on test scores for admission purposes, an expanded definition of academic preparedness, and reform of standardized tests to eliminate bias.

An abstract is a block paragraph of 100–120 words.

Standardized Testing   3

1-inch
margins;
page header
1 inch from
top of page

The Problems of Standardized Testing

Each year, out of the millions applying to college, many are denied admission to the school of their choice because of poor performance on entrance examinations like the SAT and ACT. Have these students not done well because they are not as gifted as those who are accepted? Or have disadvantaged or nontraditional backgrounds failed to provide many with the skills necessary to do well on admissions tests? What do these tests measure, exactly? Are they fair? How well do they predict college success?

An introduction that states a problem and poses research questions

❶ Background

❷ *History*

Headings: (1) primary centered, (2) secondary flush left, (3) tertiary run-in

❸ *The Scholastic Aptitude Test* (renamed the *Scholastic Assessment Test* and now simply *SAT*). Among the millions of students who take educational achievement tests each year, the largest number takes the SAT, approximately 2 million. First used in 1926, it was developed, according to the Educational Testing Service, to measure "abilities in quantitative and verbal reasoning that develop over a long period of time" (FairTest, *Different Tests, Same Flaws,* Purpose according to the test-makers, para. 1). Taken by 12th graders in one of several new forms introduced each year, it is used for college admissions and counseling (Dejnozka, Kapel, & Gifford, 1997, p. 456).

APA citation of an Internet source without page numbers

Citation of a source with three authors, names linked by an ampersand

The American College Test. Founded in 1959, The American College Testing Program (ACT) is currently the second largest testing organization in the country, with 1.3 million students tested annually. Overlapping traditional aptitude and achievement tests (Anastasi & Urbina, 1996), the ACT Assessment Battery measures

Two citations of summaries from sources

Standardized Testing   4

preparedness in English, math, the social sciences, and
natural sciences (The American College Test [ACT], 2004).

Important Definitions

Achievement test. A standardized test measuring what
students have actually learned.

Aptitude test. A standardized test measuring "the
capacity or potentiality of an individual for a
particular kind of behavior" (Nairn, 1980, p. 55).

A quotation
identified
by a specific
page number

Bias. In the popular sense, a biased test favors
some test takers and penalizes others. In its statistical
sense, bias designates "constant or systematic error as
opposed to chance errors" (Anastasi 1996, p. 194).

Reliability. A test is reliable when the same test
taker earns consistent scores on the same or equivalent
versions of the test.

Standardization. Preparing a "standardized test" to
make it a reliable and valid measure for all test takers.
When a test has been "standardized," the value of an
individual's score can be determined by comparing it to
established norms (Anastasi & Urbina, 1996, pp. 25-26).

Validity. The extent to which "a test actually
measures what it purports to measure" (Anastasi & Urbina,
1996, p. 26). If an aptitude or achievement test measures
class membership or economic status instead of
educational preparedness or achievement, it is invalid.

Results and Discussion

Reduced Reliance on Standardized Tests

Even though standardized tests continue to be
popular college admissions tools and have received a
recent boost in popularity from the "No Child Left
Behind" Act, they have lost favor at over 700 academic

Cause/effect
organization
of the body
of the report:
The writer
examines
why stan-
dardized
tests are los-
ing favor as a
method for
determining
college
admissions.

Standardized Testing   5

institutions of all kinds, from small colleges like Bates and Bowdoin to public universities like those in California and Oregon (FairTest, *The SAT: Questions and answers*, 2004), to highly selective institutions like Harvard and Princeton. There is now a trend away from one method of selecting students (selection "by the numbers" according to test scores) toward another method that relies on judgments (selection involving comprehensive, holistic review of a candidate's credentials) (Rigol, 2003, p. 9). What are the reasons for these changing admissions methods?

The Skills Measured by Standardized Tests

One reason standardized tests now receive failing grades is that they measure only a narrow range of skills, factual recall, and "shallow thinking" (Kohn, 2001, p. 348), not such qualities as judgment, motivation, academic commitment, honesty, and altruism. According to William Sedlacek, professor of education and director of testing at the University of Maryland (Rooney, 1998, p. 44), and according to an ETS survey of 3,400 teachers reported by Elert (2003), these are the qualities that have most to do with college and career success.

The current thinking about human intelligence is that there are, in fact, "multiple intelligences." If this view is accurate, Paris and McEvoy argued (2000, p. 148), then "a few numbers [standardized test scores] cannot capture the level or rates of [student] achievements." Among education experts, there is now "virtually unanimous agreement . . . that no single measure should decide a student's academic fate"

Margin annotations:

Topic sentence to introduce a paragraph

Author and credentials in a signal statement

Brackets and ellipsis points used to fit a quotation into the context of the writer's paragraph

Standardized Testing   6

(Kohn, 2001, p. 350). By disregarding standardized test
scores and making admissions decisions holistically,
based on a range of assessment instruments, institutions
such as Bates, Bowdoin, California State University, and
the University of Texas have actually improved the
quality of their student bodies. Incoming students
without standardized admissions test scores come from
more diverse backgrounds yet have performed academically
as well as or better than those with scores and, equally
important, have taken on more responsibilities of campus
leadership than tested students (Rooney, 1998; Elert,
2003).

Predictive Failures

Perhaps because standardized tests measure so few
traits essential to academic success, they are not
particularly accurate predictors of it. According to a
FairTest review of the ACT's and ETS's own research ("SAT
I: A Faulty Instrument," 2003), their tests have such
"weak predictive ability" that a score on either test is
a "virtually worthless" piece of information, no better
at predicting college freshman grades or future success
"than a pair of dice" (Elert, 2003). After years of
arguing that standardized tests like the SAT could
recognize merit and predict achievement, even the ETS
itself has now recognized that "it is a myth that a test
will provide a unitary, unequivocal yardstick for ranking
on merit" (Rooney, 1998, p. 74). What will predict
student success? Both the ACT and ETS have admitted "that
class rank, high school grades, and rigor of classes
taken are better tools for predicting college success
than any standardized test" (Elert, 2003).

Margin notes:
A reference to a specific part of source to cite a quotation

The use of examples to support a point

Two sources within the same citation

Quotations blended into the writer's sentences

Bias

A third cause of the decline in the popularity of standardized tests is their bias against test takers who might be considered "different": the poor, minorities, and women. Kohn (2001, p. 348) explained that when schools, towns, or states are compared for the test scores of their students, "an overwhelming proportion of the variance" in these scores can be accounted for by the socioeconomic status (SES) of the test takers (see the table below). In other words, students from wealthier backgrounds tend to score better than those from less wealthy families. It would be more honest, said Harvard professor Lani Guinier, to call a standardized test a

SAT score	M	F	20	30	50	100	100+	Wht	Asn	NtAm	Hisp	AfAm
1150							1123					
1100								1060	1070			
1050						1068						
1000	1041	1002										
950					997					962		
900				931							910	
850			888									857
800												
	Gender		Annual Income x 100					Ethnicity				

Note. The data in this table list SAT scores for 2002 college-bound seniors. From the *College-Board National Seniors National Report, 2002.* FairTest: The National Center for Fair & Open Testing. Retrieved April 14, 2004, from http://www.fairtest.org/univ/2002SAR%20Sccores.html

"wealth test" (Zwick, 2001, p. 34). Peter Sacks,
describing what he calls the "rigged game" of
standardized testing, explains: "The data [correlating
wealth with high test scores] is so strong . . . that one
could make a good guess about a child's standardized test
scores by simply looking at how many degrees her parents
have and what kind of car they drive" (2000, p. 6). Such
disparity exists, Zwick reasoned, because "students who
come from wealthier families are more likely to have
achievement-oriented environments and to attend resource
rich schools staffed by better-trained teachers" (p. 34).
In addition, Owen and Doerr (1999) noted that it is the
wealthy students who are able to pay the $1,000 tuition
for test coaching schools to help them prepare for the
supposedly "uncoachable" ACT and SAT tests.

Involved with this economic bias, as both symptom
and result, are ethnic, gender, and geographic biases
that "stack the deck" against women, minorities, and
rural students (Northwest Regional Educational Laboratory
Equity Center, 2001). It is widely recognized that
African-American and Hispanic students tend to score
lower than whites or Asians (Zwick, 2001, p. 33). Why?
Jay Rosner (2003), Executive Director of the Princeton
Review, a test-coaching service, explained:

> If you look at all of the SAT questions on the test,
> every question is pretested and preselected, and they
> just happen to favor whites over blacks. That is,
> higher percentages of whites answer every SAT
> question correctly than blacks, and the test makers
> know this before they choose the questions to appear
> on the test.

A quotation
longer than
40 words is
indented ½
inch from
the left mar-
gin; quota-
tion marks
are omitted.

Standardized Testing 9

The gap between male and female test takers is less pronounced than that between white and minority test takers but just as constant: "despite the fact that girls earn higher grades throughout both high school and college, they consistently receive lower scores on [ACT and SAT tests] than do their male counterparts" (FairTest, "Gender Bias," 2003). Again the question, why? Weaver (1997) explained that "standardized tests are biased in favor of those whose culture and upbringing most closely resemble that of the test makers--typically white middle-class males who live in metropolitan areas."

Proponents of standardized testing argue that it is a way both to eliminate the bias of affirmative action and recognize the achievements of those who are different. But Paris and McEvoy (2000, p. 146) examined the discrepancies in student scores from standardized testing and concluded that standardized testing "does not level the playing field for ['different' students]; it tilts it further." And they quote Peter Sacks (2000) who used an even more critical metaphor, calling this testing "meritocracy's crooked yard stick."

Conclusions

The narrow focus, predictive failures, and significant bias of standardized tests make them unreliable instruments for evaluating students. This fact is recognized by the more than 700 colleges and universities that no longer require the SAT or ACT as an admissions requirement. Because such tests contribute so little to our national goal of excellence in education, other schools should follow their lead. Instead of using standardized test scores, admissions officials should

The writer's conclusion, based on information and expert opinion in the "Results and Discussion" section

Standardized Testing   10

adopt assessment tools such as essay questions,

portfolios, and observations that focus on the

achievements and personal traits shown to predict success

in college and afterward (Northwest Regional Educational

Laboratory Equity Center, 2001). As postsecondary

education is increasingly required of greater and greater

numbers, the emphasis should change from measuring

students to fit a particular pattern to enlarging the

pattern to accommodate diverse student needs.

The writer's
proposal of a
solution to
the problem
uncovered by
the report

Standardized Testing   11

References

The American College Test. (2004). *ACT assessment: Frequently asked questions.* Retrieved April 15, 2004, from http://www.act.org/aap/faq/general.html

Anastasi, A., & Urbina, S. (1996). *Psychological testing* (7th ed.). New York: Prentice Hall.

Dejnozka, E. L., Kapel, D. E., & Gifford, C. S. (1997). *American educators' encyclopedia.* Westport, CT: Greenwood.

Elert, G. (2003). *The SAT: Aptitude or demographics?* Retrieved April 14, 2004, from http:// hypertextbook.com/eworld/sat.shtml

FairTest: National Center for Fair & Open Testing (2003, September 16). *Different tests, same flaws.* Retrieved April 13, 2004, from http://www.fairtest.org/facts/ univtestcomparison.html

FairTest. (2003, September 16). *Gender bias in college admissions tests.* Retrieved April 17, 2004, from http://www.fairtest.org/facts/genderbias.htm

FairTest. (2003, September 16). *The SATI I: A faulty instrument for predicting college success.* Retrieved April 17, 2004, from http://www.fairtest.org/facts/ satfact.htm

FairTest. (2003, September 16). *The SAT: Questions and answers.* Retrieved April 17, 2004, from http://www.fairtest.org/facts/satfact.htm

Kohn, A. (2001, January). Fighting the tests. *Phi Delta Kappan 82,* (5), 348-57.

Nairn, A. (1980). *The reign of ETS: The corporation that makes up minds.* Washington, DC: Ralph Nader.

Northwest Regional Educational Laboratory Equity Center. (2001, September 6). *Educate America: Student*

For APA Reference List guidelines, see 55b.

Institutional publication available on the Internet

Book citation

Source by three authors

Internet source

Multiple sources by one author or organization are arranged, first, chronologically and then alphabetically by title.

URL divided following a slash

Journal with volume and issue numbers

Standardized Testing   12

assessment and testing. Retrieved April 20, 2004, from

http://nwrel.org/cnorse/booklets/educate/index.html

Owen, D. & Doerr, M. (1999). *None of the Above.* Lanham,

MD: Rowman & Littlefield.

Paris, S. G., & McEvoy, A. P. (2000). Harmful and enduring

effects of high-stakes testing. *Issues in Education 6,*

(1-2), 145-59.

Rigol, G. W. (2003). *Admissions decision-making models.*

The College Board. Retrieved April 19, 2004, from

http://www.collegeboard.com

Rooney, C. (1998). *Test scores do not equal merit.*

Cambridge, MA: National Center for Fair and Open

Testing.

Rosner, J. (2003, April 1). How affirmative action impacts

standardized testing [Interview]. In *Tavis Smiley*

[radio broadcast]. Washington, DC: National Public

Radio.

Sacks, P. (2000). *Standardized minds: The high price of*

America's testing culture and what we can do to change

it. Cambridge, MA: Perseus.

Weaver, C. (1997). Facts: On standardized test and

assessment alternatives [Electronic version]. In C.

Weaver, L. Gillmeister-Krause, G. Vento-Zogby (Eds.),

Creating support for effective literacy education.

Portsmouth: Heinemann. Retrieved April 23, 2004, from

http://www.heinemann.com/product/08894.asp

Zwick, R. (2001, March/April). What causes the test-score

gap in higher education. *Change,* pp. 32-37.

Work with
2 authors

An organiza-
tion report
posted on
the Internet

An interview

An Internet
source based
on a print
document

Other Styles

56 Using Endnotes or Footnotes (The Chicago Style)

In business, history, and the fine arts, a system of endnotes or footnotes plus a bibliography, referred to as the Chicago style or CMS (after *The Chicago Manual of Style,* 15th edition), is often used to document the sources of borrowed materials. If you use endnotes or footnotes, you may not even need a bibliography; check with your instructor. If a bibliography is required, see 56c.

56a Choose an endnote or footnote format

Use endnotes at the end of your paper unless you are instructed to place footnotes at the bottom of a page of text.

- *Numbering.* Number notes consecutively from the beginning to the end of your paper. Do not assign each source its own number. Use a new number for each citation even if several notes refer to the same source. In the text, at the first sentence or clause break after a summary, paraphrase, or quotation, write a raised, or superscript, arabic numeral outside all punctuation except dashes.

    Charlotte Perkins Gilman described her nomadic childhood as "thick with railroad journeys."[14]

- *Placement.* Endnotes appear on a separate "Notes" page at the end of your paper, following the text and preceding the bibliography. Double-space between and within endnotes. If you must use footnotes, quadruple-space after the last line of text and place them at the bottom of the page. Single-space footnotes; double-space between them. If a footnote continues onto the next page, skip two lines below the text on the new page and type a short solid line 1–2 inches long across the page; then double-space and continue the note. Place new notes immediately after it.

COMPUTER TIP: Creating Notes with Your Word Processor

Use the end notes or footnotes function of your word processor to format your notes for you.

- *Indentations.* Indent the first line the same number of spaces as you are indenting paragraphs in your paper, generally one-half inch or 5 spaces. Make second and succeeding lines flush with the left margin.

- *Formatting note numbers.* The number preceding each note should *not* be a superscript. Use the same numerals that you use elsewhere in your text, for dates and so forth. After the number, put a period followed by one character space.

- *The first reference to a source.* When you cite a source for the first time, give complete publication information in the note. Begin each note with a capital letter and end with a period. Do not use internal periods. Give the author's first, then last names. For books, enclose the place of publication, publisher, and date of publication in parentheses following the book title. Always give the exact page number(s) of a borrowing.

  1. Aldo Leopold, *A Sand County Almanac* (New York: Oxford University Press, 1987), 204.

- *Subsequent references to a source.* In second and later references to a source, give the author's last name, or a short form of the title if no author's name is given, followed by the page numbers of the borrowing. This information will allow readers to locate complete information for a source in an earlier note or in the bibliography.

  2. Leopold, 169.

  3. "Report," 14.

- *Subsequent references to an author of more than one source.* If you use more than one source by an author, use the author's last name and a short form of the title in subsequent references to distinguish one source from another.

  23. Coates, "Crowds," 16.

  24. Coates, "Creature Comforts," 14.

- *A reference to the source in the preceding note.* Use *Ibid.* (an abbreviation of *ibidem*, "in the same place") to refer to a source cited in the immediately preceding note. Follow with a page number if different from that in the preceding note.

  24. Coates, "Creature Comforts," 14.

  25. Ibid., 15.

56b Make a full first reference to a source

1 ▪ Citing books

Basic reference to a book. Cite two or more authors in the order given on the title page of the book. Use commas to separate the names of three or more authors. Use *and* before the second or final author's name. For a corporate publication, cite the corporation as the author. After the book title, include information such as the names of translators or editors (if any), the number or description of the edition (if other than the first), and the series name (if any). Cite a pamphlet as you would a book.

When citing publisher names, you may give the publisher's name in full (*Random House*) or in a shortened form (*Random*), omitting words not essential to identifying the publisher and abbreviations such as *Co.* and *Inc.* or initials before a family name. However, retain words such as *Books* (*Basic Books*) and *Press* (*Free Press*). Accompany the city of publication with the state, province, or country if the place of publication may be unfamiliar to readers; use old-style state abbreviations with periods (*Del., Fla., N.J.*).

1. Barry Lopez, *Arctic Dreams: Imagination and Desire in a Northern Landscape* (New York: Scribner's, 1986), 104.

■ *A book with three authors*

2. Gary B. Nash, Charlotte Crabtree, and Ross E. Dunn, *History on Trial: Culture Wars and the Teaching of the Past* (New York: Alfred A. Knopf, 1997), 35.

■ *A corporate author*

3. Southwest Parks and Monuments Association. *Chaco Culture* (Tucson, Ariz.: Southwest Parks and Monuments Association, 2003), 31.

■ *An introduction, foreword, preface, or afterword*

4. David McCullough, foreword to *The Book of Abigail and John: Selected Letters of the Adams Family,* ed. L. H. Butterfield, Marc Friedlaender, and Mary-Jo Kline (Boston: Northeastern University Press, 2002), xi-xiii.

■ *One volume from a multivolume work.* Place the volume number after the general title. If a particular volume is titled separately, include the individual title after the volume number.

5. Joseph Blotner, *Faulkner: A Biography,* vol. 2 (New York: Random House, 1976), 426.

■ *Titled parts of a book*

6. Bao-Tran Truong, "Stepping Stones in America," in *Where Coyotes Howl and Wind Blows Free: Growing Up in the West,* ed. Alexandra R. Haslam and Gerald W. Haslam, pp. 150-158 (Reno: University of Nevada Press, 1995), 155.

■ *An encyclopedia or dictionary.* Begin with the name of the reference work followed by the edition, the abbreviation *s.v.* (for *sub verbo,* "under the word"), and the item cited, which is capitalized if a proper noun and otherwise written in lowercase letters.

> 7. *Encyclopaedia Britannica,* 11th ed., s.v. "Mexico."

2 ■ Citing periodicals and newspapers

Write out the names of months in publication dates. Capitalize the names of seasons: (*Fall 1996*).

■ *Article in a weekly or monthly magazine*

> 8. Katherine Boo, "The Churn: Creative Destruction in a Border Town," *New Yorker,* March 29, 2004, 62-63.

■ *Article in a scholarly journal.* If the periodical is paged by issue, include the issue number after the volume number of the journal.

> 9. Harriet Ritvo, "Animal Planet," *Environmental History* 9, no. 2 (2004): 217.

■ *Review of a book, movie, play*

> 10. David Denby, review of *Troy* (Warner Brothers movie), *New Yorker,* May 17, 2004, 109.

■ *Newspaper article.* To cite a signed newspaper article, begin with the author's name. To cite an unsigned newspaper article, begin with the title. When appropriate, include the edition, section number, and page number.

> 11. Kim Campbell, "'Send in the Historians,' Cry Critics of Sound-Bite News," *The Christian Science Monitor,* October 4, 2001, sec. 1, p. 18.

■ *An editorial*

> 12. "Privatizing Warfare," editorial, *New York Times,* April 21, 2004, late edition, sec. A, p. 22.

3 ■ Citing Internet sources

The Chicago Manual of Style, 15th edition, provides the following general guidelines for citing Internet sources: (1) When sources exist in both print and online versions, cite only the source consulted. (2) Do not surround URLs with angle brackets; when they come at the end of a note, add a period at the end. (3) Divide URLs after a double or single slash; before a tilde (~), a period, comma, hyphen, underline (_), question mark, number sign, or percent sign; and before or after an equals sign or ampersand (&). (4) For time-sensitive materials or those that are periodically updated, provide your access date at the end of the note (e.g., *accessed August 24, 2004*).

■ *A book published online*

author   title of the book

13. Frederick Douglass, *The Narrative of the Life of Frederick*

original publication date   electronic publisher

Douglass, an American Slave (1845; Eserver: Iowa State University,

posting date   part of the work cited   URL followed by a period

1998), chap. 1, http://eserver.org/books/narrative.

■ *A source in an online database.* A database is any online collection of information. Databases include collections of records, texts, and public documents; archives; online library information services like EBSCO; and online issues of journals and newspapers.

two authors   title of the work

14. William G. Thomas and Edward L. Ayers, "The Differences

Slavery Made: A Close Analysis of Two American Communities,"

name of the database   date of electronic publication

American Historical Review: Electronic Projects, December 2003,

URL followed by one space, the access date, and a period

http://www.vcdh.virginia.edu/AHR (accessed June 23, 2004).

■ *An article in an online journal*

author   title of the work

15. Charles M. Payne, "'The Whole United States Is Southern!':

online journal title

Brown v. Board and the Mystification of Race," *Journal of American*

volume number, issue number, and publication date

History 106, no. 1 (Spring, 2004), http://www.historycooperative.org/

access date

journals/jah/91.1 (accessed June 20, 2004).

■ *Article in an online magazine*

16. David Roberts, "The Secrets of the Maya: Deciphering Tikal,"

Smithsonian Magazine, July 2004, http://www.smithsonianmag.si.edu/

smithsonian/issues04/jul04/pdf/tikal.pdf.

■ *Article in an online newspaper*

17. Alessandra Stanley, "Revisiting the Drama of the Longest

publication date   URL divided after a slash

Day," *New York Times*, June 4, 2004, http://www.nytimes.com/2004/

access date

06/23/arts/television/23STAN.html (accessed June 23, 2004).

■ *An online government document*

Sponsoring government agency   title of document

18. National Park Service: Navajo National Monument, "Anasazi,"

publication date

July 1, 2004, http://www.nps.gov/nava/ana.htm.

■ *Electronic mail*

> 19. Jennifer Loster, e-mail message to the author, September 1, 2004.

■ *Informally published Internet material: newsgroup and listserv posts, chat room posts, and Weblog comments.* Include the author, the name of the newsgroup, listserv, chat group, or Weblog, the date of the posting, the URL for archived material, and the access date.

> 20. Ethel Flores, e-mail to Illinois Immigrant History mailing list, January 30, 2004, http://www.ilimhist.org/issues/01/30/04/21.txt (accessed June 15, 2004).

4 ■ Citing other sources

■ *Government publications.* The format for government publications follows this sequence: government body, subsidiary body, title of document, individual author if given, identifying numbers, publication information (in parentheses), page number(s). Include as much information as you have available.

> 21. House Subcommittee on Science, Research and Technology, *Genetic Engineering, Human Genetics and Cell Biology*, 96th Cong., 2nd sess., May 14, 1980, 47.

■ *A dissertation.* Treat published dissertations like books. Follow the publication information with the form of publication (e.g., microfilm) and the page of the citation. If you are citing an abstract, give details of the original dissertation as well as the abstract.

> 22. Elaine Marie Cullen, "Women Coming to Voice through Writing"
> date of dissertation acceptance
> (Ph.D. diss. University of Minnesota, 1999), abstract in *Dissertation*
> volume number   publication date and item number
> *Abstracts International* 60 (2000): 2473A.

■ *A letter*

> 23. Troy M. Linville, letter to the author, June 4, 2003.

■ *Lecture, speech, or publication of an oral presentation.* To cite the actual presentation, describe the occasion, including the place and the date. Treat a published presentation as you would the chapters in a book.

> 24. Indira Gandhi, "What Educated Women Can Do" (speech given at the Golden Jubilee Celebrations of the Indraprastha College for Women, Delhi, India, November 23, 1974).

■ *Interview*

> 25. Paul C. Light (Senior Fellow, Governance Studies, Brookings Institution), interview by Neal Conan, *Talk of the Nation*, NPR, June 15, 2004.

■ *Film, DVD, or Videocassette*

> 26. Fred Astaire and Ginger Rogers, *Shall We Dance*, VHS, produced by Pandro S. Berman (1937; Los Angeles: Fox Hills Video, 1987).

> 27. Ken Burns, *The Civil War*, DVD (Washington, DC: PBS Home Video, 2002).

■ *Sound Recordings*

> 28. Edward Kennedy ["Duke"] Ellington, "Harlem Airshaft," *The Duke Ellington Carnegie Hall Concerts*, Prestige 24075.

56c Prepare a bibliography

If a bibliography is required to accompany your project, follow these guidelines.

■ *Placement.* Start the bibliography on a new page immediately following the endnotes or, if you used footnotes, following the text of the paper. Center the heading "Bibliography" 1 inch from the top of the page. Continue page numbering from the notes page or text of the paper.

■ *Spacing.* Double-space throughout.

■ *Indentation.* Do not indent the first line of an entry. Indent following lines one-half inch or 5 spaces.

■ *Alphabetical order.* Do not number the entries of a bibliography. Arrange them in alphabetical order according to the author's last name or the first word of the title, ignoring *A, An,* and *The.*

> Anaya, Rodolfo, and Francisco Lomeli, eds. *Aztlán: Essays on the Chicano Homeland*. Albuquerque: Academia, 1989.

> Mahfouz, Naguib. *Arabian Nights and Days*. Translated by Denys Johnson-Davies. New York: Doubleday, 1995.

■ *Punctuation.* Separate the major parts of an entry with a period and 1 space.

■ *A titled part of a book.* Cite the pages of the part immediately after the title and the editor.

Tolstoy, Leo. "The Three Hermits." In *Short Shorts: An Anthology of the Shortest Stories,* edited by Irving Howe and Ilana Wiener Howe, 3-11. New York: Bantam, 1983.

57 Using the CSE Style and Other Styles

57a Use the CSE style for scientific writing

In *Scientific Style and Format,* 6th edition, The Council of Science Editors (CSE) recommends two styles for writing in the life sciences: biology, botany, zoology, anatomy, and physiology. One is an author-date system similar to the APA style (see Chapter 55). The other system, illustrated here, is a citation-sequence system that uses numbers in the text of the paper to refer to numbered entries in a reference list at the end of the paper. For citing online materials, the Council of Science Editors follows the guidelines of the National Library of Medicine, *Recommended Formats for Bibliographic Citation; Supplement: Internet Formats.* (See < http://www.nlm.nih.gov/pubs/formats/internet.pdf > .)

1 ▪ Citing sources in the text of your writing

▪ Use raised, superscript numbers after each use of source material to refer readers to entries in the reference list. Begin with "1" and give each source its own number.

The increase of childhood asthma during the last twenty years is attributed to environmental rather than genetic factors.[1] Chief among these factors is air pollution.[2]

▪ If you cite two or more sources at once, place a comma but no space between citation numbers. If you refer to a source cited earlier, reuse the original number.

Studies of asthma in developing nations have noted that exposure to firewood smoke is a frequent cause of obstructive airways disease.[2,3]

2 ▪ Preparing the reference list

At the end of your paper provide a list of all sources that you refer to in your paper, including sources cited in notes, tables, and figures. Follow these format guidelines:

▪ *Heading.* Use the heading "References."

▪ *Spacing.* Single-space each entry; double-space between entries.

- *Arrangement.* Arrange entries in the numerical order of their first citation in the paper, not alphabetically.

- *Indentation.* Type the number of each entry on the line of type (not raised) and flush with the left margin (not indented). Follow with a period and 1 space. Indent the second and successive lines of an entry to align beneath the first word in the first line.

- *Author names.* Invert all author names, typing last name first followed by 1 space and initials for the first and middle names. Do not use periods or spaces between initials—for example, *Conroy LB*. If a source has two or more authors, place a comma between author names—for example, *Conroy LB, Jameson RN.*

- *Punctuation.* Use a period and 1 space to separate major parts of an entry: "Author name. Title. Publication information."

- *Titles.* Do not underline, italicize, or use quotation marks for the titles of books and articles. Capitalize only the first letter of the first word and proper nouns.

3 ▪ Sample citations

- *A book.* Use a colon and 1 space between the place of publication and the publisher. Use a semicolon and 1 space between the publisher and year. Conclude with the total number of pages in the book.

  1. Pollan M. The botany of desire: a plant's-eye view of the world.

     New York: Random; 2001. 271 p.

- *An article in scholarly periodical.* After the journal title, provide the year of publication, a semicolon, the volume number, a colon, and the inclusive pages. No space precedes or follows the semicolon and colon.

  2. Thurston GD, Bates DV. Air pollution as an underappreciated cause

     of asthma symptoms. JAMA Oct 2003;290:1915-17.

- *A magazine article*

  3. Glasser RJ. We are not immune: influenza, SARS, and the collapse of

     public health. Harper's 2004 Jul;35-42.

- *An article in a newspaper.* Provide the date, the newspaper section, page, and column numbers.

  4. O'Connor A. Panel finds mold in buildings is no threat to most

     people. New York Times 2004 May 26; Sect A:14(col 5).

■ *An online serial article.*

two authors   title of the work

5. Pianosi PT, Davis HS. Determinants of physical fitness in children

publication date of
journal title medium publication access date

with asthma. Pediatrics [Internet]. 2004 [cited 2004 June 30];

page numbers   URL

113:225-9. Available from: http://pediatrics.aappublications.org/

cgi/content/full/113/3/e225

■ *An online file in a database or retrieval system*

three authors   title of the work

6. Harik-Khan RI, Muller DC, Wise RA. Serum vitamin levels and the

print source

risk of asthma in children. Am J Epidemiol 2004 Feb 15;159(4): 351-7.

database   database owner

In: Medline [Internet]. Washington (DC): National Library of

access date   length of article

Medicine (US); [cited 22 2004 May 3]. [about 12 screens]. Available

URL with no period following

from: http://www.ncbi.nlm.nih.gov/entrez/

■ *Online newspaper article*

7. Janofsky M. Toxic release increased in 2002, study says. The New

York Times Online [Internet]. 2004 Jun 23 [cited 2004 Jun 28]: [14

paragraphs]. Available from: http://www.nytimes.com/2004/06/23/

politics/23toxic.html

■ *E-mail message*

author   subject of the messaage   medium

8. Winegarden O. Hodgkins disease therapies [Internet]. Message

recipient of the e-mail posting date and time   date of access

to: Lawrence Barnet. 2003 Feb 9,1:18 pm [cited 2003 Feb 10].

length of message

[about 2 screens].

57b Choose a style manual appropriate for your subject

■ *Biology.* Huth, Edward J., ed. *Scientific Style and Format: The CBE Manual for Authors, Editors, and Publishers.* 6th ed. New York: Cambridge UP, 1994.

■ *Chemistry.* Dodd, Janet S., ed. *The ACS Style Guide: A Manual for Authors and Editors.* 2nd ed. Washington: ACS, 1997.

- ■ *English and the humanities.* Gibaldi, Joseph. *MLA Handbook for Writers of Research Papers.* 6th ed. New York: Modern Language Association, 2003.

- ■ *Engineering.* Michaelson, Herbert B. *How to Write and Publish Engineering Papers and Reports.* 3rd ed. Phoenix: Oryx, 1990.

- ■ *Geology.* United States Geological Survey. *Suggestions to Authors of the Reports of the United States Geological Survey.* Ed. Wallace R. Hansen, 7th ed. Washington: GPO, 1991.

- ■ *Law.* *The Bluebook: A Uniform System of Citation.* Comp. Editors of Columbia Law Review et al. 17th ed. Cambridge: Harvard Law Review, 2000.

- ■ *Linguistics.* Linguistic Society of America. *LSA Bulletin,* Dec. issue.

- ■ *Mathematics.* American Mathematical Society. *A Manual for Authors of Mathematical Papers.* 8th rev. ed. Providence: AMS, 1990.

- ■ *Medicine.* Iverson, Cheryl, et al. *American Medical Association Manual of Style.* 9th ed. Baltimore: Williams, 1997.

- ■ *Music.* Holoman, D. Kern, ed. *Writing about Music: A Style Sheet from the Editors of* 19th-Century Music. Berkeley: U of California P, 1988.

- ■ *Physics.* Scott, J. T. *AIP.* American Institute of Physics *Style Manual.* 4th ed. New York: Springer-Verlag Telos, 1990.

- ■ *Psychology.* American Psychological Association. *Publication Manual of the American Psychological Association.* 5th ed. Washington: APA, 2001.

- ■ *General.* *The Chicago Manual of Style.* 15th ed. Chicago: U of Chicago P, 2003. United States. Government Printing Office. *Style Manual.* 29th ed. Washington: GPO, 2000.

PART XI

Argument and Persuasion

FOCUS ON . . . Logical Argument

- Identifying the point of an argument—four kinds of claims   444
- Collecting evidence and establishing warrants   445 and 446
- Building an argument (choosing the appropriate strategy)   448
- Testing and modifying your argument   452

ON THE WEB   www.ablongman.com/dodds

XI Argument

Argument and Persuasion

58 Creating Logical Arguments

In many people's minds, argument involves anger and other heated emotions. But here, and in most academic writing, it is nothing more—and nothing less—than a process of reasoning about an issue whose truth or plausibility is in doubt. In its simplest form, **argument** consists of an assertion supported by factual information and logic.

Consider, for example, two friends planning a vacation. One says, "If it's real wilderness you want, let's go to Capitol Reef National Park, in Utah. You'll see few tourists, fewer RVs and buses, and no souvenir stands cluttering the landscape. That's as close to my definition of wilderness as we're going to get." What we have here is a capsule argument (and note that in its classic definition an argument requires only one participant):

- *Assertion.* "If it's real wilderness you want, let's go to Capitol Reef National Park, in Utah."

- *Factual information.* Capitol Reef has "few tourists, fewer RVs and buses, and no souvenir stands cluttering the landscape."

- *Logic.* A definition of *wilderness* shows that the factual information supports the assertion.

As you will see in this chapter, this process of reasoning in a more fully developed form is a feature of many kinds of writing you do, in school, on the job, in public. In essays, reports, business writing, and elsewhere, it provides a way to determine the truth, make sound judgments, and decide on the best course of action.

58.1
Aids to
practical
reasoning:
Web link

🌎 WRITING IN THE USA Argument and Culture

Cultures vary in their attitudes toward argument. The American academic community tends to value originality, analysis, and proof more than consensus or harmony. Cultures differ, too, in the way in which arguments are presented. In academic arguments in English, readers prefer deductive organization (the presentation of main points followed by supporting detail), directness (no major digressions from the main point), and the use of objective evidence (facts, statistics, expert commentary). Americans writing for other cultural audiences need to be sensitive to the potential preference for less step-by-step argument, and writers fluent in other languages may find the organization of American academic essays spare or unadorned. The thesis/support essay presented in this handbook (see 4f) is the basic format of most American academic argument.

58a Write arguable claims

1 ▪ Identifying the point of an argument

An argument begins when someone makes an assertion—a claim—needing support before others will accept it. Like the thesis of an essay, a **claim** is the point of an argument, what it is all about. Just as the content of an essay provides support for the thesis, the factual information and logic of an argument provide support for the claim. There are four kinds of claims. Knowing what they assert will help you see how to support them.

- ▪ A **factual claim** asserts that something about a subject is true or plausible. For example: *Standardized achievement tests are biased against racial minorities, the poor, and rural students.* The subject of this claim is *standardized tests.* The claim asserts that these tests are biased. To prove the truth of this claim, an argument would have to provide factual information about standardized test scores and logic showing that these scores reveal bias.

- ▪ A **cause-effect claim** makes an assertion about the causes of an effect or, conversely, the effects resulting from a cause. For example: *Television advertising targeted to children raises unattainable expectations and promotes their unhappiness.* This claim asserts that a cause, television advertising, has two effects on children. An argument supporting it would have to show that young viewers of television advertising are affected in these ways.

- ▪ A **value judgment** is a claim that evaluates a subject for its usefulness, beauty, desirability, or rightness or wrongness. For example: *The Dynacomp Personal Computer has the internal memory, disk space, and speed to meet the needs of most college students.* An argument supporting this evaluation of a computer's usefulness would have to present information about the needs of college students and then show that the features of this computer meet those needs.

- ▪ A **proposal** is a claim advocating a course of action or a policy. It may assert a need for action, the benefits of action, or both. For example: *To protect endangered park environments, the National Park Service should begin restricting admissions at parks most threatened by visitor overcrowding.* An argument supporting this proposal would have to show a need for action with information about the conditions of national parks, the benefits of reduced park use, and the practicality of restricting admission.

2 ▪ Writing a tentative claim

When you have a project requiring an argument, begin by writing a tentative claim that you hope to support. Write it as you would a tentative thesis, beginning with the words *My point is that* (see 2d).

My point is that bilingual education is the most effective and economical method for teaching English to nonnative speakers.

As you gather support for your claim, revise the claim to fit that support. Later, as you write the actual argument, remove the formula phrase. For example: *Bilingual education is the most effective and economical method for teaching English to nonnative speakers.*

3 ■ Converting a tentative claim to an arguable assertion

As you write a claim, make it an arguable assertion, one whose truth or plausibility is in doubt but which can be supported by factual information and logic. Follow these guidelines.

■ *Avoiding subjective assertions.* Avoid subjective assertions of personal preference. An arguable claim is more than an expression of personal preference or taste.

~~I think our~~ ^Our^ national parks are ~~too crowded.~~ ^so overcrowded that visitor enjoyment and the environment are suffering.^

[The original claim may have meant only that the writer doesn't like all those other visitors visiting national parks. The revision makes a value judgment claim that can be supported by factual information and logic.]

■ *Avoiding easily verifiable statements.* Avoid easily verifiable statements of fact. Statements that are obviously true or easily shown to be true do not require argument.

The smog from auto pollution is ~~as bad in many national parks as in downtown Los Angeles or Denver.~~ ^killing the forests of many national parks.^

[The original claim is an easily verifiable statement of fact. The revision is a cause-effect claim whose truth must be established by an argument showing that smog is killing the forests.]

■ *Avoiding vague language.* Use exact, specific language. You and your audience must know exactly what your words refer to.

The US Park Service must ~~act now to save the treasures of our national parks.~~ ^devote more funds to protect wildlife and restore historic monuments.^

[The meaning of the words *save* and *treasures* is imprecise and vague. The revision makes a proposal in which the subject of the argument is well focused and clear.]

58.2
Writing
arguable
claims:
Exercises

58b Gather two kinds of support for your claim

1 ■ Collecting evidence

Evidence consists of factual information presented to support a claim. (For methods of research to help you gather evidence, see Chapters 47, 48, and 49.) You'll probably collect three kinds.

■ **Data** may be facts, statistics, experimental data, research findings, or reliable observation.

Note: If you're writing an essay about a work of literature, the data that you'll use to prove your point will be the words of the poem, story, novel, or play.

■ **Examples, anecdotes, and precedent.** *Examples* are specific instances or illustrations of the point being made; for example, the levels of pollution in a specific US National Park may illustrate pollution throughout the national park system (see 6b5). *Anecdotes* are brief stories that help to illustrate a point. *Precedent* refers to past events that have a bearing on subsequent or future events, as successful actions taken to reduce the impact of auto traffic in one national park may provide a precedent for taking the same actions in other parks.

■ You may use as evidence the **opinion of an expert** based on an examination of the facts, unless the opinion is challenged. In that case, the truth must be established independently.

Note: In academic arguments, your most important support for a claim will be your words and your reasoning. Increasingly, however, photographs, charts, and graphs are used to present the facts of a case, offer examples, explain a point, or dramatize it. Consider Eric Martínez's argument concerning overcrowding in US national parks (Chapter 54). He uses photographs to dramatize his point about overcrowding in our most popular national parks. Later, he uses a map of the United States to show the extent of the threat to national parks. If your arguments would be strengthened by the use of photographs, charts, or graphs, check with your instructor to see whether they're appropriate for the assignment.

🌎 **WRITING IN THE USA** What Counts as Evidence

In American academic argument, the amount of relevant factual information provided in support of a claim is typically what counts most. In more personal argument in English—about politics, sports, or religion, for example—stories, communal wisdom, and appeal to sacred texts tend to count more.

---

2 ■ Establishing warrants

A **warrant** makes a connection between evidence and a claim, showing how or why the two connect. For an argument to be effective, there must be a link, and it must be clear and logical. Suppose two people are driving down a busy street, late for a concert. As they approach an intersection, the passenger says, "Here, turn right on Highland Avenue. There's less traffic, and it's shorter." In a diagram of this passenger's argument, the evidence is connected to the claim by the warrant, an assumption travelers make when choosing a route.

| **Evidence:** Highland Avenue is the shorter route and has less traffic. | **Unspoken implicit warrant:** The best route is the shortest one with the least traffic. | **Claim:** Turn right on Highland Avenue. |

In simple arguments like this, the logic is so clear that the warrant need not be explicitly stated. In other arguments, however, the link between evidence and claim may not be clear or more than one warrant may be at work, and people who have trouble following the line of reasoning will say, "I don't see the connection."

Consider another argument:

EVIDENCE	CLAIM
During the last fifty years, canals have been dug through the Florida Everglades, and vast amounts of water have been diverted for human consumption. The result is that many species of animals, fish, and birds have disappeared, vegetation is dying, and the region is beginning to resemble a desert.	The National Park Service should allocate resources to repair damage to the Everglades and restore the park as much as possible to its original state.

Even if the claim is one you could agree with, it may not be clear why the evidence calls for the action the claim proposes, so the link must be identified. Here is the way this argument looks written out, with several warrants connecting the evidence to the claim.

Evidence		**Complete claim**
During the last fifty years, canals have been dug through the Florida Everglades, and vast amounts of water have been diverted for human consumption. The result is that many species of animals, fish, and birds have disappeared, vegetation is dying, and the region is beginning to resemble a desert.	**Warrant 1:** *an ecological principle.* If the Everglades is destroyed, the surrounding environments will also suffer. **Warrant 2:** *the principle of self-interest.* Our way of life may be threatened. **Warrant 3:** *a standard of judgment.* Besides, the natural world is beautiful and valuable in itself, and deserves protection. **Warrant 4:** *a law.* And there's no alternative, really, because the National Parks Act requires that parks should be preserved "unimpaired for future generations."	Therefore, the National Park Service should allocate resources to repair damage to the Everglades and restore the park as much as possible to its original state.

Singly and together, these warrants reveal the logic of the argument, showing how evidence and claim are related.

As this example shows, we take warrants from many sources: natural laws (such as gravity or photosynthesis), scientific and mathematical formulas (πr^2), theories (evolution), human laws, institutional policies, standards of artistic taste, moral values, principles of human nature, rules of thumb, proverbs ("Waste not, want not"), basic assumptions ("All people are created equal"), and precedent (the assumption that past events may be a guide to future events).

3 ▪ Building logic into your argument

As you construct an argument and look for warrants linking evidence to your claim, follow these guidelines.

▪ *Writing a claim based on evidence.* If you have a body of evidence but are unsure what to claim about it, ask yourself what laws, policies, principles, assumptions, or procedures apply to that evidence. They will act as warrants leading you to a logical claim.

▪ *Identifying the link between evidence and claim.* If you already have a claim and supporting evidence but need a link tying the two together, ask what laws, policies, principles, assumptions, or procedures explain the connection. These are your warrants.

▪ *Stating warrants in an argument.* As you design an argument for an audience, ask whether the connection between evidence and claim is clear and logical. If you have doubts, express your warrant or warrants directly in your argument. If you're certain the relationship is clear, they can remain unstated.

58c Build an argument that fits your purpose

1 ▪ Establishing the truth

The aim of many arguments is to show that one view, stated by a claim, best fits the facts of the matter. You can establish the truth of your arguments in three ways.

▪ *Presenting evidence.* You can show that your opinion makes the best sense of the facts simply by presenting those facts. This is one strategy taken by Eric Martínez, the student writer of the research paper in Chapter 54. Among other things, he aims to show that US national parks, supposedly nature sanctuaries, in fact suffer from high levels of pollution (one of his claims). He supports this claim with evidence of all kinds: the visual evidence available on national park Web cams, expert and eyewitness testimony about the effects of air pollution, and statistics showing by how many miles smog has reduced visibility at mountain top and canyon vistas. Presenting sufficient amounts of evidence is the easiest way to build an argument.

- *Applying key terms.* Sometimes arguments seem to be about words as much as evidence and truth. Consider Ashley Sheffer, the student whose report on standardized testing is presented in 55d. If she used her research to argue that standardized tests such as the SAT and ACT are ineffective for college admissions decisions, she'd probably claim that these tests are "invalid." To make her case, she'd begin by defining *validity*, the extent to which a test measures what it is supposed to measure. Then she would offer factual evidence showing that standardized tests do not always measure what they are supposed to. That is, the evidence from standardized testing does not fit her definition of *validity*. In this way, she would prove her claim.

  Arguments often proceed in this manner. First, an arguer defines key terms to set the boundaries of an argument—what it's about and what must be proven. Then he or she presents evidence showing that something either fits or does not fit within the boundaries set by those terms. As you plan an argument, look for key terms whose definitions will help you see what you have to prove and what kind of evidence you have to present.

- *Comparing and contrasting.* You may also establish the truth about something by comparing it with something else. The procedure is to look for points of similarity or difference between the subject of your argument and something else that everyone already knows about. This is another procedure Eric Martínez follows to prove that US National Parks are affected by air pollution (see Chapter 54). He compares selected parks to cities throughout the US, such as Los Angeles and Boston, known for high pollution levels. By showing that parks and cities have approximately the same number of pollution-alert days, he helps to prove the fact of pollution in the parks. As you gather materials for your arguments, look for comparisons to make. Ask, "How is my subject like or unlike another subject that my readers and I already know about?"

Note: Arguers often invent analogies, nonliteral comparisons, to help them dramatize a point. Here, for example, is a former director of the FBI arguing that the death penalty deters potential murderers and should not be abolished.

> A judge once said, "The death penalty is a warning, just like a lighthouse throwing its beams out to sea. We hear about shipwrecks, but we do not hear about the ships the lighthouse guides safely on their way. We do not have proof of the number of ships it saves, but we do not tear the lighthouse down."

See the comparisons? Death penalty = lighthouse, those who may or may not commit murder = ships. Analogies are powerful because they offer such vivid pictures. But because they are nonliteral comparisons, they don't really prove anything; they only suggest resemblances. Use them in your arguments, but make sure the resemblances are logical as well as dramatic.

2 ■ Identifying causes and effects

When you build a cause-effect argument, you support your claim by establishing links between causes and effects. For example, when the student Ashley Sheffer (see 55d) set out to show that standardized tests are biased against certain test takers, she had to link facts of family income, gender, and ethnicity (causes) with reduced scores on these tests (effects). She had to show that these causes, not lack of intelligence, determine the test scores. Thus, the tests are biased. To make a good argument, she had to perform several operations you'll perform when you make a cause-effect argument.

- *Recognizing multiple causes.* In most situations, more than one cause produces a particular effect. Strengthen your argument by showing all the causes involved.

- *Identifying underlying causes.* Sometimes the most important causes are difficult to see. To argue successfully, trace the causal chain all the way to the remote, underlying causes of an effect. For example, to show why US national parks face an environmental crisis, Eric Martínez traces the cause of that crisis back to the funding decisions of particular government officials. These human causes of events are called the **responsible cause**.

- *Distinguishing "true" causes from contributory and false causes.* Some causes are more important than others. To argue effectively, with appropriate emphasis, you must show which causes, by themselves, produce an effect and which only contribute to that effect. You must also expose false causes, which only seem to produce an effect. Consider the debate over capital punishment. Does the presence of the death penalty (cause) reduce murder rates (effect)? To find out, those interested in the question have considered murder rates in similar death penalty and non–death penalty states. They've discovered little difference in murder rates and so have concluded that the death penalty is not a "true" cause of reduced crime.

3 ■ Supporting value judgments

Arguments are sometimes not about the truth of something but about whether something has value, whether it is good or bad in a moral sense, whether it is pleasing or desirable (such as a good movie or a beautiful house), or whether it works as it is supposed to. These three kinds of value judgments are classified as moral, aesthetic, or utilitarian. To make an effective value judgment argument, you first have to identify appropriate standards of value: relevant criteria that you and others use to evaluate something as good or not so good. Then you introduce evidence to show whether your subject measures up to those standards. This is the procedure Ashley Sheffer follows (55d) to show that standardized tests are unfair (a moral value judgment) and that Eric Martínez follows (54) to show that crowded US national parks offer visitors unpleasant experiences (an aesthetic and utilitarian value judgment).

4 ▪ Proposing action or policy

Propositional arguments aim to change people's behavior or the policies that regulate behavior. Eric Martínez's research paper in Chapter 54 argues for a change in US national parks admission policy. He proposes that the most overcrowded and environmentally damaged parks institute a reservation procedure to control park access. In a later argument (see 59d), he proposes an action, that outdoor enthusiasts should consider other places, such as state parks and federal wilderness areas, for their vacation destinations in order to help reduce the harm to national parks.

The form of his arguments is one you should follow to propose action or policy. First establish a need for action; then argue for a particular action, show why this is the right response, and, if necessary, dramatize the benefits of action. Along the way, if your proposal is complex, you may need to explain how to do or how to pay for what you want done.

Note: *a fortiori* arguments. *A fortiori,* from Latin, means "all the stronger." To make such an argument, you show that what you want is similar to what has already been done. Therefore, what you want is certainly feasible. For example, to argue that standardized tests should be dropped as part of the college admissions procedure, Ashley Sheffer shows how many colleges, from small to large, from public to private schools, have dropped these tests without negative consequences. *A fortiori,* "all the stronger," other schools can do the same.

5 ▪ Making rebuttals

In some situations, you'll not only present your own case, you'll also show why others' arguments aren't as strong as yours. Your rebuttal will take the form of a point-by-point critique of opposing positions. To reveal weaknesses in your opponents' arguments, consider the following:

- ▪ *Your opponents' evidence.* Is everything true and relevant to the case being made? Has everything been collected with reliable methods from trustworthy sources? Is anything missing?

- ▪ *Your opponents' logic.* Does everything make sense (see the fallacies in 58e)? Do your opponents make the simplest case possible? Have they oversimplified? Is their case practical? Is the presentation vague at any points?

WRITING IN THE USA Rebuttal

In American college classrooms, academic readers will want a full, fair rebuttal of your opponent's positions. They want to understand why your case is better than your opponent's. Nonacademic readers form a more diverse audience. If you believe that they share your opponents' position, you should make your rebuttal with special tact (see 59a).

58d Test your argument; modify it, if necessary

1 ■ Testing an argument

Throughout the process of building an argument, check its accuracy, logic, and strength by applying the following critical thinking tests (see also 1a).

- *The truth test.* Is everything supporting your claim true or plausible?

- *Relevance.* Do your evidence and warrants actually apply to the case you're arguing? Your support must be relevant to your claim.

- *Timeliness.* Do your evidence and warrants represent the most recent or up-to-date information?

- *Sufficiency.* Do you have enough support to make your claim convincing?

- *Representativeness.* Have you gathered your support from a variety of sources—more than just one or a few? Your support should broadly represent the facts of your case.

- *Occam's razor.* Named for a medieval theologian, *Occam's razor* is the principle that the simplest argument is usually the best. What is the simplest case you can make for your claim and still support it convincingly?

- *Utility.* Apply this test to proposal arguments. Is your proposal practical and workable? How confident can you be that it will achieve your aims?

- *The counter-case test.* Try to create an argument opposite your own or one in rebuttal (see the guidelines in 58c5). Use these arguments to test the strength or logic of your own argument. Modify your original argument as necessary.

2 ■ Modifying an argument

As you apply the preceding tests, you may find that an argument has fatal flaws of truth or logic. To be reasonable, you'll have to abandon it in favor of a better alternative. Or you may find a weak argument that needs strengthening. The following modifications will help clarify or strengthen your case.

- ▪ *Citing sources.* If your audience may not accept the truth of your evidence or warrants at face value, citing their sources may improve your credibility. In academic writing especially, cite your sources by name and document them appropriately. (For MLA citations, see Chapters 52 and 53; for APA citations, see Chapter 55.)

- ▪ *Adding qualifiers.* Qualifiers are words that indicate degrees of strength, confidence, or certainty: *may, must, certainly, probably, necessarily, it is unlikely, as far as the evidence goes, it seems, as nearly as I can tell,* and so forth. Rarely will you be able to argue with ironclad proof and reach absolute certainty. Add qualifiers to assertions to show the degree of confidence you have in their truth or logic.

Tourists ~~are~~ ^{may be} responsible for the loss of Alpine vegetation in Rocky
∧
Mountain National Park.

[The original version expresses complete confidence in the truth of the assertion; the revision reflects incomplete or inconclusive evidence.]

- ▪ *Identifying exceptions.* Rarely will an argument apply to all situations, so explain where it applies and where it doesn't by stating the exceptions. An argument that appears to cover many situations when it really covers only a few will lack credibility.

To protect national park environments, the National Park Service should begin regulating park admissions/ *at those parks most affected by overcrowding.*

[The original seems to apply to all parks without exception. The revision limits the case to parks needing protection; others are exceptions to the claim.]

58e Identify logical fallacies

You'll improve your ability to test an argument if you can recognize errors in reasoning, known as **logical fallacies**. The following are the most common.

58.3
A glossary
of fallacies:
Web link

- ▪ *Against the person (ad hominem).* Attacking a person instead of rebutting an argument, often through name-calling, as in "those weak-kneed, do-good liberals." Attacking a person's character is justified only when self-interest or incapacity may affect that person's ability to argue truthfully or logically.

- ▪ *Appeal to the people (ad populum).* Appealing irrelevantly to the attitudes of an audience instead of convincing them with argument. "Reelect Representative Hamm! Born and raised here in Pleasantville, in the good old USA, he's a freedom-loving veteran who will oppose every attempt to pick your pocket with new taxes." Evidence should support a claim rather than play to an audience's personal sympathies.

- *Bandwagon.* Arguing that one should accept a claim because everyone else does. Consider: "You still don't have a Dynacomp 68040 Computer? Why, you're the only person in the dorm without one!" The value of a claim does not depend on how widely it is supported.

- *Begging the question.* Assuming the truth of a statement without proof, arguing in a circle. "State U. should drop its literature requirement. So much literature is bad for growing minds, filled as it is with sex and violence." This argument uses as evidence the unproven—"begged"—statement that literature containing sexual subjects and violence is bad for growing minds. Until a statement has been proven to be true or plausible, it cannot be used to support a claim.

- *Either/or.* Arguing that only two alternatives exist when there may be more and, often, rejecting one as inappropriate. "Either we provide weapons for the freedom fighters of Santa Costa, or we abandon them to dictatorship." In fact, there are many kinds of aid one country can give to another. The alternatives in argument are often more than two.

- *Faulty analogy or comparison.* Comparing two subjects that are not really similar in order to force a conclusion. "We must reform schools to make them more like businesses. In business, employees are held accountable for the products they produce. The same should be true of schools, whose product is educated youngsters." Students are more than raw materials to be shaped into products, so the analogy is false.

- *False cause (post hoc).* The post hoc fallacy (which comes from the Latin *post hoc ergo propter hoc*, "after this, therefore because of this") assumes that because one thing precedes another, the first caused the second. But sequence does not always signal a cause-effect relation. "Most people who succeed in business wear suits. If you want to succeed, you'll wear a suit, too." Events may be coincidental, or one may only be an insignificant cause of another.

- *Hasty generalization.* A generalization about a group is hasty when based on insufficient, unrepresentative, or irrelevant evidence. "Walking around campus, I see students with stereo headphones on, students reading comic books or playing computer games, students lying on the grass sunning themselves. Obviously, today's students are illiterates!" A generalization this broad must depend on more evidence than the casual observations of one person.

- *Irrelevant emotional appeals.* Appealing to emotion rather than reason. "Please don't give us a final exam, Professor Moore. It's been a long semester. We've worked so hard, and we're tired. Besides, you're such a hard grader." Irrelevant appeals to fear, pleasure, or pity (as in the "sob story") are used to coerce, seduce, or mislead rather than persuade.

- *Irrelevant authorities (testimonial).* Using an opinion that comes from outside that person's area of expertise. Consider political ads in which actors endorse politicians or other ads in which athletes sell motor oil or clothing. This fallacy of irrelevancy attempts to transfer prestige and authority from one area to another.

- *Non sequitur ("it does not follow").* Making false assumptions based on signs or symptoms. "Fred loves to read. I see him in bookstores and the library all the time. With his thick glasses, he even looks like the studious type. He must get straight A's." These traits do not necessarily signal a person's academic success. The support for an argument must lead logically to the claim.

- *Red herring.* Hunters long ago used to drag strong-smelling herring across the path of dogs to divert them from their prey. An arguer uses a red herring when he or she purposely introduces irrelevant issues to divert an audience from the real issues. "Sure, you support raising admission fees to US national parks. You're wealthy and retired, your children all grown, and you have no financial worries." The status of the audience has nothing to do with support for the claim. A red herring is a way of ducking issues.

58.4
Visual
fallacies:
Exercises

- *Visual fallacies.* Using photographs, graphs, charts, or other visuals to distort, mislead, or exaggerate. Consider the photo of the girl in the rocking chair on p. 16. The relaxed impression she conveys is misleading because the photograph has been cropped from the one on p. 14, omitting the impoverished circumstances in which she sits. Consider, too, the tuition graph on p. 17, in which the shrinking dollar bills suggest that tuition for low-income students is half what it was a few years earlier, when the truth is that tuition fees have declined for this group by only two percent. Both of these images present visual fallacies.

58.5
Identifying
logical
fallacies:
Exercises

59 Arguing Persuasively

59.1
Persuasive
strategies:
Web link

If the audience for an argument were all like Mr. Spock, the thoroughly rational Vulcan of *Star Trek* fame, a logical argument would be persuasive by itself. But audiences naturally bring their own interests, understanding, and priorities to an issue, which means that they use more than reason alone to make up their minds. To win your audience's agreement involves adapting an argument to their priorities, building their trust in you, and rousing their desire to accept your position.

59a Adapt your argument to your audience's needs and interests

1 ▪ Knowing your audience

Arguments often fail because people make cases that would persuade themselves but not necessarily their audiences. As you build an argument, think of your audience and what it will take to persuade them.

- *Audience profile.* Construct a profile of what you know about your audience (see 1d3).

- *Audience knowledge.* Decide what your audience knows or believes about your subject. Are they opponents or potential allies, skeptical or merely undecided?

- *Interests and priorities.* Identify your audience's interests and priorities. Where your subject is concerned, are your readers interested in fairness, justice, effectiveness, efficiency, health, safety, pleasure, or some other priority? Do they have a hidden agenda about your topic—fears or motives they may be reluctant to acknowledge?

2 ▪ Building a persuasive argument

As much as possible, make a claim that respects your audience's interests, needs, and capacities. Be clear about what, exactly, you want from them. Avoid claims that may leave them asking, "So? What should be done? By whom? How?" An effective claim answers these questions.

> ~~Overcrowding~~ *Because visitor overcrowding* threatens plant and animal life in our most popular
>
> national ~~parks.~~ *parks,* *environmentally minded tourists should take their vacations elsewhere.*
>
> [The original claim does not involve the audience. The revision proposes their action in response to the environmental threat.]

As you build your argument, avoid issues that may distract your audience or work against you. For example, if you intended to persuade people concerned with fairness that visits to overcrowded national parks must be reduced, you would probably avoid a quota system as one solution. This audience may become resentful at the thought of being denied access to a park their tax dollars support.

HOW TO . . . Plan an Effective Persuasion

Complete the following questionnaire.

1. Who is the audience I want to persuade?
2. What do they know about my topic? What opinions do they have?
3. What moral, emotional, or practical priorities influence these opinions?
4. What omissions, factual errors, or mistakes in reasoning may cloud their thinking?
5. What part of my argument will be most appealing to them, given their priorities?
6. What is my opponents' position? What do my readers think of it?
7. What are the strengths or merits of my opponents' position that I'll have to acknowledge? What compromises should I propose? What are the weaknesses of their case?
8. What can I do to appear trustworthy to my readers?
9. What stories, examples, or descriptions will be most moving to my readers, given their priorities?

---

3 ■ Organizing persuasively

Organize your argument for greatest clarity and logical impact on your readers. You can adapt or combine the following common patterns of argument.

- *Thesis/support.* Putting your claim first, followed by your support, is an effective strategy if your claim is especially strong.

- *Emphatic order.* Generally, the most emphatic arrangement of ideas from a reader's point of view is to place the most important last, the next most important in the beginning, the least important in the middle.

- *Warrants first (deductive order).* Begin with the warrants linking your evidence to your claim, follow with the evidence covered by them, and conclude with your claim. This design is effective when an audience may not understand how your evidence supports your claim or when they will accept your warrants without question. If they accept these warrants without question and if you can show that your evidence is covered by them, you've made your case.

- *Evidence first (inductive order).* Place your evidence before your claim. Use this pattern when your evidence is dramatic and leads clearly and logically to your claim, or when your audience might reject your claim if you put it first.

- *The pro/con pattern.* Begin by summarizing the arguments for and against a position, follow with a claim that chooses between the positions, and conclude by defending your claim as the best choice.

- *The classical argument.* Begin with a summary of the problem and at least a partial statement of the claim. Follow with an argument supporting the claim, a rebuttal answering opponents, and a conclusion that makes new appeals or summarizes your case.

- *The needs/benefits and problem-solution patterns.* First, show that change is necessary. Follow with a claim proposing change or a solution. To conclude, show the benefits of your proposal, explain why it is the best, and, if necessary, explain how to implement it. (See the sample essay in 59d for an illustration of this pattern.)

- *The narrative pattern.* An argument in story form is most effective when you are offering your own experiences as proof for your claim. But be sure your audience keeps sight of your claim, and remember that anecdotal evidence is the weakest, least convincing kind. If you can add evidence from other sources as you tell your story, you'll strengthen your case.

- *Rogerian argument.* This model of argument proposed by psychiatrist Carl Rogers aims at building understanding between opponents when no agreement is currently possible. Begin by summarizing your opponents' position fairly in words they can accept. Then summarize your position in words that won't alienate them, while at the same time being fair to your beliefs. Point out key differences dividing you and your opponents, and what common ground (values, priorities, interests) you share. If possible, conclude by proposing compromise or interim activities to foster relations, maintain communication, and lead to eventual resolution.

59b In your introduction, present yourself as trustworthy

An argument may be entirely logical, but if an audience doesn't know or trust the person making it, it will not, by itself, be persuasive. For this reason most persuasions open with what the philosopher Aristotle called *ethos*, an introduction of the person making the case. If you present yourself in the beginning as someone your audience can trust, you'll have an easier time winning them to your position. Here are ways to build trust in your introduction.

- *Presenting your credentials.* Present your credentials for writing about your chosen subject. What knowledge, experience, or expertise qualifies you? How can you work these qualifications into your opening without seeming to brag?

- *Establishing common ground.* If yours is a "friendly persuasion," addressed to people with whom you share values and experiences and who are likely to become your allies, plan an introduction that establishes common ground with them. Identify common experiences or values creating a bond between you. Show that you speak their language; create a persona they will feel comfortable listening to. (See 2c.)

- *Being fair.* If you're addressing people with whom you have little in common, win their trust by showing fairness to all involved, concern for others instead of yourself, willingness to compromise, and respect for others' opinions.

- *Building trust in academic audiences.* Most academic writing does not require special efforts to build trust. Your knowledge of your subject, fairness, and documentation of your sources will build academic readers' trust. (For more on introductions, see 6c.)

59c Conclude with suitable emotional appeals

Most academic writing has little room for emotion; objectivity is the required point of view. But when the occasion permits—in school or out—you can give an argument additional power by including relevant emotional appeals to audience feelings, which Aristotle called *pathos*. Persuasions often conclude with such appeals. Aim to make your position attractive or your opponents' position unattractive. How can you rouse an audience's feelings? Use the following strategies.

- *Anecdotes.* Tell a moving story that illustrates your point.

- *Description.* Describe an emotionally charged scene that helps your audience see things as they were, are, or could be.

- *Quotations.* End with a dramatic quotation, especially a quotation by someone your audience finds sympathetic.

- *Figurative language.* End with a fresh, vivid metaphor or simile that expresses feeling and understanding (see 26c).

- *Visuals* When appropriate, use photographs or other visuals to dramatize your argument or rouse your readers' emotions.

Note: Appealing irrelevantly to your readers' feelings, as in a "sob story" or name-calling, is a logical fallacy (see 58e).

HOW TO . . . Revise and Edit Persuasive Writing

Use these questions to guide your revision and editing. Or ask peer reviewers to read your draft with these questions in mind and answer the most important. (For more on revision, see 4b and c.)

1. Does this paper have a clearly identifiable and arguable claim? What revisions would make the claim clearer or more arguable? (See 58a3.)

2. Does the paper support the claim with factual, relevant, timely, representative, and sufficient evidence? Does the paper supply warrants showing the connection between the evidence and claim? What changes will strengthen its argument? (See 58d.)

3. Who is the audience for this paper? Will its argument appeal to their interests and priorities? What changes would strengthen its appeal? (See 59a1.)

4. What does this paper do to earn readers' trust? Consider the writer's credentials, persona, establishment of common ground, and fairness. What changes would increase readers' trust? (See 59b.)

5. What does this paper do to make its case emotionally appealing? Look for moving stories, description, and figurative language. Are they relevant to the argument? What changes would improve the appeal of this case? (See 59c.)

59.2
Analyzing
audiences:
Exercises

59d Sample persuasive essay

The student author of the following persuasive essay, Eric Martínez, wrote his paper in a composition course focusing on argument and persuasion. He first conducted research into the issue of overcrowding in US national parks and wrote a research project (see the paper in Chapter 54). For his persuasive paper, he was assigned to use this research in an argument attractive to a clearly identifiable audience. In the earlier paper, Eric wrote objectively about the environmental threats to national parks and the need for a reservations system to regulate use. Here he writes more personally, addresses outdoor enthusiasts like himself, and tries to persuade them to change their vacation plans and, in so doing, reduce the problems of overcrowding in national parks. The general subjects of the two papers are similar, but the differing purposes and audiences have led to distinctly different projects. (See 46a for guidelines to the manuscript form for academic writing. See 46d for the Modern Language Association documentation format used in this paper and appropriate for college English classes. See 46e for the American Psychological Association documentation format.)

On Not Seeing the Forests for the People

59.3
Good
electronic
arguments:
Web link

An anecdote that dramatizes a problem and presents the writer as an eyewitness

What a disappointment! For months my friend Peter and I had been planning a trip to US national parks in Utah and Colorado. Our high point was to be Rocky Mountain National Park and Trail Ridge Road winding across the summit of the Rockies at over 12,000 feet. The air might be thin and the weather chill, but what views! Snowy peaks. Subalpine valleys. Forests and streams. Arctic tundra. Wildlife. What we didn't anticipate was how many others had the same plans.

Emotionally charged language to describe the effects of over-crowding

Trail Ridge Road was jammed bumper to bumper with cars and RVs. Medicine Bow Curve, the visitor center at Fall River Pass, and the Gore Range Overlook might as well have been New York City at rush hour. I could see the mountains, all right—through a forest of other people's heads, elbows, and camera straps. Peter and I ended up as two of the more than 3 million visitors who yearly stand where we stood and like us, probably, wondered whether there were more people than trees in these mountains. One of my keenest memories is of two park workers straining to lift a barrel of garbage into their truck as the wind sent candy wrappers and hamburger bags scudding in an ugly blizzard across the snow fields. This was the high point of my vacation? Next year I'm doing something different.

Ethos: the writer's values that establish common ground with the audience and establish a warrant

Now, I'm no hermit. People and the pace of city life suit me fine. But from time to time I want something underfoot besides concrete—I long for the wind in trees, wildflowers, colors that are not dyed, the feel of rock and leaf and moss, the sight of animals not tamed into pets. And, like most people these days, I consider myself an environmentalist and believe with Henry David Thoreau that "in wildness is the preservation of the world" (qtd. in Stegner 37).

MLA in-text citation of sources

The writer's credentials: research

Evidence: statistics

So my disappointment at Rocky Mountain National Park comes from more than irritation that I wasn't first in line at the sightseeing overlook. Since my vacation I've done some reading, and what I've discovered is that my experience is not uncommon. Our fifty-five national parks, America's most popular nature preserves, are overcrowded and becoming more so each year. In 2003, 58 million people visited them, more than two for each of the National Park System's 25 million acres. This figure will swell to 90 million by 2010 (United States). Consider the consequences: Each park has what ecologists call a "carrying capacity." That is, each can accommodate only so many visitors before they and park environments begin to suffer. And that is what is happening at the most popular national parks, which are crowded beyond capacity. Increasingly, America's "pleasuring grounds," as Yellowstone National Park was once called, are no longer providing pleasure, and the environment is being devastated.

Warrant: a definition of "carrying capacity" used to link evidence to the claim

From Acadia National Park in Maine, to the Great Smoky Mountains in Tennessee, to Arches in Utah, and Olympic in Washington state, park roads are as filled with traffic as they were on my journey through Rocky Mountain National Park. At many parks, cars are lined up at entrances, and overflowing in parking lots, where visitors wait sometimes half a day for entrance. At Grand Canyon, up to 6,000 cars a day vie for just 2,500 parking spaces (Hill par. 10). At Bryce and Grand canyons, a "crush" of hikers crowds along the canyon rims, blocking other visitors from the views. Down into Grand Canyon hike 70,000 hikers annually, while 100,000 more fly over to admire the view. At the heart of the canyon, in the Colorado River, float 22,000 rafters, some who have waited two years for their place on a raft (Wilkinson, "At More Parks").

These visitors probably come to the national parks for their "tranquility, peace, and silence" (Mace, Bell, and Loomis 229), but what they get instead is a nearly endless roar. "On a daily basis," observes Wes Henry, senior National Park Service wilderness management expert,

> airplanes and helicopters buzz wilderness areas in the Grand Canyon previously reached only by foot and raft; cellular telephones ring on top of Mount Rainier; snowmobiles whine throughout Yellowstone's winter wonderland; and chain saws roar in isolated corners of parks as trail crews clear fallen trees from the paths of hiking trails. (Wilkinson, "Promised Land" 22)

According to a Park Service official at Rocky Mountain National Park, many visitors now complain that the quality of their "national park experience" is less like wilderness and more like Times Square on New Year's Eve (National).

With the increasing number of visitors, argues Alan Ewert, more and more "natural landscapes are being turned into theme parks" (64). They are becoming what Rob Smith, representative for the Sierra Club, calls "a venue for entertainment" (Graham 2), filled with stores, hotels, fast food, groomed trails, and other amusements—"manicured, manipulated, and increasingly regimented" (Ewert 64). Increasingly, park rangers report vacationers more interested in park services and amenities than in the natural environments surrounding them (National).

What many of these distracted visitors may not see is that virtually every one of the national parks has been harmed in some way. Air pollution from automobiles and snowmobiles is destroying national forests (Hill 26). Hikers, horses, and mountain bikes are causing park trail erosion. The water in park streams and lakes is everywhere polluted. Climbers are destroying rock faces. And other visitors are destroying vegetation, disrupting habitats, and endangering wildlife (Hill par. 3). As the nineteenth-century naturalist and author George Perkins Marsh declared, "Man is

Marginal notes (left column):

A factual claim

Factual evidence cited from sources: one consequence of national parks' popularity

Citation of an author who provides more than one source for this paper

A source with more than one author

Citation of a source's credentials

Block quotation of a quotation more than four lines long

Evidence: a second consequence of national parks' popularity (their transformation into "theme parks")

Evidence: a third consequence of national parks' popularity (environmental damage)

Reference to two sources in one citation

everywhere a disturbing agent. Wherever he plants his foot, the harmonies of nature are turned to discords" (qtd. in Stegner 38).

Enough! America's national parks, "the best idea America ever had," according to Britain's Lord Bryce, deserve better. Certainly, they need more money. It's true that the current federal administration has promised the National Park Service an additional $4.9 billion. Unfortunately, 98% of this money is promised for roads, buildings, and other commercial development, only 2% for plants, animals, and historic artifacts, and the administration has yet to deliver most of this funding ("Fixing"). What parks may need most from us nature lovers, then, at least some of us, is a rest.

I say, give the harried park staff, the trampled landscape, and the threatened wildlife a rest. With reduced pollution and use, the air will clear, the scars will heal themselves, the plants will regenerate, the animals return. Where to go instead? Consider state parks, Bureau of Land Management lands, or National Forests. Any good map, atlas, or travel guide will identify them. Better yet, go to the Internet and check out the "Best of the Best State Parks" Web site at < http://usparks.about.com/blbestparks.htm >. Instead of the Great Smoky Mountains, there is the Joyce Kilmer Wilderness in North Carolina. In Arizona, instead of Grand Canyon, there are Red Rock and Tonto Natural Bridge state parks. In Alaska, instead of Denali National Park and Preserve, consider Denali State Park, 324,240 acres, with a great trail system, abundant wildlife, and wonderful views of the Alaska range (Smith). Most alternative vacation spots offer their own attractive vistas and activities made more so without all those other vacationers to block the view or clog roads and trails. What will you find off the beaten track? Here's an example.

This summer, after nearly a week of weaving through crowds at Utah's Zion and Bryce Canyon National Parks, my friend Peter and I headed across Utah toward Arches National Park. Along the way, east of Escalante, we happened upon Dry Hollow, the tiny town of Boulder (population 65), and Boulder Mountain. Before we arrived, they were just names on a map, unremarked by us and most other vacationers. But surprise! This became the best part of our trip. Except for the welcoming residents of Boulder glad for two new faces, we were alone, away from the crowds, the enticements of *un-natural* "theme park" activities, and the souvenir stands packed with trinkets stamped out who knows where.

Over two days a wonderful experience opened to us. The cliffs of the hollow were as sheer and deeply red as Zion or Bryce, the textures of rock as sharp to the touch and the eye, the rush of wind as constant, the road even steeper in its hairpin turns dropping to the canyon floor. On the floor of the hollow, not dry at all, rippled a muscular ribbon of creek flowing into the Escalante River. Everywhere were flowers: desert marigold, thornapple, Sego lily, desert paintbrush, blue flax, Tahoka daisy, and wild rose. Up on Boulder Mountain, aspens shimmered, streams sang, snow glistened. And there was this: in purple dusk, in the middle of Boulder, deer bounded in silent arcs from the playground of the one-room school, across a meadow, over a fence, and into the evening. Above them in the distance, like sentinels watching over our two-days' travel, stood the Henry Mountains. To be in such a place and have such experiences was, in the words of Chief Luther Standing Bear of the Oglala Sioux, to live "surrounded with the blessing of the Great Mystery" (qtd. in Stegner 35). The pleasure of this mystery is there for you, too, out there somewhere along a road less traveled.

A concluding quotation from a sympathetic source to emphasize the value of accepting the writer's proposal

MLA documentation of the writer's sources

Works Cited

A journal article

Ewert, Alan W. "Outdoor Recreation and Natural Resource Management: An Uneasy Alliance." *Parks & Recreation* 34.7 (July 1999): 58-67.

A newspaper editorial

"Fixing Up the National Parks." Editorial. *New York Times.* 26 June 2004. NYTimes.Com. 1 Sept. 2004 < http://www.nytimes.com/2004/06/26/opinion/26sat2.html >.

A newspaper story

Graham, Judith. "The Grand Canyon Has Grand Woes." *Chicago Tribune* 11 Apr. 2001, sec 1: 1-2.

An Internet source

Hill, Rebecca. "National Parks in Peril." *WildSites.* 20 July 2004. 15 pars. 30 July 2004 < http://www.wildsite.org/hill/peril .html >.

A source with three authors

Mace, Britton L., Paul A. Bell, and Ross J. Loomis. "Aesthetic, Affective, and Cognitive Effects of Noise on Natural Landscape Assessment." *Society & Natural Resources* 12.3 (Apr./May 1999): 225-41.

An interview

National Park Service Information Office (Rocky Mountain National Park). Telephone interview. 25 Sept. 2004.

An Internet source

Smith, Darren. "Best of the Best State Parks." *US/Canadian Parks.* 2004. About.com. 20 Oct. 2004 < http://usparks. about.com/blbestparks.htm >.

A magazine article

Stegner, Wallace. "It All Began with Conservation." *Smithsonian.* Apr. 1990: 34-43.

A government document

United States. Department of the Interior. National Park Service. Public Use Statistics Office. *Statistical Abstract: 2003.* (Denver: WASO-TNT, 2004) 1.

Two sources by the same author

Wilkinson, Todd. "At More Parks, Visitors Leave the Car Behind." *Christian Science Monitor* 24 May 2001: 3.

---. "Promised Land." *National Parks* Sept. 1999: 22-25.

PART XII

Special Writing Projects

FOCUS ON . . . Electronic Communication

- Preparing a scannable résumé   486
- Using electronic media in a business or professional environment   489
- How to format an e-mail message   492
- Writing effectively online: Netiquette   493
- Designing Web pages and Web sites   498

Web Links

Writing about Literature

60 Writing about Literature

60a Reading the elements of literature

See 1b for general guidelines for critical reading. The following additional guidelines will increase your pleasure in reading literature and add to your insights. As you read, look for the literary elements that writers use to create their art.

- *Characters.* Greet literary characters as you greet real people you're meeting for the first time—with healthy skepticism. Don't believe everything they say. What do they know, exactly? Are they reliable observers? Compare words to deeds and to other characters' remarks.

- *The narrator.* Every work of fiction and poetry has a narrator, a person who tells the story or presents the poem, even if there is no *I* in the work. Narrators do not necessarily speak for the author. Unless they earn your trust, view narrators with the same healthy skepticism with which you view any other character in the work.

- *Stylistic devices.* Look for the stylistic devices writers use to dramatize their message: **irony** (discrepancies between words and deeds, between your expectation and what actually happens, between what a character says and what you know to be true), **symbols** (things, places, or people that have meaning beyond themselves), and **figurative language** (metaphor and simile). (See 26c.)

- *Mood.* As you read, be sensitive to the feeling expressed in the work toward the subject (serious, humorous, mocking, amused, and so forth). Mood is expressed by the narrator's point of view, details of characterization, the course of events, and the way events and setting are described.

- *The title.* Decide what the title suggests about the mood, subject, or message of the work.

- *Key passages.* Look for key passages in which the narrator or another character seems to step back and comment on the subject or action.

- *Layout and staging.* Consider white space between passages and stanzas as clues to structure or meaning.

Note: Use stage directions and descriptions of set design to help you imagine setting, events, and the personality of the characters. Note the instructions for characters' actions or speeches that suggest personality, motivation, and conflict.

60b Choose your options for writing about literature: analysis and interpretation

Analysis is the systematic description of literary elements (character, setting, plot, imagery, and so forth) and the way they work together to form your opinions as you read. **Interpretation** focuses on elements that are not immediately apparent (for example, the hidden causes of an event or the reasons for two characters' conflict) and then, using evidence and logic, tries to clarify these elements (see 1a1 and 2).

1 ▪ Selecting literary elements to analyze and interpret

Adapt the questions after each of the following elements to your chosen literary work. Your answers will provide materials for your writing.

- *Character.* What kind of person is this? Consider appearance, dress, speech, action, thoughts, feelings, flaws, relationships, and motives. Does this character change? If so, how? What is the secret of the relationship between this character and another? Why do these characters engage in conflict? How are conflicts resolved? What is this character's role in the work: main character (protagonist), antagonist, confidant(e), or foil (a minor character whose personality sheds light on a main character's personality)? Begin to express your thinking by completing this formula: "_____ is a person who _____ [identify this character's most important traits] ."

- *Setting.* Describe the setting of the work—natural, social, political, or cultural. What does setting contribute to the mood, your understanding, or your evaluation? What force does it exert on the characters? Begin to express your thinking by completing this formula: "_____ is a place where _____ [identify the most important feature of this setting] ."

- *Plot and structure.* Describe the change taking place in the course of the narrative. What are the causes and consequences of this change? Begin to express your thinking by completing this formula: "_____ [write the protagonist's name here] 's is a story about how _____ [tell what happens to this person and why] ."

- *Symbols.* Identify and explain literary symbols. What characters or details of setting seem to be symbolic? What ideas, values, or conditions do they symbolize?

- *Mood.* Explain the overall feeling or attitude expressed in the work about its subject. What do the characters, setting, plot, imagery, and style contribute to this mood?

- *Style.* Describe the style of the work and the contributions of this style to the work's mood or theme. Consider formal or informal word choice (see 27a), metaphor and simile (see 26c), and complex or simple sentence structure (see 10c).

- *Point of view.* **Point of view** is the narrator's vantage point for presenting the action of a literary work. Who is the narrator: an actual character in the work (an *I* telling his or her story or someone else's) or a disembodied voice writing in the third person (*he* or *she*)? What does the narrator know or not know? Do you trust the narrator? Why or why not? How do the narrator's knowledge, values, and relationships with other characters affect the structure, mood, and message of the work?

- *A key passage.* Explain how a brief key passage sums up the mood or message of a work.

2 ■ Defending a theme

In a broad sense, a **theme** is the message of a work but more than simply a moral. A moral says, "Do this; don't do that." A theme says, "Life is like that." Theme is a message or judgment that a work dramatizes about its subject. Present the theme of a work and show how it is embodied by the characters, plot, imagery, mood, and style—for example, *Eudora Welty's short story "Death of a Travelling Salesman" portrays materialistic human beings prevented by the fear and mistrust born of their materialism from fulfilling their desire for human companionship.*
Follow these guidelines for writing theme statements:

- *A formula for writing theme statements.* Use this formula to write a tentative theme statement: "The message of ___[the name of the work]___ is that. . . ."

- *A generalization.* A theme is a generalization about life; therefore, it does not identify characters by name but makes statements about people in general or certain types of people.

- *A complete sentence.* A theme is a complete declarative sentence, not a fragment or question.

- *A stated or implied theme.* A theme may sometimes be located in an actual statement in a work. Or it may only be implied, and you'll express it in your own words.

- *An insightful statement.* A theme statement for a serious work of literature will always be more insightful than pronouncements on "the moral of the story" or a trite saying ("Love conquers all").

■ *A unifying statement.* As a unifying statement, a theme should not be contradicted by any major details of a work.*

60c Choose your options for writing about literature: the review

A **review** *evaluates* a literary work or some part of it. But a review does more than present one reader's personal preferences. Skillful reviewers rely on widely shared standards of value and recognized points of comparison to decide the value of their subjects (see 1a3).

1 ■ Applying standards of value

There are three kinds of standards for evaluating literature.

■ Reviewers apply **technical and aesthetic standards** to judge how well a work achieves its intended effects. Is a humorous story humorous; is a tragedy tragic? What explains a work's success or failure in achieving its aims: point of view, structure, plot, characterization, style? How well constructed is a work in comparison with others of its type?

■ Reviewers use **psychological and social standards of personality and behavior** to evaluate the plausibility of characters and their world. How "real" are these characters? Or how well do they express the conventions of their literary type?

■ Reviewers use **ethical standards** to evaluate the morality of a work and its contents. What values does this work seem to endorse? Do you share them?

2 ■ Writing a review

The thesis for a review is your **dominant impression**, your overall judgment of the work or the feature you've chosen to evaluate. You may focus your review in two ways, drawing from the standards described in 60c1 to make your judgment.

60.1
Writing a
review:
Web link

1. Evaluate a literary work or some feature of it. How effectively does the writer handle characters, setting, plot, structure, or style? Is the work believable, consistent, appropriate to its type, well constructed?

2. Evaluate the ideas or values expressed in a literary work. What does the work dramatize as useful, valuable, desirable, or virtuous? What does the work suggest about the way things should be?

---

*For these guidelines to theme statements, I am grateful to Thomas Arp and Laurence Perrine's *Literature*, 8th ed. (New York: Heinle, 2001).

Consider description, dialogue, and the narrator's comments. Do you agree with what the work seems to favor? Why or why not?

60d Choose your options for writing about literature: the personal or creative response

1 ■ Writing a personal response

- ■ *The responsive essay.* Write an essay in which you explain your responses to a literary work. Answer these questions: What in the literary work prompted your responses? What were your feelings, memories, or associations as you read? What personal experiences, observations, or beliefs explain these responses?

- ■ *The relation between art and life.* Explore the relationship between art and life by writing a comparison. Use your experiences to help you explain something in a literary work: character, setting, plot, theme. Or use something from the work to help make sense of something in your own life.

- ■ *Then and now.* Responses and opinions change as readers reread and discuss a literary work. Trace the evolution in your thinking by answering these questions: What did I originally think or feel and why? What made me change? What do I now think and feel?

2 ■ Writing a creative response

Use literary techniques to dramatize your feelings or opinions about a work or some part of it. Imagine a revealing scene that the author has not presented. Or dramatize the thoughts of a character in a soliloquy (a monologue in which a character expresses thoughts or feelings that would otherwise be unspoken). Or narrate events that might have occurred "offstage." Or present an episode in a character's life from before or after the events described in the literary work. Whichever strategy you choose, try to remain faithful to the characters, plot, mood, theme, and style as the original author expressed them.

60e Choose your options for writing about literature: the research project

Many literature classes require some form of research paper. (For guidelines, see Chapters 47–51.)

- ■ *Writing a review of research.* Your project may expand on one of the preceding options, using scholars' interpretations to enrich your own. With whom do you agree? Why? How has your research changed your thinking?

- ■ *Writing a biographical project.* Investigate a writer and his or her work. How does this writer's work reflect his or her life? How did he or she come to write this work? What is the history of the work's reputation?

- ■ *Writing about historical context.* Investigate the historical context of a work or some part of it. What does this work reveal about the culture and period in which it was written? How accurately does it present historical figures, conditions, or events?

60f Write a literary paper, using these guidelines

1 ■ Preparing to write

- ■ *Focusing.* Write a key question about your topic or a tentative thesis to provide focus as you reread your chosen work and gather ideas for your paper. (See 2b3 and 2d.)

- ■ *Taking notes.* To support your thesis, take notes as you reread. Provide a context for each note: Who is speaking to whom? What is happening where and when? (See 49c and d.)

- ■ *Refocusing your thesis.* When you've finished rereading and taking notes, reconsider your thesis to see whether it fits what you've discovered. (See 3a.) Beware of "So?" statements, incomplete assertions. Revise to make assertions about the causes, consequences, or importance of your topic.

Laura Sheridan, in Katherine Mansfield's short story "The Garden Party," lives in a dream world/ *until her visit to the grieving Scott family, when she awakens from her dream and discovers what it means to be fully alive.*

[The original is a "So?" thesis: So what's the point about Laura and her dream world? The revision answers the question.]

- ■ *Organizing to support your thesis.* In an important sense, your paper is not about your chosen literary work. It's about your thesis. Organize so that everything in your paper follows from or leads to your thesis.

2 ■ Writing and revising

- ■ *Identifying author and title.* Identify the author and title of your literary work early in your essay, even in the first sentence. Use quotation marks around the titles of poems and short stories ("The Garden Party"). Italicize or underline the titles of novels, plays, and films (*Hamlet* or Hamlet). (For quotation marks, see 38d; for italics or underlining, see 41a.)

- *Avoiding an all-summary paper.* Unless instructed otherwise, assume that the audience for your paper is your instructor and the other members of your class. They've probably read your chosen work and won't want to read a book report–style summary. But they may not understand the work as you do or remember the small details you have in mind. Summarize briefly to present evidence supporting your opinions.

- *Using the present tense for summaries.* Use the present tense to write about an author's work and to summarize action in the work. The original may read: *As Laura walked up to the workmen, she blushed and tried to look severe.* But you would write: *As Laura **walks** up to the workmen, she **blushes** and **tries** to look severe.* Events occurring before the opening of a work should be summarized in the past tense. (See 13b1.)

60.2
Student
examples:
Web link

- *Using quotations.* Quote often but briefly to explain and illustrate. (See 38a and b.) Indent long quotations of more than four typed lines. (See 50d.) Use ellipsis points to signal omissions from quotations (see 39d) and brackets to insert clarifications (see 39c).

- *Following the proper format.* Format the final draft of your paper according to Modern Language Association guidelines for writing in the humanities (see 46d).

HOW TO . . . Revise and Edit a Literary Essay

Use the following questions to guide your revision and editing. Or ask peer reviewers to read your draft with these questions in mind and answer the most important. (For more on revision, see 4b and c.)

1. A question for peer reviewers: Describe the thoughts and feelings you had as you read this paper. Do your responses to the literary work agree with the writer's? If not, where do you differ? Can you explain the differences?

2. What is this paper's purpose: analysis, interpretation, evaluation, or personal response? Point out any passages that may not fit this purpose.

3. Point out or summarize the thesis of this paper. Does it seem to be a "So?" thesis? Does the paper include another version at the end? Is that statement clearer? Does it better fit the evidence of the paper? (See 4b4.)

4. Does the paper present enough evidence (quotation, summary, and explanation) to support the thesis? Point out places where more support is needed.

(continued)

5. Can readers follow this essay from beginning to end? Does its design follow the order of events in the original literary work (summary order) or the order of ideas in the thesis (logical order)? What design is clearest and most appropriate?

6. Does this paper follow the format for literary essays? (See 60f.)

60g Sample literary essay

In an Introduction to Literature course, student-author Leslie Kelly was assigned to write an essay analyzing the narrator of William Stafford's poem "Traveling Through the Dark." To make her analysis, she considers the narrator's personality and the poem's setting, imagery, and style. She concludes by explaining how the narrator embodies the poem's theme. (For guidelines to the format of a literary essay, see 60f2.)

"Traveling Through the Dark" by William Stafford

Traveling through the dark, I found a deer
dead on the edge of the Wilson River road.
It is usually best to roll them into the canyon:
that road is narrow; to swerve might make more dead.

By glow of the tail-light I stumbled back of the car
and stood by the heap, a doe, a recent killing;
she had stiffened already, almost cold.
I dragged her off; she was large in the belly.

My fingers touching her side brought me the reason—
her side was warm; her fawn lay there waiting,
alive, still, never to be born.
Beside that mountain road I hesitated.

The car aimed ahead its lowered parking lights;
under the hood purred the steady engine.
I stood in the glare of the warm exhaust turning red;
around our group I could hear the wilderness listen.

I thought hard for us all—my only swerving—
then pushed her over the edge into the river.

Dark Necessity

An opening that identifies the author and title of the literary work

On a first reading of William Stafford's "Traveling Through the Dark," the narrator of the poem appears admirable, a hero, even. He is a good Samaritan, sensitive but in control of his feelings, thoughtful, and capable of decisive action. Who wouldn't trust him to be the driver on a journey down a dark, dangerous, lonely road? And yet a careful rereading reveals that there is more to this man and his actions than first appears.

Make no mistake. He is a good man doing the right thing for the right reasons. From the first stanza, as soon as he sees the dead deer, he shows his concern for others and their safety. You or I might whiz by, unseeing, indifferent, or pressed for time. But he sees that if he does not act, because the "road is narrow; to swerve might make more dead." Other travelers might swerve to avoid the carcass and turn into the path of oncoming traffic or over the edge into the river. Three times he acts. He "dragged her [the dead doe] off the road." He "thought hard for" "our group" about what should be done after he discovers that the dead doe's unborn fawn is alive. Then, deciding what must be done, he "pushed her over the edge into the river."

He acts decisively, in part, because he thinks so clearly. Nearly every stanza reveals his logic. In the first, he reasons about what he has discovered—the dead deer, the narrow road, and the potential consequences of a swerve. In stanzas 2 and 3 he reasons inductively. Already stiffened, "almost cold," the deer was a "recent killing." But "large in the belly," "her side [still] warm," "her fawn lay there waiting." He knows from common sense that there is no saving this fawn. Reasoning by analogy, he knows that to pause in pity is a "swerving" as dangerous as the actual swerve of a car.

Throughout, however, his logic is tempered by sensitivity. "Her fawn lay there waiting, alive, still, never to be born." The word "still" seems to mean both "yet," as in "yet alive," and "quiet" or "unmoving," as one might expect of an animal connected by umbilical cord to its dead mother. There is paradox and enormous awareness in these lines. As he thinks of what to do, he personifies the silence of the wilderness into listening attention. In these connections between life and death, self and wilderness, he understands the importance of his decision. How often do we think and act so decisively but with such understanding and awareness?

And yet . . . even if the narrator is as admirable as these details make him appear, there are other details to be accounted for. Consider the title. The narrator is not driving through the dark; he's "traveling." This word suggests more than a drive in the country, not the fact of a journey so much as its condition. He may be driving his car, but to no near destination.

Here is a man whose condition is being in the dark. In such darkness, some things are difficult to see. One is the world of the poem. It is a pair of parallel universes existing simultaneously in the same space. There is, first of all, the natural world of night, mountain, river, canyon, dead doe,

An interpretation of the setting that reveals a contrast between the narrator's civilized world and the natural world

and dying fawn. The other world penetrates, dominates, and finally destroys the former. Its features are the human name for the river, the road, the man, the darkness of the poem's title that refers to more than night, and, most vivid of all, the narrator's car. In contrast to doe and fawn, it lives in images of "the steady engine" that "purred" "under the hood," in the breath of "warm exhaust turning red," in its readiness for purposeful action as it "aimed ahead its lowered parking lights." Given these powerful differences, the human, technological world must displace the natural as it does in the narrator's last, symbolic act, when, with an energy not called for in the first stanza, he does not "roll" the [deer] into the canyon, he *pushed* [emphasis added] her over the edge into the river."

The narrator's behavior explained in terms of the values of his world

He pushes despite his feelings for the fawn because he stands apart from the natural world. His first response, in stanza 1, is to the social code covering such encounters with the natural world: "It is usually best to roll them into the canyon." The deer is a "heap" *before* it is a "doe" ("the heap, a doe"), the descriptive word suggesting debris more than a "recent killing." He does not perceive the presence of the fawn directly. Instead, "my fingers touching her side brought me the reason," as if his fingers were intermediaries between the natural world and human world of reason and technology. Throughout, of course, he thinks and acts "by the glow of the tail-light." The only sound the wilderness can hear as he thinks and it listens is the purr of the car, the sound of the life that directs his life and decides his choice.

A conclusion that states the theme of the poem as the writer of the essay understands it

Given his character and the nature of his world, what other choice does he have? He may think hard, but his concern for the fawn is only a "swerving"—a dangerous reflex from a civilized point of view. Viewed in the dim tail-lights of the car, "roll" comes naturally to "push," and "shove" is not far behind. "Traveling Through the Dark" dramatizes the force of civilized life in the natural world. However much human pity may give it pause, its effects are inevitably disregarding, brutal, destructive. For travel through the dark must continue.

—Leslie Kelly (student)

Essay Examinations

61 Essay Examinations

Essay exams usually ask you to demonstrate three skills:

- *Recall.* You'll show your grasp of the facts by recalling information.

- *Clarification.* You'll demonstrate your understanding of facts (their meaning, causes, consequences, sequences, relationships, points of comparison, and priorities) by clarifying and organizing information.

- *Argument.* You'll apply your knowledge to new situations by constructing arguments that use factual information to prove a point (see Chapter 58).

Note: Your instructors may know more than you do about the subject of the examination. But don't take their knowledge for granted and leave out information because you assume they know it. Treat them as intelligent, curious readers interested in your subject. Provide them with what they need to understand you.

61.1
Writing
essay
exams:
Web link

61a Deciding what a question calls for

When you receive an essay exam, study each question carefully before you begin writing.

- Look for **topical terms** identifying the subjects you'll cover in your answer. Frequently nouns, they identify people, events, issues, and concepts.

List the most prominent abolitionists of the pre–Civil War era. Discuss their contributions to the abolitionist movement.

[Topical terms here are *abolitionists, pre–Civil War era, contributions*, and *abolitionist movement.*]

- Locate **operators** to decide what skills the question calls for. Frequently verbs, these terms will tell you what to do with your information: inform, clarify, or argue. In the sample question above, students are asked to list (recall) and discuss (recall and clarify)—in other words, to describe what each abolitionist did, identify influence, and evaluate achievement or importance. Here is a list of operators that appear frequently on essay exams. Note the accompanying definitions and synonyms:

Analyze: divide into parts, explain features, describe the structure or operations.

Argue: make a point and prove it with evidence.

Classify: divide into groups based on shared characteristics.

Comment: describe, analyze, or explain.

Compare: show similarities.

Contrast: show differences.

Criticize: evaluate positively or negatively, giving your reasons.

Defend: support a statement with facts, statistics, authorities, and logic.

Define: tell what something is, how it works.

Describe: present features, parts, or details about a subject.

Develop: explain, analyze, or present details involved with the subject.

Discuss: explain, trace, analyze, or make a subject clear.

Enumerate: list.

Evaluate: present and defend a judgment about a subject.

Exemplify: present examples that illustrate or explain a subject.

Explain: make clear by description, definition, or enumerating.

Identify: describe, list, explain, or offer examples.

Illustrate: present examples.

Interpret: analyze, explain, or present and defend your opinion.

Judge: evaluate.

Justify: explain, prove, or defend.

List: recall.

Outline: give steps or stages; identify major points or topics.

Persuade: argue; support a statement with evidence and reasoning.

Prove: argue.

Provide information: give facts and figures.

Rebut: oppose a statement with evidence and reasoning.

Refute: oppose.

Review: summarize, explain, or provide information.

Show: explain, illustrate, or prove.

Summarize: give the main points of your reading, observation, or study.

Trace: identify the steps or stages in a process; describe causes or effects.

■ Look for **modifiers** indicating how to organize or focus your answer. Usually these will be adjectives or adverbs: *most important, primary, briefly, thoroughly,* and so forth. In the sample question above, *most prominent* indicates that students must decide who were the most important abolitionists and focus on their *contributions.*

■ Here are some more essay questions. Before you read the accompanying analysis of each question, try to identify their topical terms, operators, and modifiers.

Describe the operation of the adrenal glands.

[This recall question requires students to define the adrenal glands before describing their operation.]

Briefly define and illustrate the concept of determinism.

[This question's first word, *briefly*, provides a clue that this is primarily a test of recall and understanding. Students are being asked to state the meaning of a key term—presented in class discussion or a textbook—and summarize examples that illustrate the way determinism works.]

Analyze the characters of the Duke and Duchess of Ferrara in Robert Browning's poem "My Last Duchess." Trace the Duke's growing disenchantment with his wife; evaluate his reasons for his actions.

[To answer this question successfully, students must do more than summarize the poem. To *analyze*, they must describe the personalities of the Duke and Duchess and then support their opinions with details from the poem. To *trace*, they must describe a process. To *evaluate*, they must judge the quality of a character's reasoning.]

61b Planning and writing your answer

If scratch paper is available, use it. If you're writing with a computer, create a "notes" file to plan your writing. Even if you're well prepared, the answer to a complex question may not spring to mind fully formed.

- *Brainstorming and freewriting.* Make lists, jot down ideas, freewrite.

- *Noting your main idea or thesis.* Write out the main idea or thesis of your essay. Be sure that this most important part of your essay includes key topical terms from the question to keep you on course as you write. Consider this thesis:

Determinism is the philosophical doctrine that every event, human or natural, can be explained as the result of earlier events. Everything is caused; there is no such thing as free will; no event is purely accidental.

[This thesis gives the definition called for by the question. The following explanatory sentence clarifies the definition by telling what *determinism* is not and lists the areas from which the writer will draw the examples called for by the question: examples of causality, the absence of free will, and the absence of chance.]

- *Writing a sketch outline.* To complete your plans, sketch an outline of your answer. Think of your answer as a pyramid with the thesis or main idea at the top and your facts and explanations spreading out beneath, following a line of reasoning and providing support.

- *Manuscript form.* If permitted, write in pencil so that you can erase. Write on every other line, allowing generous margins.

  Note: Check with your instructor before bringing a laptop computer to the exam.

- *Organization.* Don't waste time with introductions. Get to the point. Follow your outline.

■ *Rereading.* If you have time, read your answer twice—once to make sure you've actually answered the question, a second time to check grammar, punctuation, spelling, and legibility.

Business Writing

62 Business and Professional Writing

🖥 **COMPUTER TIP** Creating Templates for Business Documents

Your word processing program may already have a "templates file," containing a variety of templates for familiar business documents such as letters and memos. Customize them to suit your needs or create your own templates using the fonts, styles, header, and format commands of your word processor. Note, however, that ornate, "over-produced" documents will distract readers.

62a Write effective business letters

1 ■ "Inventing" business letters

62.1
Professional
writing tips:
Web link

Give business letters the same careful preparation that any important writing deserves. Begin with research and note taking. Who is your reader, by name, title, and position? What can he or she do for you—or what can you do for him or her? Do the profile described in the "How to Profile an Audience" box on p. 20. Use the Internet, your library, friends, colleagues, or telephone calls to learn about your reader's organization. Look for facts relevant to your reasons for writing. Gather the materials you'll present in your letter so that they're at your fingertips as you type.

Focus your letter by deciding which of the four types of business letters you're going to write:

■ *Letter of application:* Your aim is a job, scholarship, grant, or a favor. To earn positive results, describe exactly what you want and why you deserve it (your qualifications)—but without pressing or bragging. If necessary, explain the information in an accompanying résumé or dossier, but avoid tedious restatement. Distinguish yourself from other applicants, and link your qualifications to those required. Close with a request for an interview and instructions for reaching you. If possible, keep your letter to less than a page. See the sample application letter on p. 481.

■ *Letter of inquiry:* You are requesting services or information. If possible, learn the name of the audience you're addressing before you write: a person, office, or agency. Anticipate what information readers will need to respond to you. Provide background information and be specific about what you want, itemizing if possible.

■ *Response letter:* The range of response letters is broad, from a letter to the editor to a letter in response to another letter. You may write to offer an opinion, answer a query, or promote good will toward the organization you represent. Aim to sound courteous, responsible, understanding, concerned, and fair. Be clear about what readers can do for you and what you can do for them.

■ *Letter of adjustment,* popularly known as a "complaint letter": You are trying to solve a problem. The person you address will probably not be the individual responsible for causing your problem. Writing in anger will do little good. Be polite but firm. Provide the background and explanation your reader will need to take action on your behalf.

2 ■ Organizing business letters

Your letter should contain appropriate elements from those illustrated in the sample letter on p. 481. For the body, adopt the standard three-part design. Open by identifying your subject and purpose and providing the necessary background. In your middle paragraphs, provide information, explanation, and reasons. Conclude by describing the action you want your audience to take. If you have bad news, save it until you've presented all the information and reasons explaining it.

3 ■ Writing in a professional, readable style

Whatever your reasons for writing, your readers will appreciate anything in your letter that makes their work easier, including layout, detailed information, and style. Be businesslike. Be as serious as the occasion requires without sounding stuffy. Avoid the features of an informal style: slang, most contractions, sentence fragments, and inappropriately charged language. (For more on persona, see 2c and 27a.)

Whenever possible, adopt what business writers call a "you" attitude. Try to see things from your readers' point of view, keeping their interests, needs, and benefits uppermost in mind. Most public letters are, after all, persuasive. You'll be persuasive if your readers know you're thinking of them as you write. (See 59b.)

HOW TO . . . Write Effectively to International Readers

With the increase of global communication, you may have to write to readers whose language and culture differ from yours.

1. Before you write, learn about your reader's country or culture.

2. Without being condescending, choose common, easy-to-understand words. Choose synonyms to replace hard words. Your thesaurus will help.

3. Avoid ambiguous words that have more than one meaning, for example, *conceive*. Don't change words merely to avoid repetition, as with *home/residence*. Make sure nothing can be misinterpreted.

4. Be careful with technical words. Provide definitions, if necessary.

5. Be careful with metaphors and similes whose meanings might be unfamiliar to readers from another culture. Avoid idiomatic expressions such as *get a handle on it*.

6. Adapt units of measure (e.g., distance or money) to those used by your readers.

7. Be careful about references to people, places, and events unfamiliar to your readers.

8. Write simple, easy-to-understand sentences. Prefer the active voice of verbs.

---

4 ▪ Formatting and sending your letter

▪ *Paper.* Use good-quality, heavy, white bond paper of at least 20 lb. weight. Letterhead paper makes the best impression.

▪ *Typing and printing.* Choose a professional-looking font such as Times Roman in the 10 or 12 point size. If possible, use a laser printer with a fresh toner cartridge. (See 46a.)

▪ *Length.* When possible, limit letters to one page. If you write a longer letter, put second and successive pages on plain white paper. One inch from the top, type a heading: the addressee's name flush left, the page number centered, and the date flush right.

▪ *Balance.* Make your letter look easy to read by centering it on the page. Keep paragraphs relatively brief; double-space between them. Provide ample white space surrounding your text. Use margins of at least an inch. To help readers keep track of important information, use indented lists, bullets, or enumeration. (See 46b2.)

▪ *Format.* Among letter formats, one of the most common and attractive is the modified block, illustrated by the sample letter on page 481. Near the right margin, place the return address (unless you're

1201 W. Chase Avenue, Apt. 2C
East Lansing, MI 48824
April 14, 200-

Maria L. Mohammed
Director of Student Services
Harley Williams School
Institute of Child Psychiatry
709 W. Greenleaf Avenue
Chicago, IL 60626

Dear Ms. Mohammed:

Professor Gerald Ashby, Chair of the Psychology Department at Michigan State University, has informed me that you have three openings for Child Care Worker-Summer Interns. I wish to apply for one of these positions.

As my enclosed résumé indicates, I am now a college sophomore studying for a degree in child psychology. I plan a career as a child psychologist working with institutionalized children. Most of my work so far has been with children.

> For two years I worked as a summer counselor at a camp for children with developmental disabilities. My responsibilities were to provide tutoring, physical therapy, and recreational supervision.

> For one year I worked as a Boys Club Recreation Supervisor. Besides my supervisory and coaching duties, I was assigned to five boys to act as their "big brother."

> My current position as a hospital orderly not only helps me pay for tuition, books, room, and board but also provides a valuable introduction to institutional work.

I believe I am qualified by education and work experience to be a Child Care Worker-Summer Intern at Harley Williams School. I can be available for an interview at your convenience; if you wish, I will have my references and academic records sent to you. I can be reached by mail at the above address, at (517) 555-1541, or <mleigh@aol.com>. I look forward to hearing from you.

Sincerely,

Matthew Leigh

Matthew Leigh

Enclosure: Résumé

Heading (return address omitted with letterhead stationery) and date

Modified block business letter format

Inside address

Salutation followed by a colon

Itemized information

Block paragraphs

Complimentary close

Reference area: enclosures, typist's initials, copies, and so forth

using letterhead stationery), the date, complimentary close, and signature section. All other parts begin at the left margin.

- *Nonsexist address.* Use nonsexist forms of address. Address readers by name or specific title: *Dear Mr., Ms., Mrs., Dr., Professor,* and so forth. Call ahead to find out your readers' names. When you do not know their names, address them by title alone: *Dear Editor, Service Manager, Director of Admissions,* and so forth. Do not use first names unless you know your reader personally. (See 27e.)

- *Proofreading and previewing.* Proofread your letter carefully. Before you print, use your computer's print-preview command to make sure everything looks professional.

- *Envelopes.* Mail business letters in standard business-size envelopes, 4 × 9 1/2 inches. If you don't know a Zip code, find it on the Internet at < http://www.usps.gov > .

62b Write effective memos, faxes, and e-mail

1 ▪ Memos

A **memo** is a written document sent within an organization to specific persons or departments. Its purposes are to inform, summarize, record, raise a question, ask permission, or call for action. Even with the widespread use of e-mail, memos remain important methods of communication when a permanent record or confidentiality is important.

62.2
Memo tips:
Web link

Effective memos are sensitive to writer-reader relations as equals, as subordinate to superior, or vice-versa. In style, they are less formal than letters, and as brief and precise as possible. Present yourself as a friendly, cooperative colleague. (See 2c for guidelines to creating a persona.) Often customized to suit the needs of a particular organization, memos vary widely in their formats. The sample memo on p. 483 illustrates standard memo parts and a common pattern of organization.

As you write a memo, use your first sentence to link its body to the subject line. Also, present any necessary background; be clear about your reasons for writing. In the middle of your memo, state the why, what, when, or how of your topic. Conclude by indicating the response you want from your reader. If necessary, provide recommendations to be accepted, rejected, or revised. To clarify your ideas, use italics, boldface, lists, bullets, or headings.

2 ▪ Faxes

Because faxes are easily lost, advise the recipient by telephone or e-mail that one is coming. To compensate for the poor image quality of faxes, prepare the document to be faxed using a 12- or 14-point font; avoid marginal comments that might be lost in transmission. Include a cover sheet that gives the recipient's name, company, fax number, date,

Memo

Block format
memo

TO: Laura Chin, Selection Committee, State
               College Student Anthology

FROM: Beth Logan, Editor *BL*

Writer's
initials

DATE: December 10, 200-

SUBJECT: Reading this year's submissions to the student
               literary anthology

Triple-space
after the
subject line
and begin
the body of
the memo
flush left.

Enclosed are the submissions to be evaluated for the next
issue of the anthology. Read them in the usual way:

Do not
indent memo
paragraphs.

  1) Award each entry from 1 to 5 points (1 low, 5 high).

Single-space
within para-
graphs, dou-
ble-space
between.

  2) If you discover incomplete or misassembled entries,
     let me know, and I'll try to get you good copies.

  3) Record your votes beneath your initials on the
     enclosed alphabetized list.

Whenever
possible, use
lists for
clarity and
emphasis.

We'll meet to discuss our evaluations at the end of
January. Thanks for all your efforts on last year's
issue. It was first-rate. I know we can make this year's
even better.

Enclosures: Anthology submissions
               Author list

Reference
area

time, subject, your name, fax number, and the total number of pages,
including the cover sheet.

3 ▪ E-mail

E-mail messages are less formal than business letters or even memos;
sometimes, even in a business environment, they seem closer to speech
than to writing. But if your business or professional communication is
important, plan before you write, edit after you write, and check your
spelling. And note that two-thirds of US companies conduct electronic
surveillance of their employees; e-mail is not confidential. (For a detailed
discussion of e-mail, see 63a.)

62c Write a winning résumé

The résumés you write may be printed on paper, attached to an e-mail, or posted on the Internet. Whatever the format, your aim is the same: to convince a prospective employer that your background, education, experiences, skills, achievements, and references qualify you for the job you want.

1 ▪ Preparing a résumé

Begin with "the-power-of-positive-thinking" brainstorming. In freewriting, describe all that makes you a good job candidate: your best classes in school, what assignments you did the best, your technical skills, "people skills," awards you've won, jobs you've had that have prepared you for the job you want, important life experiences that make you an "added-value" candidate, special activities that show your abilities. Read this freewriting from your prospective employers' point of view. What will they see that you can do for them? In their eyes, how will you compare to other candidates? Then choose your five or six most job-worthy strengths and list them accurately, precisely, and clearly.

62.3
Résumé
guidelines:
Web link

As you prepare your résumé, be brief but complete. Choose specific nouns and action verbs to bring your education, work, skills, and achievements to life. Write in clipped phrases and clauses rather than complete sentences: *Career objective: A child psychologist caring for autistic children in an instutional setting.* If necessary, add brief explanations showing how your education, work, responsibilities, or experiences qualify you for the position you seek. Give specific numbers if your GPA is over 3.0. Be sure to include academic honors and scholarships. For work experience, begin with your most recent experience, giving attention to the most relevant jobs. Avoid stringing out a series of part-time jobs; group them in one brief statement.

2 ▪ Formatting a résumé

The formats for résumés are varied. It should be no longer than one or two pages, with the length depending upon your degrees and experience. If you have important achievements, list them first. Follow a chronological order, with most recent job first; or describe the functions of your job, with the most important first. If you're a recent graduate or still in school, place your education before your work experience, beginning with your most recent schooling. Omit salary expectations, work schedule preferences, benefit requests, travel restrictions, reasons for leaving your last job, a photograph, or personal information. While preparing your final draft, remember that your prospective employers will be looking for résumés that are attractive, well organized, accurate, current, and relevant. Use the following guidelines for the final draft and see the sample résumé on p. 485.

MATTHEW R. LEIGH
1201 W. Chase Avenue
East Lansing, MI 48824
Voice: (517) 555-1541
Fax: (517) 555-6039
mleigh@aol.com

Position Desired: Child Care Worker-Summer Intern
Career Objective: Child psychologist working with autistic
children in an institutional setting

Education:
200- to present: Michigan State University, BS in
psychology expected June, 200-
Major: Child Psychology
Related courses: Child Psychology,
Abnormal Psychology, The Brain and
Behavior, The Psychology of
Language, Psychobiology, Social and
Emotional Development
Minor: English
Grade Point Average: 3.75 (Possible 4.0)
Honors: Dean's List, 200- to 200-
Leonard E. Frank Scholarship, 200-

Academic
history to
highlight
training

Honors
listed

200- to 200-: William Rainey Harper College
Phi Theta Kappa Honor Society
Editor, The Harbinger, Campus Newspaper
Basketball and Track Teams, 200- and 200-

Experience:
200- to present: Orderly, Weldon Memorial Hospital, East
Lansing, MI
Duties: tutoring long-term adolescent
patients, providing physical care and
recreational therapy

Work
experience
listed in
reverse
chronological
order

200- and 200-: Camp Counselor, Camp Onewata, Schroon
Lake, NY
Duties: tutored and supervised
recreation at this camp for
developmentally disabled children,
ages 8-14

199- to 200-:	East Lansing Boys Club, East Lansing, MI
	Duties: supervised group recreation
Skills and Interests:	Languages: Spanish and English
	Computers and Word Processing:
	Microsoft Word, WordPerfect, Adobe
	PageMaker
	Campus organizer: US congressional
	campaign of Alma Washington, 200-
References:	References and credentials available
	upon request

Relevant activities or accomplishments

- Allow for an appropriate amount of white space. Too little white space produces a difficult-to-read document; too much suggests you have few qualifications.

- Use boldface or italic type for highlights. Avoid fancy fonts and visual effects.

- Proofread your résumé repeatedly to be sure it's letter perfect.

- Choose good quality white or off-white paper of at least 20 lb. weight. Use a laser printer.

- Send print originals rather than photocopies. Never send a traditional and a scannable résumé in the same envelope. Use a $9^1/_2 \times 12$ inch envelope.

- Always send a cover letter of approximately one page in which you explain the position you want and why you're a good candidate. Emphasize the connection between your qualifications and the position, but avoid merely repeating your résumé.

3 ■ Preparing a scannable résumé

You may need to prepare a résumé to be scanned into a computer database, or wish to send one on disk, attach it to an e-mail, or post it on a Web site. In such cases, your first reader will be, not a human being, but a computer. Follow these guidelines to create a machine-friendly résumé.

- List the key words for which your résumé will be scanned. Choose nouns to refer to your qualifications and the job you want, for example, *child care worker* rather than *worked extensively with children*. Study company publications to find the right words to use. Repeat these words two or three times in your résumé or put them in a separate section at the beginning.

- If you'll send a print copy of a scannable résumé, use plain white paper.

- Make your résumé easy to scan: Left justify all lines. Use plain (ASCII) text and a simple sans serif font, such as Geneva, in 10–14 point size, using the larger fonts for headings. Avoid bullets, italics, underlining, and fancy fonts; if you must emphasize, use asterisks (*) or plus (+) signs. Avoid punctuation as much as possible. Keep your lines short, with sixty-five to seventy characters.

- For a file name, use your last name followed by your first.

- Place your name on top on its own line, followed by your address, phone number, and e-mail address, each on its own line.

- Test your format by sending your résumé to a friend as an e-mail and as an attachment. If you will mail your scannable résumé, print it on a laser printer; do not fold or staple it. If you send it electronically, send a separate print version. In either case, add a cover letter.

The opening of a scannable résumé:

```
Matthew R. Leigh
1201 W. Chase Avenue
East Lansing, MI 48824
Phone: (517) 555-1541
Fax: (517) 555-6039
E-mail: mleigh@aol.com


Keywords: child care worker, summer intern, child
psychologist, child psychology, autism, English, Phi Theta
Kappa, editor, orderly, tutor, recreational supervisor,
institutional setting


POSITION DESIRED
Child Care Worker-Summer Intern


CAREER OBJECTIVE
Child psychologist working with autistic children in an
institutional setting


EDUCATION
Michigan State University, 200- to 200-, Child Psychology
major, English minor
```

62.4
Career sites:
Web link

62d Make effective oral presentations

1 ■ Speaking in public

If you're among the large group of people who report that public speaking is one of life's most nerve-wracking experiences, you can calm your nerves by recognizing three things: (1) Most audiences that you appear before will be sympathetic, wishing you well and probably not even noticing whatever nervousness you might feel. (2) In many respects, public speaking has much in common with writing; what you know about good writing is also true about effective oral presentations. (3) The key to your success as both writer and speaker is preparation.

Preparing an oral presentation

62.5
Preparing
and
delivering
an oral
presenta-
tion:
Web link

- Begin your preparation by considering the audience who will hear you.

- Decide on your goal for your audience.

- As you gather the materials for your speech, look for things that will make you interesting to listen to: surprising facts or statistics, thought-provoking assertions, challenging questions, interesting stories that dramatize your point, illuminating quotations.

- Organize your speech in the traditional three-part design. Your **introduction** should announce your goal, provide a sketch outline of your speech, and earn credibility for what you'll say. (For tips on earning credibility, see 59b.) The **body of your speech** should have a clear order; one might be to anticipate reader questions and then answer them one by one. Your **conclusion** should answer the question, "So what?" Why have your listeners listened to you? What should they remember? What should they do now?

- Prepare an outline from which you'll speak. Keep it to one page if possible. Writing out a speech to read or trying to memorize a speech will only hinder your effectiveness.

- Practice your presentation. Review your outline several times; record your speech and listen to your tone of voice, clarity, speaking pace, and the way your speech holds together.

Delivering your presentation

- If you can, make an advance check of the room where you'll speak. What are the conditions that will influence how you sound? What equipment will you need? If the lights will be dimmed, bring a small flashlight to adjust equipment or to read from your speaking outline.

- As you speak, make eye contact with your audience, use natural gestures, and aim to project your feelings for your subject. Speak slowly but conversationally. Keep your sentences short but varied. Make your language "pictorial" to help listeners "see" what you mean. Use frequent repetition of key words and transitions to link ideas and guide your listeners, point by point, through your presentation. Remember: readers can reread a difficult text, but listeners cannot rehear a speech that is unclear or difficult to follow.

2 ■ Using presentation media to support your speech

Presentation media range from simple overhead transparencies, posters, and slides, all the way to multimedia software such as Microsoft's PowerPoint. They help speakers to organize, illustrate, and dramatize the main points of a speech. If you have occasion to use multimedia for a presentation, remember that listening is more difficult than reading. Design your presentation to help your audience follow your spoken words.

- Be sure that visuals are clear, legible, and instantly recognizable from the farthest part of the room in which you will be speaking.

- Each visual should have one main point. Use visuals to add impact, tone, or a frame of reference (the "big picture") to what you are saying. Never use visuals merely for decoration.

- Make visuals simple, but beware of using visuals that oversimplify your ideas.

- Use bullets or outlines to highlight main points; limit each visual to just a few lines of text. Choose simple, easy-to-see sans serif fonts.

- Use only a few colors; choose them for their emotional associations.

- Design each visual with natural eye movement in mind. (For more on layout, font selection, and color, see 46a.)

62e Write persuasive proposals

A **proposal** is a detailed plan of action sent to a reader or readers for their approval. Proposals may be solicited, written in response to a "Request for a Proposal" statement (an RFP) that specifies guidelines for the proposal, or they may be unsolicited, prompted by the writer's desire to initiate action. In either case, approach a proposal as a problem-solving activity: a problem exists at work or in some other organization, and you're going to show interested readers how to solve it. Regard these readers as skeptical; they won't accept your proposal unless you're persuasive. Therefore, you should investigate the problem and your solution thoroughly. Consider counterproposals. What makes yours better? Prove to your readers that your proposal is workable and financially realistic.

Proposals vary in style and format, but are similar to arguments and formal reports. (See Chapters 58, 59, and 62f.) Divide your presentation into the following parts: purpose statement (what you're proposing), a statement of the problem (proving that it exists and that its effects must be dealt with), your solution (including the implementation, those involved with the solution, and the costs), and a conclusion (a reminder of the serious nature of the problem, why action needs to be taken, and why your proposal is the best response).

62.6
How to
write a
proposal:
Web link

62f Choose your options for writing an effective report

A **report** is a systematic presentation of information to a specific audience for a specific purpose. The reports you'll write in college and on the job may take several forms: informal memo or letter reports, technical field or lab reports, informative reports, problem-solution reports, progress reports, proposals, and case studies.

1 ▪ Preliminary activities

Your preliminary preparations will be similar to those for other investigative writing: surveying the situation (see 1d), posing key questions or describing the problem, and identifying your purpose (see 47a2). You will gather the information for your report from appropriate sources: interviews, minutes, letters, questionnaires, surveys, experimentation, direct observation, published reports, and other documents. (For guidelines to research, see Chapters 47–49.) When you finish your investigation, write out your **conclusion**, the point of your report supported by your information (see 2d4).

2 ▪ Organizing a report

62.7
Writing
reports:
Web link

Prepare an informal report as you would a letter, memo, or essay, with an appropriate beginning, middle, and end. Formal reports generally consist of (1) prefatory parts such as a cover, title page, letters of authorization or acceptance, acknowledgments, a table of contents, an abstract, and an executive summary; (2) the text of the report, including an introduction, body, and conclusion; (3) supplementary parts such as an appendix, bibliography, or index. Include all parts relevant to your report and required by your readers. Follow these guidelines to organize the text of your report:

▪ *Introduction.* The introduction includes all elements necessary to orient your readers and help them understand your information: a statement of the problem or key questions, a description of materials and methods, background or history, definitions, a review of relevant published research, or an overview of the presentation to follow.

- *Body.* The body of a report is often labeled *Results, Data, Findings,* or *Discussion.* The results and discussion may be separated or combined, depending on their relationship, the length of the report, and your readers' needs. Organize the body of a report according to topics, chronology, importance, or other logical patterns. (See 6b.)

- *Conclusion.* A conclusion summarizes information, makes generalizations about it (comparisons, causes and effects, classifications, estimations, predictions), poses solutions to problems, makes evaluations and recommendations, or proposes action.

- *Inductive or deductive organization.* For readers who need detailed explanation or who may resist your recommendations without a full presentation of the case, organize the text of your report in an *inductive* or conclusion-last order: introduction, body, conclusion. For busy readers who may not read the entire report, who will agree with you, or who want your opinion promptly, use a *deductive* or conclusion-first order: introduction, conclusion, body.

3 ▪ Formatting and style

- *Headings.* Informal reports are usually written as continuous documents, undivided except for paragraphing. The text of formal reports is usually divided by headings into clearly labeled parts: *Introduction, Background, Discussion, Conclusion,* and so forth. (For guidelines to effective headings, see 46b1.)

- *Visual aids.* Use lists, tables, and graphics to illustrate and group information as well as to help your readers understand it (see 46b and c).

- *Style.* Generally write in the present tense unless you have a good reason for using the past tense: *This report recommends . . .* (see 13b1). Choose concrete, specific words as specialized as the subject requires and reader understanding will allow (see 26a and b). Except in conclusions, avoid generalities. Also avoid emotionally charged words that may make your report sound biased (see 25b).

- *Documentation.* Cite the sources of borrowed information in an appropriate format. (For Modern Language Association guidelines, see Chapters 52 and 53; for American Psychological Association guidelines, see 55a–c; for other formats, see the style manuals listed in Chapter 57.)

4 ▪ Sample formal report

For a sample formal report written in the American Psychological Association style, see 55d.

Writing Online

63 Writing Online

63a Communicate by e-mail

1 ■ Writing effective e-mail messages

Writing and reading e-mail messages has become as much a feature of everyday life as deleting the spam that too often clutters e-mail in-boxes and makes it difficult to distinguish important messages from the unsolicited mail. To make sure your e-mail gets read and not trashed by your intended readers, begin by writing a clear "subject" line of three to four words that identifies the contents of your message. Then, if possible, begin your message with its most important part, or announce the point of your e-mail. Conclude with an electronic signature: your name, title when appropriate, e-mail address, and important numbers (fax, telephone, voice mail). Your mail software will probably enable you to create a signature file (called a *sig. file*), inserted automatically at the end of your message.

HOW TO . . . Format an E-Mail Message

1. *Text.* Write in plain text (ASCII text). Many e-mail programs lack the full features of word processors. Avoid tabs and other computer commands you would normally use to format text.

2. *Line length.* Keep your lines short, about 60 to 70 characters, to avoid inappropriate line wrap.

3. *Paragraph length.* Write brief, letter-style paragraphs. Double space between them.

4. *Message length.* When possible, keep your message brief, about 250 words or one screen.

5. *Underlining.* Use a single underlining mark before and after text that you would italicize or underline in a print document.

    Henry David Thoreau's_Walden_recommends simple living but not poverty.

6. *Asterisks to replace italics and underlining.* If your e-mail application does not support italics or underlining, use asterisks.

    Poverty is *not* what Thoreau had in mind.

7. *Hyphens and Internet addresses (URLs).* Never add a hyphen when you break an Internet address at the end of a line. The MLA guideline is to break only after a slashmark (/). (See also 48a4.)

8. *Angle brackets (< ... >) and Internet addresses (URLs).* In the text of your message, enclose Internet addresses, including e-mail, in angle brackets: < http://www.nps.gov >. Do not add additional punctuation within the angle brackets.

9. *All-capitals format.* Avoid writing in ALL CAPITALS, a difficult-to-read and emotionally intense style known as "shouting."

10. *Deleting original messages from replies.* When you reply to an e-mail, some programs automatically reproduce the sender's message at the beginning of your reply. Except for passages you wish to quote, delete the original message, especially the header.

11. *Using emoticons and abbreviations.* Use emoticons (typographic images) and e-mail abbreviations only in casual communication with people you know well. (See 63a3.)

2 ▪ Attaching files to e-mail

The attachments feature of most e-mail programs enables you to link a file to an e-mail message and send the file with its own formatting intact. This feature is valuable for sending papers to instructors or graphics to friends and family. To ensure a successful transfer, keep the process as simple as possible. Send text files in plain (ASCII) text or in Rich Text Format (RTF). Use the SAVE AS feature of your word processor and the format option to make this translation. When attaching images, keep the file sizes small to facilitate downloading.

If you're communicating across computer platforms, between a Macintosh and a PC, things may get tricky. To ensure compatibility between computers, you may need a translator program like MacLink Plus. In any case, always include information about an attachment within your e-mail message: file type, its size, and the program that created it.

When you receive an e-mail with an attachment, open it only if you know the sender. It may contain a virus that could damage your files or computer. Anti-virus software, such as Norton AntiVirus, will scan attachments before you open them. Save your downloaded attachments in a special "My Documents" or "Downloads" directory (folder).

3 ▪ Writing effectively online: Netiquette

To communicate effectively, successfully, and happily on the Internet, observe the following guidelines, often referred to as **Netiquette**.

- *Subject lines.* Use e-mail subject lines to identify your topic and to guide your reader's response. Use these abbreviations: FYI for nonurgent messages, URGENT for time-sensitive messages, LONG for long messages. Change the subject line when replying.

- *Openers and closers.* Begin your message with a brief greeting to set the tone: *Hi Annie* or *Dear Dr. Masood.* Include a brief appropriate closing (*Bye* or *Sincerely*) followed by your signature file.

- *Brevity.* Keep your messages short and to the point. However, there is no need to have a "telegram" style of clipped sentences and lots of abbreviations.

63.1
Netiquette:
Web link

- *Formality.* Adjust your formality to fit the occasion. Online messages addressed to friends and coworkers are often as informal as casual conversation, with all the slang, abbreviations, and sentence fragments you would expect to hear in speech. Online messages addressed to strangers or anonymous readers should sound somewhat more formal, suitable to your topic and purpose for communicating. To achieve the appropriate degree of formality for your messages, follow the guidelines in 27a–d.

- *Confidentiality.* E-mail is public. Never use it to send confidential messages.

- *Editing.* Edit online communication as the occasion requires. With informal online communication, readers are generally tolerant of minor errors and typos. But always reread your messages to see that you've said what you intended. Then check to see that your writing is relatively free of error. And if your e-mail program has a spell checker, run it.

- *Writing in anger.* Never send a message when angry or upset.

- *Expressing your attitude.* Irony, sarcasm, and humor are often difficult to decipher in e-mail. Use them carefully. In informal messages, emoticons will convey your attitude.

- *Emoticons and abbreviations.* For informal online messages, the following emoticon symbols and abbreviations help to convey the meanings behind your words. Beware of overuse.

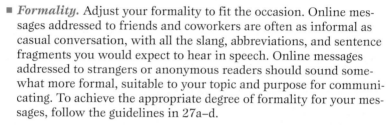

:-)	smile	AFAIK	as far as I know
;-)	wink	IMO	in my opinion
:-(	frown	IMHO	in my humble opinion
< g >	grin	BTW	by the way
< vbg >	very big grin	OTOH	on the other hand
		CU	see you

- *Responding to e-mail.* Reply promptly. Change the subject lines of the original message and, if necessary, delete the original message. Obtain the sender's permission before forwarding an e-mail.

63b Contribute to—or create—online discussions

1 ▪ Newsgroups

To find Internet newsgroups whose discussions you'd like to join, see 48c1. To participate, you may need to download special software or to register. The individual newsgroup or the newsgroup host, such as Google Groups, will give you information. Responding to newsgroup postings or starting your own discussion is much like sending any other e-mail. Observe the tips in "How to Format an E-Mail Message," pp. 492–493, the Netiquette section (63a3), and the following additional guidelines.

- *Lurking.* Before participating in a newsgroup, familiarize yourself with the discussion by reviewing the postings, a process known as "lurking." Follow the group's own Netiquette.

- *Audience.* Be courteous to the group, and keep your comments relevant. Because participants may come from many countries, make sure your cultural and geographic references are clear.

- *Off-subject messages and personal replies to questions.* Reply privately to off-subject messages by responding to the sender's personal e-mail address. So, too, with questions: reply to the questioner's personal e-mail rather than the whole group.

- *Focus.* Limit each message to one topic.

- *Quotations.* When you quote, edit the quotation down to what's relevant to your message. Use quotation marks and give the source of all quotations.

- *Empty replies.* Avoid mere agreement or disagreement or sending out what is already well known.

- *Spamming.* Avoid cross-posting to multiple groups.

- *Attachments.* To direct your readers to Web sites, simply include the addresses (URLs) in your message. Avoid attachments to e-mail newsgroup postings.

2 ▪ Listservs

To identify and join subscription discussion groups (listservs), see 48c2. You'll participate in a listserv via e-mail, as you would a regular newsgroup. Observe the tips in "How to Format an E-Mail Message," pp. 492–493, the Netiquette sections (63a3 and 63b1), and the following additional guidelines.

- *Using personal addresses.* Subscribe to a listserv using your personal e-mail address rather than a shared group address.

- *Using the subscription address.* Subscribe to the subscription address rather than the posting address. A subscription address looks like this: < LISTSERV@[the name of the host] >.

- *Letter of confirmation.* For future reference, save your letter of subscription confirmation and its important information.

- *Unsubscribing.* If you're going to be away from your computer for more than a week, unsubscribe or suspend mail delivery. Your subscription letter will explain how.

3 ▪ Weblogs

A Weblog (or "blog") is, literally, a "log" posted on the World Wide Web, a series of dated entries compiled by an individual writer (a "blogger"), writing about a topic of personal or professional interest. Weblogs differ from regular Web pages in the frequency with which they are updated. In their effect, they are a cross between an online journal and a diary, or as someone has remarked, because Weblogs invite replies from readers, they might be considered a cross between a newspaper column and talk radio.

The uses of Weblogs. As a student, you might encounter a Weblog as part of a college course, by which an instructor expands on classroom remarks, updates course information, makes assignments, provides links to online resources, or invites student comments. You might even be asked to create your own Weblog to develop a public writing voice, gather the materials for writing assignments, post drafts of your assignments for peer review and commentary, or create a portfolio of your work during a course.

Features of a Weblog. All Weblogs generally have the same features: a series of posts (anything from brief statements to full-length essays) arranged in reverse chronological order, most recent first; headers or footers for each post, giving the date and time of the posting; a title for each post; a "permalink" address (often the time of the post) that links to an archived version of each post; the name or nickname of the writer of the post; comments on individual posts; space for new comments to be made; often a series of links to other sites (the "blogroll") of interest to the "blogger"; and sometimes a calendar that enables readers to search the sites's archives for a specific post. See the sample post from John Chen's Weblog about bicycle commuting on p. 497.

Creating your own Weblog. One reason Weblogs are growing so quickly in popularity (nearly 2.5 million blogs by 2004) is that they are easy to create. You have several options, but the easiest and least expensive is to use a hosted Weblog service such as Blogger (< http://www.blogger.com >), Pitas.com (< http://www.pitas.com >), or Manila Sites (< http://www .manilasites.com >).

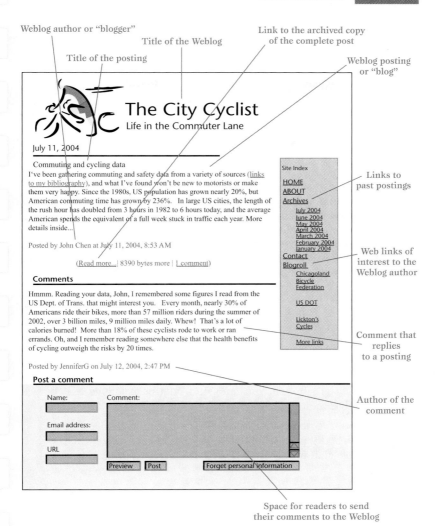

Weblog author or "blogger"

Title of the Weblog

Title of the posting

Link to the archived copy
of the complete post

Weblog posting
or "blog"

The City Cyclist
Life in the Commuter Lane

July 11, 2004

Commuting and cycling data

I've been gathering commuting and safety data from a variety of sources (links to my bibliography), and what I've found won't be new to motorists or make them very happy. Since the 1980s, US population has grown nearly 20%, but American commuting time has grown by 236%. In large US cities, the length of the rush hour has doubled from 3 hours in 1982 to 6 hours today, and the average American spends the equivalent of a full week stuck in traffic each year. More details inside...

Posted by John Chen at July 11, 2004, 8:53 AM

(Read more... | 8390 bytes more | 1 comment)

Comments

Hmmm. Reading your data, John, I remembered some figures I read from the US Dept. of Trans. that might interest you. Every month, nearly 30% of Americans ride their bikes, more than 57 million riders during the summer of 2002, over 3 billion miles, 9 million miles daily. Whew! That's a lot of calories burned! More than 18% of these cyclists rode to work or ran errands. Oh, and I remember reading somewhere else that the health benefits of cycling outweigh the risks by 20 times.

Posted by JenniferG on July 12, 2004, 2:47 PM

Post a comment

Name:

Email address:

URL

Comment:

[Preview] [Post]   [Forget personal information]

Site Index

HOME
ABOUT
Archives
  July 2004
  June 2004
  May 2004
  April 2004
  March 2004
  February 2004
  January 2004
Contact
Blogroll
  Chicagoland
  Bicycle
  Federation

  US DOT

  Lickton's
  Cycles

  More links

Links to
past postings

Web links of
interest to the
Weblog author

Comment that
replies
to a posting

Author of the
comment

Space for readers to send
their comments to the Weblog

Writing a successful Weblog.

- A successful Weblog not only expresses the blogger's ideas and opinions but gathers a group of interested readers. Whether you're writing to fellow students or a wider audience, begin with a definite audience in mind.

- A successful Weblog has a distinctive voice. Find a voice and online writing style that you feel comfortable with and that are suitable for writing about the topics that interest you. (See 2c for tips to create an effective writer's persona.)

- A successful Weblog is "reader friendly," with frequent updates, links to fresh and original sites, navigational cues, brief posts, and links to longer archived documents.

- The style of a successful Weblog is personal, precise, brief, vivid, and edited for grammar, punctuation, and spelling (unlike informal e-mail).

4 ▪ "Real-Time" Communication

E-mail, newsgroups, listservs, and Weblogs are examples of **asynchronous** communication. That is, the sender and the receiver of a message may not necessarily be online at the same time. But when you use instant messaging software or when you participate in an online class discussion through such software as WebCT or Blackboard, it's as if you're talking on the telephone. Writers and readers are all online at the same time, and you're engaged in **synchronous**—or "real-time"—communication. To participate in these "chat room" discussions, follow the Netiquette guidelines (63a3 and 63b1), as well as the following.

- Even though the software may announce your arrival or your departure from the group, when a break is appropriate, introduce yourself or say good-bye.

- Online discussions can sometimes be chaotic or fragmented. Use your remarks to give helpful replies to others' questions and to develop and test your own ideas. Stay on topics that interest you; don't lose sight of what you can gain from this exchange. See the sample chat room exchange on p. 24.

- "Chat room" conversation is usually pretty informal. Don't worry too much about producing flawless typing. Focus on your ideas. (See the sample chat room discussion in 2a3.)

63c Create Web documents

Creating documents for the Web has become an increasingly popular assignment in writing classes. Your project may be as straightforward as reformatting a paper for posting on a class Web site, or you may be involved in something more elaborate, such as designing a Web page or even a complete Web site, containing a number of related pages. (See the sample Web pages on p. 499 and p. 502.) Whatever your project, the following guidelines will introduce you to successful Web design.

1 ▪ Understanding HTML

The code used to produce a Web page, called HyperText Markup Language (HTML), tells an Internet browser how and where to display text, graphics, colors, and video on a computer screen. HTML is not dif-

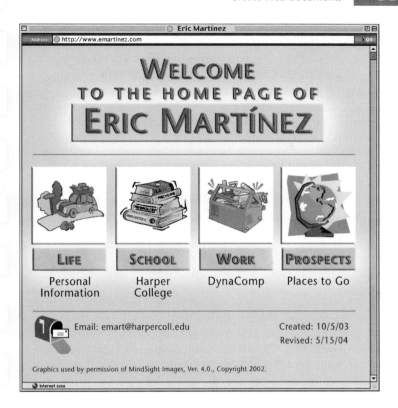

http://www.emartinez.com

WELCOME
TO THE HOME PAGE OF
ERIC MARTÍNEZ

LIFE	SCHOOL	WORK	PROSPECTS
Personal Information	Harper College	DynaComp	Places to Go

Email: emart@harpercoll.edu

Created: 10/5/03
Revised: 5/15/04

Graphics used by permission of MindSight Images, Ver. 4.0., Copyright 2002.

ficult to learn, but it's easier to use a Web layout program (called a Web page editor) to produce your page. The best known are Adobe PageMill, ClarisWorks, Netscape Composer, and Microsoft's FrontPage; some are free over the Internet. You may even be able to use your own word processor. Such programs enable you to make a page look the way you want it to, and the software writes the necessary HTML code for you.

2 ▪ Analyzing your project

- *Audience.* Begin planning a Web document as you would any writing project, by identifying your audience: their interests, reading skills, computer skills, and time for reading your Web page.

- *Purpose.* What do you want viewers to get from your document: information about you or about some topic, instruction, persuasion, entertainment?

- *Unity.* What theme, thesis, or main idea will hold the parts of your document together, both text and visuals?

- *Visual design.* Think about the visual nature of the medium. What can you do with visuals, color, and layout to focus visitors on what's important? (See the guidelines in 46a.) Explore the World Wide Web for pages like the one you have in mind. What makes them successful or not? Use your browser to reveal the page's HTML code.

■ *An ISP.* You'll need an Internet service provider (ISP) to display your Web document. If you're just getting started, you'll upload your document to your class Web site or use your school's server. See your instructor, your computer center, or the computer center's help desk. However, you may also use an Internet service provider like America Online or Microsoft Network or an Internet hosting site such as GeoCities (< http://www.geocities.com >).

3 ■ Formatting papers for posting online

If you're asked to post a paper at a class Web site or on an online bulletin board, you'll have to reformat it for online viewing and save it as an HTML document.

■ *Background.* Use a light background for ease of reading.

■ *Chunking.* Chunk your text for ease of reading. Provide headings to subdivide your paper into manageable parts. Then divide your text into brief paragraphs that can be easily read on a screen. Use the block paragraph format: do not indent first lines, leave space between paragraphs. To facilitate skimming and locating particular passages, put a paragraph number within brackets at the beginning of each paragraph, like so: *[12]*.

■ *Fonts and line length.* For ease of on-screen reading, choose a standard sans serif font like Geneva and a line length of 70–80 characters.

■ *Links.* If you provide a table of contents or an outline, provide internal (or "relative") links that connect headings in this preliminary matter to specific parts of your paper. In your works cited, provide external (or "absolute") links that connect individual citations to the actual online sources (see the note in 52b14).

■ *Saving your paper as an HTML document.* After you have reformatted your paper, save it as an HTML document. Use the SAVE AS feature of your word processor or copy and paste your paper into an HTML editor such as Adobe PageMill or Microsoft's Front Page.

4 ■ Designing Web pages and Web sites

■ *Design for visual coherence.* As you design your Web page, sketch it out on paper as a story board or flow chart. Include a "content list" identifying each piece of information you'll include on your page. Which pieces of information should come early, which later?

■ *Focus.* Give your page focus by making all images and text relate in some direct way to the topic and purpose of the page. No matter how striking the visual, if it doesn't contribute to fulfilling your purpose, it will only distract.

- *Size.* Keep your page brief, if possible. Format so that it fits comfortably on a thirteen-inch monitor. Also, keep your text brief. If you have lots to say, break it into screen-size chunks, each with its own heading. Leave space around blocks of text. If your document is large and you expect readers will want to print all of it, provide a "printer-friendly" option or format it as a single Web page rather than a series of pages.

- *Web writing style.* Write in a style that's easy to read on screen: Summarize first or put your main points in your first paragraph, so readers who skim won't miss your main idea. Be concise and brief. Use highlighting, headings, and lists to aid readers looking for your main idea, but avoid cluttering your text with too many different textual features.

- *Fonts.* Choose one or only a few easy-to-read fonts. (See 46a3.) Use sans-serif fonts for text, serif fonts for headings (the opposite of writing for a print environment). Size your fonts so text is easy to read on screen.

- *Visuals.* Keep the file size of graphics or video small so they will load quickly. And allow for a text-only viewing option for your page.

- *Color.* Use color consistently and "lightly." Avoid many different colors; avoid dark colors for backgrounds and very light colors for text. Use one color for headings, another for text. (See also 46a5.) Be sure to choose from the 216 "browser-safe" colors that display reliably on Web browsers. Programs like Color Schemer or Color Wheel Pro will help you use colors effectively.

- *Arrangement.* Lay out your page so that it is visually appealing and aids reading. (See 46a1.) You may wish to divide a complex page into frames, each with its own scroll bar, but note that such pages are difficult for visually impaired viewers to use.

- *Navigation buttons.* If your page is more than two or three screens, use navigation buttons at the top, bottom, and sides to aid reader movement through the document.

- *Links.* Decide what other pages or sites you want to link to yours. Avoid cluttering a page with too many links. Consider creating subordinate, intermediate pages with branching links to subtopics. And clearly label your links so that readers know where they're going before they click.

Note: It is courteous to ask other Web page owners' permission before linking to their pages. (See the sample links Web page on p. 502.)

One major principle of site design is consistency. If you wish to combine a series of related pages into a Web site, begin by drawing a site map identifying each page and its relation (coordinate or subordinate) to the others. All pages should have a similar appearance and work together harmoniously. Your home page will probably act as a template, guiding your choice of background, colors, fonts, graphics, and links to other pages.

Once you've decided what pages will comprise your site, plan how to link them:

- *Back and forth links.* Link your home page individually to each subordinate page.

- *Cascading links.* Link your home page to a second page, which has a link to a third page, which is linked to another, and so forth.

- *Pyramid links.* Link so that readers can move two or more pages from your home page and then return.

- *Full linkage.* Every page is linked to every other.

63.3
Publishing
on the
Web:
Web link

5 ■ Creating, testing, and publishing your page

Compose a draft of your Web page in your regular word processing program rather than in HTML. You'll find it easier to revise. When the

63.4
Web design
resources:
Web link

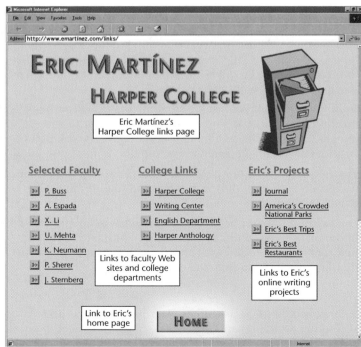

text of your page satisfies you, compose the window in which it'll appear, transfer the text to it, and save your page as an HTML document using your word processor or an HTML editor program. If you're creating a Web site, repeat the process for each page.

If you intend to display graphics that you've taken from the Internet or other copyrighted source, you'll have to get permission to use them, unless they are accompanied by an explicit "free-use" statement. (See 51c for permission procedures.) As you incorporate graphics, accompany them with a credit line, for which HTML code has a specific tag. For anything you borrow under "fair use" conventions, credit its source. (See 51a.)

When you've created and revised your page or site, ask peer reviewers to critique it. Is it easy to use? Appealing? Does it fulfill your purpose? Open your pages in different browsers and on both Macintosh and Windows computers to see how everything looks. Do your images appear where you want them? Make sure that everything loads accurately and quickly. Test your links. Check with your Internet service provider for procedures for transferring your page or site to a computer server. Then, once you've published your work, update it regularly and recheck all links.

Appendix: Answers to Exercises

Part II: Sentence Editing

11.1—FIXING FRAGMENTS

1. The causes of social status are many: the possession of money, education, relationship to political power, the accidents of birth or geography, even physical appearance.
2. Strategies in chess are determined by the designated movements of each piece as well as the initial arrangement of the pieces on the board.
3. Correct
4. The majority of smokers begin to smoke as teenagers, seventy-five percent by age seventeen, eighty-nine percent by age nineteen.
5. Gena lay awake throughout the storm, listening to the branches of the ancient crabapple scratching the side of her house.

12.1—FIXING COMMA SPLICES

1. As we stood at the grave side, we had no words to share with one another. We had only our silent sorrow.
2. I was involved in a serious accident during my sophomore year of high school; ironically, it occurred on the last day of driver's ed.
3. Correct
4. Women and girls have little reason to fear hemophilia, or bleeder's disease; usually only males are affected.
5. Correct

12.2—FIXING FUSED SENTENCES

1. Pessimists never hope for the best; they always expect the worst.
2. Losing her second job in six months didn't seem to bother Charlene. She took the disappointment with her usual wisecrack and a grin.
3. When they were less than two years old, the Fox children were put in a foster home and grew up knowing nothing of what had happened to their parents.
4. My background is similar to Irene's. My mother is Spanish and came to the US just before I was born.
5. Correct

13.1—EDITING VERB TENSES

1. We returned home from California by the same route that had taken us there.
2. More movies have been made of *Romeo and Juliet* than any other Shakespeare play.
3. At Matt and Joe's funeral, we laughed as much as we cried, remembering all the good times we had had with them.
4. Correct
5. Throughout the history of the United States, minorities and women have been discriminated against.

14.1—EDITING SUBJECT-VERB AGREEMENT

1. People who have been laid off or downsized know why economics is referred to as "the dismal science."
2. John Knudsen's paintings and sculpture are varied in technique but always devoted to urban themes.
3. The silence of the brooding, majestic pines and firs creates a somber mood in the park's visitors.
4. In recent months, there have been several cases of Dengue fever reported in Texas.
5. Commerce Secretary Ron Brown, in addition to his staff and the plane's crew, was killed in the crash.

15.1—EDITING PRONOUN-ANTECEDENT AGREEMENT

1. When my parents sat me down to tell me of their divorce, I heard their words, but none of them made any sense.
2. Everyone experiences depression at some point in his or her life.
3. Hideaway Resort is widely known for its inexpensive but comfortable and activity-filled vacations.
4. Correct
5. Unable to speak the language and knowing little about local customs, we did what anyone would do for protection from con artists and thieves.

16.1—EDITING PRONOUN REFERENCE

1. Karen had no desire to taste the goat's milk, and she was certain she didn't want to milk the goat.
2. Betty shared the exciting news about her winning lottery ticket with Adele.
3. Morale at my company is low because employees don't know one another or understand any job besides their own. This situation makes it difficult to increase productivity.
4. Avid readers should stop at the Book Nook for the weekly specials on adult and children's books of all kinds.
5. In today's highly mobile society, a person can easily lose touch with family members who have been forced to relocate as part of their jobs.

17.1—EDITING PRONOUN CASE FORMS

1. Correct
2. Janet, Jeffrey, Patricia, and I will be pleased to help with the Oxfam Fund Drive.
3. As my two friends and I were setting up our tents at sunset, we looked up and saw four or five black bears near the edge of the woods.
4. We will sell the antique telephone to whoever makes us the best offer.
5. I was delighted when Edward gave my husband and me two tickets to the new Tom Stoppard play.

18.1—EDITING ADJECTIVES AND ADVERBS

1. Correct
2. The man in the clown suit and greasy makeup looked at me peculiarly.
3. Correct
4. Joshua had the happiest of childhoods.
5. On the balance beam, Sharon performed well.

19.1—EDITING FAULTY PARALLELISM

1. The campsites in many national parks have electricity and running water.
2. According to a recent Canadian study, the keys to financial success are education, hard work, and the avoidance of risks.
3. Today, many college students use the Internet to register for classes and to reserve seats for special on-campus events.
4. As my father's cancer worsened, he debated whether to end the painful chemotherapy or continue to battle his terrible disease.
5. Erin would rather spend her weekend surfing the Internet on her computer than dancing the night away at a fancy club.

20.1—EDITING THE ACTIVE AND PASSIVE VOICE

1. Writers of arguments should take care to use only facts and generally accepted truths.
2. Correct [present perfect tense, intransitive verbs]
3. Correct [present tense, passive voice]
4. Genetic engineers have inserted a polyester gene into a cotton plant in order to grow wrinkle-free fibers as warm as wool.
5. Between 1900 and 1972, more than 150 innocent men were condemned to die by US courts, and at least 23 of them were executed.

20.2—EMPHASIZING WITH SUBORDINATION AND COORDINATION

1. In one version of the story of Lady Godiva, she was observed by only one person, a tailor, the original Peeping Tom, who was struck blind by what he saw.
2. Although lightning is usually associated with thunderstorms, it may also be produced by snowstorms, sandstorms, even the clouds over erupting volcanoes.
3. Ball lightning, a spherical flash, varies in size from three to three hundred feet in diameter and lasts less than five seconds.
4. The abominable snowman, also known as the "yeti," is a giant creature that supposedly roams the mountains at night looking for victims.
5. It is described as having an upright posture, a covering of black to reddish hair, and the appearance of a bear, ape, or human.

23.1—EDITING MISPLACED MODIFIERS

1. Albert intended to eat only one chocolate-covered doughnut.
2. As the months passed, dust began to thicken on bookcases, file cabinets, and desks.
3. After paddling our canoes for twelve hours, none of us thought night would ever come.
4. On the walls of the restaurant are large frames containing records and tapes of famous musical artists plated with silver, gold, and platinum.
5. After a lunch break, I was walking back to the courthouse where I was serving on jury duty.

23.2—EDITING DANGLING MODIFIERS

1. Chef Edgar has served diners throughout Europe, including royalty.
2. From watching people toss a frisbee around in the park, I think playing with it must be very relaxing.

3. When the championship game is over, we hope the victory flag will be hoisted over our stadium.
4. Life becomes more difficult for most young people after they reach what lawyers call the age of accountability.
5. Some jobs are not satisfying or glamorous but do pay good wages, working in a supermarket, for instance.

27.1—EDITING FOR WORDS APPROPRIATE TO ACADEMIC AND PUBLIC WRITING

1. The years following the stock market crash of 1929 were difficult for almost all Americans.
2. Cynical politicians profess their support for election finance reform—until they are elected.
3. My low aptitude test scores almost denied me admission to college. I was accepted at two state schools, however.
4. The writer Oscar Ramírez explores the way in which American culture interacts with immigrant cultures and is transformed.
5. By installing tape recorders in his White House office, President Richard Nixon made his impeachment and the conviction of his friends possible.

28.1—EDITING FOR WORDINESS

1. Some elderly people resist seeing themselves as old.
2. When the Christmas holidays come, I purchase all of my gifts from catalogs.
3. Bide-a-Wee Resort has a wide variety of campsites: pull-through sites with electricity and water, electricity-only sites, and primitive sites carved into bluffs.
4. Many kinds of waste toxins linger in landfills, polluting the soil and ground water for dozens, even hundreds of years.
5. An executive secretary is more an administrative assistant than clerk or typist.

30.1—EDITING ARTICLES AND QUANTIFIERS

1. After hiking two more miles, we found an easy way down the mountain.
2. Territorial behavior is expressed by humans and animals alike.
3. Finally, soccer is becoming a popular game in the United States.
4. Every Friday evening I go out to eat with several of my friends.
5. Although I'm not a musician, I enjoy music very much, and the music I enjoy most is jazz.

31.1—EDITING FOR CORRECT VERB FORMS

1. By the time I received my flu shot I had already had the flu twice this year.
2. When the hurricane struck, our car was sitting under two huge palm trees.
3. Hasn't anyone ever told you that cigars can be as deadly as cigarettes?
4. When handling HIV patients, you are not supposed to work with your bare hands.
5. We would have loved to attend the party.

31.2—EDITING CONDITIONAL SENTENCES

1. Whenever I am most absorbed by my work, the telephone rings.
2. If Carol were less outspoken, she would offend fewer people.
3. Yueng would be a better musician if he spent more time practicing.
4. If I leave my house by six o'clock, I will arrive at your house by seven.
5. You would have seen a spectacular meteor shower if you had gone for a walk with us.

31.3—EDITING INFINITIVES AND GERUNDS

1. After the way they embarrassed me, I refuse to speak to them any more.
2. Correct
3. My family and I are planning to go to the Grand Canyon next summer.
4. We are looking forward to seeing lions, elephants, and zebras in the wild game parks of Kenya.
5. Correct

31.4—COMPLETING TWO-WORD VERBS

1. Please turn in your assignments by Friday afternoon at the latest.
2. Shut off the engine so that we don't run out of gas.
3. I was so angry that I tore up the letter and threw it away.
4. Timothy and Angela left an hour ago; we'll never catch up with them.
5. When my best friends come home in the evenings, the first thing they do is turn on their stereo and turn up the volume so that all their neighbors can hear them.

32.1—EDITING OMISSIONS AND REPETITIONS

1. I know this is true because it has happened to me.
2. There are many orchards and gardens in the Nile River valley.
3. In some parts of Saudi Arabia, ten years may pass without rainfall.
4. Because all of Nigeria lies within the tropics, there are only two seasons, wet and dry.
5. The Amazon Valley of eastern Ecuador constitutes about half the country's area.

32.2—EDITING DEPENDENT CLAUSES FOR CORRECT LINKING WORDS

1. I like Seyung's research project because he used so many quotations to support his opinions.
2. To strangers, I usually present myself as someone who is afraid of nothing.
3. Correct
4. Barbara returned to the Ukraine, while the rest of her family remained in the United States.
5. When Darina arrived at the airport, a kind police officer showed her where her departure gate was located.

32.3—EDITING SUMMARIZED QUESTIONS AND SPEECH

1. When I called, Natalia told me she was getting dressed and would be ready in fifteen minutes.
2. An old man sitting next to me on a park bench said that once he had been wealthy and powerful.

3. After the plane had been in the air for an hour, Sergio nervously asked how long it would be before he arrived in Los Angeles.
4. In my environmental ethics class we spent a whole week debating whether the federal government should act to preserve wetlands.
5. Yesterday, my supervisor asked me whether I would like to attend this year's COMDEX computer convention in Las Vegas.

32.4—CHOOSING CORRECT WORD ENDINGS

1. Ana is a person who is usually able to give good reasons for her beliefs.
2. Couples today marry at a later age than they did two or three decades ago.
3. Unfortunately, the victims of many crimes choose to keep silent and not call the police.
4. The time and energy that farmers devote to advanced fertilization techniques will go far to reducing world hunger.
5. Ironically, just one little mistake or misjudgment by the tragic hero is responsible for his death.

32.5—EDITING *-ING* AND *-ED* ADJECTIVES (PARTICIPLES)

1. I had just finished eating breakfast when the telephone rang.
2. She thought he was the most fascinating person she had ever met.
3. Casey said she was not interested in attending the urban planning lecture.
4. Correct
5. After the police used riot control gas, the demonstrators were nauseated for several hours.

32.6—ARRANGING CUMULATIVE ADJECTIVES AND PLACING ADVERBS

1. When my rich aunt comes to visit, she often brings little gifts to remind us just how rich she is.
2. Some kind of thick yellow slime was oozing rapidly from a pipe into the small stream.
3. Correct
4. Waiters like to see Armand stroll through a restaurant door because he always leaves large tips.
5. During the Vietnam War, several devout Buddhist monks burned themselves to death to protest the conflict.

32.7—EDITING PREPOSITIONS

1. I meet so many interesting people at work.
2. For four long blocks a suspicious person followed me on the other side of the street.
3. Happy people are usually content with the things they have, whether a little or a lot.
4. The phrase "age of accountability" refers to the age when children are treated as responsible for themselves.
5. In most American restaurants, smokers and non-smokers are seated in different areas.

33.1—EDITING END PUNCTUATION

1. Was Thomas Jefferson the first to declare that human beings have the right to "life, liberty, and the pursuit of happiness"?

2. Because most of the Earth is covered in a liquid mantle, science writer Dava Sobel says a more appropriate name for our planet would be "Water."
3. Correct
4. The Japanese fliers began their surprise attack on Pearl Harbor at 7:50 a.m. and concluded their devastating bombardment by 10 a.m.
5. Most Americans believe that the federal government has hidden proof of UFOs from the public (a surprising twenty percent believe UFOs represent alien life forms).

34.1—COMMAS

1. Ralph reached for his pocket calculator, which he carried everywhere, and quickly added up the long list of figures.
2. Correct
3. Francis Bacon said, "Some books are to be tasted, others to be swallowed, and some few to be chewed and digested."
4. Des Moines, Iowa, the state capital, was founded in 1843 and originally called Fort Des Moines.
5. Some of the most intricately designed oriental rugs actually come from Kurdistan, a region of northern Iraq and southern Turkey.

34.2—EDITING FOR MISSING AND MISUSED COMMAS

1. Most people associate bagpipes with Scotland, but they originated in Greece and Asia.
2. If the "big bang" theory is correct, the universe is about 10 billion years old.
3. According to the Catholic doctrine of papal infallibility, the Pope is an imperfect human being, but he cannot lead the church into religious error.
4. Air pollution is severe in Albuquerque because the city is located in a broad, shallow valley.
5. To challenge someone in authority who disagrees with me is not easy to do.

35.1—EDITING COMMAS AND SEMICOLONS

1. The old log cabin stood five feet from the ground on a stone foundation, its log steps leading up to an open doorway.
2. Vince pulled into the gas station for a fill-up, and as he stood at the pump, his eyes fell on the huge dent in his rear fender.
3. People with heart disease are strongly cautioned to control their anger instead of venting their emotions and risking a heart attack.
4. According to the Center on Addiction and Substance Abuse, women get drunk more quickly than men, become addicted to drugs more quickly, and develop substance-abuse illnesses more quickly.
5. Correct

36.1—EDITING COMMAS, SEMICOLONS, AND COLONS

1. Barbara's allergies make her so sensitive to food that she can eat only one kind: beige food.
2. Some of the most dangerous sports include climbing, cycling, swimming, skiing, and football.

3. Where is it stated in the Constitution that all Americans are guaranteed happiness and a life as comfortable as the next person's?
4. Correct
5. Victims of AIDS suffer a variety of symptoms, such as coughing, shortness of breath, skin lesions that do not heal, seizures, cramps, diarrhea, and memory loss.

37.1—EDITING APOSTROPHES

1. Gresham's Law refers to people's preference for spending overvalued currency and hoarding undervalued currency.
2. Stacy's sister works as a field investigator in the FBI's Dallas office.
3. The summers of '88 and '89 were America's driest since the dust-bowl years of the Great Depression.
4. The children's delighted cries echoed from the playground.
5. The Old Mill Inn's best menu items are fresh catfish, steak, and tacos.

38.1—EDITING QUOTATIONS

1. The beggar asked Jeff whether he had any spare change.
2. "Are these bags yours or his?" the ticket agent asked.
3. The funeral director indicated that cremation was not as expensive as burial.
4. Midwives provide assistance with what is called "natural childbirth," a process involving no anaesthesia or surgery.
5. "All rise," the bailiff called out to the courtroom.

39.1—EDITING THE DASH, PARENTHESES, BRACKETS, ELLIPSIS, AND SLASH

1. Ernest Wynder identifies the paradoxical goal of modern medicine as helping "people die young as late in life as possible."
2. Correct
3. The terrain of China rises almost like steps from the lowlands of the east coast to the high mountains of the west.
4. Reducing welfare payments to poor families—without providing funds for job creation, job training, and day care—will do nothing to reduce the number of poor people.
5. The aurora australis (the southern lights) glow as brightly and dynamically in the southern hemisphere as the aurora borealis glow in the northern hemisphere.

40.1—EDITING CAPITAL LETTERS

1. Many Hispanics would prefer to be referred to as Latinos or Latinas.
2. My aunt and uncle have invited me to live with them if I attend school near their home.
3. This evening's speech on anti-drug legislation will be given by Attorney General Alberto Gonzalez.
4. Zachary Taylor, twelfth president of the United States, died of cholera after serving for less than one year.
5. The country town where I grew up was so small that its downtown consisted of only a general store and a tiny post office.

41.1—EDITING ITALICS/UNDERLINING

1. NASA's *Pathfinder* spacecraft is scheduled to land on Mars on July 4, 1997.
2. Willa Cather's most popular novel is probably *My Antonia*.
3. Correct
4. Correct
5. The first three books of the New Testament—Matthew, Mark, and Luke—are believed to be based on an earlier account of Jesus's life.

42.1—EDITING ABBREVIATIONS

1. Correct
2. According to Dr. Herman Tyroler, heart disease is no longer an illness primarily afflicting the affluent.
3. Returning from a night reconnaissance following the Battle of Chancellorsville, General Jackson was wounded by some of his own men, who mistook him for the enemy.
4. Correct
5. Correct

43.1—EDITING NUMBERS

1. Montana has imposed a 75 mph speed limit on its highways.
2. The most prolific builder of ancient Egyptian temples was probably King Ramses II.
3. Correct
4. Correct
5. A Chia bust of the late Jerry Garcia of the Grateful Dead rock group, already seeded to grow green hair, sells for $21.95.

44.1—EDITING HYPHENS

1. The "either/or" fallacy treats a many-sided issue as if it had only two sides.
2. Seated in front of me at the theater last night was a well-known television actor.
3. Correct
4. When a reward was offered for information about the escaped prisoners, the police switchboard was flooded with calls.
5. One problem with modern housing developments is that street layout prevents the formation of genuine neighborhoods.

Credits

Adler, Mortimer, "How to Mark a Book." *Saturday Review* 6 July 1940. Reprinted by permission of The Saturday Review © 1940, S.R. Publications, Ltd.

Ambrose, Stephen, *Crazy Horse and Custer: The Parallel Lives of Two American Warriors.* New York: Doubleday, 1986. Reprinted with permission from Doubleday, a division of Bantam Doubleday Dell Publishing Group, Inc.

American Heritage Dictionary. Copyright © 1996 by Houghton Mifflin Company. Reproduced by permission from *American Heritage College Dictionary, Third Edition.*

Angelou, May, introduction to "Champion of the World." From *I Know Why the Caged Bird Sings* by Maya Angelou. Copyright © 1969 by Maya Angelou. Reprinted by permission of Random House, Inc.

Bettelheim, Bruno, *Johnny Wants to Read.* Copyright © 1982 by Bruno Bettelheim. New York: Alfred A. Knopf Inc., 1982.

Britt, Suzanne, "Neat People vs. Sloppy People " from *Show and Tell.* Copyright © 1982 by Suzanne Britt. Reprinted by permission of the author.

Burwell, Rex. "A Nation of Poets' at War with the United States." Reprinted by permission of the author.

Carson, Rachel, "A Fable for Tomorrow" from *Silent Spring.* Copyright © 1962 by Rachel L. Carson, renewed 1990 by Roger Christie. Reprinted by permission of Houghton Mifflin Co. All rights reserved.

Cole, K.C. "Entropy." *The New York Times,* 18 Mar. 1982. © 1982 by The New York Times Company. Reprinted by permission of Houghton Mifflin Co. All rights reserved.

Cousins, Norman, "Who Killed Benny Paret?" *Saturday Review,* 1962. Reprinted by permission of *The Saturday Review* © 1962, S. R. Publications Ltd.

Daly, Christopher B., adapted from "How the Lawyers Stole Winter." *The Atlantic,* March 1995. Reprinted by permission of the author.

Dillard, Annie, excerpt from "In the Jungle" from *Teaching a Stone to Talk: Expeditions and Encounters* by Annie Dillard. Copyright © 1982 by Annie Dillard. Reprinted by permission of HarperCollins Publishers, Inc.

Durning, Alan Thein, "The Consumer Society," excerpt from *How Much Is Enough? The Consumer Society and the Future of the Earth* by Alan Durning. Copyright © 1992 by Worldwatch Institute, www.worldwatch.org. Reprinted by permission of W. W. Norton & Company, Inc.

Ehrlich, Gretel, "Rules of the Game: Rodeo," from *The Solace of Open Spaces* by Gretel Ehrlich. Copyright © 1985 by Gretel Ehrlich. Used by permission of Viking Penguin, a division of Penguin Group Inc.

Eiseley, Loren, "The Cosmic Prison." Reprinted with permission of Scribner, a Division of Simon & Schuster Adult Publishing Group, from *The Invisible Pyramid* by Loren Eiseley. Copyright © 1970 by Loren Eiseley.

FirstSearch screens are used with the permission of OCLC Online Computer Center, Inc. FirstSearch is a registered trademark of OCLC Online Computer Library Center, Inc.

Google screen copyright 2000. Used with permission.

Haines, John, excerpt from "Snow." Copyright 1989 by John Haines. Reprinted from *The Stars, The Snow, The Fire* with the permission of Graywolf Press, Saint Paul, Minnesota.

Hayakawa, S. I., "How Dictionaries Are Made." Excerpt from *Language in Thought and Action,* Fourth Edition by S. I. Hayakawa, copyright © 1978 by Harcourt Brace & Company, reprinted by permission of the publisher.

Hoffman, Banesh, "Unforgettable Albert Einstein." Reprinted from the January 1968 *Reader's Digest.* Copyright 1967 by The Reader's Digest Assn., Inc.

Hubbell, Sue, "Summer," *A Country Year.* Copyright © 1983, 1984, 1985, 1986 by Sue Hubbell. Reprinted by permission of Random House, Inc.

King, Martin Luther, Jr., excerpt from "I Have a Dream." Reprinted by arrangement with the Estate of Martin Luther

Index

A Guide to Correction and Editing Symbols

Numbers refer to chapters in the book

abbr	incorrect abbreviation, 42
adj	incorrect adjective, 18
adv	incorrect adverb, 18
agr	faulty agreement: subject-verb, 14; pronoun-antecedent, 15
art	incorrect articles (ESL), 30
aud	audience unclear, 1c3
awk	awkward: emphasis needed, 20; variety needed, 21; mixed and incomplete messages, 22
case	incorrect case form, 17
cap	incorrect capitalization, 40
cliché	cliché, 26d
coh	coherence needed, 7
cs	comma splice, 12a–b
comp	incorrect comparisons, 18d
coord	ineffective coordination, 20c, 21b2
dm	dangling modifier, 23b
d	ineffective diction (word choice): exact words, 25; vivid words, 26; appropriate words, 27
db neg	double negative, 18e
dev	inadequate subject development, 6
det	concrete details needed, 6a; concrete and specific words, 26a–b
doc	incorrect documentation: MLA, 52a–b; APA, 54a–c; CMS, 55a–c; CSE, 56a
emph	emphasis needed, 20
exact	imprecise or inexact word, 25
fig	inappropriate figure of speech, 26c–d
frag	sentence fragment, 11
fs	fused sentence, 12c
hyph	misused hyphen, 44
ind quot	indirect quotation: 24e; ESL, 32d
-ing	-ing error (ESL), 31f
ital	italics: 41; for emphasis, 41e
jar	jargon, 27c
lc	lower case: 40; misuse of capitals, 40d
log	incorrect or faulty logic (fallacies), 58e
mixed	mixed construction, 22b
mm	misplaced modifier, 23a
ms	incorrect manuscript form (format): 46a; MLA format, 46d; APA format, 46e
nonst	nonstandard: 27b; nonstandard reflexive pronouns, 17g
num	incorrect use of numbers, 43
org	ineffective organization, 3

p	punctuation error: end punctuation, 33; comma, 34; semicolon, 35; colon, 36; apostrophe, 37; quotation marks, 38; dash, 39a; parentheses, 39b; brackets, 39c; ellipsis points, 39d; slash, 39e
pass	ineffective passive voice: 20a; 28c4
prep	preposition error: 25f3; ESL, 32h
quot	quotation error: 38; 50c–d
ref	faulty pronoun reference, 16
rep	needless repetition (redundancy), 28a
run-on	run-on sentence: fused sentence, 12c
-s	error in -s ending, 13c
shift	faulty shift: point of view, 24a; number, 24b; tense, 24c; mood and voice, 24d; direct and indirect discourse, 24e
sl	inappropriate use of slang, 27b
sp	spelling error, 45
sub	ineffective subordination: 20b; combining choppy sentences, 21b
t	incorrect verb tense: 13b; ESL, 31a–c
trans	ineffective transition, 7b
us	usage error (incorrect use of a troublesome word or phrase), 29
stet	stet ("let it stand as written"), 4d2
v or vb	verb error: 13; ESL, 31
var	variety needed, 21
w or wdy	wordiness, 28
wo	incorrect word order: misplaced modifiers, 23a; ESL, 32g
ww	wrong word, 25; a guide to usage, 29

Symbol	Meaning
??	unclear or illegible: 4d; format: 46a
¶ or no ¶	begin a new paragraph or no paragraph required: 4d2
//	faulty parallelism: 19
⌒	close up space: 4d2
#	add space: 4d2
∧	insert: 4d2
ℯ	delete: 4d2
∩∪	transpose: 4d2
x	obvious error
.?!	end punctuation misuse
∧	comma misuse
∨̌	apostrophe misuse
;	semicolon usage
--/( )/[ ]	other punctuation usage as marked

A Brief Contents and Browsing Guide